(Continued on back endpaper)

SEVENTH EDITION

FUNDAMENTALS OF
BEHAVIORAL
STATISTICS

Richard P. Runyon
Audrey Haber

Garden State Rehabilitation Hospital

McGraw-Hill, Inc.
New York St. Louis San Francisco Auckland Bogotá
Caracas Lisbon London Madrid Mexico City Milan
Montreal New Delhi San Juan Singapore
Sydney Tokyo Toronto

This book is printed on acid-free paper.

Fundamentals of Behavioral Statistics

Copyright © 1991, 1988, 1984, 1980, 1976, 1971, 1967 by McGraw-Hill, Inc. All rights reserved.
Printed in the United States of America. Except as permitted under the United States
Copyright Act of 1976, no part of this publication may be reproduced or distributed in any
form or by any means, or stored in a data base or retrieval system, without the prior written
permission of the publisher.

    7 8 9 0 DOC DOC 9 5

ISBN 0-07-054326-7

This book was set in Zapf Book Light by Monotype Composition Company.
The editors were Maria E. Chiappetta, Jane Vaicunas, and James R. Belser;
the designer was Wanda Siedlecka;
the production supervisor, was Janelle S. Travers.
R. R. Donnelley & Sons Company was printer and binder.

Library of Congress Cataloging-in-Publication Data

Runyon, Richard P.
    Fundamentals of behavioral statistics / Richard P. Runyon, Audrey
  Haber. — 7th ed.
      p.   cm.
    Includes bibliographical references and index.
    ISBN 0-07-054326-7
    1. Social sciences—Statistical methods.   2. Statistics.
  I. Haber, Audrey.   II. Title.
    [DNLM: 1. Psychometrics. 2. Statistics. BF 39 R943f]
  HA29.R85   1991
  519.5—dc20
  DNLM/DLC
  for Library of Congress   90-13426
                         CIP

Contents

PART III
INFERENTIAL STATISTICS: PARAMETRIC TESTS OF SIGNIFICANCE   253

PART IV
INFERENTIAL STATISTICS: NONPARAMETRIC TEST
OF SIGNIFICANCE 449

Preface

It is difficult for us to believe that this text is going into its seventh edition, almost a quarter of a century after it took its first halting steps in the groves of academe. The widespread and continued acceptance of this text in its many editions has been a source of deep satisfaction to its authors.

Reflect for a moment on what has happened to the processing of data during this past quarter century. We have gone from mostly manual calculations, with occasional assistance from slide rules and noisy, recalcitrant mechanical calculators, to large and expensive calculators and computers, to compact, "throw away" pocket calculators and small, inexpensive computers with tremendous data storing and data-processing capabilities. As our grandchildren would say, "It's awesome!"

These changes have, of course, placed different requirements on the teaching of statistics. Less time need be spent on the mechanics of computation, and more time can be devoted to the rationale for research designs and statistical analysis. Our various editions have reflected these changes. But let's not throw out the baby with the bath. Some users of our texts have suggested that the explosion in the availability of sophisticated calculators and computers has made obsolete the use of grouping techniques in descriptive statistics. In some areas, this may well be so. However, vital statistics and census summaries, to name but two, are almost always presented in the form of grouped frequency distributions. Knowledge of grouping techniques is still required for a variety of reasons: to permit comprehension and understanding of both the advantages and the pitfalls of these widely used data summaries. One of our goals, as authors of statistical texts, has been to encourage statistical literacy. In our view, students unfamiliar with grouping techniques have gaps in this literacy.

The advent of the computer is not necessarily an unmixed blessing. Along with all the obvious benefits of the computer, there also arise some risks. There is a temptation to collect the data, then enter them immediately, and with cursory examination at best, into computer data files. In doing so, we lose contact with our raw data and may overlook important aspects of these data. It is for this reason that we have added a section on exploratory data analysis. We hope that this brief introduction to EDA will stimulate our colleagues and their students to delve deeper into these important recent statistical developments.

It was a concern for the scarcity of raw data that prompted us, while preparing the previous edition, to contact several authors of recently published research and request that they make their raw data available to us. We are happy to say that we have continued to use their data, which we incorporated into a feature: "Statistics in Action." We wish to renew our expression of deep appreciation to S. R. Anthony, H. L. Wagner, and C. J. MacDonald at the University of Manchester, Manchester, England; Deems F. Ortega and Janet E. Pipal at Patient and Family Services, Iowa Lutheran Hospital, Des Moines, Iowa; Kenneth A. Perkins at the University of Pittsburgh and Western Psychiatric Institute and Clinic, Pittsburgh, Pennsylvania; and Norman E. Rosenthal at the National Institute of Mental Health, Clinical Psychobiology Branch, Bethesda, Maryland.

We have also added a feature to this edition: Putting It All Together. This appears at the end of most chapters and ties together the many disparate sections of the chapter. In some cases, a single set of data is subjected to the statistical procedures that were featured in the chapter. In others, some contemporary issue of importance is discussed in the light of a statistical perspective.

Those who desired greater coverage of analysis of variance (ANOVA) should not be disappointed. Chapters 13 and 14 of the previous editions were combined into a single chapter, and the new Chapters 14 and 15 cover ANOVA. All three chapters have a parallel structure—independent-samples designs followed by correlated-measures designs. Thus, Chapter 13 includes Student's t-ratio for independent and correlated samples (including before-after measures). Chapter 14 explores one-way ANOVA with both independent and correlated measures (randomized block designs). Finally, Chapter 15 covers two-way ANOVA, including factorial and randomized block factorial designs. For those who use this text in the first course at the graduate level, these two chapters should provide a sound introduction to more advanced statistical procedures.

Nor have the supplementary materials been neglected. The *Study Guide and Solutions Manual* has been expanded to include a greater emphasis on detailed worked solutions. This has been done to assist the student who, after spending considerable time on obtaining the answer, discovers that he or she has made an error. In some cases, the values of computations at varying stages in the analysis are shown so that the student can pinpoint where the error was made. In other instances, detailed solutions are shown. A supreme effort was made to achieve accuracy in the *Study Guide*. The solutions were checked and double-checked, using two independent sets of statistical software.

The *Study Guide* continues its sections on "guesstimating" a statistic on the basis of an examination of raw data, rather than using formal computational procedures. These guesstimating techniques yield rapid results that are often astonishingly close to the computed solution. Their use often helps the student better understand some abstruse point. Moreover, a sizable difference between the guesstimate and the computed solution alerts the student to a possible error in the values entered into the computation or the subsequent analysis of the data.

In addition, statistical routines for use with IBM (and IBM-compatible) and Apple personal computers are available for application in instructional settings where computers are used.

In particular, the MYSTAT computer package is available for use with this book; its major features include:

● Available for both Macintosh and IBM-type microcomputers.

● Fits on a single floppy disk; works without a hard disk and without changing disks; not copy protected.

● Outstanding freedom from rounding error, far surpassing mainframe SAS.

● Automatic reporting of the tolerance and exact significance level p for each independent variable, along with its slope, standard error of slope, standardized slope, and t.

● The CATEGORY command, which works like the CLASS command in SAS. For instance, if *religion* is represented by categories numbered 1–8, the commands

> > category religion = 8
> > model attitude = constant + age + religion
> > estimate

are all that is necessary to produce an analysis of covariance testing the differences in attitude among the 8 religious groups with age controlled statistically.

● The * operator to represent interaction and power terms. For instance, the commands

> > category religion = 8
> > model attitude = constant + age + religion + age*age + age*religion
> > estimate

add to the previous model a square term for age, and a term for the interaction between age and religion.

● A full-screen data editor that includes the ability to make logarithmic and many other data transformations and combinations, search for specific values, and generate uniform or normal random numbers.

● Ability to find the exact significance level p for any F, including F's calculated by hand or by other packages; see Appendix 2.

● Ability to find slopes and their standard errors for numerical variables even when some variables are categorical; see Section 10.1.6.

● Tests on sets of variables; see Section 5.3.1.

● A full range of regression diagnostics, including leverage, Cook's measure of influence, and studentized residuals. Unlike similar options in SAS, these can be used with both categorical and numerical variables.

● Ability to detect cases with unusual leverage or influence on a particular regression slope. Such cases may not be detected by overall measures of leverage and influence. See Section 14.1.7.

- A structure that discourages the inappropriate use of what SAS calls "Type I" sums of squares and also what Cohen and Cohen (1983) call "Model II" error terms. This structure has been considered a disadvantage by some writers who don't understand the dangers in these models; see Section 7.5.3.

A textbook of this sort is a collaboration of many individuals, with their contributions meriting more than a mention in the Preface. First, there are those who write unsolicited letters to us to bestow compliments for a job well done or to chastise us whenever we drop the ball. We appreciate both the praise and the censure; the first for boosting our egos and the second for helping to improve our performance of our shared mission—instruction in one of the most important courses in the curriculum. A second group of individuals agree to subject themselves to the agony, without the ecstasy. In short, they read the entire text and make detailed suggestions, many of which are incorporated into the text. They have our undying admiration and appreciation.

We wish to thank the following reviewers for their most generous contribution of their time and talents: Kay Coleman, Boston University; Robert Cudeck, University of Minnesota; Richard Serkes, Tulsa Junior College; James Starr, Howard University; and Lois Tetrick, Wayne State University.

Finally, we would be remiss if we did not acknowledge the exceptionally fine support of our co-producers at McGraw-Hill, Inc. James R. Belser calmly and amiably supervised the production of the book; Maria E. Chiappetta and Jane Vaicunas provided valuable help and support during the revision stages of the manuscript.

We are grateful to the Literary Executor of the late Sir Ronald A. Fisher, F.R.S., to Dr. Frank Yates, F.R.S., and the Longman Group Ltd., London, for permission to reprint Table III from their book *Statistical Tables for Biological, Agricultural, and Medical Research (Sixth Edition, 1974)*.

RICHARD P. RUNYON
AUDREY HABER

FUNDAMENTALS OF
BEHAVIORAL STATISTICS

PART I

INTRODUCTION

Statistical Analysis

1.1 WHAT IS STATISTICS?

Think for a moment of the thousands of incredibly complex things you do during the course of a day, and then stand in awe at the marvel you represent. You are absolutely unique. No one else possesses your features, your intellectual makeup, your personality characteristics, or your value system. Yet, like billions of others of your species, you are the most finely tuned and enormously sophisticated statistical instrument ever devised by natural forces. Every moment of your life provides mute testimony to your ability to receive, integrate, and process a wealth of sensory data and then to act upon this information in an instant to generate a spectrum of probabilities relating to possible courses of action. To illustrate, imagine that you are driving in heavy traffic. You are continuously scanning the road conditions, noting the speed of cars in front of you relative to your speed, the position and rate of approach of vehicles to your rear, and the presence of automobiles in the oncoming lane. If you are an alert driver, you are constantly summarizing this descriptive information—usually without words or awareness. Imagine next that, without warning, the driver in front of you suddenly jams on the brakes. In an instant, you are summoned to act upon this prior descriptive information. You must brake the car, turn left, turn right, or pray. Your probability mechanism instantly assesses alternative courses of action. If you jam on the brakes, what is the likelihood that you will stop in time? Is the car behind you sufficiently distant to avoid a rear-end collision? Can you prevent an accident by turning into the left lane or onto the right shoulder? Most of the time, the decision made from sensory data is correct. It is for this reason that most of us live to reach a ripe old age. In this situation, as in many others during the course of a lifetime, you have accurately assessed the probabilities and taken the right course of action. And we make such decisions uncounted thousands of times each and every day of our lives. It is for this reason that you should regard yourself as a sublime mechanism for generating statistical decisions. In this sense, you are already a statistician.

In daily living, our statistical functioning is usually informal and loosely structured. We *behave* statistically, although we may be totally unaware of the formal laws of probability.

In this course, we shall attempt to provide you with some of the procedures for collecting and analyzing data, and making decisions or inferences based upon these analyses. Since we shall frequently be building upon your prior experiences, you will often feel you are in familiar territory: "Why, I have been calculating arithmetic means almost all my life—whenever I determine my test average in a course or the batting average of my favorite baseball player!" If you constantly draw upon your previous knowledge and relate course materials to what is familiar in daily life, statistics need not, and should not, be the bugaboo it is often painted to be.

What, then, is statistics all about? To many people, statistics is merely a collection of numerical facts that are expressed in terms of a summarizing statement such as: "Seven out of ten doctors prescribe the pain reliever that is contained in Product X," or "During his current hitting streak, Wade Boggs hit safely in 20 of his last 45 times at bat," or "During the 4th of July weekend, 1986, more than 6 million New Yorkers and visitors participated in the centennial celebration of the unveiling of the Statue of Liberty."

Statistics: A method for dealing with data; a tool for organizing and analyzing numerical facts or observations in accordance with a systematic plan.

Research Design: The systematic plan for collecting data in order to provide answers to specific questions.

However, this is not the way scientists regard statistics. Rather, **statistics** is a method for dealing with data; it involves the organization and analysis of numerical facts or observations that are collected in accordance with a systematic plan. The plan for collecting data is called the **research design**. Broadly speaking, the design of the study is structured to provide answers to specific questions. Some of these go to the heart of contemporary problems.

For example, AIDS is potentially the most devastating disease that has ever struck our species. The AIDS virus uses the very system designed by the body to prevent infection (the immune system) as the breeding ground for its own reproduction. In doing so, it renders the immune system incapable of waging a successful war against a host of other viral invaders. The disease is fatal. There is as yet no cure, although some treatments have been found to slow its progress. It is not known when, if ever, a successful vaccine may be developed.

With all this uncertainty about the timetable for a successful medical treatment of AIDS, many governmental and private agencies have launched educational programs aimed at increasing knowledge about the disease and at encouraging those types of behaviors that lessen the risk of transmitting AIDS. Box 1.1 presents a graph of the results of interviews conducted on two randomly selected groups of approximately 3500 adults (18 years and over) in August of 1987 and August of 1988. The purpose of this aspect of the survey was to ascertain if there was an increase, over time, in the percentage of adults responding correctly to true and false statements about AIDS.

A distinction may be made between the two functions of the statistical method: **descriptive** statistical techniques and **inferential** or **inductive** statistical techniques.

The major concern of descriptive statistics is to present information in a convenient, usable, and understandable form. Inferential statistics, on the other hand, is concerned with generalizing this information or, more specifically, with making inferences about populations that are based upon samples taken from those populations.

In describing the functions of statistics, we have already presented certain terms with which you may or may not be familiar. Before we elaborate on the differences between descriptive and inductive statistics, you need to learn the meaning of certain terms that will be employed repeatedly throughout the text.

Descriptive Statistics: Procedures employed to organize and present data in a convenient, usable, and communicable form.

Inferential or Inductive Statistics: Procedures employed to arrive at broader generalizations or inferences from sample data to populations.

1.2   DEFINITIONS OF TERMS COMMONLY USED IN STATISTICS

Variable   Any characteristic of a person, environment, or experimental situation that can vary from person to person, environment to environment, or experimental situation to experimental situation. Thus weight, IQ, and sex are variables since they may take on different values when different individuals are observed. A variable is contrasted with a constant, the value of which never changes; for example, pi = 3.1416.

Variable: A characteristic or phenomenon that may take on different values.

Data   Numbers or measurements that are collected as a result of observations. They may be head counts (frequency or enumerative data), as, for example, the number of individuals stating a preference for the Republican presidential candidate; they may be rankings, such as the "pecking order" among birds in an aviary; or they may be scores, as on a psychological or educational test.

Data: Numbers or measurements that are collected as a result of observations.

Population   A complete set of individuals, objects, or measurements having some common observable characteristic. Thus, all babies born in a particular year may constitute a population. However, a population may also be a *theoretical* set of *potential* observations, rather than a "complete set." For example, we may expand the above population to include *all* babies regardless of when they were born or will be born.

Population: A complete set of individuals, objects, or measurements having some common observable characteristic, or a theoretical set of potential observations.

BOX 1.1

HUMAN IMMUNODEFICIENCY VIRUS EPIDEMIC AND AIDS: TRENDS IN KNOWLEDGE— UNITED STATES, 1987 AND 1988

Statistics is one of the most widely used tools in the behavioral, social, health, and physical sciences. Statistical information is collected on virtually every aspect of life and death. The resulting data are then subjected to various levels of statistical processing, inferences are drawn, and decisions are made that directly and indirectly affect our daily lives.

Frequently, observations are made at varying times to permit the comparison of changes over time.

The records of these observations are then analyzed, and the results are often displayed graphically. Figure 1.1 shows the percentage of interviewees in 1987 and 1988 who correctly identified statements that are definitely true (above) and definitely false (below).

It would appear that the messages are getting through, but not uniformly. Most adults knew in both years that AIDS can lead to death and that there is no cure at present. A greater percentage knew in 1988 than in 1987 that it is an infectious disease caused by a virus, but relatively few knew in either year that AIDS can damage the brain. By 1988, almost 80% of those interviewed knew that there is no vaccine available, but less than 20% were able to identify as false the statement that AIDS leads to heart disease.

FIGURE 1.1 Provisional estimates of percentage of adults responding correctly to selected AIDS knowledge items—United States, August 1987 and August 1988. (*Source*: From "HIV Epidemic and AIDS: Trends in Knowledge—United States, 1987 and 1988 (1989), *Morbidity and Mortality Weekly Report*, **38**(20), 353–358.)

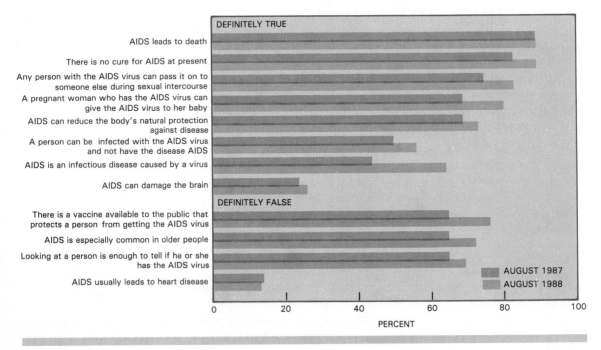

Some statisticians prefer to distinguish between a population and a source. They use population to refer only to numerical measurements or observations and source as the origin of these observations. According to this distinction, voters in a national election are a source and their votes are the population. We do not differentiate between population and source in this book. The slight ambiguity does not usually constitute a problem as long as we are aware of the fact that statistical statements are expressed in terms of numerical values.

Parameter   A value summarizing a measurable characteristic of a population, for example, the true proportion of television viewers watching the first episode of a new situation comedy. In this book, we shall follow the generally accepted practice of using Greek letters to represent population parameters. For example, the Greek letter μ (pronounced mew) represents a population mean, whereas $\bar{X}$ (pronounced X bar) symbolizes the sample mean.

Parameter: A value summarizing a measurable characteristic of a population, e.g., the proportion of neonates who are female.

Sample   A subset of a population selected in accordance with the research design. To illustrate, if we wished to estimate the number of viewers of a new situation comedy, we might select a subset of television viewers during the hours the sitcom is airing.

Sample: A subset of a population selected in accordance with the research design.

Random Sample   A subset of a population selected in such a way that each member of the population has an equal opportunity to be selected. Random sampling permits inferences about characteristics of the population from which the sample is selected.

It should be noted that random sampling is not an end in itself, but merely a means to an end. The goal is that the sample accurately reflect all the characteristics of the population from which it was drawn. Random sampling is only one way to achieve this goal. Randomization is the backbone of probability theory, as is explained in Chapter 10.

Random Sample: A subset of a population or universe selected in such a way that each member of the population has an equal opportunity to be selected.

Statistic   A number resulting from manipulation of sample data according to certain specified procedures or rules. For example, if we want to express the number of patients in a care facility diagnosed "schizophrenic" as a proportion, we follow the rule: divide the number diagnosed as schizophrenic by the total number of patients. Thus, if there are 880 patients and 356 are diagnosed schizophrenic, the proportion is 356/880 = 0.40 (rounded to the second decimal place). Commonly, we use a statistic that is calculated from a sample in order to estimate the population parameter; for example, a sample of Americans of voting age is employed to estimate the proportion of Democrats in the entire population of voters. It should be noted that for every statistic that describes some aspect of a sample there is a corresponding parameter that describes the same aspect of a population. Thus, for the statistic "mean of a sample" there is a parameter "mean of the population." We shall employ italic letters (e.g., $\bar{X}$ sample mean) to represent sample statistics. Thus, by looking at statistical notation, we can distinguish

Statistic: A value summarizing a measurable characteristic of a sample, e.g., the proportion of female neonates in a sample of newly delivered infants.

between samples and populations. More will be said about the fascinating problem of sampling later in the text.

Example Imagine that you have been hired as a statistical consultant by the governing body of a large metropolitan region. Your first assignment is to obtain statistical information on a medico-psychological problem that has surfaced over the past decade or so, namely, drug addiction among newborn infants. Treatment of these innocent victims of drug abuse requires some specialized equipment and round-the-clock medical supervision. Your immediate task is to estimate the extent and types of neonatal drug addiction so that the various clinics and hospitals in the city may make informed decisions about equipment and personnel needs for the coming year. Typically, your operating budget and the availability of trained assistants are limited. Therefore, there is no way you can hope to study the medical records of *all* the children born during the preceding year. At best, you can select only a small portion of the total records and subject these to intensive scrutiny. These selected records constitute the sample. If the sample is selected in such a way that each record has an equal probability of being chosen, we speak of the selection process as *random selection*. The *variable* of interest is the drug addiction status of each neonate. For our purposes we shall assume that each record reveals either the presence or the absence of drug addiction. The *data* consist of the number of drug-addicted and non-drug-addicted infants in the sample. When the data are manipulated according to certain rules to yield summary statements (such as the proportion of drug-addicted neonates), the resulting numerical value constitutes a *statistic*. The *population* to which we are interested in generalizing is all the infant births occurring in the metropolitan region during the preceding year. The "true" proportion of neonatal addicts in the population is the *parameter* (see Figure 1.2). Note that it is highly unlikely that the parameter will ever be known, for to find it would require the examination of the medical records of every infant born in the region over a time period of one year. Since it is difficult, time-consuming, and expensive to locate all members of a population, exhaustive studies of populations are not frequently undertaken. Consequently, parameters are rarely known, but as we shall see, they are commonly estimated from sample statistics.

It is, of course, possible to define a very small population by narrowing the definition of "common observable characteristic" to something like "all students attending their Psych 91 class at Pitzer College today." In this event, calculating a parameter (such as the class mean on the examination given today) would pose no difficulty. For such small populations, there is no reason to select samples and calculate sample statistics.

From the point of view of the instructor, observations on the students in Psych 91 at Pitzer College may be of supreme importance. However, such limited populations would be of little theoretical interest. Usually, in

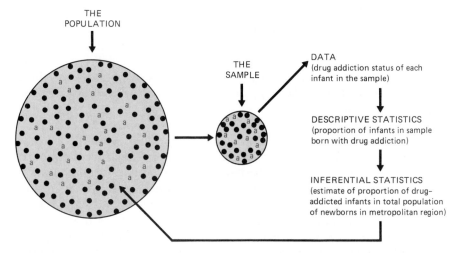

FIGURE 1.2   The population consists of many thousands of neonates born in a given metropolitan region over a specific time period. Some of these neonates are addicted (a) and others are not (●). Because of cost or logistic reasons, the large size of the population rules out the possibility of a complete **census.** Thus, the parameter (the true proportion of addicted neonates in the population) is not knowable. A sample is selected from the population in such a way that it is likely to mirror the population. The *data* are collected, and various descriptive statistics are obtained. In inferential statistics, we attempt to estimate one or more population parameters, such as the proportion of drug-addicted neonates among all newborn children in the metropolitan region.

the real workaday world, the behavioral scientist is interested in making statements having general validity over a wider domain and thus must *estimate* the (population) parameter. This estimate is based on the statistic that is calculated on the sample. Thus, we might use the observations on the students at Pitzer College as a basis for estimating parameters of the larger population.

Let us return to the two functions of statistical analysis for a closer look.

1.3   DESCRIPTIVE STATISTICS

When a behavioral scientist conducts a study, he or she characteristically collects a great deal of numerical information or data about the problem at hand. The data may take a variety of forms: frequency data (head counts of voters preferring various political candidates) or scale data (the weights of the contents of a popular breakfast cereal, ratings or rankings such as the order of preference of breakfast cereals, or the IQ scores of a group of college students). In their original form, as collected, these data are usually a confusing hodge-podge of scores. In performing the descriptive function, statisticians formulate rules and procedures for presentation of the data in a more usable and meaningful form. Thus, statisticians state rules by which data may be represented graphically. They also formulate rules for calculating various *statistics* from masses of data.

Let us imagine that, as a behavioral scientist, you administered a number of measuring instruments (e.g., intelligence tests, personality inventories, aptitude tests) to a group of high school students. What are some things you may do with the resulting measurements or scores to fulfill your descriptive functions?

1. You may rearrange the scores and group them in various ways, in order to be able to see at a glance an overall picture of your data (Chapter 3, "Frequency Distributions and Graphing Techniques").

2. You may construct tables, graphs, and figures to permit visualization of the results (Section 3.3, "Graphing Techniques," in Chapter 3).

3. You may convert raw scores to other types of scores that are more useful for specific purposes. Thus, you may convert these scores into either percentile ranks, standard scores, or grades. Other types of conversion will also be described in the text (Chapter 4, "Percentiles," and Chapter 7, "Standard Deviation/Standard Normal Distribution").

4. You may calculate averages, to learn something about the typical performances of your subjects (Chapter 5, "Measures of Central Tendency").

5. Employing the average as a reference point, you may describe the dispersion, or spread, of scores about this central point. Statistics that quantify this dispersion are known as measures of variability or measures of dispersion (Chapter 6, "Measures of Dispersion").

6. A relationship between two different measuring instruments may be obtained. The statistic for describing the extent of the relationship is referred to as a *correlation coefficient*. Such coefficients are extremely useful to the behavioral scientist. For example, you may wish to determine the relationship between intelligence and classroom grades, personality measures and aptitudes, or interests and personality measures. Once these relationships are established, you may employ scores obtained from one measuring instrument to predict performance on another (Chapter 8, "Correlation," and Chapter 9, "Regression and Prediction").

1.4 INFERENTIAL STATISTICS

As a behavioral scientist, your task has just begun when you have completed your descriptive function. In fact, you are often nearer to the beginning than to the end of your task. The reason for this is obvious when we consider that the purpose of your research is often to explore hypotheses of a general nature, rather than simply to compare limited samples.

Let us imagine that you are interested in determining the effects of a given drug upon the performance of a task involving psychomotor coordination. Consequently, you set up a study involving two conditions, *experimental* and *control*. You administer the drug to the experimental subjects at specified time periods before they undertake the criterion task. To rule out "placebo effects," you administer a pill containing inert ingredients to the control subjects. After all subjects have been tested, you perform your descriptive function. You find that "on the average" the experimental subjects did not perform as well as the controls. In other words, the arithmetic mean of the experimental group was lower than that of the control group. You then ask the question, "Can we conclude that the drug produced the difference between the two groups?" Or, more generally, "Can we assert that the drug has an adverse effect upon the performance of the criterion task under investigation?" For us to answer these questions, it is not sufficient to rely solely upon *descriptive statistics*.

"After all," you reason, "even if the drug had *no effect*, it is highly improbable that the two group means would have been *identical*. Some difference would have been observed." The operation of uncontrolled variables (sometimes referred to rather imprecisely as "chance factors") is certain to produce some disparity between the group means. The critical question, from the point of view of inferential statistics, becomes: Is the difference great enough to rule out uncontrolled variation in the experiment as a sufficient explanation? Stated another way, if we were to repeat the experiment, would we be able to predict with confidence that the same differences (i.e., the control group mean is greater than the experimental group mean) would systematically occur?

As soon as we raise these questions, we move into the fascinating area of statistical analysis that is known as *inductive* or *inferential statistics*. As you will see, much of the present text is devoted to procedures that the researcher employs to arrive at conclusions that extend beyond the sample statistics themselves.

1.5 THE GOALS OF RESEARCH

Behavioral scientists engage in a rich variety of differential activities in diverse settings that involve the collection and analysis of numerical observations or data. These activities are generally subsumed under the label "research." The goals of these research activities may be classified into three broad categories: information gathering, describing relationships, and establishing causality. It should be noted that these goals are not mutually exclusive. All three are common components of many research efforts.

Information Gathering

The focus of many statistical activities is to provide information about some aspect of our professional activities that arouses our interest. For example, we may wish to know whether the proportion of women entering the field of psychology is changing over the years, or the average starting salary of recent Ph.D.s accepting positions at academic institutions, or the proportion of clinical psychologists using the 3d edition of the *Diagnostic and Statistical Manual (DSM III)* as a means of classifying the presenting behaviors of clients. In these information-gathering activities, the emphasis is to provide accurate descriptions of the situations studied. The information is considered valuable in its own right. Therefore, there may not be any effort to relate the data to other events or situations. For example, we may make no attempt to answer the question, why are the starting salaries of new Ph.D.s in academia *X* dollars?

CASE EXAMPLE 1.1

Sexual Attraction to Clients in Psychotherapy

The survey is one means of collecting timely information on topics of interest. One issue of considerable concern in recent years involves sexual intimacy between help-givers (physicians, psychotherapists, counselors, nurses, etc.) and their clients. Such intimacy is unethical, is possibly harmful to the therapeutic process, and exposes the therapist to censure and possible malpractice action. Although there is now a considerable body of knowledge concerning sexual intimacy between psychotherapists and their clients, little has been done to document the extent to which therapists are attracted to their clients and why. The present survey attempts to fill some of that void.

Data from 575 psychotherapists showed that 87% reported being attracted (rarely, occasionally, or frequently) to their clients, but only a minority (9.4% of men and 2.5% of women) acted out their feelings. Considering the importance of the therapist-client relationship, it may come as a surprise that approximately half the therapists did not receive any training on this issue and only 9% found the training and/or supervision adequate.

Figure 1.3 shows the percentage of male and female therapists who never, rarely, occasionally, or frequently felt attracted to male and female clients. As you can see, the majority of male therapists felt at least occasionally attracted to their female clients (50.9% occasionally and 15.7% frequently). In contrast, fewer female therapists felt at least an occasional attraction to their male clients (30.9% occasionally and 1.2% frequently).

Surveys of this sort often exert a profound influence on public policy. Look for the future training of psychotherapists to include considerable training and supervision on dealing with their sexual feelings toward their clients.

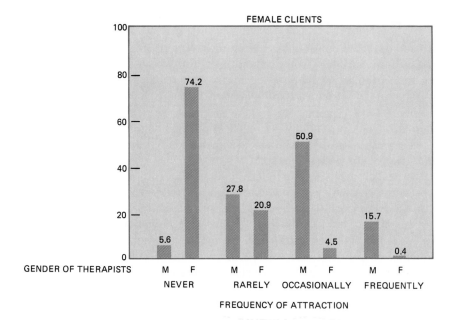

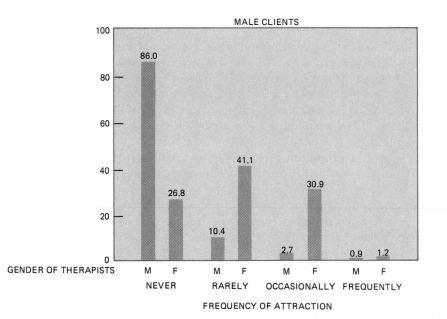

FIGURE 1.3 Frequency of attraction of male and female psychotherapists to their male and female clients. (Based on Kenneth S. Pope, Patricia Keith-Spiegel, and Barbara G. Tabachnick (1986), ''Sexual Attraction to Client: The Human Therapist and the (Sometimes) Inhuman Training System,'' *American Psychologist*, **41**(2), 147–158.)

Describing Relationships

In the course of conducting research, we often obtain measurements on two or more variables from each subject, and we wish to know whether or not the variables go together, or covary. Does academic performance vary in relation to measured intelligence? Is there a relationship between temporal lobe epilepsy and aggressiveness, as some researchers have claimed? Does our ability to recall childhood experiences relate to the pleasantness or unpleasantness associated with these experiences at the time they occurred?

Studies of this sort are referred to as correlational. They attempt to ascertain whether or not two variables are related (i.e., correlated—think of them as co-related) or vary together and, if so, to measure the direction and strength of the relationship. To illustrate, if we have measurements on two variables for each individual, we may raise such questions as: As the values of one variable increase (e.g., measured intelligence), do the paired measures on the second variable also increase (e.g., academic performance)? Or are increases in one variable (e.g., anxiety) associated with decreases in a second variable (e.g., score on a complex problem-solving task)? Or does there not appear to be any detectable relationship between the two variables (e.g., length of big toe and score on an intelligence test)?

It is important to note that correlation between naturally occurring variables such as intelligence, gender, racial/ethnic backgrounds, or learning scores do not, as such, permit us to claim that changes in one variable *cause* changes in a second variable. They merely establish whether or not the two variables vary together. Many serious misinterpretations of data have occurred because people have ignored this fact. Thus, at various times in our history as a nation, members of various minority groups (e.g., blacks, Italians, Poles, Jews, etc.) have labored under the stigma of inferiority because their low positions on the educational and socioeconomic ladders have been attributed to their racial and/or ethnic backgrounds. The point is that these groups differed from the majority in many ways other than their ethnic/racial backgrounds—for example, command of the English language, educational and economic opportunities, and life-styles—to name a few. To focus on a single characteristic (such as ethnic background) that distinguished each of these groups from the majority and to attribute their social and economic position to this characteristic is to ignore the wealth of other ways in which they differ.

Establishing Causality

One of the paramount goals of any science is to go beyond statements of relationships (e.g., if the value of A is high, then the value of B is also high) to those of causality (e.g., increases in the values of A *cause* the values of B to increase also). In spite of hundreds of years of speculating, thinking, and writing about causality, it remains a somewhat elusive term. Not all scientists agree on the procedures for establishing cause-effect relationships. Indeed, some even doubt its feasibility, and others question its necessity. However, the vast majority of scientists appear to agree that a statement such as "*A* causes *B*" is among the most powerful that a scientist can make and should be at the core of scientific inquiry.

Although there are advocates of several different strategies for establishing causality, we shall limit our discussion to the **"true" experiment.** In the typical true experiment, we are concerned primarily with two different types of variables—*independent* and *dependent*. The **independent variable** is usually some feature of the individual's external environment (type of incentive, instructional materials, pharmaceutical compound), although it may also be an internal state, such as motivational level. The purpose of the experiment is to assess the effects of variations in the independent variable on some response measure (the **dependent variable**). Response variables include diverse measures such as scores on a test, the time required to demonstrate mastery of a task or skill, attitudes toward a political candidate or proposed piece of legislation, electrical conductivity of the skin, or time required to react to the introduction of a visual or auditory stimulus. The key to qualifying as a true experiment is that *the independent variable must be under the control of the experimenter*. To illustrate, different types of incentives, instructional materials, or pharmaceutical compounds can all be independently manipulated and varied by an experimenter. Consequently, they can all qualify as independent variables in a true experiment. If our data analyses yield convincing evidence that variations in the independent variable lead to systematic and predictable variations in the dependent measure, we are justified in concluding that the manipulation of the independent variable caused the changes in the response variable.

This is not necessarily the case with all independent variables. Often the independent variable is a state of nature or of the organism that is not under the experimenter's control (**organismic variable**). To illustrate, we may have observed that people's moods appear to be different on cloudy days as opposed to sunny days. We design the following study: We administer a mood scale to two randomly selected groups of subjects. Half take the test on sunny days and half on cloudy days. Let's suppose we find that the moods are clearly better on the sunny days. Can we conclude that sunshine causes the favorable moods? No necessarily. It is quite possible that mood is unaffected by sunshine, as such, but reflects the effects of variables that covary with sunshine. For example, when it is sunny, more people are present outdoors, and the presence of others may be a source of a positive mood; when it is sunny, people are more active, and increased activity levels may enhance mood; and when it is not sunny, people are more likely to stay indoors, and staying indoors all day may be depressing.

To conclude that sunshine causes better moods, we would be required to manipulate sunshine (or full-spectrum artificial light) independent of these other variables. The same considerations apply when we use orga-

True Experiment: A study in which the independent variable is under the control of the experimenter.

Independent Variable: A variable that is examined in order to determine its effects on an outcome of interest (the dependent variable).

Dependent Variable: An outcome of interest (e.g., some characteristic of behavior) that is being observed and measured in order to assess the effects of the independent variable.

Organismic Variables: Naturally occurring characteristics of the organism such as nationality, age, and gender. They are often used as "independent" variables but are not under the control of the researcher.

STATISTICS IN ACTION 1.1

Seasonal affective disorder: Designing an experiment

There are a number of individuals who experience marked mood swings and behavioral changes that are tied to the seasons of the year. Depression, "characterized by fatigue, lethargy, oversleeping, overeating, and carbohydrate craving" (Rosenthal et al., 1984–85, p. 1), sets in during the fall and winter and is followed by a remission of symptoms in the spring and summer. Many different lines of evidence suggested the possibility that the timing of episodes of Seasonal Affective Disorder (SAD) may be related to seasonal variations in the daily amount of sunlight—depression with smaller amounts of sunlight in the fall and winter, and feelings of well-being accompanying the greater amount of sunlight in the spring and summer.

To test this notion, it would seem to be obvious that an experiment should be conducted in which people suffering from SAD could be exposed to varying amounts of sunlight during the fall and winter months (the independent variable) and the changes in mood (the dependent measure) could be assessed. But how can the amount of sunlight be used as an independent variable? It is a naturally occurring variable that is not under the experimenter's control. Rosenthal and his associates found an elegant solution to this dilemma. They exposed clients suffering with SAD to daily doses of full-spectrum artificial light before dawn and after dusk. Dim light was used as the control condition and bright light was used as the experimental condition.

The design of the experimental (referred to as a "crossover study") had some unique features. Some clients were exposed to bright light for a week, followed by a week of withdrawal (no exposure to artificial light), then dim light for a week, which was again followed by a week of withdrawal. For other clients, dim light was used during the first week and bright light during the third week, thus controlling for any possible effects of the order in which the experimental and control conditions were administered. The clients' moods were rated prior to the study (baseline measures) and following each week of "treatment" by two raters using The Hamilton Rating Scale. The raters were purposely kept in the dark (usually referred to as "blind") concerning the interventions used with each subject so that their ratings would not be influenced by their knowledge of the condition administered during the preceding week.

We shall be looking at and analyzing the data of Rosenthal and his associates throughout this text and see how they arrived at the conclusion that 5 to 6 hours of daily light treatment produces an antidepressant effect in the majority of clients with SAD.

Source: Based on Rosenthal et al. (1984–1985), "Antidepressant Effects of Light in Seasonal Affective Disorder," *American Journal of Psychiatry,* **21**, 234–239.

nismic variables as independent measures. To illustrate, suppose we conducted a study in which we formed two groups—schizophrenic and normal subjects. The diagnosis would constitute the independent variable. Next, suppose we measured the levels of a particular neurotransmitter (the dependent variable) at a specific site in the central nervous system and found consistently lower levels among schizophrenics. Could we conclude that schizophrenia causes reduced levels of the neurotransmitter? As with the sunshine example, we could not. There are numerous other variables that covary with schizophrenia (e.g., dietary habits, life-styles, activity levels, etc.), any number of which could cause the drop in the neurotransmitter level. It is also possible that the level of neurotransmitter is a cause of the schizophrenia, but this study would not provide the answer.

To summarize, the key to ascertaining whether a study can qualify as a true experiment resides in the degree of control the researcher has over the manipulation of the independent variable. If the investigator can randomly assign the experimental conditions (the independent variable) to the subjects, the study is a true experiment and strong conclusions of causality may be drawn. If the independent variable cannot be manipulated by the researcher but is a naturally occurring variable that forms the basis for constituting the experimental groups, strong inferences of causality cannot be drawn. Although superficially resembling a true experiment, such investigations have more in common with the correlational study (see "Describing Relationships" earlier in this chapter). Moreover, they share both the assets and liabilities of correlational research.

Case examples are found throughout this book. Some will be correlational research; others will be correlational studies that have the surface appearance of an experiment; and still others will be true experiments. Much emphasis will be placed on the types of conclusions that can be drawn from such research.

1.6   A WORD TO THE STUDENT

The study of statistics need not and should not become a series of progressive exercises in calculated tedium. If it is approached with the proper frame of mind, statistics can be one of the most exciting fields of study; it has applications in virtually all areas of human endeavor and cuts across countless fields of study. H. G. Wells, the nineteenth-century prophet, remarked, "Statistical thinking will one day be as necessary for efficient citizenship as the ability to read and write." Keep this thought constantly in mind. The course will be much more interesting and profitable to you if you develop the habit of "thinking statistically."

A common misconception held by laypersons is that statistics is merely a rather sophisticated method for fabricating lies or falsifying our descriptions of reality. The authors do not deny that some unscrupulous individuals employ statistics for just such purposes. However, such uses of statistics are anathema to the behavioral scientist who is dedicated to the establishment of truth. From time to time, references will be made to various techniques that are used for lying with statistics. However, the purpose is not to instruct you in these techniques but to make you aware of the various *misuses* of statistical analysis so that you do not inadvertently "tell a lie," and so that you may be aware when others do.

When you see statistical information being exhibited, develop a healthy attitude of skepticism. Ask pertinent questions. When a national magazine sends a physically fit reporter to ten different diet doctors and he or she receives an unneeded prescription from each, do not jump to the conclusion that all diet doctors are frauds. Do not say, "After all, ten out of ten is a rather high proportion" and dismiss further inquiry at this point. Ask how the reporter obtained the sample. Was it at random, or is it possible that the doctors were selected on the basis of prior information indicating they were rather careless in their professional practices? Question constantly, but reserve judgment until you have the answers.

If you wish to enjoy statistical chicanery and not be victimized by it, watch commercials on television and turn a more jaundiced eye toward newspaper advertisements; scrutinize more labels on packaged products. It's a jungle of deceptive statistics out there. For example, in 1989, JONNY CAT litter had a large promise emblazoned on its 10-pound package: "25% MORE." In fine print, it modified the claim with "than 8 Lb. Bags."* This is an absolute truth, but what was the purpose? To elevate the minds of the purchasers by teaching them to calculate percentages? Or to raise false expectations that the customer would obtain a greater amount of cat litter at no cost increase?

There is also something you can do to maximize the benefits derived from this course. You should set aside a separate section of your notebook to keep permanent records of your solutions to exercises. You will find that these solutions will provide an invaluable review of statistical procedures. For some of you, their use will long outlive the completion of this course. Of more immediate concern, however, it will be necessary to refer back to these solutions as you explore more advanced terrains in the statistical landscape. Your notebook will reflect an important fact of statistical life: Researchers do not simply collect data, conduct a single statistical analysis of the data, and then share their results with others in the form of a published paper. Rather, they typically subject the same set of data to many levels of statistical analysis. It is hoped that this course will reflect the continuity among the various phases of ongoing research: Research design, descriptive and inferential data processing, and the ensuing conclusions are part of an organic whole. Something fundamental is lost if they are treated like discrete, independent elements of a jigsaw puzzle. To impart a flavor of real-world research, we shall follow a number

* Cited in *Consumer Reports*, September 1989, p. 603.

of research studies through all phases of their development, from their conception to a statement of conclusions that appear to be warranted by the statistical facts.

If you make statistical thinking an everyday habit, you will find not only that the study of statistics becomes more interesting, but also that the world you live in appears different and, perhaps, more interesting.

1.7 PUTTING IT ALL TOGETHER*

A dentist practicing in Charlottesville, Virginia, made an unusual observation. Two unrelated patients, 17 and 28 years of age, exhibited extensive pitting and erosion of the enamel on a number of their teeth. Such pitting is commonly found among individuals exposed to acid. An examination of their case histories revealed no medical, occupational, or dietary exposure to acid. However, they both shared one known characteristic in common: They were swimmers who trained regularly at the same club.

Wisely, the dentist reported his observations to what is widely recognized as the finest statistical-medical-behavioral sleuthing agency in the world, the Atlanta Center for Disease Control. In an attempt to identify additional cases, a survey questionnaire was mailed to all club members. Although the investigators would have preferred a census, not all members replied. The sample consisted of a total of 747 replies. The population to which the investigators wished to generalize was all members of the club. The data consisted of their self-observations. Members were considered to have indications of enamel erosion if they reported one or more of the following symptoms "a lot" or two or more of these symptoms "sometimes": "1) gritty or rough teeth; 2) transparent or yellow teeth; 3) 'chalky' white teeth; 4) painful teeth when chewing. Members were also considered cases if their dentists had clinically diagnosed enamel erosion during or after the summer of 1982." (p. 601)

Note that the sample consisted of two groups, those who met the various criteria of enamel erosion and those who did not. Since this variable is self-selected (the subjects are not randomly assigned to conditions by the investigator), the variable of interest is an organismic variable. Therefore, the study is not a true experiment. The data subjected to statistical analysis consisted of "head counts," that is, the number of members who presented evidence of enamel erosion versus the number who did not. Subsequently, different groups were identified in the sample (such as frequent swimmers versus nonfrequent swimmers), appropriate sample statistics were calculated, and inferential statistics were then invoked to ascertain if broad conclusions could be drawn concerning a possible cause of the pitting of dental enamel.

* Based on "Erosion and dental enamel among competitive swimmers—Virginia" (1983), *Morbidity and Mortality Weekly Report* **32**(28).

We will continue with this fascinating case of statistical sleuthing in Chapter 2.

CHAPTER SUMMARY

In this chapter, we saw that many people regard statistics as merely a collection of numerical facts. Scientists, however, stress the use of statistics as a method or tool concerned with the collection, organization, and analysis of numerical facts.

A distinction is made between two functions of the statistical methods, descriptive and inferential statistical analyses. The former is concerned with the organization and presentation of data in a convenient, usable, and communicable form. The latter addresses the problem of making broader generalizations or inferences from sample data to populations.

We also looked at the goals of research, which included gathering information, describing relationships, and establishing causality. We noted the important role of a systematic plan (the design of the study) in accomplishing these goals.

A number of terms commonly employed in statistical analysis were defined.

Finally, it was pointed out that statistics is frequently employed for the purpose of "telling lies." Such practices are inimical to the goal of establishing a factual basis for our conclusions and statistically based decisions. However, you should be aware of the techniques for telling statistical lies, so that you do not inadvertently tell one yourself or fail to recognize one when someone else does.

New terms or concepts that have been introduced in a chapter will be listed at the end of each chapter as well as in the margins at the points where they first appear. Some of these terms will be more precisely defined in other chapters and consequently may appear again.

TERMS TO REMEMBER

census	**population**
data	**random sample**
dependent variable	**research design**
descriptive statistics	**sample**
independent variable	**statistic**
inferential or inductive	**statistics**
statistics	**true experiment**
organismic variable	**variable**
parameter	

EXERCISES

1. Indicate whether each of the following constitutes a statistic, data, or an inference from statistics:

   a. A sample of 250 wage earners in Carlthorp City yielded a per-capita income of $14,460.

   b. Based on a random sample of 250 wage earners in Carlthorp City, it is believed that the average income of all wage earners in this city is about $14,500.

   c. Slugs from a .22 rifle traveled 0.8, 0.96, and 1.1 miles.

   d. My tuition payment this year was $4580; Sally's was $5285.

   e. The number of people viewing Monday night's television special was 23,500,000.

2. Many populations studied in experimental situations are theoretical in nature. Give some examples of theoretical populations that may be dealt with in research.

3. Indicate whether each of the following represents a variable or a constant:

   a. Number of days in the month of August.

   b. Number of shares traded on the New York Stock Exchange on various days of the year.

   c. Age of freshman entering college.

   d. Time it takes to complete an assignment.

   e. Age at which an individual is first eligible to vote in a national election.

   f. Scores obtained on a 100-item multiple-choice examination.

   g. Maximum score possible on a 100-item multiple-choice examination.

   h. Amount of money spent on books per year by students.

4. Professor Norman Yetman of the University of Kansas has concerned himself with possible economic discrimination against black athletes by the media.* He has analyzed their opportunities to appear on commercials, make guest appearances, and obtain off-season jobs. Two of the findings follow:

   a. In 351 commercials associated with New York sporting events in the autumn of 1966, black athletes appeared in 2.

   b. An analysis of media advertising opportunities of athletes on a professional football team in 1971 revealed that in a sample of 11 whites, 8 had an opportunity; 2 of 13 black athletes had a similar opportunity.

   Indicate whether these examples provide parameters, data, or inferences from statistics.

* *Source:* Gary Lehman, AP sports writer, August 22, 1975.

5. Football telecasters frequently point to tables like the following and offer comments such as: "Here are the half-time statistics. They really tell the story of this game!"

	Team A	Team B
First downs	6	10
Passes attempted	12	8
Passes completed	7	4
Yards passing	62	30
Yards running	78	104
Total yards	140	134
Turnovers	2	1
Time of possession	12'04"	17'56"

Are these numbers in fact statistics? If not, what are they? Data

Exercises 6 through 11 are based on the following: Imagine an industrial firm engaged in the production of hardware for the space industry. Among its products are machine screws that must be maintained within fine tolerances with respect to width. As part of its quality-control procedures, a number of screws are selected from the daily output and are carefully measured.

6. The screws selected for study constitute the
   a. Population.   **b.** Statistic.   **c.** Parameter.   **d.** Sample.

7. The width of a screw in such a sample constitutes the
   a. Statistic.   **b.** Variable.   **c.** Parameter.   **d.** Sample

8. The measurement of each screw constitutes the
   a. Data.   **b.** Sample.   **c.** Statistic.   **d.** Population.

9. The average width of the screws in the sample constitutes the
   a. Parameter.   **b.** Statistic.   **c.** Variable.   **d.** Data.

10. We wish to generalize the output of the sample to the
   a. Data.   **b.** Variable.   **c.** Statistic.   **d.** Population.

11. The average width of all screws produced in a day constitutes the
   a. Parameter.   **b.** Variable.   **c.** Data   **d.** Population.

12. Identify the sample and the population in the "Seasonal Affective Disorder" study (Statistics in Action 1.1).

13. Classify each of the following independent variables as (a) under the control of the experimenter, (b) organismic, or (c) a naturally occurring physical variable: 1) the amount of drug administered; 2) the season of the year; 3) the time of day; 4) the diagnostic categories of clients participating in a study; 5) the gender of experimental subjects 6) the amount of noise in an experimental setting;

7) the method of instruction; 8) the hours of food deprivation; 9) the scores on an IQ test; 10) the age at which toilet training will be introduced during infancy; 11) the age in infancy at which toilet training was previously introduced in adult subjects; 12) the mood of experimental subjects.

Basic Mathematical Concepts

2.1 INTRODUCTION

"I'm not much good in math. How can I possibly pass statistics?" The authors have heard these words from the lips of countless undergraduate students. For many, this is probably a concern that legitimately stems from prior discouraging experiences with mathematics. A brief glance through the pages of this text may only serve to increase this anxiety, since many of the formulas appear quite imposing to the novice and may seem impossible to master. Therefore, it is most important to set the record straight right at the beginning of the course.

You do not have to be a mathematical genius to master the statistical principles enumerated in this text. The amount of mathematical sophistication necessary for a firm grasp of the fundamentals of statistics is often exaggerated. As a matter of fact, statistics requires a good deal of arithmetic computation, sound logic, and a willingness to stay with a point until it is mastered. To paraphrase Carlyle, success in statistics is an infinite capacity for taking pains. Beyond these modest requirements, little is needed but the mastery of several algebraic and arithmetic procedures that most of you learned early in your high school careers. In this chapter, we review the grammar of mathematical notation, discuss several types of numerical scales, and adopt certain conventions for the rounding of numbers.

If you wish to brush up on your basic mathematics, Appendix A contains a review of all the math necessary to master this text.

2.2   THE GRAMMAR OF MATHEMATICAL NOTATION

Throughout this textbook, you will be learning new mathematical symbols. For the most part, we define these symbols when they first appear. However, there are three notations that will appear so frequently that their separate treatment at this time is justified. These notations are Σ (pronounced *sigma*), X, and N. However, while defining these symbols and showing their use, let's also review the grammar of mathematical notation.

It is not surprising to learn that many students become so involved in the forest of mathematical symbols, formulas, and operations, they fail to realize that mathematics has a form of grammar that closely parallels the spoken language. Thus, mathematics has its nouns, adjectives, verbs, and adverbs.

Mathematical Nouns   In grammar, we use nouns to represent persons, places, things, and ideas. In mathematics, our nouns are commonly quantities. The notation we use most frequently in statistics to represent quantity (or a score) is X, although we occasionally employ Y. In addition, X and Y are employed to identify variables; for example, if weight and height were two variables in a study, X might be used to represent weight and Y to represent height. Other frequently used "nouns" are the symbol c, which represents a constant, and the symbol N, which represents the number of scores or quantities with which we are dealing. Thus, if we have ten quantities,

$$N = 10$$

Mathematical Adjectives   In grammar, we use adjectives to describe or modify nouns. When we want to modify a mathematical noun, to identify it more specifically, we commonly employ subscripts. Thus, if we have a series of scores or quantities, we may represent them as X_1, X_2, X_3, X_4, and so on. We shall also frequently encounter X_i, in which the subscript may take on any value that we desire.

Mathematical Verbs   In grammar, we use verbs to denote actions related to nouns. In mathematics, notations that direct the reader to do something have the same characteristics as verbs in the spoken language. One of the most important "verbs" is the symbol already alluded to as Σ. This notation directs us to sum all quantities or scores following the symbol. Thus

$$\Sigma(X_1, X_2, X_3, X_4, X_5)$$

indicates that we should add together all these quantities from X_1 through X_5. Other "verbs" we encounter frequently are $\sqrt{}$, which directs us to find

BOX 2.1

VICTIMIZED BY VIOLENT CRIME: INCOME AND RACE

| | Race | |
Income Level	White (%)	Black (%)
Under $3,000	6.26	5.57
$3,000–7,499	4.12	5.18
$7,500–9,999	3.67	4.06
$10,000–14,999	3.53	4.12
$15,000–24,999	2.87	3.04
$25,000 & above	2.50	2.74

Much of data collected in the behavioral and social sciences consist of head counts—the number of people falling in one category as opposed to another category. We commonly use percentages or proportions to summarize such data. Various agencies of the criminal justice system rely heavily on the "head count" technique to summarize data on crimes and victims of crimes.

The accompanying table shows the rates of victimization by violent crime (rape, robbery, or assault) during 1982, broken down in terms of race and income level. The data are based on interviews with about 60,000 households and represent 128,000 occupants of age 12 and over. Note that, with the exception of the lowest income category, a greater percentage of blacks are victims of crime within each income level. Note also that there appears to be an inverse relationship between income level and victimization rate: the higher the income level is, the lower the rate of victimization is. This relationship appears to hold for both blacks and whites.

Source: P. A. Langan and C. A. Innes (1985), "The Risk of Violent Crime," Bureau of Justice Statistics Special Report, NCJ-97119.

the square root, and exponents (X^a), which tell us to raise a quantity to the indicated power. In mathematics, mathematical verbs are commonly referred to as *operators*.

Mathematical Adverbs In grammar, adverbs are used to describe or modify verbs. Likewise, in mathematics, adverbial notations are used to modify the verbs. We frequently find that the summation signs are modified by adverbial notations. Let's imagine that we want to indicate that the following quantities are to be added:

$$X_1 + X_2 + X_3 + X_4 + X_5 + \cdots + X_N$$

Symbolically, we would present these operations as follows:

$$\sum_{i=1}^{N} X_i$$

The notations above and below the summation sign indicate that i takes on the successive values from 1, 2, 3, 4, 5 up to N. Stated verbally, the notation reads: We should sum all quantities of X starting with $i = 1$ (that is, X_1) and proceeding through to $i = N$ (that is, X_N).

Sometimes this form of notation may direct us to add only selected quantities. Thus, if $X_1 = 7, X_2 = 5, X_3 = 9, X_4 = 8, X_5 = 11$, and $X_6 = 4$,

$$\sum_{i=2}^{5} X_i = X_2 + X_3 + X_4 + X_5$$
$$= 5 + 9 + 8 + 11 = 33$$

At other times, the notation may direct us to square each indicated value of the variable prior to summing. Thus,

$$\sum_{i=2}^{5} X_i^2 = X_2^2 + X_3^2 + X_4^2 + X_5^2$$
$$= 5^2 + 9^2 + 8^2 + 11^2$$
$$= 25 + 81 + 64 + 121 = 291$$

At still other times, we may be directed to sum all the values of the variable and then square this sum. Thus,

$$(\sum_{i=2}^{5} X_i)^2 = (X_2 + X_3 + X_4 + X_5)^2$$
$$= (5 + 9 + 8 + 11)^2$$
$$= 33^2$$
$$= 1089$$

Example   For all the values of X shown in the preceding examples, find

$$\text{a. } \sum_{i=1}^{N} X_i; \quad \text{b. } \sum_{i=1}^{N} X_i^2; \quad \text{c. } (\sum_{i=1}^{N} X_i)^2$$

$$\text{a. } \sum_{i=1}^{N} X_i^* = 7 + 5 + 9 + 8 + 11 + 4 = 44$$

$$\text{b. } \sum_{i=1}^{N} X_i^2 = 7^2 + 5^2 + 9^2 + 8^2 + 11^2 + 4^2$$

$$= 49 + 25 + 81 + 64 + 121 + 16 = 356$$

$$\text{c. } (\sum_{i=1}^{N} X_i)^2 = (7 + 5 + 9 + 8 + 11 + 4)^2 = (44)^2 = 1936$$

---

*When all values of the variable are to be summed, the usual practice is to drop the $i = 1$ below the summation sign and the N above the summation sign. It is understood that all values are included in the summation.

2.3 SUMMATION RULES

The summation sign is one of the most frequently used operators in statistics. Let's summarize a few of the rules governing the use of the summation sign.

Generalization 1   *The sum of a constant added together N times is equal to N times that constant.* Symbolically,

$$\sum_{i=1}^{N} c = Nc$$

Let c be a constant. Thus, if $c = 10$ and $N = 5$,

$$\sum_{i=1}^{N} c = (10 + 10 + 10 + 10 + 10) = 5(10) = 50$$

Similarly, if $\overline{X}$ is the constant and $\overline{X} = 20$, $N = 15$

$$\sum_{i=1}^{N} \overline{X} = N\overline{X} = (15)(20) = 300$$

Generalization 2   *Multiplying each value of a variable by a constant and then summing the products yields the same result as first summing the values and then multiplying the sum by the constant.* Symbolically,

$$\sum_{i=1}^{N} cX_i = c \sum_{i=1}^{N} X_i$$

Thus, if $c = 5$, and $X_1 = 2, X_2 = 3, X_3 = 4$

$$\sum_{i=1}^{N} cX_i = (5)(2) + (5)(3) + (5)(4) = 45$$

Also,

$$c \sum_{i=1}^{N} X_i = 5(2 + 3 + 4) = 45$$

Generalization 3   *Adding a constant to each value of a variable and then summing these new values yields the same result as first summing the values of the variable and then adding that sum to N times the constant.* Symbolically,

$$\sum_{i=1}^{N} (X_i + c) = \sum_{i=1}^{N} X_i + Nc$$

Imagine a sample in which $N = 3$ and $X_1 = 3$, $X_2 = 4$, and $X_3 = 6$. The sum of the values of the variable may be shown by

$$\sum_{i=1}^{N} X_i = X_1 + X_2 + X_3$$
$$= 3 + 4 + 6$$

To show the sum of the values of a variable when a constant $(c = 2)$ has been added to each

$$\sum_{i=1}^{N} (X_i + c) = (3 + c) + (4 + c) + (6 + c)$$
$$= 3 + 4 + 6 + (c + c + c)$$
$$= 3 + 4 + 6 + (2 + 2 + 2)$$
$$= 13 + 3c = 13 + 3(2)$$
$$= 19$$

Generalization 4 *Subtracting a constant from each value of a variable and then summing these new values yields the same result as first summing the values of the variable and then subtracting N times the constant from that sum. Symbolically,*

$$\sum_{i=1}^{N} (X_i - c) = \sum_{i=1}^{N} X_i - Nc$$

To show the sum of the values of a variable when a constant has been subtracted from each, let $X_1 = 3$, $X_2 = 4$, $X_3 = 6$, and $c = 2$.

$$\sum_{i=1}^{N} (X_i - c) = (3 - c) + (4 - c) + (6 - c)$$
$$= 3 + 4 + 6 - (c + c + c)$$
$$= 3 + 4 + 6 - 3c$$
$$= 13 - 3(2) = 7$$

Example These generalizations are often useful in statistics, particularly when we want to sum numbers with large quantitative values, for example,

$$X_1 = 100{,}465 \qquad X_2 = 100{,}467 \qquad X_3 = 100{,}469 \qquad X_4 = 100{,}472$$

To sum these four numbers, you can subtract 100,000 from each quantity, sum the remainder, and then add 4 times 100,000. Thus

$$\sum_{i=1}^{N} X_i = 465 + 467 + 469 + 472 + 4(100{,}000)$$
$$= 1873 + 400{,}000$$
$$= 401{,}873$$

2.4 TYPES OF NUMBERS AND SCALES

Cultural anthropologists, psychologists, and sociologists have repeatedly called attention to the common human tendency to explore the world that is remote from our primary experiences long before we have investigated that which is closest to us. Thus, while we were probing distant stars and describing with striking accuracy their apparent movements and interrelationships, we virtually ignored the very substance that gave us life: air (which we inhale and exhale over four hundred million times a year). In the authors' experience, a similar pattern exists in relation to the student's familiarity with numbers and his or her concepts of them. In our quantitatively oriented Western civilization, a student, Cory, employs and manipulates numbers long before he is expected to calculate the batting averages of the latest baseball hero. Nevertheless, ask him to define a number, or to describe the ways in which numbers are employed, and you are likely to be met with expressions of consternation and bewilderment. "I've never thought about it before," he will frequently reply. After a few minutes of soul searching and deliberation, he will probably reply something to the effect that numbers are symbols denoting amounts of things that can be added, subtracted, multiplied, and divided. These are all familiar arithmetic concepts, but do they exhaust all possible uses of numbers? At the risk of reducing our student to utter confusion, you may ask: "Is the symbol 7 on a baseball player's uniform such a number? What about your home address? Channel 2 on your television set? Do these numbers indicate amounts of things? Can they reasonably be added, subtracted, multiplied, or divided? Can you multiply the number on any football player's back by an other number and obtain a meaningful value?" A careful analysis of our use of numbers in everyday life reveals a very interesting fact: Most of the numbers we employ do not have the arithmetical properties we usually ascribe to them; they cannot be meaningfully added, subtracted, multiplied, and divided. A few examples are the serial number of a home appliance, a zip code number, a telephone number, a home address, an automobile registration number, and the numbers on a book in the library.

The important point is that numbers are used in a variety of ways to achieve many different ends. Much of the time, these ends do not include the representation of an amount or a quantity. In fact, there are three fundamentally different ways in which numbers are used.

1. To name (**nominal numbers**)
2. To represent position in a series (**ordinal numbers**)
3. To represent quantity (**cardinal numbers**)

Measurement is the assignment of numbers to objects or events according to sets of predetermined (or arbitrary) rules. The different levels of measurement that we shall discuss represent different levels of numerical

Nominal Numbers: Numbers used to name.

Ordinal Numbers: Numbers used to represent position, or order, in a series.

Cardinal Numbers: Numbers used to represent quantity.

Measurement: The assignment of numbers to objects or events according to sets of predetermined (or arbitrary) rules.

information contained in a set of observations (data), such as a series of house numbers, the order of finish in a horse race, a set of IQ scores, or the price per share of various stocks. The type of scale obtained depends on the kinds of mathematical operations that can be legitimately performed on the numbers. In the social sciences, we encounter measurements at every level.

It should be noted that there are other schemes for classifying numbers and the ways they are used. We use the nominal–ordinal–cardinal classification because it best handles the types of data we obtain in the behavioral sciences. As you will see, we count, we place in relative position, and we obtain quantitative scores. We should also note that assignment to categories is not always clear-cut or unambiguous. There are times when even experts cannot agree. To illustrate: Is the number in your street address nominal or ordinal? The answer depends on your need. For certain purposes it can be considered nominal, such as when it is used as the *name* of a dwelling. At other times it can be considered ordinal, since the numbers place your house in a position relative to other houses on the block. Thus 08 may be to the left of 12 and to the right of 04.

The fundamental requirements of observation and measurement are acknowledged by all the physical and social sciences as well as by any modern-day corporation interested in improving its competitive position. The things we observe are often referred to as **variables.** Any particular observation is called the *value of the variable*. If we are studying the number of days of hospitalization among different kinds of patients, we are looking at two different variables—the classification of the patients (an organismic variable used as the independent variable) and the time each patient remained hospitalized. As we can see, the classification variable is identified by name rather than by a numerical value. On the other hand, the time variable is expressed as a numerical value. Thus, if a patient spends 8½ days in the hospital, the value of the variable is 8.50. As we have seen, this time measure is identified as the dependent variable.

> **Variable:** A characteristic or phenomenon that may take on different values.

Nominal Scales

When the majority of people think about measurement, they probably conjure up mental images of wild-eyed men in white suits manipulating costly and incredibly complex instruments in order to obtain precise measures of the variable they are studying. Actually, however, not all measurements are this precise or this quantitative. If we were to study the sex of the offspring of female rats that had been subjected to atomic radiation during pregnancy, sex would be the variable we would observe. There are only two possible values of this variable: male and female (barring an unforeseen mutation that produced a third sex!). If we were using a computer to analyze our results, we might assign a number to each value of the variable. Thus, male might be assigned a zero and female a one. Our data would consist of the number of observations in each of these two classes. Note that we do not think of this variable as representing an ordered series of values, such as height, weight, speed, and so on. An organism that is female does not have any more of the variable, sex, than one that is male.

Observations of unordered variables constitute a very low level of measurement and are referred to as a **nominal scale** of measurement. As previously seen, we may assign numerical values to represent the various classes in a nominal scale, but these numbers have no quantitative properties. They serve only to identify the class.

The data employed with nominal scales consist of frequency counts or tabulations of the number of occurrences in each class of the variable under study (see Box 2.2). In the aforementioned radiation study, our frequency counts of male and female progeny would comprise our data. Such data are often referred to interchangeably as **frequency data, enumerative data, attribute data,** or **categorical data.** The only mathematical relationships germane to nominal scales are those of equivalence (=) or of nonequivalence (≠). Thus, a particular person or object either has the characteristic that defines the class (=) or does *not* have that characteristic (≠).

Nominal Scale: Observations of unordered variables.

Frequency Data (Attribute Data, Categorical Data, Enumerative Data): Tabulations of the number of occurrences in each class of a given variable.

Ordinal Scales

When we move into the next higher level of measurement, we encounter variables in which the classes *do* represent an ordered series of relationships. Thus, the classes in **ordinal scales** not only are different from one another (the characteristic defining nominal scales) but also stand in some kind of *relation* to one another. More specifically, the relationships are expressed in terms of the algebra of inequalities; a is less than b ($a < b$) or a is greater than b ($a > b$). Thus, the relationships encountered are: greater, faster, more intelligent, more mature, more prestigious, more disturbed, and so on. The numerals employed in connection with ordinal scales contain more quantitative information than nominal scales but less than interval or ratio scales. They indicate position in an ordered series, not "how much" of a difference exists between successive positions on the scale.

Ordinal Scale: Scale in which the classes stand in a relationship to one another that is expressed in terms of the algebra of inequalities: a is less than b or a is greater than b (this statement in albegraic notation is written $a < b$ or $a > b$).

We shall be looking at these data again in Chapter 8 when we obtain the correlation between the rankings of response strategies of these two occupational groups.

Examples of ordinal scaling include the following: rank ordering of baseball players according to their "value to the team," rank ordering of potential candidates for political office according to their "popularity" with people, and rank ordering of officer candidates in terms of their "leadership" qualities. Note that the ranks are assigned according to the ordering of individuals within the class. Thus, the most popular candidate may receive the rank of 1, the next most popular may receive the rank of 2, and so on, down to the least popular candidate. It does not in fact make any difference whether or not we give the most popular candidate the highest numerical rank or the lowest, *so long as we are consistent in placing the individuals*

BOX 2.2

PARADOXICAL PERCENTAGES

Hypothetical Data Showing the Number of Male and Female Applicants for Various Categories, the Number Accepted, and the Percent Accepted.

Job Category Teacher	No. Appl.	Male No. Accp.	% Accp.	No. Appl.	Female No. Accp.	% Accp.
Grades 13–14 (2-yr coll)	150	30	20	40	16	40
Grades 11–12	200	70	35	50	35	70
Grades 9–10	100	15	15	50	15	30
Grades K–8	50	2	4	600	48	8
Total	500	117	23	740	114	15

A common form of data collection involves the "head count" technique, i.e., recording the number of individuals, objects, or observations that fall into various categories. To make sense of these data, the head counts are frequently converted to proportions or percentages. However, under certain circumstances, these percentages can be deceptive and misleading.

The following is an excerpt from *Winning with Statistics* that illustrates the problem of the Paradoxical Percentages.

Let me show you some hypothetical data in which the proportion of females accepted in each job category is actually higher than the proportion of males accepted in each of these

---

Interval Scale:
Quantitative scale that requires a constant unit of measurement and permits the use of arithmetic operations. The zero point in this scale is arbitrary.

Ratio Scale: Same as interval scale, except that there is a true zero point.

accurately with respect to their relative position in the ordered series. By popular usage, however, the lower numerical ranks (1st, 2d, 3d) are usually assigned to those "highest" on the scale. Thus, the winning candidate receives the rank of "first" in a Miss America or Mr. America pageant; the pennant winner is "first" in its respective league. The fact that we are not completely consistent in our ranking procedures is illustrated by such popular expressions as "first-class idiot" and "first-class scoundrel."

Interval and Ratio Scales

Finally, the highest level of measurement in science is achieved with scales employing cardinal numbers (**interval** and **ratio scales**). The numerical categories. Nevertheless, when the proportions of males and females accepted for the various positions are combined over all of the categories, it is found, as if by magic, that the females have a much lower overall proportion of acceptances. So if you were to look at the overall figures you'd be led inexorably to the conclusion that there is discrimination against females. However, if you looked at the same evidence category by category you'd be led to precisely the opposite conclusion, namely, that there is discrimination against males. Let's look at these data in the table above.

Take a careful look at the table. It has been purposely constructed so that in every single category the precentage of women accepted is double the percentage of men accepted. Nevertheless, when all of the applicants among the males are combined, and the number is divided into the number of males accepted, and the same thing is done with the female category, you find that in fact the overall percentage of males accepted (23%) is higher than the overall percentage of females accepted (15%). How is it possible to obtain this sort of numerical sleight-of-hand? Very simple. If you look at

the table again you will find that most of the female applications, 600, were for positions in Grades K through 8. Conversely, very few of the male applicants competed for those positions. It turns out that the number of openings for grades K through 8 is the smallest. What you have then is a situation in which an overwhelming majority of the women were applying for "difficult-to-get" positions. On the other hand, most of the men were applying for positions that were more plentiful. When you combine all of these categories in which there are different numbers of applicants for different positions, the lower percentage of females in the K–8 group is devastating to the female teachers. Why? Better than 80% of the female teachers applied for the very positions where the number of openings was extremely low in relation to the number of applicants.

There is a moral here. Better to apply for a position where few are called but many (relatively speaking) are chosen than to seek entrance where many are called but few are chosen.

Source: R. P. Runyon, *Winning with Statistics.* Reading, Mass.: Addison-Wesley, 1977.

values associated with these scales are truly quantitative and therefore permit the use of arithmetic operations such as adding, subtracting, multiplying, and dividing. Interval and ratio scales require a constant unit of measurement, such as inches, pounds, or seconds. Thus, equal differences between points on any part of the scale are equal. For example, the difference between 4 feet and 2 feet is the same as the difference between 9231 and 9229 feet.

In ordinal scaling, as you will recall, we cannot claim that the *difference* between first and second place is the same as the *difference* between second and third place.

There are two types of scales based upon cardinal numbers: interval scales and ratio scales. The interval scale differs from the ratio scale in

CASE EXAMPLE 2.1

Help Is Where You Find It

Psychological help and counseling is not the exclusive province of people specifically trained to give such help. Members of some occupational categories are necessarily involved in interpersonal relationships with their clients, often involving intimate revelations by the clients and attempts to render verbal assistance by the help-giver. One aspect of this study dealt with the response strategies of four different occupational groups (hairdressers, lawyers, supervisors, and bartenders) when clients sought help and advice concerning personal problems. The various strategies employed by members of each of these groups were rank-arranged in an ordinal scale from most frequent to least frequent. Table 2.1 shows the ordinal ranking of 11 different strategies among hairdressers and bartenders.

Table 2.1 reveals some interesting differences as well as similarities in the help-giving strategies of these two professions. Both rate offering support, trying to be lighthearted, and just listening high on their hierarchy of response strategies. The most notable disagreement involves telling the clients to count their blessings. Hairdressers are more inclined to adopt this strategy than bartenders.

TABLE 2.1 Ordinal Position of Response Strategies of Hairdressers and Bartenders when Clients Seek Advice and Counsel. A Rank of 1 Corresponds to the Most Frequently Used Strategy and 11 to the Least Frequently Used Strategy

Strategy	Hairdressers	Bartenders
Offer support and sympathy	1	3
Try to be lighthearted	2	2
Just listen	3	1
Present alternatives	4	4
Tell person to count blessings	5	10
Share personal experiences	6	5
Try not to get involved	7	6
Give advice	8	7
Ask questions	9	9
Try to get person to talk to someone else	10	11
Try to change topic	11	8

Source: Based on Emory L. Cowen (1982), "Help Is Where You Find It," *American Psychologist,* **37**(4), 385–395.

terms of the location of the zero point. In an interval scale, the zero point is arbitrarily determined. It does not represent the complete absence of the attribute being measured. Our calendar is an example of an interval scale; the year zero does not mean that there was no time before this year. We refer to the years prior to zero as B.C. and to those after zero as A.D. In contrast, the zero in a ratio scale does represent the complete absence of the attribute of interest. Zero length means no length. As a consequence of this difference in the location of the zero point, only the ratio scale permits us to make statements concerning the ratios of numbers in the scale; for example, 4 feet are to 2 feet as 2 feet are to 1 foot. The difference between these scales can be clarified by examining a well-known interval scale, for example, the Celsius scale of temperature. Incidentally, the Fahrenheit scale of temperature is also an interval scale with zero set at 32 degrees below the freezing point of water at sea level.

The zero point on the Celsius scale does not represent the complete absence of heat. In fact, it is merely the point at which water freezes at sea level and therefore has an arbitrary zero point. Actually, the true zero point is known as *absolute zero*, which is approximately $-273°$ Celsius. Now, if we were to say that 40°C is to 20°C as 20°C is to 10°C, it would appear that we were making a correct statement. Actually, we are completely wrong, since 40°C really represents $273° + 40° = 313°$ of temperature; 20°C represents $273° + 20° = 293°$ of temperature; and 10°C represents $273° + 10° = 283°$ of temperature. The ratio of 313 is to 293 as 293 is to 283 clearly does not hold. These facts may be better appreciated graphically. In Figure 2.1 we have represented all three temperature readings as distances from the true zero point, which is $-273°C$. From this graph we see that the distance from $-273°C$ to 40°C is not twice as long as the distance from $-273°C$ to 20°C. Thus, 40°C is not twice as warm as 20°C, and the ratio 40°C is to 20°C as 20°C is to 10°C does not hold.

Apart from the difference in the nature of the zero point, interval and ratio scales have the same properties and will be treated alike throughout the text.

It should be clear that one of the most sought-after goals of the behavioral scientist is to achieve measurements that are at least interval in nature. Indeed, interval scaling is assumed for most of the statistical tests reported

FIGURE 2.1 Relationships of various points on the Celsius scale to absolute zero.

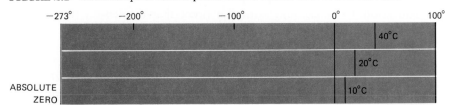

in this book. Although whether many of our scales achieve interval measurement is debatable, most behavioral scientists are willing to make the assumption that they do.

One of the characteristics of higher-order scales is that they can readily be transformed into lower-order scales. Thus, the outcome of a 1-mile foot race may be expressed as time scores (ratio scale), for example, 3:56, 3:58, and 4:02. The time scores may then be transformed into an ordinal scale, for instance, first-, second-, and third-place finishers. However, the reverse transformation is not possible. If we know only the order of finishing a race, for example, we cannot express the outcome in terms of a ratio scale (time scores). Although it is permissible to transform scores from higher-level to lower-level scales, it is not usually recommended, since precise quantitative information is lost in the transformation.

2.5 CONTINUOUS AND DISCONTINUOUS VARIABLES

Imagine that you are given the problem of trying to determine the number of children per American family. You scale of measurement would start with zero (no children) and would proceed by *increments of 1* to perhaps 15 or 20. Note that in moving from one value on the scale to the next, we proceed by *whole numbers* rather than by fractional amounts. Thus, a family has either 0, 1, 2, or more children. In spite of the statistical abstraction that the American family averages approximately one and three-quarters children, the authors do not know a single couple that has achieved this marvelous state of family planning. Such variables are referred to as

Discontinuous Variables (Discrete Variables): Variables that contain gaps where no real values of the variable occur, such as 2.63 children.

discontinuous or **discrete.** They are characterized by gaps in which no real values of the variable are found. Discrete variables are characterized by equality of *counting units*. Thus, if we are studying the number of children in a family, each child is equal with respect to providing one counting unit. Such variables involve cardinality insofar as they permit arithmetic operations such as adding, subtracting, multiplying, and dividing. Thus, we can say that a family with four children has twice as many children as a family with two children. Observations of discrete variables are always exact so long as the counting procedures are accurate. Examples of discontinuous variables are the pulse rate (number of beats per minute) of human adults, the number of white blood cells counted in one square centimeter, the number of alpha particles observed in a second, and so on.

You should not assume from the preceding discussion that discrete variables necessarily involve *only* whole numbers. However, most of the discontinuous variables used by behavioral and social scientists are usually expressed in terms of whole numbers. For example, a psychologist tabulates the number of people with varying pulse rates, or the number of kindergarten children from family units of different sizes. In each of these examples we are clearly dealing with values that proceed by whole numbers.

In contrast, a **continuous variable** is one in which there are no gaps in the values of the variable; there are an unlimited number of *possible* values between any two adjacent values on the scale. Thus, if the variable is height measured in inches, then 4 inches and 5 inches would be two adjacent values of the variable. However, there can be an infinite number of intermediate values, such as 4.5 inches or 4.7 inches. If the variable is height measured in tenths of inches, then 4.5 inches and 4.6 inches are two adjacent values of the variable, but there can *still* be an infinite number of intermediate values, such as 4.53 inches or 4.59 inches.

Is is important to note that, although our measurement of discrete variables is always exact, our measurement of continuous variables is always approximate. If we are measuring the height of American males, for example, any particular measurement is inexact because it is always possible to imagine a measuring stick that would provide greater accuracy. Thus, if we reported the height of a man to be 68 inches, we would mean 68 inches give or take one-half an inch. If our scale is accurate to the nearest tenth, we can always imagine another scale providing greater accuracy, say, to the nearest hundredth or thousandth of an inch. The basic characteristic of continuous variables, then, is equality of *measuring units*. Thus, if we are measuring in inches, 1 inch is always the same throughout the scale. Examples of continuous variables are length, velocity, time, weight, and so on.

Let's consider one additional point. Often, continuous variables are expressed as whole numbers and therefore appear to be discontinuous. Thus, you may say that you are 5′8″ tall and weigh 150 pounds, your father is 5′9″ and weighs 193 pounds, and your mother is 5′3″ and weighs 123 pounds. However, the decision to express heights to the nearest inch and weights to the nearest pound was yours. You could just as easily have expressed height to the nearest fraction of an inch and weight to the nearest ounce. You do not have such a choice when reporting things such as the number of children in a family. These *must* occur as whole numbers.

Continuous Variables, Errors of Measurement, and "True Limits" of Numbers

In our preceding discussion, we pointed out that continuously distributed variables can take on an unlimited number of intermediate values. Therefore, we can never specify the exact value for any particular measurement, since it is possible that a more sensitive measuring instrument can slightly increase the accuracy of our measurements. For this reason, we stated that numerical values of continuously distributed variables are always approximate. However, it is possible to specify the limits within which the true value falls; for example, the **true limits** of a value of a continuous variable are equal to that number plus or minus one-half of the unit of measurement. Let's look at examples. You have a bathroom scale that is calibrated in

Continuous Variables: Variables in which values of the variable can occur at *any* point along the scale of values, such as 22.5634 pounds.

True Limits of a Number: The true limits of a value of a continuous variable are equal to that number plus or minus one-half of the unit of measurement.

terms of pounds. When you step on the scale, the pointer will usually be a little above or below a pound marker. However, you report your weight to the nearest pound. Thus, if the pointer were approximately three-quarters of the distance between 212 pounds and 213 pounds, you would report your weight as 213 pounds. It would be understood that the "true" limit of your weight, assuming an accurate scale, falls between 212.5 pounds and 213.5 pounds. If, on the other hand, you are measuring the weight of whales, you would probably have a fairly gross unit of measurement, say, 100 pounds. Thus, if you reported the weight of a whale at 32,000 pounds, you would mean that the whale weighed between 31,950 pounds and 32,050 pounds. If the scale were calibrated in terms of 1000 pounds, the true limits of the whale's weight would be between 31,500 pounds and 32,500 pounds.

2.6 ROUNDING

Imagine that you have some data that, in the course of conducting a statistical analysis, require that you divide one number into another. There will be innumerable occasions in this course when you will be required to perform this arithmetic operation. In some cases, the answer will be a value that extends to an endless number of decimal places. For example, if you were to express the fraction 1/3 in decimal form, the result would be 0.33333 + . It is obvious that you cannot extend this series of numbers *ad infinitum*. You must terminate at some point and assign a value to the last number in the series that best reflects the remainder. When you do this, two problems will arise:

1. To how many decimal places do we carry the final answer?
2. How do we decide on the last number in the series?

The answer to the first question is usually given in terms of the number of significant figures. However, there are many good reasons for not following the mathematical stricture to the letter. For simplicity and convenience, we have adopted the following policy with respect to rounding.

> In obtaining the final answer, we should round to two more places than were in the original data. We should not round the intermediate steps.*

Thus, if the original data were in whole-numbered units, we would round our answer to the second decimal. If in tenths, we would round to the third decimal, and so forth.

* Since many of you will be using calculators, you should be aware of minor differences that may occur in the final answer. These differences may be attributed to the fact the different calculators will carry the intermediate steps to a different number of decimal places. Thus, a calculator that carries the intermediate steps to 4 places will probably produce a slightly different final answer from one that carries to 14 places.

Once we have decided the number of places to carry our final figures, we are still left with the problem of representing the last digit. Fortunately, the rule governing the determination of the last digit is perfectly simple and explicit. If the remainder beyond that digit is greater than 5, increase that digit to the next higher number. If the remainder beyond that digit is less than 5, allow that digit to remain as it is. Let's look at a few illustrations. In each case, we shall round to the second decimal place:

6.546 becomes 6.55
6.543 becomes 6.54
1.967 becomes 1.97
1.534 becomes 1.53

You may ask, "In those illustrations, what happens if the digit at the third decimal place is 5?"

You should first determine whether or not the digit is exactly 5. If it is 5 plus the slightest remainder, the preceding rule holds and you must add one to the digit at the second decimal place. If it is almost, but not quite 5, the digit at the second decimal place remains the same. If it is *exactly 5 with no remainder*, then an arbitrary convention that is accepted universally by mathematicians applies: Round the digit at the second decimal place to the *nearest even* number. If this digit is already even, then it is not changed. If it is odd, then *add* 1 to this digit to make it even. Let's look at several illustrations in which we round to the second decimal place:

6.545001 becomes 6.55 Why?
6.545000 becomes 6.54 Why?
1.9652   becomes 1.97 Why?
0.00500 becomes 0.00 Why?
0.02500 becomes 0.02 Why?
16.89501 becomes 16.90 Why?

2.7 RATIOS, FREQUENCIES, PROPORTIONS, AND PERCENTAGES

Of all the statistics in everyday use, perhaps the most misunderstood and misused involve the representation of ratios, proportions, and percentages. These statistics also provide the most fertile grounds for misleading and outright fraudulent statements. It is possible for a congressman, seeking to impress "the people back home" with his vital interest in consumer affairs, to charge that a given drug company is making a 300% profit on its sales to retail outlets, while the drug company, looking at precisely the same statistical facts, may reply with righteous indignation that its profit is only 75%. How could this come about? Let's see.

Assume that the cost to manufacture a given drug is $2 per gross. In turn, a gross is sold to the retailer at $8. The ratio of profit ($8 − $2 = $6)

STATISTICS IN ACTION 2.1

Curiosity is dangerous to more than cats: Finding percentage in terms of total, column, and rows

Take the problem of the seemingly insatiable curiosity of children. Their explorations of the worlds of sight, smell, sound, and touch often get them into serious difficulties. Look at the following table. Here we find a summary of a study conducted on 950 children who had ingested products containing hydrocarbons (Anas et al., 1981). From the results, we can learn what dangerous hydrocarbons are most commonly ingested by children and how often hospitalization is required. Armed with such knowledge, community agencies can often undertake educational and preventive programs that are targeted toward both careless adults and offending substances.

By looking down the "row totals" column, we see that furniture polish is the most frequent offender, with gasoline and lighter fluid running a rather distant second and third. Reading across the column totals, we see that most cases (800) do not require hospitalization.

Frequency of Children Hospitalized and Not Hospitalized Following Ingestion of Substances Containing Hydrocarbons

Substance Ingested	Not Hospitalized Frequency	Hospitalized Frequency	Row Totals
Cleaning fluids	24	6	30
Furniture polishes	312	48	360
Gasoline	128	28	156
Kerosene	72	12	84
Lighter fluid	112	23	135
Paint thinner	88	23	111
Other	64	10	74
Column totals	800	150	950

Prepare a table showing:

a. The percentage of the grand (or overall) total in each cell of this two-variable frequency table.

b. The percentage of cases within each column subcategory.

c. The percentage of cases within each row subcategory.

d. Looking at the raw data, identify the substance that accounts for the largest number of hospitalization cases. Which accounts for the least number?

e. Looking at table a in the answers, identify the substance that accounts for the greatest percentage of hospitalization cases. Which accounts for the lowest percentage?

f. Looking at table b, identify the substance that produces the highest rate of hospitalization. Which produces the lowest rate?

g. Now look at table c. Relative to the number ingesting each substance, which leads to the greatest percentage of hospitalizations? Which leads to the lowest percentage of hospitalizations?

h. Considering all the ways of finding percentages, which substances does it appear to be most important to "keep out of the reach of children"?

ANSWERS
a. Percentages in terms of totals

Substance Ingested	Not Hospitalized, Percentage	Hospitalized, Percentage	Row Percentage
Cleaning fluids	3	1	3
Furniture polishes	33	5	38
Gasoline	13	3	16
Kerosene	8	1	9
Lighter fluid	12	2	14
Paint thinner	9	2	12
Other	7	1	8
Column percentage	85	15	100

b. Percentages in terms of columns

Substance Ingested	Not Hospitalized, Percentage	Hospitalized, Percentage	Row Percentage
Cleaning fluids	3	4	3
Furniture polishes	39	32	38
Gasoline	16	19	16
Kerosene	9	8	9
Lighter fluid	14	15	14
Paint thinner	11	15	12
Other	8	7	8
Column percentage	100	100	100

c. Percentages in terms of rows

Substance Ingested	Not Hospitalized, Percentage	Hospitalized, Percentage	Row Percentage
Cleaning fluids	80	20	100
Furniture polishes	87	13	100
Gasoline	82	18	100
Kerosene	86	14	100
Lighter fluid	83	17	100
Paint thinner	79	21	100
Other	86	14	100

d. Furniture polish produces the greatest number of hospitalizations and cleaning fluids the least. Looking only at the raw data, we might be tempted to assert that furniture polish is the most dangerous substance and cleaning fluid the least.

e. Furniture polish produces the greatest percentage of hospitalizations and cleaning fluids the least.

f. When we find percentages in terms of the column variable, "Hospitalized percentage," we still find that ingesting furniture polish leads to the greatest number of hospitalizations and cleaning fluids the least.

g. When we look at the rates of hospitalization *relative to the number ingesting each substance* (percentages across), the picture of potential danger suddenly reverses itself. We now see that cleaning fluids are a close second to paint thinner in terms of rate of hospitalization (20% and 21% respectively). In contrast, furniture polishes lead to the lowest rate of hospitalization relative to the large number of children who ingest furniture polishes.

h. From the point of view of accessibility, it is apparent that many children have easy access to furniture polishes (38% of all cases involved furniture polishes). However, furniture polishes produced a relatively low rate of hospitalization among children ingesting these products (13%). Paint thinner is both fairly readily accessible (12% of all cases) and leads to a higher rate of hospitalization among those who ingest it (21%). Cleaning fluids are least accessible (3% of all ingestions) but lead to a high rate of hospitalization among children who ingest them (20%). So, you see, there is no simple answer except "All these substances are potentially dangerous—some because of the sheer numbers of children who ingest them and others because of their inherent danger once ingested."

Source: N. Anas, V. Namasonthi, and M. Ginsburg (1981), "Criteria for Hospitalizing Children Who Have Ingested Products Containing Hydrocarbons," *Journal of the American Medical Association,* **246,** 8.

to manufacturing cost is 6:2 or 3:1. Stating this ratio as a percentage (multiplying by 100), we get 300%. It would appear that the congressman is correct. But the drug company replies, "The selling price is $8 and our profit is $6, the ratio of profit to selling price is 6:8 or 0.75. Stated as a percentage, our profit is 75% of the selling price. When considering the cost of research and development and all the inherent financial risks, the profit is not excessive."

Which statement better describes the facts? Actually, both statements are correct. The confusion stems from the fact that two different values ($2 and $8) have been employed as the base, or denominator, in arriving at the final percentage figures. There is nothing wrong with either procedure *as long as it is made perfectly clear* which base has been employed in the initial calculations. Knowing the base, we can freely move from one to the other with little confusion. Thus, if we know that the congressman has used the production cost as the base, we can employ elementary algebra to translate this statement to one employing selling price as a base: Let

$$x = \text{production cost} = \$2$$
$$y = \text{selling price} = \$8$$

The following equation represents the percentage of profit, employing production cost as a base:

$$\frac{y - x}{x} \times 100 = \text{percent of profit (employing production cost as a base)}$$

Using these values and substituting in the equation, we find that

$$\frac{y - x}{x} \times 100 = \frac{8 - 2}{2} \times 100 = 300\%$$

The formula for calculating percentage of profit employing *selling price* as a base is

$$\frac{y - x}{y} \times 100 = \text{percent of profit (related to selling price)}$$

Substituting into the preceding formula, we obtain

$$\frac{y - x}{y} \times 100 = \frac{6}{8} \times 100 = 75\%$$

CASE EXAMPLE 2.2

Do We Help Beauty or the Beast?

Much research has been done on the effects of physical attractiveness on various aspects of our behavior. In this field study, the objective was to ascertain whether favoritism toward the physically attractive generalizes to behavioral

TABLE 2.2   Number Helping When the Applicant Is an Attractive or Unattractive Female (Whites and Blacks Combined) and the Subject Is a Male

Helping Response	Characteristics of Target		
	Attractive	Unattractive	Total
Helped	52	35	87
Did not help	62	71	133
Total	114	106	220

helping responses. Graduate school applications, complete with mailing address, envelope, and stamps, were "inadvertently" left in a number of telephone booths at a busy metropolitan airport. Pictures of the applicant were prominently displayed, some chosen to be physically attractive and others to be unattractive. Thus, physical attractiveness was the independent variable. The dependent response was whether or not the subject engaged in helping behavior, defined as "mailing the application or taking the envelope to one of the airport ticket counters." The results of one aspect of the study are summarized in Table 2.2.

In this study, these are two nominal categories—the characteristics of the target person (either attractive or unattractive) and the nature of the helping response (either the subject engaged in or did not engage in helping behavior). Three distinctively different sets of proportions or percentages may be constructed from these two-variable frequency tables, namely

1. Proportions or percentages in terms of the total
2. Proportions or percentages within each class of the column variable
3. Proportions or percentages within each class of the row variable

Let's look at each.

When we divide each frequency count in Table 2.2 by the total number of cases (N), we obtain a proportion of the total within each cell as well as the proportions within each class of both the row and column variables. If we wish to obtain the corresponding percentages, we multiply each proportion by 100. Percentage expressed in terms of totals are useful in providing an overall picture of the way the cases are distributed within each cell and within each variable. To illustrate, an examination of Table 2.3 shows that 40% of the total sample received help. Looking down the column headed by "Unattractive," we find that 16% of the total sample was both unattractive and helped, whereas double that percentage (32%) was both unattractive and not helped. However, caution should be observed when interpreting this difference. The substantially higher percentage of subjects who did not help *unattractive subjects* could merely reflect the difference in the *total sample* of subjects who did not help *any* target person, regardless of attractiveness.

TABLE 2.3   Relative Frequency Table in Which We Have Taken Percentages in Terms of Totals, Dividing Each Cell and Marginal Frequency by N and Multiplying the Resulting Proportions by 100*

	Characteristics of Target Person		
Helping Response	**Attractive (%)**	**Unattractive (%)**	**Row Percentage (%)**
Helped	24 (52)	16 (35)	40 (87)
Did not help	28 (62)	32 (71)	60 (133)
Column percentage	52 (114)	48 (106)	100 (220)

* The number of subjects in each cell, row, and column total is given in parentheses.

To obtain a handle on how the helping response is distributed in terms of attractiveness, we would calculate the percentages *within* each class of the column variable (see Table 2.4). To do this, we divide the cell frequency within each column by the corresponding column total and multiply by 100. Thus, for the cell corresponding to "attractive–helped," the percentage is 52/114 × 100 = 46%. This means that, among the 114 subjects who found the application of an attractive target person, 46% provided help and 54% did not.

Now contrast these percentages with those in the unattractive subcategory. Here we see that of 116 subjects who found the application of an unattractive target person, only 33% provided help, whereas 67% did not. Noting these apparently large differences, we might be tempted to go beyond the sample findings and conclude that the likelihood of receiving help depends on the physical attractiveness of the target person. However, we shall reserve this judgment until Chapter 17, when we ask the inferential question, "Is this difference in sample percentages sufficiently large to justify the conclusion that the general population of attractive people are more likely than their unattractive counterparts to receive help?"

TABLE 2.4   Relative Frequency Table in Which We Obtain the Percentages Within Each Column by Dividing Each Cell Frequency by Its Corresponding Column Total and Multiplying by 100*

	Characteristics of Target Person	
Helping Response	**Attractive (%)**	**Unattractive (%)**
Helped	46 (52)	33 (35)
Did not help	54 (62)	67 (71)
Column percentage	100 (114)	100 (106)

* The number of subjects in each cell and column is given in parentheses.

TABLE 2.5   Relative Frequency Table in Which We Obtain the Percentages Across Each Row by Dividing Each Cell Frequency by Its Corresponding Row Total and Multiplying by 100*

| | Characteristics of Target Person | | |
Helping Response	Attractive (%)	Unattractive (%)	Row Percentage (%)
Helped	60 (52)	40 (35)	100 (87)
Did not help	47 (62)	53 (71)	100 (133)

* The number of subjects in each cell and row are given in parentheses.

Finally, given the subcategory of subjects who helped (row 1, Table 2.5), we may wish to know the percent of subjects who found the application of a target person who was attractive versus unattractive. Alternatively, given those who did not help (row 2), we may ask how the percentages are distributed in each of the subcategories of attractiveness. We obtain answers to these queries by finding the percentages across rows. As we can see, among the 87 subjects who helped, almost 60% were directed toward attractive ($52/87 \times 100 = 59.77\%$) target persons and 40% toward unattractive applicants. In contrast, among the 133 subjects who did not help, 47% involved attractive target persons ($62/133 \times 100 = 46.62\%$) and 53% those who were unattractive ($71/133 \times 100 = 53.38\%$).

Source: Based on Peter L. Benson, Stuart A. Karabenick, and Richard M. Lerner (1976), "Pretty Pleases: The Effects of Physical Attractiveness, Race, and Sex on Receiving Help," *Journal of Experimental Social Psychology*, **12,** 409–415.

2.8 PUTTING IT ALL TOGETHER

Recall the statistical detective work introduced in Chapter 1, which might best be named "the mysterious case of erosion of dental enamel among members of a private club."

After all the questionnaires of the sample of 747 respondents were returned, it became obvious that two groups could be separated out—frequent and nonfrequent swimmers. The number of individuals in each group evidencing dental enamel erosion could be tabulated. The two dependent measures (Yes versus No) represent a nominal scale of measurement. Table 2.6 presents these results in tabular form.

TABLE 2.6   Relative Frequency Table of Frequent and Nonfrequent Swimmers Evidencing and Failing to Evidence Erosion of Dental Enamel*

| | Evidence of Dental Enamel Erosion | | |
	No	Yes	Row Totals
Frequent swimmers	383 (85)	69 (15)	452 (100)
Nonfrequent swimmers	286 (97)	9 (3)	295 (100)
Column totals	669 (90)	78 (10)	747 (100)

* Row percentages and column total percentages are shown in parentheses.
Source: "Erosion and dental enamel among competitive swimmers—Virginia" (1983), *Morbidity and Mortality Weekly Report,* **32,** 28.

As we can see, the descriptive statistics show that about 10% of all respondents met the criteria for erosion of dental enamel. However, this was not uniformly distributed among frequent and nonfrequent swimmers. Fully 15% of the frequent swimmers and only 3% of the nonswimmers met the criteria. Inferential statistics are then calculated to ascertain whether this difference in rate of erosion might reasonably be dismissed as a chance occurrence. So that you'll not be left hanging until later in the text, let it be noted that the investigators formed the conclusion that the rate of dental erosion represented a genuine effect of some variable. Frequent swimmers were experiencing a higher rate of enamel erosion. We shall look later at follow-up studies that included measurement of the level of pool acid.

Following this analysis, a follow-up questionnaire was mailed to all 452 frequent swimmers, of whom 294 (65%) replied. The results were then divided into two groups—those who swam 5 or more days a week, and those who swam less than 5 days a week. The data and sample statistics are shown in Table 2.7.

These descriptive statistics are in line with those presented in Table 2.6 and provide further data to be subjected to inferential statistical analysis.

TABLE 2.7   Relative Frequency Table of Frequent Swimmers Who Swam 5 or More Days a Week Versus Those Who Swam Less Than 5 Days a Week Who Showed or Failed to Show Evidence of Erosion of Dental Enamel

| | Evidence of Dental Enamel Erosion | | |
	No	Yes	Row Totals
5 or more days a week	97 (73)	35 (27)	132 (100)
Fewer than 5 days a week	148 (91)	14 (9)	162 (100)
Column totals	245 (83)	49 (17)	294 (100)

* Row percentages and column total percentages shown in parentheses.

Note that the dependent measures in this study consisted of nominal scales of measurement. The researchers could have achieved an ordinal scale of measurement by having experts (dental practitioners) observe the subjects' teeth and rate the degree of erosion, such as 1 for no evidence up to 4 or 5 for an advanced degree of pitting. Such ordinal scales are in common use in psychology, sociology, business, and economics (for example, on a survey, rate your degree of agreement with some specific statement from strongly agree, to agree, to neutral, to disagree, to strongly disagree). In medicine, disease processes are commonly ranked from 1 to 4 (from early to advanced stages), and outcomes are characteristically predicted on the basis of the stage. Finally, by devising some physical apparatus that plots the total area of pitting, it would be possible to develop an interval or a ratio scale of measurement. The decision often depends on the degree of precision necessary, the availability of measuring instruments, and the funds allocated for the research. Broadly speaking, the more precise the measurements required, the more expensive the research.

CHAPTER SUMMARY

In this chapter, we pointed out that advanced knowledge of mathematics is not a prerequisite for success in this course. A sound background in high school mathematics plus steady application to assignments should be sufficient to permit mastery of the fundamental concepts put forth in this text.

To aid the student who may not have had recent contact with mathematics, we have attempted to review some of the basic concepts of mathematics. Included in this review are: (1) the grammar of mathematical notation, (2) types of numbers, (3) types of numerical scales, (4) continuous and discontinuous scales, (5) rounding, and (6) frequencies, proportions, and percentages. Students requiring a more thorough review of mathematics may refer to Appendix A.

TERMS TO REMEMBER

cardinal numbers
continuous scales
discontinuous scales (discrete scales)
frequency data (attribute data, categorical data, enumerative data)
interval scale

nominal numbers
nominal scale
measurement
ordinal numbers
ordinal scale
ratio scale
true limits of a number
variable

EXERCISES

The following exercises are based on this chapter and Appendix A.

1. It has been speculated that Californians cope with earthquake hazards by avoidance—simply not thinking about them. Professor Ralph H. Turner, a sociologist and the director of UCLA's Institute for Social Science Research, has collected data that bear on this common belief. Shown below are the data collected on a number of survey questions concerned with media coverage of earthquake-related information.

Find the proportion and percentage of individuals responding in each category to each of the questions raised in the survey.

Do the responses appear to support the common view that Californians avoid thinking about earthquakes?

a. Do the media provide too little, too much, or sufficient coverage about what to do if an earthquake strikes?

	Number Responding
Too little	386
About right	103
Too much	8
No opinion	3

b. How about the news media's coverage on preparations for an earthquake?

	Number Responding
Too little	357
About right	121
Too much	14
No opinion	8

c. Do the media provide sufficient information about what the government is doing to prepare for an earthquake?

	Number Responding
Too little	413
About right	67
Too much	10
No opinion	10

d. How about the attention the media pay to the nonscientific earthquake predictions?

	Number Responding
Too little	126
About right	142
Too much	215
No opinion	17

2. Find a when $b = 10$, $c = 4$, and $a + b + c = 19$.

3. Find y when $N = 4$ and $20 + N = y + 2$.

4. Find ΣX when $N = 20$ and $\overline{X} = 60$, where $\overline{X} = \Sigma X/N$.

5. Find N when $\overline{X} = 90$ and $\Sigma\, X = 360$, where $\overline{X} = \Sigma\, X/N$.

6. Find N when

$$\sum (X - \overline{X})^2 = 640 \qquad s^2 = 16 \qquad \text{where } s^2 = \frac{\Sigma(X - \overline{X})^2}{N}$$

7. Find s^2 when

$$\sum (X - \overline{X})^2 = 240 \qquad N = 12 \qquad \text{where } s^2 = \frac{\Sigma(X - \overline{X})^2}{N}$$

8. Round the following numbers to the second decimal place:

   a. 99.99500   **b.** 46.40501   **c.** 2.96500   **d.** 0.00501

   e. 16.46500   **f.** 1.05499   **g.** 86.2139   **h.** 10.0050

9. The accompanying table shows the number of suicides in the United States during 1981, broken down in terms of gender and race.

   a. Find the percent of male and female suicides among blacks.

   b. Find the percent of white suicides among males.

   c. Find the percent of male and female suicides among whites.

   d. Can you think of a serious problem in interpreting the percent figures in part (b)?

	Gender	
Race	**Male**	**Female**
Black	1,315	343
White	19,166	6,286

10. In 1982 in the United States, the deaths of 19,309 murder victims were caused by: guns, 11,721; cutting or stabbing, 4,065; blunt object, 957; strangulation, 1,657; drowning or arson, 279; all other, 630. Find the proportions attributable to each cause of death (round to the second decimal place).

11. In 1973, there were 20,465 suicides and 17,123 homicides. Find the proportion of the total attributable to suicide and then find the proportion attributable to homicide (round to the fourth decimal place).

12. The following table shows the number of male and female victims of homicide between the years 1968 and 1973.

Year	Number of Male Victims of Homicide	Number of Female Victims of Homicide
1968	5106	1700
1969	5215	1801
1970	5865	1938
1971	6455	2106
1972	6820	2156
1973	7411	2575

a. Of the total number of male homicide victims during the years 1968 through 1973, find the percentage for each year.

b. Of the total number of female homicide victims during the years 1968 through 1973, find the percentage for each year.

13. Determine the value of the following expressions, in which $X_1 = 4$, $X_2 = 5$, $X_3 = 7$, $X_4 = 9$, $X_5 = 10$, $X_6 = 11$, $X_7 = 14$:

a. $\sum_{i=1}^{4} X_i = 25$ **b.** $\sum_{i=1}^{7} X_i = 60$ **c.** $\sum_{i=3}^{6} X_i = 37$

d. $\sum_{i=2}^{5} X_i = 31$ **e.** $\sum_{i=1}^{N} X_i = 60$ **f.** $\sum_{i=4}^{N} X_i = 44$

14. Express the following in summation notation:
a. $X_1 + X_2 + X_3 = \sum_{i=1}^{3} X_i$ **b.** $X_1 + X_2 + \cdots + X_N$
c. $X_3^2 + X_4^2 + X_5^2 + X_6^2$ **d.** $X_4^2 X_5^2 + \cdots + X_N^2$

15. The answers to the following questionnaire items are based upon what scale of measurement?
a. What is your height?
b. What is your weight?
c. What is your occupation?
d. How does this course compare with others you have taken?

16. In the following examples, identify the scale of measurement of the italicized variable and determine whether it is continuous or discontinuous
a. *Distance* traveled from home to school by 50 different students.
b. Number of infants born at *varying times of the day*.
c. Number of votes compiled by each of *three candidates* for a political office.

17. Determine the square roots of the following numbers to two decimal places:
a. 160   **b.** 16   **c.** 1.60   **d.** 0.16   **e.** 0.016

18. State the true limits of the following numbers:
a. 0   **b.** 0.5   **c.** 1.0   **d.** 0.49   **e.** −5   **f.** −4.5

19. Using the values of X_i given in Exercise 13, show that

$$\sum_{i=1}^{N} X_i^2 \neq \left(\sum_{i=1}^{N} X_i \right)^2$$

20. Which of the following italicized variables represent continuous scales and which represent discrete scales of measurement?
a. The *number of light bulbs* sold each day in a hardware store
b. The *monthly income* of graduate students
c. The *temperatures* recorded every 2 hours in the meat department of a supermarket
d. The *weights of pigeons* recorded every 24 hours in an experimental laboratory
e. The *lengths of newborns* recorded at a hospital nursery
f. The *number of textbooks* found in the college bookstore

21. Using the figures for the number of students, by sex, majoring in each of five academic areas shown in the following table, answer the following questions:

a. Of all the students majoring in each academic area, what percentage is female?

b. Considering only the males, what percentage is found in each academic area?

c. Considering only the females, what percentage is found in each academic area?

d. Of all students majoring in the five areas, what percentage is male? What percentage is female?

e. Among those majoring in business administration, what percentage is female?

Academic Area	**Male**	**Female**
Business administration	400	100
Education	50	150
Humanities	150	200
Science	250	100
Social science	200	200

f. What percentage is male among students majoring in science?

22. Indicate which of the following variables represent discrete or continuous scales:

a. The time it takes you to complete these problems.

b. The number of newspapers sold in a given city on December 19, 1991.

c. The amount of change in weight of 5 women during a period of 4 weeks.

d. The number of home runs hit by each of 10 randomly selected batters during the 1991 baseball season.

e. The number of stocks on the New York Stock Exchange that increased in selling price on January 3, 1991.

23. At left is a list showing the number of births in the United States (expressed in thousands) between 1950 and 1970. (*Source: The World Almanac*, 1975, adapted. Published by Newspaper Enterprise Association Inc., p. 951.) Calculate the percentage of males and females for each year.

Year	Males	Females
1950	1824	1731
1955	2074	1974
1960	2180	2078
1965	1927	1833
1970	1915	1816

24. Eugene J. Kanin[*] has studied various aspects of the behavior of sexually aggressive males. Sexually aggressive was defined as "a quest for coital access of a rejecting female during the course of which physical coercion is utilized to the degree that offended responses are elicited from the female" (p. 429). When his findings were compared with those for a sample of nonaggressive males, if was hypothesized that nonaggressive males might attempt *exploitative* rather than aggressive techniques more often than their aggressive counterparts as a means of achieving sexual access.

The data from a high school sample of 254 nonaggressive and 87 aggressive males reveals the following frequencies with which the subjects admitted to the use of exploitative techniques.

[*] *Source:* Kanin, E. J. (1967), "An Examination of Sexual Aggression as a Response to Sexual Frustration," *Journal of Marriage and the Family,* **29,** 428–433. Copyright © 1967 by the National Council on Family Relations. Reprinted by permission.

	Nonaggressive Males†	Aggressive Males†
Attempted to get girl intoxicated	23	33
Falsely promised marriage	19	7
Falsely professed love	37	39
Threatened to terminate relationship	9	8
Total number of males interviewed	$N = 254$	$N = 87$

† The sum of the frequencies does not equal N, since some subjects admitted to employing more than one technique and others claimed never to use such techniques.

a. Find the percentages of aggressive and nonaggressive males admitting to the use of each exploitative technique.

b. Does it appear that the hypothesis is supported?

25. Shown below are the methods of suicide used by students at University of California at Berkeley (1952–1961) and at Yale (1920–1955). (*Source*: R. H. Seiden (1966), "Campus Tragedy: A Story of Student Suicide," *Journal of Abnormal and Social Psychology*, **71,** 389–399.)

	Berkeley	Yale
Firearms	8	10
Poisoning	6	3
Asphyxiation	4	5
Hanging	2	6
Jumping from high places	2	1
Cutting instruments	1	0
Total suicides	$N = 23$	$N = 25$

Calculate the percentage of suicides in which the various means of self-destruction were employed at each institution. Round to the nearest percent.

26. Refer to Exercise 4, Chapter 1.

a. What are the proportion and the percentage of commercials in which black athletes appeared?

b. In 1971, what proportion of white and black professional football players sampled had an opportunity to appear in advertising?

27. In the study of attractiveness and helping behavior (Case Example 2.2), the table that follows shows the number of male subjects choosing to help attractive and unattractive female applicants (whites and blacks combined). Calculate:

a. The percentage of females rendering help regardless of the attractiveness of the target.

b. The percentage rendering help and not rendering help when the target is attractive.

c. The percentage helping and not helping when the target is physically unattractive.

Helping Response	Characteristics of Target		
	Attractive	Unattractive	Total
Helped	17	13	30
Did not help	24	27	51
Total	41	40	81

28. Refer to Exercise 27 and Case Example 2.2.
   a. What is the population for this study?
   b. Is it likely to be representative of the general population?

29. Black and white male and female voters were polled concerning their willingness to vote for black and/or female candidates for the office of President of the United States (Sigelman and Welch, 1984). The results of their study are shown in the following table.

Would Vote For:	White Males	White Females	Black Males	Black Females	Row Totals
Neither a black nor a female	87	114	0	5	206
A female but not a black	119	115	1	6	241
A black but not a female	106	156	28	19	309
Both a black and a female	811	981	99	151	2042
Column totals	1123	1366	128	181	2798

Source: Adapted from L. Sigelman and S. Welch (1984), "Race, Gender, and Opinion toward Black and Female Presidential Candidates," *Public Opinion Quarterly,* **48,** 467–475.

   a. Find the percentages in terms of totals.
   b. Find the percentages in terms of rows.
   c. Find the percentages in terms of columns.
   d. Is there any factor that could lead to confusion concerning the interpretation of the percentages in terms of totals and rows? Explain your answer.

30. Within recent years, a disabling type of physical disorder has surfaced that appears to be work-related—that is, related to the physical activities required by the hands and arms in performing a particular job. Referred to as repetitive strain disorder (RSI), it is placing the workers compensation system in Australia in jeopardy because of the large number of employees in computer keyboard types of jobs that are afflicted. The following table shows the number of operators and number of cases reported in 14 occupational categories in Western Australia. (Cited in S. Kiesler and T. Finholt (1988), "The Mystery of RSI," *American Psychologist*, **43**(12), 1004–1015.)

Cases of RSI Reported Among Government Employees through January 1985

Employment Category	Number of Operators	Reported Cases
Secretary stenographers	397	70
Typists	1163	137
Clerk typists	838	60
Word processing operators	340	99
Data processing operators	379	84
Telephonists	172	6
Accounting machinists	72	7
Computer programmers	749	9
Clerks	1190	40
Clerical assistants	193	9
Telex operators	49	0
Journalists	12	0
Hansard/court reporters	32	7
Other keyboard operators	938	32

a. Find the total number of operators and the total number of reported cases.
b. Find the percentage of cases in each occupational category.
c. Find the percentage of cases for the total sample.

DESCRIPTIVE STATISTICS

3

Frequency Distributions and Graphing Techniques

3.1 GROUPING OF DATA

In the middle 1960s, a team of researchers headed by R. H. Rosenman described a class of individuals who, in response to environmental challenge, tended to display a pattern of behaviors that are characterized by extreme hostility, competitiveness, impatience, and time-consciousness (Rosenman et al., 1975; Jenkins et al., 1967). They also reported that individuals displaying these Type A behaviors are particularly prone to coronary heart disease. These initial observations unleashed a veritable flood of research aimed at confirming or disconfirming the initial research findings and at describing other behavioral and/or physiological characteristics that distinguish Type A individuals from their more relaxed Type B counterparts.

The typical strategy of this research involves the administration of a psychological scale (often the Jenkins Activity Survey or JAS) to a pool of potential subjects to distinguish between individuals who are characterized by Type A as opposed to Type B behaviors. Then a challenging task is administered to both groups of subjects, and some aspect of their behavioral and/or physiological responses is measured. In these studies, the type of behavior (A vs. B) is typically one of two or more independent variables, and various responses to challenge—for example, challenge-seeking behavior, heart-rate measures, blood pressure, to name a few—are the

TABLE 3.1 Diastolic Blood Pressures of 120 Subjects, 60 Classified as Type A* and 60 as Type B*†

53	**57**	**58**	**59**	**59**	**60**	**60**	**60**	**60**	**61**
61	**61**	**61**	**79**	**81**	**81**	**78**	**77**	**74**	**74**
74	**62**	**62**	**62**	**73**	**73**	**73**	**63**	**63**	**63**
63	**71**	**71**	**71**	**64**	**64**	**64**	**64**	**70**	**70**
70	**70**	**65**	**65**	**65**	**65**	**65**	**68**	**68**	**68**
68	**66**	**66**	**66**	**67**	**67**	**67**	**67**	**67**	**80**
93	51	80	80	80	80	59	59	79	79
60	60	60	78	61	61	76	76	62	62
62	74	63	63	63	63	63	73	73	73
64	64	64	72	72	72	65	65	65	65
65	65	65	71	71	71	67	67	67	70
70	70	70	68	68	68	68	68	52	69

* Boldface = Type A; lightface = Type B.
† Each score is the average of five separate measurements.
Source: Based on data from Ortega and Pipal (1984), "Challenge Seeking and Type A Coronary-Prone Behavior Pattern," *Journal of Personality and Social Psychology* **46**(6), 1328–1334.

dependent measures. It should be noted that the type of behavior is not a "true" independent variable because it is a preexisting condition of the subjects that is not under the control of the researcher.

In a study by Deems Ortega and Janet Pipal (1984), both behavioral and physiological dependent measures were used. Among the physiological measures were systolic blood pressure (when the heart is contracting) and diastolic blood pressure (when the heart is filling with blood). Table 3.1 shows the average diastolic blood pressure of 120 subjects, 60 classified as Type A and 60 as Type B.

As you mull over these BP measures, it soon becomes obvious that you cannot "make heads or tails" out of them unless you organize them in some systematic fashion. It may occur to you to list all scores from the highest to the lowest and then place a slash mark alongside each score every time it occurs (Table 3.2). The number of slash marks, then, represents the frequency of occurrence of each score.

Frequency Distribution: When the values of a variable are arranged in order according to their magnitudes, a frequency distribution shows the number of times each score occurs.

When you have done this, you have constructed an ungrouped **frequency distribution** of scores. Note that in the present example the scores are widely spread out, a number of scores have a frequency of zero, and there is no "visually" clear indication of central tendency. Under these circumstances, it is customary for most researchers to *group* the scores into what is referred to as *classes* and then obtain a frequency distribution of "grouped scores."

TABLE 3.2 **Frequency Distribution of Diastolic Blood Pressure Scores of 120 Subjects, Combining 60 Classified as Type A and 60 as Type B**

X	f	X	f	X	f
93	1	78	2	63	9
92	0	77	1	62	6
91	0	76	2	61	6
90	0	75	0	60	7
89	0	74	4	59	4
88	0	73	6	58	1
87	0	72	3	57	1
86	0	71	6	56	0
85	0	70	8	55	0
84	0	69	1	54	0
83	0	68	9	53	1
82	0	67	8	52	1
81	2	66	3	51	1
80	5	65	12		
79	3	64	7		

Source: Based on data from Ortega and Pipal, 1984.

Grouping into Classes

Grouping involves a sort of "collapsing the scale" wherein we assign scores to **mutually exclusive** classes in which the classes are defined in terms of the grouping intervals employed. The reasons for grouping are (1) Unless automatic calculators are available, it is uneconomical and unwieldy to deal with a large number of cases spread out over many scores. (2) Some of the scores have such low frequency counts that we are not justified in maintaining these scores as separate and distinct entities. (3) Grouping makes the display more comprehensible; that is, there is less information to overwhelm the reader.

On the negative side, of course, there is the fact that grouping inevitably results in the loss of information. For example, individual scores lose their identity when we group them into classes, and some small errors in statistics based upon grouped scores are unavoidable.

The question now becomes, "On what basis do we decide upon the grouping intervals that we will employ?" Obviously, the intervals selected must not be so wide that we lose the discrimination provided by our original measurement. For example, if we were to divide the previously collected diastolic BPs into two classes, those below 72 and those 72 and above, practically all the information inherent in the original scores would be lost. On the other hand, the width of the classes should not be so narrow that the purposes served by grouping are defeated. In answer to

Mutually Exclusive:

Events *A* and *B* are said to be mutually exclusive if both cannot occur simultaneously.

our question, there is unfortunately no general prescription that can be applied to all data. Much of the time the choice of the number of classes must represent a judgment based upon a consideration of the relative effects of grouping upon discriminability and presentational economy. However, it is generally agreed that most data in the behavioral sciences can be accommodated by 10 to 20 classes. For uniformity, we aim for approximately 15 classes for the data that we discuss in this textbook.

Having decided upon the number of classes that is appropriate for a set of data, we find that the procedures for assigning scores to classes are quite straightforward. Although any of several different techniques may be used, we employ only one, for the sake of consistency. The procedures to be employed are as follows:

Step 1. Find the difference between the highest and the lowest score values contained in the original data. Add 1 to obtain the total number of scores or potential scores. In the present example, this result is $(93 - 51) + 1 = 43$.

Step 2. Divide this figure by 15 to obtain the number of scores or potential scores in each class. If the resulting value is not a whole number, and it usually is not, we prefer to round to the nearest odd number so that a whole number will be at the middle of the class. However, this practice is far from universal, and you would not be wrong if you rounded to the *nearest number*. In the present example, the number of scores for each class is 43/15, or 2.87. This rounds to 3. We designate the width of the class by the symbol i. In this example, $i = 3$.

Step 3. Take the lowest score in the original data as the minimum value in the lowest class. Add to this $i - 1$ to obtain the maximum score of the lowest class. Thus, the lowest class of the data on hand is 51–53.

Step 4. The next higher class begins at the integer following the maximum score of the lower class. In the present example, the next integer is 54. Follow the same steps as in (3) to obtain the maximum score of the second class. Follow these procedures for each successive higher class until all the scores are included in their appropriate classes.

Step 5. Assign each obtained score to the class within which it is included. The **grouped frequency distribution** of Table 3.3 was obtained by employing the preceding steps.

Grouped Frequency Distribution: A frequency distribution in which the values of the variable have been grouped into classes.

Note that by grouping we may obtain an immediate "picture" of the distribution of diastolic BPs among our subjects. For example, note that there is a clustering of frequencies in the classes between the scores of 60 and 80. It is also apparent that the number of scores in the extremes

TABLE 3.3   Grouped Frequency Distribution of Diastolic Blood Pressure Measures Based on Data Appearing in Table 3.2

Class	f	Class	f	Class	f
93–95	1	78–80	10	63–65	28
90–92	0	75–77	3	60–62	19
87–89	0	72–74	13	57–59	6
84–86	0	69–71	15	54–56	0
81–83	2	66–68	20	51–53	3

tends to dwindle off. Thus, we have achieved one of our objectives in grouping: to provide a systematic, economical, and manageable arrangement of scores.

The stem-and-leaf diagram is a related and useful way of displaying Frequency and grouped Frequency data, particularly if N is not large (see Box 3.1).

One word of caution: Most scores with which the behavioral scientist deals are expressed as whole numbers rather than as decimals. It is for this reason that our examples employ integers. However, occasionally scores are expressed in decimal form (e.g., reaction time). The simplest procedure is to treat the scores as if the decimal points did not exist. In other words, treat each score as a whole number. The decimals can then be reinserted at the final step. If, in the preceding example, the highest score had been 9.3 and the lowest 5.1, the calculations would have been exactly the same. At the last step, however, the highest class would have been changed to 9.3 to 9.5 and the lowest to 5.1 to 5.3, with corresponding changes in between. The width of the class would have been 0.3. See the Study Guide for a worked example.

The True Limits of a Class

In our prior discussion of the "true limits" of a number in Section 2.5, we pointed out that the "true" value of a number is equal to its apparent value plus and minus one-half of the unit of measurement. Of course, the same is true of these values even after they have been grouped into classes. Thus, although we write the limits of the lowest class as 51 to 53, the true limits of the class are 50.5 to 53.5 (i.e., the lower real limit of 51 and the upper real limit of 53, respectively).

It is important to keep in mind that the true limits of a class are not the same as the *apparent limits*. Later, when calculating the median and percentile ranks for grouped data, we shall make use of the *true limits* of the class.

BOX 3.1

EXPLORATORY DATA ANALYSIS (EDA)

While few would question the tremendous strides in speed, depth, and comprehensiveness of data analyses ushered in by the widespread availability of the computer, there is also a downside to this data-processing revolution. Specifically, researchers are strongly tempted to rush the data into a computer file and then command the computer to start printing out the bottom lines of various outcomes of pro- grammed statistical analyses. In this dash to the bottom line, the raw data themselves may receive little or no attention.

Advocates of exploratory data analysis (EDA) are justifiably unhappy with this situation. They favor, metaphorically, investing time and effort getting their hands "dirty on data" before conducting traditional data analyses. They argue cogently that EDA "can serve as the foundation stone—as the first step" (Tukey, 1977, p. 3). If you don't familiarize yourself with the data and examine them from a variety of different perspectives, you may overlook subtle and important facets of the data that will not be brought to light in traditional statistical analyses. While it is beyond the scope of this text to delve deeply into EDA, a few key techniques may be helpful.

Much attention is directed toward stem-and-leaf displays, such as in Table 3.4. Each line is a stem, and each item of information on a stem is a leaf. In this exhibit, the class boundaries are shown in the left column and the second digits are shown by the leaves. To illustrate, take the stem and leaf 78-80 8899900000. We read these entries as 78, 78, 79, 79, 79, 80, 80, 80, 80, 80. The value of such stem- and-leaf displays is that they provide economy of space while reminding us of the actual data values. Moreover, the final product is a graph, which is a powerful aid to thinking about data.

TABLE 3.4   Stem-and-Leaf Exhibit of the Diastolic Blood Pressures Shown in Table 3.3.

Digit-Reminder Display

93–95	3
90–92	
87–89	
84–86	
81–83	11
78–80	8899900000
75–77	667
72–74	2223333334444
69–71	900000000111111
66–68	666777777777888888888
63–65	333333333344444445555555555555
60–62	0000000111111222222
57–59	789999
54–56	
51–53	123

3.2   CUMULATIVE-FREQUENCY AND CUMULATIVE-PERCENTAGE DISTRIBUTIONS

Cumulative-Frequency:
The number of cases (frequencies) at and below a given point.

It is often desirable to arrange the data from a frequency distribution into a **cumulative-frequency** distribution. Besides aiding in the interpretation of the frequency distribution, a **cumulative-frequency distribution** is of great value in obtaining the median and the various percentile ranks of scores, as we shall see in Chapter 4. A cumulative-frequency distribution shows the cumulative frequency below the upper real limit of the corresponding class. If, for example, we want the people with the fastest reaction times to be our champions at the PAC-MAN tournament, we select those in the bottom 10 percent of the reaction time distribution.

The cumulative-frequency distribution is obtained in a very simple and straightforward manner. Look at the data in Table 3.5. The entries in the frequency distribution indicate the number of BP measures falling within each of the classes. Each entry within the cumulative frequency distribution indicates the number of all cases or frequencies *below the upper real limit* of that class. Thus, in the third class from the bottom in Table 3.5, the entry "9" in the cumulative frequency distribution indicates that a total of nine subjects obtained a diastolic BP lower than the upper real limit of that class, which is 59.5. The entries in the cumulative frequency distribution are obtained by a simple process of successive addition of the entries in the frequency column. Thus, the cumulative frequency corresponding to the upper real limit of the class 65.5 to 68.5 is obtained by successive addition of $3 + 0 + 6 + 19 + 28 + 20 = 76$. Note that the top entry in the cumulative-frequency column is always equal to N. If you fail to obtain this result, you know that you have made an error in cumulating frequencies and should check your work.

The **cumulative-proportion distribution,** also shown in Table 3.5, is obtained by dividing each entry in the cumulative frequency column by N.

Cumulative-Frequency Distribution: A distribution that shows the cumulative frequency below the upper real limit of the corresponding class.

Cumulative-Proportion Distribution: A distribution that shows the cumulative proportion below the upper real limit of the corresponding class.

Cumulative Proportion: The proportion of cases (frequencies) at and below a given point.

Cumulative Percentage: The percentage of cases (frequencies) at and below a given point.

Cumulative-Percentage Distribution: A distribution that shows the cumulative percentage below the upper real limit of the corresponding class.

TABLE 3.5 **Grouped Frequency and Cumulative and Percentage Distributions of Diastolic Blood Pressure Measures Based on Data Appearing in Table 3.3**

Class	f	Cumulative f	Cumulative Proportion	Cumulative Percentage $(CP \times 100)$
93–95	1	120	1.000	100.0
90–92	0	119	0.992	99.2
87–89	0	119	0.992	99.2
84–86	0	119	0.992	99.2
81–83	2	‸119	0.992	99.2
78–80	10	117	0.975	97.5
75–77	3	107	0.892	89.2
72–74	13	104	0.867	˙86.7
69–71	15	91	0.758	75.8
66–68	20	76	0.633	63.3
63–65	28	56	0.467	46.7
60–62	19	28	0.233	23.3
57–59	6	9	0.075	7.5
54–56	0	3	0.025	2.5
51–53	3	3	0.025	2.5

Baseline heart-rate measures of subjects classified as Type A and Type B subjects: Preparing grouped frequency distributions

In another study of Type A and B behaviors, A and B types were identified by extreme scores (high = Type A; low = Type B) on the Jenkins Activity Survey (Perkins, 1984). In the challenging task, the subjects were required to detect the onset of one of five lights arranged in a semicircle and to press a button corresponding to that light, thereby turning it off. There were other aspects to the design that will be elaborated upon later. The dependent variable in this study was the heart-rate (HR) change resulting from practicing a challenging task. The measures shown in Table 3.6 are baseline scores. They were taken during a rest period following the second administration of the JAS and prior to the introduction of the challenging task.

a. Prepare a grouped frequency distribution by combining the HR measures of both groups of subjects, using 41.5–46.4 as the apparent limits of the lowest class. (*Note*: The fact that the HR measures are to the first decimal place does not prevent you from using an interval width that is a whole number. In the present example, i = 46.4 − 41.5 + 0.1 = 5.)

b. What are the true limits of the lowest class?

c. Based on the grouped frequency distribution, prepare cumulative-frequency, cumulative-proportion, and cumulative-percentage distributions of the HR measures.

TABLE 3.6 Baseline heart-rate measures of two groups of subjects (N = 140) during a rest period*

69.3	**62.0**	**58.0**	**78.0**	**93.3**	**69.6**	**71.3**	**65.3**	**52.6**	**88.6**
63.3	**86.6**	**79.3**	**61.3**	**60.6**	**67.3**	**84.6**	**74.6**	**70.0**	**90.6**
68.0	**59.3**	**84.6**	**73.3**	**78.0**	**56.6**	**62.6**	**72.0**	**76.6**	**42.0**
74.0	**73.3**	**60.0**	**68.6**	**74.6**	**72.6**	**78.6**	**74.6**	**80.0**	**76.6**
72.0	**73.3**	**84.6**	**54.0**	**78.6**	**69.3**	**72.0**	**80.0**	**56.6**	**73.3**
84.6	**91.3**	**76.0**	**95.3**	**76.6**	**71.3**	**76.6**	**46.6**	**101.3**	**54.6**
64.0	**80.0**	**62.0**	**59.3**	**67.3**	**76.6**	**70.6**	**68.0**	**79.3**	**66.6**
72.0	110.6	80.6	62.0	60.6	61.3	66.6	102.0	87.3	73.3
65.3	86.6	86.6	76.6	96.0	59.3	86.6	60.6	82.6	70.0
71.3	62.6	96.6	69.3	66.0	84.6	104.0	80.6	73.3	86.0
93.3	69.3	86.0	88.6	56.6	106.0	72.6	69.3	84.6	66.6
68.6	75.3	79.3	82.6	84.6	97.3	90.6	64.6	69.3	71.3
74.0	92.0	71.3	68.0	73.3	65.3	83.3	80.6	77.3	70.0
75.3	80.6	79.3	62.6	64.6	77.3	82.6	47.3	68.0	88.6

* Boldface = Type A; lightface = Type B

Source: Based on data from Perkins (1984), "Heart Rate Changes in Type A and Type B Males as a Function of Response Cost and Task Difficulty," *Psychophysiology*, **21**, 14–21.

d. Using the same classes as in the preceding grouped frequency distribution, prepare separate grouped frequency distributions of baseline HR measures of both groups of subjects.

e. Examine both frequency distributions in part d. Do they appear to be similarly distributed in both groups? In later chapters, we shall examine inferential procedures that will help us decide if it is likely that both groups of subjects were drawn from the same population.

ANSWERS

a., c.	Class	f	Cumulative f	Cumulative Proportion	Cumulative Percentage
	106.5–111.4	1	140	1.000	100.0
	101.5–106.4	3	139	0.993	99.3
	96.5–101.4	3	136	0.971	97.1
	91.5– 96.4	5	133	0.950	95.0
	86.5– 91.4	11	128	0.914	91.4
	81.5– 86.4	13	117	0.836	83.6
	76.5– 81.4	23	104	0.743	74.3
	71.5– 76.4	20	81	0.579	57.9
	66.5– 71.4	28	61	0.436	43.6
	61.5– 66.4	14	33	0.236	23.6
	56.5– 61.4	13	19	0.136	13.6
	51.5– 56.4	3	6	0.043	4.3
	46.5– 51.4	2	3	0.021	2.1
	41.5– 46.4	1	1	0.007	0.7

b. 41.45–46.45.

d.	Class	Type A Subjects	Type B Subjects
	106.5–111.4	0	1
	101.5–106.4	0	3
	96.5–101.4	1	2
	91.5– 96.4	2	3
	86.5– 91.4	4	7
	81.5– 86.4	4	9
	76.5– 81.4	14	9
	71.5– 76.4	12	8
	66.5– 71.4	14	14
	61.5– 66.4	6	8
	56.5– 61.4	8	5
	51.5– 56.4	3	0
	46.5– 51.4	1	1
	41.5– 46.4	1	0
		$n = 70$	$n = 70$

BOX 3.2

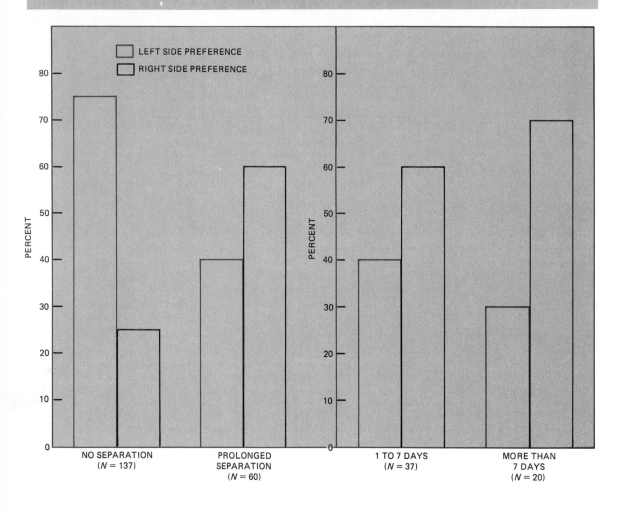

JUST A HEARTBEAT AWAY

Psychologists have often speculated that the heartbeat of the mother is comforting to the infant. If a child is held on the mother's left side, the sound of the heartbeat is more pronounced. One investigator explored the various circumstances under which mothers show a preference for holding their infants on the left or right side. Some mothers have access to their infants immediately after birth (no separation),

whereas others do not have their first contact for at least a period of 24 hours (prolonged separation). The graphs summarize the findings in a sample of 197 mothers.

Mothers of firstborns who were not separated from their infants at birth showed a marked preference for holding their baby on the left side. In contrast, mothers of firstborns who did not have early contact tended to prefer the right side. (See graph above.)

Any separation (for a day or more) appears to

lead to a right-side preference. The separation, the greater is the right-side preference, as shown in the second graph. This is based on data for 57 mothers who did not have access to their infants immediately after birth.

When each **cumulative proportion** is multiplied by 100, we obtain a **cumulative-percentage distribution.** Note that the top entry must be 100%, since all cases fall below the upper real limit of the highest class (i.e., 95.5).

3.3 GRAPHING TECHNIQUES

We have just examined some of the procedures involved in making sense out of a mass of unorganized data. As we pointed out, your work is usually just beginning when you have constructed frequency distributions of data. The next step usually is to present the data in pictorial form so that readers may readily apprehend the essential features of a frequency distribution and compare one with another if they desire. Such pictures, called graphs, should *not* be thought of as substitutes for statistical treatment of data, but rather as *visual aids* for thinking about and discussing statistical problems. (See Box 3.2.)

3.4 MISUSE OF GRAPHING TECHNIQUES

As you are well aware, graphs are often employed in the practical world of commerce to mislead the reader. For example, by the astute manipulation of the vertical (**Y-axis** or **ordinate**) and horizontal (**X-axis** or **abscissa**) axes of a graph, it is possible to convey almost any impression that is desired. Figure 3.1 illustrates this misapplication of graphing techniques. Two bar graphs are shown (based on the same data) in which the *X*- and *Y*-axes are respectively elongated to produce two distinctly different impressions.

Note that graph (a) tends to exaggerate the difference in frequency counts among the three classes, whereas graph (b) tends to minimize these differences.

Y-axis (ordinate): Vertical axis of a graph.

X-axis (abscissa): Horizontal axis of a graph.

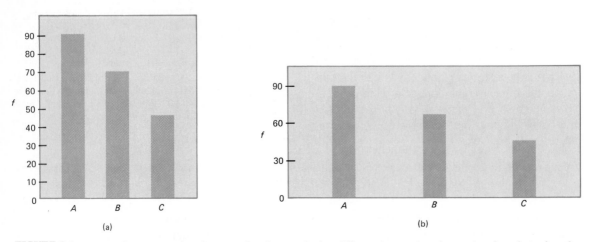

FIGURE 3.1   Bar graphs representing the same data but producing different impressions by varying the relative lengths of the Y- and X-axes.

The differences might be further exaggerated by use of a device called the "Gee Whiz!" chart by Darrell Huff and Irving Geis in their excellent book, *How to Lie with Statistics*. This procedure consists of eliminating the zero frequency from the vertical axis and beginning with a frequency count greater than zero. Figure 3.2, borrowed from the *How to Lie* book, illustrates quite dramatically the way in which graphs may be employed for purposes of deception.

It is obvious that the use of such devices is inimical to the aim of the statistician, which is to present data with such clarity that misinterpretations are reduced to a minimum. We may overcome the second source of error illustrated in Figure 3.2 by making the initial entry of the Y-axis a zero frequency. The first problem, however, remains: the selection of scale units to represent the horizontal and vertical axes. Clearly, the choice of these units is an arbitrary affair, and anyone who decides to make the Y-axis twice the length of the X-axis is just as correct as one who decides upon the opposite representation. In order to avoid graphic anarchy, however, it is necessary to adopt a convention designed to minimize bias. Most statisticians agree that the height of the vertical axis should be approximately 0.75 the length of the horizontal axis, with any proportion between 0.70 and 0.80 being acceptable.

The advantage of this convention is that it prevents subjective factors and, possibly, personal biases from influencing decisions concerning the relative proportions of the X-axis and the Y-axis in graphic representations. The use of this convention is illustrated in the forthcoming section dealing with bar graphs. This rule has also been applied to all the graphs appearing in the remainder of the chapter.

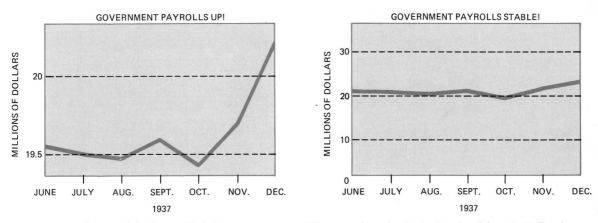

FIGURE 3.2   The use of the "Gee Whiz!" chart to exaggerate differences along the Y-axis. (Reprinted from D. Huff and I. Geis, *How to Lie with Statistics*. New York: W. W. Norton, 1954, with permission.)

3.5 NOMINALLY SCALED VARIABLES

The **bar graph,** illustrated in Figure 3.3, is a graphic device employed to represent data that are either nominally or ordinally scaled. A vertical bar is drawn** for each category, and the *height* of the bar represents the number of members of that class. If we arbitrarily set the width of each bar at one unit, the *area* of each bar may be used to represent the frequency for that category. Thus, the total area of all the bars is equal to *N*.

Bar Graph: A form of graph that employs bars to indicate the frequency of occurrence of observations within each nominal or ordinal category.

In preparing frequency distributions of nominally scaled variables, you must keep two things in mind:

1. No order is assumed to underlie nominally scaled variables. Thus, the various categories can be represented along the abscissa in any order you choose. The authors prefer to arrange the categories alphabetically, in keeping with their desire to eliminate any possibility of personal factors entering into the decision.
2. The bars should be separated rather than touching, so that any implication of continuity among the categories is avoided.

3.6 ORDINALLY SCALED VARIABLES

As you will recall, the scale values of ordinal scales carry the implication of an ordering that is expressible in terms of the algebra of inequalities

** Bar graphs are sometimes drawn horizontally [this has an advantage in cases where the number of cases (or classes) is large and the list may occupy a full page in length]. Nevertheless, the vertical array (as shown in Figure 3.3) is more often used (and more easily understood at sight) because of its adaptability to a histogram or a frequency curve (see Figures 3.6 and 3.7).

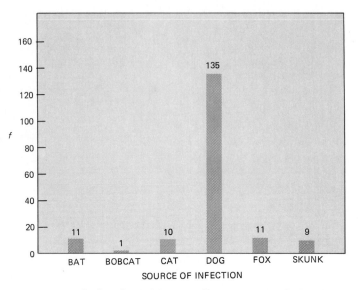

FIGURE 3.3   Shades of Cujo.* Between the years 1946 and 1983, there were 268 confirmed cases of human rabies in the United States. Of these, the most probable source was known in 175 cases. The bar graph shows the number attributable to each of six different animal sources. It is readily apparent that "our best friend" was the major source of infection. However, it should be noted that canine vaccination has successfully abolished this route of infection in the United States. Between 1966 and 1983, there were only 12 cases of human rabies in the United States, all due to exposures outside the continental United States. (*Source*: Table 3 of "Rabies in the United States and Canada, 1983," *Morbidity and Mortality Weekly Report*, 1985, **34**(1SS), 11SS–27SS).

(greater than, less than). In terms of our preceding discussion, ordinally scaled variables should be treated in the same way as nominally scaled variables, except that the categories should be placed in their naturally occurring order along the *X*-axis. Figure 3.4 illustrates the use of the bar graph with an ordinally scaled variable.

3.7 INTERVAL- AND RATIO-SCALED VARIABLES

Histogram

Recall the fact that interval- and ratio-scaled variables differ from ordinally scaled variables in one important way. Equal differences in scale values are equal. This means that we may permit the vertical bars to touch one another in graphic representations of interval- and ratio-scaled frequency

* A rabid dog in the Stephen King novel "Cujo."

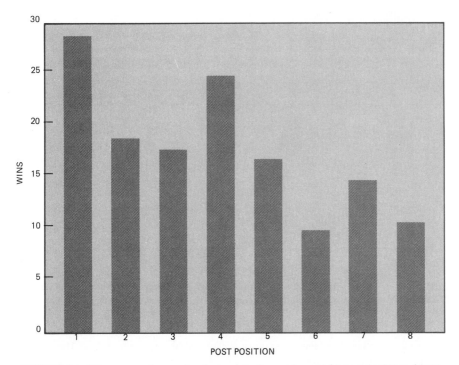

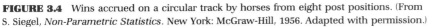

FIGURE 3.4 Wins accrued on a circular track by horses from eight post positions. (From S. Siegel, *Non-Parametric Statistics*. New York: McGraw-Hill, 1956. Adapted with permission.)

distributions. Such a graph is referred to as a **histogram** and replaces the bar graph employed with nominal and ordinal variables. Figure 3.5 illustrates the use of the histogram with a discretely distributed ratio-scaled variable.

We previously noted (Section 3.5) that frequency may be represented either by the area of a bar or by its height. However, there are many graphic applications in which the height of the bar may give misleading information concerning frequency. Consider Figure 3.6, which shows the histogram that results when the data are grouped into classes with unequal widths. The use of unequal class widths is most commonly found when there are relatively few scores at one or another extreme end of a distribution. For example, income figures commonly contain a few very extreme cases, such as annual incomes in the upper hundreds of thousands to millions of dollars. It is common to lump these extreme values into a single broad category.

If you think of frequency in terms of the height of the ordinate, you might erroneously conclude that the class 15 to 25 includes only two cases. However, if we represent each score by one unit on the scale of frequency and an equal unit on the scale of scores, the total area for each score is

Histogram: A form of bar graph used with interval- or ratio-scaled frequency distributions.

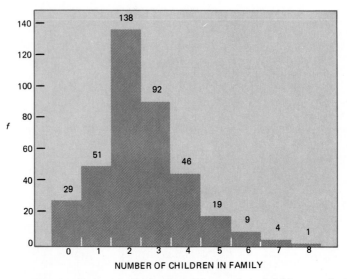

FIGURE 3.5 Frequency distribution of the number of children per family among 389 families surveyed in a small suburban community (hypothetical data).

FIGURE 3.6 Histogram employing unequal class widths (hypothetical data). The squares have been added for illustrative purposes. Each square represents one frequency at a given score. The total number of squares equals N (the sum of all the frequencies).

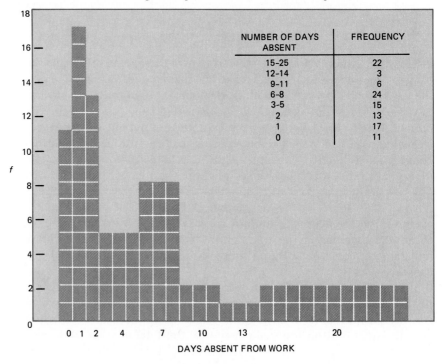

NUMBER OF DAYS ABSENT	FREQUENCY
15–25	22
12–14	3
9–11	6
6–8	24
3–5	15
2	13
1	17
0	11

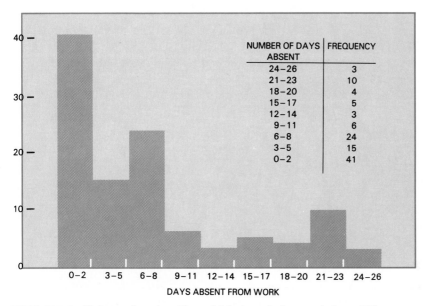

NUMBER OF DAYS ABSENT	FREQUENCY
24–26	3
21–23	10
18–20	4
15–17	5
12–14	3
9–11	6
6–8	24
3–5	15
0–2	41

FIGURE 3.7   Histogram based on Figure 3.6, but employing equal class widths.

equal to one. In the class 15 to 25, there are 22 frequency units distributed over 11 score units; thus, for this class the height of the ordinate will be 22/11 or 2 score units. Similarly, in the class 6 to 8, there are 24 frequency units distributed over 3 score units. Thus, the height of the ordinate must equal 8 units.

This problem with classes of unequal widths can readily be avoided by using equal widths wherever possible. Figure 3.7 shows the days-absent-from-work graph when equal widths of classes are used.

In general, it is advisable that we consider frequency in terms of area whenever we are dealing with variables in which an underlying continuity may be assumed.

Frequency Curve

We can readily convert the histogram into another commonly employed form of graphic representation, the **frequency curve,** by joining the midpoints of the bars with straight lines. However, it is not necessary to construct a histogram prior to the construction of a frequency curve. All you need to do is place a dot where the tops of the bars would have been, and join these dots. In practice, we prefer to reserve the use of the histogram for discrete distributions and the frequency curve for distributions in which underlying continuity is explicit or may be assumed. When two or more frequency distributions are compared, the frequency curve provides a

Frequency Curve: A form of graph representing a frequency distribution, in which a continuous line is used to indicate the frequency of the corresponding scores.

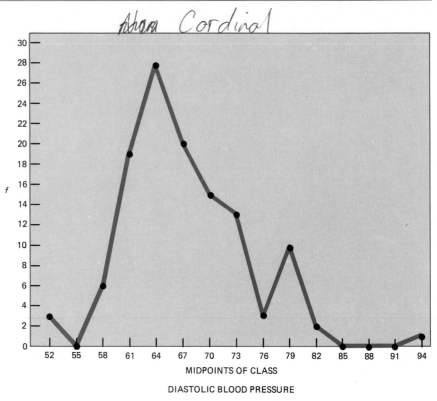

FIGURE 3.8   Frequency curve based on the grouped frequency distribution of diastolic blood pressure measures of 120 Type A and Type B subjects (Table 3.3).

clearer picture. Figure 3.8 shows a frequency curve based upon the grouped frequency distribution appearing in Table 3.3.

Cumulative-Frequency Curve

In Section 3.2, we demonstrated the procedures for constructing cumulative-frequency and cumulative-percentage distributions. The corresponding graphic representations are the cumulative-frequency curve and the cumulative-percentage curve. These are combined in Figure 3.9, with the left-hand Y-axis showing cumulative frequencies and the right-hand axis showing cumulative percentages.

There are three important points to remember: (1) The cumulative frequency or percentage is plotted against the *upper real limit* of each class; (2) the maximum value on the Y-axis in the cumulative-frequency curve is N, and that in the cumulative-percentage curve is 100%; and (3) the cumulative-frequency curve never decreases as you read from left to right.

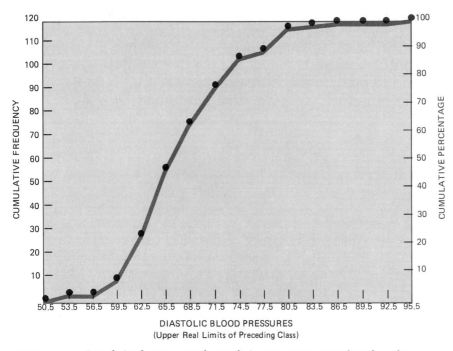

FIGURE 3.9 Cumulative-frequency and cumulative-percentage curve based on the cumulative-frequency and cumulative-percentage distributions shown in Table 3.4.

3.8 FORMS OF FREQUENCY CURVES

Frequency curves may take on an unlimited number of forms. However, many of the statistical procedures discussed in the text assume a particular form of distribution, namely, the "bell-shaped" **normal curve.**

In Figure 3.11, several forms of bell-shaped distributions are shown. Curve (a), which is characterized by a piling up of scores in the center of the distribution, is referred to as a **leptokurtic distribution.** In curve (c), where the opposite condition prevails, the distribution is referred to as **platykurtic.** And finally, curve (b) takes on the ideal form of the normal curve and is referred to as a **mesokurtic distribution.**

The normal curve is referred to as a symmetrical distribution, since, if it is folded in half, the two sides will coincide. Not all symmetrical curves are bell-shaped, however. A number of different symmetrical curves are shown in Figure 3.12.

Certain distributions have been given names; that in Figure 3.12(a) is called a *rectangular distribution*, and that in Figure 3.12(b), a *U-distribution*. Incidentally, a *bimodal distribution*, such as appears in Figure 3.12(c), for example, is often found when the frequency distributions of two different populations are represented in a single graph. For example, a frequency

Normal Curve: A hypothetical frequency curve with a characteristic bell-shaped form in which the curve never touches the horizontal axis.

Leptokurtic Distribution: Bell-shaped distribution characterized by a piling up of scores in the center of the distribution.

Platykurtic Distribution: Frequency distribution characterized by a flattening in the central portion.

Mesokurtic Distribution: Bell-shaped distribution; "ideal" form of normal curve.

STATISTICS IN ACTION 3.2

Comparing heart-rate measures of Type A and Type B subjects: Preparing frequency and percentage graphs

In Statistics in Action 3.1 we looked at the distribution of baseline scores of 70 subjects who were classified as Type A and another 70 who were classified as Type B. When we constructed separate frequency distributions of each group of subjects, we found that the distribution of heart-rate measures of the Type B subjects contained fewer low HR and a greater number of high HR measures. To compare the two distributions graphically, we might consider constructing two separate frequency distributions on the same graph and comparing the resulting curves. This comparison is shown in Figure 3.10.

Inspection of the frequency curves confirms that, for the sample of 140 baseline HR measures, there are a greater number of subjects with high heart rates among Type B than among Type A subjects. When we get to inferential statistics, we shall ask whether this sample difference is likely to represent a population difference; that is, Are the resting heart rates of Type B individuals in the general population greater, on the average, than those of Type A subjects?

FIGURE 3.10 Two frequency curves based on two grouped frequency distributions of baseline heart-rate measures of 70 Type A and 70 Type B subjects.

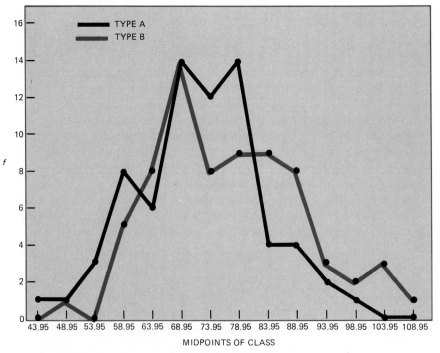

a. Another way to compare two distributions visually is to convert each frequency distribution to a percentage distribution and plot them on the same graph. Do this with the baseline HR data.

b. There is one circumstance under which it is almost essential that we convert frequency distributions to percentage distributions in order to compare them graphically—when the number of cases in each sample is not equal. The greater the difference in sample size is, the greater is the need for this conversion to percentages. Why so?

c. To illustrate the difficulty of comparing frequency distributions when sample sizes differ, prepare a frequency curve on the graph showing baseline HR measures for all 140 subjects and baseline HR measures for Type A subjects.

d. Now convert both to percentage curves.

ANSWERS

a.

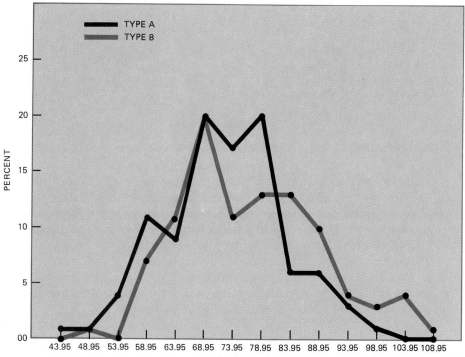

b. If two distributions are identical in form but one contains twice as many cases as the other, the frequencies of the group with the larger N will appear twice as high as those in the group with the smaller N. By converting to percentages, we can express all the frequencies relative to 100%. Direct visual comparisons then become possible.

c.

MIDPOINTS OF CLASS

Skewed Distribution:
Distribution that departs
from symmetry and tails
off at one end.

**Positively Skewed
Distribution:** Distribution
that has relatively fewer
frequencies at the high
end of the horizontal axis.

**Negatively Skewed
Distribution:** Distribution
that has relatively fewer
frequencies at the low
end of the horizontal axis.

distribution of male and female adults of the same age would probably
yield a curve similar to Figure 3.12(c) on a strength-of-grip task.

When a distribution is not symmetrical, it is said to be **skewed.** If we
say that a distribution is **positively skewed,** we mean that the distribution
tails off at the high end of the horizontal axis and there are relatively fewer
frequencies at this end. If, on the other hand, we say that the distribution
is **negatively skewed,** we mean that there are relatively fewer scores
associated with the left-hand, or low, side of the horizontal axis. Figure
3.13 presents several forms of skewed distributions.

Figure 3.13(a) is referred to as a J-curve, and Figure 3.13(b) is referred to
as an **ogive.** A cumulative-frequency distribution of data that are distributed
in a bell-shaped fashion will yield an ogive or S-shaped distribution. Note
that, even though the data in Table 3.5 only approximate a bell-shaped
distribution, the cumulative curve takes on the form of an ogive (see Figure
3.9).

d.

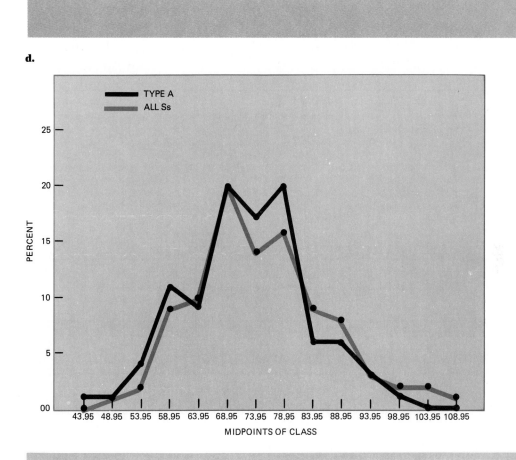

Figure 3.13(c) is positively skewed. Incidentally, Figure 3.13(a) illustrates an extreme *negative skew*.

It is not always possible to determine by inspection whether or not a distribution is skewed. There is a precise mathematical method for determining both direction and magnitude of skew. It is beyond the scope of this book to go into a detailed discussion of this topic. In Chapter 5, however, we outline a procedure for determining the *direction*, if not the magnitude, of skew. A quantitative measure of skew is shown in Section 6.6

Ogive: A cumulative-frequency distribution of bell-shaped data.

3.9 OTHER GRAPHIC REPRESENTATIONS

As noted in Section 1.5, we are often interested in comparing various groups or conditions with respect to a given characteristic. The groups or conditions

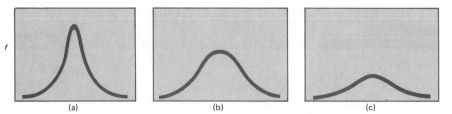

FIGURE 3.11 Three forms of bell-shaped distributions (a) leptokurtic, (b) mesokurtic, and (c) platykurtic.

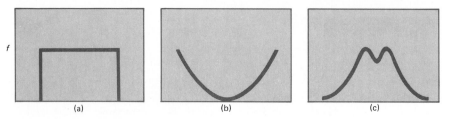

FIGURE 3.12 Illustrations of several nonnormal symmetric frequency curves.

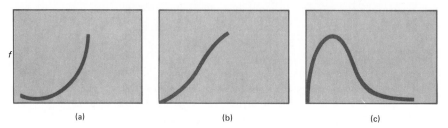

FIGURE 3.13 Illustration of skewed frequency curves.

are defined by the independent variable that is administered to them, whereas the characteristic we measure in order to judge the impact of the independent variable is called the dependent measure. Case Example 3.1 shows the use of graphic representations to illuminate the results of an experiment. Note that the independent variable is represented along the X-axis (horizontal) and the dependent variable along the Y-axis (vertical).

3.10 PUTTING IT ALL TOGETHER

Overcrowding of prisons was at the core of one of the great social, political, and financial controversies of the 1980s. Should society mete out harsher mandatory sentences to criminal offenders (particularly those pushing drugs) and make plea bargaining and parole more difficult to negotiate? If this tack is taken, more prisons will have to be built, at great cost to society.

CASE EXAMPLE 3.1

CASE EXAMPLE 3.1

Mood and Memory

"Mood and Memory," an article in *American Psychologist*, describes a series of studies in which hypnosis was used to induce moods in subjects in order to ascertain the influence of emotions on learning and memory. In one part of the investigation, the subjects were asked to keep a diary in which they recorded emotional incidents: time, place, participants, the gist of what happened, and a rating of each incident as pleasant or unpleasant on a 10-point scale. One week after submitting the diaries, the subjects returned to the laboratory. Hypnosis was used to induce a pleasant mood in half the subjects and an unpleasant mood in the remaining half. They were then asked to recall all the incidents they could that were reported in their diaries. The results are graphically displayed in Figure 3.14.

A glance at Figure 3.14 suggests a complex effect of mood on the recall of pleasant and unpleasant experiences. Specifically, when the mood is unpleasant, a greater percentage of unpleasant incidents is recalled. In contrast, when the mood is pleasant, the percentage of pleasant incidents recalled is greater than that of unpleasant incidents. However, a note of caution is in order. The graph does not, in and of itself, prove the effects of mood on recall. It merely summarizes, in a readily grasped form, the findings for the sample used in the study. To draw broad inferences about the data requires the use of inferential statistical analyses.

Source: Based on Gordon H. Bower (1981), "Mood and Memory," *American Psychologist*, **36**(2), 129–148.

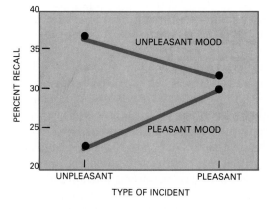

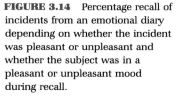

FIGURE 3.14 Percentage recall of incidents from an emotional diary depending on whether the incident was pleasant or unpleasant and whether the subject was in a pleasant or unpleasant mood during recall.

TABLE 3.7 Estimated Numbers of White and Black Prison Inmates in Various Age Groupings and Number of Deaths Due to Illness Within Each Racial Grouping and Age Group

Age	Estimated Number of White Inmates	Number of Deaths Due to Illness	Estimated Number of Black Inmates	Number of Deaths Due to Illness
15–24	49,312	12	46,375	18
25–34	77,669	38	80,686	106
35–44	37,326	56	30,540	126
45–54	12,065	62	6,032	71
55–64	4,147	65	2,639	68
65–74	1,131	42	754	34
Totals	181,650	275	167,026	423

Based on R. B. Ruback and C. A. Innes (1988), "The Relevance and Irrelevance of Psychological Research: The Example of Prison Crowding," *American Psychologist*, **43**(9), 683–702.

If the cost of building and maintaining prisons is unacceptably high, prison overcrowding may increase to the breaking point. As an alternative to increased rates of incarceration, should society's emphasis be on social and rehabilitation services in which such programs as work furloughs and halfway houses are encouraged? Informed answers to these questions should depend, at least in part, on the results of coherent research.

One avenue of exploration has focused on the mortality rates of prisoners in various age groups. Table 3.7 shows two frequency distributions, grouped by age, of white and black male prison inmates in 1984. Also shown are the approximate number of deaths due to illness in each age group for both white and black inmates.

By dividing the estimated number of inmates within each age group by its column total, we obtain the proportion within each class. However, death rates per age groups are obtained by dividing the number of deaths within each age group by the number of inmates within that group (for example, for the death rate of whites in class 15–24, you obtain 12/49,312 = 0.00024). Because the rates of mortality statistics are typically low, they are often expressed in terms of deaths per thousand or deaths per hundred thousand. To express these proportions as rates of death per thousand, multiply the proportion of deaths in each age group by 1000; for rates of death per hundred thousand, multiply each proportion by 100,000. Thus, for whites in age group 15–24, the deaths per 100,000 = 0.00024 × 100,000 = 24 (rounded). Table 3.8 shows the proportion of inmates within each age group, by race, and the rates of death per hundred thousand, also by race.

The relative frequency distributions of proportions of whites and blacks in each age class are shown in Figure 3.15. It is clear that the greatest

TABLE 3.8 **Estimated Proportions of White and Black Prison Inmates in Various Age Classes and Mortality Rates (Deaths per Hundred Thousand) Due to Illness Within Each Racial Grouping and Age Class**

Age	Proportion of White Inmates	Rates of Death per 100,000 Due to Illness	Proportion of Black Inmates	Rates of Death per 100,000 Due to Illness
15–24	0.2715	24	0.2777	39
25–34	0.4276	49	0.4831	131
35–44	0.2055	150	0.1828	413
45–54	0.0664	514	0.0361	1177
55–64	0.0228	1567	0.0158	2577
65–74	0.0062	3714	0.0045	4509

Based on R. B. Ruback and C. A. Innes (1988), "The Relevance and Irrelevance of Psychological Research: The Example of Prison Crowding," *American Psychologist*, **43**(9), 683–702.

proportions of white and black inmates are drawn from 25 to 34 year olds, and that the graphs are similar for whites and blacks.

As would be expected, the death rates due to illness increased with increasing age among both whites and blacks (see Figure 3.16). However, it is apparent that the rates of death per 100,000 are higher among blacks in

FIGURE 3.15 Relative frequency curve of white and black male prison inmates within different age classes.

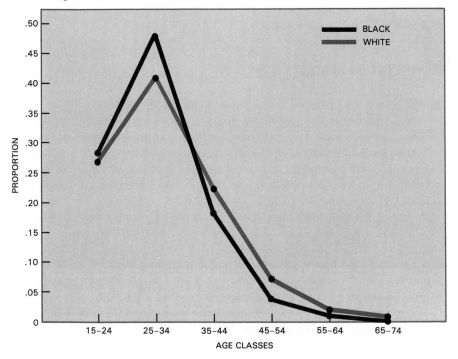

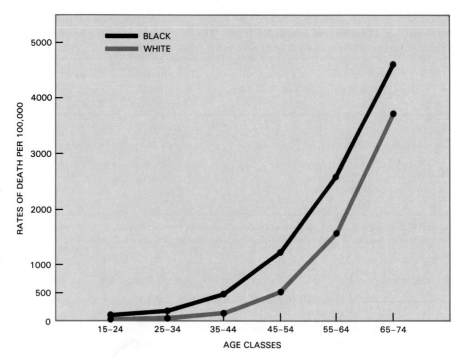

FIGURE 3.16 Rates of death from illness per hundred thousand prison inmates for white and black male prisoners in various age classes.

all age classes. Findings of this sort beg for follow-up studies to account for the differential death rates.

CHAPTER SUMMARY

This chapter was concerned with the techniques employed in "making sense" out of a mass of data. We demonstrated the construction of frequency distributions of scores and presented various graphing techniques. When the scores are widely spread out, many have a frequency of zero; and when there is no clear indication of central tendency, it is customary to group scores into classes. The resulting distribution is referred to as a grouped frequency distribution.

The basis for arriving at a decision concerning the grouping units to employ and the procedures for constructing a grouped frequency distribution were discussed and demonstrated. We saw that the true limits of a class are obtained in the same way as the true limits of a score. We also demonstrated procedures for converting a frequency distribution into a cumulative-frequency or cumulative-percentage distribution.

We reviewed the various graphing techniques employed in the behavioral sciences. The basic purpose of graphical representation is to provide visual aids for thinking about and discussing statistical problems. The primary objective is to present data in a clear, unambiguous fashion so that the reader may apprehend at a glance the relationships that you want to portray.

1. Devices employed by unscrupulous individuals to mislead the unsophisticated reader.
2. The use of the bar graph with nominally and ordinally scaled variables.
3. The use of the histogram and the frequency curve with continuous and discontinuous ratio- or interval-scaled variables.
4. Various forms of normally distributed data, nonnormal symmetrical distributions, and asymmetrical or skewed distributions.
5. Graphic representations of data, other than frequency distributions, commonly employed in the behavioral sciences.

TERMS TO REMEMBER

bar graph	histogram
cumulative frequency	leptokurtic distribution
cumulative-frequency	mesokurtic distribution
distribution	mutually exclusive
cumulative percentage	negatively skewed distribution
cumulative-percentage	normal curve
distribution	ogive
cumulative proportion	platykurtic distribution
cumulative-proportion	positively skewed distribution
distribution	random
frequency curve	skewed distribution
frequency distribution	X-axis (abscissa)
grouped frequency	Y-axis (ordinate)
distribution	

EXERCISES

1. Give the true limits, the midpoints, and the width of the class for each of the following classes:
   a. 8 to 12   **b.** 6 to 7   **c.** 0 to 2   **d.** 5 to 14
   e. (-8) to (-2) **f.** 2.5 to 3.5   **g.** 1.50 to 1.75   **h.** (-3) to $(+3)$

2. For each of the following sets of measurements, state (a) the best width of the class (i) (b) the apparent limits of the lowest class, (c) the true limits of that class, (d) the midpoint of that class:
   i. 0 to 106   **ii.** 29 to 41   **iii.** 18 to 48
   iv. -30 to $+30$ **v.** 0.30 to 0.47   **vi.** 0.206 to 0.293

3. Given the following list of scores in a statistics examination, use $i = 5$ for the classes and (a) set up a frequency distribution; (b) list the true limits and the midpoint of each class: (c) prepare a cumulative-frequency distribution; and (d) prepare a cumulative-percentage distribution.

Scores on a Statistics Examination									
63	88	79	92	86	87	83	78	40	67
68	76	46	81	92	77	84	76	70	66
77	75	98	81	82	81	87	78	70	60
94	79	52	82	77	81	77	70	74	61

4. Using the data in Exercise 3, set up frequency distributions with the following:
   a. $i = 1$ (ungrouped frequency distribution)　　**b.** $i = 3$
   c. $i = 10$　　　　　　　　　　　　　　　　　　**d.** $i = 20$
   Discuss the advantages and the disadvantages of employing these widths.

5. Given the following list of numbers, (a) construct a grouped frequency distribution; (b) list the true limits and the midpoint of each class (indicate the width employed); and (c) compare the results with those of Exercises 3 and 4.

6.3	8.8	7.9	9.2	8.6	8.7	8.3	7.8	4.0	6.7
6.8	7.6	4.6	8.1	9.2	7.7	8.4	7.6	7.0	6.6
7.7	7.5	9.8	8.1	8.2	8.1	8.7	7.8	7.0	6.0
9.4	7.9	5.2	8.2	7.7	8.1	7.7	7.0	7.4	6.1

6. Several apparent class limits in a frequency distribution showing the yield of corn per acre of land are 15 to 21, 8 to 14, 1 to 7.
   a. What is the width of each class?　　**b.** What are the lower and upper real
   c. What is the midpoint of each class?　　　　limits of each of these three classes?

7. Construct a grouped frequency distribution, using 5 to 9 as the lowest class for the following list of numbers. List the width, midpoint, and real limits of the highest class.

67	63	64	57	56	55	53	53	54	54
45	45	46	47	37	23	34	44	27	44
45	34	34	15	23	43	16	44	36	36
35	37	24	24	14	43	37	27	36	26
25	36	26	5	44	13	33	33	17	33

8. Do Exercise 7 again, using 3 to 7 as the lowest class. Compare the resulting frequency distribution with those of Exercise 7, 9, and 10.

9. Repeat Exercise 7, using 4 to 5 as the lowest class.

10. Repeat Exercise 7, using 0 to 9 as the lowest class.

11. Give an example of each of the following distributions:
   a. normal distribution　　　　　　　**b.** U-shaped distribution
   c. positively skewed distribution　　**d.** negatively skewed distribution
   e. rectangular distribution　　　　　**f.** bimodal distribution

12. Given the following frequency distribution of the weights of 96 students, draw a histogram.

Class	M	f	Class	M	f
160–164		1	130–134		17
155–159		3	125–129		11
150–154		10	120–124		8
145–149		6	115–119		3
140–144		14	110–114		1
135–139		22			

13. Take a pair of dice, toss 100 times, and record the sum (on the face of the two dice) for each toss. Prepare a bar graph, showing the number of times each sum occurs.

14. Given the following monthly sales by five salespeople in a large appliance store, draw graphs to perpetrate lies or distort facts to accomplish the following:
a. The sales manager wants to impress upon the owner of the store that all members of his sales force are functioning at a uniformly high level.
b. The sales manager wants to spur Mr. Richard to greater efforts.
c. The store owner wants to spur the sales manager to greater efforts.

Sales Person	Sales, $	Sales Person	Sales, $
Ms. Amy	22,500	Mr. Tommy	22,100
Mr. Richard	17,900	Ms. Maribeth	20,700
Ms. Nancy	21,400		

15. Draw a graph of the data representing the true state of affairs in Exercise 14.

16. The following table gives the scores of two groups of fourth-grade students on a test of reading ability.

Class	Group A f	Group B f	Class	Group A f	Group B f
50–52	5	2	29–31	9	22
47–49	12	3	26–28	6	11
44–46	18	5	23–25	4	9
41–43	19	8	20–22	3	6
38–40	26	12	17–19	1	4
35–37	19	24	14–16	2	2
32–34	13	35			
				137	143

a. Construct a frequency curve for each of these groups on the same axis.

b. Describe and compare each distribution.

17. Describe the types of distributions you would expect if you were to graph each of the following:

a. annual incomes of U.S. families

b. the heights of adult U.S. males

c. the heights of adult U.S. females

d. the heights of U.S. males and females combined in one graph

18. Consider the table to the left. Given this frequency distribution of the score results of 73 students on a midterm exam, draw a frequency curve.

Class	f	Class	f
95–99	2	65–69	11
90–94	2	60–64	6
85–89	5	55–59	3
80–84	9	50–54	0
75–79	16	45–49	1
70–74	18		

19. For the data in Exercise 18, draw a cumulative frequency curve.

20. A team of researchers at New York Metropolitan Medical Center (Zelon, Rubio, and Wasserman, 1971) has been collecting data on the incidence of drug addiction among mothers of newborn infants as well as among the infants themselves. The following table shows the total live births over a ten-year period and the number of mothers found to be drug-addicted. Calculate the percentage of drug-addicted mothers for each year. Graph the percent incidence over the ten-year period. Does there appear to be any change in the incidence of drug addiction of mothers over this ten-year period?

Year	Total Live Births	Total Drug-Addicted Mothers
1960	4284	26
1961	4396	36
1962	4290	43
1963	4335	44
1964	3923	31
1965	3615	28
1966	3089	31
1967	2688	47
1968	2283	46
1969	2367	50

21. In addition to being addicted at birth, many infants of drug-addicted mothers appear to display other physical deviations from infants born to nonaddicted mothers. The following table shows the percentage of drug-addicted infants whose birth weight was less than 2500 grams. The hospital incidence of weights less than 2500 grams is also shown. Prepare a graph showing the percent of incidence of infants with low weight among neonates of drug-addicted mothers and among all children born in the hospital during the ten-year period. Does there appear to be any consistent differences in the two rates of incidence?

	Percent of Neonates with Birth Weight under 2500 Grams	
Year	Infants of Drug-Addicted Mothers	Hospital Incidence*
1960	69.0	13.9
1961	52.7	15.9
1962	56.8	15.8
1963	40.9	15.1
1964	29.0	14.4
1965	50.0	12.6
1966	54.8	14.2
1967	52.0	14.7
1968	45.6	14.6
1969	48.0	12.7

* Includes drug-addicted infants.

22. Following are the number of quarts of milk sold at a supermarket on 52 consecutive Saturdays.

67	75	63	71	65	73	71	88	61
65	56	62	58	72	66	76	77	75
61	70	64	71	63	61	63	64	62
69	60	66	78	92	64	64	69	64
65	75	72	67	88	74	65	73	
78	62	68	69	67	57	65	58	

a. The manager of the dairy department decides to limit the number of quarts of milk on sale each Saturday to 70. Assuming that the sales figures will be the same the following year, what is the likelihood (i.e., the percentage of time) that the department will be caught short?

b. Group the sales figures into a frequency distribution with lower-class limits of 56 to 58.

c. Prepare a cumulative-frequency distribution and a cumulative-percentage distribution based upon the preceding frequency distribution.

d. Group the sales figures into a frequency distribution with lower-class limits of 55 to 59. Prepare a cumulative-frequency distribution and a cumulative-percentage distribution based upon this frequency distribution. Compare the resulting distributions with those obtained previously.

23. Draw a frequency curve for the frequency distribution obtained in Exercise 7.

24. Draw a frequency curve for the frequency distribution obtained in Exercise 8. Compare this distribution with that of Exercise 23.

25. Draw a cumulative-frequency distribution of Exercise 7.

26. Draw a cumulative-frequency curve for the frequency distribution obtained in Exercise 8. Compare this distribution with that of Exercise 25.

27. Figures on birth rates are usually given in terms of the number of births per thousand in the population. This table shows the birth rate data at the end of

Year	Number of Births per 1000 Population
1900	32
1910	30
1920	28
1930	21
1940	19
1950	24
1960	24
1970	18

each decade since the turn of the century, rounded to the nearest whole number. (*Source:* Commission on Population Growth and the American Future.)

a. Plot these data on a line chart.

b. Is any general trend in birth rate discernible?

*28. Imagine that you have a population consisting of seven scores: 0, 1, 2, 3, 4, 5, 6. You write each of these numbers on a paper tab and place them in a hat. Then you draw a number, record it, place it back in the hat, and draw a second number. You add the second number to the first to obtain a sum. You continue drawing pairs of scores and obtaining their sums until you have obtained all possible combinations of these seven scores, taken two at a time.

The following table shows all possible results from drawing samples of $N = 2$ from this population of seven scores. The values within each cell show the sum of the two scores.

First Draw

		0	**1**	**2**	**3**	**4**	**5**	**6**
Second Draw	0	0 + 0 = 0	1 + 0 = 1	2 + 0 = 2	3 + 0 = 3	4 + 0 = 4	5 + 0 = 5	6 + 0 = 6
	1	0 + 1 = 1	1 + 1 = 2	2 + 1 = 3	3 + 1 = 4	4 + 1 = 5	5 + 1 = 6	6 + 1 = 7
	2	0 + 2 = 2	1 + 2 = 3	2 + 2 = 4	3 + 2 = 5	4 + 2 = 6	5 + 2 = 7	6 + 2 = 8
	3	0 + 3 = 3	1 + 3 = 4	2 + 3 = 5	3 + 3 = 6	4 + 3 = 7	5 + 3 = 8	6 + 3 = 9
	4	0 + 4 = 4	1 + 4 = 5	2 + 4 = 6	3 + 4 = 7	4 + 4 = 8	5 + 4 = 9	6 + 4 = 10
	5	0 + 5 = 5	1 + 5 = 6	2 + 5 = 7	3 + 5 = 8	4 + 5 = 9	5 + 5 = 10	6 + 5 = 11
	6	0 + 6 = 6	1 + 6 = 7	2 + 6 = 8	3 + 6 = 9	4 + 6 = 10	5 + 6 = 11	6 + 6 = 12

a. Obtain an ungrouped frequency distribution of the 49 sums.

b. Construct a histogram from the frequency distribution.

c. Note that the original distribution of scores was rectangular, since each score occurred with the same frequency. Compare the form of the original distribution with the form of the frequency distribution of sums.

29. Refer to Exercise 24 in Chapter 2. Prepare a bar graph to show the percentages of aggressive and nonaggressive males who employ exploitive techniques in order to gain "coital access to a female."

30. In another aspect of the study reported in Case Example 3.1, the subjects were asked to recall events from childhood when they were in a neutral mood and to classify each incident as pleasant, unpleasant, or neutral. At a later time, they were induced into either a happy or a sad mood and were asked to recall incidents from their childhood. When their mood was happy, they recalled approximately 1 unpleasant event, on the average, and approximately 26 pleasant incidents. When their mood was sad, they recalled about 10 unpleasant events, on the average, and 8 pleasant events. Construct a graph to summarize these findings.

---

* All exercises that are used to lay the groundwork for future discussion are preceded by an asterisk.

31. Paradoxically, hyperactive children are often treated with a stimulant in order to *reduce* their activity. In one study, 20 hyperactive boys were treated with a stimulant (methylphenidate). A number of behaviors were then studied, including activity levels and interactions with their mothers [R. A. Barkley and C. E. Cunningham (1979), "The Effects of Methylphenidate on the Mother-Child Interactions of Hyperactive Children," *Arch. Gen. Psychiatry*, **36,** 201–208]. In one facet of the study, wrist and ankle actometers recorded the time that wrists and ankles were active. Under the placebo condition, the wrist activity was approximately 1600 minutes, on the average, and the ankle activity was about 1700. Under the drug, the average number of minutes were about 900 for the wrist and 1000 for the ankle. Prepare a graph to show these findings.

32. The table below shows the estimated numbers of white and black prison inmates who died in prison as a result of suicide and homicide.
   a. Find the proportion of deaths in each age class due to suicide among white and black prisoners.
   b. Find the proportion of deaths in each age class due to homicide among white and black prisoners.
   c. Prepare a graph of the proportions of deaths due to suicide and homicide for each class of white and of black prisoners.

Age	Number of White Suicides	Number of White Homicides	Number of Black Suicides	Number of Black Homicides
15–24	10	6	5	33
25–34	20	13	16	100
35–44	9	5	5	20
45–54	3	1	1	4
55–64	1	0	0	1
65–74	1	0	0	0
Totals	44	25	27	158

Source: Ruback, R. B. and C. A. Innes (1988), "The Relevance and Irrelevance of Psychological Research: The Example of Prison Crowding," *American Psychologist*, **43**(9), 683–702.

33. Refer to Exercise 30 in Chapter 2. Prepare a bar graph of the percentage of reported cases of RSI in the 14 employment categories. Because of the large number of categories, it is recommended that a horizontal graph be constructed.

4

Percentiles

4.1 INTRODUCTION

Suppose a younger brother came home from school and announced, "I received a score of 127 on my scholastic aptitude test." What would be your reaction? Commend him for obtaining such a fine score? Criticize him for not getting a higher one? Or reserve judgment until you learned more about the distribution of scores within your sibling's class or group? If you have passed the course up to this point, you have undoubtedly selected the last of these three alternatives.

It should be clear that a score by itself is meaningless. It takes on meaning only when it can be compared to some standard scale or base. Thus, if your younger sibling were to volunteer the information, "Seventy-nine percent of the students scored lower than I," he would be using **percentiles** as a frame of reference for interpreting the score. Indeed, he would have been citing the **percentile rank** of his score. The *percentile rank* of a score, then, *represents the percent of cases in a comparison group that achieved scores at or lower than the one cited*. Thus, to say that a score of 127 has a percentile rank of 79 is to indicate that 79% of the comparison group scored at or below 127. Incidentally, each score is considered to be a hypothetical point without dimension, so that it would be equally meaningful to say that 21% of the comparison group scored higher than 127.

Percentiles: Numbers that divide a distribution into 100 equal parts.

Percentile Rank: A number that represents the percent of cases in a comparison group that achieved scores equal to or lower than the one cited.

97

4.2 CUMULATIVE PERCENTILES AND PERCENTILE RANK

Obtaining the Percentile Rank of Scores from a Cumulative-Percentage Graph

In Chapter 3 we constructed cumulative-frequency and cumulative-percentage distributions. If we were to graph a cumulative-percentage distribution, we could read the percentile ranks directly from the graph, since the cumulative percentage corresponding to a given score is the same as the percentile rank of that score. Note that the reverse is also true; that is, given a percentile rank, we could read the corresponding score.

Look at Figure 4.1 You may recall that this is the cumulative-percentage graph of baseline diastolic BPs of 120 Type A and Type B subjects. Suppose we wanted to determine the percentile rank of a BP reading of 65. First, we locate 65 along the horizontal axis and draw a perpendicular line that intercepts the curve. From that point on the curve, we read directly across to the scale on the vertical axis, and see that the percentile rank is

FIGURE 4.1   Using a cumulative-percentage curve to estimate the percentile rank of a blood pressure reading of 65 and the blood pressure measure corresponding to the 90th percentile. (*Note*: The cumulative percentage corresponding to a given score is the same as the percentile rank of that score.)

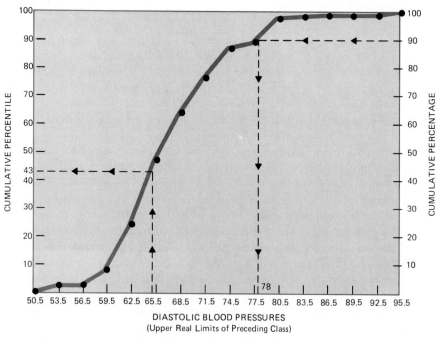

DIASTOLIC BLOOD PRESSURES
(Upper Real Limits of Preceding Class)

approximately 43. On the other hand, if we wanted to know the score at a given *percentile*, we could reverse the procedure. For example, what diastolic BP reading is at the 90th percentile? We locate the 90th percentile on the vertical axis, then read directly to the left until we meet the curve; at this point, we draw a line perpendicular to the horizontal axis, and read the value on the scale of BP measures. In the present example, it can be seen that a diastolic BP at the 90th percentile is approximately 78.

Obtaining the Percentile Rank of Scores Directly

We are often called upon to determine the percentile rank of scores without the assistance of a cumulative-percentage curve, or with greater precision than is possible with a graphical representation. To do this, we usually need to interpolate within the cumulative-frequency column to determine the precise cumulative frequency corresponding to a given score.

Using the grouped frequency distribution found in Table 4.1, let's determine directly the percentile rank of a BP of 65 that we previously approximated by the use of the cumulative-percentage curve.

TABLE 4.1   Grouped Frequency Distribution and Cumulative-Frequency Distribution of Baseline Diastolic BPs of 120 Subjects Participating in a Study of Type A and Type B Behaviors

Class (Real Limits)	f	Cumulative f
92.5–95.5	1	120
89.5–92.5	0	119
86.5–89.5	0	119
83.5–86.5	0	119
80.5–83.5	2	119
77.5–80.5	10	117
74.5–77.5	3	107
71.5–74.5	13	104
68.5–71.5	15	91
65.5–68.5	20	76
62.5–65.5	28	56
59.5–62.5	19	28
56.5–59.5	6	9
53.5–56.5	0	3
50.5–53.5	3	3
$N = 120$		

BOX 4.1

THE STRESS OF THE BEGINNING

It has frequently been maintained that suicides among college students result from the stresses of final examinations. A long-term study at the University of California, Berkeley, investigated various factors related to student suicides. The figure at right shows that the percentage of suicides was greatest in the opening weeks of the semester, leveled off at mid-semester (no suicides during weeks 6 to 12), and showed a moderate increase during the last third of the semester. Thus, contrary to popular opinion, the period of greatest danger appears to be the beginning, rather than the end of the semester.

A cumulative-percentage graph shows the percentages of cases falling below any selected value of the variable of interest. The accompanying graph shows that almost two-thirds of student suicides occur by the sixth week of the semester.

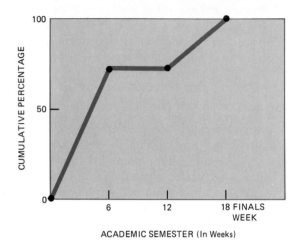

ACADEMIC SEMESTER (In Weeks)

Source: R. H. Seiden (1966), "Campus Tragedy: A Story of Student Suicide," *Journal of Abnormal Social Psychology,* **71,** 389–399. Copyright © by the American Psychological Association, Reprinted by permission.

Formula (4.1) presents a generalized formula for calculating the percentile rank of a given score.

$$\text{Percentile rank} = \frac{\text{cum}\, f_{ll} + \left(\dfrac{X - X_{ll}}{i}\right)(f_i)}{N} \times 100 \qquad (4.1)$$

where

$\text{cum}\, f_{ll}$ = cumulative frequency at the lower real limit of the class containing X

X = given score (BP in the present example)

X_{ll} = score at lower real limit of the class containing X

i = width of class

f_i = number of cases within the class containing X

N = number of scores in the distribution

The first thing we should note is that a BP of 65 falls within the class 62.5 to 65.5. The total cumulative frequency below that class is 28. Our task is to find the precise cumulative frequency corresponding to a BP of 65. It is clear that the cumulative frequency corresponding to a BP of 65 lies somewhere between the 28th and the 56th cases, the cumulative frequencies at both extremes of the class. We must now interpolate within the class 62.5 to 65.5 to find the exact cumulative frequency of a BP of 65. In doing this, we are actually trying to determine the proportion of distance that we must move into the class in order to find the number of cases included up to a BP of 65.

A BP of 65 is 2.5 score units above the lower real limit of the class (that is, $65 - 62.5 = 2.5$). Since there are 3 score units within the class, a BP of 65 is 2.5/3 of the distance through the class. We now make a very important assumption: *The cases or frequencies within a particular class are evenly distributed throughout that class.* Since there are 28 cases within the class, we may now calculate that a BP of 65 is $(2.5/3) \times 28$, or the 23.33 case within the class. In other words, the frequency 23.33 in the class corresponds exactly to a BP of 65. We have already seen, however, that 28 cases fall at or below the lower real limit of the class. Adding the two together, we find that a BP of 65 has a cumulative frequency of exactly 51.33. Substituting into Formula (4.1), we obtain the following:

$$\text{Percentile rank of } 65 = \frac{51.33}{120} \times 100 = 42.78$$

Note that this answer, when rounded to the nearest percentile, agrees with the approximation obtained by the use of the graphical representation of a cumulative percentage distribution (Figure 4.1).

Figure 4.2 summarizes graphically the procedures involved in finding the cumulative frequency of a given score. You will note that the class 62.5 to 65.5 is divided into 3 equal units corresponding to the scores within that class, whereas the frequency scale is divided into 28 equal units corresponding to the 28 frequencies within that class. What we are accomplishing, in effect, in finding the frequency corresponding to a score, is a *linear transformation* from a scale of scores to a scale of frequencies;

FIGURE 4.2 Graphic representation of the procedures involved in finding the cumulative frequency corresponding to a given score.

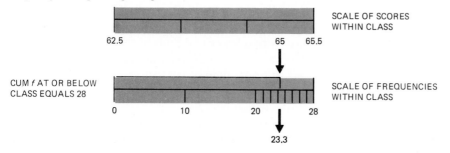

this is analogous to converting Fahrenheit readings to values on a Celsius scale, and the converse.

It should be noted that the percentile rank of a score and the score corresponding to a given percentile rank will not always agree with the values obtained from ungrouped frequency distributions or from stem-and-leaf diagrams. The disparity is due to the fact that some quantitative precision is lost during the process of grouping. One of the virtues of stem-and-leaf diagrams is the fact that this precision is not lost, since all the original data remain intact. To illustrate, refer back to the stem-and-leaf diagram in Table 3.4. Note that there are 12 values of 65 in the class 63 to 65. Assuming that half of these are above the desired score and half are below, count 6 values of 65 and all values below 65. The total comes to 50. Thus, the score corresponding to a percentile rank of 65 equals $(50/120) \times 100 = 41.67$. There is a disparity of 1.11 $(42.78 - 41.67 = 1.11)$ between these two methods of determining the score corresponding to a given percentile rank. This disparity may be attributed to grouping error.

Finding the Score Corresponding to a Given Percentile Value

Suppose you learned that the percentile rank of a male subject's BP was 90 and you wished to learn his diastolic BP corresponding to this percentile.

To obtain the answer, we must interpolate in the reverse direction, from the cumulative-frequency scale to the scale of scores. The first thing we must learn is the cumulative frequency corresponding to the 90th percentile. This may be obtained by multiplying the percentile rank by N and dividing by 100. In other words,

$$\operatorname{cum} f = \frac{\text{percentile rank} \times N}{100} \tag{4.2}$$

Since we are interested in a score at the 90th percentile and our N is 120, the cumulative frequency of a score at the 90th percentile is

$$\operatorname{cum} f = \frac{90 \times 120}{100} = 108$$

Referring to Table 4.1, we see that the frequency 108 is in the class with real limits of 77.5 to 80.5. Indeed, it is 1 frequency into the class, since the cum f at the lower real limit of the class is 107, which is 1 less than 108. There are 10 cases in all within the class. Thus, the frequency 108 is 1/10 of the way through a class with a lower real limit of 77.5 and an upper real limit of 80.5. In other words, it is 1/10 of the way through 3 score units. Expressed in terms of score units, then, it is $(1/10) \times 3$ or 0.3 score units above the lower real limit of the class. By adding 0.3 to 77.5, we obtain the score at the 90th percentile, which is 77.8.

Figure 4.3 represents graphically the procedures involved in the linear transformation from units of the frequency scale to units of the scale of

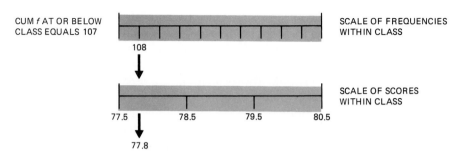

FIGURE 4.3 Graphic representation of the procedures involved in finding the score corresponding to a given frequency within the class.

scores. For those of you who desire a generalized method for determining scores corresponding to a given percentile, Formula (4.3) should be helpful:

$$\text{Score at a given percentile} = X_{ll} + \frac{i(\text{cum}\,f - \text{cum}\,f_{ll})}{f_i} \qquad (4.3)$$

where

X_{ll} = score at lower real limit of the class containing cum f
i = width of the class
cum f = cumulative frequency of the score
cum f_{ll} = cumulative frequency at the lower real limit of the class containing cum f
f_i = number of cases within the class containing cum f

[Note that Formula (4.3) requires the use of Formula (4.2) to calculate cum f.]

To illustrate the use of the formula, let's employ an example with which we are already familiar. What BP is at the 42.78th percentile? First, by employing Formula (4.2), we obtain

$$\text{cum}\,f = \frac{42.78 \times 120}{100} = 51.34^*$$

The score at the lower real limit of the class containing the frequency 51.34 is 62.5; i is 3; cum f to the lower real limit of the class is 28; and the number of cases within the class is 28. Substituting the above values into Formula (4.3), we obtain

$$\text{Score at 42.78th percentile} = 62.5 + \frac{3(51.34 - 28)}{28}$$
$$= 62.5 + 2.5 = 65$$

Note that this is the score from which we previously obtained the percentile rank 42.78 and that this formula illustrates a good procedure for checking the accuracy of our calculations. In other words, whenever you find the

* Note that cum f = 51.34 differs slightly from 51.33, found on page 101, due to rounding.

percentile rank of a score, you may take that answer and determine the score corresponding to that percentile value. You should obtain the original score. Similarly, whenever you obtain a score corresponding to a given percentile rank, you may take that answer and determine the percentile rank of that score. You should always arrive at the original percentile rank. Failure to do so indicates that you have made an error. It is preferable to repeat the solution without reference to your prior answer rather than to attempt to find the mistake in your prior solution. Such errors are frequently of the "proofreader" type that defy detection, are time-consuming to locate, and are highly frustrating.

TABLE 4.2 Raw-Score Equivalents of Selected Percentile Points on the Miller Analogies Test for Eight Graduate and Professional School Groups

Per-centile	Physical Sciences	Agri-culture	Medical Science	Biological Sciences	Social Sciences	Social Work	Languages and Literature	Law-School Freshmen	Per-centile
99	93	89	92	88	90	81	87	84	99
95	91	86	83	87	85	76	84	79	95
90	88	77	78	86	82	67	80	73	90
85	85	72	76	80	79	64	76	66	85
80	82	67	74	76	76	61	74	63	80
75	80	64	71	70	74	60	73	60	75
70	78	61	67	68	69	58	68	58	70
65	76	59	64	67	67	57	66	55	65
60	74	57	60	65	64	54	65	53	60
55	70	56	58	63	63	52	61	51	55
50	68	54	57	61	61	50	59	49	50
45	65	51	55	58	58	47	56	47	45
40	63	50	53	55	56	46	53	45	40
35	60	48	50	53	53	45	51	42	35
30	58	43	47	52	51	41	46	40	30
25	55	40	45	50	49	39	43	37	25
20	51	37	43	48	46	37	41	35	20
15	47	34	41	47	44	32	38	32	15
10	43	31	34	41	39	27	35	30	10
5	39	26	30	37	32	22	29	25	5
1	28	5	24	28	18	9	7	18	1
N	251	125	103	84	229	116	145	558	N
Mean	66.7	53.6	57.6	61.5	60.2	49.4	57.7	49.6	Mean
SD	16.6	17.3	16.2	15.6	16.0	15.2	17.4	16.1	SD

4.3 PERCENTILE RANK
AND REFERENCE GROUP

Just as a score is meaningless in the abstract, so also is a percentile rank. A percentile rank must always be expressed in relation to some reference group. Thus, if a friend claims that she obtained a percentile rank of 93 in a test of mathematical aptitude, you might not be terribly impressed if the reference group were made up of individuals who completed only the eighth grade. On the other hand, if the reference group consisted of individuals holding a doctorate in mathematics, your attitude would unquestionably be quite different.

Many standardized tests employed in psychology, education, and industry publish separate norms for various reference groups. Table 4.2 shows the raw-score equivalents for selected percentile points on a test widely employed for graduate-school admissions. You will note that a person obtaining a raw score of 50 on this test would obtain a percentile rank of 25, 35, 40, and 50 when compared successively with reference groups in the biological sciences, medical science, agriculture, and social work.

CASE EXAMPLE 4.1

One Person's Normal Is Another's Hypertension

Hypertension is a condition in which the blood pressure—either systolic (when the heart pumps blood through the arteries) and/or diastolic (when the heart is at rest between beats)—is chronically elevated. In about two-thirds of all cases, the cause of the condition is unknown, giving rise to speculation that psychological factors (work pressures, anxiety, etc.) may be involved. What is not widely known is that many adolescent boys and girls have abnormally high systolic and/or diastolic blood pressures for their age.

In "Adolescent Hypertension," Klein presents blood pressure (BP) readings (systolic/diastolic) at the 50th percentile (the median, discussed in Chapter 5) and the 95th percentile for boys and girls from ages 10 through 18 (see Table 4.3). Three readings at or above the 95th percentile, taken at least a week apart at a single health clinic, are sufficient for a diagnosis of adolescent hypertension.

Note that as the subject's age increases, the BP reading at the 95th percentile also increases. Thus, an 18-year-old female with BP readings of, for example,

TABLE 4.3 Percentiles of Blood Pressure (mm Hg) Taken from the Right Arm, with the Subject Seated

Age	Male		Female	
	50th %ile	95th %ile	50th %ile	95th %ile
10	109/72	130/86	110/73	132/87
11	112/73	134/87	113/74	134/88
12	115/74	137/87	115/75	136/89
13	117/75	137/89	117/76	138/89
14	120/76	143/91	119/76	140/90
15	122/76	146/92	120/77	142/91
16	124/77	148/93	121/77	143/91
17	126/78	150/94	122/78	144/92
18	128/79	153/95	123/79	145/92

135/88 would be considered within the high "normal" range. For a female of 10 years of age, however, these readings would be above the 95th percentile on both systolic and diastolic measures.

Source: Based on Arthur Klein (1981), "Adolescent Hypertension," *Therapaeia,* Sept., 37–41.

4.4 PUTTING IT ALL TOGETHER

In Section 3.10, we looked at data concerning the numbers of black and white male prison inmates and the causes of death during incarceration. Table 4.4 shows the combined black and white frequency and cumulative-frequency distributions for the numbers of prisoners in six age classes.

Let us suppose that we wanted to know the age at and below which 60% of all prisoners fall. This age would correspond to the 60th percentile.

Steps in finding the age corresponding to a given percentile rank: the 60th percentile:

1. Sum the f column to obtain N. $N = 347,976$
2. Cumulative frequencies by successive addition of frequencies from the lowest to the highest class. The last cumulative frequency *must* equal N.
3. Multiply the percentile rank in which we are interested (60) by N and divide by 100. Thus,

$$\frac{60 \times 347,976}{100} = 208,785.6$$

TABLE 4.4 Estimated Combined Numbers of White and Black Male Prison Inmates in Various Age Groupings in 1984

Class (Age)	Estimated Number of Inmates (f)	Cum f
65–74	1,185	347,976
55–64	6,786	346,791
45–54	18,097	340,005
35–44	67,866	321,908
25–34	158,355	254,042
15–24	95,687	95,687
N	347,976	

Based on R. B. Ruback and C. A. Innes (1988), "The Relevance and Irrelevance of Psychological Research: The Example of Prison Crowding," *American Psychologist*, **43**(9), 683–702.

4. Find the class containing the 208,785.6th cumulative frequency. This is the class with the apparent limits of 25 to 34 and the real limits of 24.5 to 34.5.
5. Subtract from the value obtained in step 3 the cumulative frequency at the upper real limit of the adjacent lower class; that is, 208,785.6 − 95,687 = 113,098.6.
6. Divide the value found in step 5 by the frequency within the class (158,355) and multiply by the width of the class ($i = 10$). Thus, the number of years within the class corresponding to the 60th percentile is (113,098.6/158,355) × 10 = 7.14.
7. Add the value found in step 6 to the score (age) at the lower real limit of the class containing the 208,785.6th cumulative frequency. Thus, 24.5 + 7.14 = 31.64. We may conclude that 60 percent of all male prisoners were 31.64 years of age or less.

Now, if we were to find the percentile rank of age 31.64, we should obtain our original percentile rank of 60. The following are the steps in obtaining the percentile rank of a score:

1. Sum the f column to obtain N. $N = 347,976$
2. Cumulate frequencies by successive addition of frequencies from the lowest to the highest class. The last cumulative frequency *must* equal N.
3. Identify the class containing the score (age): 31.64.
4. Subtract the age at the lower real limit of that class from 31.64: 31.64 − 24.5 = 7.14.

5. Note the frequency within that class: 158,355.
6. Divide the value found in step 4 by the width of the class and multiply by the frequency noted in step 5. Thus, $(7.14/10) \times 158,355 = 113,065.5$.* This value represents the frequency within the class 24.5 to 34.5 corresponding to an age of 31.64.
7. Note the cumulative frequency appearing in the adjacent lower class: cum $f = 95,687$.
8. Add the value found in step 6 to the value found in step 7. Thus, $113,075.5 + 95,687 = 208,752.5$.
9. Divide the value found in step 8 by N and multiply by 100. Thus, $(208,752.5/347,976) \times 100 = 60$.

CHAPTER SUMMARY

In this chapter, we saw that a score, by itself, is meaningless unless it is compared to a standard base or scale. Scores are often converted into units of the percentile-rank scale in order to provide a readily understandable basis for their interpretation and comparison.

We saw that

1. Percentile ranks of scores and scores corresponding to a given percentile may be approximated from a cumulative-percentage graph.
2. Direct computational methods permit a more precise location of the percentile rank of a score and the score corresponding to a given percentile. These methods were discussed and demonstrated in the text. See Table 4.1 and the illustrative solutions that accompany it.
3. A percentile rank is meaningless in the abstract. It must always be expressed in relation to some reference group.

TERMS TO REMEMBER

percentile rank   **percentiles**

EXERCISES

1. Estimate the percentile rank of the following BPs, employing Fig. 4.1:
   a. 60   **b.** 70   **c.** 80

2. Calculate the percentile rank of the BPs in Exercise 1, employing Table 4.1.

3. Estimate the BPs corresponding to the following percentiles, employing Fig. 4.1:
   a. 25   **b.** 50   **c.** 75

* The slight disparity from step 5 in the previous illustration is due to rounding error.

4. Calculate the BPs corresponding to the percentiles in Exercise 3, employing Table 4.1.

5. A younger sibling claims to have obtained a score of 130 on a standard vocabulary test. What additional information might you seek in order to interpret this score?

6. Refer to Chapter 3, Exercise 16.
   a. A student in group A obtained a score of 45 on the test of reading ability. What is his or her percentile rank in the group?
   b. What is the percentile rank of a student in group B who also obtained a score of 45?
   c. Combine both groups into an overall frequency distribution and obtain the percentile rank of a score of 45. What happens to the percentile rank of the student in group A? group B? Why?

*7. If we were to place all the BPs shown in Table 4.1 into a hat, what is the likelihood (percentage of times) that, selecting at random, we would obtain
   a. a BP equal to or higher than 73?
   b. a BP equal to or lower than 73?
   c. a BP equal to or below 58?
   d. a BP equal to or above 83?
   e. a BP between 60 and 80?
   f. a BP equal to or greater than 75, or equal to or less than 57?

8. The following questions are based on Table 4.2.
   a. John H. proudly proclaims that he obtained a "higher" percentile ranking than his friend Howard. Investigation of the fact reveals that his score on the test was actually lower. Must it be concluded that John H. was mistaken, or is some other explanation possible? Explain.
   b. Jean H. obtained a percentile rank of 65 on the social-work scale. What was her score? What score would she have had to obtain to achieve the same percentile rank on the physical sciences scale?
   c. World Law School employs the Miller Analogies Test as an element of the admissions procedure. No applicants obtaining percentile ranks below 75 are considered for admission, regardless of their other qualifications. Thus, the 75th percentile might be called a "cutoff" point. Which reference group is most likely to be involved in the decision? What score constitutes the cutoff point for this distribution?
   d. Foster Medical School also employs the 75th percentile as a cutoff point. Lee F. obtained a raw score of 62. What are Lee's chances of being considered for admission?

The following table shows a frequency and cumulative-frequency distribution of 140 baseline heart-rate (HR) measures (Perkins, 1984). In Exercises 9–14, we provide the HR measures of six subjects. Determine the percentile rank of each HR.

9. 72 **10.** 53 **11.** 95 **12.** 62 **13.** 101 **14.** 81

* All exercises that are used to lay the groundwork for future discussion are preceded by an asterisk.

Class (Real Limits)	f	Cumulative f
106.45–111.45	1	140
101.45–106.45	3	139
96.45–101.45	3	136
91.45– 96.45	5	133
86.45– 91.45	11	128
81.45– 86.45	13	117
76.45– 81.45	23	104
71.45– 76.45	20	81
66.45– 71.45	28	61
61.45– 66.45	14	33
56.45– 61.45	13	19
51.45– 56.45	3	6
46.45– 51.45	2	3
41.45– 46.45	1	1

Using the same table, find the HR measures corresponding to the percentile ranks provided in Exercises 15–20.

15. Percentile rank of 10

16. Percentile rank of 25

17. Percentile rank of 75

18. Percentile rank of 18

19. Percentile rank of 84

20. Percentile rank of 16

21. Suppose a manager were interested in comparing the scores of 25 employees on a mathematical test. Assigning one person to each letter, he records the following scores:

A. 55	F. 40	K. 50	P. 40	U. 40
B. 50	G. 60	L. 45	Q. 35	V. 30
C. 35	H. 45	M. 25	R. 25	W. 45
D. 45	I. 50	N. 35	S. 20	X. 35
E. 40	J. 30	O. 55	T. 30	Y. 40

Calculate the percentile rank for each person, employing $i = 5$ and assuming that the lowest class is 20 to 24.

22. In addition, the manager studies the number of mathematical problems the employees solve per day. He finds the following number of units completed per day for the same 25 employees (the employees were designated by the same letters as above):

A. 45	F. 30	K. 40	P. 30	U. 30
B. 40	G. 50	L. 35	Q. 25	V. 20
C. 25	H. 35	M. 15	R. 15	W. 35
D. 35	I. 40	N. 25	S. 10	X. 25
E. 30	J. 20	O. 45	T. 20	Y. 30

Calculate the percentile rank for each person and compare it to the ranks in Exercise 21. Employ $i = 5$ and a lowest class of 10 to 14.

*23. Refer to Exercise 28, Chapter 3, and construct both a cumulative-frequency and a cumulative-percentage distribution of the 49 sums.

*24. Review the sampling experiment demonstrated in Exercise 28, Chapter 3. Then return to the cumulative-percentage distribution in Exercise 23, above. Answer the following questions:
   a. What is the likelihood (what is the percentage of times) that a sum equal to or less than 11 would have been drawn in a sample of $N = 2$ from the original population of seven numbers?
   b. What is the likelihood (what is the percentage of times) that a sum greater than 5 or less than 10 would have been obtained? [*Hint:* The cumulative percentage to the upper real limit of 9 is 88; below the upper limit of 5 is 43.]
   c. What percentage of times would a sum equal to or less than 2 be obtained?
   d. What percentage of times would a sum equal to or greater than 10 be obtained?
   e. What percentage of times would a sum equal to or less than 2 or equal to or greater than 10 be obtained?

25. Refer to Case Example 4.1. Which of the following systolic blood pressures would be at or above the 95th percentile?
   a. Charles, age 15/99.   b. Maria, age 13/139.
   c. Matthew, age 10/133.   d. Bob, age 18/145.
   e. Alicia, age 14/140.   f. Karen, age 17/143.

26. Given the accompanying table, calculate the percentile rank for the following size families:
   a. 3   b. 5   c. 8
   In what way does this table violate the procedures outlined for constructing a frequency distribution?

Size of U.S. Families of Spanish Origin in 1977

Size	Number (in Thousands)
2	662
3	636
4	625
5	408
6	218
7 or more persons	216

Source: U.S. Bureau of Census, *Current Population Reports*, Series P-20, No. 339, U.S. Government Printing Office.

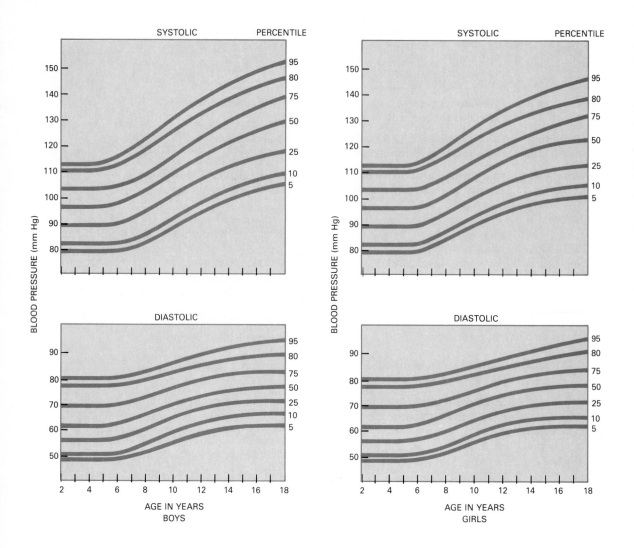

Percentiles of distribution of blood pressure measurements (taken at the right arm, subject seated) are shown plotted against age for boys and girls. (From National Heart, Lung, and Blood Institute (1977), "Report of the Task Force on Blood Pressure Control in Children" *Pediatrics* **59**(2), 797–820. Reprinted with permission.)

27. The percentile bands corresponding to systolic and diastolic blood pressures of boys and girls between 2 and 18 years of age are shown above. Using these figures, find the approximate percentile rank of each of the following:

a. boy, age 6, systolic BP = 90. **b.** girl, age 6, systolic BP = 90.
c. boy, age 18, systolic BP = 103. **d.** girl, age 18, systolic BP = 103.
e. girl, age 8, diastolic BP = 78. **f.** girl, age 17, diastolic BP = 80.

5

Measures of Central Tendency

5.1 INTRODUCTION

One of the greatest sources of confusion among lay people, and perhaps a cause for their suspicion that statistics is more of an art than a science, revolves around the ambiguity in the use of the term "average." Unions and management speak of average salaries and frequently cite numerical values that are in sharp disagreement with each other; television programs and commercials are said to be prepared with the average viewer in mind; politicians are deeply concerned about the views of the average voter; the average family size is frequently given as a fractional value, a statistical abstraction that is ludicrous to some and absurd to others; the term "average" is commonly used as a synonym for the term "normal"—if the temperatures for a given day approach the long-term average for the day, the TV meteorologist tells us that the day was normal. Indeed, the term average has so many popular connotations that many statisticans prefer to drop it from the technical vocabulary and refer, instead, to **measure of central tendency.** We define a measure of central tendency as an *index of central location employed in the description of frequency distributions.* Since the center of a distribution may be defined in different ways, there will be a number of different measures of central tendency. In this chapter, we concern ourselves with three of the most frequently employed measures of central tendency; the mean, the median, and the mode.

Measure of Central Tendency: Index of central location employed in the description of frequency distributions.

BOX 5.1

THE AMBIGUITY OF "AVERAGE"

Annual salaries of XYZ Company (in dollars)

30,000
24,000
14,000
10,000 ◄——— Mean
9,000
9,000
9,000
7,000 ◄——— Median
6,000
6,000
6,000
5,000 ⎫
5,000 ⎬ ◄— Mode
5,000 ⎪
5,000 ⎭

The term "average" is frequently used by mass media, labor unions, corporations, hucksters, politicians, and students to describe scores or numerical values in the central part of a distribution. Unfortu-

nately, there are three different measures of central tendency, which, for a given distribution, may deviate substantially from one another. This disparity often gives rise to heated disagreements among individuals who focus their attention upon one or another measure of central tendency. Many people are confused by all this bickering and the endless citation of conflicting statistics. They may conclude, in dismay, "Statistics are meaningless. You can do anything you want with them."

In the accompanying table we show an array of annual salaries of a hypothetical small business that employs 15 individuals, including the president and the vice-president. The company has recently gone on strike. The leader of the strike cites the poor wages—pointing to the most frequently occurring wage (the mode). "The average salary is five thousand dollars," shouts the leader, in a controlled rage. Management, looking at the arithmetic average (mean) of all the salaries, replies with righteous indignation, "Nonsense! The average salary is ten thousand dollars." A mediator, looking at exactly the same data but concentrating on the middle salary (the median), expostulates contemptuously, "Balderdash! Both of you are wrong. The average salary is seven thousand dollars."

Thus doth statistics make liars of us all!

Why Describe Central Tendency?

In the first four chapters of the book, we were concerned primarily with organizing data into a meaningful and useful form. Beyond this, however, we want to describe our data so that we can make quantitative statements. A frequency distribution represents an organization of data, but it does not, in itself, permit us to make quantitative statements either describing the distribution or comparing two or more distributions.

There are two features of many frequency distributions that statisticians have noted and have developed quantitative methods for describing: (1) Data often cluster around a central value that lies between the two extreme values of the variable under study, and (2) data may tend to be dispersed or distributed about the central value in a way that can be specified quantitatively. The first of these features—central tendency—is the topic of the present chapter; the second—dispersion—will be discussed in Chapter 6.

The ability to locate a point of central tendency, particularly when coupled with a description of the dispersion of scores about that point, can be very useful to behavioral scientists. For example, they may be able to reduce a mass of data to a simple quantitative value that can be communicated to and understood by other scientists.

We have already stated that the behavioral scientist is frequently called upon to compare the measurements obtained from two or more groups of subjects for the purpose of drawing inferences about the effects of an independent variable. Measures of central tendency greatly simplify the task of drawing conclusions.

5.2 THE ARITHMETIC MEAN

Methods of Calculation

You are probably intimately familiar with the arithmetic mean, for whenever you obtain an average of grades by summing the grades and dividing by the number of grades, you are calculating the arithmetic **mean.** In short, *the mean is the sum of the scores or values of a variable divided by their number.* Stated in algebraic form,

Mean: Sum of the scores or values of a variable divided by their number.

$$\overline{X} = \frac{X_1 + X_2 + \cdots + X_N}{N} = \frac{\Sigma X}{N} \tag{5.1}$$

where

$\overline{X}$ = the mean and is referred to as X bar*
N = the number of scores
Σ = the mathematical verb directing us to sum all the measurements

Thus, the arithmetic mean of the scores 8, 12, 15, 19, 24 is $\overline{X}$ = 78/5 = 15.60.

Obtaining the Mean from an Ungrouped Frequency Distribution   You will recall that we constructed a frequency distribution as a way of eliminating the constant repetition of scores that occur with varying frequency, in order to permit a single entry in the frequency column to

---

* In Section 1.2, we indicated that italic letters are employed to represent sample statistics and Greek letters to represent population parameters. The Greek letter μ is used to represent the population mean.

Emotional contrast and mood: Calculating the mean

January 28, 1986 is a day that will remain etched in the memory of many witnesses to the tragic events of that day. Following many days of frustrating delays in the launch of *Challenger* with seven astronauts aboard, the shuttle soared skyward in an apparently perfect launch. The successful launch was greeted with great joy throughout the nation, including numerous classrooms where children and teachers cheered for the first teacher in space. A little more than a minute into the flight, joy was suddenly transformed into horror as the shuttle was demolished by a massive blast. In the days afterward, many observers reported feelings of great sadness and depression. Is it possible that the sharp contrast in emotions (from joy to horror in a matter of moments) contributed to the emotional aftermath of this tragedy?

Long before the events of this day, a team of researchers at the University of Manchester, England, had been investigating the effects of intense prior emotions on our subsequent emotional reactions to situations that evoke contrasting emotional states. Is horror more unpleasant when it is preceded by humor? Is humor funnier when preceded by horror?

The following ratings of unpleasantness were obtained on ten male subjects when five televised scenes of horror were preceded by six humorous scenes and on ten other male subjects for whom the horror scenes were not preceded by humorous scenes. The higher the score was, the greater was the reported unpleasantness.

Horror Preceded by Humor	Horror First
36	29
31	34
36	27
20	33
41	10
34	28
32	26
34	31
32	30
33	35
$\Sigma X = 329$	$\Sigma X = 283$
$\overline{X} = 32.9$	$\overline{X} = 28.3$

a. The following ratings of unpleasantness were obtained on ten female subjects when horror was preceded by humor and on ten other female subjects for whom horror was not preceded by humor. The higher the score was, the greater was the reported unpleasantness. Calculate the mean for each condition.

b. Prepare a graph showing the means of the males and females under each condition.

Horror Preceded by Humor	Horror First
42	30
26	33
40	37
31	32
37	30
37	31
43	45
43	36
44	38
41	38

c. Do the results of the study appear to support the contrast hypothesis? That is, do emotionally contrasting experiences tend to exaggerate the extent of the emotional swing?

ANSWERS

a. $\Sigma X = 384$ $\bar{X} = 38.4$ $\Sigma X = 350$ $\bar{X} = 35.0$

b.

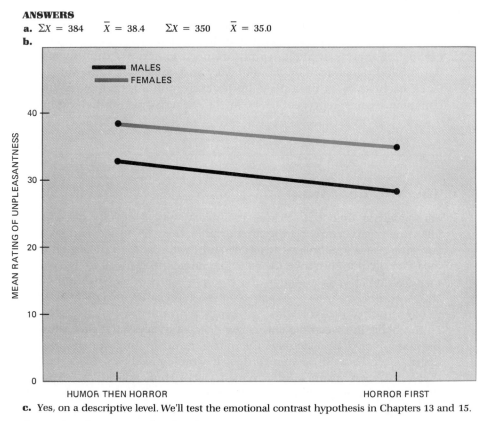

c. Yes, on a descriptive level. We'll test the emotional contrast hypothesis in Chapters 13 and 15.

Source: Based on Manstead et al., 1983.

TABLE 5.1 Computational Procedures for Calculating the Mean with Ungrouped Frequency Distributions. Scores Made by Type B Subjects, Active Condition, on a Standard Challenging Task (SCT)

X	f	fX	Computation
10	4	40	
9	2	18	$\bar{X} = \Sigma fX/N$
8	6	48	
7	2	14	$\bar{X} = 155/20$
6	5	30	
5	1	5	$\bar{X} = 7.75$

$$N = 20 \; \Sigma fX = 155$$

Source: From Ortega and Pipal, 1984.

represent the number of times a given score occurs. Thus, in Table 5.1, we know from the column headed *f* that the score of 8 occurred six times. In calculating the mean, then, we do not need to add 8 six times, since we may multiply the score by its frequency and obtain the same value of 48. Since each score is multiplied by its corresponding frequency prior to summing, we may represent the mean for frequency distributions as follows:

$$\bar{X} = \frac{\Sigma fX}{N} \qquad (5.2)$$

The Weighted Mean

Let's imagine that four classes in introductory sociology obtained the following mean scores on the final examination: 75, 78, 72, and 80. Could you sum these four means together and divide by 4, to obtain an overall mean for all four classes? This could be done *only if* the N in each class is identical. What if, as a matter of fact, the mean of 75 is based on an N of 30, the second mean is based on 40 observations, the third on N = 25, and the fourth on N = 50?

To obtain the weighted mean, we need only apply the procedures we previously used to calculate the mean from an ungrouped frequency distribution. To do this, we regard each sample mean as if it is a score and the N for each mean as its frequency. We then make up a frequency distribution of means and follow the procedures that are already familiar. This frequency distribution of means is shown in Table 5.2. *Note:* It is not necessary to arrange these means in ascending or descending order unless you wish to calculate the median of the sample means. This is not often done.

CASE EXAMPLE 5.1

Endorphins and Sudden Infant Death: A Link?

The occurrence of sudden, unexplained deaths in infants (SIDS, or Sudden Infant Death Syndrome) has been a source of great concern in the health-care professions. Mental health professionals are specifically concerned with SIDS because the death of a child often leaves a deep residue of guilt in the parents. Compounding this problem is the fact that one parent often blames the other for the catastrophe.

A seemingly unrelated series of developments in physiological research might provide a clue to the cause of at least some SIDS. In recent years, it has been discovered that the body produces its own narcotic-like substances, endorphins and enkephalins. In a study by Orlowski, the research team measured the β-endorphin levels in the cerebrospinal fluid of eight infants who had experienced near-SIDS (a cessation of breathing for more than 20 seconds). These levels were as follows: 52, 52, 66, 54, 47, 66, 90, 50. The β-endorphin levels of two control infants were 10 and 1.

The mean of the experimental subjects is $\overline{X} = 477/8 = 59.62$. The mean of the two control subjects is $\overline{X} = 11/2 = 5.5$. The difference between these two means is $59.62 - 5.5 = 54.12$. We shall reexamine these data in Chapter 13 to see if this large a difference in means could reasonably be attributed to chance. Note, however, that this study is not a true experiment. The high endorphin levels were not randomly assigned to the near-SIDS infants. Rather, they occurred naturally. It is altogether possible that the elevated endorphin levels were a bodily reaction to the cessation of breathing rather than a cause of the cessation.

Source: Based on James P. Orlowski (1982), "Endorphins in Infant Apnea," *New England Journal of Medicine,* **307**(3), 186–187.

TABLE 5.2 Obtaining the Weighted Mean by Regarding Each Sample Mean as a Score and Its Associated *N* as a Frequency, and Using the Same Procedures We Used for Calculating the Mean from an Ungrouped Frequency Distribution. X_w Is the Weighted Mean and N_t Is the Sum of All the Sample *N*'s

Sample Mean ($\overline{X}$)	Frequency (*f*)	*f*$\overline{X}$	Computation
75	30	2250	$\overline{X}_w = \Sigma f\overline{X}/N_t$
78	40	3120	
72	25	1800	$\overline{X}_w = 11{,}170/145$
80	50	4000	$\overline{X}_w = 77.03$
	$N_t = 145$	$\Sigma f\overline{X} = 11{,}170$	

BOX 5.2

THE WILL ROGERS PARADOX

Will Rogers was a colorful, often sardonic, social commentator of the 1920s and 1930s who often brought smiles to a public whose spirit was otherwise weighed down by The Great Depression. Noting the mass migration of Oklahomans to California in search of employment (see Steinbeck's *The Grapes of Wrath),* Rogers is reported to have said, "When the Okies left Oklahoma and moved to California, they raised the average intelligence of both states."

This observation derives its humor largely from the fact that is appears to be totally absurd. How could the average IQ of both states increase as a result of the one-way migration from one state to another? Surprisingly, it is possible. Take a few moments and see if you can construct a scenario that would permit this to happen.

Here it is. Suppose that the mean IQ of those migrating from Oklahoma is below the mean IQ for the state but above the mean IQ of Californians. This reverse "brain drain" would raise the mean IQ of Oklahomans left behind. Now, since the mean IQ of the migrating hoards was higher than the mean IQ of Californians, the migration would raise the mean IQ of that state. Now such a situation will occur only under one set of circumstances: If the mean IQ of Oklahomans is greater than the mean IQ of Californians. The paradox was the indirect way Will Rogers chose to tweak the egos of Californians.

No doubt, this was all said by ole Will with a twinkle in his eye. But the biggest surprise of all is the recent resurrection of the Will Rogers paradox by a team of medical researchers (Feinstein et al., 1985) who believe it provides a clue to an important source of misleading survival statistics. Let's see how this works.

Patients with progressive disorders are frequently assigned to categories according to the physician's assessment of how advanced the disorder is at that time. Thus, a patient in the early stages of a disease is assigned to Stage I, a "good" category. An advanced case is assigned to one of the two progressively "bad" categories, Stage II or Stage III. As might be expected, if the disorder is generally terminal, the patients in the earlier stages will typically live longer than those in the later stages *regardless of treatment interventions.*

But tremendous advances in diagnostic techniques have occurred in recent years, resulting in the assignment of patients to stages that are different from what would have occurred a few years earlier. One example is cancer that originates in the lungs. Patients with "silent" or "early" phases of a spreading disease (previously Stage I) are now routinely detected with new diagnostic methods. These patients are now assigned to a bad category (Stage II or Stage III). However, since the silent spread is in its early phases and unaccompanied by overt symptoms, the expected survival time of these patients who have migrated to more advanced stages would be longer than patients in these stages who have overt symptoms. *This migration would raise the mean observed survival times of patients in advanced stages of lung cancer, even if the treatments were totally ineffective.* Moreover, since the higher risk patients are now removed from Stage I, the average survival time for the remaining Stage I patients would also be increased, even without effective treatment. To summarize this startling medical application of the Will Rogers paradox: Because of enormously improved diagnostic techniques, patients without overt symptoms migrate from lower to higher stages, thereby increasing the average survival time of patients in both the good and the bad stages of lung cancer without in any way affecting the overall survival times. Under these circumstances, it would be easy to ascribe the apparent prolongation of life in each category, taken separately, to the medical treatment used, even if completely ineffective.

Source: From Feinstein et al., 1985.

As you see, the **weighted mean** is 77.03. Had we merely summed the sample means and divided by 4, we would have obtained an incorrect value of 305/4 = 76.25. Weighted means are frequently used when we want to obtain the "average" amount we paid per share on several different purchases of a given stock, when we calculate the lifetime batting average of a baseball player throughout his career, or when we wish to ascertain the overall mean we paid per pound (or gallon) for some product we purchased in different amounts over different times, to name but a few.

Weighted Mean: Sum of the mean of each group multiplied by its respective weight (the N in each group), divided by the sum of the weights (total N).

5.3 THE MEDIAN

With grouped frequency distributions, the **median** is defined as *that score or potential score in a distribution of scores that divides the distribution so that the same number of scores lie on each side of it.* If this definition sounds vaguely familiar to you, it isn't surprising. The median is merely a special case of a percentile rank. Indeed, the median is the score at the 50th percentile. It should be clear that the generalized procedures discussed in Chapter 4 for determining the score at various percentile ranks may be applied to the calculation of the median.

Median: Score or potential score in a distribution of scores that divides the distribution so that the same number of scores lie on each side of it.

Modifying Formula (4.3) for application to the special case of the median, we obtain the following:

$$\text{Median} = X_{ll} + i \left[\frac{(N/2) - \text{cum} f_{ll}}{f_i} \right] \qquad (5.3)$$

where

X_{ll} = score at lower real limit of the class containing X

i = width of class

$\text{cum} f_{ll}$ = cumulative frequency at the lower real limit of the class containing X

f_i = number of cases within the class containing X

Applied to the data in Table 4.1, the median becomes

$$\text{Median} = 65.5 + 3 \left[\frac{120/2) - 56}{20} \right]$$

$$= 65.5 + 3 \left[\frac{(60 - 56)}{20} \right] = 65.5 + 3 \left(\frac{4}{20} \right)$$

$$= 65.5 + 0.6 = 66.1$$

The Median of an Array of Scores

Occasionally it will be necessary to obtain the median when the N is not sufficient to justify casting the data into the form of a frequency distribution or a grouped frequency distribution. Consider the following array of scores: 5, 19, 37, 39, 45. Note that the scores are arranged in order of magnitude and that N is an odd number. A score of 37 is the median, since two scores fall above it and two scores fall below it.* If N is an *even* number, the median is the arithmetic mean of the *two middle values.* The two middle values in the array of scores 8, 26, 35, 43, 47, 73 are 35 and 43. The arithmetic mean of these two values is $(35 + 43)/2$, or 39. Therefore, the median is 39.

Occasionally the middle score in an array of scores is tied with other scores. How do we specify the median when we encounter tied scores?

Consider the following array of 20 scores: 2, 3, 3, 4, 5, 7, 7, 8, 8, 8, 8, 9, 10, 12, 14, 15, 17, 19, 19, 20. The easiest procedure is to convert the array to an ungrouped frequency distribution (see Table 5.3) and apply Formula (5.3). However, the i may be eliminated, since it is equal to 1.

$$\text{Median} = X_{ll} + \frac{(N/2) - \text{cum} f_{ll}}{f_1}$$

$$= 7.5 + \frac{(20/2) - 7}{4}$$

$$= 7.5 + \frac{3}{4} = 8.25$$

5.4 THE MODE

Mode: Score that occurs with the greatest frequency.

Of all measures of central tendency, the **mode** is the most easily determined, since it is obtained by inspection rather than by computation. The mode is simply *the score that occurs with greatest frequency.* For grouped data, the mode is designated as the midpoint of the interval containing the highest frequency count. In Table 4.1 the mode is a score of 64, since it is the midpoint of the class (62.5 to 65.5) containing the greatest frequency.

In some distributions, which we do not consider here, there will be two high points, which produce the appearance of two humps, as on a camel's back. Such distributions are referred to as being *bimodal.* A distribution containing more than two humps is referred to as being *multimodal.*

5.5 COMPARISON OF MEAN, MEDIAN, AND MODE

Given the choice of three different measures of central tendency, how does one decide which is appropriate for a given set of data? Before considering the various facets of this question, we will dispense with the mode as a

---

* When you work with an array of numbers where N is odd, the definition of the median does not quite hold; that is, in the preceding example, in which the median is 37, two scores lie below it and two above it, as opposed to one-half of N. If the score of 37 is regarded as falling one-half on either side of the median, this disparity is reconciled.

TABLE 5.3 An Ungrouped Frequency Distribution of 20 Scores Arranged in Descending Order

X	f	Cum f	X	f	Cum f
20	1	20	10	1	13
19	2	19	9	1	12
18	0	17	8	4	11
17	1	17	7	2	7
16	0	16	6	0	5
15	1	16	5	1	5
14	1	15	4	1	4
13	0	14	3	2	3
12	1	14	2	1	1
11	0	13			

leading candidate for use in the behavioral sciences. Since the mode is obtained by inspection rather than by computation, it is the appropriate statistic whenever a quick, rough estimate of central tendency is desired or when only the typical case is of interest. The mode may also be useful in obtaining a quick estimate of the mean and median, particularly if the distribution of scores is unimodal and relatively symmetrical. Otherwise, it is rarely used in the behavioral sciences.

Apart from these considerations, we restrict our discussion to the pros and cons of the mean and median as measures of central tendency. Specifically, we compare them in terms of the following five features: ease of computation, algebraic properties, sensitivity to skewness, utility when there are indeterminate values, and stability.

Ease of Computation

As we have seen, every piece of data in a data set contributes toward the calculation of the mean. Consequently, all values must be entered into the equation of the mean before its value may be computed. This is not the case with the median. In fact, all we need are the sample size (N), the upper and lower real limits of the class that contains the median, the cumulative frequency up to the lower limit of that class, and the number of cases within that class. Thus, if you know that $N = 60$, the class containing the median is 105.5 to 110.5, the cumulative frequency to the lower limit of the class is 24, and the number of cases within the class is 12, the median is readily calculated:

$$\text{Median} = 105.5 + 5(30 - 24)/12 = 108$$

The determination of the median is even easier if the data are in the form of an array, since the primary requirement is counting.

However, paradoxically, if you have access to a computer and the data have all been entered into a sophisticated statistical system, the mean may be obtained by giving a few simple commands. This may or may not be the case with the median. We do not know of a single instance of statistical software that ignores the mean. The same cannot be said about the prevalence of the median in statistical software.

Algebraic Properties and Sensitivity to Skewness

One of the most important properties of the mean is that *it is the point in a distribution of measurements or scores about which the summed deviations are equal to zero.* In other words, if we were to subtract the mean from each score and then sum or add the resulting deviations from the mean, this sum would equal zero. Symbolically,

$$\Sigma(X - \overline{X}) = 0 \tag{5.4}$$

The algebraic proof of this statement is

$$
\begin{aligned}
\Sigma(X - \overline{X}) &= \Sigma X - \Sigma \overline{X} \\
&= N\overline{X} - N\overline{X} \\
&= 0
\end{aligned}
$$

In following this algebraic proof, we should note (1) that since

$$\overline{X} = \frac{\Sigma X}{N}$$

it follows that $\Sigma X = N\overline{X}$ and (2) that summing the mean over all the scores $(\Sigma \overline{X})$ is the same as multiplying $\overline{X}$ by N—that is, $N\overline{X}$ (see Generalization 1, Chapter 2).

Therefore, the mean is a score or a potential score that balances all the scores on either side of it. In this sense it is analogous to the fulcrum of a seesaw. In playing on seesaws, you may have noticed that it is possible for a small individual to balance a heavy individual if the latter moves closer to the fulcrum. Thus, if you wanted to balance a younger brother or sister (presumably lighter than you) on a seesaw, you would move yourself toward the center of the board. This analogy leads to a second important characteristic of the mean; that is, *the mean is very sensitive to extreme measurements when these measurements are not balanced on both sides of it.*

Array: Arrangement of data according to their magnitude, from the smallest to the largest value, or vice versa.

Observe the two **arrays** of scores in Table 5.4 An *array is an arrangement of data according to their magnitude from the smallest to the largest value or from the largest to the smallest.* Note that all the scores in both distributions are the same except for the very large score of 33 in column X_2. This one extreme score is sufficient to double the size of the mean. The sensitivity of the mean to extreme scores is a characteristic that has important implications governing our use of it.

TABLE 5.4   Comparison of the Means of Two Arrays of Scores, One of which Contains an Extreme Value

Group 1 Score, X_1	Group 2 Score, X_2
2	2
3	3
5	5
7	7
8	33
$\Sigma X_1 = 25$	$\Sigma X_2 = 50$
$\overline{X}_1 = 5.00$	$\overline{X}_2 = 10.00$

In contrast to the mean, an outstanding characteristic of the median is its *insensitivity* to extreme scores. Consider the scores in column 2 of Table 5.4. The median is 5 in spite of the presence of a very high score ($X = 33$). It would remain 5 even if that score were *any* value greater than 5. Thus, when a distribution is markedly skewed, the mean provides a misleading estimate of central tendency, whereas the median better reflects the central region of that distribution. Annual income is a commonly studied variable in which the median is preferred over the mean, since the distribution is distinctly skewed in the direction of high incomes. The incomes of multimillionaires exert a much stronger upward pull on the mean than the incomes of paupers exert a downward pull. Income does not go below zero, but there is no similar restraint on the upper end of the scale.

A third important characteristic of the mean is that *the **sum of squares** of deviations from the arithmetic mean is less than the **sum of squares** of deviations about any other score or potential score.*

Sum of Squares: Deviations from the mean, squared and summed.

This characteristic of the mean is illustrated in Table 5.5, which shows the squares and the sum of squares when deviations are taken from the mean and various other scores in a distribution. It can be seen that the sum of the squared deviations is smallest in column 4, where deviations are taken from the mean.

This property of the mean provides us with another definition; that is, *the mean is the measure of central tendency that makes the sum of squared deviations around it minimal.* The method of locating the mean by finding the minimum sum of squares is referred to as the **least-squares method.** The least-squares method is of considerable value in statistics, particularly when it is applied to curve fitting.

Least-Squares Method: Method of locating the mean by finding the minimum sum of squares.

Indeterminate Values

There are a number of different occasions when values of the variable are indeterminate. The highest class (and sometimes the lowest) in many

TABLE 5.5   The Squares and Sum of Squared Deviations Taken from Various Scores in a Distribution

1 X	2 $(X - 2)^2$	3 $(X - 3)^2$	4 $(X - \bar{X})^2$	5 $(X - 5)^2$	6 $(X - 6)^2$
2	0	1	4	9	16
3	1	0	1	4	9
4	4	1	0	1	4
5	9	4	1	0	1
6	16	9	4	1	0
Totals	30	15	10	15	30

$N = 5$
$\bar{X} = 4$

summaries of health and age-related statistics does not include either an upper or lower boundary. If age is the variable of interest, the highest class may be 80 and above; if income is the variable, the lowest class may be under $2,500 and the highest class may be $50,000 and over. Since we are unable to specify the limits of these classes, we cannot ascertain the midpoint. Consequently, a mean cannot be calculated. (See Statistics in Action 5.2)

The inability, on occasion, to specify a value of a variable can also have important implications for the study of the environment. Many electronic and chemical tests for toxic substances in the environment (such as groundwater and air) are unable to detect quantities below certain values. It is not that these substances do not exist at these lower values but that the test procedures are simply unable to find them. To illustrate, if a given substance is measured in parts per million per cubic meter and the available technology cannot measure amounts less than 50 parts per million, then samples containing 49, 48, 47, and fewer parts per million would not be detected. If there are many of these undetected values and they are all recorded as zero, the mean would be an inappropriate statistic, since all the recorded zeros would draw the mean toward them. The resulting sample mean could seriously underestimate the actual amount of the toxic substance in the environment studied. Under these circumstances, the median might provide a better estimate of central tendency, since it would be unaffected by the spurious zeros—unless, of course, the majority of the readings are in the undetectable range.

The Mean and Median as Estimators

As previously noted, one important function of inferential statistics is to provide estimates of parameters. If we take a number of different samples from a symmetrical population with a single mode and wish to estimate

STATISTICS IN ACTION 5.2

AIDS in Europe, classified by age and gender: Calculating measures of central tendency with open-ended classes

Statistical information concerned with disease and matters of life and death (vital statistics) is often presented in the form of age-related grouped frequency distributions. The class widths may or may not be equal, and the highest age class is commonly open-ended. These features are exemplified in Table 5.6, where the four lowest classes have a width of 5, the next four have a width of 10, and the upper limit of the highest class is left undefined. The use of unequal widths and open-ended classes can be justified: We may wish to have a more precise look at certain age categories, and there may be too few cases in the higher age brackets to warrant separate classes. However, these procedures complicate the calculation of measures of central tendency. When a class is open-ended, we cannot locate the midpoint of the class. Consequently, the mean cannot be ascertained. But we can obtain the median and the percentile rank of any age except for those included in the open-ended class. We need only pay particular attention to each class width when calculating either the median and percentile ranks of scores or finding the score corresponding to a specific percentile rank.

    a. If you wish to compare graphically the male and female distributions of the ages at which AIDS is diagnosed, what type of distribution would be most appropriate and why?

TABLE 5.6 AIDS Cases by Age and Gender—21 European Countries through September 30, 1985

Age Group (Real Limits)	Males	Females
60 & above	21	4
50–60	103	9
40–50	375	12
30–40	622	36
20–30	277	57
15–20	8	0
10–15	3	0
5–10	3	1
0– 5	15	14
	$N = 1427$	$N = 133$

b. Based on your answer to (a), construct the graph that permits the visual comparison of AIDS cases by age category. Do there appear to be differences in the ages at which AIDS is diagnosed in males and females?

c. Prepare cumulative-frequency and cumulative-percentage distributions for males alone, females alone, and males and females combined.

d. What is the median age at which AIDS is first diagnosed in males? females?

e. What is the mean age at which AIDS is first diagnosed in males? females?

ANSWERS

a. Grouped percentage distributions because of the enormous difference in the number of males versus females infected (almost 11 to 1).

b.

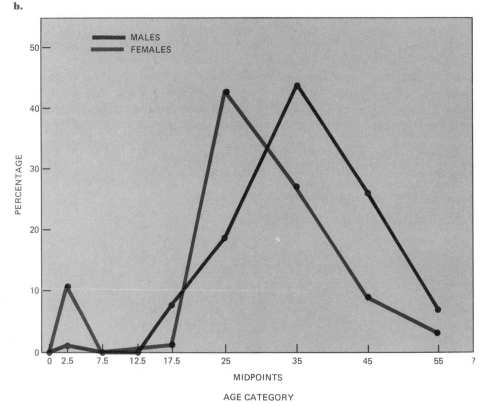

Diagnosed cases of AIDS appear to peak in the 20s in females and in the 30s in males.

c.

Age Group (Real Limits)	Males			Females			Combined		
	f	Cum f	Cum %	f	Cum f	Cum %	f	Cum f	Cum %
60 & above	21	1427	100.00	4	133	100.00	25	1560	100.00
50–60	103	1406	98.53	9	129	96.99	112	1535	98.40
40–50	375	1303	91.31	12	120	90.23	387	1423	91.22
30–40	622	928	65.03	36	108	81.20	658	1036	66.41
20–30	277	306	21.44	57	72	54.14	334	378	24.23
15–20	8	29	2.03	0	15	11.28	8	44	2.82
10–15	3	21	1.47	0	15	11.28	3	36	2.31
5–10	3	18	1.26	1	15	11.28	4	33	2.12
0– 5	15	15	1.05	14	14	10.53	29	29	1.86
	$N = 1427$			$N = 133$			$N = 1560$		

d. The cumulative frequency of the score is 713.5

$N = 1427$ $i = 10$; score at lower limit $= 30$; score units within class $= 6.55145$

The score at the 50th percentile equals 36.5515

The cumulative frequency of the score is 66.5

$N = 133$ $i = 10$; score at lower limit $= 20$; score units within class $= 9.03509$

The score at the 50th percentile equals 29.0351

e. Neither mean can be calculated because the highest class is open-ended.

Source: From "Acquired Immunodeficiency syndrome—Europe," *Morbidity and Mortality Weekly Report* (1986), **35**(3), 35–46.

the population mean from these samples, the mean would be a better estimator than the median for sample sizes greater than 2. The size of the error of any given estimate using the mean of the sample is likely to be less than an estimate using the sample median.

5.6 THE MEAN, MEDIAN, AND SKEWNESS

In Chapter 3, we demonstrated several forms of skewed distributions. We pointed out, however, that skew cannot always be determined by inspection. If you understood the differences between the mean and the median, you

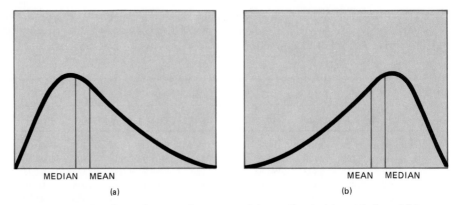

FIGURE 5.1 The relation between the mean and the median in (a) positively and (b) negatively skewed distributions.

should be able to suggest a method for determining whether or not a distribution is skewed and to determine the direction of the skew, if one exists. The basic fact to keep in mind is that the mean is pulled in the direction of the skew, whereas the median, unaffected by extreme scores, is not. Thus, when the mean is higher than the median, the distribution may be said to be positively skewed; when the mean is lower than the median, the distribution is negatively skewed. Figure 5.1 demonstrates the relation between the mean and the median in positively and negatively skewed distributions. In Chapter 6, we present a useful index of skew.

5.7 PUTTING IT ALL TOGETHER

In Section 4.4, we used the prisoner data to illustrate the calculation of the score (age) corresponding to a given percentile rank and the percentile rank of a given score (age). In this chapter, we'll use the same data to demonstrate the calculation of the mean and median and to estimate the direction of skew, if any.

Table 5.7 shows the entries necessary to calculate each of the two statistics, the mean and the median.

Finding the mean of a grouped frequency distribution.

Step 1. Multiply the midpoint of each class by the number of cases (frequencies) within that class. Enter each value in the column headed fX.

Step 2. Obtain ΣfX, which is the sum of all the values in the column headed fX.

Step 3. Calculate the mean by dividing ΣfX by N:

$$\overline{X} = 10{,}600{,}002/347{,}976 = 30.46$$

TABLE 5.7 Estimated Combined Numbers of White and Black Male Prison Inmates in Various Age Groupings in 1984. Tabular Entries Necessary to Calculate the Mean and the Median of a Grouped Frequency Distribution

Class (Age)	Midpoint of Class (X)	Estimated Number of Inmates (f)	fX	Cum f
65–74	69.5	1,185	82,357.5	347,976
55–64	59.5	6,786	403,767.0	346,791
45–54	49.5	18,097	895,801.5	340,005
35–44	39.5	67,866	2,680,707.0	321,908
25–34	29.5	158,355	4,671,472.5	254,042
15–24	19.5	95,687	1,865,896.5	95,687

$$N = 347,976 \quad \Sigma fX = 10,600,002$$

Finding the median of a grouped frequency distribution.

Follow the procedures illustrated in Section 5.3 for finding the age corresponding to the median. You should find that the median equals 29.44. Note that the median is quite close to the mode (29.5), which is the midpoint of the class with the greatest frequency.

Finding the direction of skew, if any.

Since the mean is higher than the median (30.46 vs. 29.44), the direction of skew is positive. In other words, the distribution is skewed toward the higher ages.

CHAPTER SUMMARY

In this chapter, we discussed, demonstrated the calculation of, and compared three indices of central tendency that are frequently employed in the description of frequency distributions: the mean, the median, and the mode. We saw that the mean may be defined variously as the sum of scores divided by their number, the point in a distribution about which the summed deviations are equal to zero, or the point in the distribution that makes the sum of the squared deviations around it minimal. The median divides the area under the curve into halves, so that the number of scores below the median equals the number of scores above it. Finally, the mode is defined as the most frequently occurring score. We demonstrated the method for obtaining the weighted mean of a set of means when each of the individual means is based on a different N.

Because it possesses special properties, the mean is the most frequently employed measure of central tendency. However, the sensitivity of the mean to extreme scores that are not balanced on both sides of the distribution makes the median the usual measure of choice when distributions are markedly skewed. The mode is rarely employed in the behavioral sciences.

Finally, we demonstrated the relationship between the mean and the median in negatively and positively skewed distributions.

TERMS TO REMEMBER

array	median
least-squares method	mode
mean	sum of squares
measure of central tendency	weighted mean

EXERCISES

1. Find the mean, the median, and the mode for each of the following sets of measurements. Show that $\Sigma(X - \bar{X}) = 0$.
   a. 10, 8, 6, 0, 8, 3, 2, 5, 8, 0   b. 1, 3, 3, 5, 5, 5, 7, 7, 9
   c. 119, 5, 4, 4, 4, 3, 1, 0

2. In which of the sets of measurements in Exercise 1 is the mean a poor measure of central tendency? Why?

3. For each of the sets of measurements in Exercise 1, show that *the sum of squares of deviations from the arithmetic mean is less than the sum of squares of deviations about any other score or potential score.*

4. You have calculated the maximum speed of various automobiles. You later discover that all the speedometers were set 5 miles per hour too fast. How will the measures of central tendency based on the corrected data compare with those calculated from the original data?

5. You have calculated measures of central tendency on the weights of barbells, expressing your data in terms of ounces. You decide to recompute after you have divided all the weights by 16 to convert them to pounds. How will this affect the measures of central tendency?

6. Calculate the median and mode for the data in Chapter 3, Exercises 12 and 18.

7. In Exercise 1(c), if the score of 119 were changed to a score of 19, how would the various measures of central tendency be affected?

8. On the basis of the following measures of central tendency, indicate whether or not there is evidence of skew and, if so, what its direction is.
   a. $\bar{X} = 56$ Median = 62   Mode = 68
   b. $\bar{X} = 68$ Median = 62   Mode = 56
   c. $\bar{X} = 62$ Median = 62   Mode = 62
   d. $\bar{X} = 62$ Median = 62   Mode = 30, Mode = 94

9. What is the nature of the distribution in Exercise 8(c) and (d)?

10. Calculate the mean of the following array of scores: 3, 4, 5, 5, 6, 7.

    a. Add a constant, say, 2, to each score. Recalculate the mean.
       Generalize: What is the effect on the mean of adding a constant to all scores?

    b. Subtract the same constant from each score. Recalculate the mean.
       Generalize: What is the effect on the mean of subtracting a constant from all scores?

    c. Alternately add and subtract the same constant, say, 2, from the array of scores (that is, 3 + 2, 4 − 2, 5 + 2, etc.). Recalculate the mean.
       Generalize: What is the effect on the mean of adding and subtracting the same constant an equal number of times from an array of scores?

    d. Multiply each score by a constant, say, 2. Recalculate the mean.
       Generalize: What is the effect on the mean of multiplying each score by a constant?

    e. Divide each score by the same constant. Recalculate the mean.
       Generalize: What is the effect on the mean of dividing each score by a constant?

11. Refer to Exercise 16, Chapter 3. Which measure of central tendency might best be used to describe group A? group B? Why?

12. In Section 5.5 we stated that the mean is usually *more reliable* than the median, that is, less subject to fluctuations. Suppose we conduct an experiment consisting of 30 tosses of three dice, obtaining the following results:

6, 6, 2	5, 4, 3	4, 3, 2	2, 1, 1	6, 5, 3	6, 5, 4
4, 1, 1	4, 4, 3	6, 4, 1	5, 4, 3	5, 1, 1	6, 2, 1
6, 5, 5	6, 6, 4	6, 4, 2	5, 4, 4	6, 5, 2	5, 4, 3
6, 4, 3	5, 3, 2	5, 1, 1	4, 3, 1	6, 3, 3	5, 4, 1
4, 2, 1	6, 3, 3	6, 5, 4	4, 2, 2	6, 6, 5	6, 3, 1

    a. Calculate the 30 means and 30 medians.

    b. Starting with the real limits of the lower class of 0.5 to 1.5, group the means and medians into separate frequency distributions.

    c. Draw histograms for the two distributions. Do they support the contention that the mean is a more stable estimator of central tendency? Explain.

    d. Assume that we place the medians and means into two separate hats and draw one at random from each. What is the likelihood that
       i. a statistic greater than 5.5 would be obtained?
       ii. a statistic less than 1.5 would be obtained?
       iii. a statistic greater than 5.5 or less than 1.5 would be obtained?

13. If we know that the mean and median of a set of scores are equal, what can we say about the form of the distribution?

14. Give examples of data in which the preferred measure of central tendency would be the
    a. mean   **b.** median   **c.** mode

15. In a study of Grinspoon (1969), nine naive subjects were tested on the Digit Symbol Substitution Test. The scores were considered the baseline measures. The subjects were tested 15 minutes after smoking a heavy dose of marijuana in one test session, and 15 minutes after smoking a placebo in another session. The baseline scores were subtracted from the baseline scores made in these sessions. The resulting difference scores are shown below. A negative sign means that the test score was lower than the baseline score.

Subject	1	2	3	4	5	6	7	8	9
Placebo	−3	10	−3	3	4	−3	2	−1	−1
Heavy dose	5	−17	−7	−3	−7	−9	−6	1	−3

Source: From Grinspoon, 1969.

Find the mean difference scores under (a) the placebo condition and (b) the heavy-dose condition.

16. In the same study cited in Exercise 15, eight chronic users were tested 15 minutes after a heavy-dose session. The difference scores are shown here:

Subject	1	2	3	4	5	6	7	8
Difference score	−4	1	11	3	−2	−6	−4	3

Source: From Grinspoon, 1969.

Find the mean difference score for this group.

17. In a study on the effects of operant conditioning on systolic blood pressure (Benson et al., 1971), the investigators recorded the following blood pressures* of seven subjects during control sessions (no feedback or reinforcement given).

Subject	1	2	3	4	5	6	7
Systolic blood pressure	139.6	213.3	162.3	166.9	157.8	165.7	149.0

Source: From Benson et al., 1971.

Calculate the mean blood pressure of these seven subjects during the control session.

18. In the same study cited in Exercise 17, the blood pressure of these same subjects was recorded during conditioning sessions (feedback and rewards given for lowering systolic blood pressure).

Subject	1	2	3	4	5	6	7
Systolic blood pressure	136.1	179.5	133.1	150.4	141.7	166.6	131.7

Source: From Benson et al., 1971.

Calculate the mean blood pressure of these seven subjects during the conditioning sessions.

---

* The measures were actually the median blood pressure during the last five control and last five conditioning sessions.

19. The difference scores (control minus conditioning sessions) for each subject are given as follows:

Subject	1	2	3	4	5	6	7
Difference score	−3.5	−33.8	−29.2	−16.5	−16.1	0.9	−17.3

    a. Calculate the mean difference score for the seven subjects.
    b. Find the difference between the means in Exercise 17 and Exercise 18, and *16.5* compare this to the mean difference found here. What do you discover?

20. On the basis of examination performance, an instructor identifies the following groups of students:
    a. Those with a percentile rank of 90 or higher.
    b. Those with a percentile rank of 10 or less.
    c. Those with percentile ranks between 40 and 49.
    d. Those with percentile ranks between 51 and 60.

      Which group would the instructor work with if he wished to raise most easily the *median* performance of the total group? Which group would he work with if he wished to raise most easily the *mean* performance of the total group?

21. Which of the measures of central tendency is most affected by the degree of skew in the distribution? Explain.

22. What can we say about the relationships between the mean and the median in a negatively skewed distribution? In a positively skewed distribution?

23. Shown at the end of this exercise are the population and the annual rate of growth for six geographical regions. Calculate the weighted percent of growth over all six regions.

Region	Present Population (in Millions)	Annual Rate of Growth (Percent)
North America	225	1.1
South America	276	2.9
Europe	456	0.8
USSR	241	1.0
Africa	344	2.4
Asia	1990	2.0

Source: L. Rocks and R. P. Runyon, *The Energy Crisis.* New York: Crown Publishers, 1972.

24. What is the mean number of cleaners sold per sales agent per day?
    Mr. A sells a mean of 1.75 vacuum cleaners per day in 4 days.
    Ms. B sells a mean of 2.0 per day in 5 days.
    Mr. C sells a mean of 2.4 per day in 5 days.
    Ms. D sells a mean of 2.5 per day in 4 days.
    Mr. E sells a mean of 2.0 per day in 3 days.
    Ms. F sells a mean of 1.67 per day in 3 days.

25. Suppose that a given merchant sells the following number of apples from Monday through Saturday:
  a. 30,   30,   30,   30,   30,   30
    What are the mean, median, and mode?
  b. 25,   30,   35,   30,   35,   25
    What are the mean, median, and mode?
  c. 10,   25,   30,   36,   25,   30
    Calculate the mean, median, and mode.

26. Work the following problems:
  a. In Exercise 25(c), show that $\Sigma (X - \bar{X}) = 0$.
  b. Show that the sum of the deviations from the median and from the mode do not equal zero.
  c. Why do the deviations from the mean equal zero, whereas the deviations from the median and mode do not?

27. Determine the mean, median, and mode for the following array:

  4,   4,   5,   5,   6,   7,   7,   7,   8,   8

28. A freelance writer earns a mean of $15.00 per hour for 4 hours of work, $17.50 per hour for 2 hours of work, $13.33 per hour for 3 hours, and $14.00 per hour for 1 hour. What are the writer's mean earnings per hour?

29. Two manufacturers state that the average life of their refrigerators is seven years. However, upon drawing a random sample of durations, a person finds that the life (in years) of 20 machines from manufacturer A is as follows:

  5, 5, 5, 6, 6, 6, 6, 7, 7, 7, 7, 7, 7, 8, 8, 8, 8, 9, 9, 9

A sample of machines from manufacturer B shows durations of:

  2, 3, 4, 5, 5, 5, 5, 6, 6, 6, 7, 7, 7, 7, 7, 8, 8, 20, 20, 20

What measurement of average was each manufacturer reporting? Which machine would probably be the best investment? With which machine would you feel more confident in stating that the average life is seven years?

30. At the beginning of 1972, there were 27 nuclear power plants in the United States, with a mean output of 436.5 megawatts. An additional 54 plants, with a mean output of 847.8 megawatts, were being built. Finally, 52 additional plants were planned, with a mean output of 991.7 megawatts.
  a. What is the anticipated mean output, in megawatts, of all 133 nuclear power plants?
  b. What will be the total output of all 133 power plants?

*31. In Chapter 3, Exercise 28, we described a sampling experiment in which samples of $N = 2$ were drawn from a population of seven scores. We constructed a table of sums of all possible combinations of seven scores, taken two at a time. Since $N = 2$ in each sample, that sum can be converted to a mean by dividing by 2. Construct a table showing all 49 means.

*32. Construct a frequency distribution of the means calculated in Exercise 31.

* All exercises that are used to lay the groundwork for future discussion are preceded by an asterisk.

*33. Selecting samples of $N = 2$ as we did in Exercise 28 of Chapter 3, what percentage of the time would we expect to obtain (round to nearest percent):
  a. A mean equal to 6?
  b. A mean of 5.5 or greater?
  c. A mean of 2.5 or less?
  d. A mean equal to or greater than 5.5, or equal to or less than 0.5?

*34. Calculate the mean of the sample means in Exercise 33, above. (*Hint:* Treat each mean as a score, and follow the computational procedures for calculating the mean with ungrouped frequency distributions.) How does the mean of the sample means compare with the original population mean?

35. In the study involving Type A and Type B behaviors (see Section 3.1), the investigators (Ortega and Pipal, 1984) assessed the effects of prior activity on behavioral measures among subjects classified in terms of Type A and Type B behaviors.

  The 60 Type A subjects and 60 Type B subjects were randomly assigned to a *relaxed* condition, a *passive* condition, and an *active* condition. Thus, there were 20 Type A's in the relaxed condition, 20 in the passive condition, and 20 in the active condition. The Type B subjects were similarly subdivided, 20 subjects per group.

  Following one of these activities, the subjects were given the opportunity to select problems from four different sets of tasks of increasing difficulty (4IDP). The more difficult the problem selected was, the higher was the presumed level of challenge seeking. Note that the subjects were not required to solve these problems. Rather, they selected the level of difficulty that they were prepared to solve.

  Following are the scores (table on page 140) on the level of challenge seeking (4IDP).* (Footnote with Table) Calculate the means for all six groups.

36. Refer to Exercise 35. Prepare a graph showing the means of active, passive, and relaxed groups for subjects classified in terms of Type A and Type B behaviors.

37. Refer to the data in Exercise 35.
  a. Combine the scores in the first three columns (Type A), construct an ungrouped frequency distribution, and calculate the mean and median.
  b. Combine the scores in the second three columns (Type B), construct an ungrouped frequency distribution, and calculate the mean and median.

38. In the study described in Exercise 35, the subjects were administered a standard challenging task (SCT), consisting of various perceptual, verbal, and arithmetic items of moderate difficulty. The following scores on the SCT provided a measure of their actual performance on these tasks. Calculate the mean for all six groups (please see table at top of page 141).

39. Refer to Exercise 38. Prepare a graph showing the means of active, passive, and relaxed groups for subjects classified in terms of Type A and Type B behaviors.

40. In Statistics in Action 1.1, we introduced the work of Rosenthal and his associates in which clients suffering from seasonal affective disorder (SAD) were treated with light therapy. Recall that bright light was the independent variable, with dim light and withdrawal serving as controls. The dependent measure was provided by the Hamilton Rating Scale, in which a high score indicated

Type A Behaviors			Type B Behaviors		
Active	**Passive**	**Relaxed**	**Active**	**Passive**	**Relaxed**
24	23	26	19	17	23
24	21	23	18	22	23
25	23	21	13	11	21
26	24	22	24	23	17
22	13	20	19	20	22
26	24	22	23	20	21
25	24	26	10	23	18
27	22	25	17	16	20
28	21	19	18	20	16
26	25	26	14	23	17
21	21	25	21	25	23
20	21	16	21	16	19
24	26	17	19	13	19
21	25	19	24	25	18
26	24	23	22	18	25
23	24	19	24	21	22
24	21	18	25	19	23
25	23	24	14	18	23
22	26	18	18	28	17
25	27	20	15	18	19

* Subjects examined four different sets of problems of increasing difficulty and indicated which level they would like to complete at a later time. The higher the 4IDP score was, the greater was the challenge sought by the subject.
Source: Based on data from Ortega and Pipal, 1984.

depression. The following table shows the scores obtained by six subjects for whom bright light was introduced in the first week and dim light in the third.
a. Find the mean and standard deviation for each column (baseline and ratings at the end of each of four weeks).
b. Plot the means of each group using the column headings as the categories along the horizontal axis.

Bright Light First					
		Week No.			
Subject	**Baseline**	**1** **Bright**	**2** **WD-1**	**3** **Dim**	**4** **WD-2**
1	30.0	17.0	20.0	13.0	27.5
2	25.0	18.0	25.0	28.0	19.0
3	26.0	27.0	15.5	31.0	26.0
4	20.0	12.0	13.0	17.0	20.0
5	31.0	17.0	22.5	29.5	17.0
6	28.5	10.0	21.0	21.0	25.0

Source: Based on data from Rosenthal et al., 1985.

Type A Behaviors			Type B Behaviors		
Active	**Passive**	**Relaxed**	**Active**	**Passive**	**Relaxed**
9	9	7	9	9	9
9	10	9	8	7	10
10	10	6	10	9	3
10	10	9	8	6	8
10	9	10	7	10	8
10	8	9	8	10	10
4	9	10	6	9	9
10	8	8	6	9	8
9	9	10	5	9	9
10	10	10	8	9	7
10	9	10	6	10	6
6	10	8	6	9	7
7	10	8	6	9	10
10	10	10	10	2	10
10	9	9	10	10	9
5	10	8	9	10	9
9	7	10	10	4	7
8	10	8	8	10	10
10	7	6	7	9	8
10	10	10	8	5	8

Source: Based on data from Ortega and Pipal, 1984.

41. The following table shows the scores obtained by seven subjects for whom dim light was introduced in the first week and bright light in the third.

   a. Find the mean and standard deviation for each column (baseline and ratings at the end of each of four weeks).

   b. Plot the means of each group using the column headings as the categories along the horizontal axis.

Dim Light First					
		Week No.			
		1	**2**	**3**	**4**
Subject	**Baseline**	**Dim**	**WD-1**	**Bright**	**WD-2**
7	35.5	32.0	31.5	2.0	32.5
8	25.0	30.0	31.0	29.0	15.5
9	31.0	25.0	28.0	10.0	13.0
10	32.5	23.0	24.5	2.5	8.0
11	24.0	19.0	21.0	8.0	17.0
12	15.0	6.0	16.0	8.0	11.0
13	25.0	28.0	23.0	9.0	22.0

Source: Based on data from Rosenthal et al., 1985.

42. Using Table 3.7 in Section 3.10, calculate the mean and median age of white prisoners.

43. Using Table 3.7 in Section 3.10, calculate the mean and median age of black prisoners.

6

Measures of Dispersion

6.1 INTRODUCTION

In the introduction to Chapter 4, we saw that a score by itself is meaningless
and takes on meaning only when it is compared with other scores or other
statistics. Thus, if we know the mean of the distribution of a given variable,
we can determine whether a particular score is higher or lower than the
mean. But how much higher or lower? It is clear at this point that a
measure of central tendency such as the mean provides only a limited
amount of information. To describe a distribution more fully, or to interpret
a score more fully, we require additional information concerning the
dispersion of scores about our measure of central tendency.

Consider Figure 6.1, parts (a) and (b). In both examples of frequency
curves, the mean of the distribution is exactly the same. However, note the
difference in the interpretations of a score of 128. In (a), because the scores
are widely dispersed about the mean, a score of 128 may be considered
only moderately high. Quite a few individuals in the distribution scored
above 128, as indicated by the proportion of area to the right of 128. In (b),
on the other hand, the scores are compactly distributed about the same
mean. This is a more *homogeneous* distribution. Consequently, the score
of 128 is now virtually at the top of the distribution, and therefore it may
be considered a very high score.

> **Dispersion:** The spread
> or variability of scores
> about the measure of
> central tendency.

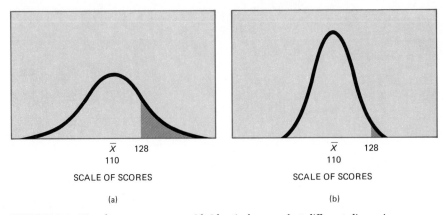

$\overline{X}$ 128
110

SCALE OF SCORES

(a)

$\overline{X}$ 128
110

SCALE OF SCORES

(b)

FIGURE 6.1   Two frequency curves with identical means but different dispersion or variability.

As can be seen, then, in interpreting individual scores, we must find a companion to the mean or the median. This companion must in some way express the degree of dispersion of scores about the measure of central tendency. We discuss five such measures of dispersion or variability: the **range,** the **semi-interquartile range,** the **mean deviation,** the **variance,** and the **standard deviation.** Of the five, we shall find the standard deviation to be our most useful measure of dispersion in both descriptive and inferential statistics. In advanced inferential statistics, such as the analysis of variance (Chapters 14 and 15), the variance will become a most useful measure of variability.

6.2   THE RANGE

When we calculated the various measures of central tendency, we located a *single point* along the scale of scores and identified it as the mean, the median, or the mode. When our interest shifts to measures of dispersion, however, we must look for an index of variability which indicates the *distance* along the scale of scores.

Crude Range: Measure of dispersion: The scale distance between the largest and the smallest score.

One of the first measures of distance that comes to mind is the so-called **crude range.** The range is by far the simplest and the most straightforward measure of dispersion. It consists simply of the scale distance between the largest and the smallest score; that is, range = highest score − lowest score. Thus, if the highest score is 140 and the lowest is 30, the range is 110.

Although the range is meaningful, it is of little use because of its marked instability. Note that if there is one extreme score in a distribution, the dispersion of scores will appear to be large when in fact the removal of that score may reveal an otherwise "compact" distribution. Several years ago, a long-term resident of an institution for retarded persons was found to have an IQ score in the 140s. Imagine the erroneous impression that would result if the range of scores for the residents was reported as, say, 140–20 or 120! Stated another way, the range reflects only the two most extreme scores in a distribution.

6.3   THE SEMI-INTERQUARTILE RANGE (SIR)

In order to overcome the instability of the crude range as a measure of dispersion, one sometimes employs the **semi-interquartile range.** The semi-interquartile range is calculated simply by subtracting the score at the 25th percentile (referred to as the first quartile or Q_1) from the score at the 75th percentile (the third quartile or Q_3) and dividing by 2 (see Figure 6.2).

> **Semi-interquartile Range:** A measure of variability obtained by subtracting the score at the 25th percentile from the score at the 75th percentile and dividing by 2.

If the distribution takes on that bell-shaped form we previously identified as normal, the median plus and minus the semi-interquartile range (SIR) cuts off the middle 50% of all cases in the distribution. Thus, if the median is 70 and the SIR is 10, we can provide a useful summarizing statement, namely, 70 ± 10 includes the middle 50% of all cases. Even with markedly skewed distributions (Figure 6.2), the median plus and minus the SIR provides a crude approximation to the values that include the middle 50% of the cases. Thus, 65 ± 6.5 would yield 58.5 and 71.5 as the values that bracket the middle 50% of the cases. For this reason, the SIR is most frequently used in conjunction with the median when extreme skew rules out the use of the mean as the measure of central tendency and the standard deviation as the measure of dispersion. In the behavioral sciences we find that reaction-time scores, heart-rate measures, and income figures are typically sufficiently skewed to justify the use of the median and the semi-interquartile range as measures of central tendency and dispersion, respectively. In addition, both are often used with ordinally scaled data. Although this measure of variability of scores is far more meaningful than

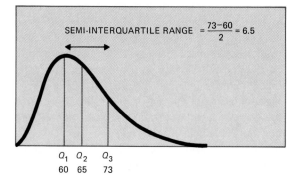

$$\text{SEMI-INTERQUARTILE RANGE} = \frac{73-60}{2} = 6.5$$

Q_1 Q_2 Q_3
60   65   73

FIGURE 6.2   The semi-interquartile range and a skewed distribution. Like the median (Q_2), the semi-interquartile range is not sensitive to extreme scores at one or the other end of the distribution.

BOX 6.1

SHAVING PEAK IS REDUCING VARIABILITY

When we have found a measure of central tendency, we have taken a first and important step in describing a distribution. To complete our description, we must find some comparison measure that tells us something about how widely the scores are dispersed or spread about the central value. Interest in dispersion is more than a mere academic exercise engaged in by statisticians during their leisure hours. The following adaptation from *Winning with Statistics* makes the point that a consideration of variability is of fundamental importance in the everyday affairs of the real world.

At times our preoccupation with averages can cause us to lose sight of the fact that many of the most important workday decisions are based on considerations of the extremes, rather than on the middle of a distribution. Imagine what life would be like if:

- Our highways were constructed to accommodate the average traffic load of vehicles of average weight.
- Mass transit systems were designed to move only the average number of passengers (i.e., total passengers per day divided by 24 hours) during each hour of the day.
- Bridges, homes, and industrial and commercial buildings were constructed to withstand the average wind or the average earthquake.
- Telephone lines and switchboards were sufficient in number to accommodate only the average number of phone calls per hour.
- Your friendly local electric utility calculated the year-round average electrical demand and constructed facilities to provide only this average demand.
- Emergency services provided average personnel and facilities during all hours of the day and all seasons of the year.

- Our space program provided emergency procedures for only the average type of failure.

Chaos is the word for it. Utter chaos. The fact of the matter is that virtually all of human endeavor must gear itself to meet the extreme conditions known as peak load. If you don't mind my digressing a bit, let me say that the peak load problem is, at once, one of the great challenges and monumental opportunities that we face today. It is because of peak load that many community facilities and services are barely used during certain time periods and are swamped at others. Assuming that the years ahead are sure to place a continued stress on resources, both natural and human, we shall not long be able to sustain the luxury of "gearing up to peak."

The alternative is to raise the valleys and lower the peaks of demand. In statistical terms, the goal is to obtain the same average while reducing the variability. By doing so, we are able to increase and improve our use of existing facilities.

To illustrate with another example, Tucson lies at the edge of the great Sonora desert which covers much of southern Arizona and extends into northern Mexico. The combination of a burgeoning population and the annual influx of both winter visitors (snowbirds) and summer tourists has placed heavy and uneven demands on its water supply, all of which is presently drawn from wells extending deep into the aquifer. The peak demand occurs during the summer months, especially in midday and afternoons, when temperatures regularly soar above 100 degrees. If left unabated, meeting the peak demand for water would require the continuous drilling of many additional wells, with consequent depletion of the aquifer and enormous financial burdens for the taxpayer. Some years ago, the mayor of Tucson proclaimed the summer months a "beat the peak" period. In a completely voluntary effort, residents were encouraged to landscape with native flora (cactus and the like) and to water only in early mornings and late evenings. The result has been a dramatic balancing of the demand for water, accompanied by a lower overall consumption.

Look for many electrical utilities to find ways to even out both the diurnal and seasonal demands for electricity as an alternative to constructing new facilities to meet peak demand.

Source: Adapted from R. P. Runyon, *Winning with Statistics.* Reading, Mass.: Addison-Wesley, 1977.

the crude range, it has two significant shortcomings: (1) like the crude range, it does not by itself permit the precise interpretation of a score within a distribution, and (2) like the median, it does not enter into any of the "higher" mathematical relationships that are basic to inferential statistics. Consequently, we shall not devote any more discussion to the semi-interquartile range.

6.4 THE MEAN DEVIATION

As pointed out in Chapter 5, when we are dealing with data from normally distributed populations, the mean is our most useful measure of central tendency. We obtain the mean by adding together all the scores and dividing them by N. If these procedures were carried one step further, we could subtract the mean from each score, sum the deviations from the mean, and thereby obtain an estimate of the typical amount of deviation from the mean. By dividing by N, we would have a measure that would be analogous to the arithmetic mean except that it would represent the dispersion of scores from the arithmetic mean.

If you think for a moment about the characteristics of the mean, which we discussed in the preceding chapter, you will encounter one serious difficulty. The sum of the deviations of all scores from the mean must add up to zero. Thus, if we defined the **mean deviation** (MD) as this sum divided by N, the mean deviation would have to be zero. You will recall that we employed the fact that $\Sigma(X - \bar{X}) = 0$ to arrive at one of several definitions of the mean.

Now, if we were to add all the deviations *without regard to sign* and divide by N, we would still have a measure reflecting the mean deviation from the arithmetic mean. The resulting statistic would, of course, be based on the **absolute value** of the deviations. The absolute value of a positive number or of zero is the number itself. The absolute value of a negative number can be found by changing the sign to a positive one. Thus, the absolute value of $+3$ or -3 is 3. The symbol for an absolute value is $|\ |$. Thus, $|-3| = 3$.

Mean Deviation (Average Deviation): Sum of the deviations of each score from the mean, without regard to sign, divided by the number of scores.

Absolute Value of a Number: The value of a number without regard to sign.

TABLE 6.1   Computational Procedures for Calculating the Mean Deviation from an Array of Scores Made by Type B Subjects, Active Condition, on a Standard Challenging Task

X	$\bar{X}$	$X - \bar{X}$
10	7.75	$\mid$ 2.25$\mid$
10	7.75	$\mid$ 2.25$\mid$
10	7.75	$\mid$ 2.25$\mid$
10	7.75	$\mid$ 2.25$\mid$
9	7.75	$\mid$ 1.25$\mid$
9	7.75	$\mid$ 1.25$\mid$
8	7.75	$\mid$ 0.25$\mid$
8	7.75	$\mid$ 0.25$\mid$
8	7.75	$\mid$ 0.25$\mid$
8	7.75	$\mid$ 0.25$\mid$
8	7.75	$\mid$ 0.25$\mid$
8	7.75	$\mid$ 0.25$\mid$
7	7.75	$\mid - 0.75\mid$
7	7.75	$\mid - 0.75\mid$
6	7.75	$\mid - 1.75\mid$
6	7.75	$\mid - 1.75\mid$
6	7.75	$\mid - 1.75\mid$
6	7.75	$\mid - 1.75\mid$
6	7.75	$\mid - 1.75\mid$
5	7.75	$\mid - 2.75\mid$

$$\Sigma|(X - \bar{X})| = 26$$

$\Sigma X = 155$

$N = 20$

$\bar{X} = 7.75$

$$\text{MD} = \frac{\Sigma|(X - \bar{X})|}{N} \qquad (6.1)$$

$$= \frac{26}{20} = 1.3$$

Source: From Ortega and Pipal, 1984.

The calculation of the mean deviation is shown in Table 6.1.

As a basis for comparison of the dispersion of several distributions, the mean deviation has some value. For example, the greater the mean deviation is, the greater is the dispersion of scores. However, for interpreting scores within a distribution, the mean deviation is less useful, since there is no precise mathematical relationship between the mean deviation, as such, and the location of scores within a distribution.

You may wonder why we bother demonstrating the mean deviation when it is of so little use in statistical analysis. As we shall see, the standard deviation and the variance, which have great value in statistical analysis, are very close relatives of the mean deviation.

6.5 THE VARIANCE (s^2) AND STANDARD DEVIATION (s)*

Following a perusal of Table 6.1, you might be tempted to make this speculation: "We had to treat the values in the column headed ($X - \overline{X}$) as absolute numbers because their sum was equal to zero. Why could we not square each ($X - \overline{X}$) and then add the squared deviations? In this way we would legitimately rid ourselves of the minus signs, while still preserving the information that is inherent in these deviation scores."

The answer: We could, if by so doing we arrived at a statistic of greater value in judging dispersion than those we have already discussed. It is most fortunate that the standard deviation, based on the squaring of these deviation scores, is of immense value in three different respects.

1. The standard deviation reflects dispersion of scores, so that the variability of different distributions may be compared in terms of the standard deviation (s).
2. The standard deviation permits the *precise* interpretation of scores within a distribution.
3. The standard deviation, like the mean, is a member of a *mathematical system* that permits its use in more advanced statistical considerations. Thus, we employ measures based on s when we advance into inferential statistics.

An understanding of the meaning of the standard deviation hinges on a knowledge of the relationship between the standard deviation and the normal distribution. Thus, in order to be able to interpret the standard deviations that are calculated in this chapter, we need to explore the relationship among raw scores, the standard deviation, and the normal distribution. This material is presented in the following chapter.

Calculation of Variance and Standard Deviation, Mean Deviation Method, with Ungrouped Scores

The **variance** is defined as *the sum of the squared deviations from the mean, divided by N.* Symbolically, it is represented as

Variance: Sum of the squared deviations from the mean, divided by N.

$$s^2 = \frac{\Sigma(X - \overline{X})^2}{N}$$

(6.2)

*We remind you that italic letters are used to represent sample statistics, and Greek letters to represent population parameters; for example, σ^2 represents the population variance, and σ represents the population standard deviation. The problem of estimating population parameters from sample values will be discussed in Chapter 12.

Sum of Squares:
Deviation of each score
from the mean, squared
and then summed.
Represented as SS.

You will recall that the sum of the $(X - \overline{X})^2$ column, that is, $\Sigma(X - \overline{X})^2$, is known as the **sum of squares** and that this sum is minimal when deviations are taken about the mean. From this point on in the course, we encounter the sum of squares with regularity. It will take on a number of different forms, depending on the procedures that we use for calculating it. However, we should remember that, whatever the form, the sum of squares represents the *sum of the squared deviations from the mean*. Since it is more convenient, we use the symbol SS to represent $\Sigma(X - \overline{X})^2$. Thus

$$ SS = \Sigma(X - \overline{X})^2 \tag{6.3} $$

The variance then becomes

$$ s^2 = \frac{SS}{N} \tag{6.4} $$

A word of caution must be interjected at this point. Formulas (6.2) and (6.4) yield the variance of a sample. There is another formula, similar to Formula (6.2), that is used to provide an unbiased *estimate of the population variance*, namely, $\hat{s}^2 = SS/(N - 1)$. Note that the only difference between the two is that when we estimate the population variance, $N - 1$ replaces N in the denominator of the formula for the sample variance. We shall discuss this important distinction between biased and unbiased estimators in Chapter 12. The immediate importance of the distinction is that the two formulas are not interchangeable. Many of you may have statistical calculators that compute the variance and standard deviation at the touch of a button once the raw data have been entered. Some of these use N in the denominator, some use $N - 1$, and some provide a choice between the two. You should check your calculator to see which is the case. If your calculator uses $N - 1$ in the denominator of the variance, it is relatively simple to convert your answer so that it reflects the variance based on N in the denominator. This conversion is shown in Chapter 6 of the *Study Guide*.

Standard Deviation:
Extremely useful measure
of dispersion, defined as
the square root of the
sum of the squared
deviations from the mean
divided by N.

The **standard deviation** is the *square root* of the variance and is defined as

$$ s = \sqrt{\frac{SS}{N}} \tag{6.5} $$

The computational procedures for calculating the standard deviation, utilizing the mean deviation method, are shown in Table 6.2.

The mean deviation method was shown only to impress you with the fact that the standard deviation is based on the deviation of scores from the mean. This method is extremely unwieldy for use in calculation, particularly when the mean is a fractional value, which is usually the case. Consequently, in the succeeding paragraphs, we shall examine a num-

TABLE 6.2   Computational Procedures for Calculating the Variance and Standard Deviation, Mean Deviation Method, from an Array of Scores

X	$\overline{X}$	$X - \overline{X}$	$(X - \overline{X})^2$	Computation
10	7.75	2.25	5.0625	$s^2 = \dfrac{\Sigma(X - \overline{X})^2}{N} = \dfrac{SS}{N}$
10	7.75	2.25	5.0625	
10	7.75	2.25	5.0625	$= \dfrac{47.75}{20}$
10	7.75	2.25	5.0625	
9	7.75	1.25	1.5625	$= 2.3875$
9	7.75	1.25	1.5625	
8	7.75	.25	.0625	$s = \sqrt{s^2}$
8	7.75	.25	.0625	$= 1.5452$
8	7.75	.25	.0625	
8	7.75	.25	.0625	
8	7.75	.25	.0625	
8	7.75	.25	.0625	
7	7.75	$-.75$	.5625	
7	7.75	$-.75$	.5625	
6	7.75	-1.75	3.0625	
6	7.75	-1.75	3.0625	
6	7.75	-1.75	3.0625	
6	7.75	-1.75	3.0625	
6	7.75	-1.75	3.0625	
5	7.75	-2.75	7.5625	

$\Sigma X = 155$ $\quad\quad\quad \Sigma (X - \overline{X}) = 0 \quad\quad SS = 47.7500$
$N = 20$
$\overline{X} = 7.75$

Source: From Ortega and Pipal, 1984.

ber of alternative ways of calculating the sum of squares and standard deviation.

Calculation of Standard Deviation, Raw Score Method, with Ungrouped Scores

It can be shown mathematically that

$$SS = \sum X^2 - \frac{(\Sigma X)^2}{N} \tag{6.6}$$

where

$$SS = \Sigma(X - \overline{X})^2 = \Sigma X^2 - 2 \Sigma X\overline{X} + \Sigma \overline{X}^2$$

TABLE 6.3   Computational Procedures for Calculating the Variance and Standard Deviation, Raw Score Method, from an Array of Scores

X	X²	Computation
10	100	$SS = \sum X^2 - \dfrac{(\sum X)^2}{N}$
10	100	
10	100	$= 1249 - \dfrac{(155)^2}{20}$
10	100	
9	81	$= 47.75$
9	81	$s^2 = \dfrac{SS}{N}$
8	64	
8	64	
8	64	$= \dfrac{47.75}{20}$
8	64	
8	64	$= 2.3875$
8	64	$s = \sqrt{s^2}$
8	64	
7	49	$= 1.5452$
7	49	
6	36	
6	36	
6	36	
6	36	
6	36	
5	25	

$\sum X = 155 \qquad \sum X^2 = 1249$
$N = 20$

Source: From Ortega and Pipal, 1984.

However, $\sum X = N\bar{X}$,* and summing the mean square over all values of $\bar{X}$ is the same as multiplying by N (see Generalization 1, Chapter 2). Thus

$$SS = \sum X^2 - 2N\bar{X}^2 + N\bar{X}^2$$

$$= \sum X^2 - N\bar{X}^2 = \sum X^2 - N\left(\frac{\sum X}{N}\right)^2$$

$$= \sum X^2 - \frac{N(\sum X)^2}{N^2}$$

$$= \sum X^2 - \frac{(\sum X)^2}{N}$$

Dividing the sum of squares by N yields the variance

$$s^2 = \frac{SS}{N}$$

* Since $\bar{X} = \sum X/N$, it follows that $\sum X = N\bar{X}$.

CASE EXAMPLE 6.1

The Light at the End of the Tunnel

In Statistics in Action 1.1 we reported on the research of Rosenthal and his associates on the use of light treatment on patients suffering from an autumn and winter depression known as Seasonal Affective Disorder (1985). Prior to their exposure to the various treatment and control conditions, baseline scores were obtained on the Hamilton Rating Scale. The higher the scale value is, the greater is the indication of a depressed mood. Table 6.4 shows the baseline scores of seven outpatients who were characterized as "typical."

The mean baseline value of the seven outpatients is: $\overline{X} = 176/7 = 25.14$. The sum of squares is

$$SS = 4655.5 - (176)^2/7$$
$$= 230.3572$$

Therefore, the variance (s^2) is $230.3572/7 = 32.908$ and the standard deviation (s) is $\sqrt{32.908} = 5.74$.

TABLE 6.4 Baseline Scores of Seven Outpatients Characterized as Typical

Patient No.	Score on Hamilton Rating Scale *X*	*X²*
4	20	400
5	31	961
6	28.5	812.25
17	32.5	1056.25
18	24	576
19	15	225
20	25	625
	$\Sigma X = 176$	$\Sigma X^2 = 4655.5$

Source: From Rosenthal et al., 1985.

In turn, extracting the square root of the variance yields the standard deviation

$$s = \sqrt{\frac{SS}{N}}$$

Table 6.3 summarizes the computational procedures. Note that the result agrees with the answer we obtained by the mean deviation method.

Calculation of Standard Deviation, Raw Score Method, from an Ungrouped Frequency Distribution

If we take the data in Table 6.2 and arrange them into an ungrouped frequency distribution, we obtain

X	f
10	4
9	2
8	6
7	2
6	5
5	1

To calculate SS, multiply each score by its corresponding frequency and then sum. This yields $\sum fX$. Next, to find $\sum fX^2$, square each score, multiply by its corresponding frequency, and sum. Place these values in the formula for sum of squares:

$$SS = \sum fX^2 - \frac{(\sum fX)^2}{N}$$

Finally, substitute this value in the formula for the standard deviation:

$$s = \sqrt{\frac{SS}{N}}$$

Table 6.5 summarizes the procedure for obtaining the standard deviation from an ungrouped frequency distribution.

TABLE 6.5   Computational Procedures for Calculating the Variance and Standard Deviation from an Ungrouped Frequency Distribution

X	f	fX	fX²	Computation
10	4	40	400	$SS = \sum fX^2 - \dfrac{(\sum fX)^2}{N}$
9	2	18	162	
8	6	48	384	$= 1249 - \dfrac{(155)^2}{20}$
7	2	14	98	
6	5	30	180	$= 1249 - 1201.25 = 47.75$
5	1	5	25	$s^2 = \dfrac{SS}{N} = \dfrac{47.75}{20} = 2.3875$
				$s = \sqrt{2.3875} = 1.5452$
$N = 20$	$\sum fX = 155$	$\sum fX^2 = 1249$		

Source: From Ortega and Pipal, 1984.

Errors to Avoid

In using the raw score method of calculating the standard deviation, students commonly confuse the similar-appearing terms ΣX^2 (or ΣfX^2) and $(\Sigma X)^2$ [or $(\Sigma fX)^2$]. It is important to remember that the former represents the *sum of the individually squared* scores, whereas the latter represents the *square of the sum* of the scores. By definition, it is impossible to obtain a negative sum of squares or a negative standard deviation. In the event that you obtain a negative value under the square root sign, you have probably confused these two terms.

A rule of thumb for estimating the standard deviation is that the ratio of the range to the standard deviation is rarely smaller than 2 or greater than 6. In the preceding example, the ratio is 5/1.55 = 3.23. If we obtain a standard deviation that yields a ratio greater than 6 or smaller than 2, we have almost certainly made an error.

6.6 THE MEAN, MEDIAN, STANDARD DEVIATION, AND PEARSON'S COEFFICIENT OF SKEW

In Section 5.6, we noted that the direction of skew can be judged by the position of the mean relative to the median. When the mean is higher than the median, that is, when $(\overline{X} - \text{Mdn})$ is a positive value, the distribution of scores is positively skewed. Conversely, when $(\overline{X} - \text{Mdn})$ is a negative value, the scores are negatively skewed. However, these indices of *direction* of skew tell us little about the *amount* of skew. E. S. Pearson, whom many consider the founder of modern statistics, proposed the following coefficient of skew (sk):

$$sk = \frac{3(\overline{X} - \text{Median})}{s} \qquad (6.7)$$

Let's apply this formula to the data presented in Case Example 6.1, where we found the mean to be 25.14, the standard deviation to be 5.74, and the median to be 25. Thus, the index of skew is

$$sk = \frac{3(25.14 - 25)}{5.74}$$
$$= +0.073$$

The positive sign indicates that the scores are positively skewed. If the distribution is symmetrical, the mean and median are the same. Therefore, $sk = 0$. However, it is widely accepted that data sets with indices of skew ranging between ± 0.50 may be considered sufficiently symmetrical for most practical applications. Since the skew of the data in Case Example 6.1 does not exceed $|0.50|$, the distribution of scores is regarded as symmetrical.

STATISTICS IN ACTION 6.1

Heart-rate data on subjects who received no feedback and were not penalized for failure: Means, ranges, variances, and standard deviations.

Ortega and Pipal investigated the effects of ongoing activity on physiological measures of Type A and Type B males as well as the effects of these prior activities on challenge-seeking behavior and actual performance on challenging tasks.

In another study (Perkins, 1984), Type A and Type B male subjects were placed before a display of five lights arranged in a semicircle and were required to press a button that turned off the one light that was lit. The experimental subjects received different types of feedback and were penalized for failure.

There were ten Type A and ten Type B control subjects who received no feedback and were not penalized for failure. Table 6.6 shows the heart rate (in beats per minute) data on one practice trial and four test trials for the ten Type A control subjects. The bottom and the right-hand **marginals** show the corresponding means, ranges, variances, and standard deviations.

If you have ever pondered the fact of human variability in performance (i.e., individual differences), take a few moments to look over the data and the various statistics calculated from these data. As you look down the columns, note the large ranges in HR measures

Marginals: The values shown in the margins of the table, usually referred to as the right-hand or row marginals and the bottom or column marginals.

TABLE 6.6 Heart-Rate Data, One Practice and Four Additional Trials for Ten Type A Subjects Who Received No Feedback and Were Not Penalized for Failure

Subject	Practice	Trial no. 1	2	3	4	Mean	Range	s^2	s
1	86.0	82.6	82.6	82.6	80.6	82.88	5.4	3.03	1.74
2	109.3	112.6	110.0	107.3	106.6	109.16	6.0	4.51	2.12
3	73.3	70.0	73.3	70.6	68.6	71.16	4.7	3.47	1.86
4	80.6	76.6	72.6	76.0	72.6	75.68	8.0	8.83	2.97
5	86.6	84.0	82.6	82.6	83.3	83.82	4.0	2.20	1.48
6	85.3	86.0	87.3	85.3	87.3	86.24	2.0	0.81	0.90
7	83.3	82.6	83.3	84.6	84.6	83.68	2.0	0.63	0.79
8	78.6	81.3	77.3	78.0	76.6	78.36	4.7	2.61	1.62
9	92.0	86.6	88.0	88.6	88.0	88.64	5.4	3.25	1.80
10	76.0	75.3	75.3	76.6	74.6	75.56	2.0	0.47	0.68
Mean	85.10	83.76	83.23	83.22	82.28				
Range	36.0	42.6	37.4	36.7	38.0				
s^2	92.41	116.58	106.64	89.83	103.07				
s	9.61	10.80	10.33	9.48	10.15				

of these ten subjects. As a case in point, look at the column labeled "Practice." Note the contrast in heart rates of subjects 2 and 3: 109.3 versus 73.3. Subject 2's heart rate was almost 50% faster than that of subject 1 [$(109.3 - 73.3)/73.3 \times 100 = 49.11\%$]. It might appear that one subject was engaged in aerobic exercises while the other was at rest! Note the generally high variances and standard deviations of these subjects on all the trials.

The summary statistics appearing in the bottom marginals are based on the measurements between and among ten different subjects. For this reason, the variance between independent subjects is often referred to as the **between-subject variance.** Contrast these with the variances shown in the right-hand marginals. The variances based on measures within a single individual are called **within-subject variance.** Note that, in general, all measures of variability are substantially less when based on repeated measures of the same subject. What does this mean? Briefly, it suggests that there is less variability of performance within a single individual than there is between different individuals. Look at the record of subject 2 as an example. Although his mean HR is quite high (109.16), his range, variance, and standard deviation are much smaller than *any* of the corresponding between-subject measures of variability. This is due to the fact that his heart rate is consistently high.

Table 6.7 shows the heart-rate data on one practice trial and four test trials for the ten Type B control subjects.

Between-subject Variance: The variance computed on the scores of different subjects.

Within-subject Variance: The variance computed on the scores of a single subject.

a. Calculate the between-subject measures of variability on all five trials and the within-subject measures of variability for all ten subjects.

b. Are the within-subject measures of variability generally larger than the between-subject measures?

c. Construct a graph showing the mean heart-rate measures of both Type A and Type B subjects on the practice and four test trials.

TABLE 6.7 Heart-Rate Data, One Practice and Four Additional Trials for Ten Type B Subjects Who Received No Feedback and Were Not Penalized for Failure

Subject	Practice	1	2	3	4
1	103.3	85.3	82.0	80.0	78.6
2	98.6	94.0	93.3	92.6	92.6
3	88.6	93.1	88.0	88.0	86.0
4	85.3	89.3	84.6	81.3	77.3
5	90.6	85.3	76.6	78.0	76.0
6	98.6	98.0	94.0	94.6	94.0
7	120.6	118.6	114.6	112.0	120.6
8	62.6	63.3	58.6	56.0	54.6
9	109.3	106.6	97.3	93.3	88.0
10	106.6	98.6	99.3	96.0	98.0

ANSWERS

a. Type B behaviors

Subject	Practice	Trial No. 1	2	3	4	Mean	Range	s^2	s
1	103.3	85.3	82.0	80.0	78.6	85.84	24.7	81.28	9.02
2	98.6	94.0	93.3	92.6	92.6	94.22	6.0	5.07	2.25
3	88.6	93.1	88.0	88.0	86.0	88.74	7.1	5.53	2.35
4	85.3	89.3	84.6	81.3	77.3	83.56	12.0	16.27	4.03
5	90.6	85.3	76.6	78.0	76.0	81.30	14.6	32.71	5.72
6	98.6	98.0	94.0	94.6	94.0	95.84	4.6	4.12	2.03
7	120.6	118.6	114.6	112.0	120.6	117.28	8.6	11.77	3.43
8	62.6	63.3	58.6	56.0	54.6	59.02	8.7	11.99	3.46
9	109.3	106.6	97.3	93.3	88.0	98.90	21.3	64.04	8.00
10	106.6	98.6	99.3	96.0	98.0	99.70	10.6	13.11	3.62
Mean	96.41	93.21	88.83	87.18	86.57				
Range	58.0	53.3	56.0	56.0	66.0				
s^2	227.35	191.16	202.08	195.90	266.59				
s	15.08	13.83	14.22	14.00	16.33				

b. Yes, the between-subject measures of variability were all higher than their corresponding within-subject measures.

c.

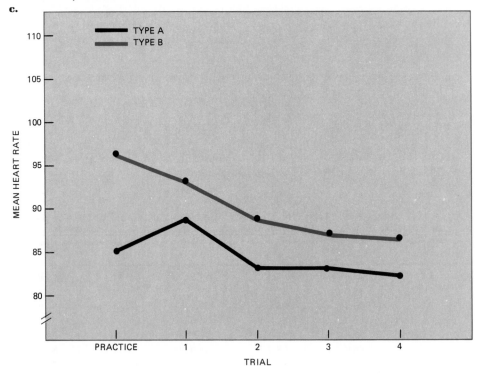

Source: Based on Perkins, 1984.

6.7 PUTTING IT ALL TOGETHER

We previously calculated the mean and median ages of prison inmates from the grouped frequency distribution appearing in Section 5.7. Let us now look at the procedures used to calculate the variance and standard deviation of a grouped frequency distribution. We will then demonstrate the calculation of Pearson's coefficient of skew using the following statistics: the mean, the median, and the standard deviation.

Step 1. Sum the values in the frequency column of Table 6.8 to obtain N. $N = 347,976$.

Step 2. Square each midpoint of class (X) and place the result in the column headed X^2.

Step 3. Multiply the midpoint of each class (X) by its corresponding frequency to obtain fX.

Step 4. Sum the values in the fX column to obtain ΣfX. $\Sigma fX = 10,600,002$. The mean equals $10,600,002/347,976 = 30.46$.

Step 5. Multiply each frequency (f) by its corresponding X^2 and place the result in the column headed fX^2.

Step 6. Sum the values in the column headed fX^2 to obtain ΣfX^2. In the present example, $\Sigma fX^2 = 353,443,404$.

Step 7. Using the values obtained in steps 2, 4, and 6, substitute in the following formula for the variance:

$$s^2 = \frac{\Sigma fX^2}{N} - X^2$$
$$= 353,443,404/345,976 - (30.46)^2$$
$$= 1021.58 - 927.93$$
$$= 93.65$$

TABLE 6.8 Estimated Combined Numbers of White and Black Male Prison Inmates in Various Age Groupings in 1984. Tabular Entries Necessary to Calculate the Variance and the Standard Deviation of a Grouped Frequency Distribution

Class (Age)	Midpoint of Class (X)	Estimated Number of Inmates (f)	fX	X²	fX²
65–74	69.5	1,185	82,357.5	4,830.25	5,723,846.25
55–64	59.5	6,786	403,767.0	3,540.25	24,024,136.50
45–54	49.5	18,097	895,801.5	2,450.25	44,342,174.25
35–44	39.5	67,866	2,680,707.0	1,560.25	105,887,926.50
25–34	29.5	158,355	4,671,472.5	870.25	137,808,438.75
15–24	19.5	95,687	1,865,896.5	380.25	36,384,981.75
		$N = 347,976$	$\Sigma fX = 10,600,002$		$\Sigma fX^2 = 353,443,404.00$

Step 8. To obtain the standard deviation, find the square root of s^2 (step 7). $s = \sqrt{93.65} = 9.68$.

Calculating Pearson's coefficient of skew, using the median (29.44) calculated in Section 5.7:

$$sk = 3(30.46 - 29.44)/9.68 = 0.32$$

Although there is some positive skew, the value is within the range ($+0.50$ to -0.50) where the distribution may be considered symmetrical for most practical purposes.

CHAPTER SUMMARY

We have seen that to describe fully a distribution of scores, we require more than a measure of central tendency. We must also be able to describe how these scores are dispersed about the measure of central tendency. In this connection we discussed five measures of dispersion: the range, the semi-interquartile range, the mean deviation, the standard deviation, and the variance. (See Table 6.9.)

For normally distributed variables, the two measures based on the squaring of deviations about the mean (the variance and the standard deviation) are maximally useful. We discussed and demonstrated the procedures for calculating the standard deviation employing the mean

TABLE 6.9 Summary Procedures: Calculating the Variance and the Standard Deviation from an Array of Scores

X	X^2	Steps
7	49	**1.** Count the number of scores to obtain N. $N = 12$.
6	36	**2.** Sum the scores in the X column to obtain ΣX. $\Sigma X = 48$.
6	36	**3.** Square each score and place it in the adjacent column.
5	25	**4.** Sum the X^2 column to obtain $\Sigma X^2 = 242$.
5	25	**5.** Substitute the values found in steps 2 and 4 in the formula for the sum of
5	25	squares.
4	16	
4	16	$$SS = \sum X^2 - \frac{(\Sigma X)^2}{N} = 242 - \frac{2304}{12} = 50$$
3	9	
2	4	**6.** Substitute SS in the formulas for s^2 and s.
1	1	
0	0	$$s^2 = \frac{SS}{N} = \frac{50}{12} = 4.17 \qquad s = \sqrt{4.17} = 2.04$$

$\Sigma X = 48 \qquad \Sigma X^2 = 242$

$(\Sigma X)^2 = 48^2$

$\qquad = 2304$

deviation method and the raw score method with ungrouped frequency distributions. We also pointed out several of the errors commonly made in calculating standard deviations.

While examining the HR data (Perkins, 1984), which involved repeated measures on the same subjects, we noted that the within-subject measures of variability were substantially lower than the corresponding between-subject measures. These observations are in line with the view that there is a greater diversity in performance between different individuals than there is within a given individual.

Finally, we looked at a useful measure of skew, Pearson's *sk*.

TERMS TO REMEMBER

absolute value of a number   **semi-interquartile range**
between-subject variance   **standard deviation**
crude range   **sum of squares**
dispersion   **within-subject variance**
marginals   **variance**
mean deviation (average
  deviation)

EXERCISES

1. Calculate s^2 and s for the following array of scores: 3, 4, 5, 5, 6, 7.
   a. Add a constant, say, 2, to each score. Recalculate s^2 and s. Would the results be any different if you had added a larger constant, say, 200?
   Generalize: What is the effect on s and s^2 of adding a constant to an array of scores? Does the variability increase as we increase the magnitude of the scores.
   b. Subtract the same constant from each score. Recalculate s^2 and s. Would the results be any different if you had subtracted a larger constant, say, 200?
   Generalize: What is the effect on s and s^2 of subtracting a constant from an array of scores?
   c. Alternately add and subtract the same constant from each score (i.e., 3 + 2, 4 − 2, 5 + 2, etc.). Recalculate s and s^2. Would the results be any different if you had added and subtracted a larger constant?
   Generalize: What is the effect on s and s^2 of adding and subtracting a constant from an array of scores? (*Note:* This generalization is extremely important with relation to subsequent chapters where we discuss the effect of random errors on measures of variability.)
   d. Multiply each score by a constant, say, 2. Recalculate s and s^2.
   Generalize: What is the effect on s and s^2 of multiplying each score by a constant?
   e. Divide each score by the same constant. Recalculate s and s^2.
   Generalize: What is the effect on s and s^2 of dividing each score by a constant?

2. Compare your generalizations with those you made in relation to the mean (see Exercise 10, Chapter 5).

3. A rigorous definition of a measure of variation as a descriptive statistic would involve the following properties: (a) if a constant is added to or subtracted from each score or observation, the measure of variation remains unchanged; (b) if each score is multiplied or divided by a constant, the measure of variation is also multiplied or divided by that number. Check the following for the satisfaction of these conditions:

  i. the mean   **ii.** the median   **iii.** the mode
  iv. the mean deviation   **v.** the standard deviation   **vi.** the variance

If the properties defining measures of dispersion were extended to include *powers* of the constant by which each score is multiplied, would the variance qualify as a measure of dispersion?

4. How would the standard deviation be affected by the situations described in Exercises 4 and 5, Chapter 5?

5. What is the nature of the distribution if $s = 0$?

6. Calculate the standard deviations for the following sets of measurements:
  a. 10, 8, 6, 0, 8, 3, 2, 2, 8, 0   **b.** 1, 3, 3, 5, 5, 5, 7, 7, 9
  c. 20, 1, 2, 5, 4, 4, 4, 0   **d.** 5, 5, 5, 5, 5, 5, 5, 5, 5, 5

7. Why is the standard deviation in part (c) of Exercise 6 so large? Describe the effect of extreme deviations on s.

8. Determine the range for the sets of measurements in Exercise 6. For which of these is the range a misleading index of variability, and why?

9. In Exercises 15 and 16, Chapter 5, find the variances and standard deviations of the difference scores made by the naive subjects, (a) placebo and (b) heavy dose, and those made by the (c) chronic users in the marijuana study by Grinspoon. (*Hint:* To expedite calculations when there are negative scores, add a constant to all scores that is equal to or greater than the absolute value of the largest negative score.)

10. Calculate the mean and standard deviation for the set of 40 scores found in Exercise 5, Chapter 3.

11. A comparison shopper compares prices of plums at a number of different supermarkets. She finds the following prices per pound (in cents): 56, 65, 48, 73, 59, 72, 63, 65, 60, 63, 44, 79, 63, 61, 66, 69, 64, 71, 58, 63.
  a. Find the mean.
  b. Find the range, semi-interquartile range, and mean deviation.
  c. Find the standard deviation and variance.

12. Give one advantage of the standard deviation over the variance. Give an example.

13. Referring to Exercise 22, Chapter 3, find the mean and standard deviation of the number of quarts of milk sold at the supermarket.

14. List at least three specific instances in which a measure of variability was important in describing a group.

15. List at least three specific instances in which a measure of variability was important in comparing a group of people.

16. In Statistics in Action 5.1, we calculated the mean unpleasantness ratings made by four groups of subjects: males in which horror was preceded by humor, females in which horror was preceded by humor, males in which horror was first, and females in which horror was presented first.
   a. Find the range, variance, and standard deviation for each group.
   b. Combine the male and female groups in which humor preceded horror and find the mean, range, variance, and standard deviation.
   c. Combine the male and female groups in which horror was presented first and find the mean, range, variance, and standard deviation.
   d. Note that the measures of variability for the combined groups are usually larger than those for the four groups taken separately. See if you can devise a rationale for this difference.

17. Suppose merchant A sold a quart of milk for $0.40 and the standard deviation of this price was 0 during the last month. What was the price on the third day of the month? on the fifteenth day?

18. Calculate the crude range, variance, and standard deviation for both manufacturers in Exercise 29, Chapter 5.

19. Monthly normal precipitation (in inches) for four urban areas.
   a. It is possible to calculate means and measures of variability by columns (months of the year) or by community. Which corresponds to a within-subject measure of variability and which is a between-subject measure? Explain.
   b. Determine the yearly mean, range, variance, and standard deviation of precipitation for each city.
   c. Find the mean, range, variance, and standard deviation of the precipitation during each month.
   d. Which seems to yield the higher measures of variability—the within- or between-subject?
   e. Which cities have the most and the least consistent monthly precipitation data?

Stations	Jan	Feb	Mar	Apr	May	June	July	Aug	Sept	Oct	Nov	Dec
Barrow, Alaska	0.2	0.2	0.1	0.1	0.1	0.4	0.8	0.9	0.6	0.5	0.2	0.2
Burlington, Vt.	2.0	1.8	2.1	2.6	3.0	3.5	3.9	3.4	3.3	3.0	2.6	2.1
Honolulu, Hawaii	3.8	3.3	2.9	1.3	1.0	0.3	0.4	0.9	1.0	1.8	2.2	3.0
Seattle–Tacoma, Washington	5.7	4.2	3.8	2.4	1.7	1.6	0.8	1.0	2.1	4.0	5.4	6.3

Source: Based on data from National Climatic Center, NOAA, U.S. Department of Commerce.

20. Refer to Exercise 32, Chapter 5. Calculate the standard deviation of the frequency distribution of sample means. (*Hint:* Treat each mean as a score, and employ the raw score method for obtaining the standard deviation from an ungrouped frequency distribution.)

21. Find the variances and standard deviations of the systolic blood pressure scores (Benson *et al.*, 1971) appearing in Exercises 17–19, Chapter 5:
  a. Control sessions
  b. Conditioning sessions
  c. Difference scores

22. Refer to Case Example 5.1. Calculate the standard deviation of the
  a. β-endorphin levels of the near SIDS infants.
  b. Control infants.

23. Refer to Case Example 5.1. Calculate *sk* for the β-endorphin levels of the near-SIDS infants.

24. In the study described in Statistics in Action 5.1, the rating of pleasantness of humor was obtained on male and female subjects when humorous scenes alone were shown (humor first) or when humorous scenes were preceded by five scenes of horror (one minute excerpts from the movie *Halloween*).

The following table presents the pleasantness ratings made by the four groups of subjects (the lower the score was, the greater was the pleasantness).

Humor First		Humor Preceded by Horror	
Male	**Female**	**Male**	**Female**
17	9	17	10
24	12	11	15
13	20	25	14
13	18	20	7
24	23	6	10
18	18	10	13
21	21	6	6
28	32	31	6
12	12	8	11
9	12	17	14

Source: Based on data from Manstead et al., 1983.

  a. Calculate the mean, median, range, variance, and standard deviation for each of the four groups.
  b. Combine the male and female scores in humor first and find the mean, median, range, variance, and standard deviation.
  c. Combine the male and female scores in humor preceded by horror and find the mean, median, range, variance, and standard deviation. Are the means consistent with the emotional contrast hypothesis that would predict lower scores when humor is preceded by horror?
  d. Determine the measure of skew for each of the groups in (a).

25. Refer to Exercise 24. We have noted that the range, variance, and standard deviation are all measures of the dispersion or variability of scores in a distribution. For each of the four groups in Exercise 24(a):

   a. Plot the values of the range on the X-axis and the values of the corresponding standard deviation on the Y-axis.

   b. Do low values of the range appear to be associated with low values of the standard deviation?

   c. In the absence of knowledge of the standard deviation, does it appear that the range can provide information on the relative dispersion of different distributions?

26. Referring back to Exercise 42 in Chapter 5, calculate the variance and standard deviation of the ages of white prisoners.

27. Referring back to Exercise 43 in Chapter 5, calculate the variance and standard deviation of the ages of black prisoners.

28. Calculate Pearson's coefficient of skew for white and black prisoners, respectively. Is there a sufficient degree of skew in either case to regard either distribution as nonsymmetrical?

Standard Deviation/ Standard Normal Distribution

7.1 INTRODUCTION

We previously noted that to the behavioral scientist, scores derived from scales are generally meaningless by themselves. To take on meaning, they must be compared to the distribution of scores from some reference group. Indeed, the scores derived from any scale, including those employed by the physical scientists, become more meaningful when they are compared to some reference group of objects or persons. Thus, if we were to learn that a Canadian fisherman caught a northern pike weighing 50 pounds, we might or might not be impressed, depending on the extent of our knowledge concerning the usual weight of this type of fish. However, once a reference group is established, the measurement becomes meaningful. Since most northern pike weigh under 10 pounds and only rarely achieve weights as high as 20 pounds, the achievement of our apocryphal fisherman must be considered Bunyanesque.

7.2 THE CONCEPT OF z-SCORES

In interpreting a single score, we want to place it in some position with respect to a collection of scores from some reference group. In Chapter 4, you learned to place a score by determining its percentile rank. It will be recalled that the percentile rank of a score tells us the percentage of scores that are of lower scale value. Another approach to interpretation of a single score might be to view it with reference to some central point, such as the mean. Thus, a score of 20 in a distribution with a mean of 23 might be reported as -3. Finally, we might express this deviation score in terms of standard deviation units. Therefore, if our standard deviation is 1.5, the score of 20 would be two standard deviations below the mean (i.e., $-3/1.5 = -2$). This process of dividing a deviation of a score from the mean by the standard deviation is known as the transformation to **z-scores.** Symbolically, z is defined as

z-Score: A score that represents the deviation of a specific score from the mean and is expressed in standard deviation units.

$$z = \frac{X - \bar{X}^*}{s} \quad \text{or} \quad z = \frac{X - \mu}{\sigma} \tag{7.1}$$

when dealing with parameters.

Note that every score in the distribution may be transformed into a z-score, in which case each z will represent the *deviation of a specific score from the mean, expressed in standard deviation units.*

Now suppose we were to take all the scores in a distribution, subtract the mean from each $(X - \bar{X}$, the familiar deviation score), and then divide each deviation score by the standard deviation of the distribution. Would the transformed distribution possess any characteristics that are common to *all* distributions transformed in this way? The answer is "Yes."

As we'll see, *the mean of such a transformed distribution is always zero, the sum of the squared z-scores always equals N, and the standard deviation is always 1.* Why is this so? To begin with, the mean of the z-scores

$$\bar{z} = \sum z/N = \sum \frac{(X - \bar{X})}{Ns}$$

since each $z = (X - \bar{X})/s$. However, since N and s are constants throughout this summation, we may rewrite the mean of the z-scores as follows:

$$\bar{z} = \frac{1}{Ns} \sum (X - \bar{X})$$

We have previously shown that $\Sigma(X - \bar{X}) = 0$. Therefore, $\bar{z} = 0$.

The fact that the sum of the squared z-scores (Σz^2) equals N may be demonstrated mathematically:

$$\sum z^2 = \frac{\Sigma(X - \bar{X})^2}{s^2} = \frac{1}{s^2} \cdot \sum (X - \bar{X})^2$$

$$= \frac{N}{\Sigma(X - \bar{X})^2} \cdot \sum (X - \bar{X})^2$$

$$= N$$

---

* It is sometimes useful to go from a z-score to a raw score: $X = zs + \bar{X}$, or $X = z\sigma + \mu$.

Finally, the standard deviation and the variance of z-scores is 1. Thus

$$s_z = s_z^2 = 1 \qquad (7.2)$$

To demonstrate, we have

$$s_z^2 = \frac{\Sigma(z - \bar{z})^2}{N}$$

Since $\bar{z} = 0$, then

$$s_z^2 = \frac{\Sigma z^2}{N}$$

Since $\Sigma z^2 = N$, then

$$s_z^2 = \frac{N}{N} = 1$$
$$s_z = \sqrt{s_z^2} = \sqrt{1} = 1$$

What is the value of transforming to a z-score? The conversion to z-scores always yields a mean of 0 and a standard deviation of 1, but it does not "normalize" a nonnormal distribution. However, if the *population of scores* on a given variable is normal, we may express any score as a percentile rank by referring our z to the *standard normal distribution*. In addition, since z-scores represent abstract numbers, as opposed to the concrete values of the original scores (inches, pounds, IQ scores, etc.), we may compare an individual's position on one variable with his or her position on a second. To understand these two important characteristics of z-scores, we must make reference to the *standard normal distribution*.

7.3 THE STANDARD NORMAL DISTRIBUTION

As we noted previously, many variables are distributed in such a way that most observations are concentrated near the center of the distribution. As the distance between the values of the variable and the center of the distribution increases, the frequency of actual observations decreases, both above and below the central concentration of frequencies. This yields a bell-shaped distribution that is commonly referred to as the normal distribution.

As a matter of fact, the normal distribution is a mathematical abstraction that is not found in the real world. It consists of a family of distributions in which the curves approach but never touch the horizontal axis. This is another way of saying that no matter how distant a given value of the variable is from the central concentration, there are other values, both negative and positive, that are more distant. In contrast, empirical distributions have upper and lower limits beyond which no real measurements

BOX 7.1

SO YOU WANT TO INTERPRET A TEST SCORE?

As we previously noted, a score in and of itself is meaningless. In this chapter, we see that the z-score transformation provides a precise means of interpreting any value of a variable when the scores are normally distributed. The following excerpt from *Winning with Statistics* illustrates the use of the z-score transformation in the interpretation of test scores on standard psychological and educational tests.

Here are the step-by-step procedures for taking all of the mystery out of the interpretation of test scores on standard psychological and educational tests.

1. Determine the mean and the standard deviation of the test. Sometimes different means and standard deviations are given for different age groups. Be sure to find these two measures for the age group in which you are interested. Sources of this information are the Administration Booklet for the particular test and the Buros Mental Measurement Yearbook. Since the Administration Booklets are not usually available to nonprofessionals, the Mental

Percent of Scores Above and Below a Given z-Score

A	B	C
z	Percent of cases below	Percent of cases above
−2.2	1	99
−2.1	2	98
−2.0	2	98
−1.9	3	97
−1.8	4	96
−1.7	4	96
−1.6	5	95
−1.5	7	93
−1.4	8	92
−1.3	9	91
−1.2	12	88
−1.1	14	86
−1.0	16	84
−0.9	18	82
−0.8	21	79
−0.7	24	76
−0.6	27	73
−0.5	31	69
−0.4	34	66
−0.3	38	62
−0.2	42	58
−0.1	46	54
0.00	50	50

are found. If we are measuring height, weight, and age of humans, for example, we shall find no real-world negative values for these variables (such as −50 pounds, −4 years of age) nor will there be any real observations beyond some upper limit (e.g., according to the 1990 edition of the Guinness Book of Records, the heaviest person on record weighed 1400 pounds, give or take a few).

The value of the normal distribution lies in the fact that many real-world distributions—including values of a variable as well as values of sample statistics (e.g., means, variances, standard deviations)—approach the form of the theoretical distribution. This enables us to use the characteristics of the theoretical model to advantage in real-world applications. The **standard normal distribution** has a μ of 0, a σ of 1, and a total area equal to 1.00*

Standard Normal Distribution: A normal distribution that has a mean of 0, a standard deviation of 1, and a total area equal to 1.00.

* It will be recalled that the Greek letters μ and σ represent the population mean and the standard deviation, respectively. The equation of the normal curve is

Measurement Yearbook is your best bet. If it is not found in your local library, it is almost certain to be in the collection of your nearest college and university library.

2. Transform the score you are interested in interpreting to a z-score using the following formula:

$$z = \frac{\text{Score} - \text{Mean}}{\text{Standard deviation}}$$

If you interested in interpreting a score of 40 and you know that the mean and standard deviation are 30 and 9, respectively, you would have

$$z = \frac{40 - 30}{9} = \frac{10}{9} = 1.1$$

3. Look up a positive value of 1.1 under column B of the accompanying table. Here we find an entry of 86. This means that 86 percent of a comparison group with which this score is being compared obtained scores lower than 86. Only 14 percent (column C) scored higher.

There it is. It's as easy as that.

Source: Excerpted from R. P. Runyon, *Winning with Statistics*. Reading, Mass.: Addison-Wesley, 1977.

Percent of Scores Above and Below a Given z-Score (*Continued*)

A	B	C
z	Percent of cases below	Percent of cases above
0.1	54	46
0.2	58	42
0.3	62	38
0.4	66	34
0.5	69	31
0.6	73	27
0.7	76	24
0.8	79	21
0.9	82	18
1.0	84	16
1.1	86	14
1.2	88	12
1.3	91	9
1.4	92	8
1.5	93	7
1.6	95	5
1.7	96	4
1.8	96	4
1.9	97	3
2.0	98	2
2.1	98	2
2.2	99	1

There is a fixed proportion of cases between a vertical line (ordinate) erected at any one point and an ordinate erected at any other point. Taking

$$Y = \frac{Ni}{\sigma \sqrt{2\pi}} e^{\frac{-(X - \mu)^2}{2\sigma^2}}$$

in which

Y = the frequency at a given value of X
σ = the standard deviation of the distribution
π = a constant equaling approximately 3.1416
e = approximately 2.7183
N = total frequency of the distribution
μ = the mean of the distribution
i = the width of the class
X = any score in the distribution

It should be clear that there is a family of curves that may be called normal. By setting $Ni = 1$, a distribution is generated in which $\mu = 0$ and total area under the curve equals 1.

a few reference points along the normal curve, we can make the following statements:

1. Between the mean and 1 standard deviation above the mean there are 34.13% of all cases. Similarly, 34.13% of all cases fall between the mean and 1 standard deviation below the mean. Stated in another way, 34.13% of the *area* under the curve is found between the mean and 1 standard deviation above the mean, and 34.13% of the *area* falls between the mean and −1 standard deviation.

2. Between the mean and 2 standard deviations above the mean there are 47.72% of all cases. Since the normal curve is symmetrical, 47.72% of the area also falls between the mean and −2 standard deviations.

3. Finally, between the mean and 3 standard deviations above the mean there are 49.87% of all the cases. Similarly, 49.87% of the cases fall between the mean and −3 standard deviations. Thus, we see that 99.74% of all cases fall between ±3 standard deviations. These relationships are shown in Figure 7.1.

Now, by transforming the scores of a normally distributed variable to z-scores, we are, in effect, expressing these scores in units of the standard normal curve. For any given value of X with a certain proportion of area beyond it, there is a corresponding value of z with the same proportion of area beyond it. Thus, if we have a population in which $\mu = 30$ and $\sigma = 10$, the z of a score at the mean ($X = 30$) will equal zero, and the z of scores 1 standard deviation above and below the mean ($X = 40$ and $X = 20$) will be +1.00 and −1.00, respectively.

Finding Area Between Given Scores

For expositional purposes, we confined our preceding discussion of area under the standard normal curve to selected points. As a matter of fact, however, it is possible to determine the percent of areas between *any* two points by making use of the tabled values of the area under the normal curve (see Table A in the table section of this book.). The left-hand column headed by z represents the deviation from the mean expressed in standard deviation units. *By referring to the body of the table, we can determine the*

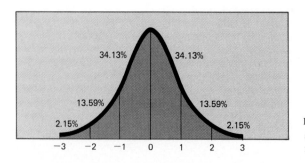

FIGURE 7.1   Areas between selected points under the normal curve.

proportion of total area between a given score and the mean, column (B), *and the area beyond a given score*, column (C). Thus, if an individual obtained a score of 24.65 on a normally distributed variable with $\mu = 16$ and $\sigma = 5$, her z-score would be

$$z = \frac{24.65 - 16}{5} = 1.73$$

Referring to column (B) in Table A, we find that 0.4582 or 45.82%* of the area lies between her score and the mean. Since 50% of the area also falls below the mean in a symmetrical distribution, we may conclude that 95.82% of all the area falls below a score of 24.65. Note that we can now translate this score into a percentile rank of 95.82.

Let us suppose that another individual obtained a score of 7.35 on the same normally distributed variable. His z-score would be

$$z = \frac{7.35 - 16}{5} = -1.73$$

Since the normal curve is symmetrical, only the areas corresponding to the positive z-values are given in Table A. Negative z-values will have precisely the same proportions as their positive counterparts. Thus, the area between the mean and a z of -1.73 is also 45.82%. The percentile rank of a score below the mean may be obtained either by subtracting 45.82% from 50%, or directly from column (C). In either case, the percentile rank of a score of 7.35 is 4.18.

You would carefully note that these relationships apply *only to scores from normally distributed populations*. Transforming the raw scores to standard scores does not in any way alter the form of the original distribution. The only change is to convert the mean to zero and the standard deviation to one. Thus, if the original distribution of scores is nonnormal, *the distribution of z-scores* will be nonnormal. In other words, our transformation to z's will *not* convert a nonnormal distribution to a normal distribution.†

Figure 7.2 further clarifies the relationships among raw scores, z-scores, and percentile ranks of a normally distributed variable. It assumes that the mean = 50 and the standard deviation = 10.

7.4 ILLUSTRATIVE PROBLEMS

Let's take several sample problems in which we assume that the mean is equal to 100 on a standard IQ test and the standard deviation is 16. It is assumed that the variable is normally distributed.

---

* The areas under the normal curve are expressed as proportions of area. To convert to a percentage of area, multiply by 100 or merely move the decimal two places to the right.
† Appendix B summarizes the procedures for transforming a nonnormal frequency distribution into a normal distribution.

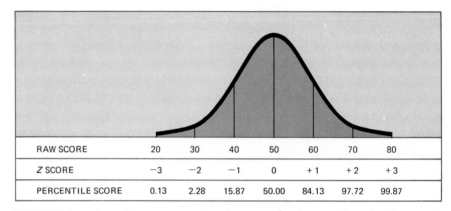

RAW SCORE	20	30	40	50	60	70	80
Z SCORE	−3	−2	−1	0	+1	+2	+3
PERCENTILE SCORE	0.13	2.28	15.87	50.00	84.13	97.72	99.87

FIGURE 7.2   Relationships among raw scores, z-scores, and percentile ranks of a normally distributed variable in which the mean = 50 and the standard deviation = 10.

Problem 1.   John Doe obtained a score of 125 on an IQ test. What percent of cases fall between his score and the mean? What is his percentile rank in the general population?

At the outset, it is wise to construct a crude diagram representing the relationships in question. Thus, in the present example, the diagram would appear as shown in Figure 7.3. To find the value of z corresponding to X = 125, we subtract the population mean from 125 and divide by 16. Thus

$$z = \frac{125 - 100}{16} = 1.56$$

Looking up 1.56 in column (B), Table A, we find that 44.06% of the area falls between the mean and 1.56 standard deviations above the mean. John Doe's percentile rank is therefore 50 + 44.06 or 94.06.

Problem 2.   Mary Jones scores 93 on an IQ test. What is her percentile rank in the general population (Figure 7.4)?

$$z = \frac{93 - 100}{16} = -0.44$$

The minus sign indicates that the score is below the mean. Looking up 0.44 in column (C), we find that 33.00% of the cases fall below her score. Thus, her percentile rank is 33.00.

Problem 3.   What percent of cases fall between a score of 120 and a score of 88 (Figure 7.5)?

Note that to answer this question we do *not* subtract 88 from 120 and divide by σ. The areas in the normal probability curve are designated in relation to the mean as a fixed point of reference. We must therefore separately calculate the area between the mean and a score of 120 and the

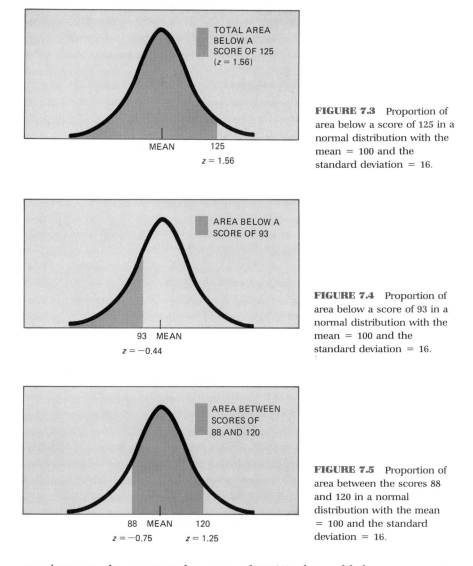

FIGURE 7.3 Proportion of area below a score of 125 in a normal distribution with the mean = 100 and the standard deviation = 16.

FIGURE 7.4 Proportion of area below a score of 93 in a normal distribution with the mean = 100 and the standard deviation = 16.

FIGURE 7.5 Proportion of area between the scores 88 and 120 in a normal distribution with the mean = 100 and the standard deviation = 16.

area between the mean and a score of 88. We then add the two areas to answer our question.

Procedure:

Step 1. Find the z corresponding to $X = 120$:

$$z = \frac{120 - 100}{16} = 1.25$$

Step 2. Find the z corresponding to $X = 88$:

$$z = \frac{88 - 100}{16} = -0.75$$

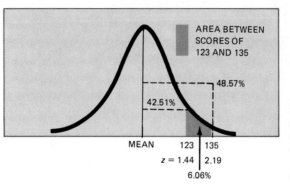

FIGURE 7.6 Proportion of area between the scores 123 and 135 in a normal distribution with the mean = 100 and the standard deviation = 16.

Step 3. Find the required areas by referring to column (B), Table A:

Area between the mean and z = 1.25 is 39.44%
Area between the mean and z = − 0.75 is 27.34%

Step 4. Add the two areas together.

Thus, the area between 88 and 120 = 66.78%.

Problem 4. What percent of the area falls between a score of 123 and 135 (Figure 7.6)?

Again, we cannot obtain the answer directly; we must find the area between the mean and a score of 123 and subtract this from the area between the mean and a score of 135.

Procedure:

Step 1. Find the z corresponding to X = 135:

$$z = \frac{135 - 100}{16} = 2.19$$

Step 2. Find the z corresponding to X = 123:

$$z = \frac{123 - 100}{16} = 1.44$$

Step 3. Find the required areas by referring to column (B):

Area between the mean and z = 2.19 is 48.57%
Area between the mean and z = 1.44 is 42.51%

Step 4. Subtract to obtain the area between 123 and 135. The result is

$$48.57 - 42.51 = 6.06\%$$

Problem 5. We stated earlier that our transformation to z-scores permits us to compare an individual's position on one variable with his or her position on another. Let us illustrate this important use of z-scores.

BOX 7.2

DESIGNING SEAT SIZE IN COMMERCIAL CARRIERS: FOR COMFORT OR PROFIT?

Are you one of those rather wide-of-beam travelers who must gird your spirits for the next commercial airline flight (or take a trip on an intracity or intercity bus) because the seat width always seems to be about 2 inches shy of your comfort zone? Although measuring beam widths may not seem to be the most significant human enterprise, fortunes may be won or lost by common carriers by a seemingly minor shift in the width of the passenger seats. To illustrate, if a given aircraft has 50 rows, 4 across, it can accommodate a maximum load of 200 passengers. However, if it can trim a few inches from each seat and a few more from the aisle, one more seat per row can be added, bringing the passenger capacity up to 250. That is a 25% increase [(250 − 200)/200 × 100 = 25%] in seating capacity!

Let's assume that the beam width of airline passengers (including elbows) is normally distributed with a mean of 20 inches and a standard deviation of 2. Cheapflight Airlines finds that by reducing each seat by 3 inches and the aisle by 5 inches, it can accommodate five seats to a row. By doing so, it can reduce ticket fares considerably and increase the number of flights running at or near capacity.

Taking the opposite tack, Broadbeam Airlines decides to emphasize passenger comfort in its advertising campaign. By trimming 8 inches off the

aisle, it can increase the seat width to 22 inches. However, its passenger capacity remains 200. Broadbeam justifies its higher fares in terms of its luxurious seating.

What percentage of the passengers in each airline will find the seat width within their comfort zone?

Broadbeam Airlines: $z = (22 − 20)/2 = 1.00$. Presumably, all passengers with a $z \leq 1.00$ will luxuriate in posterior comfort. This comes to a generous 84.13% (50% + 34.13%).

Cheapflight Airlines: $z = (17 − 20)/2 = −1.5$. Only passengers with a $z \leq −1.50$ will find the seating capacity adequate. Referring to Table A, we find that the area beyond z is 0.0668. Thus, only about 7% of Cheapflight's passengers will emerge from the flight without severely pinched posteriors. About 93% will be at their wits' end.

Now, suppose another airline wanted to join the battle of the beams and base their advertising pitch on the claim that 97.5% of its passengers could sit in total comfort. How wide would the seats have to be to justify this claim?

Notice that the problem here is the same as in Problem 6. We are given the desired percentage of area and would like to know the value of the variable that yields this percentage. The first step is to find the value of z that excludes 0.0250 (2.5%) of the area. Referring to column C in Table A, we find that the area beyond a z of 1.96 equals 0.0250. Using the formula $X = z\sigma + \mu$ (see footnote in Section 7.2 p. 168), we find $X = 1.96 \times 2 + 20 = 23.92$. In other words, the seats would have to be about 24 inches wide.

On a standard aptitude test, John G. obtained a score of 245 on the verbal scale and 175 on the mathematics scale. The means and the standard deviations of each of these normally distributed scales are as follows: verbal, $\overline{X} = 220$, $s = 50$; math, $\overline{X} = 150$, $s = 25$. On which scale did John score higher?

All that we need to do is compare John's z-score on each variable. Thus

$$\text{Verbal } z = \frac{245 - 220}{50} \qquad \text{Math } z = \frac{175 - 150}{25}$$
$$= 0.50 \qquad\qquad\qquad = 1.00$$

We conclude, therefore, that John scored higher on the math scale of the aptitude test. Of course, if we so desire, we may express these scores as percentile ranks. Thus, John's percentile rank is 84.13 on the math scale and only 69.15 on the verbal scale.

Problem 6. In each of the preceding problems, we knew the mean, the standard deviation, and the value of the variable for which we wanted the corresponding percentage of area. There are numerous occasions when we are given the desired percentage of area and wish to know the value of the variable that yields that percentage. To illustrate, imagine that you wish to join a highly selective intellectual society that requires members to be in the upper 2% of the population in intelligence. The IQ test used for selection has a mean of 100 and a standard deviation of 16.

The first step to find the value of z that cuts off the upper 2% of area in the standard normal curve, that is, 0.0200 of the area. Referring to column (C) in Table A, we find that the area beyond a z of 2.05 excludes 2.02% of area in the normal curve. This is sufficiently close so that we'll use this value in our calculations. Using the formula $X = z\sigma + \mu$ when parameters are known or $X = zs + \overline{X}$ for normally distributed variables in which the sample standard deviation and mean are known (see footnote in Section 7.2, p. 168), we find $X = 2.05 \times 16 + 100 = 132.8$. Thus, a minimum IQ of 133 would be needed to qualify for membership in this society.

7.5 THE STANDARD DEVIATION AS AN ESTIMATE OF ERROR AND PRECISION

In the absence of any specific information, what is our best single basis for predicting a score that is obtained by any given individual? If the data are drawn from a normally distributed population, we find that the mean (or *any* measure of central tendency) is our best single predictor. The more compactly our scores are distributed about the mean, the smaller *our errors* in prediction will be, on the average. Conversely, when the scores are widely spread about the mean, we will make larger errors in prediction, on the average, when we use the mean to predict scores. To illustrate, suppose that the star forwards on two different women's basketball teams score the following number of points during a seven-game period:

	A	B
	14	10
	15	18
	12	9
	15	19
	14	14
	15	6
	13	22
Sum	98	98

Note that both players obtained precisely the same mean ($\overline{X}$ = 14), but look how much more variable is B's performance! You would surely feel much more confident in predicting that A rather than B would score around 14 points in any given game. Since the standard deviation reflects the dispersion of scores, it becomes, in a sense, an estimate of error. For the same reasons, the smaller standard deviation provides more precise measures (i.e., measures closer to the mean), on the average.

To take another example, imagine that we are comparing two artillery units, Battery A and Battery B. A zero score means that the shell was on target; a positive score means that the shell went beyond the target, and a negative score indicates that it fell short of the target. Table 7.1 summarizes the results.

TABLE 7.1   Hypothetical Scores Made by Two Artillery Batteries when Firing at Designated Target

	Frequency	
Distance from Target (in Meters)	**Battery A**	**Battery B**
200	2	0
150	4	1
100	5	5
50	7	10
0	9	13
−50	7	10
−100	5	5
−150	4	1
−200	2	0
$\overline{X}$ =	0	0
s =	102.74	65.83*

* Note that, although the mean accuracy of both batteries was identical, the shelling of Battery B showed less dispersion or scattering.

"I have some good news and some bad news, Captain. The bad news is that first we were 150 meters past the target; then 150 meters under; next 75 meters under and, then, 75 meters over. Not a single #*!#* shell on target. The good news is that, on the average, we were right on target!"

Although both batteries achieved the same mean, it is clear that more of the shells of Battery B landed close to the target than did the shells of Battery A. In other words, the firing of Battery B was more precise. This greater precision is reflected in the lower standard deviation of Battery B.

7.6 THE TRANSPORTATION TO *T*-SCORES

Many psychological and educational tests have been purposely constructed to yield a normal distribution of z-scores. Moreover, procedures are available for transforming nonnormal distributions into a standard normal distribution. These procedures are shown in Appendix B. Recall, however, that z-scores include many negative values and are expressed in decimal form. Since it is often inconvenient and sometimes confusing to deal with negative numbers and decimals, the z-scores of normally distributed variables are frequently converted to *T*-scores, employing the following transformation equation:

$$T^* = 100 + 10z$$

---

* The *T*-transformation may involve the substitution of any desired constants into the equation. Thus, if a mean of 100 and a standard deviation of 20 is desired, the transformation equation becomes 100 + 20z. There is a *T*-score transformation that normalizes nonnormal distributions. The procedures are beyond the scope of this book. For reference, see Helen M. Walker and Joseph Lev, *Elementary Statistical Methods*, 3d ed. New York: Holt, Rinehart and Winston, 1969.

This transformation now yields a distribution with a mean of 100 and a standard deviation of 10. It eliminates all negative values. Thus, a score with a z corresponding to -1.52 becomes

$$T = 100 + 10(-1.52)$$
$$= 100 - 15.2 = 84.8$$

It is traditional to round to the nearest whole number, thereby eliminating the decimal.

We may readily convert T-scores to units of the standard normal curve:

$$z = \frac{T - \bar{T}}{10}$$

Thus, a person obtaining a T of 84.8 would have a corresponding z of

$$z = \frac{84.8 - 100}{10} = -\frac{15.2}{10} = -1.52$$

Employing the standard normal curve, we find that this score has a corresponding percentile rank of 6.43.

To eliminate the decimals entirely, we could use a transformation such as

$$T = 500 + 100z$$

A z of -1.52 would become

$$T = 500 + 100(-1.52)$$
$$= 500 - 152$$
$$= 348$$

7.7 PUTTING IT ALL TOGETHER

Table 7.2 shows the scores of Mary Cardinale on six scales of a standardized aptitude test. Also shown are the mean and standard deviation for each of these scales.

TABLE 7.2 The Mean and Standard Deviation on Six Scales of a Standardized Test and the Scores Made by a Single Individual on Each of These Scales.

	Clerical Ability	Logical Reasoning	Mechanical Ability	Numerical Reasoning	Spatial Relations	Verbal Fluency
Score	41	47	100	105	90	70
Mean	50	40	120	100	70	60
S.D.	15	4	25	10	20	6

Converting each of Mary's raw scores into a z-score and then expressing each as a percentile rank:

Scale	z		Percentile Rank
Clerical ability	$(41 - 50)/15 =$	-0.6	27
Logical reasoning	$(47 - 40)/4 =$	1.75	96
Mechanical ability	$(100 - 120)/25 =$	-0.80	21
Numerical reasoning	$(105 - 100)/10 =$	0.50	69
Spatial relations	$(90 - 70)/20 =$	1.00	84
Verbal fluency	$(70 - 60)/6 =$	1.67	95

Take note of the fact that Mary's raw score on logical reasoning is the second to lowest of all her scores. Nevertheless, her percentile rank on this scale is her highest, exceeding 96% of the group against which this test was standardized. Conversely, her highest raw score was on the Numerical Reasoning scale, but her percentile rank (69) was considerably lower than her rank on the Logical Reasoning scale. How can this be?

This example illustrates that performance is not necessarily judged on the basis of raw scores. What must also be taken into account is the mean and the standard deviation of the comparison group on each scale of the aptitude test. Converting each score to a common scale of values (the z-scale) and a common reference standard (the standard normal curve) enables us to compare an individual's relative performance on a diverse spectrum of abilities. Figure 7.7 shows a bar graph of both Mary's raw scores and her relative performance (percentile rank) on all six scales of the aptitude test. Note how misleading your estimate of Mary's abilities would be if you were to base your conclusions on her raw scores. For instance, you would judge her second best on mechanical ability (raw score = 100). In reality, when a measure of relative performance is used, such as z-score or percentile rank, you would conclude that she performed poorest on this scale: at the 21st percentile. On this scale, 79% of the standardization group scored higher than she.

CHAPTER SUMMARY

In this chapter, we demonstrated the value of the standard deviation for comparison of the dispersion of scores in different distributions of a variable, the interpretation of a score with respect to a single distribution, and the

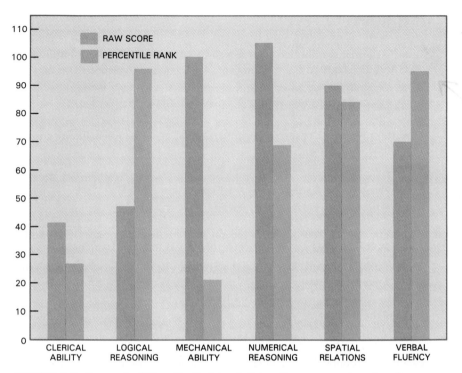

FIGURE 7.7 Bar graph of Mary Cardinale's relative performance on six scales of an aptitude test. The hatched bars show her raw scores, whereas the solid bars represent a measure based on relative performance (percentile rank).

comparison of scores on two or more variables. We showed how to convert raw scores into units of the standard normal curve (transformation to z-scores), and explained the various characteristics of the standard normal curve. A series of problems demonstrated various ways to convert normally distributed variables to z-scores.

Finally, we discussed the standard deviation as an estimate of error and as an estimate of precision. We demonstrated the use of the T-transformation as a convenient method for eliminating the negative values occurring when scores are expressed in terms of z.

TERMS TO REMEMBER

standard normal distribution   **standard score (z)**

EXERCISES

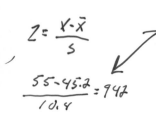

$$z = \frac{x - \bar{x}}{s}$$

$$\frac{55 - 45.2}{10.4} = .942$$

1. Given a normal distribution with a mean of 45.2 and a standard deviation of 10.4, find the standard score equivalents for the following scores:

a. 55   **b.** 41   **c.** 45.2

d. 31.5   **e.** 68.4   **f.** 18.9

2. Find the proportion of area under the normal curve between the mean and the following z-scores:

a. -2.05 **b.** -1.90 **c.** -0.25

d. $+0.40$ **e.** $+1.65$ **f.** $+1.96$

g. $+2.33$ **h.** $+2.58$ **i.** $+3.08$

3. Assume a normal distribution based on 1000 cases with a mean of 50 and a standard deviation of 10.

a. Find the proportion of area and the number of cases *between* the mean and the following scores:

$$60 \qquad 70 \qquad 45 \qquad 25$$

b. Find the proportion of area and the number of cases *above* the following scores:

$$60 \qquad 70 \qquad 45 \qquad 25 \qquad 50$$

c. Find the proportion of area and the number of cases *between* the following scores:

$$60{-}70 \qquad 25{-}60 \qquad 45{-}70 \qquad 25{-}45$$

4. Below are Spiegel's scores, the mean, and the standard deviation on each of three normally distributed tests.

Test	μ	σ	Spiegel's Score
Arithmetic	47.2	4.8	53
Verbal comprehension	64.6	8.3	71
Geography	75.4	11.7	72

a. Convert each of Spiegel's test scores to standard scores.

b. On which test did Spiegel stand the highest? On which the lowest?

c. Spiegel's score in arithmetic was surpassed by what proportion of the population? Her score in verbal comprehension? In geography?

5. On a normally distributed mathematics aptitude test, for females,

$$\mu = 60 \qquad \sigma = 10$$

and for males,

$$\mu = 64 \qquad \sigma = 8$$

   a. Arthur obtained a score of 62. What is his percentile rank on both the male and the female norms?

   b. Helen's percentile rank is 73 on the female norms. What is her percentile rank on the male norms?

6. If frequency curves were constructed for each of the following, which would approximate a normal curve?

   a. Heights of a large representative sample of adult American males

   b. Means of a large number of samples with a fixed N (say, $N = 100$) drawn from a normally distributed population of scores

   c. Weights, in ounces, of ears of corn selected randomly from a cornfield

   d. Annual income, in dollars, of a large number of American families selected at random

   e. Weight, in ounces, of all fish caught in a popular fishing resort in a season

7. In a normal distribution with $\mu = 72$ and $\sigma = 12$:

   a. What is the score at the 25th percentile?

   b. What is the score at the 75th percentile?

   c. What is the score at the 90th percentile?

   d. Find the percent of cases scoring above 80.

   e. Find the percent of cases scoring below 66.

   f. Between what scores do the middle 50 percent of the cases lie?

   g. Beyond what scores do the most extreme 10 percent lie?

   h. Beyond what scores do the most extreme 1 percent lie?

8. Answer Question 7 (a) through (h) for:

   a. $\mu = 72$ and $\sigma = 8$

   b. $\mu = 72$ and $\sigma = 4$

   c. $\mu = 72$ and $\sigma = 2$

9. Using the following information, determine whether Larry did better on Test I or Test II. On which test did Mindy do better?

	Test I	Test II
μ	500	24
σ	40	1.4
Larry's scores	550	26
Mindy's scores	600	25

10. Are all sets of z-scores normally distributed? Why?

11. Is there more than one normal distribution?

12. Transform the following z-scores to T-scores, using $T = 50 + 10z$. Round to the nearest whole number.

    a. -2.43 **b.** 1.50 **c.** -0.50 **d.** 0.00

13. The transformation to T-scores yields the following values when $T = 500 + 100z$. Convert back to the original z-scores.

    a. 230   **b.** 500   **c.** 780   **d.** 640   **e.** 460

14. In what sense can the standard deviation be regarded as a measure of precision?

15. Refer to Box 7.2. The values of μ and σ were given for the populations and included both males and females. Suppose the mean beam width is 18 for females and 22 for males, with $\sigma = 2$ for both populations.

    a. What percentage of males and females flying Cheapflight will achieve their comfort zone?

    b. What percentage of males and females flying Broadbeam will be comfortable?

16. How wide would the seats have to be in order to achieve the comfort zone for 90.32% of the

    a. females?

    b. males?

17. Following are the means and standard deviations of five different normally distributed educational tests:

Variable	μ	σ
A	50	10
B	50	20
C	100	15
D	100	10
E	120	30

a. Relative to which variable is a score of 70 the highest?

b. Relative to which variable is a score of 85 the lowest?

18. Refer to Exercise 17. Monica obtained the following scores on each of the variables: $A = 60, B = 80, C = 115, D = 112, E = 145$.

a. Find her percentile rank on each variable.

b. On which variable did she score the highest?

c. On which variable did she score the lowest?

8

Correlation

8.1 THE CONCEPT OF CORRELATION

Thus far in the course, we have been interested in calculating various statistics that permit us to describe thoroughly the distribution of the values of a single variable and to relate these statistics to the interpretation of individual scores. However, as you are well aware, many of the problems in the behavioral sciences go beyond the description of a single variable in its various and sundry ramifications. We are frequently called upon to determine the relationships among two or more variables. For example, college administration officers are vitally concerned with the relationship between high school grade averages or Scholastic Aptitude Test (SAT) scores and performance at college. Do students who do well in high school or who score high on the SAT also perform well in college? Conversely, do poor high school students or those who score low on the SAT perform poorly at college? Do parents with high intelligence tend to have children of high intelligence? Is there a relationship between the declared dividend on stocks and their paper value on the exchange? Is there a relationship between socioeconomic class and recidivism in crime?

As soon as we raise questions concerning the relationship among variables, we are thrust into the fascinating area of **correlation.** In order to express quantitatively the extent to which two variables are related, we

Correlation: Relationship between two variables.

189

TABLE 8.1 Several Different Types of Correlation Coefficients and Numerical Scales with Which They Are Used

Scale	Symbol	Used With
Nominal	r_{phi}* (phi coefficient)	Two dichotomous variables.
	r_b* (biserial r)	One dichotomous variable, with underlying continuity assumed; one variable that can take on more than two values.
	r_t* (tetrachoric r)	Two dichotomous variables in which underlying continuity can be assumed.
Ordinal	r_s (Spearman r)	Ranked data. If one variable is inherently ordinal and the second is interval/ratio, both must be expressed as ranks prior to calculating Spearman r.
	τ† (Kendall's tau, or rank correlation coefficient)	Ranked data.
Interval/Ratio	Pearson r	Both scales interval and/or ratio.
	Multiple R‡	Three or more interval- and/or ratio-level variables.

* See A. L. Edwards, *Statistical Methods*, 3d ed. New York: Holt, Rinehart and Winston, 1973.
† See S. Siegel, *Nonparametric Statistics*. New York: McGraw-Hill, 1956.
‡ See A. Haber and R. P. Runyon, *Business Statistics*. Homewood, Ill.: Irwin, 1982.

Correlation Coefficient: A measure that expresses the extent to which two variables are related.

need to calculate a **correlation coefficient.** There are many types of correlation coefficients. The decision to employ one of them with a specific set of data depends on factors such as (1) the type of scale of measurement in which each variable is expressed, (2) the nature of the underlying distribution (continuous or discrete), and (3) the characteristics of the distribution of the scores (linear or nonlinear). Table 8.1 shows some of the correlation coefficients that are available for use with various types of scales. We present two correlation coefficients in this text: the *Pearson r*, or the *Pearson product-moment correlation coefficient*, employed with interval- or ratio-scaled variables, and r_s or the *Spearman rank-order correlation coefficient*, employed with ordered or ranked data.

No matter which correlational technique we use, all have certain characteristics in common.

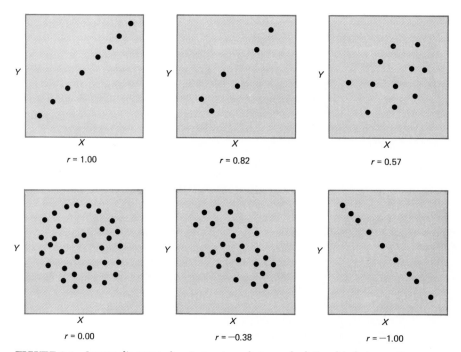

FIGURE 8.1   Scatter diagrams showing various degrees of relationship between two variables.

1. Two sets of measurements are obtained on the same individuals (or events), or on pairs of individuals who are matched on some basis.
2. The values of the correlation coefficients vary between −1.00 and +1.00. Both extremes represent perfect relationships between the variables, and 0.00 represents the *absence* of a relationship.
3. A **positive relationship** means that individuals obtaining high scores on one variable tend to obtain high scores on a second variable. The converse is also true; that is, individuals scoring low on one variable tend to score low on a second variable.*
4. A **negative relationship** means that individuals scoring low on one variable tend to score high on a second variable. Conversely, individuals scoring high on one variable tend to score low on a second variable.*
5. A high correlation between variables does not, as such, establish a causal link between variables. Rural dwellers will testify to the high degree of relationship between the rooster's crow and the rising of the sun. Few would argue that the rooster *causes* the sun to rise.

Positive Relationship: Variables are said to be positively related when a high score on one is accompanied by a high score on the other. Conversely, low scores on one variable are associated with low scores on the other.

Negative Relationship: Variables are said to be negatively related when a high score on one is accompanied by a low score on the other. Conversely, low scores on one variable are associated with high scores on the other.

---

* These characteristics are true for correlation coefficients that measure linear relationship, but not for all correlation coefficients.

BOX 8.1

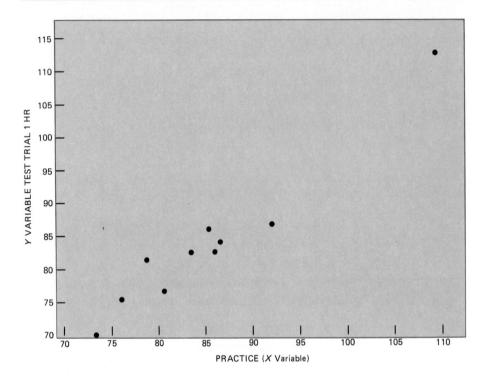

PRACTICE (*X* Variable)

THE CONSISTENCY (RELIABILITY) OF HEART-RATE MEASURES

In Chapter 6, we examined the heart-rate measures of ten Type A and ten Type B subjects, obtained over one practice and four test trials (Perkins, 1984). We noted that the measures of variability based on individual subjects (within-subject variability) were generally much lower than the measures of variability based on between-subject measures. We interpreted these results to mean that there appears to be considerable consistency among the HRs of individual subjects. Stated another way, there appears to be a high relationship between HR measures of a given subject taken at one time and that same subject's HR measures taken at another time.

The following table shows the HR measures of ten Type A subjects on one practice trial and the first test trial. We have called these variables *X* and

Y, where *X* is the HR observed on the practice trial and *Y* is the HR observed on the first test trial. Note that each subject has two HR measures—one for the *X* and the other for the *Y* variable.

Subject	Practice	Trial No. 1
1	86.0	82.6
2	109.3	112.6
3	73.3	70.0
4	80.6	76.6
5	86.6	84.0
6	85.3	86.0
7	83.3	82.6
8	78.6	81.3
9	92.0	86.6
10	76.0	75.3

Visualize these results in the scatter diagram. It is traditional to represent the values of the *X*-variable along the horizontal axis (also called the X-axis) and the Y-variable along the vertical axis (also called the Y-axis). The points shown on the scatter diagram represent the paired X and Y heart rates for each subject. Here is the procedure for constructing such a scatter diagram.

Note that the X-value of the first subject is 86.0 and the corresponding Y-value is 82.6. Follow the X-axis until a value of 86 is located. Draw a line at a right angle to the X-axis at this point. Now locate a value of 82.6 on the Y-axis. The point where the two variables meet represents the values of each variable, X and Y, for the first subject.

Scatter diagrams are useful for depicting the relationship between two variables. The preceding diagram shows a positive relationship between X and Y (i.e., low scores on X are generally associated with low scores on Y; high scores on X are associated with high scores on Y). Stated another way, a person with a low HR on the practice trial had a low HR on the first test trial. Conversely, a subject with a high HR on the practice trial also had a high HR on the first test trial. It also appears that the relationship is linear (straight-line) rather than curvilinear.

There is another point on which we shall elaborate further. Often we are tempted to interpret a correlation between two variables as causation. The fact that the values of two variables go together is *not* sufficient to justify the conclusion that one causes another. Without further evidence of a noncorrelational nature, we could not conclude that a high heart rate on the practice trial causes a high rate on the first test trial.

Source: From Perkins, 1984.

Figure 8.1 shows a series of **scatter diagrams** illustrating various degrees of relationships between two variables, X and Y. In interpreting the figures, we must remember that every dot represents two values: an individual's score on the X-variable and the same person's score on the Y-variable. As indicated earlier (Section 3.4), the X-variable is represented along the X-axis and the Y-variable along the Y-axis.

Scatter Diagram: Graphic device employed to represent the variation in two variables.

8.2 PEARSON *r*- AND *z*-SCORES

A high positive Pearson *r* indicates that each individual obtains approximately the same *z*-score on both variables. In a *perfect* positive correlation ($r = 1.00$), each individual obtains *exactly* the same *z*-score on both variables.

With a high negative *r*, each individual obtains approximately the same *z*-score on both variables, but opposite in sign.

Remembering that the *z*-score represents a measure of relative position on a given variable (i.e., a high positive *z* represents a high score relative to the remainder of the distribution, and a high negative *z* represents a low score relative to the remainder of the distribution), we may now generalize the meaning of the Pearson *r*.

Pearson *r* represents the extent to which the same individuals or events occupy the same relative position on two variables.

TABLE 8.2   Raw Scores and Corresponding z-Scores Made by Seven Subjects on Two Variables (Hypothetical Data)

Subject	X	$X - \bar{X}$	$(X - \bar{X})^2$	z_x	Y	$Y - \bar{Y}$	$(Y - \bar{Y})^2$	z_y	$z_x z_y$
A	1	−6	36	−1.5	4	−9	81	−1.5	2.25
B	3	−4	16	−1.0	7	−6	36	−1.0	1.00
C	5	−2	4	−0.5	10	−3	9	−0.5	0.25
D	7	0	0	0	13	0	0	0	0
E	9	2	4	0.5	16	3	9	0.5	0.25
F	11	4	16	1.0	19	6	36	1.0	1.00
G	13	6	36	1.5	22	9	81	1.5	2.25

$$\Sigma X = 49 \qquad SS_x = 112 \qquad \Sigma Y = 91 \qquad SS_y = 252 \qquad \Sigma z_x z_y = 7.00$$
$$\bar{X} = 7.00 \qquad s_x = \sqrt{\frac{112}{7}} = 4.00 \qquad \bar{Y} = 13.00 \qquad s_y = \sqrt{\frac{252}{7}} = 6.00$$

In order to explore the fundamental characteristics of the Pearson r, let us examine a simplified example of a perfect positive correlation. In Table 8.2, we find the paired scores of seven individuals on the two variables, X and Y.

Note that the scale values of X and Y do not need to be the same for the calculation of a Pearson r. In the example, we see that X ranges from 1 through 13, whereas Y ranges from 4 through 22. This independence of r from specific scale values permits us to investigate the relationships among an unlimited variety of variables. We can even correlate the length of the big toe with the IQ if we feel so inclined!

Note also, as we have already pointed out, that the z-scores of each subject on each variable are identical in the event of a perfect positive correlation. Had we reversed the order of either variable, that is, paired 1 with 22, paired 3 with 19, and so on, the z-scores would still be identical, but would be opposite in sign. In this latter case, our correlation would be a maximum *negative* ($r = -1.00$).

If we multiply our paired z-scores and then sum the results, we obtain maximum values only when our correlation is 1.00. Indeed, as the correlation approaches zero, the sum of the products of the paired z-scores also approaches zero. Note that when the correlation is perfect, the sum of the products of the paired z-scores is equal to N, where N equals the number of pairs or the number of measurements of either the X- or the Y-variable. These facts lead to one of the many different but algebraically equivalent formulas for r:

$$r = \frac{\Sigma(z_x z_y)}{N} \tag{8.1}$$

In Section 7.2, we pointed out that $\Sigma z^2 = N$. You will note that when the correlation is perfect, each z-score on the X-variable is identical to its corresponding z-score on the Y-variable. Thus, $\Sigma z_x z_y = \Sigma z_x^2 = \Sigma z_y^2$ when $r = 1.00$. In other words, in a perfect correlation, $\Sigma z_x z_y = N$. The Pearson r then becomes N/N or 1.00.

Try taking the data in Table 8.2, rearranging them in a number of different ways, and calculating r, employing the Formula (8.1). You will arrive at a far more thorough understanding of r by working the problems than by reading the text (not that we are discouraging the latter).

It so happens that the formula is unwieldy in practice, since it requires the calculation of separate z's for each score of each individual. Imagine the Herculean task of calculating r when N exceeds 50 cases, as it often does in behavioral research!

For this reason, a number of different computational formulas are employed. In this text, we shall illustrate the use of two: (1) the mean deviation formula and (2) the raw score formula.

8.3 CALCULATION OF PEARSON r

Mean Deviation Method

The mean deviation method for calculating a **Pearson r,** like the preceding z-score formula, is not often employed by behavioral scientists because it involves more time and effort than other computational techniques. It is presented here primarily because it sheds further light on the characteristics of the Pearson r. However, with small N's, it is as convenient a computational formula as any, unless an automatic calculator is available. The computational formula for the Pearson r, employing the mean deviation method, is

Pearson r (Product-Moment Correlation Coefficient): Correlation coefficient employed with interval- or ratio-scaled variables.

$$r = \frac{\Sigma(X - \bar{X})(Y - \bar{Y})}{\sqrt{SS_x \cdot SS_y}} \qquad (8.2)$$

TABLE 8.3   Computational Procedures for Pearson r Employing Mean Deviation Method (Hypothetical Data)

Subject	X	$(X - \bar{X})$	$(X - \bar{X})^2$	Y	$(Y - \bar{Y})$	$(Y - \bar{Y})^2$	$(X - \bar{X})(Y - \bar{Y})$
A	1	-6	36	7	-6	36	36
B	3	-4	16	4	-9	81	36
C	5	-2	4	13	0	0	0
D	7	0	0	16	3	9	0
E	9	2	4	10	-3	9	-6
F	11	4	16	22	9	81	36
G	13	6	36	19	6	36	36

$$SS_x = 112 \qquad SS_y = 252 \qquad \Sigma(X - \bar{X})(Y - \bar{Y}) = 138$$

$$r = \frac{\Sigma(X - \bar{X})(Y - \bar{Y})}{\sqrt{SS_x \cdot SS_y}} = \frac{138}{\sqrt{(112)(252)}} = \frac{138}{168.00} = 0.82$$

Let us illustrate the mean deviation method, employing the figures in Table 8.2 but arranging them in a different sequence (Table 8.3).

The computational procedures, employing the mean deviation method, should be perfectly familiar to you. You have already encountered the SS_x and the SS_y when you studied the standard deviation. In fact, in calculating r, only one step has been added, namely, the one to obtain the sum of the cross products $\Sigma(X - \overline{X})(Y - \overline{Y})$. This is obtained easily enough by multiplying the deviation of each individual's score from the mean of the X-variable by its corresponding deviation on the Y-variable and then summing all of the cross products. Incidentally, you should notice the similarity of $\Sigma(X - \overline{X})(Y - \overline{Y})$ to $\Sigma(z_x z_y)$, which is discussed in Section 8.2. Everything that has been said with respect to the relationship between the variations in $\Sigma(z_x z_y)$ and r holds also for $\Sigma(X - \overline{X})(Y - \overline{Y})$ and r. Notice that if maximum deviations in X had lined up with maximum deviations in Y and so on down through the array, $\Sigma(X - \overline{X})(Y - \overline{Y})$ would have been equal to 168.00, which is the same as the value of the denominator, and would have produced a correlation of 1.00.

Raw Score Method

We have already seen that the raw score formula for calculating the sum of squares is

$$SS_x = \sum X^2 - \frac{(\sum X)^2}{N}$$

and

$$SS_y = \sum Y^2 - \frac{(\sum Y)^2}{N}$$

By analogy,* the raw score formula for the sum of the cross products is

$$\sum (X - \overline{X})(Y - \overline{Y}) = \sum XY - \frac{(\sum X)(\sum Y)}{N} \qquad (8.3)$$

---

* See Section 6.5 on variance and standard deviation for the proof of $SS = \sum X^2 - (\sum X)^2/N$. By analogy,

$$\Sigma(X - \overline{X})(Y - \overline{Y}) = \Sigma XY - \Sigma X\overline{Y} - \Sigma Y\overline{X} + \Sigma \overline{X}\overline{Y}$$

Since

$$\Sigma X = N\overline{X} \qquad \Sigma Y = N\overline{Y}$$

and

$$\Sigma \overline{X}\overline{Y} = N\overline{X}\overline{Y} \qquad \text{(Generalization 1, Chapter 2)}$$

it follows that

$$\Sigma(X - \overline{X})(Y - \overline{Y}) = \Sigma XY - N\overline{X}\overline{Y} - N\overline{Y}\overline{X} + N\overline{X}\overline{Y}$$
$$= \Sigma XY - NXY$$
$$= \Sigma XY - N\left(\frac{\Sigma X}{N}\right)\left(\frac{\Sigma Y}{N}\right)$$
$$= \Sigma XY - \frac{(\Sigma X)(\Sigma Y)}{N}$$

In calculating the Pearson r by the raw score method, you have the option of calculating all the preceding quantities separately and substituting them into Formula (8.2), or defining r in terms of raw scores as in Formula (8.4) as follows:

$$r = \frac{\sum XY - (\sum X)(\sum Y)/N}{\sqrt{[\sum X^2 - (\sum X)^2/N][\sum Y^2 - (\sum Y)^2/N]}} \qquad (8.4)$$

A useful alternative formula for calculating the Pearson r when the means and standard deviations have already been calculated for other purposes is

$$r = \frac{\sum XY/N - \overline{X}\,\overline{Y}}{s_x s_y} \qquad (8.5)$$

The procedures for calculating r by the raw score method are summarized in Table 8.4. Here we find exactly the same coefficient as we did before. As with the mean deviation method, all the procedures, except those of obtaining the cross products, are familiar to you from the earlier use of the raw score formula to obtain the standard deviation. The quantity $\sum XY$ is obtained very simply by multiplying each X-value by its corresponding Y and then summing these products.

8.4 A WORD OF CAUTION

When low correlations are found, we are strongly tempted to conclude that there is little or no relationship between the two variables under study. However, it must be remembered that the Pearson r reflects only the *linear* relationship between two variables. The failure to find evidence of a relationship may be due to one of two possibilities: (1) the variables are in fact unrelated or (2) the variables are related in a *nonlinear* fashion. In the latter instance, the Pearson r would not be an appropriate measure of the degree of relationship between the variables. To illustrate, if we were plotting the relationship between age and strength of grip, we might obtain a picture somewhat like that in Figure 8.2.

It is usually possible to determine whether there is a substantial departure from linearity by examining the scatter diagram. If the distribution of points in the scatter diagram is elliptical, without the decided bending of the ellipse that occurs in Figure 8.2, it may safely be assumed that the relationship is linear. Any small departures from linearity will not greatly influence the size of the correlation coefficient.

On the other hand, where there is marked curvilinearity, as in Figure 8.2, the Pearson r could be misleading. The overall linear relationship might be extremely low (if not 0.00) because the positive and negative components of each side of the curve would be antagonistic, and would tend to cancel each other out. A curvilinear coefficient of correlation would better reflect the relationship of the two variables under investigation. Although it is

TABLE 8.4 Computational Procedures for Pearson r Employing Raw Score Method (Hypothetical Data)

Subject	X	X^2	Y	Y^2	XY
A	1	1	7	49	7
B	3	9	4	16	12
C	5	25	13	169	65
D	7	49	16	256	112
E	9	81	10	100	90
F	11	121	22	484	242
G	13	169	19	361	247
	$\Sigma X = 49$	$\Sigma X^2 = 455$	$\Sigma Y = 91$	$\Sigma Y^2 = 1435$	$\Sigma XY = 775$

1. Using Formula (8.2),

$$r = \frac{\Sigma(X - \bar{X})(Y - \bar{Y})}{\sqrt{SS_x \cdot SS_y}}$$

$$\Sigma(X - \bar{X})(Y - \bar{Y}) = \Sigma XY - \frac{(\Sigma X)(\Sigma Y)}{N}$$

$$= 775 - 637$$

$$= 138$$

$$SS_x = \Sigma X^2 - \frac{(\Sigma X)^2}{N}$$

$$= 455 - \frac{(49)^2}{7}$$

$$= 112$$

$$SS_y = \Sigma Y^2 - \frac{(\Sigma Y)^2}{N}$$

$$= 1435 - \frac{(91)^2}{7}$$

$$= 252$$

$$r = \frac{\Sigma(X - \bar{X})(Y - \bar{Y})}{\sqrt{SS_x \cdot SS_y}}$$

$$= \frac{138}{\sqrt{112 \cdot 252}} = \frac{138}{168}$$

$$= 0.82$$

2. Or, using Formula (8.4),

$$r = \frac{\Sigma XY - (\Sigma X)(\Sigma Y)/N}{\sqrt{[\Sigma X^2 - (\Sigma X)^2/N][\Sigma Y^2 - (\Sigma Y)^2/N]}}$$

$$= \frac{775 - (49)(91)/7}{\sqrt{(455 - (49)^2/7)(1435 - (91)^2/7)}}$$

$$= \frac{775 - 637}{\sqrt{(112)(252)}}$$

$$= \frac{138}{168}$$

$$= 0.82$$

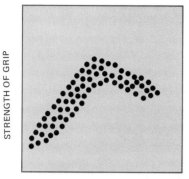

FIGURE 8.2   Scatter diagram of two variables that are related in a nonlinear fashion (hypothetical data). Note that there appear to be two components in the scatter diagram: a positive component from birth to the middle years and a negative component thereafter.

CASE EXAMPLE 8.1

Craning and Gawking at Nothing

Bibb Latané proposed a theory of social impact that specifies the effect of other persons on an individual. Basing these conclusions on many different avenues of social research, the author states ". . . when other people are the source of impact and the individual is the target, impact should be a multiplicative function of the strength, immediacy, and number of other people." He presents considerable evidence that the relationship between impact and the number of people is not linear. In fact, the impact of each additional person added to the group is less than the impact of the preceding individual. This produces a curvilinear relationship between the number of people and social impact.

Have you ever been on a crowded city street and seen people craning and gawking at some nonexistent event? Figure 8.3 (a) shows that as the size of the crowd increases, the percent of passersby who imitate craning and gawking behavior increases. Figure 8.3 (b) shows that, similarly, in an Asch type of study in which confederates gave incorrect answers to a length-of-line judging task, conformity increased with the size of the incorrect majority. Finally, in Figure 8.3 (c) the size of the tip, in percent of total, decreases with the number of people seated at the table. Note that all describe curvilinear relationships between the independent variable (the number of people involved) and the dependent measure.

Source: Based on Bibb Latané (1981), "The Psychology of Social Impact," *American Psychologist,* **36**(4), 342–356.

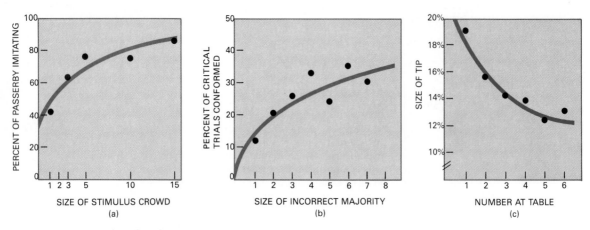

FIGURE 8.3   Several studies showing curvilinear relationships among variables, (a) Data from S. Milgram, L. Bickman, and L. Berkowitz (1969), "Note on the Drawing Power of Crowds," *Journal of Personality and Social Psychology*, **13,** 79–82; (b) data from H. B. Gerard, R. A. Wilhelmy, and E. S Conolley (1968), "Conformity and Group Size," *Journal of Personality and Social Psychology*, **8,** 79–82; (c) data from S. Freeman, M. R. Walker, R. Borden, and B. Latané (1975), "Diffusion of Responsibility and Restaurant Tipping. Cheaper by the Bunch," *Personality and Social Psychology Bulletin*, **1**, 584–587.

beyond the scope of this text to investigate nonlinear coefficients of correlation, you should be aware of this possibility and, as a matter of course, construct a scatter diagram prior to calculating the Pearson r.

The assumption of linearity is the most important requirement to justify the use of the Pearson r as a measure of relationship between two interval- or ratio-scaled variables. It is not necessary that r be calculated only with normally distributed variables. So long as the distributions are unimodal and relatively symmetrical, a Pearson r may legitimately be computed.

Another situation giving rise to spuriously low correlation coefficients results from restricting the range of values of one of the variables. For example, if we were interested in the relationship between age and height for children from 3 to 16 years of age, we would undoubtedly obtain a rather high coefficient of correlation between these two variables. However, suppose that we were to restrict the range of one of our variables. What effect would this have on the size of the coefficient? That is, let us look at the same relationship between age and height but only for those children between the ages of 9 and 10. We would probably end up with a rather low coefficient. Let us look at this graphically.

You will note that the overall relationship illustrated in Figure 8.4 is rather high. The inset illustrates what happens when we restrict our range. Note that the scatter diagram contained in the inset represents a very low correlation. This restriction of the range is frequently referred to as the **truncated range.** The problem of truncated range is not uncommon in behavioral research, since much of this research is conducted in the colleges and universities, where subjects have been preselected for intelligence and related variables. Thus, they represent a fairly homogeneous group with

Truncated Range:
Restriction of the range of one or both variables, resulting in a deceptively low correlation between these variables.

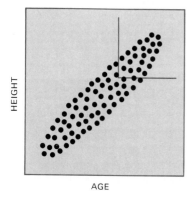

FIGURE 8.4 Scatter diagram illustrating high correlation over entire range of *X*- and *Y*-values, but low correlation when the range is truncated (hypothetical data).

respect to these variables. Consequently, when an attempt is made to demonstrate the relationship between variables like SAT scores and college grades, the resulting coefficient may be lowered because of the truncated range. Furthermore, the correlations would be expected to be lower for colleges that select their students from within a narrow range of SAT scores.

8.5 ORDINALLY SCALED VARIABLES AND r_s

Imagine that you are a grade school teacher. After long years of observation in the classroom, you have developed a strong suspicion that intelligence and leadership are related variables. In an effort to test this hypothesis, you obtain IQ estimates on all the children in your class. However, you discover that no scales are available to measure classroom leadership and you can think of no satisfactory way to quantify this variable. Nevertheless, from numerous observations of the children in different leadership situations, you feel confident that you are able to *rank* the children from those who are the highest in leadership to those who are the lowest in this quality. The resulting measurements constitute, of course, an ordinal scale. Although we could obtain a Pearson *r* with ranked data, a variant of the product-moment correlation coefficient, which is referred to as the **Spearman** *r*, *r_s*, or the **rank correlation coefficient,** gives precisely the same answer but reduces the computational task involved in obtaining the correlation. The Spearman *r* is appropriate when one scale constitutes ordinal measurement and the remaining scale is either ordinal or interval/ratio. However, prior to applying the r_s formula, *both* scales must be expressed as ranks.

Realizing that your knowledge of the children's IQ scores might "contaminate" your estimates of their leadership qualities, you ask a fellow teacher to provide ranks for his or her children based on leadership

Spearman *r* (*r_s* or Rank Correlation Coefficient): Correlation coefficient employed with ordered or ranked data.

Correlations among HR measures:
Preparing a correlational matrix

Recall that in the Perkins study of Type A and Type B behaviors, five different HR measures were obtained on each individual—one practice and four test trials. In Box 8.1, we looked at the scatter diagram involving the practice trial and the first test trial for ten Type A subjects. But what about all the other intercorrelations that are possible with these data, that is, the practice trial versus test trials 2, 3, and 4 or test trial 1 versus test trials 2, 3, and 4, and so on? The total number of intercorrelations between and among these five variables equals the number of variables ($\#v$) times the number of variables minus 1 ($\#v - 1$) divided by 2. In other words, the number of possible intercorrelations equals $\#v \cdot (\#v - 1)/2$. In the present example, this comes to $5 \cdot 4/2 = 10$.

When all the intercorrelations are calculated, it is helpful to display them in the form of a correlational matrix (which follows). Note that each variable is represented in both the columns and rows. The correlation between any two variables is shown at their intersection. Thus, to find the correlation between practice and trial 4, locate practice in the first row and read across to the last column (trial 4). Here we see that the correlation is 0.96. Note that the intercorrelations are all in the 0.90s, with the smallest being 0.960 between practice and trial 4. As we'll see, these are extremely high correlations that permit high levels of predictability from trial to trial.

Correlation Matrix

Variable No.

	Practice	Trial 1	Trial 2	Trial 3	Trial 4
Practice	(10)	0.970	0.963	0.979	0.960
Trial 1	(10)	(10)	0.977	0.985	0.971
Trial 2	(10)	(10)	(10)	0.986	0.985
Trial 3	(10)	(10)	(10)	(10)	0.991
Trial 4	(10)	(10)	(10)	(10)	(10)

Note: r's are in the upper triangle; N's are in parentheses.

The following table shows the heart-rate measures of ten Type B subjects on one practice trial and four test trials.

a. Prepare scatter diagrams showing: practice versus trial 2; trial 1 versus trial 3; and trial 2 versus trial 4.

Subject	Practice	1	2	3	4
1	103.3	85.3	82.0	80.0	78.6
2	98.6	94.0	93.3	92.6	92.6
3	88.6	93.1	88.0	88.0	86.0
4	85.3	89.3	84.6	81.3	77.3
5	90.6	85.3	76.6	78.0	76.0
6	98.6	98.0	94.0	94.6	94.0
7	120.6	118.6	114.6	112.0	120.6
8	62.6	63.3	58.6	56.0	54.6
9	109.3	106.6	97.3	93.3	88.0
10	106.6	98.6	99.3	96.0	98.0

b. Find the intercorrelations between and among all five trials and prepare a correlation matrix showing these intercorrelations.

ANSWERS
a.

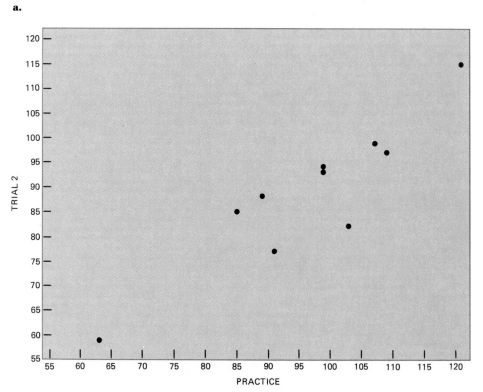

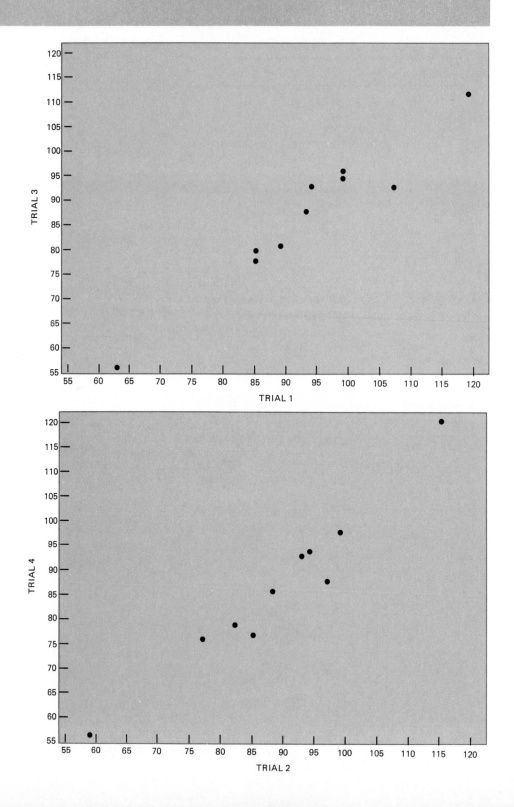

b. CORRELATION MATRIX

Var No.	1	2	3	4	5
1	(10)	0.912	0.914	0.907	0.886
2	(10)	(10)	0.979	0.974	0.941
3	(10)	(10)	(10)	0.992	0.975
4	(10)	(10)	(10)	(10)	0.983
5	(10)	(10)	(10)	(10)	(10)

Note: *r*'s are in the upper triangle; *N*'s are in parentheses.

Source: Based on Perkins, 1984.

qualities. You then obtain, independent of ranks, an estimate of their IQ's. Following this, you rank the IQ's from the highest to lowest.

The rank correlation coefficient requires that you obtain the differences in the ranks, square and sum the squared differences, and substitute the resulting values into the formula

$$r_s = 1 - \frac{6\Sigma D^2}{N(N^2 - 1)} \tag{8.6}$$

in which D = rank X − rank Y.

Table 8.5 on page 206 shows the hypothetical data and the procedures involved in calculating r_s.

As a matter of course, ΣD should be obtained even though it is not used in any of the calculations. It constitutes a useful check on the accuracy of your calculations up to this point, since ΣD must equal zero. If you obtain any value other than zero, you should recheck your original ranks and the subsequent subtractions.

Tied Ranks

Occasionally, when it is necessary to convert scores to ranks, you will find two or more tied scores.* In this event, assign the mean of the tied ranks to each of the tied scores. The next score in the array receives the rank normally assigned to it. Thus, the ranks of the scores 128, 122, 115, 115, 115, 107, 103 would be 1, 2, 4, 4, 4, 6, 7, and the ranks of the scores 128, 122, 115, 115, 107, 103 would be 1, 2, 3.5, 3.5, 5, 6.

---

* When there are numerous tied ranks on either or both the *X*- and *Y*-variables, the Spearman formula tends to yield a spuriously high coefficient of correlation. When there are many ties, it is preferable to apply the Pearson *r* formula to the *ranked data*.

TABLE 8.5 Computational Procedures for Calculating r_s from Ranked Variables (Hypothetical Data)

IQ Rank	Leadership Rank	D	D²	
1	4	−3	9	$r_s = 1 - \dfrac{6\sum D^2}{N(N^2 - 1)}$
2	2	0	0	
3	9	−6	36	
4	1	3	9	$= 1 - \dfrac{6 \cdot 204}{15(224)}$
5	7	−2	4	
6	10	−4	16	
7	8	−1	1	$= 1 - \dfrac{1224}{3360}$
8	13	−5	25	
9	5	4	16	$= 1 - 0.36$
10	3	7	49	
11	11	0	0	$= 0.64$
12	6	6	36	
13	12	1	1	
14	15	−1	1	
15	14	1	1	

$$\Sigma D = 0 \qquad \Sigma D^2 = 204$$

If you use a statistical calculator or a computer to obtain correlations and there is no program for r_s, you may use the Pearson r to obtain the rank correlation. However, you enter the ranks rather than the values of the variable. If there are no ties, the Pearson formula will yield the same correlations as the Spearman formula. If there are many ties, the Pearson formula will be more accurate.

CASE EXAMPLE 8.2

Help Is Where You Find It!

We previously examined some of the data in Cowen's report when we discussed ordinal scales of measurement (Case Example 2.1). Table 8.6 presents the rankings of four different occupational groups in terms of how frequently they use various help-giving strategies when engaged with clients. We want to learn the extent to which they agree or disagree in their use of the 11 different strategies.

TABLE 8.6 Ordinal Position of Response Strategies of Four Different Occupations when Clients Seek Advice and Counsel. A Rank of 1 Corresponds to the Most Frequently Used Strategy and 11 to the Least Frequently Used Strategy

Strategy	Hairdressers	Bartenders	Lawyers	Supervisors
Offer support and sympathy	1	3	1	1.5
Try to be lighthearted	2	2	8	8
Just listen	3	1	5	1.5
Present alternatives	4	4	4	4
Tell person to count blessings	5	10	7	9
Share personal experiences	6	5	6	5
Try not to get involved	7	6	9.5	10
Give advice	8	7	3	7
Ask questions	9	9	2	3
Try to get person to talk to someone else	10	11	9.5	6
Try to change topic	11	8	11	11

We must now find all possible intercorrelations among the four occupational groups. All told, six different correlations must be calculated: hairdressers versus bartenders, lawyers, and supervisors (three comparisons), bartenders versus lawyers and supervisors (two comparisons), and lawyers versus supervisors (1 comparison). We'll show the calculation of r_s only for hairdressers versus bartenders (Table 8.7) and shall summarize all their intercorrelations in Table 8.8.

TABLE 8.7 Ordinal Position of Response Strategies of Two Different Occupations when Clients Seek Advice and Counsel. A Rank of 1 Corresponds to the Most Frequently Used Strategy and 11 to the Least Frequently Used Strategy

Strategy	Hairdressers	Bartenders	Difference	Difference Squared
Offer support and sympathy	1	3	-2	4
Try to be lighthearted	2	2	0	0
Just listen	3	1	2	4
Present alternatives	4	4	0	0
Tell person to count blessings	5	10	-5	25
Share personal experiences	6	5	1	1
Try not to get involved	7	6	1	1
Give advice	8	7	1	1
Ask questions	9	9	0	0
Try to get person to talk to someone else	10	11	-1	1
Try to change topic	11	8	3	9

$$\Sigma D^2 = 46$$

TABLE 8.8 **Intercorrelations among Four Occupational Groups on Strategies for Help-Giving to Clients**

	Hairdressers	Bartenders	Lawyers	Supervisors
Hairdressers	—	0.79	0.43	0.46
Bartenders	—	—	0.30	0.43
Lawyers	—	—	—	0.78
Supervisors	—	—	—	—

The Spearman rank correlation for these data is

$$r_s = 1 - \frac{6(46)}{1320}$$
$$= 0.79$$

Table 8.8 shows the intercorrelations among all four occupational groups in terms of their help-giving strategies displayed in a correlation matrix.

Examination of Table 8.8 reveals that hairdressers and bartenders intercorrelate more than either does with lawyers and supervisors. The r_s of 0.79 is the highest of the 6 intercorrelations. Moreover, lawyers and supervisors intercorrelated more with each other than they do with hairdressers and bartenders.

Source: Based on Emory L. Cowen (1982), "Help Is Where You Find It," *American Psychologist,* **37**(4), 385–395.

8.6 PUTTING IT ALL TOGETHER

As we approach the twenty-first century, concerns about global warfare have receded into the background as we begin to ponder the quality of the habitat we are bequeathing to future generations. We are witnessing the beginning of what could become a pervasive deterioration of our environment—the destruction of the Amazon and other rain forests that renew our oxygen supplies; the release of industrial byproducts that endanger health into the air, ground, and water supplies; and the emission of enormous quantities of carbon dioxide into the air by the burning of fossil fuels, which could usher in global warming (the greenhouse effect), to name a few.

In the industrial nations, the automobile is like a triple-threat halfback—it emits carbon dioxide, it contains many potentially harmful byproducts of combustion, and it burns enormous quantities of petroleum products, which are themselves coming into short supply. For this reason, Congress and numerous state legislatures have enacted laws that establish standards

TABLE 8.9   Car Length, City mpg, and Highway mpg among Twenty-One 1988 Automobiles with Automatic Transmission

Car Model	Length	City mpg	Highway mpg
Acura Legend	189	15	33
Audi 500S	193	14	28
BMW 3251	177	16	31
Buick Regal	192	16	37
Buick Skyhawk	180	19	38
Cadillac Cimarron	178	15	28
Chevrolet Cavalier	172	19	38
Chevrolet Corsica	183	17	36
Dodge Lancer	180	16	31
Ford Taurus	188	14	33
Honda Accord	180	19	40
Lincoln Mark VII	203	12	35
Mercedes-Benz 300E	187	16	28
Nissan Maxima	182	15	32
Nissan Stanza	178	16	34
Oldsmobile Delta 88	197	13	33
Pontiac Bonneville	199	13	33
Saab 900	182	13	32
Sterling 825	189	15	30
Toyota Cressida	188	15	29
Volkswagon Quantum	180	14	26

for fuel consumption and auto emissions. In many cases, these laws have forced automobile manufacturers to go to smaller cars, on the grounds that they require less fuel and, therefore, can meet the standards more readily. But how valid is the claim that small cars use less fuel? Table 8.9 identifies twenty-one 1988 model cars and provides information on three variables: their length (size), their miles per gallon (mpg) in city driving, and their mpg on highways.

Figure 8.5 shows the scatter diagram of two variables, length and mpg in city driving. By inspection, there is an ellipse that leans from the lower left-hand corner to the upper right-hand corner. It is clear, then, that there is a negative relationship between length of automobile and city mpg. In other words, shorter cars get better mileage and longer cars obtain poorer mileage. But how large is the correlation between these two variables? The steps in obtaining the correlation are shown below.

Step 1. Square each value of X and place the result in the column labeled X^2 (See Table 8.4).

Step 2. Sum the values in X^2 to obtain $\Sigma X^2 = 724{,}449$.

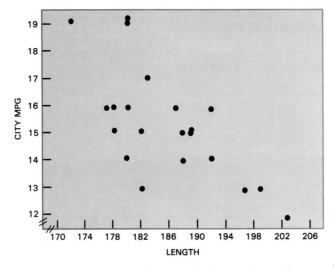

FIGURE 8.5 Scatter diagram of length of car and city miles per gallon among twenty-one 1988 model cars with automatic transmission.

Step 3. Square each value of Y and place the result in the column labeled Y^2.

Step 4. Sum the values in Y^2 to obtain $\Sigma Y^2 = 5016$.

Step 5. Multiply each value of X by its corresponding value of Y to obtain $\Sigma XY = 59{,}537$.

Step 6. Find $\Sigma XY - (\Sigma X)(\Sigma Y)/N = 59{,}537 - (3897)(322)/21 = -217$.

Step 7. Find $SS_X = 724{,}449 - (3897^2/21) = 1277.14$.

Step 8. Find $SS_Y = 5017 - (322^2/21) = 78.67$.

Step 9. Find r by substituting the values found in steps 6, 7, and 8 in Formula (8.2). Thus, $r = -217/\sqrt{1277.14 \cdot 78.67} = -0.68$.

As we can see, there is a negative relationship between length of car and city mpg ($r = -0.68$). How large a correlation is this? In Chapters 9 and 12, we'll examine ways to evaluate the magnitude of the correlation coefficient.

If we obtain all three possible correlations between the three variables, we have the correlational matrix found in Table 8.10.

In contrast to the length of car and city mpg correlation, note that the negative correlation between length of car and highway mpg is quite close to zero ($r = -0.07$). These findings are at the descriptive level and do not permit us to draw definitive conclusions at this time. Nevertheless, they should provoke a number of questions that might well be addressed by inferential statistics. Here are a few: Are the correlation coefficients reliable, that is, likely to hold up with different samples and different sample sizes? Since the data suggest that the size of the car (length) may have a more adverse affect on mpg obtained in city driving, should people who do most

TABLE 8.10   Correlation Matrix Involving Three Variables: Length of Automobile, City mpg, and Highway mpg

Variable	Length	City mpg	Highway mpg
Length	(21)	−0.68	−0.07
City mpg	(21)	(21)	0.54
Highway mpg	(21)	(21)	(21)

of their driving in cities pay particular attention to the size of the cars they drive? Questions such as these may legitimately be raised, and research may advantageously be designed to obtain answers.

CHAPTER SUMMARY

In this chapter we discussed the concept of correlation and demonstrated the calculation of two correlation coefficients, i.e., the Pearson r employed with interval- or ratio-scaled data, and r_s used with ordinally scaled variables.

We saw that correlation is concerned with determining the extent to which two variables are related or tend to vary together. The quantitative expression of the extent of the relationship is given in terms of the magnitude of the correlation coefficient. Correlation coefficients vary between values of -1.00 and $+1.00$; both extremes represent perfect relationships. A coefficient of zero indicates the absence of a relationship between two variables.

We noted that the Pearson r is appropriate only for variables that are related in a linear fashion. With ranked data, the Spearman rank correlation coefficient is the exact counterpart of the Pearson r. The various computational formulas for the Pearson r may be employed in calculating r_s from ranked data. However, a computational formula for r_s was demonstrated that considerably simplifies the calculation of the rank correlation coefficient.

TERMS TO REMEMBER

correlation
correlation coefficient
negative relationship
Pearson r (product-moment correlation coefficient)

positive relationship
scatter diagram
Spearman r (r_s or rank correlation coefficient)
truncated range

EXERCISES

1. The following data show the scores obtained by a group of 20 students on a college entrance examination and a verbal comprehension test. Prepare a scatter diagram and calculate a Pearson r for these data.

Student	College Entrance Exam (X)	Verbal Comprehension Test (Y)	Student	College Entrance Exam (X)	Verbal Comprehension Test (Y)
A	52	49	K	64	53
B	49	49	L	28	17
C	26	17	M	49	40
D	28	34	N	43	41
E	63	52	O	30	15
F	44	41	P	65	50
G	70	45	Q	35	28
H	32	32	R	60	55
I	49	29	S	49	37
J	51	49	T	66	50

2. The data in the following table represent scores obtained by ten students on a statistics examination and their final grade-point averages. Prepare a scatter diagram and calculate a Pearson r for these data.

Student	Score on Statistics Exam, X	Grade-Point Average, Y	Student	Score on Statistics Exam, X	Grade-Point Average, Y
A	90	2.50	F	70	1.00
B	85	2.00	G	70	1.00
C	80	2.50	H	60	0.50
D	75	2.00	I	60	0.50
E	70	1.50	J	50	0.50

3. A psychological study involved the ranking of rats along a dominance-submissiveness continuum in which a low numeral rank means high in dominance. In order to determine the reliability of the rankings, we tabulated the ranks given by two different observers. Are the rankings reliable? Explain your answer.

Animal	Rank by Observer A	Rank by Observer B	Animal	Rank by Observer A	Rank by Observer B
A	12	15	I	6	5
B	2	1	J	9	9
C	3	7	K	7	6
D	1	4	L	10	12
E	4	2	M	15	13
F	5	3	N	8	8
G	14	11	O	13	14
H	11	10	P	16	16

4. Explain in *your own words* the meaning of correlation.

5. In each of the examples presented below, identify a possible source of contamination in the collection and/or interpretation of the results of a correlational analysis.

a. The relationship between age and reaction time for subjects from three months to 65 years of age.

b. The correlation between IQ and grades for honor students at a university.

c. The relationship between vocabulary and reading speed among children in an economically disadvantaged community.

6. For a group of 50 individuals, $\Sigma z_x z_y$ is 41.3. What is the correlation between the two variables?

7. The following scores were made by five students on two tests. Calculate the Pearson r (using $r = \Sigma z_x z_y / N$). Convert to ranks and calculate r_s.

Student	Test X	Test Y
A	5	1
B	5	3
C	5	5
D	5	7
E	5	9

Generalize: What is the effect of tied ranks on r_s?

8. Show algebraically that

$$\sum (X - \bar{X})(Y - \bar{Y}) = \sum XY - \frac{\Sigma X \Sigma Y}{N}$$

9. What effect does a departure from linearity have on the Pearson r?

10. How does the range of scores sampled affect the size of the correlation coefficient?

11. Following are data showing scores on college entrance examinations and college grade-point averages following the first semester. What is the relationship between these two variables?

Entrance Examinations	Grade-Point Averages	Entrance Examinations	Grade-Point Averages
440	1.57	528	2.08
448	1.83	550	2.15
455	2.05	582	3.44
460	1.14	569	3.05
473	2.73	585	3.19
485	1.65	593	3.42
489	2.02	620	3.87
500	2.98	650	3.00
512	1.79	690	3.12
518	2.63		

12. The data in the table on page 215 show the latitude of 35 cities in the northern hemisphere and the mean high and mean low annual temperatures.
   a. What is the correlation between the latitude and mean high temperature?
   b. What is the correlation between the latitude and mean low temperature?
   c. What is the correlation between the mean high and mean low temperatures?

13. In Exercise 17 and 18 of Chapter 5, we presented data on the systolic blood pressures of seven subjects during control and conditioning sessions.
   a. Find the Pearson r between these two measures.
   b. Transform both sets of scores to ranks and calculate r_s.

14. Throughout the blood pressure study, the patients remained on drugs to control hypertension. Shown below are the rank order of the amount of medication received by each subject (from the lowest to highest) and the difference score (conditioning minus control) for each subject.

Subject	1	2	3	4	5	6	7
Rank of amount of drug	7	2	6	1	5	3	4
Difference score	−3.5	−33.8	−29.2	−16.5	−16.1	0.9	−17.3

Rank-order the difference scores from the lowest (0.9) to the highest (−33.8) reduction in systolic blood pressure, and find r_s.

15. Explain the difference between $r = 0.76$ and $r = -0.76$.

16. Suppose you wanted to study the relation between the efficiency of labor-saving machinery a manufacturer possesses and the mean price of the leather belts he produces. Because it is difficult to order the quality of machinery on a ratio scale, you rank the machines on an ordinal scale, with a rank of 15 indicating the most advanced machinery. You find the relation of price and type of the machines to be as follows:

15	$3.50	10	$4.25	5	$4.95
14	$3.75	9	$4.50	4	$5.50
13	$3.50	8	$4.45	3	$5.75
12	$4.00	7	$4.75	2	$5.45
11	$3.95	6	$5.00	1	$6.00

Determine the r_s between the quality of machinery and the price.

City	Latitude to Nearest Degree	Mean High Temperature	Mean Low Temperature
Acapulco	17	88	73
Accra	6	86	74
Algiers	37	76	71
Amsterdam	52	54	46
Belgrade	45	62	45
Berlin	53	55	40
Bogota	5	66	50
Bombay	19	87	74
Bucharest	44	62	42
Calcutta	22	89	70
Casablanca	34	72	55
Copenhagen	56	52	41
Dakar	15	84	70
Dublin	53	56	42
Helsinki	60	46	35
Hong Kong	22	77	68
Istanbul	41	64	50
Jerusalem	32	74	54
Karachi	25	87	70
Leningrad	60	46	33
Lisbon	39	67	55
London	52	58	44
Madrid	40	66	47
Manila	15	89	73
Monrovia	6	84	73
Montreal	46	50	35
Oslo	60	50	36
Ottawa	45	51	32
Paris	49	59	43
Phnom Penh	12	89	74
Prague	50	54	42
Rangoon	17	89	73
Rome	42	71	51
Saigon	11	90	74
Shanghai	31	69	53

17. A store owner recorded the number of times consumers bought or asked for a given item. She called this amount the demand. Each month she had 15 of the items to sell. In addition, the owner recorded the price of the item each month.

    a. Determine the relation between the demand and price, using the Pearson r.

    b. Determine the relation between the demand and price, using r_s.

Month	Demand	Price	Month	Demand	Price
Jan.	25	$0.50	July	13	$0.80
Feb.	10	.90	Aug.	19	.70
Mar.	12	.80	Sept.	18	.72
April	18	.75	Oct.	16	.74
May	11	.85	Nov.	15	.75
June	20	.70	Dec.	15	.75

18. Referring to Exercise 12 (this chapter), determine the correlation between the latitude and mean high temperature for those areas with a latitude on or below 25 degrees. Compare this correlation with that obtained in Exercise 12(a). Why are the correlations different?

19. Again referring to Exercise 12, determine the correlation between the latitude and mean high temperature for those areas with a latitude on or above 45 degrees. Compare this correlation with those obtained in Exercises 12(a) and 18. Why are they different?

20. Demonstrate that $\Sigma D^2 = 0$ for the following paired ranks:

    1   1
    2   2
    3   3
    4   4
    5   5
    6   6
    7   7
    8   8

21. Calculate r_s for Exercise 20.

22. Construct a scatter diagram for each of the sets of data listed in the table at the top of page 217.

23. By inspecting the scatter diagrams for the data in Exercise 22, determine which one represents

    a. A curvilinear relation between X and Y

    b. A positive correlation between X and Y

    c. Little or no relation between X and Y

    d. A negative correlation between X and Y

24. In the study reported in Case Example 8.2, the investigator ascertained the frequency with which various feelings were experienced when people raised problems with them. The following are the rankings associated with 11 different feelings by members of the four occupations. Calculate the intercorrelations among all four occupational groups listed in the second table on page 207.

a. X	Y	b. X	Y	c. X	Y	d. X	Y
1.5	0.5	0.5	5.0	0.5	0.5	0.5	1.0
1.0	0.5	0.5	4.5	1.0	1.0	0.5	2.5
1.0	2.0	1.0	3.5	1.0	1.5	0.5	4.5
1.5	1.5	1.5	4.0	1.5	2.5	1.0	3.5
1.5	2.0	1.5	2.5	1.5	3.5	1.5	1.0
2.0	2.0	2.0	3.0	2.0	2.5	1.5	2.5
2.5	2.5	2.5	2.0	2.0	3.5	1.5	4.0
2.5	3.2	2.5	3.5	2.5	4.5	2.0	1.0
3.0	2.5	3.0	2.5	3.0	3.5	3.0	2.0
3.0	3.5	3.0	2.0	3.5	3.0	3.0	3.5
3.5	3.5	3.5	2.0	3.5	2.5	3.0	4.5
3.5	4.5	3.5	2.5	3.5	2.0	3.5	1.0
4.0	3.5	4.0	1.5	4.0	2.5	3.5	1.0
4.0	4.5	4.0	0.7	4.0	2.0	3.5	3.5
4.5	4.5	5.0	0.5	4.5	1.0	4.0	3.5
5.0	5.0			5.0	1.0	4.0	4.5
				5.0	0.5	4.5	2.5
						4.5	1.0

Feelings	Hairdressers	Lawyers	Supervisors	Bartenders
Gratified	1	4	4	4
Sympathetic	2	1	3	3
Encouraging	3	3	1	1
Supportive	4	2	2	2
Puzzled	5	7	5.5	7
Helpless	6	5	5.5	5.5
Uncomfortable	7	6	7	9
Bored	8	8	8	8
Trapped	9.5	11	9	5.5
Depressed	9.5	10	11	10
Angry	11	9	10	11

25. In the study reported in Case Example 8.2, the investigator ranked problems raised in order of their frequency of occurrence. The rankings are shown in the table at the top of page 218.

a. What is the correlation between the two occupational groups in terms of the problems raised?

b. How do you account for the low correlation when previous correlations have been so high?

Problem	Hairdressers	Bartenders	Difference	Difference Squared
Difficulties with children	1	7		
Physical health	2	6		
Marital problems	3	2		
Depression	4	5		
Anxiety, nervousness	5	8.5		
Jobs	6	1		
Financial	7	3		
Sex	8	4		
Drugs	9	10		
Alcohol	10	8.5		

26. How well do you remember the names of the seven dwarfs from Disney's animated classic *Snow White and the Seven Dwarfs?* The following table shows the order in which they were recalled, the percent of subjects recalling the names of each of them, and the percent who correctly identified them in a recognition task.

Dwarf	Order of Recall	Recalled %	Recognized %
Sleepy	1	86	91
Dopey	2	81	95
Grumpy	3	75	86
Sneezy	4	78	93
Doc	5	58	80
Happy	6	62	70
Bashful	7	38	84

Source: Based on Meyer and Hildebrand, 1984.

a. What is the measure of relationship appropriate for these data?

b. Prepare a correlation matrix showing the intercorrelation of these three variables.

27. Sleep studies continue to provide a wealth of surprising findings. For example, in one study (Sewich, 1984), the subjects were awakened from sleep (as defined by the electroencephalograph or EEG) by a ring of a telephone. The experimenter recorded the time required for the subject to make a verbal response. Each subject was asked if he or she was awake or asleep when the telephone rang. Surprisingly, a number of subjects reported having been awake when, according to the EEG record, they were asleep. The table below shows the mean reaction times over a number of trials for each of ten subjects when they perceived themselves as being awake or asleep. For purposes of this analysis, we'll treat each subject's mean as a score.

a. Calculate the mean and standard deviation for awake reports and for sleep reports.

b. What type of correlation is appropriate for these data?

c. Prepare a scatter diagram for these data.

d. Find the correlation between awake reports and asleep reports.

e. Note that the performance of subject 9 appears to be considerably different from that of the other subjects. Such observations are termed "outliers" and often initiate an inquiry into the reasons for the difference, for example, errors in collecting, coding, or data entry, or some specific characteristics of the subject. Recalculate the Pearson r, deleting the scores of subject 9.

	Mean Reaction Times (in Seconds)	
Subject No.	**Subject Reported Being Awake**	**Subject Reported Being Asleep**
1	5.7	6.2
2	8.6	4.3
3	1.9	2.2
4	3.7	5.2
5	2.2	4.7
6	7.8	12.9
7	3.4	7.3
8	2.2	4.2
9	4.0	25.1
10	3.4	4.1

Source: Based on data from Sewich, 1984.

9

Regression and Prediction

9.1 INTRODUCTION TO PREDICTION

If we know Janet's IQ, what can we say about her prospects of satisfactorily completing a college curriculum? Knowing Frank's prior voting record, can we make any informed guesses concerning his vote in the coming national elections? Maureen is enrolled in a statistics course. If we know her score on the midterm exam, can we make a reasonably good estimate of her grade on the final?

Let's look at an example of an approach we might take toward answering questions such as these. Suppose the semester is beginning to wind down. Maureen has completed all the assignments in statistics. The only hurdle remaining is the final examination. She sets about the task of trying to predict her score on the final.

Based on discussions with her instructor, she learns that the exam is designed to yield a mean of 75. If this is the only information available, her best guess is that she will score 75 on the final.* But she does have

---

* See Section 5.5 "Comparison of the Mean, Median, and Mode," in which we demonstrated that the sum of the deviations from the mean is zero and that the sum of squares of deviations from the arithmetic mean is less than the sum of squares of deviations about any other score or potential score.

additional information. She knows that she obtained a score of 62 on the midterm. How can she use this information to make a better prediction of her performance on the final? If she knows that the class mean on the midterm was 70, she could reason that a score below the mean on the midterm would probably be followed by a score below the mean on the final. At this point, she appears to be closing in on a more accurate prediction of her expected performance. However, simply knowing that she scored below the mean on the midterm would not provide a clear picture of her relative standing on that exam. How might we introduce even more precision in specifying her performance on the midterm?

Following further investigation, Maureen learns that the scores on the midterm were approximately normally distributed with a standard deviation of 4 $(s_x = 4)$. Since Maureen scored two standard deviations below the mean on the midterm $(z_x = -2.00)$, would she be justified in "guestimating" that she will score 2 standard deviations below the mean on the final $(z_y = -2.00)$? That is, if $s_y = 8$, should she predict a failing score of 59 [predicted $Y = (-2)(8) + 75 = 59$]?

Not necessarily. You may have noted that an important piece of information is missing—the correlation between the midterm and the final. You may recall from our discussion of correlation* that the Pearson r represents the extent to which the same individuals or events occupy the same relative position on two variables. Thus, we are justified in predicting a score of exactly 59 on the final exam only when the correlation is perfect (i.e., when $r = +1.00$). Suppose that the correlation is equal to zero. Then it should certainly be obvious that we are not justified in predicting a score of 59; rather, we are once again back to our original prediction of 75 (i.e., $\overline{Y}$).

In summary, when $r = 0$, our best prediction is 75 $(\overline{Y})$; when $r = +1.00$, our best prediction is 59 $(z_y = z_x)$.† It should be clear that predictions for intermediate values of r will fall somewhere between 59 and 75.

An outstanding advantage, then, of a correlational analysis stems from its application to problems involving predictions from one variable to another. Psychologists, educators, biologists, sociologists, and economists are constantly called upon to perform this function. To provide an adequate explanation of r and to illustrate its specific applications, we need to digress into an analysis of linear regression.

9.2 LINEAR REGRESSION

To simplify our discussion, let us start with an example of two variables that are usually perfectly or almost perfectly related: monthly salary and yearly income. In Table 9.1 we have listed the monthly income of eight

---

* See Section 8.2

† We are assuming that the correlation is positive. If the correlation were -1.00, our best prediction would be a score of 91, that is, $z_y = -z_x$.

TABLE 9.1   Monthly Salaries and Annual Income of Eight Wage Earners in an Electronics Firm (Hypothetical Data)

Employee	Monthly Salary	Annual Income
A	1,400	16,800
B	1,450	17,400
C	1,500	18,000
D	1,575	18,900
E	1,600	19,200
F	1,625	19,500
G	1,650	19,800
H	1,675	20,100

wage earners in a small electronics firm. These data are shown graphically in Figure 9.1. It is customary to refer to the horizontal axis as the X-axis and to the vertical axis as the Y-axis. If the variables are temporally related, the prior one is represented on the X-axis. It will be noted that all salaries are represented on a straight line extending diagonally from the lower left-hand corner to the upper right-hand corner.

Formula for Linear Relationships

The formula relating monthly salary (X) to annual salary (Y) may be represented as

$$Y = 12X$$

FIGURE 9.1   Relation of monthly salaries to annual income for eight employees in an electronic firm.

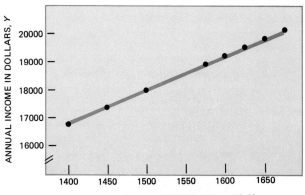

MONTHLY SALARY IN DOLLARS, X

BOX 9.1

THE HEAVYWEIGHT CHAMPIONS OF GAS-GUZZLING

One of the benefits of correlated data is that mathematicians have worked out ways of predicting values of one variable from knowledge of the values of a correlated variable. The method is *regression analysis*.

The following, adapted from *Winning with Statistics*, shows how correlated data may be used to guide decision making when you are purchasing the latest dream machine.

Living with Regression Analysis

The beauty of correlated data, particularly when the relationship is high, as in the case of weight of auto and miles per gallon, is that mathematicians have worked out ways of predicting values on one variable from knowledge of the values of a correlated variable. The method is known as *regression analysis*. Please don't let the term throw you. We can arrive at a pretty fair comprehension of regression without stumbling about in the arcane caverns of mathematics.

Take a look at the accompanying figure. It shows a scatter diagram of weight of automobile and miles per gallon. Note that I have drawn a line connecting the mean miles per gallon at each weight of car. The resulting line is a pretty good *approximation* to what mathematicians call the regression line for predicting Y-values (miles per gallon) from knowledge of X-values (auto weight). For purposes of discussion, we'll treat that line as if it were the regression line. In mathematical shorthand, it is called the line of regression of Y on X. But that is not important. What is important is that when the relationship between X and Y is high, we can use the regression line to predict Y-values from known X-values, achieving startling degrees of accuracy.

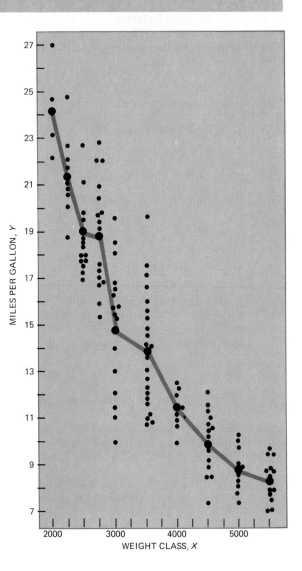

Let's see how this works. Let us say that you are considering buying one of two cars. Brand A is flaming red and weighs 3200 pounds when equipped. The second, brand B, is a metallic gold and weighs 2400 pounds. You can make your best guess about the overall performance of brand A by looking at the figure and drawing a vertical line at 3200 pounds until it intersects the regression line. Now look left to find the corresponding value for miles per gallon.

You may substitute any value of X into the formula and obtain the value of Y directly. For example, if another employee's monthly salary were 1700, his annual income would be

$$Y = 12 \cdot 1700 = 20{,}400$$

Let's add one more factor to this linear relationship. Suppose that the electronics firm had an exceptionally good year and that it decided to give each of its employees a Christmas bonus of $500. The equation would now read

$$Y = 500 + 12X$$

Perhaps, thinking back to your days of high school algebra, you will recognize the preceding formula as a special case of the general formula for a straight line; that is,

$$Y = a + b_y X \qquad (9.1)$$

in which Y and X represent variables that change from individual to individual and a and b_y represent constants for a particular set of data. More specifically, b_y represents the slope of a line relating values of Y to values of X. This is referred to as the regression of Y on X. In the present example, the slope of the line is 12, which means that Y changes by 12 for each change of one unit in X. The letter a represents the value of Y when $X = 0$.

Note also that Formula (9.1) may be regarded as a method for predicting Y from known values of X. When the correlation is 1.00 (as in the present case), the predictions are perfect.

Predicting X and Y from Data on Two Variables

In behavioral research, however, the correlations we obtain are almost never perfect. Therefore, we must find a straight line that best fits our data and make predictions from that line. But what do we mean by "best fit"? You will recall that when discussing the mean and the standard deviation, we defined the mean as that point in a distribution that makes the sum of squares of deviations from it minimal (least sum of squares). When applying the least-sum-of-squares method to correlation and regression, the *best-fitting straight line* is defined as that line which makes the squared deviations around it minimal. This straight line is referred to as a **regression line.**

Regression Line (Line of "Best Fit"): Straight line that makes the squared deviations around it minimal.

We might note at this time that the term "predict," as employed in statistics, does not carry with it any necessary implication of futurity, but simply refers to the fact that we are using information about one variable to obtain information about another. Thus, if we know students' college grade-point averages, we may use this information to predict their intelligence (which in our more generous moods we assume preceded their entrance into college).

At this point we introduce two new symbols: X' and Y'. These may be read as "X prime and Y prime," "X predicted and Y predicted," or "estimated X and estimated Y." We use these symbols whenever we employ the regression line or the regression equation to estimate or predict a score on one variable from a known score on another variable.

Returning to the formula for a straight line ($y = a + b_y X$), we are faced with the problem of determining b and a for a particular set of data so that Y' may be obtained.

The formula for obtaining the slope of the line relating Y to X, which is known as the line of regression of Y on X, is

$$b_y = \frac{\Sigma(X - \overline{X})(Y - \overline{Y})}{SS_x} \tag{9.2}$$

From Formula (9.2) we may derive another useful formula for determining the slope of the line of Y on X: Since [Formula (8.2)]

$$r = \frac{\Sigma(X - \overline{X})(Y - \overline{X})}{\sqrt{SS_x \cdot SS_y}}$$

it follows that

$$\Sigma(X - \overline{X})(Y - \overline{X}) = r\sqrt{SS_x \cdot SS_y}$$

and from Formula (6.4), where $s^2 = SS/N$, it follows that

$$SS_x = Ns_x^2 \qquad SS_y = Ns_y^2$$

Thus

$$b_y = \frac{r\sqrt{N^2 s_x^2 \cdot s_y^2}}{Ns_x^2}$$

$$= r\frac{Ns_x s_y}{Ns_x^2} \tag{9.3}$$

$$= r\frac{s_y}{s_x}$$

The constant a is given by the formula

$$a = \bar{Y} - b_y\bar{X} \qquad (9.4)$$

In the computation of Y', it is unwieldy to obtain each of these values separately and to substitute them into the formula for a straight line. However, by algebraically combining Formulas (9.3) and (9.4) and relating the result to Formula (9.1), we obtain a much more useful formula for Y':

$$Y' = \bar{Y} + r\frac{s_y}{s_x}(X - \bar{X})^* \qquad (9.5)$$

Concentrating our attention upon the second term on the right of Formula (9.5), we can see that the larger the r, the greater will be the magnitude of the entire term. This term also represents the *predicted deviation from the sample mean resulting from the regression of Y on X.* Thus, we may conclude that the greater the correlation is, the greater will be the predicted deviation from the sample mean. In the event of a perfect correlation, the entire predicted deviation is maximal. On the other hand, when $r = 0$, the predicted deviation is also zero. Thus, when $r = 0$, we have $Y' = \bar{Y}$. All of this is another way of saying that, in the absence of a correlation between two variables, our best prediction of any given score on a specified variable is the mean of the distribution of that variable.

Thus far, we have concentrated our attention on the regression of Y on X; that is, we have been predicting values of Y (Y') from known values of X. There is also a separate regression formula for predicting **scores on the** X-variable from values of the Y-variable. Thus, the slope of the regression line X on Y may be expressed as

$$b_x = \frac{\Sigma(X - \bar{X})(Y - \bar{Y})}{\text{SS}_y} \qquad (9.6)$$

or

$$b_x = r\frac{s_x}{s_y} \qquad (9.7)$$

Therefore, the regression formula for predicting scores on the X-variable from values of the Y-variable is

$$X' = \bar{X} + r\frac{s_x}{s_y}(Y - \bar{Y})\dagger \qquad (9.8)$$

---

* Since $Y' = a + b_yX$, $a = \bar{Y} - b_y\bar{X}$, and $b_y = r(s_y/s_x)$, then

$$Y' = \bar{Y} - r\left(\frac{s_y}{s_x}\right)\bar{X} + r\left(\frac{s_y}{s_x}\right)X = \bar{Y} + r\left(\frac{s_y}{s_x}\right)(X - \bar{X})$$

† Note that the prediction formulas could also be expressed in terms of z-scores. Thus,

$$X' = \bar{X} + r\frac{s_x}{s_y}(Y - \bar{Y})$$

$$\left(\frac{Y - \bar{Y}}{s_y}\right) = z_y$$

but

Therefore $$X' = \bar{X} + (r)(s_x)(z_y)$$

Similarly $$Y' = \bar{Y} + (r)(s_y)(z_x)$$

The following raw score formulas are often more convenient, especially because all the quantities shown are readily obtained in the course of calculating the Pearson r.

$$Y' = \bar{Y} + \frac{N\sum XY - (\sum X)(\sum Y)}{N\sum X^2 - (\sum X)^2}(X - \bar{X}) \qquad (9.9)$$

Similarly, the raw score formula for predicting X is

$$X' = \bar{X} + \frac{N\sum XY - (\sum X)(\sum Y)}{N\sum Y^2 - (\sum Y)^2}(Y - \bar{Y}) \qquad (9.10)$$

Midterm (X-Variable)	Final (Y-Variable)
$\bar{X} = 70$	$\bar{Y} = 75$
$s_x = 4$	$s_y = 8$
$r = 0.60$	

Illustrative Regression Problems

Here are two sample problems employing the data introduced in Section 9.1.

Problem 1. Maureen, you will recall, scored 62 on the midterm examination. What is our prediction concerning her score on the final examination? The relevant statistics are reproduced above.

Employing Formula (9.5), we find

$$Y' = 75 + 0.60 \left(\frac{8}{4}\right)(62 - 70) = 75 - 9.60 = 65.40$$

Problem 2. Hugh, on the same midterm test, scored 76. What is our prediction concerning his score on the final examination? Employing the tabular data of Problem 1, we obtain the following results:

$$Y' = 75 + 0.60 \left(\frac{8}{4}\right)(76 - 70) = 75 + 7.20 = 82.20$$

Had our problem been to predict X-scores from known values of Y, the procedures would have been precisely the same as above, except that Formula (9.8) would have been employed.

A reasonable question at this point is, "Since we know $\bar{Y}$ and s_y in the two problems, we presumably have all the observed data at hand. Therefore, why do we want to predict Y from X?" It should be pointed out that the purpose of these examples is to acquaint you with the prediction formulas. In actual practice, however, correlational techniques are most commonly employed in making predictions about future samples where Y is unknown.

For example, let us suppose that Ms. Holiday, the admissions officer of a college, has constructed an entrance examination that she has administered to all the applicants over a period of years. During this time, she has accumulated much information concerning the relationship between entrance scores and subsequent quality point averages in school. She finds that it is now possible to use scores on the entrance examination (X-variable) to predict subsequent quality point averages (Y-variable), and then use this information to establish an entrance policy for future applicants.

Since we have repeatedly stressed the relationship between Pearson r and z-scores, it should be apparent that the prediction formulas may be expressed in terms of z-scores. Mathematically, it can be shown* that

$$z_y' = rz_x \tag{9.11}$$

where $z_y' = Y'$ expressed in terms of a z-score.

Returning to Problem 1, we see that Maureen's score of 62 on the midterm can be expressed as $z = -2.00$. Thus, $z_y' = 0.60(-2.00) = -1.20$.

To assure yourself of the comparability of the two prediction formulas— Formulas (9.5) and (9.11)—you should translate the z_y' -score into a raw score, Y'. Thus,

$$Y' = \bar{Y} + z_{y'} \cdot s_y$$
$$= 75 + (-1.20)(8)$$
$$= 75 - 9.60 = 65.40$$

Constructing Lines of Regression

Let us return to the problem of constructing regression lines for predicting scores on the variables X and Y. As we have already pointed out, the regression line will not pass through all the paired scores except when $r = 1.00$ or $r = -1.00$. It will in fact pass among the paired scores in such a way as to minimize the squared deviations between the regression line (predicted scores) and the obtained scores. Earlier we pointed out that the mean is the point in a distribution that makes the squared deviations around it minimal. In discussing regression, we say that the regression line is analogous to the mean, since the sum of deviations of scores around the

---

*$Y' = \bar{Y} + r(s_y/s_x)$ $(X - \bar{X})$. By transposing terms:

$$\frac{Y' - \bar{Y}}{s_y} = r\frac{(X - \bar{X})}{s_x} \quad \text{but} \quad \frac{X - \bar{X}}{s_x} = z_x \quad \text{and} \quad \frac{Y' - \bar{Y}}{s_y} = z_y'$$

Therefore $z_y' = rz_x$.

Type A and Type B behaviors and heart-rate data: Constructing regression lines

In Box 8.1, we prepared a scatter diagram of HR measures of ten Type A subjects during practice and the first test trial. Now let's superimpose the line of regression for predicting Y (test trial 1) from known values of X (practice). This line is called the regression line of Y on X.

We previously calculated the following statistics:

	Practice	**First Test Trial**
Mean	85.10	83.76
Standard deviation	9.61	10.80
Pearson r	0.97	

First, we must write the equation for the straight line that minimizes the squared deviations around the regression line. Specifically, we may wish to calculate the constants for these data, b_y and a.

$$b_y = r\frac{s_y}{s_x} = 0.97\frac{10.80}{9.61} = 1.09$$

$$a = \bar{Y} - b_y\bar{X} = 83.76 - (1.09)(85.10) = -9.0$$

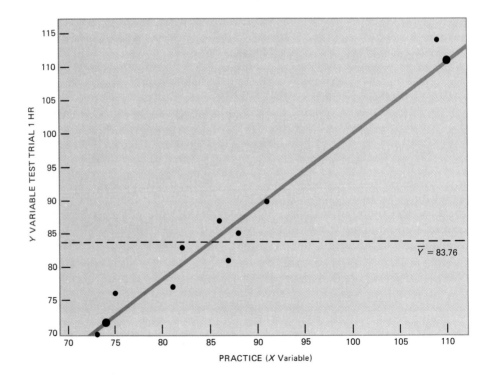

Thus, for any given value of X, $Y' = a + b_yX$. To illustrate, if $X = 74$, $Y' = -9.0 + (1.09)(74) = 71.7$. We may now plot this point on the scatter diagram. It will be the lower left-hand anchor point in the graph of the regression line. To obtain the upper right-hand anchor point, select a high value of X, say, $X = 110$, and find the corresponding Y'.

Thus, when $X = 110$, $Y' = -9.0 + (1.09)(110) = 110.9$. By joining these two points and extending the resulting straight line, we have constructed the regression line for predicting values of Y from values of X.

Let's consider one important word of caution. The two constants in the equation (a and b_y) represent sample statistics rather than parameters and may or may not faithfully reflect the parameters. Since the predictions from a given sample data set are "customized" for that set, predictions for other data sets are unlikely to be as accurate.

 a. Apply Formula (9.5) to obtain Y' from $X = 74$ and $X = 110$. Verify that the same predicted values are found.

 b. Referring to the scatter diagrams you prepared for Statistics in Action 8.1, superimpose regression lines on practice versus trial 2, trial 1 versus trial 3, and trial 2 versus trial 4. (*Note:* These are based on Type B behaviors.)

ANSWERS

a. When $\underline{X} = 74$, $Y' = 83.76 + 1.09(74 - 85.10) = 83.76 - 12.10 = 71.7$.
 When $\overline{X} = 110$, $Y' = 83.76 + 1.09(110 - 85.10) = 83.76 + 27.14 = 110.9$.

b.

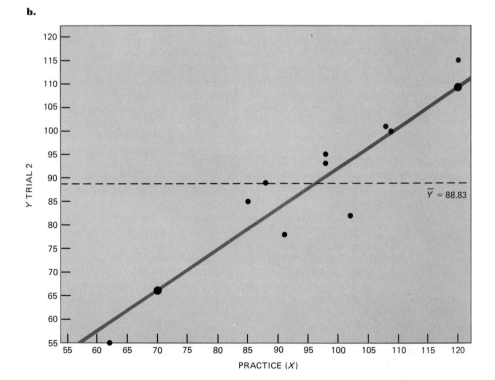

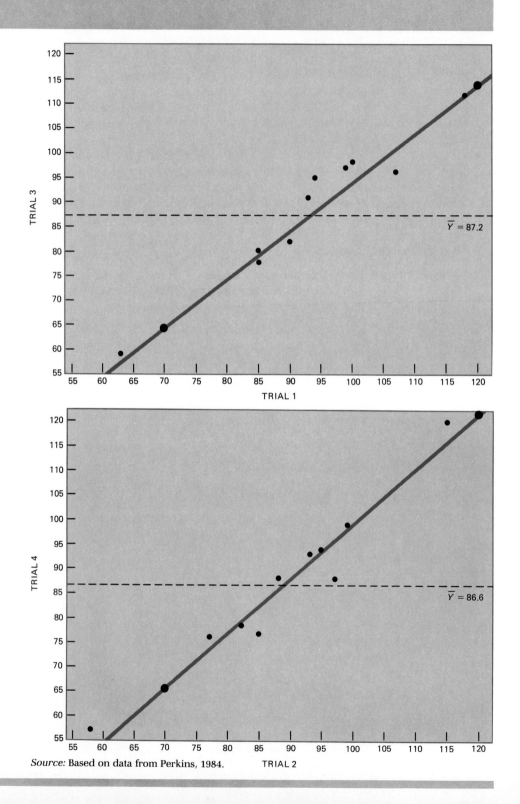

Source: Based on data from Perkins, 1984.

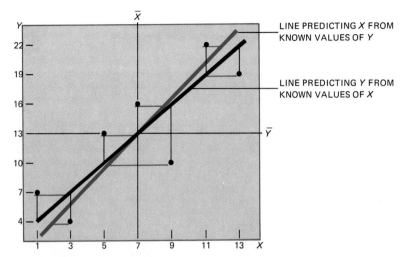

FIGURE 9.2   Scatter diagram representing paired scores on two variables and regression lines for predicting X from Y and Y from X. Note that the line predicting Y from X minimizes the vertical or Y-axis deviations of the data points (black lines). In contrast, the line predicting X from Y minimizes the horizontal or X-axis deviations (color lines).

regression line is zero and the sum of squares of these deviations is minimal, as we shall demonstrate.

Recall that all the values required to calculate predicted scores are readily found during the course of calculating r, that is, $\overline{X}$, $\overline{Y}$, s_x, s_y. Now to construct our regression line for predicting Y from X, all we need to do is take two extreme values of X, predict Y from each of these values, and then join these two points on the scatter diagram. The line joining these points represents the regression line for predicting Y from X, which is also referred to as the line of regression of Y on X. Similarly, to construct the regression line for predicting X from Y, we take two extreme values of Y, predict X for each of these values, and then join these two points on the scatter diagram. This is precisely what was done in Figure 9.2 to construct the two regression lines from the data in Table 8.2.

Note that both regression lines intersect at the means of X and Y. In conceptualizing the relationship between the regression lines and the magnitude of r, we shall find it helpful to think of the regression lines as rotating about the joint means of X and Y. When $r = 1.00$, both regression lines will have identical slopes and will be superimposed upon one another, since they pass directly though all the paired scores. However, as r becomes smaller, the regression lines rotate away from each other, so that in the limiting case when $r = 0$, they are *perpendicular* to each other. At this point the regression line for predicting X from known values of Y is $\overline{X}$, and the regression line for predicting Y from known values of X is $\overline{Y}$.

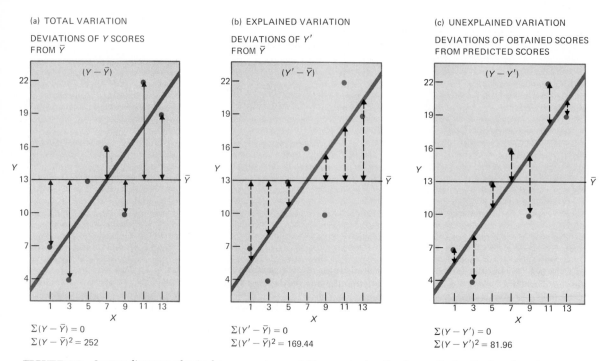

(a) TOTAL VARIATION

DEVIATIONS OF Y SCORES FROM $\bar{Y}$

$\Sigma(Y - \bar{Y}) = 0$
$\Sigma(Y - \bar{Y})^2 = 252$

(b) EXPLAINED VARIATION

DEVIATIONS OF Y' FROM $\bar{Y}$

$\Sigma(Y' - \bar{Y}) = 0$
$\Sigma(Y' - \bar{Y})^2 = 169.44$

(c) UNEXPLAINED VARIATION

DEVIATIONS OF OBTAINED SCORES FROM PREDICTED SCORES

$\Sigma(Y - Y') = 0$
$\Sigma(Y - Y')^2 = 81.96$

FIGURE 9.3   Scatter diagrams of paired scores on two variables, regression line for predicting Y-values from known values of X, and the mean of the distribution of Y-scores ($\bar{Y}$): $r = 0.82$ (from data in Table 8.3). (a) Deviations of scores ($Y - \bar{Y}$) from the mean of Y (total variation). (b) Deviations of predicted scores ($Y' - \bar{Y}$) from the mean of Y (explained variation). (c) Deviations of scores ($Y - Y'$) from the regression line (unexplained variation).

9.3 RESIDUAL VARIANCE AND STANDARD ERROR OF ESTIMATES

Figure 9.3 shows a series of scatter diagrams, each reproduced from Figure 9.2, showing only one regression line: the line for predicting Y from known values of X. Although our present discussion will be directed only to this regression line, all the conclusions we draw will be equally applicable to the line predicting X from known values of Y.

The regression line represents our best basis for predicting Y scores from known values of X. As we can see, not all the obtained scores fall on the regression line. However, if the correlation had been 1.00, all the scores *would* have fallen right on the regression line. The deviations ($Y - Y'$) in Figure 9.3 represent our errors in prediction.

You will note the similarity of $Y - Y'$ (the deviation of scores from the regression line) to $Y - \bar{Y}$ (the deviation of scores from the mean). The algebraic sum of these deviations around the regression line is equal to zero. Earlier, we saw that the algebraic sum of the deviations around the mean is also equal to zero. In a sense, then, the regression line is a sort of "floating mean": one that takes on different values depending on the values of X that are employed in prediction.

You will also recall that in calculating the variance, s^2, we squared the deviations from the mean, summed, and divided by N. Finally, the square root of the variance provided our standard deviation. Now, if we were to square and sum the deviations of the scores from the regression line, $\Sigma(Y - Y')^2$, we would have a basis for calculating another variance and standard deviation. The variance around the regression line is known as the **residual variance** and is defined as follows:

$$s^2_{\text{est}\,y} = \frac{\Sigma(Y - Y')^2}{N - 2} \tag{9.12}$$

Residual Variance: Variance around the regression line.

When the predictions are made from Y to X, the residual variance of X is

$$s^2_{\text{est}\,x} = \frac{\Sigma(X - X')^2}{N - 2} \tag{9.13}$$

The standard deviation around the regression line (referred to as the **standard error of estimate**) is, of course, the square root of the residual variance. Thus

$$s_{\text{est}\,y} = \sqrt{\frac{\Sigma(Y - Y')^2}{N - 2}} \tag{9.14}$$

Standard Error of Estimate: Standard deviation of scores around the regression line.

When predictions are made from Y to X, the standard error of estimate of X is

$$s_{\text{est}\,x} = \sqrt{\frac{\Sigma(X - X')^2}{N - 2}} \tag{9.15}$$

You may be justifiably aghast at the amount of computation that is implied in the preceding formulas for calculating the standard error of estimate. However, as has been our practice throughout this text, we have shown the basic formulas so that you may have a conceptual grasp of the meaning of the standard error of estimate. It is, as we have seen, the standard deviation of scores around the regression line rather than around the mean of the distribution.

Fortunately, as in all previous illustrations in the text, there is a simplified method for calculating $s_{\text{est}\,y}$ and $s_{\text{est}\,x}$.

$$s_{\text{est}\,y} = s_y \sqrt{\frac{N(1 - r^2)}{N - 2}} \tag{9.16}$$

and

$$s_{\text{est}\,x} = s_x \sqrt{\frac{N(1 - r^2)}{N - 2}} \tag{9.17}$$

You will note that when $r = \pm 1.00$, $s_{est\,y} = 0$, which means that there are no deviations from the regression line, and therefore no errors in prediction. On the other hand, when $r = 0$, the errors of prediction are maximal for that given distribution and will approach s_y, that is, $s_{est\,y} = s_y$ $\sqrt{N/(N-2)}$. For large Ns, the quantity $\sqrt{N/(N-2)} \cong 1$ and $s_{est\,y} \cong s_y$.

With the data in Exercise 1, Chapter 8, the following statistics were calculated:

College Entrance Exam (X Variable)	Verbal Comprehension Exam (Y Variable)
$\overline{X} = 47.65$	$\overline{Y} = 39.15$
$s_x = 13.82$	$s_y = 12.35$
$r = 0.8466$	

Thus

$$s_{est\,y} = 12.35 \sqrt{\frac{20(1 - 0.8466^2)}{18}}$$
$$= 12.35(0.5610) = 6.93$$

We noted earlier that the regression line is analogous to the mean and shares its properties: The sums of the deviations about the mean and about the regression line are zero, and the sums of the squared deviations about the mean and the regression line are minimal. Similarly, the standard error of estimate has properties that are similar to those of the standard deviation. Both reflect the degree of dispersion about their measures of central tendency, namely the mean and the regression line, respectively. Thus, the greater the standard error of estimate is, the greater is the dispersion of scores about the regression line. Conversely, the smaller the standard error of estimate is, the less is the dispersion of scores about the regression line.

For each value of X, there is a distribution of scores on the Y-variable. The mean of each of these distributions is Y', and the standard deviation of each distribution is $s_{est\,y}$. When the distribution of Y-scores for each value of X has the same variability, we refer to this condition as **homoscedasticity.** In addition, if the distribution of Y-scores for each value of X is normally distributed, we may state relationships between the standard error of estimate and the normal curve (see Section 7.3). We can, for example, predict a value of Y from any given X, and then describe an interval within which it is likely that the true value of Y will be found. For normally

Homoscedasticity: Homogeneous variability within the columns and the rows.

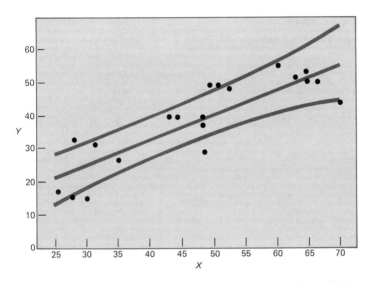

FIGURE 9.4 Line of regression for predicting Y from X with parallel lines one $s_{\text{est }y}$ above and below the regression line (from data in Exercise 1, Chapter 8). Dots indicate individual scores on X and Y.

distributed variables, approximately 68% of the time the true value of Y (i.e., Y_T) will be within the following interval:

$$\text{Interval including } Y_T = Y' \pm s_{\text{est }y} \sqrt{1 + \frac{1}{N} + \frac{(X - \overline{X})^2}{SS_x}} \qquad (9.18)$$

Thus, if we predicted a Y-value of 39.15 from $X = 25$ and $s_{\text{est }y} = 6.43$, $Y' = 22.02$, $\overline{X} = 47.65$, $SS_x = 3822.53$, and $N = 20$:

$$\text{Interval including } Y_T = 22.02 \pm 6.93 \sqrt{1 + \frac{1}{20} + \frac{(25 - 47.65)^2}{3822.53}}$$

$$= 22.02 \pm (6.93)(1.088)$$

$$\pm 7.54$$

In other words, when $X = 25$, about 68 percent of the time the true Y will be found between scores of 14.48 and 29.56.

Using these data, we draw two lines, one above and one below the regression line for predicting Y from X (Figure 9.4). For normally distributed variables, approximately 68 percent of the time the true values of Y will be found between these lines when we use Formula (9.18) to predict Y from various values of X. Note that the lines are more spread out when predicting Y from extreme values of X. The result is two slightly bowed lines, with minimum distance between them at the mean of X. (It should be noted that these relationships refer to the distributions of *both* X and Y.)

9.4 EXPLAINED AND UNEXPLAINED VARIATION*

If we look again at Figure 9.3, we see that there are three separate sums of squares that can be calculated from the data. These are

Unexplained Variation: Variation of scores around the regression line.

1. Variation of scores around the sample mean (Figure 9.3a). This variation is given by $(Y - \overline{Y})^2$ and is, of course, basic to the determination of the variance and the standard deviation of the sample.

2. Variation of scores around the regression line (or predicted scores) (Figure 9.3c). This variation is given by $(Y - Y')^2$ and is referred to as **unexplained variation.** It is the difference between the predicted score and the obtained score. The reason for this choice of terminology should be clear. If the correlation between two variables is ±1.00, all the scores fall on the regression line. Consequently, we have, in effect, explained *all* the variation in Y in terms of the variation in X and, conversely, all the variation of X in terms of the variation in Y. In other words, in the event of a perfect relationship, there is no unexplained variation. However, when the correlation is less than perfect, many of the scores will not fall right on the regression line, as we have seen. The deviations of these scores from the regression line represent variation that is not accounted for in terms of the correlation between two variables. Hence, the term "unexplained variation" is employed.

Explained Variation: Variation of predicted scores about the mean of the distribution.

3. Variation of predicted scores about the mean of the distribution (Figure 9.3b). This variation is given by $(Y' - \overline{Y})^2$ and is referred to as **explained variation.** It is the difference between the mean and the predicted score. The reason for this terminology should be clear from our discussion in the preceding paragraph and our prior reference to predicted deviation (Section 9.3). You will recall our previous observation that the greater the correlation is, the greater will be the predicted deviation from the sample mean. It follows further that the greater the predicted deviation is, the greater will be the explained variation. When the predicted deviation is maximum, the correlation is perfect; and 100 percent of variation is explained.

It can be shown mathematically that the total sum of squares consists of two components, which may be added together. These two components represent explained variation and unexplained variation, respectively. Thus

$$\Sigma (Y - \overline{Y})^2 = \Sigma (Y - Y')^2 + \Sigma (Y' - \overline{Y})^2 \qquad (9.19)$$

$$\underset{\text{Total}}{\underset{\text{variation}}{}} \qquad \underset{\text{Unexplained}}{\underset{\text{variation}}{}} \qquad \underset{\text{Explained}}{\underset{\text{variation}}{}}$$

*Although analysis of variance is not covered until Chapters 14 and 15, much of the material in this section will serve as an introduction to some of the basic concepts of analysis of variance.

The calculations are shown in Figure 9.3. You will note that the sum of the explained variation (169.44) and the unexplained variation (81.96) is equal to the total variation. The slight discrepancy found in this example is due to rounding r to 0.82 prior to calculating the predicted scores.

Now, when $r = 0.00$, then $\Sigma(Y' - \bar{Y})^2 = 0.00$. (Why? See Section 9.2.) Consequently, the total variation is equal to the unexplained variation. Stated another way, when $r = 0$, all the variation is unexplained. On the other hand, when $r = 1.00$, then $\Sigma(Y - Y')^2 = 0.00$, since all the scores are on the regression line. Under these circumstances, total variation is the same as explained variation. In other words, all the variation is explained when $r = 1.00$.

The ratio of the explained variation to the total variation is referred to as the **coefficient of determination** and is symbolized by r^2. The formula for the coefficient of determination is*

Coefficient of Determination (r^2): The ratio of the explained variation to the total variation.

$$r^2 = \frac{\text{Explained variation}}{\text{Total variation}} = \frac{\Sigma(Y' - \bar{Y})^2}{\Sigma(Y - \bar{Y})^2} \qquad (9.20)$$

Referring to Figure 9.3, we see that the proportion of explained variation to total variation is

$$r^2 = \frac{169.44}{252} = 0.67$$

It can be seen that the coefficient of determination indicates the proportion of total variation that is explained in terms of the magnitude of the correlation coefficient. When $r = 0$, the coefficient of determination, r^2, equals 0. When $r = 0.5$, the coefficient of determination is 0.25. In other words, 25% of the total variation is accounted for. Finally, when $r = 1.00$, then $r^2 = 1.00$ and all variation is accounted for.

Figure 9.5 depicts graphically the proportion of variation in one variable that is accounted for by the variation in another variable when r takes on different values.

You have undoubtedly noted that the square root of the coefficient of determination provides another definition of r. Thus

$$r = \pm \sqrt{\frac{\text{Explained variation}}{\text{Total variation}}} = \pm \sqrt{\frac{\Sigma(Y' - \bar{Y})^2}{\Sigma(Y - \bar{Y})^2}} \qquad (9.21)$$

We have previously shown that the coefficient of determination, r^2, is equal to 0.67 for the data summarized in Figure 9.3. Note that the square root of this number (i.e., $\sqrt{0.67}$) equals 0.82—which is r for these data.

---

*Table H in the table section presents a number of functions of r for various values of r, including such useful functions as r^2, $1 - r^2$, and $\sqrt{1 - r^2}$. You should familiarize yourself with this table.

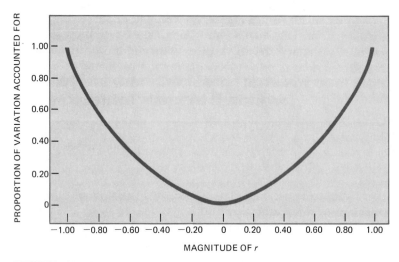

FIGURE 9.5   The proportion of the variation of one variable accounted for in terms of variations of a correlated variable at varying values of r.

Since r^2 represents the proportion of variation accounted for, $(1 - r^2)$ represents the proportion of variation that is *not* explained in terms of the correlation between X and Y. This concept is known as the **coefficient of nondetermination** and is symbolized by k^2. Thus, k^2 represents the proportion of variation in Y that must be explained by variables other than X.

Coefficient of Nondetermination: Proportion of variation not explained in terms of the correlation between the two variables.

In summary, the relationship between k^2 and r^2 is

$$k^2 = 1 - r^2 \tag{9.22}$$

or

$$k^2 + r^2 = 1 \tag{9.23}$$

For the data in Figure 9.3, k^2 may be obtained directly:

$$k^2 = \frac{\text{Unexplained variation}}{\text{Total variation}} = \frac{81.96}{252} = 0.33$$

or, by use of Formula (9.22),

$$k^2 = 1 - r^2 = 1 - 0.67 = 0.33$$

9.5 CORRELATION AND CAUSATION

You have seen that when two variables are related it is possible to predict one from your knowledge of the other. This relationship between correlation and prediction often leads to a serious error in reasoning; that is, the relationship between two variables frequently carries with it the implication that one has caused the other. This is especially true when there is a temporal relationship between the variables in question, that is, when one

CASE EXAMPLE 9.1

Why We Turn the Heat Down

With many of our key resources in jeopardy and the recently acknowledged risk of poisoning our food and water supplies with toxic substances, the field of environmental psychology is receiving increased attention. In one part of this study, the authors reviewed investigations that determined the effects of providing daily feedback on energy use. In an attempt to ascertain the role of economic factors in energy conservation practices, they related the percentage of reduction in overall energy use to (a) gross annual household income, (b) cost per month of targeted energy source, and (c) the budget share of gross monthly income expended for energy during the target month. The scatter diagrams for these data are shown in Figure 9.6, with accompanying correlation coefficients (r) and coefficients of determination (r^2).

FIGURE 9.6 Percent change in overall targeted energy use in relation to factors (a), (b), and (c).

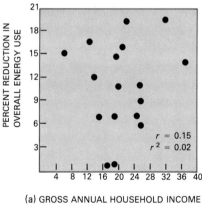
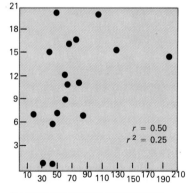
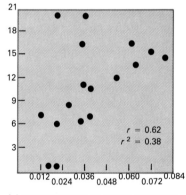

(a) GROSS ANNUAL HOUSEHOLD INCOME IN THOUSANDS OF DOLLARS

(b) LOSS PER MONTH OF TARGETED ENERGY SOURCE IN DOLLARS

(c) BUDGET SHARE OF GROSS MONTHLY INCOME EXPENDED FOR ENERGY DURING TARGET MONTH

It can be seen in Figure 9.6(a) that there is only a small relationship between the reduction in energy use and the annual household income. If $r = 0.15$ can be considered an estimate of the population correlation, annual household income accounts for only 2% of the variance in the reduction of energy use. However, when the cost of the energy source is taken into account, as in Figure 9.6(b), the correlation becomes 0.50 and 25% of the variance in the reduction of energy use is accounted for. Finally, when the proportion of the budget for energy is correlated with the reduction in energy use (Figure 9.6c), the correlation is 0.62 and approximately 38% of the variance in energy reduction is accounted for. This study suggests that economic factors play a considerable role in obtaining compliance with energy conservation strategies.

Source: Based on Robin C. Winkler and Richard A. Winett (1982), "Behavioral Interventions in Resource Conservation: A Systems Approach Based on Behavioral Economics," *American Psychologist,* **37**(4), 421–435.

---

precedes the other in time. What is often overlooked is the fact that the variables may not be causally connected in any way, but that they may vary together by virtue of a common link with a third variable. Thus, if you are a bird watcher, you may note that as the number of birds increases in the spring the grass becomes progressively greener. However, recognizing that the extended number of hours and the increasing warmth of the sun is a third factor influencing both these variables, you are not likely to conclude that the birds cause the grass to turn green, or vice versa. Unfortunately, there are many occasions, particularly in the behavioral sciences, when it is not so easy to identify the third factor.

Suppose you have demonstrated that there is a high positive correlation between the number of hours students spend studying for an exam and their subsequent grades on that exam. You may be tempted to conclude that the number of hours of study causes grades to vary. This seems to be a perfectly reasonable conclusion, and it is probably in close agreement with what your parents and instructors have been telling you for years. Let's look more closely at the implications of a causal relationship. On the assumption that a greater number of hours of study causes grades to increase, we would be led to expect that *any* student who devotes more time to study is guaranteed a high grade and that a student who spends less time with his books is going to receive a low grade. This is not necessarily the case. We have overlooked the fact that it might be the better student (by virtue of higher intelligence, stronger motivation, better study habits, etc.) who devotes more time to study and performs better simply because he or she has a greater capacity to do so.

What we are saying is that correlational studies simply do not permit inferences of causation. Correlation is a *necessary* but not a *sufficient* condition to establish a causal relationship between two variables. In short, establishing a causal relationship requires conducting an experiment in which an independent variable is randomly assigned to the subjects by the experimenter, and the effects of these assignments are reflected in the dependent, or criterion, variable. A correlational study lacks the requirement of independent random assignment.

Huff's book* includes an excellent chapter devoted to the confusion of correlation with causation. He refers to faulty causal inferences from

---

* D. Huff, *How to Lie with Statistics*. New York: W. W. Norton, 1954.

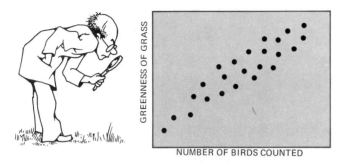

Correlation is not causation. Note that when the census count of birds is low, the grass is not very green. When there are many birds, the grass is very green. Therefore, the number of birds determines how green the grass will become. What is wrong with this conclusion?

correlational data as the *"post hoc"* fallacy. The following excerpt illustrates a common example of the **"post hoc" fallacy.**

"Post Hoc" Fallacy: Faulty causal inferences from correlational data.

> Reams of pages of figures have been collected to show the value in dollars of a college education, and stacks of pamphlets have been published to bring these figures—and conclusions more or less based on them—to the attention of potential students. I am not quarreling with the intention. I am in favor of education myself, particularly if it includes a course in elementary statistics. Now these figures have pretty conclusively demonstrated that people who have gone to college make more money than people who have not. The exceptions are numerous, of course, but the tendency is strong and clear. The only thing wrong is that along with the figures and facts goes a totally unwarranted conclusion. This is the *post hoc* fallacy at its best. It says that these figures show that if *you* (your son, your daughter) attend college you will probably earn more money than if you decide to spend the next four years in some other manner. This unwarranted conclusion has for its basis the equally unwarranted assumption that since college-trained folks make more money, they make it because they went to college. Actually we don't know but that these are the people who would have made more money even if they had *not* gone to college. There are a couple of things that indicate rather strongly that this is so. Colleges get a disproportionate number of two groups of kids—the bright and the rich. The bright might show good earning power without college knowledge. And as for the rich ones—well money breeds money in several obvious ways. Few sons of rich men are found in low-income brackets whether or not they go to college.

9.6 PUTTING IT ALL TOGETHER

In Section 8.6, we found the correlation between length of car and city mpg to be -0.68. In the present section, we'll use these data to illustrate the construction of the regression line between two variables, the prediction of the value of one variable (city mpg) from knowledge of the value of a correlated variable (length of car), and the coefficients of determination and nondetermination.

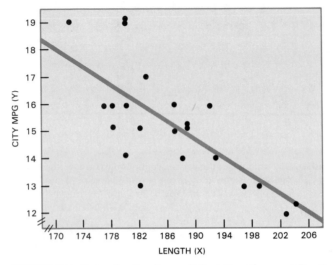

FIGURE 9.7 Regression line for predicting city miles per gallon from length of automobile.

Recall that in Section 8.6 we found SS_X to be 1277.14 and SS_Y to be 78.67. Since we'll need to know the standard deviations of each of these variables, let's obtain the respective standard deviations by dividing the sum of squares by N and extracting the square root. Thus, $s_X = \sqrt{1277.14/21} = 7.80$ and $s_Y = \sqrt{78.67/21} = 1.94$. We previously found $\bar{X} = 185.57$ and $\bar{Y} = 15.33$.

To construct a regression line for predicting city mpg (Y') from length of car (X), we take two values of X (preferably at opposite ends of the distribution) and predict corresponding values of Y'. We plot these two points on the scatter diagram (see Figure 9.7) and join them by a straight line.

Let's use the following values of X for our predictions of the corresponding values of Y': 170 and 204. Using Formula (9.5), we obtain

When $X = 170$:

$$Y' = 15.33 + (-0.68)\frac{1.94}{7.80}(170 - 185.57)$$

$$= 15.33 + 2.63 = 17.99$$

When $X = 204$:

$$Y' = 15.33 + (-0.68)\frac{1.94}{7.80}(204 - 185.57)$$

$$= 15.33 - 3.12 = 12.21$$

To obtain the coefficient of determination, square the correlation between length of car and city mpg. Thus, $r^2 = -0.68^2 = 0.46$. If we assume that the sample correlation approaches the population correlation between these two variables, 46% of the variation in city mpg is accounted for by the length of the vehicle. The coefficient of nondetermination $(1 - 0.46 = 0.54)$ tells us that 54% of the variation is not accounted for by the length of the vehicle.

CHAPTER SUMMARY

Let's briefly review what we have discussed in this chapter. We saw that it is possible to "fit" two straight lines to a bivariate distribution of scores, one for predicting Y-scores from known X-values and one for predicting X-scores from known Y-values.

We saw that when the correlation is perfect, all the scores fall upon the regression line. Thus, there is no error in prediction. The lower the degree of relationship is, the greater will be the dispersion of scores around the regression line, and the greater will be the errors of prediction. Finally, when $r = 0$, the mean of the sample provides our "best" predictor for a given variable.

The regression line was shown to be analogous to the mean: The summed deviations around it are zero, and the sums of squares are minimal. The standard error of estimate was shown to be analogous to the standard deviation.

We saw that three separate sums of squares, reflecting variability, may be calculated from correlation data.

1. Variation about the mean of the distribution for each variable. This variation is referred to as the *total sum of squares*.
2. Variation of each score about the regression line. This variation is known as *unexplained variation*.
3. Variation of each predicted score about the mean of the distribution for each variable. This variation is known as *explained variation*.

We saw that the sum of the explained variation and the unexplained variation is equal to the total variation.

Finally, we saw that the ratio of the explained variation to the total variation provides us with the proportion of the total variation that is explained. The term applied to this proportion is *coefficient of determination*. In addition, the converse concept of *coefficient of nondetermination* was discussed.

TERMS TO REMEMBER

coefficient of determination (r^2)

coefficient of nondetermination

regression line (line of "best fit")

residual variance

standard error of estimate

explained variation   **unexplained variation**
homoscedasticity
"post hoc" fallacy

EXERCISES

1. Find the equation of the regression line of Y on X for the following data.

X	1	2	3	4	5
Y	5	4	3	2	1

2. In a study concerned with the relationship between two variables, X and Y, the following was obtained:

$$\overline{X} = 119 \qquad \overline{Y} = 1.30$$
$$s_x = 10 \qquad s_y = 0.55$$
$$r = 0.70$$
$$N = 100$$

a. Sally B. obtained a score of 130 on the X-variable. Predict her score on the Y-variable.

b. A score of 1.28 on the Y-variable was predicted for Bill B. What was his score on the X-variable?

c. Determine the standard error of estimate of Y.

3. A study was undertaken to find the relationship between "emotional stability" and performance in college. The following results were obtained:

Emotional stability	College average
$\overline{X} = 49$	$\overline{Y} = 1.35$
$s_x = 12$	$s_y = 0.50$

$$r = 0.36$$
$$N = 60$$

a. Norma obtained a score of 65 on the X-variable. What is your prediction of her score on the Y-variable?

b. Determine the standard error of estimate of X and Y.

c. What proportion of total variation is accounted for by explained variation?

4. Assume that $\overline{X} = 30$, $s_x = 5$; $\overline{Y} = 45$, $s_y = 8$. Draw a separate graph for each pair of regression lines for the following values of r:

a. 0.00   **b.** 0.20   **c.** 0.40   **d.** 0.60   **e.** 0.80   **f.** 1.00

Generalize: What is the relationship between the size of r and the angle formed by the regression lines? If the values of r given in (b) through (f) above were all negative, what would be the relationship?

5. Given: The standard deviation of scores on a standardized vocabulary test is 15. The correlation of this test with IQ is 0.80. What would you expect the standard deviation on the vocabulary test to be for a large group of students with the same IQ? Explain.

6. A student obtains a score on test X that is 1.5 standard deviation above the mean. Predict the standard score for him or her on test Y, if r equals
  a. 0.00   **b.** 0.40   **c.** 0.80   **d.** 1.00   **e.** -0.50 **f.** -0.80

7. A personnel manager has made a study of employees involved in one aspect of a manufacturing process. He finds that after they have been on the job for a year, he is able to obtain a performance measure that accurately reflects their proficiency. He designs a selection test aimed at predicting their eventual proficiency, and obtains a correlation of 0.65 with the proficiency measure (Y). The mean of the test is 50, $s_x = 6$; $\overline{Y} = 100$, $s_y = 10$, $N = 1000$. Answer the following questions based on these facts (assume that both the selection test and the proficiency measure are normally distributed):

  a. Herman J. obtained a score of 40 on the selection test. What is his predicted proficiency score?

  b. How likely is it that he will score as high as 110 on the proficiency scale?

  c. A score of 80 on the Y-variable is considered satisfactory for the job; below 80 is unsatisfactory. If the X-test is to be used as a selection device, which score should be used as a cutoff point? [*Hint:* Find the value of X that leads to a prediction of 80 on Y. Be sure to employ the appropriate prediction formula.]

  d. Sonya J. obtained a score of 30 on X. How likely is it that she will achieve an acceptable score on Y?

  e. Leon M. obtained a score of 60 on X. How likely is it that he will *fail* to achieve an acceptable score on Y?

  f. For a person to have prospects for a supervisory position, a score of 120 or higher on Y is deemed essential. What value of X should be employed for the selection of potential supervisory personnel?

  g. If 1000 persons achieve a score on X that predicts a $Y = 120$, approximately how many of them will obtain Y scores below 120? Above 130? Below 110? Above 110?

8. An owner of a mail-order house advertises that all orders are shipped within 24 hours of receipt. Since personnel in the shipping department are hired on a day-to-day basis, it is important for her to be able to predict the number of orders contained in each batch of daily mail so that she can hire sufficient personnel for the following day. She hit on the idea of weighing each day's mail and correlating the weight with the actual number of orders. Over a successive 30-day period, she obtained the results shown in the following table:

Weight in Pounds	Number of Orders	Weight in Pounds	Number of Orders
20	5400	26	5400
15	4200	21	5000
23	5800	24	5400
17	5000	16	4300
12	3500	34	6700
35	6400	28	6100
29	6000	15	3600

(continued on next page)

Weight in Pounds	Number of Orders	Weight in Pounds	Number of Orders
21	5200	11	3200
10	4000	18	5300
13	3800	27	5800
25	5700	30	5900
14	4000	22	5500
18	4800	20	5200
30	6200	24	5000
33	6600	13	3700

    a. Find the correlation between the weight of mail and the number of orders. [*Hint:* In calculating the correlation, consider dropping the final two digits on the *Y*-variable.]

    b. If ten persons are required to handle 1000 orders per day, how many should be hired to handle 22 pounds of mail? 15 pounds? 30? 38? [*Note:* Assume that employees are hired only in groups of 10.]

9. Peruse the magazine section of your Sunday newspaper, monthly magazines, television, and radio advertisements for examples of the "post hoc" fallacy.

10. Assume that students take two tests for entrance into the college of their choice. Both are normally distributed tests. The college-entrance examination has a mean of 47.63 and a standard deviation of 13.82. The verbal comprehension test has a mean equal to 39.15 and a standard deviation equal to 12.35. The correlation between the two tests equals 0.85.

    a. Estelle obtained a score of 40 on her college-entrance examination. Predict her score on the verbal comprehension test.

    b. How likely is it that she will score at least 40 on the verbal comprehension test?

    c. Howard obtained a score of 40 on the verbal comprehension test. Predict his score on the college-entrance examination.

    d. How likely is it that he will score at least 40 on the college-entrance examination?

    e. REC University finds that students who score at least 45 on the verbal comprehension test are most successful. What score on the college-entrance examination should be used as the cutoff point for selection?

    f. Harris obtained a score of 55 on the college-entrance examination. Would he be selected by REC University? What are his chances of achieving an acceptable score on the verbal comprehension test?

11. On the basis of the obtained data (below), an experimenter asserts that the older a child is, the fewer irrelevant responses he or she makes in an experimental situation.

    a. Determine whether this conclusion is valid.

    b. Mindy, age 13, enters the experimental situation. What is the most probable number of irrelevant responses the experimenter would predict for Mindy?

Age	Number of Irrelevant Responses	Age	Number of Irrelevant Responses
2	11	7	12
3	12	9	8
4	10	9	7
4	13	10	3
5	11	11	6
5	9	11	5
6	10	12	5
7	7		

12. Why do we have two regression lines? Under what circumstances will the regression lines be identical?

13. The per-capita gross national product (GNP) is widely recognized as an estimate of the living standard of a nation. It has been claimed that per-capita energy consumption is, in turn, a good predictor of per-capita GNP. Shown below are the GNP (expressed in dollars per capita) and the per-capita energy consumption (expressed in millions of BTUs per capita) of various nations.

a. Construct a scatter diagram from the data below.

b. Determine the correlation between GNP and energy expenditures.

c. Construct the regression line for predicting per-capita GNP from per-capita energy consumption.

d. The following nations were not represented in the original sample. Their per-capita energy expenditures were: Chile, 21; Ireland, 49; Belgium, 88. Calculate the predicted per-capita GNP for each country. Compare the predicted values with the actual values, which are, respectively, 400; 630; 1400.

Country	Energy Consumption (in Millions of BTUs)	GNP (Dollars)
India	3.4	55
Ghana	3.0	270
Portugal	7.7	240
Columbia	12.0	290
Greece	12.0	390
Mexico	23.0	310
Japan	30.3	550
USSR	69.0	800
Netherlands	75.0	1100
France	58.0	1390
Norway	67.0	1330
West Germany	90.0	1410
Australia	88.0	1525
United Kingdom	113.0	1400
Canada	131.0	1900
United States	180.0	2900

14. Show algebraically that

$$b_y = \frac{N \sum XY - (\sum X)(\sum Y)}{N \sum X^2 - (\sum X)^2}$$

15. Show algebraically that

$$Y' = \bar{Y} + \frac{N \sum XY - (\sum X)(\sum Y)}{N \sum X^2 - (\sum X)^2}(X - \bar{X})$$

16. X 3 4 5 6 7 8 9 10 11

Y 4 3 5 6 8 7 9 9 11

a. Determine the correlation for the preceding scores.

b. Given the correlations and the computed mean for Y, predict the value of Y' for each X.

c. Calculate $\Sigma(Y - \bar{Y})^2$.

d. Calculate the unexplained variance.

e. Calculate the explained variance.

f. Calculate the coefficient of determination. Show that the square root of that value equals r.

17. A manager of a catering service found a correlation of 0.70 between the number of people at a party and the number of loaves of bread consumed.

a. For a party of 60 people, calculate the predicted number of loaves needed.

b. For a party of 35, calculate the predicted number of loaves needed.

c. What is the $s_{est\,y}$?

Number of People	Number of Loaves
$\bar{X} = 50$	$\bar{Y} = 5$
$s_x = 15$	$s_y = 1.2$

18. In a recent study, Thornton (1977) explored the relationship of marital happiness to the frequency of sexual intercourse and to the frequency of arguments. Twenty-eight married couples volunteered to monitor their daily frequency of sexual intercourse and arguments for 35 consecutive days, and then they indicated their perceived marital happiness using a 7-point scale ranging from very unhappy (1) to perfectly happy (7). Some of Thornton's results are summarized here.

	Marital Happiness	**Sexual Intercourse**	**Arguments**
Mean	5.32	13.46	6.15
s	1.66	7.32	4.19

Correlation between happiness and arguments $= -0.740$
Correlation between happiness and intercourse $= 0.705$

a. How happy would you predict a couple to be who reported having 10 arguments during the 35-day study period?

b. How happy would you predict a couple to be who reported having sexual intercourse one time each day during the 35-day study period?

c. A couple reporting that they are very unhappy (rating $= 1.0$) are most likely engaging in sexual intercourse how often?

d. What is the standard error of estimate for marital happiness when frequency of sexual intercourse is the predictor? What is the standard error of estimate when frequency of arguments is the predictor?

e. What proportion of the variability in ratings of marital happiness is accounted for by frequency of sexual intercourse? What proportion is accounted for by frequency of arguments?

f. What is the coefficient of nondetermination when marital happiness is predicted from frequency of sexual intercourse? What is the coefficient of nondetermination when marital happiness is predicted from frequency of arguments?

19. Refer to Statistics in Action 6.1. Recall that we calculated the mean, range, variance, and standard deviation of HRs for each of ten Type A subjects.

a. Prepare scatter diagrams and correlation matrices showing the relationship between and among the means, ranges, and standard deviations.

b. Superimpose a regression line on each of these scatter diagrams.

PART III

INFERENTIAL STATISTICS:
PARAMETRIC TESTS OF SIGNIFICANCE

10

Probability

10.1 AN INTRODUCTION TO PROBABILITY THEORY

In the past few chapters, we have been primarily concerned with the exposition of techniques employed by statisticians and scientists to describe and present data. Statisticians and scientists study *some* people and/or events, but they want their conclusions to hold for other people and/or events that they have *not* specifically tested. In other words, they want to generalize their results to an entire population even though they specifically tested only a small sample. Thus, scientists are not usually satisfied to report merely that the arithmetic mean of the drug group tested on variable X is higher or lower than the mean of the placebo group tested on this variable. They also want to make general statements such as, "The difference between the two groups is of such magnitude that we cannot reasonably ascribe it to chance variation. We may therefore conclude that the drug had an effect on the variable studied. More specifically, this effect was ... etc., etc."

The problem of chance variation is an important one. We all know that the variability of our data in the behavioral sciences engenders the risk of drawing an incorrect conclusion. Take a look at the following example.

From casual observations, Experimenter A hypothesizes that first-grade

BOX 10.1

THE GAMBLER'S FALLACY

Probability theory is the foundation stone of inferential statistics. Without it, our interpretation of data would progress little beyond sheer guesswork. Considering its importance, it is surprising that mistaken notions about probability pervade the thinking of many people. One is the "Gambler's Fallacy," illustrated in this excerpt from *Winning with Statistics*.

I'm Overdue for a Run of Luck

Famous last words! This one takes many forms and invades many fields. The gambler is tossing coins and loses four in a row. Reasoning that five losses in a row is exceedingly rare ($p = 0.031$, odds against $= 31.25 : 1$), he decides to increase the ante. "I'm due for a win," he proclaims confidently. Your favorite baseball player has gone 0 for 4. When he comes to bat for the fifth time, you exude confidence: "he's due for a hit." The opposing quarterback has just completed six consecutive passes against your team. You breathe a sigh of relief: "The next is bound to be incomplete or intercepted."

Although these examples are not all exactly the same, they have one thing in common—the belief that events have memories. It is as if the gambler is reasoning, "The coin will remember that it came up heads four times in a row and will try to balance out the 'law of averages' by coming up tails on the next toss." This is sheer nonsense. So long as the coin is "honest," it is just as likely to come up heads as tails on the next toss—or on any toss, for that matter. We speak of this condition as *independence*—the outcome of one trial has no effect on later trials. This is just another way of denying that coins or dice or cards or roulette wheels have memories.

It is somewhat different when dealing with activities involving behavior. Although a bat and ball have no memory, "turns at bat" are not always independent, particularly if they are against a pitcher of Tom Seaver's caliber. And your football team could have seven passes completed against it because of its porous defense. Nevertheless, it is incorrect to cite the "law of averages" as the reason for expecting something different on the next trial. The law of averages has no enforcement agency behind it, nor is there a Supreme Court to oversee the constitutionality of its "decisions." Indeed, the only thing it has in common with jurisprudence is its impartiality.

Source: Excerpted from R. P. Runyon, *Winning with Statistics*. Reading, Mass.: Addison-Wesley, 1977.

girls have higher IQ scores than first-grade boys, and administers an IQ test to four boys and four girls in a first-grade class. The mean of the girls is found to be higher: 110 to 103. Is Experimenter A justified in concluding that his or her hypothesis has been confirmed? The answer is obviously negative. Buy why? After all, there is a difference between the sample means, isn't there? Intuitively, we might argue that the variability of intelligence among first-graders is so great, and the *N* in the study so small, that *some* differences in the means are inevitable as a result of our selection procedures. The critical questions that must be answered by inferential statistics then become: (1) Is the apparent difference in intelligence among first-graders reliable? (i.e., will it appear regularly in repetitions of the study?) or (2) Is the difference the result of unsystematic factors that will vary from study to study, and thereby produce sets of differences without consistency?

A prime function of inferential statistics is to provide rigorous and logically sound procedures for answering these questions. As we shall see in this chapter and the next, *probability theory* provides the logical basis for deciding among all the various alternative interpretations of research data.

Probability theory is not so unfamiliar as many would think. Indeed, in everyday life we are constantly called upon to make probability judgments, although we may not recognize them as such. For example, let us suppose that, for various reasons, you are unprepared for today's class. You seriously consider not attending class. What are the factors that will influence your decision? Obviously, one consideration would be the likelihood that the instructor will detect your lack of preparation. If the risk is high, you decide not to attend class; if low, then you will attend.

Let us look at this example in slightly different terms. There are two alternative possibilities:

> Event A: Your lack of preparation *will* be detected.
> Event B: Your lack of preparation *will not* be detected.

There is uncertainty in this situation because more than one alternative is possible. Your decision whether or not to attend class will depend on the degree of assurance you associate with each of these alternatives. Thus, if you are fairly certain that the first alternative will prevail, you will decide not to attend class.

Suppose that your instructor frequently calls upon students to participate in class discussion. In fact, you have noted that most of the students are called upon in any given class session. This is an example of a situation in which a high degree of assurance is associated with the first alternative. Stated another way, the probability of Event A is higher than the probability of Event B. Thus, you decide not to attend class.

Although you have not used any formal probability laws in this example, you have actually made a judgment based on an *intuitive* use of probability.

You may have noted that many of the questions raised in the exercises began with, "What is the likelihood that . . . ?" These questions were in preparation for the formal discussion of probability occurring in this and the following chapters. However, before learning the elements of probability theory, you should understand one of the most important concepts in inferential statistics, that of *randomness*.

10.2 THE CONCEPT OF RANDOMNESS

Random Sampling: Samples selected in such a way that each sample of a given size has precisely the same probability of being selected.

You will recall that in discussing the role of inferential statistics we pointed out the fact that population parameters are rarely known or knowable. It is for this reason that we are usually forced to draw samples from a given population and estimate the parameters from the sample statistics. Obviously, we want to select these samples in such a way that they are representative of the populations from which they are drawn. One way to achieve representativeness is to employ simple **random sampling:** *selecting samples in such a way that each sample of a given size has precisely the same probability of being selected,* or, alternatively, *selecting the events in the sample such that each event is equally likely to be selected in a sample of a given size.*

Consider selecting samples of $N = 2$ from a population of five numbers: 0, 1, 2, 3, 4. If, for any reason, any number is more likely to be drawn than any other number, each sample would *not* have an equal probability of being drawn. For example, if for any reason the number 3 were twice as likely to be drawn as any other number, there would be a preponderance of samples containing the value of 3. Such sampling procedures are referred to as being **biased.** In the naturalistic type of study alluded to earlier, in

Bias: In sampling, when selections favor certain events or certain collections of events.

which our purpose is to describe certain characteristics of a population, the danger of bias is ever present. When we are interested in learning the characteristics of the general population on a given variable, we do not dare to select our sample from automobile registration lists or "at random" on a street corner in New York City. The dangers of generalizing to the general population from such biased samples should be obvious to you. Unless the condition of randomness is met, we may never know to what population we should generalize our results. Furthermore, with nonrandom samples we find that many of the rules of probability do not hold.

Moreover, the statistical tests presented in this text require *independent random sampling*. Two events are said to be independent if the selection of one has no effect upon the probability of selecting the other event. We can most readily grasp independence in terms of games of chance, assuming they are played honestly. Knowledge of the results of one toss of a coin, one throw of a die, one outcome of the roulette wheel, or one selection of a card from a well-shuffled deck (assuming replacement of the card after each selection) will not aid us one iota in our predictions of future outcomes.

When we are involved in conducting an experiment, we must concern ourselves with introducing randomness at two junctures of the study: *selecting* our subjects at random from the population of interest, and *assigning* these subjects at random to the experimental conditions.

It is beyond the scope of this text to delve deeply into sampling procedures, since that topic is a full course by itself. However, let us look at an illustration of the procedures by which we may achieve randomness in assigning subjects to experimental conditions.

Suppose you are interested in comparing three different methods of teaching reading readiness to preschool children. There are 87 subjects who are to be divided into 3 equal groups. The assignment of these subjects must be made in a random manner.

One method to achieve randomness would be to place each subject's name on a slip of paper. We shuffle these slips and then place them into three equal piles.

An alternative method would be to use the Table of Random Digits (Table E in the Table section of this book). Since the digits in this table have already been randomized, the effect of shuffling has been achieved. We assign to each of the 87 students a numeral from 01 to 87. We may start with any row or column of digits in Table E.

After we have selected 29 numerals that correspond to 29 different subjects, we have formed our first group. We continue until we have three groups, each consisting of 29 different subjects. For example, if we start with the fifteenth row and choose consecutive pairs of digits, we obtain the following subjects: 65, 48, 11, 76, 74, 17, and so on. If any numeral over 87 or any repeated numeral appears, we disregard it.

Finally, most present-day computers have a programmed function that generates random digits. If you have access to a computer, you will save much time by letting the computer do the selecting for you. This randomization function is at the heart of the many games that computers play.

The reason for the paramount importance of random procedures will become clear in this chapter and the next. Fundamentally, it is based on a fascinating fact of inferential statistics: *Each event may not be predictable when taken alone, but collections of random events can take on predictable forms*. The binomial distribution, which we shall discuss at greater length in Section 11.3, illustrates this fact. If we were to take, say, 20 unbiased coins and toss them into the air, we could not predict accurately the proportion that would land "heads." However, if we were to toss these 20 coins a great many times, record the number turning up heads on each trial, and construct a frequency distribution of outcomes in which the horizontal axis varies between no heads and all heads, the plot would take on a characteristic and predictable form known as the *binomial distribution* (see Figure 10.1). By employing the binomial model, we would be able to predict with considerable accuracy over a large number of trials the percentage of the time various outcomes will occur. What is perhaps more fascinating is the fact that the distribution of outcomes of this two-category variable more and more closely approximates the normal curve as N (the number of tosses of a single coin or the number of coins tossed at one time) becomes larger. Indeed, with large Ns we may use the normal curve to describe the probability of various outcomes of a binomial variable.

The same reasoning is true with respect to the normal-curve model. In the absence of any specific information, we might not be able to predict a person's status with respect to a given trait (intelligence, height, weight,

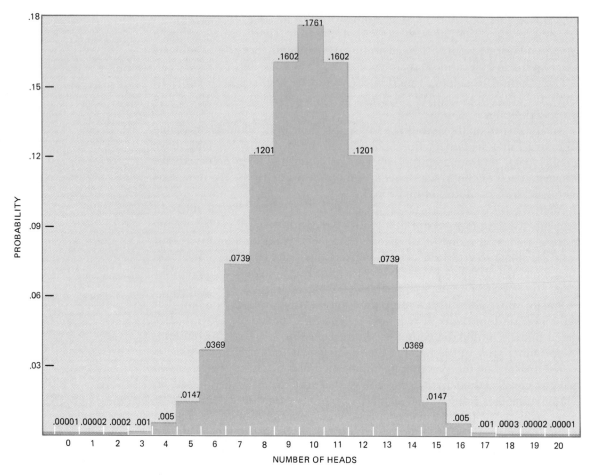

FIGURE 10.1 Probabilities of obtaining varying numbers of heads (from 0 to 20) on repeated tosses of an "honest" coin. Note how closely the histogram resembles the normal curve.

etc.). However, as we already know, frequency distributions of scores on these traits commonly take the form of the normal curve. Thus, we may predict the proportion of individuals scoring between specified score limits.

What is perhaps of more importance, from the point of view of inferential statistics, is the fact that distributions of sample statistics ($\overline{X}$, s, median, etc.) based on random sampling from a population also take on highly predictable forms. Chapter 11 deals with the concept of **sampling distributions,** which are theoretical probability distributions of a statistic that would result from drawing all possible samples of a given size from some population.

With this brief introduction to the concept of randomness, you are prepared to look at probability theory.

Sampling Distribution: A theoretical probability distribution of a statistic that would result from drawing all possible samples of a given size from some population.

10.3 APPROACHES TO PROBABILITY

Probability may be regarded as a theory that is concerned with the possible outcomes of experiments. The experiments must be potentially repetitive; that is, we must be able to repeat them under similar conditions. It must be possible to enumerate every outcome that can occur, and we must be able to state the expected relative frequencies of these outcomes.

It is the method of assigning relative frequencies to each of the possible outcomes that distinguishes the classical from the empirical approach to probability theory.

Probability: A theory concerned with the possible outcomes of experiments.

Classical Approach to Probability

The theory of probability has always been closely associated with games of chance. For example, suppose that we want to know the probability that a single card selected from a 52-card deck will be an ace of spades. There are 52 possible outcomes. We assume an ideal situation in which we expect that each outcome is equally likely to occur. Thus, the probability of selecting an ace of spades is $\frac{1}{52}$. This kind of reasoning has led to the following classical definition of probability:

$$p(A) = \frac{\text{Number of outcomes favoring event } A}{\text{Total no. of outcomes (favoring } A + \text{not favoring } A)} \quad (10.1)$$

Note that probability is defined as a proportion (p). The most important point in the classical definition of probability is the assumption of an *ideal* situation in which the structure of the population is known; that is, the total number of possible outcomes (N) is known. The expected relative frequency of each of these outcomes is arrived at by deductive reasoning. Thus, the probability of an event is interpreted as a theoretical (or an idealized) relative frequency of the event. In the preceding example, the total number of possible outcomes was 52 (all cards in the deck), and each outcome was assumed to have an equal likelihood of occurrence. Thus, $p(\text{ace of spades}) = \frac{1}{52}$; $p(\text{king of hearts}) = \frac{1}{52}$, and so on.

Empirical Approach to Probability

Although it is usually easy to assign expected relative frequencies to the possible outcomes of games of chance, we cannot do this for most real-life experiments. In actual situations, expected relative frequencies are assigned on the basis of empirical findings. Thus, we may not know the exact proportion of students in a university who have blue eyes, but we may study a random sample of students and estimate the proportion who will have blue eyes. Once we have arrived at an estimate, we may employ classical probability theory to answer questions such as, What is the probability that in a sample of ten students, drawn at random from the student body, three or more will be blue-eyed? Or, what is the probability that student Jones, drawn at random from that student body, will have blue eyes?

If, in a random sample of 100 students, we found that 30 had blue eyes, we could estimate that the proportion of blue-eyed students in the university was 0.30 by employing Formula (10.1):

$$p(\text{blue-eyed}) = \frac{30}{100} = 0.30$$

Thus, the probability is 0.30 that student Jones will have blue eyes. [*Note:* This represents an *empirical* probability; that is, the expected relative frequency was assigned on the basis of empirical findings.]

Although it is easy to assign expected relative frequencies to the possible outcomes of games of chance, we cannot do this for most real-life experiments. Take the gender of an about-to-be-born child. What is the probability that it will be a girl? On the surface, the answer would appear to be easy. Hypothetically, the birth of a boy or girl would appear to be equally likely, 0.50 in both cases. However, such is not the case. In the United States, the proportion of annual male births has been exceptionally stable for many years—0.5139 for white and 0.5071 for black (see Table 10.1).

A gambler who made his livelihood on taking bets on the gender of children about to be born could do quite well, over the long run, by giving even odds that the child will be a boy. If he bet only on white babies, on every 10,000 bets, the gambler could expect to win, on the average, 5139 times and lose 4861 times.

The fundamental feature of empirical probabilities is that they are based on actual measurements rather than on theoretical proportions. As a matter of fact, there is usually little or no basis for assigning theoretical probabilities to most of the situations confronted by the student of behavior: for example, the probability that a person will require treatment for a disorder at some time in his or her life, the probability that a convicted felon will return to crime, or the probability that a child will be born with a congenital defect. Probabilities such as these must be obtained empirically and are always subject to revision in the light of additional data.

Subjective Approaches to Probability

There are many occasions when we lack the objective data for estimating probabilities. Nevertheless, we may have strong feelings that we term "a hunch," "common sense," or an intuition. The clinician may say, "I can't tell you precisely why I feel this way, but I believe that client A is at high risk for suicide." We should not dismiss these subjective probabilities out of hand. Even though subjective probabilities cannot, by their nature, be documented and substantiated, they may nevertheless arise from a lifetime of observation and assessment of subtle cues. Indeed, it is likely that any important decision we have made in life includes subjective probabilities

TABLE 10.1   Proportion of Male Births, by Race, in the United States over the 15-Year Period 1970–1984

Year	White	Black
1970	0.5143	0.5076
1971	0.5136	0.5069
1972	0.5139	0.5059
1973	0.5138	0.5068
1974	0.5143	0.5074
1975	0.5143	0.5074
1976	0.5141	0.5067
1977	0.5141	0.5064
1978	0.5141	0.5069
1979	0.5138	0.5072
1980	0.5141	0.5072
1981	0.5138	0.5067
1982	0.5131	0.5081
1983	0.5139	0.5074
1984	0.5131	0.5076
Mean	0.5139	0.5071
Standard deviation	0.0004	0.0005

as a basic ingredient. For this reason, we accept the notion of subjective probabilities. Once made, we expect them to follow the same rules as probabilities obtained by either the classical or the empirical approach.

10.4 FORMAL PROPERTIES OF PROBABILITY

Probabilities Vary between 0 and 1.00

From the classical definition of probability, p is always between 0 and 1, inclusively. If an event is certain to occur, its probability is 1; if it is certain not to occur, its probability is 0. For example, the probability of drawing the ace of spades from an ordinary deck of 52 playing cards is $\frac{1}{52}$. The probability of drawing a *red* ace of spades is zero, since there are no events favoring this result. If all events favor a result (e.g., drawing a card with *some* marking on it), $p = 1$. Thus, for any given event, say A, $0 \leq p(A) \leq 1.00$, in which the symbol $\leq$ means "less than or equal to."[*]

[*] The symbol $\geq$ means "greater than or equal to."

Expressing Probability

In addition to expressing probability as a proportion, several other ways are often employed. It is sometimes convenient to express probability as a *percentage* or as the *number of chances in 100*.

To illustrate: If the probability of an event is 0.05, we expect this event to occur 5% of the time, or *the chances that this event will occur* are 5 in 100. This same probability may be expressed by saying that the odds are 95 to 5 *against* the event occurring, or 19 to 1 against it.

Note that when expressing probability as the *odds against* the occurrence of an event, we use the following formula:

Odds against Event A

$$= \text{(Total no. of outcomes} - \text{No. favoring A)} \; to \; \text{No. favoring A} \quad (10.2)$$

Thus, if $p(A) = 0.01$, the *odds against* the occurrence of Event A are 99 to 1.

Sample Space, Event, and Complex Experiments

So far in this chapter, we have seen that probability plays an extremely important role in our personal and professional lives. Up to this point, we have restricted our outlook to simple statistical experiments, directing our attention to finding the probability of a single outcome like selecting the ace of spades from a deck of playing cards or giving birth to a male child. In real life, our inquiry typically extends into far more complex questions. For example, if ten patients are under psychotherapeutic treatment for an anxiety disorder, what are the probabilities that all ten, or 9, or 8 . . . show improvement within some specified period? Will a target person's physical attractiveness affect the probability that help will be offered by a bystander? Or, will knowledge of a person's mood alter our assessment of that person's recollection of pleasant versus unpleasant experiences?

In dealing with complex experiments, we find it is useful to introduce the concept of **sample space.** When dealing with simple experiments, we refer to the most elementary unit as an outcome. For example, in tossing a single die, the sample space consists of the outcomes: 1, 2, 3, 4, 5, 6. All possible outcomes constitute the sample space. If we classify the results of psychotherapy into two different categories—unimproved and improved—each of these categories constitutes an outcome.

Sample Space: All possible outcomes of an experiment.

When these outcomes are combined into various subsets or collections, we have defined an event. Thus, with our patients under psychotherapy, an event might be "all patients improved," or "six improved, four unimproved," or "two improved, eight unimproved." With the die, an event may be an odd number (a collection of three outcomes), a six (a collection of

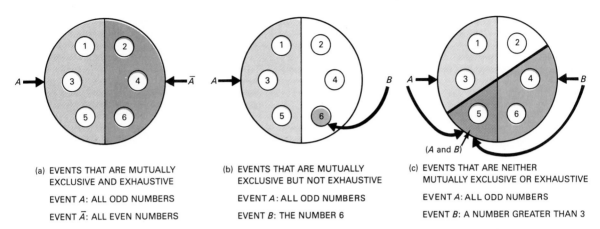

(a) EVENTS THAT ARE MUTUALLY
    EXCLUSIVE AND EXHAUSTIVE

EVENT A: ALL ODD NUMBERS

EVENT Ā: ALL EVEN NUMBERS

(b) EVENTS THAT ARE MUTUALLY
    EXCLUSIVE BUT NOT EXHAUSTIVE

EVENT A: ALL ODD NUMBERS

EVENT B: THE NUMBER 6

(c) EVENTS THAT ARE NEITHER
    MUTUALLY EXCLUSIVE OR EXHAUSTIVE

EVENT A: ALL ODD NUMBERS

EVENT B: A NUMBER GREATER THAN 3

FIGURE 10.2 Various outcomes in the sample space of a single die to yield the events of (a), (b), and (c).

one outcome), or a number greater than three (a collection of three outcomes). Suppose we call event A: an odd number. The complement of Event A (symbolized by $\overline{A}$ and read not A) consists of all outcomes not included in A. When the two events A and $\overline{A}$ exhaust all possible outcomes, $p(A) + p(\overline{A}) = 1.00$. The two events are said to be **exhaustive.** In addition, if two events cannot occur simultaneously, they are said to be **mutually exclusive.** In the example concerning a die, Events A and $\overline{A}$ are mutually exclusive since the occurrence of A on a specific trial excludes the possibility of $\overline{A}$ on the same trial.

Two useful techniques have been devised for diagramming various concepts of probability—the *Venn diagram* and the *tree diagram*. The Venn diagram is illustrated in Figure 10.2.

The tree diagram is of greatest value when the events of interest occur in stages. To illustrate, suppose we want to diagram the possible results of assessing, at three different stages, the effects of treating a single patient for an anxiety disorder. At each stage, there are two mutually exclusive and exhaustive outcomes; unimproved versus improved. The tree diagram permits us to visually display all possible events from improvement shown at all stages to no improvement shown at any stage. We later illustrate the use of the tree diagram for calculating the probabilities of various events, but for the moment, note the simplicity and utility of using it to display events visually (Figure 10.3).

Each fork in a tree diagram shows a specific outcome that can occur at each stage. For example, at stage 1 the patient can improve (upper branch) or be unimproved (lower branch). Each of these outcomes can serve as the fork for the next two possible outcomes. Thus, a patient who improves at the first stage may either improve or show no improvement at the second stage. If the patient improves again, the event that describes this result is improved. With three different stages and two outcomes at each stage, a

Exhaustive: Two or more events are said to be exhaustive if they exhaust all possible outcomes. Symbolically, p(A or B or ...) = 1.00.

Mutually Exclusive: Events A and B are said to be mutually exclusive if they cannot occur simultaneously.

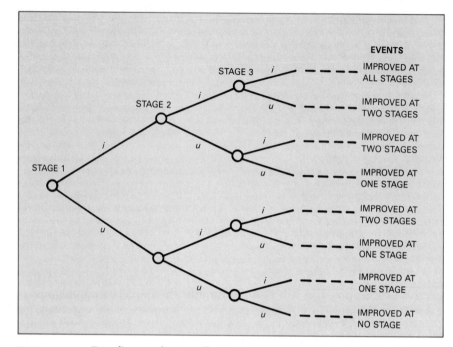

EVENTS

STAGE 3 — *i* — — — — IMPROVED AT
ALL STAGES

STAGE 2 — *u* — — — — IMPROVED AT
TWO STAGES

— *i* — — — — IMPROVED AT
TWO STAGES

STAGE 1 — *u* — — — — IMPROVED AT
ONE STAGE

— *i* — — — — IMPROVED AT
TWO STAGES

— *u* — — — — IMPROVED AT
ONE STAGE

— *i* — — — — IMPROVED AT
ONE STAGE

— *u* — — — — IMPROVED AT
NO STAGE

FIGURE 10.3 Tree diagram showing all possible consequences of treating a single patient, over three stages, for an anxiety disorder.

total of eight different branches are produced. Each end branch represents an event. To see how this works, read from left to right. The top branch at the far right represents improvement at all stages. In contrast, the bottom branch (*u, u, u*) represents unimprovement at each stage in the treatment.

10.5 ADDITION RULE

When we know the sample space of an experiment, it is possible to identify any number of different events for purposes of probability analysis. To illustrate, we may raise such questions as

1. What is the probability of obtaining one event *or* another, for example, drawing a queen *or* a club from a deck of playing cards?
2. What is the probability of obtaining two events simultaneously, for example, selecting a queen *and* a club from a deck of playing cards?

To answer the first question, we must make use of the addition rule; and, for the second, we use the multiplication rule. We shall examine the addition rule in this section and the multiplication rule in Section 10.6.

When Events Are Not Mutually Exclusive

Suppose that, in an effort to obtain data on current reasons for seeking professional help, a questionnaire was sent out to administrators at various mental health clinics throughout the country. One part of the questionnaire dealt with the abuse of drugs and alcohol among those receiving care at the clinics. The results of the questionnaires showed that out of 5900 patients, 354 abused alcohol and 236 abused drugs; of these (the abusers of alcohol and drugs) 118 abused both. Let us define Event A as the abuse of alcohol and Event B as the abuse of drugs.

Based on the replies, we can estimate the probability of each event from the sample:

$$p(A) = \frac{354}{5900} = 0.06$$

$$p(B) = \frac{236}{5900} = 0.04$$

Now, if we wished to know the probability that a given patient was either an alcohol or drug abuser, we might be tempted to add together the number of patients abusing alcohol and the number abusing drugs, and divide by N to obtain: $p(A \text{ or } B) = (354 + 236)/5900 = 0.10$. However, this probability does not take into account the 118 people who are counted twice—once as alcohol abusers and once as drug abusers. In other words, the two categories are not mutually exclusive. This is shown as the overlapping area in the Venn diagram in Figure 10.4.

To determine the probability of Event A or Event B, we must subtract the 118 cases that overlap both categories. This leads to the general case of the addition rule. It is called the general case because it applies equally to mutually exclusive and non-mutually exclusive categories:

$$p(A \text{ or } B) = p(A) + p(B) - p(A \text{ and } B) \tag{10.3}$$

where p (A and B) represents the probability associated with the overlapping events.

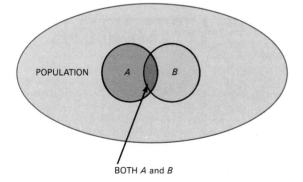

FIGURE 10.4 Venn diagram showing that the two categories, alcohol abuse and drug abuse, are not mutually exclusive. To obtain $p(A \text{ or } B)$, we must subtract out the area of overlap.

POPULATION   *A*   *B*

BOTH *A* and *B*

In the present example, $p(A \text{ or } B) = 354/5900 + 236/5900 - 118/5900 = 0.08$. Thus, according to this survey, the probability is 0.08 that a given individual seeking help at a mental health clinic is either an alcohol abuser or a drug abuser (or both).

Overlapping categories is also characteristic of many games of chance, for example, roulette or cards. To illustrate, if we want to know the probability of selecting either a heart (to fill a flush) or a jack (to fill a straight), we must take into account the fact that the jack of hearts overlaps both events. If we let Event A equal the probability of a heart, $p(A) = 13/52$. The probability of Event B (a jack) is 4/52. However, the probability of both occurring (a jack of hearts) is 1/52. Therefore, $p(A \text{ or } B) = 13/52 + 4/52 - 1/52 = 16/52 = 0.31$.

Mutually Exclusive Events

By definition, when events are mutually exclusive, there is no overlapping of the categories. Since Event A and Event B cannot occur together, the probability of Event A and Event B is 0; that is, $p(A \text{ and } B) = 0$.

Therefore, for mutually exclusive events, the last term in Formula (10.3) reduces to zero. Thus, the addition rule becomes

$$p(A \text{ or } B) = p(A) + p(B) \qquad (10.4)$$

where the events are mutually exclusive.

To illustrate, in Exercise 26 of Chapter 4, we presented census figures on the size of U.S. families of Spanish origin. These figures are reproduced in Table 10.2

What is the probability that a given family of Spanish origin has either two or three members? Using Formula (10.4), we find $p(2 \text{ or } 3) = p(2) + p(3) = 0.239 + 0.230 = 0.469$.

What is the probability that such a family will number 6 or more? $p(6 \text{ or } 7 \text{ or more}) = 0.079 + 0.078 = 0.157$.

Formula (10.4) can be extended to include any number of mutually exclusive events. Thus

$$p(A \text{ or } B \text{ or } \ldots Z) = p(A) + p(B) + \cdots + p(Z)$$

In Chapters 11 and 17, we shall be dealing with problems based on *dichotomous*, yes-no, or *two-category* populations, in which the events in question not only are mutually exclusive, but are *exhaustive*. For example, in families of Spanish origin, what is the probability of drawing either a family size equal to or greater than 5, or less than 5? Not only is it impossible to obtain both events simultaneously (i.e., they are mutually exclusive), but there is *no possible outcome other than* a family size equal to or greater than 5 or a family size less than 5. In the case of *mutually exclusive* and *exhaustive events*, we arrive at the very useful formulation

$$p(A) + p(B) = 1.00 \qquad (10.5)$$

TABLE 10.2 Size of U.S. Families of Spanish Origin in 1977

Size	Number (in Thousands)	p
2	662	0.239
3	636	0.230
4	625	0.226
5	408	0.148
6	218	0.079
7 or more persons	216	0.078

Source: U.S. Bureau of Census, *Current Population Reports*, Series P-20, no. 339, U.S. Government Printing Office.

In treating dichotomous populations, we commonly employ the two symbols P and Q to represent, respectively, the probability of the occurrence of an event and the probability of the nonoccurrence of an event. Thus, if we are flipping a single coin, we can let P represent the probability of occurrence of a head and Q the probability of the nonoccurrence of a head (i.e., the occurrence of a tail). Note that Q represents not-P($\bar{P}$). These considerations lead to three useful formulations:

$$P + Q = 1.00 \qquad (10.6)$$

$$P = 1.00 - Q \qquad (10.7)$$

$$Q = 1.00 - P \qquad (10.8)$$

when the events are *mutually exclusive and exhaustive.*

10.6 THE MULTIPLICATION RULE

In the preceding section, we were concerned with determining the probability of obtaining one event or another based on a *single* draw (or trial) from a population. In statistical inference, we are often faced with the problem of ascertaining the probability of the joint or successive occurrence of two or more events when more than one draw or trial is involved. For example, what is the probability that we shall draw a diamond and a heart on two successive draws from a deck of playing cards? Or, based on the results of the study by Benson et al. (Case Example 2.2), what is the probability that five out of five male subjects will engage in helping behavior (mailing the envelope containing the application or delivering it to an airport ticket counter)? Often our question will take on a somewhat modified form. If we assume an attractive female applicant, what is the probability that five out of five male subjects will engage in helping behavior? This last question is concerned with conditional probabilities. In this case, we are asking if the probability of obtaining helping behavior is conditional on the attractiveness of the applicant. In this section, we examine joint, marginal, and conditional probabilities as well as the multiplication rule for independent and nonindependent events.

Joint, Marginal, and Conditional Probabilities

To illustrate joint, marginal, and conditional probabilities, let's return to the data presented in Case Example 2.2 (Table 10.3).

If we divide each of the cell frequencies and the marginal (row and column) totals by N, we obtain a joint probability (Table 10.4). Note that the table provides direct answers to such questions as "What is the probability that help was provided to an attractive applicant?"

Joint Probabilities   Each cell in Table 10.4 shows the joint probability associated with the column and row variables. For example, the joint probability that the applicant was both attractive (Event A) and helped (Event B) is

$$p(\text{A and B}) = \frac{52}{220} = 0.236$$

However, the joint probability of an applicant being unattractive (Event $\overline{\text{A}}$) and helped (Event B) is

$$p(\overline{\text{A}} \text{ and B}) = \frac{35}{220} = 0.159$$

Also, the joint probability of an applicant being attractive (Event A) and not helped (Event $\overline{\text{B}}$) is

$$p(\text{A and } \overline{\text{B}}) = \frac{62}{220} = 0.282$$

TABLE 10.3   Number Helping when Applicant is an Attractive or Unattractive Female (Whites and Blacks Combined) and Subject Is Male

Helping response	Characteristics of Target		Row Totals
	Attractive	Unattractive	
Helped	52	35	87
Did not help	62	71	133
Column totals	114	106	220

TABLE 10.4   Joint Probability Table of Helping Behavior when Applicant Was either Attractive or Unattractive*

Helping Response	Attractive (A)	Unattractive ($\overline{A}$)	Marginal Probability
Helped (B)	0.236 (52/220)	0.159 (35/220)	0.395 (87/220)
Did not help ($\overline{B}$)	0.282 (62/220)	0.323 (71/220)	0.605 (133/220)
Marginal probability	0.518 (114/220)	0.482 (106/220)	1.000 (220/220)

* Cell and marginal frequencies divided by total sample size are shown in parentheses.

Marginal Probabilities   Note that each marginal probability represents a simple probability of an event and is *not* conditional on other events. For this reason, marginal probabilities are also referred to as unconditional probabilities. Thus, in Table 10.4, the right-hand or row marginals show the simple probability of a person being helped or not helped without regard to whether or not she is attractive. Thus, the unconditional probability of being helped is 0.395, whereas the unconditional probability of not being helped is 0.605.

Similarly, the column marginals show the probability that the applicant was attractive (0.518) or unattractive (0.482), whether or not she was helped.

Conditional Probabilities   When the information we have about events is limited to the marginal probabilities, our best prediction concerning the probability of a given event is similarly restricted to these marginal probabilities. Thus, if we know only that a male entered the phone booth that contained a "lost" job application, our best estimate of the probability that he will help is 0.395 and that he will not help is 0.605. But what if we are given some additional information, such as "The applicant was attractive?" Notice that the sample space is now limited to attractive applicants, rather than to all applicants, since we now have more information than we had before. Will this information permit us to "fine tune" our assessment of the probability that the male entering the phone booth will engage in helping behavior? The answer is "Yes" if helping behavior is conditional on the attractiveness of the applicant.

To illustrate, Table 10.4 provides three probabilities for each helping response—the marginal probability that help will be provided, the joint probability that the applicant is attractive and helped, and the joint probability that the applicant is attractive and not helped. Now suppose we know in advance that the applicant is attractive. Will this additional information provide a basis for a better assessment of the probability that she will be helped? Let's see.

Conditional Probability:
The probability of an event, given that another event has occurred. Represented symbolically as $p(A|B)$: the probability of A given that B has occurred.

To find the **conditional probability** that the applicant will receive help, we divide the joint probability that she is attractive and helped $p(A \text{ and } B)$ by the marginal probability that she is attractive $p(A)$. Thus, in the present example

$$p(B|A) = \frac{p(A \text{ and } B)}{p(A)} = \frac{0.236}{0.518}$$

$$= 0.456$$

where $p(B|A)$ is the conditional probability of Event B given that Event A has occurred. Similarly

$$p(A|B) = \frac{p(A \text{ and } B)}{p(B)}$$

where $p(A|B)$ is the conditional probability of Event A given that Event B has occurred.

Note that, knowing only the marginal probability, we would have assessed the applicant's chance of being helped as 0.395. Knowing that she is attractive permitted us to raise our assessment of the probability to 0.456.

Let's look at one additional example. Knowing that an applicant is unattractive, what is our assessment of the probability of her not being helped, that is, of $p(\overline{B}|\overline{A})$?

$$p(\overline{B}|\overline{A}) = \frac{p(\overline{A} \text{ and } \overline{B})}{p(\overline{A})} = \frac{0.323}{0.482}$$

$$= 0.670$$

Using only the marginal probabilities, we would have estimated the probability of any applicant not being helped as 0.605. Taking into account our knowledge of her unattractiveness, we were able to increase the probability assessment to 0.67.

Table 10.5 summarizes the conditional probabilities derived from Table 10.4

Note that the conditional probabilities shown in the two columns at the right relate to the probability of the applicant being attractive (A) and unattractive ($\overline{A}$) when the status of helping is known. Thus, we see that the probability of not being attractive when help has not been received $p(\overline{A}|\overline{B})$ is 0.534.

Similarly, the two rows at the bottom of the table show the probabilities of the applicant receiving help (B) or not receiving help ($\overline{B}$) when the status of her attractiveness is known. Thus, the probability that an attractive person receives help $p(B|A)$ is 0.456.

TABLE 10.5 Joint and Conditional Probability Table of Helping Behavior when the Applicant Was either Attractive or Unattractive. The Conditional Probabilities Are Calculated by Dividing the Joint Probability within Each Cell by its Marginal Probability

Helping Response	Attractive (A)	Unattractive (Ā)	Marginal Probability	Conditional Probability
Helped (B)	0.236	0.159	0.395	$p(A\|B)$ $p(\bar{A}\|B)$
				0.597 0.403
Did not help (B̄)	0.282	0.323	0.605	$p(A\|\bar{B})$ $p(\bar{A}\|\bar{B})$
				0.466 0.534
Marginal probability	0.518	0.482	1.000	
Conditional probability	$p(B\|A)$ 0.456	$p(B\|\bar{A})$ 0.330		
	$p(\bar{B}\|A)$ 0.544	$p(\bar{B}\|\bar{A})$ 0.670		

The Multiplication Rule for Independent Events

Consider the following conceptual experiment. You toss a single coin into the air and a head appears. Assuming an ideal coin, the probability of a head is ½ and the probability of a tail is ½. Now toss the coin a second time. Does the outcome of the first toss in any way affect the outcome of the second toss? If it does not, the two outcomes are said to be **independent.** Since we have assumed an ideal coin (i.e., it is balanced, will not stand on end, is not motivated to change its behavior, etc.), we may assume that the two outcomes are independent, so that the probability of obtaining a head remains ½, as does the probability of obtaining a tail. When outcomes or events are independent, the multiplication rule states:

Independence: The condition that exists when the occurrence of a given event will not affect the probability of the occurrence of another event.

The probability of the simultaneous or successive occurrence of two events is the product of the separate probabilities of each event.

In symbolic form,

$$p(A \text{ and } B) = p(A)p(B) \qquad (10.9)$$

Suppose we toss a single coin on three successive occasions. What is the probability of obtaining the event "all heads"? To obtain this event, *all three outcomes must be a head.* Thus

$$p(H, H, \text{ and } H) = p(H)p(H)p(H)$$

$$= (½)(½)(½)$$

$$= ⅛ \text{ or } 0.125$$

Sampling with replacement is an example of independent events. Suppose we draw a single card from a deck of playing cards and obtain a king of hearts. The probability of this outcome is $1/52 = 0.019$. If we return the card to the deck, shuffle the cards well, and make a second selection, what is the probability of selecting the king of hearts again? It remains $1/52$. When sampling with replacement, what is the probability of selecting the king of hearts twice in succession? Using the multiplication rule for independent events, we obtain $p(KH \text{ and } KH) = (1/52)(1/52) = 1/2704$ or 0.00037.

The Multiplication Rule for Nonindependent (Dependent) Events

The multiplication rule for dependent events can most readily be grasped by contrasting sampling with replacement with sampling without replacement. Imagine that we were to make two successive draws from a deck of playing cards. What is the probability that we obtain two kings?

If we use sampling with replacement, the two events are independent. Since the probability of selecting a king is $4/52$, the probability of drawing two consecutive kings $p(K \text{ and } K)$ is $(4/52)(4/52) = 0.0059$.

However, if we use sampling without replacement, the events are not independent. If we select a king on the first draw, there will be only three kings left in a deck containing 51 cards. In other words, the results of the first draw influence the possible consequences of the second draw. In fact, the conditional probability of selecting a king on the second draw assuming that a king has been selected on the first draw $p(K|K)$ is $3/51 = 0.059$.

For nonindependent or dependent events, the multiplication rule becomes

> Given two events A and B, the probability of obtaining both A and B jointly is the product of the probability of obtaining one of these events times the conditional probability of obtaining one event, given that the other event has occurred.

Stated symbolically,

$$p(A \text{ and } B) = p(A)p(B/A) = p(B)p(A|B) \qquad (10.10)$$

In the present example, the probability of selecting a king on the first draw $p(K)$ is equal to $4/52$. The probability of selecting a king on the second draw, given a king drawn on the first, is $3/51$. Thus, when using sampling without replacement, the probability of selecting two consecutive kings is

$$p(K \text{ and } K) = p(K)p(K|K)$$

$$= (4/52)(3/51)$$

$$= 0.0045$$

Figure 10.5 is a tree diagram of this statistical experiment that illustrates the calculation of the probability of all possible events.

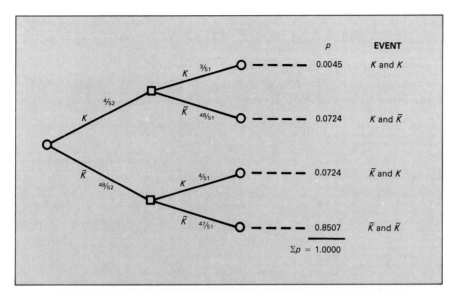

FIGURE 10.5 Tree diagram of the statistical experiment involving two draws, without replacement, from a deck of playing cards. The event of interest is the probability of selecting two consecutive kings.

Note that we can calculate the probability of each event by successively multiplying the probability associated with each branch by the probability associated with connecting branches. Thus, the probability of selecting two kings is found by multiplying the probabilities of the two K branches $(\tfrac{4}{52})(\tfrac{3}{51})$. Similarly, the two $\bar{K}$ branches provide the basis for calculating the selection of two nonkings on successive draws.

Figure 10.6 shows the tree diagram for calculating the conditional probabilities of the study concerned with physical attractiveness of the target and the helping behavior by the subjects.

10.7 PROBABILITY AND CONTINUOUS VARIABLES

Up to this point we have considered probability in terms of the expected relative frequency of an event. In fact, as we recall, probability was defined in terms of frequency and expressed as the following proportion [Formula (10.1)]:

$$p(A) = \frac{\text{No. outcomes favoring Event A}}{\text{Total no. outcomes}}$$

However, this definition presents a problem when we are dealing with continuous variables. As we pointed out in Section 3.7, it is generally

STATISTICS IN ACTION 10.1

The perceptual uncertainty of having slept: Calculating joint, marginal, and conditional probabilities*

Upon arising in the morning, how often have you been asked the question, "How did you sleep last night?"? Did you have any difficulty responding? How about the query, "How many times did you awake during the course of the night?"? How well do you think you could reply to that question? Perhaps you recall Exercise 27 in Chapter 8, in which ten subjects were awakened during the course of the night by the ring of a telephone. Each subject was asked if she or he had been awake when the telephone rang. The results are summarized in the following 2 × 2 table.

		Subject's Verbal Report		
		Awake	**Asleep**	**Totals**
True state of consciousness	Awake	200 (correct)	4 (incorrect)	204
	Asleep	161 (incorrect)	214 (correct)	375
Totals		361	218	579

Now examine the data carefully. Note that in 204 of the trials, the subjects were actually awake, and in 375 trials, they were asleep. How accurate were the subjects in reporting their states of consciousness? Note that the diagonal cells from the upper left to the lower right represent correct reports. Their sum is 200 + 214 = 414. Since there were a total of 579 trials, the proportion of correct responses was 414/579 = 0.715. In the absence of any other information, we could say that, for this sample, the empirical probability of a correct assessment by the subjects of their state of consciousness was 0.715.

* *Source:* From D. E. Sewich (1984), "The Perceptual Uncertainty of Having Slept," *Psychophysiology,* **21,** 243–259.

advisable to present frequency in terms of areas under a curve when we are dealing with continuous variables. Thus, for continuous variables, we may express probability as the following proportion:

$$p = \frac{\text{Area under portions of a curve}}{\text{Total area under the curve}} \qquad (10.11)$$

But note that we do have additional information. Looking across the first row, we see that when the subjects were awake, they were correct in judging their state of consciousness in 200 out of 204 trials. Thus, given that a subject was awake, the probability of an accurate appraisal of state of consciousness was 200/204 = 0.980. In other words, the appraisal was almost always accurate. But look what happened on the trials when the subject was actually asleep (second row across). The probability of a correct judgment fell to 214/375 = 0.571. The subject was incorrect almost 43% of the time! Thus, it appears that there is no simple answer to the question, "How well did you sleep last night?" The answer depends on how often your sleep was disturbed, whether or not you were asleep when the disturbance occurred, and how accurately you judged your state of consciousness prior to the disturbance.

The following tables summarize the joint and conditional probabilities for these data.

To find the conditional probability of the subject reporting being awake or asleep depending on his or her true state of consciousness, you divide the proportion in each cell by its corresponding right-hand marginal. Thus, the probability of the subject reporting awake when actually awake is 0.345/0.352 = 0.980. In contrast, the probability of reporting asleep when actually asleep is 0.370/0.648 = 0.571. The following table summarizes these conditional probabilities.

Joint Probability Table of Judging Sleep when Subject Was either Awake or Asleep

		Subject's Verbal Report		
		Awake	**Asleep**	**Totals**
True state of consciousness	Awake	0.345 (correct) (200/579)	0.007 (incorrect) (4/579)	0.352 (204/579
	Asleep	0.278 (incorrect) (161/579)	0.370 (correct) (214/579)	0.648 (375/579)
Totals		0.623 (361/579)	0.377 (218/579)	1.000

Since the total area in a probability distribution is equal to 1.00, we define p as the proportion of total area under portions of a curve.

Chapters 11 through 15 employ the standard normal curve as the probability model. Let's examine the probability area relationship in terms of this model.

**Probability Table of Subjects' Verbal Reports Conditional on Knowing
True State of Consciousness of Subjects**

		Subject's Verbal Report		
		Awake	**Asleep**	**Totals**
True state of consciousness	Awake	0.980 (correct)	0.020 (incorrect)	1.000
	Asleep	0.429 (incorrect)	0.571 (correct)	1.000

Finally, to find the conditional probability of the true state of consciousness when the subjects' verbal reports are known, divide the joint probability in each cell by its corresponding column marginal probability. Thus, the probability that a subject was awake when the verbal report indicated asleep equals 0.007/0.377 = 0.019. In contrast, the probability was a high 0.446 that the subject was asleep when he or she perceived his or her state of consciousness as awake (0.278/0.623 = 0.446). The following table summarizes these conditional probabilities.

**Probability Table of True State of Consciousness Conditional on
Knowing the Verbal Reports of Subjects.**

		Subject's Verbal Report	
		Awake	**Asleep**
True state of consciousness	Awake	0.554 (correct)	0.019 (incorrect)
	Asleep	0.446 (incorrect)	0.981 (correct)
Totals		1.000	1.000

a. In Statistics in Action 2.1 (Anas et al., 1981), we looked at the frequency of hospitalization versus nonhospitalization of children who had ingested substances containing hydrocarbons. Referring to the frequency table, prepare a joint probability table of substances ingested and frequency of hospitalization. Because of the small Ns in some categories, carry work to four decimal places in order to reduce rounding errors.

b. Using the same data, prepare a table showing the probability of hospitalization (four places) conditional on the substance ingested.

c. Using the same data, prepare a table showing the probability that various substances were ingested conditional on the knowledge of the hospitalization status of the child.

d. Answer the following: Knowing the child was hospitalized, what substance was most likely involved? What was least likely? Knowing the substance ingested, which is most likely to lead to hospitalization? Which is least likely?

e. Draw a tree diagram showing the calculation of the probability of all possible events conditional on the probability of ingesting each substance.

ANSWERS

a. Joint Probability Table of Children Hospitalized and Not Hospitalized Following Ingestion of Substances Containing Hydrocarbons

Substance Ingested	Not Hospitalized Probability	Hospitalized Probability	Row Totals
Cleaning fluids	0.0253	0.0063	0.0316
Furniture polishes	0.3284	0.0505	0.3789
Gasoline	0.1347	0.0295	0.1642
Kerosene	0.0758	0.0126	0.0884
Lighter fluid	0.1179	0.0242	0.1421
Paint thinner	0.0926	0.0242	0.1168
Other	0.0674	0.0105	0.0779
Column totals	0.8421	0.1579	1.000

b. Probability Table of Children Hospitalized and Not Hospitalized Conditional on Knowing Each Substance Ingested

Substance Ingested	Not Hospitalized Probability	Hospitalized Probability	Row Totals
Cleaning fluids	0.8006	0.1994	1.0000
Furniture polishes	0.8667	0.1333	1.0000
Gasoline	0.8203	0.1797	1.0000
Kerosene	0.8575	0.1425	1.0000
Lighter fluid	0.8297	0.1703	1.0000
Paint thinner	0.7928	0.2072	1.0000
Other	0.8652	0.1348	1.0000

c. Probability Table of Substance Ingested Conditional on Knowing Hospitalization Status

Substance Ingested	Not Hospitalized Probability	Hospitalized Probability
Cleaning fluids	0.0300	0.0400
Furniture polishes	0.3900	0.3200
Gasoline	0.1600	0.1867
Kerosene	0.0900	0.0800
Lighter fluid	0.1400	0.1533
Paint thinner	0.1100	0.1533
Other	0.0800	0.0667
Column totals	1.0000	1.0000

d. Furniture polishes, cleaning fluids; paint thinner, furniture polishes.

e.

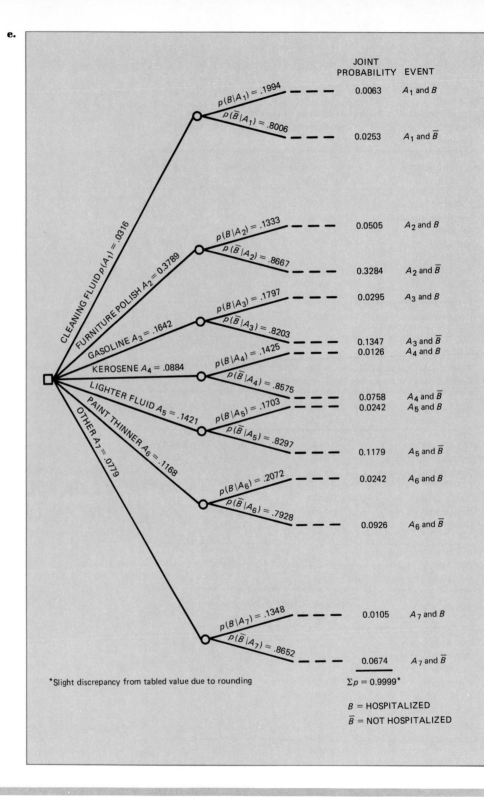

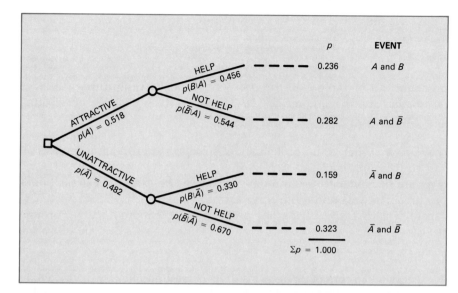

FIGURE 10.6 Tree diagram used to calculate the probability of various conditional events relating to physical attractiveness of the target and helping behavior by the subjects.

10.8 PROBABILITY AND THE NORMAL-CURVE MODEL

In Section 7.3, we stated that the standard normal distribution has a μ of 0, a σ of 1, and a total area that is equal to 1.00. We saw that when scores on a normally distributed variable are transformed into z-scores, we are, in effect, expressing these scores in units of the standard normal curve. This permits us to express the difference between any two scores as proportions of total area under the curve. Thus, we may establish probability values in terms of these proportions, as in Formula (10.11).

The following are several examples that illustrate the application of probability concepts to the normal-curve model.

Illustrative Problems*

For all problems, assume $\mu = 100$ and $\sigma = 16$.

Problem 1   What is the probability of selecting at *random* from the general population a person with an IQ score of at least 132? The answer to this question is given by the proportion of area under the curve above a score of 132 (Figure 10.7).

* See Section 7.4.

First, we must find the z-score corresponding to $X = 132$.

$$z = \frac{132 - 100}{16} = 2.00$$

In column (C) of Table A in the back of this book, we find that 0.0228 of the area lies at or beyond a z of 2.00. Therefore, the probability of selecting at random a score of at least 132 is 0.0228.

Problem 2   What is the probability of selecting at random an individual with an IQ score of at least 92?

We are dealing with two mutually exclusive and exhaustive areas under the curve. The area under the curve above a score of 92 is P; the area below a score of 92 is Q. In solving our problem, we therefore employ Formula (10.7):

$$P = 1.00 - Q$$

By expressing a score of 92 in terms of its corresponding z, we may obtain the proportion of area below $X = 92$ (i.e., Q) directly from column (C), Table A. The z-score corresponding to $X = 92$ is

$$z = \frac{92 - 100}{16} = -0.50$$

The proportion of area below a z of -0.50 is 0.3085. Therefore, the probability of selecting at random a score of at least 92 becomes

$$P = 1.00 - 0.3085 = 0.6915$$

Figure 10.8 illustrates this relationship.

Problem 3   Look at this example involving the multiplication law. Given that sampling with replacement is employed, what is the probability of drawing at random three individuals with IQs equaling or exceeding 124? For this problem, we again assume that $\mu = 100$ and $\sigma = 16$:

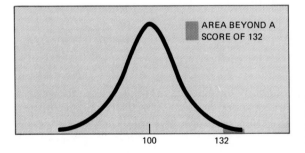

AREA BEYOND A SCORE OF 132

100   132

FIGURE 10.7 Proportion of area above a score of 132 in a normal distribution with $\mu = 100$ and $\sigma = 16$.

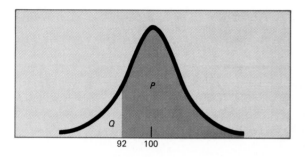

FIGURE 10.8 Proportion of area above (*P*) and below (*Q*) a score of 92 in a normal distribution with $\mu = 100$ and $\sigma = 16$.

$$z = \frac{124 - 100}{16} = 1.5$$

In column (C), Table A, we find that 0.0668 of the area lies at or beyond $z = 1.50$. Therefore

$$p(A, B, C) = (0.0668)^3 = 0.0003$$

10.9 ONE- AND TWO-TAILED *p*-VALUES

In Problem 1, we were seeking the probability of selecting at random a person with an IQ score as high as 132. We solved the problem by examining only one tail of the distribution, namely, scores as high as or higher than 132. For this reason we refer to the probability value that we obtained as being a **one-tailed *p*-value.**

One-Tailed *p*-Values: Probability values obtained by examining only one tail of the distribution.

In statistics and research, the following questions are more commonly asked: "What is the probability of obtaining a score (or statistic) this *deviant* from the mean? ... or a score (or statistic) this *rare?* ... or a result this *unusual?*" Clearly, when the frequency distribution of scores is symmetrical, a score of 68 or lower is every bit as deviant from a mean of 100 as is a score of 132. That is, both are two standard deviation units away from the mean. When we express the probability value, taking into account both tails of the distribution, we refer to the *p*-value as being *two-tailed.* In symmetrical distributions, **two-tailed *p*-values** may be obtained merely by doubling the one-tailed probability value. Thus, in problem 1, the probability of selecting a person with a score as *rare or unusual* as 132 is $2 \times 0.0228 = 0.0456$.

Two-Tailed *p*-Values: Probability values that take into account both tails of the distribution.

We may illustrate the distinction between one- and two-tailed *p*-values by referring to a sampling experiment we presented in the end-of-chapter exercises for Chapters 3, 4, 5, and 6. Figure 10.9 shows a probability histogram based on Table 10.6. This distribution was obtained by selecting,

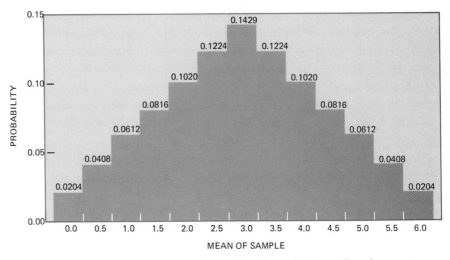

FIGURE 10.9 Probability histogram of means based on selecting, with replacement, samples of $N = 2$ from a population of seven numbers.

with replacement, all possible samples of $N = 2$ from a population of seven scores.

If we ask, "What is the probability of obtaining a mean equal to zero?" we need to refer only to the left tail of the probability histogram in order to find the answer of 0.0204. However, if we ask, "What is the probability of obtaining as deviant an outcome as a sample mean equal to zero?" we have to look at both the left and the right tails. Since a mean of 6 is equally deviant from the mean of the distribution, we use the addition rule to obtain the two-tailed value:

$$p(\overline{X} = 0 \text{ or } \overline{X} = 6) = p(\overline{X} = 0) + p(\overline{X} = 6)$$
$$= 0.0204 + 0.0204 = 0.0408$$

Let's look at two additional examples.

Example 1 What is the probability of obtaining a mean as low as 0.5 (i.e., a mean of 0.5 or lower)?

We find the probability of obtaining a mean of 0.5 and a mean of 0.0 (the only mean lower than 0.5), and add these probabilities together to obtain the one-tailed p-value:

$$p(\overline{X} \leq 0.5) = p(\overline{X} = 0.5) + p(\overline{X} = 0.0)$$
$$= 0.0408 + 0.0204 = 0.0612$$

Example 2 What is the probability of obtaining a mean as deviant or more deviant from the distribution mean as a sample mean of 0.5?

TABLE 10.6   Frequency and Probability Distribution of Means of Samples of Size *N* = 2, Drawn from Population of Seven Scores (0, 1, 2, 3, 4, 5, 6)

$\overline{X}$	f	$p(\overline{X})$
6.0	1	0.0204
5.5	2	0.0408
5.0	3	0.0612
4.5	4	0.0816
4.0	5	0.1020
3.5	6	0.1224
3.0	7	0.1429
2.5	6	0.1224
2.0	5	0.1020
1.5	4	0.0816
1.0	3	0.0612
0.5	2	0.0408
0.0	1	0.0204

$$N_{\overline{X}} = 49^* \qquad \Sigma p(\overline{X}) = 0.9997†$$

*We use $N_{\overline{X}}$ to refer to the total number of means obtained in our sampling experiment and to distinguish it from *N*, which is the number of scores upon which each mean is based.
† $\Sigma p(\overline{X})$ should equal 1.000. The discrepancy of 0.0003 represents rounding error.

The answer to this question calls for a two-tailed *p*-value obtained by applying the addition rule to

$$p(\overline{X} = 0.0) + p(\overline{X} = 0.5) + p(\overline{X} = 5.5) + p(\overline{X} = 6.0)$$

However, since the distribution is symmetrical, and means of 5.5 and 6.0 are equally as deviant as means of 0.5 and 0.0, respectively, we need only double the *p*-value obtained in Example 1:

$$p(\overline{X} \le 0.5 \text{ or } \overline{X} \ge 5.5) = 2(0.0612)$$
$$= 0.1224$$

Incidentally, the left-hand member of the preceding expression is read: *The probability of a mean equal to or less than 0.5 or equal to or greater than 5.5.*

The distinction between one- and two-tailed probability values takes on added significance as we progress into inferential statistics.

10.10 PUTTING IT ALL TOGETHER

In September 1989, a killer hurricane (Hugo) blasted the West Indies and then turned its fury on the coast of South Carolina, leaving death and devastation in its wake. Estimates of $5 billion or more do not seem excessive. Hardly a home on the Barrier Islands off Charleston was left unscathed, and destruction was extensive throughout Charleston and extended well beyond its city limits.

A number of people on the Barrier Islands vowed to rebuild, citing the odds against a recurrence of such a storm as 1 million to 1 over the next 100 years. Here's an instance in which the classical approach to probability provides no basis for assessing this optimistic claim. But what about the empirical approach? Let's see. In the late 1800s, the same area was also torn asunder by a powerful hurricane. Since both occurred within 100 years of each other, we may assign a tentative one-year hurricane probability of 0.02. If this empirical probability is even close to the true probability, then the odds are not 1 million to 1 against a recurrence within 100 years, nor even within a single year. Assuming that the probability is 2 in 100, the odds against a recurrence the following year are: $(100 - 2)$ to $2 = 49$ to 1. It sounds fairly safe, but what about the odds of at least one hurricane hitting the Charleston area over the next 10, 20, 50, 75, or 100 years? The following odds are based on the binomial using the probability of nonoccurrence in any given year of 0.98. We'll examine the calculation of these odds in Chapter 17, but the results of these calculations are quite revealing (see Table 10.7).

If the assumption is correct that the annual probability of a hurricane hitting the Charleston area is 0.02 and that of being spared is 0.98, the odds

TABLE 10.7 **The Odds Against or in Favor of Any Hurricane Striking the Charleston Area over Varying Numbers of Years, Assuming a One-Year Probability of Being Spared of $p = 0.98$ and of Being Struck of $q = 0.02$. The Empirical Probability Is Based on Only 100 Years of Data and May Be Revised Upwards or Downwards as Additional Data Are Gathered over Future Years**

Years Projected	Probability (p) of Being Spared	Odds Against or in Favor of a Recurrence
1	0.98	49:1 against
10	0.82	4.5:1 against
20	0.67	2:1 against
50	0.36	1.7:1 in favor
75	0.22	3.6:1 in favor
100	0.13	6.7:1 in favor

of another hurricane within the next 100 years are not 1 million to 1 against but almost 7 to 1 in favor of it. Misunderstanding of probabilities can have tragic consequences.

There is a common belief that, once an unusual event has occurred, a recurrence of this event is unlikely for a considerable period of time. This is not true, as long as the events in question are independent. A low-probability event is just as likely to occur again as it was likely to occur in the first place. It is inevitable that there are runs of bad or good luck.

This is not true with nonindependent events. Take earthquakes as an example. Huge plates (called tectonic plates) are constantly moving at a snail's pace underneath the earth. When they come into contact with one another (faults) and there are no minor slippages (small earthquakes) to relieve the pressure, the pressure will eventually become so great that it can no longer be contained. The result can be a fracture, a massive earthquake. Once the quake has occurred, the pressures are released and it is unlikely that another will occur in the same locality for a considerable period of time. For this reason, geologists often say, "The longer since the last big one, the shorter before the next." You may also recognize this as a statement of nonindependence.

CHAPTER SUMMARY

In this chapter, we focused our discussion on five points:

1. *The importance of the concept of randomness in inferential statistics.* Randomness refers to selecting the events in the sample in such a way that each event is equally likely to be selected in a sample of a given size. Independent random sampling refers to the fact that the selection of one event has no effect upon the probability of selecting another event. Although the individual events are unpredictable, collections of random events take on characteristic and predictable forms. The binomial distribution and the normal curve were cited in this regard.

2. *The theory of probability, which is concerned with the outcomes of experiments.* We learned to distinguish between probabilities established by assuming *idealized* relative frequencies and those established empirically by determining relative frequencies. Probability was defined as

$$p = \frac{\text{No. of outcomes favoring event}}{\text{Total no. of outcomes}}$$

3. *The formal properties of probability.*
   a. Probabilities vary between 0 and 1.00.

b. The addition rule:

If A and B are two events, the probability of obtaining either of them is equal to the probability of A plus the probability of B minus the probability of their joint occurrence. Thus

$$p(A \text{ or } B) = p(A) + p(B) - p(A \text{ and } B)$$

If Events A and B are *mutually exclusive*, the addition rule becomes

$$p(A \text{ or } B) = p(A) + p(B)$$

Allowing P to represent the probability of occurrence and Q to represent the probability of nonoccurrence, we find that three additional useful formulations for mutually exclusive and exhaustive events are

$$P + Q = 1.00 \qquad P = 1.00 - Q \qquad Q = 1.00 - P$$

c. The multiplication rule.

When events are independent. When sampling with replacement, the selection on one trial is independent of the selection on another trial. Given two events, A and B, the probability of obtaining both A and B in successive trials is the product of the probability of obtaining one of these events times the probability of obtaining the second of these events:

$$p(A \text{ and } B) = p(A)p(B)$$

When events are nonindependent. When sampling without replacement, the selection of one event affects the probability of selecting each remaining event. Thus, given two events, A and B, the probability of obtaining both A and B jointly or successively is the product of the probability of obtaining one of the events times the conditional probability of obtaining one event, *given that* the other event has occurred. Symbolically,

$$p(A \text{ and } B) = p(A)p(B|A) = p(B)p(A|B)$$

4. *The application of probability theory to continuously distributed variables.* Probability is expressed in terms of the proportion of area under a curve. Hence

$$p = \frac{\text{Area under portions of a curve}}{\text{Total area under a curve}}$$

We saw how to employ z-scores and the standard normal curve to establish various probabilities for normally distributed variables.

5. *How to distinguish between one- and two-tailed probability values.*

TERMS TO REMEMBER

bias
conditional probability
exhaustive
independence
mutually exclusive
one-tailed *p*-values

probability
random sampling
sample space
sampling distribution
two-tailed *p*-values

EXERCISES

*1. Imagine that we have a population of the following four scores: 0, 3, 6, and 9.
  a. Construct a probability distribution and histogram of all possible means when sampling with replacement, $N = 2$.
  b. Construct a probability histogram of all possible means when sampling with replacement, $N = 3$. [*Hint:* The table for finding the means appears below. The values in the cells represent the means of the three draws.]

1st Draw		0				3				6				9		
2nd Draw		**0**	**3**	**6**	**9**	**0**	**3**	**6**	**9**	**0**	**3**	**6**	**9**	**0**	**3**	**6**	**9**
3rd Draw **0**	0	1	2	3	1	2	3	4	2	3	4	5	3	4	5	6
3	1	2	3	4	2	3	4	5	3	4	5	6	4	5	6	7
6	2	3	4	5	3	4	5	6	4	5	6	7	5	6	7	8
9	3	4	5	6	4	5	6	7	5	6	7	8	6	7	8	9

*2. The original population of the four scores in Exercise 1 was rectangular (they all had the same associated frequency of 1). Compare the probability distributions in 1(a) and 1(b) and attempt to form a generalization about the form and the dispersion of the distribution of sample means as we increase the sample size.

*3. Answer the following questions based on the probability histograms obtained in Exercise 1:
  a. Drawing a single sample of $N = 2$, what is the probability of obtaining a mean equal to zero? Contrast this result with the probability of randomly selecting a mean equal to zero when $N = 3$.
  b. For each distribution, determine the probability of selecting a sample with a mean as rare or as unusual as 9.
  c. From each probability histogram, determine the probability of selecting a sample with a mean as low as 3.
  d. From each probability histogram, determine the probability of selecting a sample mean as deviant from the population mean as a mean of 3.

*4. For the probability distribution of $N = 2$ [Exercise 1(a)], find:
 a. $p(\overline{X} < 6)$ **b.** $p(\overline{X} \geq 7.5)$ **c.** $p(\overline{X} = 4.5)$

*5. For the probability distribution of $N = 3$ [Exercise 1(b)], find:
 a. $p(3 \leq \overline{X} \leq 6)$ **b.** $p(4 \leq \overline{X} \leq 5)$ **c.** $p(\overline{X} = 2 \text{ or } \overline{X} = 8)$

*6. Let's now imagine a different type of sampling experiment. You have selected all possible samples of $N = 2$ from a population of scores and obtained the following means: 1, 2, 2, 3, 3, 3, 4, 4, 5. You now place paper tabs in a hat with these means written on them. You select one mean, record it, and replace it in the hat. You select a second mean, *subtract* it from the first, and then replace it in the hat. The table for describing all possible *differences between means of N = 2* is shown below.

				First Draw of Mean						
		1	**2**	**2**	**3**	**3**	**3**	**4**	**4**	**5**
Second Draw of Mean	**1**	0	1	1	2	2	2	3	3	4
	2	−1	0	0	1	1	1	2	2	3
	2	−1	0	0	1	1	1	2	2	3
	3	−2	−1	−1	0	0	0	1	1	2
	3	−2	−1	−1	0	0	0	1	1	2
	3	−2	−1	−1	0	0	0	1	1	2
	4	−3	−2	−2	−1	−1	−1	0	0	1
	4	−3	−2	−2	−1	−1	−1	0	0	1
	5	−4	−3	−3	−2	−2	−2	−1	−1	0

 a. Construct a frequency distribution of differences between means.
 b. Construct a probability distribution of differences between means.
 c. Find the mean and the standard deviation of the differences between means.

*7. Based on the responses to Exercise 6, answer the following questions. Drawing two samples at random and with replacement from the population of means, and subtracting the second mean from the first, what is the probability that you will select
 a. a difference between means equal to zero?
 b. a difference between means equal to or less than 1 *or* equal to or greater than −1? (*Note:* −2, −3, −4 are all less than −1.)
 c. a difference between means equal to −4?
 d. a difference between means as rare or as deviant as −4?
 e. a difference between means equal to or greater than 3?
 f. a difference between means equal to or less than −3?
 g. a difference between means as rare or as unusual as −3?
 h. a difference between means equal to or less than 2 or equal to or greater than −2?

8. List all the possible outcomes of a coin that is tossed three times. Calculate the probability of
 a. 3 heads **b.** 3 tails **c.** 2 heads and 1 tail **d.** at least 2 heads

9. A card is drawn at random from a deck of 52 playing cards. What is the probability that
   a. it will be the ace of spades?   **b.** it will be an ace?
   c. it will be an ace or a face card?   **d.** it will be a spade or a face card?

10. Express the probabilities in Exercises 8 and 9 in terms of *odds against*.

11. In a single throw of two dice, what is the probability that
   a. a 7 will appear?
   b. a doublet (two of the same number) will appear?
   c. a doublet or an 8 will appear?
   d. an even number will appear?

12. On a slot machine (commonly referred to as a "one-armed bandit"), there are three reels with five different fruits plus a star on each reel. After inserting a coin and pulling the handle, the player sees that the three reels revolve independently several times before stopping. What is the probability that
   a. three lemons will appear?
   b. any three of a kind will appear?
   c. two lemons and a star will appear?
   d. two lemons and any other fruit will appear?
   e. no star will appear?

13. Three cards are drawn at random (without replacement) from a deck of 52 cards. What is the probability that
   a. all three will be hearts?
   b. none of the three cards will be hearts?
   c. all three will be face cards?

14. Calculate the probabilities in Exercise 13 if each card is replaced after it is drawn.

15. A well-known test of intelligence is constructed so as to have normally distributed scores with a mean of 100 and a standard deviation of 16.
   a. What is the probability that someone picked at random will have an IQ of 122 or higher?
   b. There are IQs so *high* that the probability is 0.05 that such IQs would occur in a random sample of people. Those IQs are beyond what value?
   c. There are IQs so *extreme* that the probability is 0.05 that such IQs would occur in a random sample of people. Those IQs are beyond what values?
   d. The next time you shop, you will undoubtedly see someone who is a complete stranger to you. What is the probability that his or her IQ will be between 90 and 110?
   e. What is the probability of selecting two people at random.
      i. with IQs of 122 or higher?
      ii. with IQs between 90 and 110?
      iii. one with an IQ of 122 or higher, the other with an IQ between 90 and 110?
   f. What is the probability that on leaving your class, the first student you meet will have an IQ below 120? Can you answer this question on the basis of the information provided above? If not, why not?

16. Which of the following selection techniques will result in random samples? Explain your answers.

   a. Population: Viewers of a given television program. Sampling technique: On a given night, interviewing every fifth person in the studio audience.

   b. Population: A home-made pie. Sampling technique: A wedge selected from any portion of the pie.

   c. Population: All the children in a suburban high school. Sampling technique: Selecting one child sent to you by each homeroom teacher.

17. In a study involving a test of visual acuity, four different hues varying slightly in brightness are presented to the subject. What is the probability that he or she will arrange them in order, from the greatest brightness to the least, by chance?

18. The proportion of people with Type A blood in a particular city is 0.20. What is the probability that

   a. a given individual, selected at random, will have Type A blood?

   b. two out of two individuals will have Type A blood?

   c. a given individual will *not* have Type A blood?

   d. two out of two individuals will *not* have Type A blood?

19. In a manufacturing process, the proportion of items that are defective is 0.10. What is the probability that

   a. in a sample of four items, none will be defective?

   b. in a sample of four items, all will be defective?

   c. one or more but less than four will be defective?

20. In the manufacture of machine screws for the space industry, millions of screws measuring 0.010 centimeter are produced daily. The standard deviation is 0.001. A screw is considered defective if it deviates from 0.010 by as much as 0.002. Assuming normality, what is the probability that

   a. one screw selected at random will be defective?

   b. two out of two screws will be defective?

   c. one screw selected at random will *not* be defective?

   d. two out of two screws will *not* be defective?

   e. one screw selected at random will be too large?

   f. two out of two screws will be too small?

21. A bag contains 6 blue marbles, 4 red marbles, and 2 green marbles. If you select a single marble at random from the bag, what is the probability that it will be

   a. red?   **b.** blue?   **c.** green?   **d.** white?

22. Selecting *without* replacement from the bag described in Exercise 21, what is the probability that

   a. three out of three will be blue?   **b.** two out of two will be green?

   c. none out of four will be red?

23. Selecting *with* replacement from the bag described in Exercise 21, what is the probability that

   a. three out of three will be blue?   **b.** two out of two will be green?

   c. none out of four will be red?

24. Forty percent of the students at a given college major in business administration.

Seventy percent of these are male and thirty percent are female. Sixty percent of the students in the school are male. What is the probability that

a. one student selected at random will be a BA major?

b. one person selected at random will be a female BA major?

c. two students selected at random will be BA majors?

d. two persons selected at random will be BA majors, one male, one female?

25. What is the probability that a score chosen at random from a normally distributed population with a mean of 66 and a standard deviation of 8 will be

a. greater than 70?

b. less than 60?

c. between 60 and 70?

d. in the 70s?

e. either equal to or less than 54 or equal to or greater than 72?

f. either less than 52 or between 78 and 84?

g. either between 56 and 64 or between 80 and 86?

26. What is meant by random sampling?

27. Refer back to Table 10.4. Construct a tree diagram of the conditional probabilities when the helping response of the subject is known.

28. In another facet of the study relating physical attractiveness to helping behavior, the target was either an attractive or unattractive male and the subjects were females. The results are shown in the following table.

Helping Response	Characteristics of Target		Row Totals
	Attractive	Unattractive	
Helped	19	13	32
Did not help	22	27	49
Column totals	41	40	81

a. Prepare a joint probability table of the results.

b. Calculate the conditional probabilities of events B and $\bar{B}$ when the attractiveness status of the subject is known.

c. Construct a tree diagram of the conditional probabilities when the attractiveness status of the target person is known.

d. Construct a tree diagram of the conditional probabilities when the helping status of the subject is known.

Introduction to Statistical Inference

11.1 WHY SAMPLE?

You are the leader of a religious denomination, and for the purpose of planning recruitment you want to know what proportion of the adults in the United States claim church membership. How would you go about getting this information?

You are an experimental psychologist, and you are interested in the relationship between the strength of drive and learning. Specifically, what are the effects of duration of food deprivation (hunger) on the number of trials that are required for a rat to learn a T-maze?

You are a sociologist, and you want to study the differences in child-rearing practices among parents of delinquent and nondelinquent children.

You are a market researcher, and you want to know what proportion of individuals prefer certain car colors and their various combinations.

You are a park attendant, and you want to determine if the ice is sufficiently thick to permit safe skating.

You are a gambler, and you want to determine if a set of dice is "dishonest."

Population: A complete set of individuals, objects, or measurements having some common observable characteristic.

What do each of these problems have in common? You are asking questions about the parameter of a population to which you want to generalize your answers, but you have no hope of ever studying the *entire* population. Earlier (Section 1.2)* we defined a **population** as a *complete* or *theoretical* set of individuals, objects, or measurements having some common observable characteristic. It is frequently impossible to study *all* the members of a given population because the population as defined either has an infinite number of members or is so large that it defies exhaustive study. Moreover, when we refer to "the population" we are often dealing with a hypothetical entity. In the typical experimental situation, the actual population does not exist. We attempt to find out something about the characteristics of that population *if it did exist*. For example, when we administer a drug to a group of subjects (the **sample**), we wish to generalize our results to everyone who could potentially receive the drug. This *population* is, of course, hypothetical.

Sample: A subset of a population or universe.

Since populations can rarely be studied exhaustively, we must depend on samples as a basis for arriving at a hypothesis concerning various characteristics, or parameters, of the population. Note that our interest is not in descriptive statistics per se, but in making inferences from data. Thus, if we ask 100 people how they intend to vote in a forthcoming election, our primary interest is not in knowing how these 100 people will vote, but in estimating how the members of the entire voting population will cast their ballots.

Almost all research involves the observation and the measurement of a limited number of individuals or events. These measurements are presumed to tell us something about the population. In order to understand how to make inferences about a population from a sample, we need to introduce the concept of sampling distributions.

11.2 THE CONCEPT OF SAMPLING DISTRIBUTIONS

In actual practice, inferences about the parameters of a population are made from statistics that are calculated from a sample of N observations drawn at random from this population. If we continue to draw samples of size N from this population, we should not be surprised if we find some differences among the values of the sample statistics that are obtained. It would be extremely unlikely that we would draw exactly the same set of observations each time. On one occasion, we might, by chance, select a set of observations in which most of the scores are high. On another, we might select mostly low scores. On still another, there might be a good mix of

---

* It is recommended that you reread Section 1.2 for purposes of reviewing several definitions of terms that will appear in this chapter.

BOX 11.1

SAMPLING: A MATTER OF SURVIVAL

We tend to think of sampling procedures as activities engaged in by only a handful of professionals—pollsters, laboratory scientists, demographers, to name a few. As the following excerpt from *Winning with Statistics* makes clear, sampling followed by decision making is among the most pervasive activities of living organisms.

We have three dogs on our ranch on the outskirts of Tucson, Arizona. The baby of the three, Millie Muffin, is an eight-month-old black and white springer spaniel. Although mischief should be her middle name, she is a sheer delight. She is constantly exploring the desert flora and fauna with the indefatigable curiosity of a three-year-old human child. When spying something that moves on its own (such as a giant spider, better known as a tarantula), she leaps about two feet off the ground—ears and feathers flapping—and retreats several feet away, all the while barking like a fierce Doberman. But I know better. In reality, she is the world's greatest coward. I'll tell you how I know.

While she is prancing mindlessly about the giant saguaro, the ocotillo, the cholla, and other assorted exotic plants of the desert, I will sneak downwind of her. Then I will raise myself on the balls of my toes, stretch my arms in front of me, and shuffle my feet as I advance toward her in my best Frankenstein-monster style. When she spies me, she lets out a startled "yip," springs into the air, and begins a barking retreat. But all the while, her nose is probing the air, sniffing constantly, desperately drawing in samples in an effort to make inferences about the nature of the intruder. While observing Millie's antics, it occurred to me that the actions involved in taking samples and drawing inferences from these samples are among the most pervasive of mammalian activities. The pet dog, the family feline, the lion in the jungle, the gorilla in the rain forest, and the wife, husband, daughter, son, businessperson, doctor, lawyer, and Indian chief have this characteristic in common. They are continuously probing aspects of their environment, assessing the risks against the benefits, making probability judgments concerning alternative avenues of behavior, and pursuing those lines of activity that appear most likely to lead to desired goals. By this I do not mean to imply that all this sampling and probability assessment is conscious or deliberate. The truth of the matter is that nature has designed us all to be exquisite probability-generating machines. Without the ability to sample and thereby judge peril, or the availability of food, or the receptivity of a sexual partner, all species presently inhabiting the earth would have come from a long line of unborn ancestors.

Source: Excerpted from R. P. Runyon, *Winning with Statistics*, Reading, Mass.: Addison-Wesley, 1977.

high and low observations. Indeed, it is this observation that has led to the concept of **sampling distributions.**

A sampling distribution is a theoretical probability distribution of the possible values of some sample statistic that would occur if we were to draw all possible samples of a fixed size from a given population.

Sampling Distributions: A theoretical probability distribution of a statistic that would result from drawing all possible samples of a given size from some population.

There is a sampling distribution for every statistic—mean, standard deviation, variance, proportion, median, and so on. It is one of the most important concepts in inferential statistics. You are already familiar with several sampling distributions, although we have not previously named them as such. Recall the various sampling problems we have introduced throughout the earlier chapters in the text. In one example, we started with a population of seven scores and selected with replacement samples of $N = 2$. We obtained all possible combinations of these scores, two at a time, and then found the mean of each of these samples. We then constructed a frequency distribution and probability distribution of means that were drawn from that population with a fixed sample size of $N = 2$.

Recall also that in Exercise 1, at the end of Chapter 10, we constructed sampling distributions based on drawing with replacement all possible samples of $N = 2$ and $N = 3$ from a population of four scores (0, 3, 6, 9). Table 11.1 shows these two sampling distributions, plus the sampling distribution of the mean when $N = 4$.

Why is the concept of a sampling distribution so important? The answer is simple. Once you are able to describe the sampling distribution of *any statistic*, be it mean, standard deviation, or proportion, you are in a position to entertain and test a wide variety of hypotheses. For example, suppose you draw four numbers from some population for which you know neither the mean or the standard deviation. You obtain a sample mean of 6.00. You

TABLE 11.1   Sampling distributions of means drawn from population of four scores (0, 3, 6, 9; $\mu = 4.5$, $\sigma = 3.94$) and sample sizes $N = 2$, $N = 3$, and $N = 4$

$N = 2$		$N = 3$		$N = 4$	
$\overline{X}$	$p(\overline{X})$	$\overline{X}$	$p(\overline{X})$	$\overline{X}$	$p(\overline{X})$
9.0	0.0625	9.0	0.0156	9.0	0.0039
7.5	0.1250	8.0	0.0469	8.25	0.0156
6.0	0.1875	7.0	0.0938	7.50	0.0391
4.5	0.2500	6.0	0.1562	6.75	0.0781
3.0	0.1875	5.0	0.1875	6.00	0.1211
1.5	0.1250	4.0	0.1875	5.25	0.1562
0.0	0.0625	3.0	0.1562	4.50	0.1719
		2.0	0.0938	3.75	0.1562
		1.0	0.0469	3.00	0.1211
		0.0	0.0156	2.25	0.0781
				1.50	0.0391
				.75	0.0156
				0.00	0.0039
$\overline{X} = 4.5$		$\overline{X} = 4.5$		$\overline{X} = 4.5$	
$s_{\overline{X}} = 2.37$		$s_{\overline{X}} = 1.94$		$s_{\overline{X}} = 1.68$	

ask, "Is it reasonable that this sample was drawn from the population of four numbers upon which the sampling distribution in Table 11.1 was based?" The mean of the sampling distribution was 4.5, and your sample mean was 6.00. Is such a departure from the population mean an extraordinary or rare event, or will departures this large occur with regularity?

In the absence of a frame of reference, these questions would be meaningless. However, if we knew the sampling distribution of the mean for the population of interest, we would have the necessary frame of reference, and the answer would be quite straightforward. If we were to tell you that the appropriate sampling distribution is given in Table 11.1, you would have little trouble in answering the question. A sample mean of 6.00 would be drawn about 12% of the time $(p = 0.1211)$, and a mean of 6.00 or greater would occur almost 26% of the time $(p = 0.1211 + 0.0781 + 0.0391 + 0.0156 + 0.0039 = 0.2578)$. Roughly 1 chance in 4 is not terribly unusual. Thus, you would have no overriding reason to suspect that the sample was selected from a population different from the one represented in Table 11.1, $N = 4$.

But what if you had selected a sample mean equal to 9.0? Referring to the same sampling distribution of means in Table 11.1, we see that such an event would be quite rare—less than 1 in 100, or, to be more precise, 39 times in 10,000 $(p = 0.0039)$. At this point, we might entertain serious doubts that the sample was drawn at random from the four scores shown in Table 11.1.

Or, to put this into everyday experiences, suppose you have (or had) a friend whom you often accompany during lunch. After the meal, when the tab is presented, your friend always produces a coin and cheerfully intones, "Heads, you pay; tails, I pay." After the toss, you friend's cheerfulness is undiminished: "Heads, bad luck, you pay." It has come up heads 10 times in a row. As with the sample mean equal to 9.00, might you not begin questioning the honesty of the coin in your friend's possession? Perhaps, with his coin, the probability of obtaining a heads and a tails are not equal. A weighted coin, or even a two-headed coin, perhaps? Rare or unusual outcomes must always alert us to the possibility that we must look elsewhere for explanations of things we observe.

Whenever we estimate a population parameter from a sample, we ask such questions as: "How good an estimate do I have? Can I conclude that the population parameter is identical with the sample statistic? Or is there likely to be some error? If so, how much?" To answer each of these questions, we compare our sample results with the "expected" results. The expected results are in turn given by the appropriate sampling distribution. But what does the sampling distribution of a particular statistic look like? How can we ever know the form of the distribution, and thus what the expected results are? Fortunately, there are known and predictable relationships between the form of the sampling distributions we shall be considering and the sample size of the statistics on which they are based. As we increase the sample size of the statistics that make up the sampling distribution, (1) the dispersion of the sample statistics becomes less (that is, the sample statistics tend to cluster closer to the parameter of interest), and (2) the form of the distribution becomes increasingly symmetrical and bell-shaped. These features are found even when the original population of scores is not distributed in a symmetrical and bell-shaped form. These points are shown in Figure 11.1.

In many of the remaining chapters, the inferences we draw imply knowledge of the form of the sampling distribution. We will be looking at two idealized models whose mathematical properties are known: the normal curve and the **binomial distribution.** Both are frequently used as models to describe particular sampling distributions. Thus, for example, if we know that the sampling distribution of a particular statistic takes the form of a normal distribution, we may raise such questions as: "How likely is it that the value of the statistic we obtained was drawn from the sampling distribution under consideration?"

The following sections should serve to clarify these important points.

Binomial Distribution: A model with known mathematical properties used to describe sampling distributions of dichotomous variables.

11.3 TESTING STATISTICAL HYPOTHESES: LEVEL OF SIGNIFICANCE

Say you have a favorite coin that you use constantly in everyday life as a basis of "either-or" decision making. For example, you may ask, "Should I study tonight for the statistics quiz, or should I relax at the movies?" Your solution: "Heads, I study; tails, I don't." Over a period of time, you have sensed that the decision has more often gone "against you" than "for you" (in other words, you have to study more often than relax!). You begin to question the accuracy and the adequacy of the coin. Does the coin come up heads more often than tails? How might you find out?

One thing is clear. The true proportion of heads and tails characteristic of this coin can never be known. You could start tossing the coin this very minute and continue for a million years (granting a long life and a remarkably durable coin) and you would not exhaust the population of possible outcomes. In this instance, the true proportion of heads and tails is unknowable because the universe, or population, is unlimited.

The fact that the *true* value is unknowable does not prevent us from trying to estimate what it is. We have already pointed out that since populations can rarely be studied exhaustively, we must depend on samples to estimate the parameters.

Returning to our problem with the coin, we clearly see that in order to determine whether or not the coin is biased, we shall have to obtain a sample of the "behavior" of that coin and arrive at some generalization concerning its possible bias. For example, if we toss our coin 10 times and obtain 5 heads and 5 tails, would we begin to suspect our coin of being biased? Of course not, since this outcome is exactly a 50–50 split, and is in

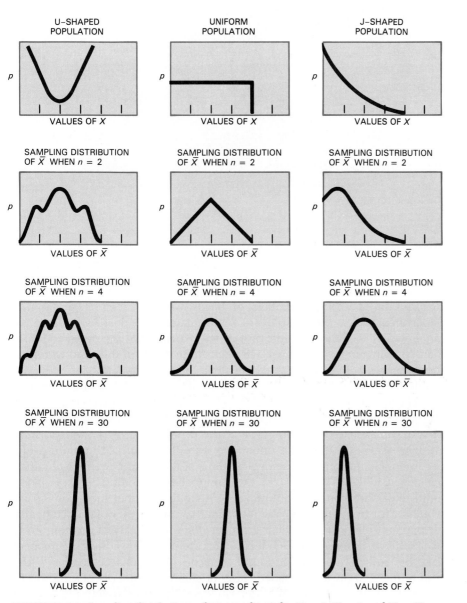

FIGURE 11.1 Sampling distributions of means of samples $N = 2$, $N = 4$, and $N = 30$ from three different types of populations. These figures illustrate the central limit-theorem by showing how, regardless of the form of the parent population, the sampling distribution of means approaches normality as N increases.

agreement with the hypothesis that the coin is not biased. What if we obtained 6 heads and 4 tails? Again, this is not an unusual outcome. In fact, we can answer the question of how often, given a theoretically perfect coin, we may expect an outcome at least this much different from a 50–50 split. Looking at Figure 11.2, which represents the theoretical probability

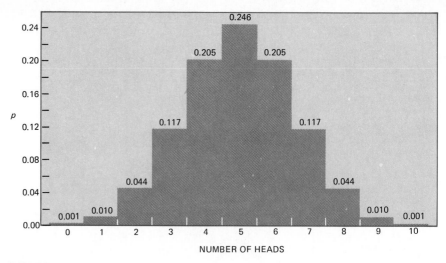

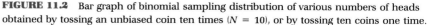

FIGURE 11.2 Bar graph of binomial sampling distribution of various numbers of heads obtained by tossing an unbiased coin ten times ($N = 10$), or by tossing ten coins one time.

distribution of various numbers of heads when $N = 10$, we see that departures from a 50–50 split are quite common. Indeed, whenever we obtain either 6 or more heads, or 4 or fewer heads, we are departing from a 50–50 split. Such departures will occur fully 75.4% of the time when we toss a perfect coin in a series of trials with 10 tosses per trial.

What if we obtained 9 heads and 1 tail? Clearly, we would begin to suspect the honesty of the coin. Why? At what point do we change from attitudes accepting the honesty of the coin to attitudes rejecting its honesty? This question takes us to the crux of the problem of inferential statistics. We have seen that the more unusual or rare the event is, the more prone we are to look for nonchance explanations of the event. When we obtained 6 heads in 10 tosses of our coin, it was not necessary to find an explanation for its departure from a 50–50 split, other than to state that such a departure would occur frequently "by chance." However, when we obtained 9 heads, we had an uncomfortable feeling concerning the honesty of the coin. Nine heads out of 10 tosses is such a rare occurrence that we begin to suspect that the explanation may be found in terms of the characteristics of the coin rather than in the so-called "laws of chance." The critical question is, where do we draw the line that determines what inferences to make about the coin?

The answer to this question reveals the basic nature of science: its probabilistic rather than its absolute orientation. In the social sciences, most researchers have adopted one of the following two cutoff points as the basis for *inferring the operation of nonchance factors*.

Significance Level: A probability value that is considered so rare in the sampling distribution specified under the null hypothesis that one is willing to assert the operation of nonchance factors. Common significance levels are 0.05 and 0.01.

1. When the event or one more deviant would occur 5% of the time or less, *by chance*, some researchers are willing to assert that the results are due to nonchance factors. This cutoff point is known variously as the 0.05 **significance level,** or the 5.00% **significance level.**

2. When the event or one more deviant would occur *1%* of the time or less, *by chance*, other researchers are willing to assert that the results are due to nonchance factors. This cutoff point is known as the 0.01 significance level, or the 1.00% significance level.

The level of significance set by the experimenter for inferring the operation of nonchance factors is known as the **alpha (α) level.** Thus, when employing the 0.05 level of significance, $\alpha = 0.05$; when employing the 0.01 level of significance, $\alpha = 0.01$.

Alpha (α) Level: The level of significance set by the experimenter for inferring the operation of nonchance factors.

In order to determine whether the results were due to nonchance factors in the present coin experiment, we need to calculate the probability of obtaining an event as *rare* as 9 heads out of 10 tosses. In determining the rarity of an event, we must consider the fact that the rare event can occur in both directions (e.g., 9 tails and 1 head) and that it includes more extreme events. In other words, the probability of an event as *rare* as 9 heads out of 10 tosses is equal to

$$p(9 \text{ heads}) + p(10 \text{ heads}) + p(1 \text{ head}) + p(0 \text{ heads})$$

Since this distribution is symmetrical,

$$p(9 \text{ heads}) = p(1 \text{ head}) \quad \text{and} \quad p(10 \text{ heads}) = p(0 \text{ heads})$$

Thus

$$p(9 \text{ heads}) + p(10 \text{ heads}) + p(1 \text{ head}) + p(0 \text{ heads})$$
$$= 2[p(9 \text{ heads}) + p(10 \text{ heads})]$$

These *p*-values may be obtained from Figure 11.1 as follows:

$$p(9 \text{ heads}) = 0.010 \quad \text{and} \quad p(10 \text{ heads}) = 0.001$$

Therefore, the *two-tailed probability* of an event as rare as 9 heads out of 10 tosses is $2(0.010 + 0.001) = 0.022$ or 2.2%.

Employing the 0.05 significance level ($\alpha = 0.05$), we would conclude that the coin was biased (i.e., the results were due to nonchance factors). However, if we employed the 0.01 significance level ($\alpha = 0.01$), we would not be able to assert that these results were due to nonchance factors.

It should be noted and strongly emphasized that you do *not* run a study, analyze the results, arrive at a probability value, and then decide on an α-level. The α-level must be specified *prior* to the study as part of the overall strategy of designing the experiment.

11.4 TESTING STATISTICAL HYPOTHESES: NULL HYPOTHESIS AND ALTERNATIVE HYPOTHESIS

At this point, many students become disillusioned by the arbitrary nature of decision making in science. Let us examine the logic of statistical inference a bit further and see if we can resolve some of the doubts. Prior to the beginning of any experiment, the researcher sets up two mutually exclusive hypotheses:

Null Hypothesis (H_0): A statement that specifies hypothesized values for one or more of the population parameters. Commonly, although not necessarily, involves the hypothesis of "no difference."

Alternative Hypothesis (H_1): A statement specifying that the population parameter is some value other than the one specified under the null hypothesis.

Directional Hypothesis: An alternative hypothesis that states the direction in which the population parameter differs from the one specified under H_0.

Nondirectional Hypothesis: An alternative hypothesis (H_1) that states only that the population parameter is different from the one specified under H_0.

Two-Tailed Probability Value: Probability values that take into account both tails of the distribution.

One-Tailed Probability Value: Probability values obtained by examining only one tail of the distribution.

1. The **null hypothesis (H_0),** which specifies hypothesized values for one or more of the *population parameters*.
2. The **alternative hypothesis (H_1),** which asserts that the *population parameter* is some value other than the one hypothesized.

In the present coin experiment, these two hypotheses read as follows:

H_0: The coin is unbiased; that is

$$P = Q = \tfrac{1}{2}$$

H_1: The coin is biased; that is

$$P \neq Q \neq \tfrac{1}{2}$$

The alternative hypothesis may be either **directional** or **nondirectional.** When H_1 asserts *only* that the population parameter is *different from* the one hypothesized, it is referred to as a *nondirectional* or **two-tailed** hypothesis; for example,

$$P \neq Q \neq \tfrac{1}{2}$$

Occasionally H_1 is **directional** or *one-tailed*. In this instance, in addition to asserting that the population parameter is different from the one hypothesized, we assert the *direction* of that difference; for example

$$P > Q \quad \text{or} \quad P < Q$$

In evaluating the outcome of an experiment, we should employ **one-tailed probability values** whenever our alternative hypothesis is directional.

Moreover, when the alternative hypothesis is directional, so also is the null hypothesis. For example, if the alternative hypothesis is that $P > Q$, the null hypothesis is that $P \leq Q$. Conversely, if H_1 is $P < Q$, H_0 reads: $P \geq Q$.

The Notion of Indirect Proof

Careful analysis of the logic of statistical inference reveals that the null hypothesis can never be proved. For example, if we had obtained exactly 5 heads on 10 tosses of a coin, would this prove that the coin was unbiased? The answer is a categorical "No!" A bias, if it existed, might be of such asmall magnitude that we failed to detect it in 10 trials. But what if we tossed the coin 100 times and obtained 50 heads? Wouldn't this prove something? Again, the same considerations apply. No matter how many times we toss the coin, we can never exhaust the population of possible outcomes. We can make the assertion, however, that *no basis exists for rejecting* the hypothesis that the coin is unbiased.

How, then, can we prove the alternative hypothesis that the coin is biased? Again, we cannot prove the alternative hypothesis directly. Think, for the moment, of the logic involved in the following problem.

Draw two lines on a paper and determine whether they are of different lengths. You compare them and say, "Well, certainly they are not equal. Therefore, they must be of different lengths." By rejecting equality (in this case, the null hypothesis), you assert that there is a difference.

Statistical logic operates in exactly the same way. We cannot prove the null hypothesis, nor can we directly prove the alternative hypothesis. However, if we can *reject* the null hypothesis, we can assert its alternative—namely, that the population parameter is some value other than the one hypothesized. Applied to the coin problem, if we can reject the null hypothesis that $P = Q = \frac{1}{2}$, we can assert the alternative—namely, that $P \neq Q \neq \frac{1}{2}$. Note that the support of the alternative hypothesis is always *indirect*. We have supported it by rejecting the null hypothesis. On the other hand, since the alternative hypothesis can be neither proved nor disproved directly, we can *never prove the null hypothesis* by rejecting the alternative hypothesis. The strongest statement we are entitled to make in this respect is that *we failed to reject the null hypothesis*. In practice, many researchers use the expressions, "fail to reject the null hypothesis" and "accept the null hypothesis" interchangeably.

What, then, are the conditions for rejecting the null hypothesis? Simply this: When employing the 0.05 level of significance, you reject the null hypothesis when a given result occurs by chance 5% of the time or less. When employing the 0.01 level of significance, you reject the null hypothesis when a given result occurs by chance 1% of the time or less. Under these circumstances, of course, you *affirm* the alternative hypothesis.

In other words, one rejects the null hypothesis when the results occur by chance 5% of the time or less (or 1% of the time or less), *assuming that the null hypothesis is the true distribution*. That is, one assumes that the null hypothesis is true, calculates the probability on the basis of this assumption, and if the probability is small, one rejects the assumption.

For reasons stated previously, the late R. A. Fisher, eminent British statistician, has affirmed:

> In relation to any experiment we may speak of this hypothesis as the "null hypothesis," and it should be noted that the null hypothesis is never proved or established, but is possibly disproved, in the course of experimentation. *Every experiment may be said to exist only in order to give the facts a chance of disproving the null hypothesis.*[*]

---

[*] (Italics supplied.) R. A. Fisher, *The Design of Experiments*. Edinburgh: Oliver & Boyd, 1935, p. 16.

11.5 TESTING STATISTICAL HYPOTHESES: THE TWO TYPES OF ERROR

You may now ask, "But aren't we taking a chance that we shall be wrong in rejecting the null hypothesis? Isn't it possible that we have in fact obtained a statistically rare occurrence by chance?"

The answer to this question must be a simple and humble "Yes." This is precisely what we mean when we say that science is probabilistic. If there is any absolute statement that scientists are entitled to make, it is that we can never assert with complete confidence that our findings or propositions are true. There are countless examples in science in which an apparently firmly established conclusion has had to be modified in the light of further evidence.

In the coin experiment, even if all the tosses had resulted in heads, it is possible that the coin was not in fact biased. By chance, once in every 1024 experiments, "on the average," the coin will turn up heads 10 out of 10 times. When we employ the 0.05 level of significance, approximately 5% of the time we shall be wrong when we reject the null hypothesis and assert its alternative.

These are some of the basic facts of the reality of inductive reasoning to which students must adjust. Students of behavior who insist on absolute certainty before they speak on issues are students who have been mute throughout all their years, and who will remain so the rest of their lives (probably).

These same considerations have led statisticians to formulate two types of errors that may be made in statistical inference.

Type I Error (Type α Error)

Back pain has become one of the most common disabling disorders of this century. In a number of cases, trauma and aging have caused the discs (shock absorbers) between the vertebrae to lose elasticity and the gap between the vertebrae to narrow. Because of speculation that surgically fusing vertebrae together might make the patient better able to absorb shock, and thereby might reduce pain, spinal fusion was introduced. The initial results of this surgical procedure were so positive that the null hypothesis (H_0: Spinal fusion does not relieve pain) was rejected. More recent evidence no longer supports the view that spinal fusion is effective in relieving back pain (i.e., there have been many failures to reject H_0). It is now a relatively rare surgical procedure. As a result of the false rejection of H_0, many people underwent expensive and temporarily incapacitating surgery without achieving any pain relief.

Type I Error (Type α Error): The rejection of H_0 when it is actually true. The probability of a Type I error is given by the α level.

In a **Type I error,** we reject the null hypothesis when it is actually true. The probability of making a Type I error is α. We have already pointed out that if we set our rejection point at the 0.05 level of significance, we shall mistakenly reject H_0 approximately 5% of the time. It would seem, then, that in order to avoid this type of error, we should set the rejection level as low as possible. For example, if we were to set $\alpha = 0.001$, we would risk a Type I error only about one time in every thousand. It should be noted that the 0.05 level is rather routinely used in the social and behavioral sciences unless there is a particular reason to be extremely conservative about making a Type I error. For example, suppose we were comparing a totally new teaching method to the technique currently in use. Suppose also that the null hypothesis was really true, that is, there was *no* difference between the two methods. If a Type I error were made and the null hypothesis falsely rejected, this could conceivably lead to an extremely costly and time-consuming changeover to a method that was in fact no better than the one being used. Similarly, in medicine a Type I error could lead to the implementation of a procedure that is costly, involves high levels of risk, and leads to severe discomfort for the patient. In situations such as these, we might want to set a more conservative level of significance (e.g., $\alpha = 0.01$). To familiarize you with the use of both α-levels, we have arbitrarily employed the $\alpha = 0.01$ and $\alpha = 0.05$ levels in examples that are presented throughout the text. However, the lower we set α, the greater is the likelihood that we shall make a Type II error.

Type II Error (Type β Error)

When DDT was first introduced into the household and on farms as an effective pesticide, there was no accumulated evidence that permitted the null hypothesis (H_0: DDT is not harmful) to be rejected. As a result of widespread use over a period of years, evidence was accumulated concerning its harmful effects on humans (cancer), domestic animals, and wildlife. Failure to reject H_0 had led to the false conclusion that DDT was not harmful (i.e., safe). Even though it is now banned, residual quantities still show up in water supplies, in ground samples, and in the food chain. The decision-making error exemplified by DDT and many later pesticides and solvents is known as a Type II error. As you can see, the consequences of such an error can be devastating.

In a **Type II error,** we fail to reject the null hypothesis when it is actually false. *Beta* (β) is the probability of making a Type II error. This type of error is far more common than a Type I error. For example, if we employ the 0.01 level of significance as the basis of rejecting the null hypothesis, and then conduct an experiment in which the result we obtained would have occurred by chance only 2% of the time, we cannot reject the null hypothesis. Consequently we cannot claim an experimental effect even though there very well may be one.

It is clear, then, that the lower we set the rejection level, the less is the likelihood of a Type I error, and the greater is the likelihood of a Type II

Type II Error (Type β Error): The probability of accepting H_0 when it is actually false. The probability of a type II error is given by β.

error. Conversely, the higher we set the rejection level, the greater is the likelihood of a Type I error, and the smaller is the likelihood of a Type II error.

The fact that the rejection level is set as low as it is attests to the conservatism of scientists, that is, the greater is the willingness on the part of the scientist to make an error in the direction of *failing* to claim a result than to make an error in the direction of *claiming* a result when he or she is wrong.

Table 11.2 summarizes the type of error made as a function of the true status of the null hypothesis and the decision we have made. We should note that Type I and Type II errors are sampling errors and refer to samples that are drawn from hypothetical populations.

Let's look at a few examples, in which for illustrative purposes we supply the following information about the underlying population: H_0, α-level, obtained p, statistical decision made, and the true status of H_0. Let's ascertain what type of error, if any, has been made.

1. $H_0: \mu_1 = \mu_2$, $\alpha = 0.05$, two-tailed test. Obtained $p = 0.03$, two-tailed value. Statistical decision: H_0 is false. Actual status of H_0: True.

Error: Type I—rejecting a true H_0.

2. $H_0: \mu_1 = \mu_2$, $\alpha = 0.05$, two-tailed test. Obtained $p = 0.04$, two-tailed value. Statistical decision: H_0 is false. Actual status of H_0: False.

Error: No error has been made. A correct conclusion was drawn, since H_0 is false and the statistical decision was that H_0 is false.

3. $H_0: \mu_1 = \mu_2$, $\alpha = 0.01$, two-tailed test. Obtained $p = 0.10$, two-tailed value. Statistical decision: fail to reject H_0. Actual status of H_0: False.

Error: Type II—failing to reject a false H_0.

TABLE 11.2   Type of Error Made as Function of True Status of H_0 and Statistical Decision Made*

		True Status of H_0	
		H_0 **True**	H_0 **False**
	Accept H_0	Correct $1 - \alpha$	Type II error β
Decision			
	Reject H_0	Type I error α	Correct $1 - \beta$

* To illustrate, if H_0 is true (column 1) and we have rejected H_0 (row 2), we have made a Type I error. If H_0 is false (column 2) and we have rejected H_0, we have made a correct decision.

STATISTICS IN ACTION 11.1

Type I and Type II errors applied to decision-making processes, including medical, psychological, sociological, economic, and other areas

Table 11.2 may be modified to exemplify an extremely broad spectrum of situations in which we must make decisions concerning one of two alternative courses of action. We may formulate two hypotheses, H_0: A given procedure will not work and H_1: A given procedure will work. If, in fact, it does not work, we have made a correct decision when we "accept" the null hypothesis. Thus, a physician who says "I will not use treatment A because it is ineffective" when the treatment is truly ineffective will have made a correct decision. But imagine that the treatment is really effective (i.e., H_0 is false), but the physician fails to reject H_0. This is analogous to a Type II error. Because of this error, the patient may be denied a treatment that will cure the disorder. Thus, you see, Type II errors *can* have serious consequences in the everyday world of decision making.

Let's look at another example. When considering the use of asbestos wrapping as an insulating material for hot water lines, the null hypothesis might be: H_0: Asbestos is not harmful. For years, we failed to reject this hypothesis and acted as if asbestos were harmless, when, in fact, the null hypothesis was false (Type II error: We failed to reject a false null hypothesis). Because of this failure to reject a false null hypothesis (i.e., H_0: Asbestos is not harmful), untold thousands of workers and others exposed to asbestos fibers are now at high risk for the development of lung cancer and other disorders of the lung. In fact, the National Institute of Occupational Safety and Health (NIOSH) has established exposure limits for well over 100 substances, many previously thought not to be harmful [NIOSH Recommendations for Occupational Safety and Health Standards, *Morbidity and Mortality Weekly Report, Supplement*, 34/(1S) 1985]. An interesting historical note in this connection is that early in his career as a medical doctor, Sigmund Freud regarded cocaine as a miracle drug. His failure to reject a false null hypothesis (H_0: Cocaine is not addicting) led to the mistaken advocacy of cocaine as a harmless way to relieve a number of disorders, including morphine addiction (cited in Dusek and Girdano, 1980).

Table 11.3 summarizes the errors that can be made as a result of accepting a false H_0 concerning the safety of a substance or incorrectly failing to reject a false H_0.

a. One of the logical problems in dealing with Type I and Type II errors is that the null hypothesis is usually expressed in the negative form. To illustrate, suppose that a pharmaceutical house is investigating the effectiveness of a new compound for the treatment of AIDS. The most likely null hypothesis is: H_0: The compound is ineffective. Rejection of H_0 involves a double negative. We do *not* accept the hypothesis that the compound is *in*effective. Two negatives make a positive. Thus,

TABLE 11.3 Types of errors and correct decisions that can be made as a function of true status of safety of substance*

| H_0: Product is not harmful | True status of H_0 | |
	Product is not harmful (H_0 true)	Product is harmful (H_0 false)
Fail to reject H_0 (treat as harmless)	Correct failure to reject The product may be used without jeopardizing public health.	Incorrect failure to reject (Type II error) Harmful substance is treated as if harmless (i.e., safe). Public health is jeopardized (e.g., DDT).
Reject H_0 (treat as harmful)	Incorrect rejection (Type I error) Harmless product is treated as harmful. Public is denied a possible treatment.	Correct rejection Product is banned. Public health is not jeopardized.

Decision

* H_0: Suspected substance is not harmful. H_1: Suspected substance is harmful. If we fail to reject H_0, we treat the substance as if it is not harmful (i.e., safe). If we reject H_0, we regard the substance as harmful (i.e., unsafe).

rejecting H_0 leads to the assertion that the compound is effective. Assuming that H_0 is true, show the consequences of a false rejection. Assuming that H_0 is false, shows the consequences of a failure to reject.

b. A parole board must decide whether or not to parole a previously dangerous prisoner. What is H_0? Show the consequences of the two types of decisions that can be made when H_0 is true and when H_0 is false.

c. A mental health team must decide whether the client's symptoms and complaints are "psychological" or "organic" before initiating treatment. The null hypothesis is that the symptoms are not organic. Show the consequences of falsely rejecting H_0 and failing to reject a false H_0.

ANSWERS

a. If H_0 is falsely rejected (the compound is found to be effective when it is not), the compound is likely to be used and discovered to be ineffective only after the continued deterioration and death of a number of patients. Its use may also preclude the adoption of other treatment regimes that may be effective. Many medical procedures, standard at one time, were dropped only after repeated failures, such as purging and blood letting. Also, the literature of medicine and psychology abounds with examples of charlatans who took advantage of the misfortunes of others to promote useless compounds and/or procedures as safe and effective treatments of serious disorders.

On the other hand, if the compound is truly effective, the failure to reject H_0 may lead to the false belief that the compound is ineffective. Thus, research on a promising compound may be abandoned and patients may be denied effective treatments for life-threatening disorders.

b. H_0: The prisoner is not dangerous. If H_0 is true and the prisoner is released, a correct decision has been made. If H_0 is true and a prisoner remains incarcerated (i.e., H_0 is rejected), society loses a possible productive individual (Type I error). If H_0 is false and the prisoner is released, a dangerous person has been let loose in society (Type II error). If H_0 is false and the prisoner is not released, a correct decision has been made.

c. If H_0 is falsely rejected (i.e., the symptoms are not organic) and the client is treated exclusively for an organic disorder, the client is unlikely to show improvement (except possibly as a result of a placebo effect). If H_0 is falsely accepted (i.e., the disorder really is organic), the root cause of the disorder is unlikely to be touched by psychotherapy, while an effective course of therapy may be neglected.

---

4. H_0: $\mu_1 = \mu_2$, $\alpha = 0.01$, two-tailed test. Obtained $p = 0.06$ two-tailed value. Statistical decision: fail to reject H_0. Actual status of H_0: True.

Error: No error has been made, since the statistical decision has been to accept H_0 when H_0 is actually true.

You may now ask, "In actual practice, how can we tell when we are making a Type I or a Type II error?" The answer is simple: We can't! If we examine once again the logic of statistical inference, we can see why. As already stated, with rare exceptions we cannot or shall not know the true parameters of a population. Without this knowledge, how can we know whether our sample statistics have approximated or have failed to approximate the true value? How can we know whether or not we have mistakenly rejected a null hypothesis? If we did know a population value, we could know whether or not we made an error. Under these circumstances, however, the need for sampling statistics is eliminated. We collect samples and draw inferences from samples only because our population values are unknowable for one reason or another. When they become known, the need for statistical inference is lost.

Is there no way, then, to know which experiments reporting significant results are accurate and which are not? The answer is a conditional "Yes." If we were to repeat the experiment and obtain similar results, we would have increased confidence that we were not making a Type I error. For example, if we tossed our coin in a second series of 10 trials and obtained 9 heads, we would feel far more confident that our coin was biased.

Parenthetically, repetition of experiments is one of the weaker areas in social science research. The general attitude is that a study is not much good unless it is "different" and is therefore making a novel contribution. Experiments designed solely to replicate results, when they are performed, frequently go unpublished. In consequence, we may feel assured that in studies employing the 0.05 significance level, approximately one out of every 20 that reject the null hypothesis is making a Type I error.*

11.6 PUTTING IT ALL TOGETHER

The concept of a sampling distribution is critical in inferential statistics. We shall encounter numerous sampling distributions in this course, including the standard normal distribution (Chapter 12), Student's t-distributions (Chapters 12 and 13), the F distributions (Chapters 14 and 15), and the chi-square distributions (Chapter 17). Although they differ in specific applications, they all share a characteristic in common—the sampling distribution provides a theoretical standard or reference against which we can weigh the probability that empirically obtained sample statistics or the differences between sample statistics were drawn from and are representative of the population of interest.

To illustrate these steps, the construction of an illustrative sampling distribution is shown in Tables 11.4 and 11.5. Table 11.4 shows 121 sample means based on selecting all possible samples of $N = 2$, with replacement, from a population of 11 numbers from 0 through 10.

We then construct a frequency distribution of these 121 means and, dividing each frequency by the number of means $(N_{\bar{x}})$, we obtain the probability of obtaining each mean from 0 through 10.00. This sampling distribution is shown in Table 11.5.

Now let's suppose we draw a sample of $N = 2$ from some unknown population. Our task involves some statistical sleuthing: We must decide whether or not it is likely that the mean we obtained was drawn from the population of numbers from which the sampling distribution in Table 11.5 was constructed.

We are next faced with the problem of formulating decision-making rules. How do we decide whether or not the sample mean was likely to have been drawn from the population of interest? Probability points the way.

---

* The proportion is probably even higher, since our methods of accepting research reports for publication are heavily weighted in terms of the statistical significance of the results. Thus, if four identical studies were conducted independently, and only one obtained results that permitted rejection of the null hypothesis, *this* one would be most likely to be published. There is virtually no way for the general scientific public to know about the three studies that *failed* to reject the null hypothesis.

TABLE 11.4   121 Sample Means Based on Selecting All Possible Samples of $N = 2$, with Replacement, from a Population of 11 Numbers

Second Draw	First Draw										
	0	**1**	**2**	**3**	**4**	**5**	**6**	**7**	**8**	**9**	**10**
0	0.0	0.5	1.0	1.5	2.0	2.5	3.0	3.5	4.0	4.5	5.0
1	0.5	1.0	1.5	2.0	2.5	3.0	3.5	4.0	4.5	5.0	5.5
2	1.0	1.5	2.0	2.5	3.0	3.5	4.0	4.5	5.0	5.5	6.0
3	1.5	2.0	2.5	3.0	3.5	4.0	4.5	5.0	5.5	6.0	6.5
4	2.0	2.5	3.0	3.5	4.0	4.5	5.0	5.5	6.0	6.5	7.0
5	2.5	3.0	3.5	4.0	4.5	5.0	5.5	6.0	6.5	7.0	7.5
6	3.0	3.5	4.0	4.5	5.0	5.5	6.0	6.5	7.0	7.5	8.0
7	3.5	4.0	4.5	5.0	5.5	6.0	6.5	7.0	7.5	8.0	8.5
8	4.0	4.5	5.0	5.5	6.0	6.5	7.0	7.5	8.0	8.5	9.0
9	4.5	5.0	5.5	6.0	6.5	7.0	7.5	8.0	8.5	9.0	9.5
10	5.0	5.5	6.0	6.5	7.0	7.5	8.0	8.5	9.0	9.5	10.0

TABLE 11.5   Frequency and Probability Distribution of All Possible Sample Means of $N = 2$, with Replacement, from a Population of 11 Numbers, 0 through 10

Mean	f	p
0	1	0.008
0.5	2	0.017
1.0	3	0.025
1.5	4	0.033
2.0	5	0.041
2.5	6	0.050
3.0	7	0.058
3.5	8	0.066
4.0	9	0.074
4.5	10	0.083
5.0	11	0.091
5.5	10	0.083
6.0	9	0.074
6.5	8	0.066
7.0	7	0.058
7.5	6	0.050
8.0	5	0.041
8.5	4	0.033
9.0	3	0.025
9.5	2	0.017
10.0	1	0.008
$N_{\bar{X}} = 121$		$p = 1.00$

1. If the event in question or an event more rare would have occurred 5% of the time or less in the sampling distribution of the statistic (Table 11.5), we shall decide that the mean was not drawn from the population of 11 scores. We shall call this the *reject decision*.
2. If the event in question or an event more rare would have occurred more than 5% of the time in the sampling distribution of the statistic, we shall entertain as possible the hypothesis that the mean was drawn from the indicated population. We shall call this the *fail to reject decision*. Note that the fail to reject decision does not lead to the positive assertion that the event was drawn from the known population. It merely acknowledges the reasonable possibility that it was.

We now select one score from the unknown population, record it, and return it to the population. We select a second score, add it to the first, divide by 2, and obtain a mean of 7.5. Referring to Table 11.5, we see that the probability of obtaining a mean equal to 7.5 or greater is $0.050 + 0.041 + 0.033 + 0.025 + 0.017 + 0.008 = 0.174$ or 17.4%. Note that the probability of obtaining a mean of 1.5 or less is also 0.174. Thus, the probability of obtaining a mean as rare as 7.5 is $0.174 + 0.174 = 0.348$. Since this probability is greater than 5%, we make the fail to reject decision. We do not reject the null hypothesis: The population from which the sample was drawn was the same as the population from which the sampling distribution was constructed.

But what if we had obtained a mean of 0.5 or 9.5? The probability of obtaining a mean this rare (0.5 or lower + 9.5 or higher) equals $0.017 + 0.008 + 0.017 + 0.008 = 0.05$. Since this probability is equal to or less than 0.05, we invoke the reject decision. We reject the null hypothesis and conclude that the sample was drawn from some population other than the one from which we constructed the sampling distribution.

Is there a chance that we have made an error? Yes, this is an inescapable fact of statistical decision making. There are two types of decision errors we can make. We may mistakenly reject the null hypothesis when it is actually true (in the sampling distribution shown in Table 11.5, we will, on the average, obtain means equal to 0.5 or lower or 9.5 or higher approximately 5% of the time, by chance). This type of decision error is known as a Type I or Type α error. There are also times when we will fail to reject the null hypothesis when it is actually false. This decision error is known as a Type II or Type β error.

Type I errors are generally regarded as more serious than Type II errors since they usually lead to the claim of a demonstrated effect, such as the operation of an experimental variable. To reduce the possibility of this type of error, some researchers prefer to use the 0.01 or 1% significance level for making the reject decision. Although adopting this significance level will provide further protection against a Type I error, it carries with it an increased risk of failing to reject the null hypothesis when it is actually false (Type II error).

CHAPTER SUMMARY

We have seen that one of the basic problems of inferential statistics involves estimating population parameters from sample statistics.

In inferential statistics we are frequently called upon to compare our *obtained* values with *expected* values. The expected values are given by the appropriate sampling distribution, which is a theoretical probability distribution of the possible values of a sample statistic.

We have seen how to use sampling distributions to interpret sample statistics.

We have seen that there are two mutually exclusive and exhaustive statistical hypotheses in every experiment: The null hypothesis (H_0) and the alternative hypothesis (H_1).

If the outcome of an experiment is rare (here "rare" is defined as some arbitrary but accepted probability value), we reject the null hypothesis and assert its alternative. If the event is not rare (i.e., the probability value is *greater* than what we have agreed upon as being significant), we fail to reject the null hypothesis. However, in no event are we permitted to claim that we have *proved* H_0.

The experimenter is faced with two types of errors in establishing a cutoff probability value that he or she will accept as significant.

Type I: Rejecting the null hypothesis when it is true.

Type II: Failing to reject ("accepting") the null hypothesis when it is false.

The basic conservatism of scientists causes them to establish a low level of significance, resulting in a greater incidence of Type II errors than of Type I errors.

Without replication of experiments, we have no basis for knowing when a Type I error has been made, and even with replication we cannot claim knowledge of absolute truth.

Finally, and perhaps most important, we have seen that scientific knowledge is probabilistic and not absolute.

TERMS TO REMEMBER

alpha- (α) level	**population**
alternative hypothesis (H_1)	**sample**
binomial distribution	**sampling distribution**

directional hypothesis
nondirectional hypothesis
null hypothesis (H_0)
one-tailed probability value

significance level
two-tailed probability value
Type I error (Type α error)
Type II error (Type β error)

EXERCISES

1. Explain in your own words the nature of drawing inferences in behavioral science. Be sure to specify the types of risks that are taken and the ways in which the researcher attempts to keep these risks within specifiable limits.

2. Give examples of experimental studies in which
   a. a Type I error would be considered more serious than a Type II error.
   b. a Type II error would be considered more serious than a Type I error.

3. After completing a study in experimental psychology, David S. concluded, "I have proved that no difference exists between the two experimental conditions." Criticize his conclusion according to the logic of drawing inferences in science.

4. Explain what is meant by the following statement: "It can be said that the purpose of any experiment is to provide the occasion for rejecting the null hypothesis."

5. An experimental psychologist hypothesizes that drive affects running speed. Assume that she has set up a study to investigate the problem employing two different drive levels. Formulate H_0 and H_1.

6. Identify H_0 and H_1 in the following:
   a. The population mean in intelligence is 100.
   b. The proportion of Democrats in Watanabe County is not equal to 0.50.
   c. The population mean in intelligence is not equal to 100.
   d. The proportion of Democrats in Watanabe County is equal to 0.50.

7. Suppose that you are a personnel manager responsible for recommending the promotion of an employee to a high-level executive position. What type of error would you be making if
   a. the hypothesis that he is qualified (H_0) is erroneously accepted?
   b. the hypothesis that he is qualified is erroneously rejected?
   c. the hypothesis that he is qualified is correctly accepted?
   d. the hypothesis that he is qualified is correctly rejected?

8. Given α and the p-values associated with the outcome of an experiment, make the decision whether or not to reject H_0.

   a. $\alpha = 0.01$, two-tailed; $p = 0.007$, one-tailed

   b. $\alpha = 0.01$, one-tailed; $p = 0.009$, one-tailed.

   c. $\alpha = 0.05$, two-tailed; $p = 0.03$, one-tailed.

9. An investigator sets $\alpha = 0.01$ for rejection of H_0, He conducts a study in which he obtains a p-value of 0.02 and fails to reject H_0. *Discuss:* Is it more likely that he is accepting a true or a false H_0?

10. *Comment:* A student of psychology has collected a mass of data to test 100 different null hypotheses. On completion of the analysis, she finds that 5 of the 100 comparisons yield p-values ≤ 0.05. She concludes: "Using $\alpha = 0.05$, I have found a true difference in five of the comparisons."

11. *Comment:* As an investigator, you have tested 500 different individuals for evidence of extrasensory perception (ESP). Employing $\alpha = 0.01$, you conclude, "I have found 6 individuals who demonstrated ESP."

12. Does the null hypothesis in a one tailed test differ from the null hypothesis in a two-tailed test?

13. Does the alternative hypothesis in a one-tailed test differ from the alternative hypothesis in a two-tailed test? Give an example.

14. In rejecting the null hypothesis for a one-tailed test, do all deviations count equally? Explain.

15. Suppose you want to test the hypothesis that there is not an equal number of male and female executives in a given large company. The appropriate null hypothesis would be as follows:

   a. There are more female than male executives.

   b. The numbers of male and female executives are equal.

   c. There are more male than female executives.

16. Suppose an efficiency expert finds a significant difference between the time it takes people to read a circular dial and the time it takes them to read a rectangular dial. Although $\alpha = 0.05$ or $\alpha = 0.01$ is traditionally applied as the level of significance, this choice is arbitrary. For each of the following levels of significance, state how many times in 1000 this difference would be expected to occur by chance.

   a. 0.001   **b.** 0.01   **c.** 0.005   **d.** 0.36

   e. 0.05   **f.** 0.095   **g.** 0.004   **h.** 0.10

17. With reference to Exercise 16, the adoption of which level of significance would be most likely to result in the following statements?

    a. There is a significant difference between the reading times of the two dials.

    b. It cannot be concluded that there is a significant difference between the reading times of the two dials.

18. Refer again to Exercise 16. The adoption of which level of significance would be most likely to result in the following errors? Identify the type of each error.

    a. There is a significant different between the reading times of the two dials. *Fact:* There is no difference.

    b. It cannot be concluded that there is a significant difference between the reading times of the two dials. *Fact:* There is a difference.

19. If $\alpha = 0.05$, what is the probability of making a Type I error?

20. Refer to Table 11.2. Suppose you are a clinician engaged in the diagnosis of individuals seeking help for emotional disorders. Assume that a person has or does not have a disorder. Construct a table that describes the types of error that a clinician might make.

21. In view of the table you constructed in Exercise 20, what are some circumstances in which a Type II error may have more serious consequences than a Type I error?

In Exercises 22 through 26, H_0, α, obtained p, and true status of H_0 are given. State whether or not an error in statistical decision has been made. If so, state the type of error.

22. $H_0: P = Q$, $\alpha = 0.01$, one-tailed test. Obtained $p = 0.008$, one-tailed value (in predicted direction). Actual status of H_0: True.

23. $H_0: P = Q$, $\alpha = 0.05$, two-tailed test. Obtained $p = 0.08$, two-tailed value. Actual status of H_0: True.

24. $H_0: P = Q$, $\alpha = 0.05$, two-tailed test. Obtained $p = 0.06$, two-tailed value. Actual status of H_0: False.

25. $H_0: P = Q$, $\alpha = 0.05$, two-tailed test. Obtained $p = 0.03$, two-tailed value. Actual status of H_0: False.

26. $H_0: P = Q$, $\alpha = 0.01$, two-tailed test. Obtained $p = 0.005$, two-tailed value. Actual status of H_0: False.

Statistical Inference and Continuous Variables

12.1 INTRODUCTION

In Chapter 11, we illustrated the use of a sampling distribution for a discrete two-category nominal variable (the binomial distribution) and for all possible means when drawing samples of a fixed N from a population of four scores. Table 11.1 showed the frequency and probability distributions of means when all possible samples of a given size were selected from the population of four scores. Figure 12.1 shows probability histograms, with superimposed curves that were obtained by connecting the midpoints of each bar.

Before proceeding with the discussion of sampling distributions for interval- or ratio-scaled variables, examine Table 11.1 and Figure 12.1 carefully. See if you can answer the following questions.

1. How does the mean of each sampling distribution of means compare with the mean of the population from which the samples were drawn?
2. How does the variability of dispersion of the sample means change as we increase the sample size on which sampling distribution is based?

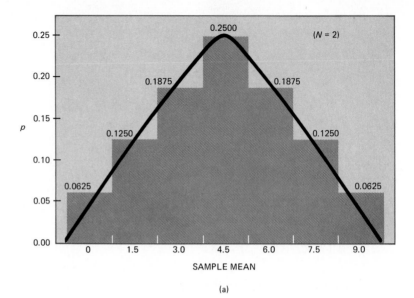

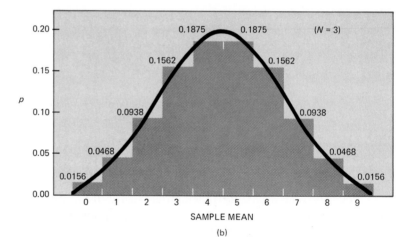

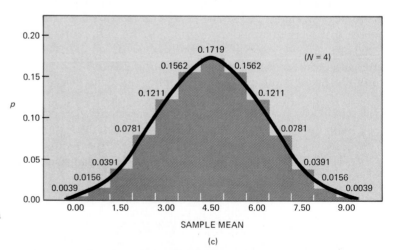

FIGURE 12.1 Probability histograms based on sampling distributions of means drawn, with replacement, from a population of four scores and sample sizes $N = 2$, $N = 3$, and $N = 4$.

Now compare your answers with ours:

1. The mean of the population of four scores is 4.5. The mean of each sampling distribution of means is 4.5. Thus, the mean of a sampling distribution of means is the same as the population mean from which the sample means were drawn. This statement is true for all sizes of N. In other words, the mean of the sampling distribution does not vary with the sample size.

2. As you increase the sample size, the dispersion of sample means becomes less. A greater proportion of means is close to the population mean and extreme deviations are rarer as N becomes larger. To verify these statements, note the probability of obtaining a mean as rare as 0 or 9 at different sample sizes. Note also that the proportion of means in the middle of the distribution becomes greater as the sample size is increased. For example, the proportion of means between and including 3 and 6 is 0.6250 when $N = 2$, 0.6874 when $N = 3$, and 0.7265 when $N = 4$.

Finally, the standard deviation of the sample means—which we'll call the **standard error of the mean** from this point forward—shows that the dispersion of sample means decreases as sample size is increased.

In the forthcoming chapters, we shall calculate many different standard errors in addition to the standard error of the mean. These standard errors represent bench marks against which we evaluate differences in means, proportions, correlations, and so forth. The smaller the standard error for a particular data set is, the more precise our estimates will become. Thus, increasing the sample size is one way of increasing the precision of our statistical decisions.

However, notice that the decrease is not linear. In going from $N = 1$ to $N = 2$ in Figure 12.2, the decrease in $s_{\bar{x}}$ equals $3.35 - 2.37 = 0.98$; from $N = 2$ to $N = 3$, the decrease is $2.37 - 1.94 = 0.43$; and from $N = 3$ to $N = 4$, the decrease is $1.94 - 1.68 = 0.26$. Thus, increasing the sample size is a curve of diminishing returns. A point will be reached when nonstatistical considerations (the difficulty of obtaining subjects, time, economics, and logistics) will outweigh the advantages of increasing N.

> **Standard Error of the Mean:** A theoretical standard deviation of sample means, of a given sample size, drawn from some specified population. When based on a known population standard deviation, $\sigma_{\bar{x}} \, \sigma/\sqrt{N}$; when estimated from a single sample, $s_{\bar{x}} = s/\sqrt{N - 1}$.

12.2 SAMPLING DISTRIBUTION OF THE MEAN

Imagine that we are conducting a sampling experiment in which we randomly draw (with replacement)* a sample of two scores from a population in which $\mu = 5.00$ and $\sigma = 0.99$ (see Table 12.1). For example, we

---

* If the population is infinite or extremely large, the difference between sampling with or without replacement is negligible.

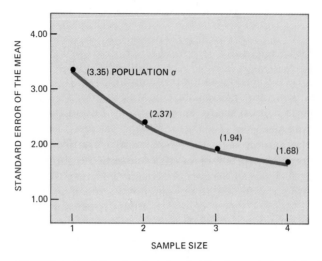

FIGURE 12.2 A line drawing showing the decreasing magnitude of $s_{\bar{x}}$ as the sample size increases. Shown are the population standard deviation of four scores and the standard error of the mean for the sampling distributions when $N = 2$, $N = 3$, and $N = 4$.

might draw scores of 3 and 6. We calculate the sample mean and find $\bar{X}$ = 4.5. Now suppose we continue to draw samples of $N = 2$ (e.g., we might draw scores of 2, 8; 3, 7; 4, 5; 5, 6; etc.) until we obtain an indefinitely large number of samples. If we calculate the sample mean for each sample drawn, and treat each of these sample means as a raw score, we may set up a frequency distribution of these sample means.

Let's repeat these procedures with increasingly larger sample sizes, for example, $N = 5$, $N = 15$. We now have three frequency distributions of sample means based on three different sample sizes.

Intuitively, what might we expect these distributions to look like? Since we are selecting at random from the population, we would expect the

TABLE 12.1 An Approximately Normally Distributed Population with $\mu = 5.00$ and $\sigma = 0.99$

X	f	p(X)
2	4	0.004
3	54	0.054
4	242	0.242
5	400	0.400
6	242	0.242
7	54	0.054
8	4	0.004
	$N = 1000$	$\Sigma\, p(X) = 1.000$

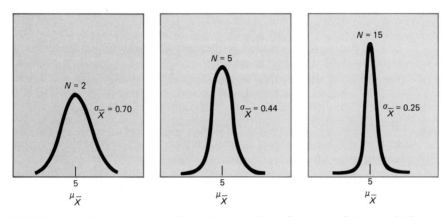

FIGURE 12.3   Frequency curves of sample means drawn from a population in which μ = 5.00 and σ = 0.99.

mean of the distribution of sample means of approximate the mean of the population.

How might the dispersion of these sample means compare with the variability in the original distribution of scores? In the original distribution, when $N = 1$, the probability of obtaining a *score* as large as, say, 8 is 4/1000 or 0.004 (see Table 12.1). The probability of obtaining a sample *mean* equal to 8 when $N = 2$ (i.e., drawing scores of 8, 8) is equal to 0.004 $\times$ 0.004 or 0.000016 [Formula (10.9)]. In other words, the probability of selecting a sample with an extreme *mean* is less than the probability of selecting a single score that is equally extreme. What if we increased our sample size to $N = 4$? The probability of obtaining results this extreme ($\overline{X} = 8$) is exceedingly small, $(0.004)^4 = 0.0000000003$. Generalizing, the probability of drawing extreme values of the sample mean is less as N increases. Since the standard deviation is a direct function of the number of extreme scores (see Chapter 6), it follows that a distribution containing proportionately fewer extreme scores will have a lower standard deviation. Therefore, if we treat each of the sample means as a raw score and then calculate the standard deviation of the means around the population mean ($\sigma_{\overline{X}}$ referred to as the *standard error of the mean**), it is clear that as the sample size increases, the variability of the sample means decreases.

If these sampling experiments were actually conducted, the frequency curves of sample means shown in Figure 12.3 would be obtained.

There are three important lessons that may be learned from a careful examination of Figure 12.3.

---

* This notation represents the standard deviation of a sampling distribution of means. This is purely a theoretical notation, since with an infinite number of sample means it is not possible to assign a specific value to the number of sample means involved.

1. The distribution of sample means drawn from a normally distributed population is bell-shaped or "normal." Indeed, it can be shown that even if the underlying distribution is skewed, the distribution of sample means will tend to be normal.
2. The mean of the sample means ($\mu_{\bar{x}}$) is equal to the mean of the population (μ) from which these samples were drawn.
3. The distribution of sample means shows less and less dispersion as we increase the size of the sample. This is an extremely important point in statistical inference, about which we shall soon have a great deal more to say.

If we base our estimate of the population mean on a *single* sample drawn from the population, our approximation to the parameter is likely to be closer as we increase the size of the sample. In other words, if it is true that the dispersion of sample means decreases with increasing sample size, it also follows that the mean of any single sample is more likely to be closer to the mean of the population as the sample size increases.

These three observations illustrate a rather startling theorem that is of fundamental importance in inferential statistics, the **central limit theorem,** which states:

Central Limit Theorem: If random samples of a fixed N are drawn from *any* population (regardless of the form of the population distribution), as N becomes larger, the distribution of the sample means approaches normality.

If random samples of a fixed N are drawn from **any** population (regardless of the form of the population distribution), as N becomes larger, the distribution of sample means approaches normality, with the overall mean approaching μ, the variance of the sample means $\sigma_{\bar{x}}^2$ being equal to σ^2/N and a standard error $\sigma_{\bar{x}}$ of $\sigma/\sqrt{N}$.

Stated symbolically:

$$\sigma_{\bar{X}}^2 = \frac{\sigma^2}{N} \tag{12.1}$$

and

$$\sigma_{\bar{X}} = \frac{\sigma}{\sqrt{N}} \tag{12.2}$$

CASE EXAMPLE 12.1

A Statistical Sampling Experiment

Most of us are aware of the information processing revolution that was ushered in by the advent of the computer. Calculations that previously took hours, days, and even weeks to perform are now completed within time frames that include

TABLE 12.2 Sample Means Obtained by Randomly Selecting 22 Samples of $N = 5$ and 22 Samples of $N = 15$ from a Uniform Population of 85 Integers from 1 through 85

$N = 5$		$N = 15$	
25.4	45.6	25.07	42.27
29.2	46.0	31.07	42.40
34.2	47.0	31.40	43.00
35.4	48.8	33.00	43.60
35.6	48.8	36.67	43.60
36.2	49.0	37.40	44.07
38.6	49.2	37.67	45.07
38.8	50.6	40.00	45.73
42.6	51.6	40.80	50.07
42.8	57.8	41.50	54.13
43.6	61.8	41.60	55.93

$$\Sigma \bar{X} = 958.6 \qquad \Sigma \bar{X} = 906.05$$
$$N_s = 22 \qquad N_s = 22$$
$$\bar{X}_{\bar{X}} = 43.47 \qquad \bar{X}_{\bar{X}} = 41.18$$
$$s_{\bar{x}} = 8.65 \qquad s_{\bar{x}} = 7.41$$

where N_s is the number of sample means, $\bar{X}_{\bar{X}}$ is the mean of the sample means, and $s_{\bar{x}}$ is the standard deviation of the sample means.

microseconds and milliseconds. Moreover, as long as the data entry is accurate and the programming is flawless, the computer simply does not make errors. For this reason, the computer has become an indispensable element of human endeavor, be it in business, education, or the sciences.

What is, perhaps, less appreciated by the general public is the fact that the computer's capabilities are not limited to high-speed computation. For example, it may be used to conduct statistical experiments that illuminate some of the "shadowy corners" of statistical thinking.

In one statistical experiment, the author had a computer select samples from a population and calculate the mean, variance, and standard deviation of each sample. The samples were selected from a population that was distributed in a completely uniform fashion—numbers from 1 to 85. The mean and standard deviation of the population were 43 and 24.54, respectively. Two sets of 22 samples were selected from this population—one with $N = 5$ and the other with $N = 15$. The results are shown in Table 12.2.

Before looking at the table, however, try answering the following questions: Do you expect that each sample mean will equal the population mean? What about the distribution of the means of each of the 22 samples based on Ns

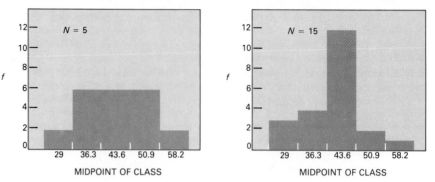

FIGURE 12.4 Grouped frequency histograms of sample means based on Ns equal to 5 and 15, respectively. The samples were randomly and independently selected from a population in which the measurements are uniformly distributed.

equal to 5 and 15, respectively? Do you expect the variability of the sample means to change in any systematic way as the sample size increases from $N = 1$ (the population distribution) to $N = 15$? What about the form of the distribution of the sample means? Does it mimic the population distribution of scores, or does it tend to change with increasing sample size? Now look at Table 12.2 and Figure 12.4 and compare your answers with the results of the sampling experiment.

When examining Table 12.2, notice that

Unbiased Estimator: An estimator that equals, on the average, the value of the corresponding parameter.

1. Each sample mean is not equal to the population mean. However, the mean of the sample means is a pretty good approximation to the population mean. It can be shown that the means of randomly selected samples, averaged over all possible samples, will yield the population mean as the average value. The means are said to be **unbiased estimators** of the population mean.

2. The variability among the sample means decreases as the sample size increases. The range and standard deviation of the population were 84 and 24.54, respectively. When $N = 5$, the range and standard deviations of the sample means were 36.4 and 8.65, respectively. Finally, with $N = 15$, the range fell to 30.86, and the standard deviation declined to 7.41.

3. The form of the distribution of means also changed with increased sample size. Remember that the population distribution was absolutely flat, with all 85 values having an associated frequency of 1. Figure 12.4 presents grouped frequency histograms of the sample means. Note how nicely they illustrate the central limit theorem. With sample sizes as small as 15, the distribution of the sample means already begins to take on the classic bell-shaped form of the normal probability distribution.

Source: Based on Richard P. Runyon, "A Statistical Sampling Experiment," Chapter 7 of *Fundamentals of Statistics in the Biological, Medical, and Health Sciences.* Boston: Duxbury Press, 1985.

12.3   TESTING STATISTICAL HYPOTHESES: POPULATION MEAN AND STANDARD DEVIATION KNOWN

Finding the Probability that a Sample Mean Will Fall Within a Certain Range

Let us briefly examine some of the implications of the relationships we have just discussed.

When μ and σ are *known* for a given population, it is possible to describe the form of the distribution of sample means that are drawn randomly from this population when N is large (regardless of the form of the original distribution). It will be a normal distribution with a mean ($\mu_{\bar{X}}$) equal to μ and a standard error $\sigma_{\bar{X}}$ equal to $\sigma/\sqrt{N}$. It now becomes possible to determine probability values in terms of areas under the normal curve. Thus, we may use the known relationships of the normal probability curve to determine the probabilities associated with any sample mean (of a given N) that is randomly drawn from this population.

We have already seen (Section 7.3) that any normally distributed variable may be transformed into the normally distributed z-scale. We have also seen (Section 10.8) that we may establish probability values in terms of the relationships between z-scores and areas under the normal curve. That is, for any given raw score value X with a certain proportion of area beyond it, there is a corresponding value of z with the same proportion of area beyond it. Similarly, for any given value of a sample mean $\bar{X}$ with a certain proportion of area beyond it, there is a corresponding value of z with the same proportion of area beyond it. Thus, assuming that the form of the distribution of sample means is normal, we may establish probability values in terms of the relationships between z-scores and areas under the normal curve.

To illustrate: Given a population with $\mu = 250$ and $\sigma = 50$, from which we randomly select 100 scores ($N = 100$), what is the probability that the sample mean $\bar{X}$ will be equal to or greater than 255? Thus, $H_0: \mu = \mu_0 = 250$.

The value of z corresponding to $\bar{X} = 255$ is obtained as follows:

$$z = \frac{\bar{X} - \mu_0}{\sigma_{\bar{X}}} \qquad (12.3)$$

where μ_0 = value of the population mean under H_0

$$\sigma_{\bar{X}} = \frac{\sigma}{\sqrt{N}} = \frac{50}{\sqrt{100}} = 5.00 \qquad \text{and} \qquad z = \frac{255 - 250}{5.00} = 1.0$$

Looking up a z of 1.00 in column (C) in Table A, at the back of this book, we find that 15.87% of the sample means falls at or above $\bar{X} = 255$. Thus, there are approximately 16 chances in 100 of obtaining a sample mean equal to or greater than 255 from this population when $N = 100$.

Testing Hypotheses about the Sample Mean

Now extend this logic to a situation in which we do not know from what population a sample is drawn. We suspect that it may have been selected from the preceding population with $\mu = 250$ and $\sigma = 50$, but we are not certain. We want to test the hypothesis that our sample mean was indeed selected from this population. Imagine that we had obtained $\overline{X} = 263$ for $N = 100$. Is it reasonable to assume that this sample was drawn from the suspected population?

Setting up this problem in formal statistical terms involves the following six steps that are common to all hypothesis testing situations:

1. *Null hypothesis (H_0):* The mean of the population (μ) from which the sample was drawn equals 250, that is, $\mu = \mu_0 = 250$.
2. *Alternative hypothesis (H_1):* The mean of the population from which the sample was drawn does *not* equal 250; $\mu \neq \mu_0$. Note that H_1 is nondirectional; consequently, a two-tailed test of significance will be employed.
3. *Statistical test:* The z statistic is used since σ is known.
4. *Significance level:* $\alpha = 0.01$. If the difference between the sample mean and the specified population mean is so extreme that its associated probability of occurrence under H_0 is equal to or less than 0.01, we shall reject H_0.
5. *Sampling distribution:* The normal probability curve.
6. *Critical region for rejection of H_0:* $|z| \geq 2.58$.* A critical region is that portion of the area under the curve that includes those values of a statistic that lead to rejection of the null hypothesis.

Critical Region: That portion of the area under the curve that includes those values of a statistic that lead to rejection of the null hypothesis.

The **critical region** is chosen to correspond with the selected level of significance. Thus, for $\alpha = 0.01$, two-tailed test, the critical region is bounded by those values of $z_{0.01}$ that mark off a total of 1% of the area. Referring again to column (C), Table A, we find that the area beyond a z of 2.58 is approximately 0.005. We double 0.005 to account for both tails of the distribution. Figure 12.5 depicts the critical region for rejection of H_0 when $\alpha = 0.01$, two-tailed test.

Therefore, in order to reject H_0 at the 0.01 level of significance, the absolute value of the obtained z must be equal to or greater than $|z_{0.01}|$ or 2.58. Similarly, if we are to be allowed to reject H_0 at the 0.05 level of

---

* Since $z_{0.01} = \pm 2.58$, $z \geq |z_{0.01}|$ is equivalent to stating $z \geq 2.58$ or $z \leq -2.58$.

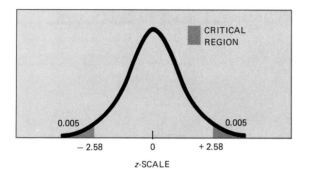

FIGURE 12.5 Critical region for rejection of H_0 when $\alpha = 0.01$, two-tailed test.

significance, the absolute value of the obtained z must be equal to or greater than $|z_{0.05}|$ or 1.96.

In the present example, the value of z corresponding to $\overline{X} = 263$ is

$$z = \frac{\overline{X} - \mu_0}{\sigma_{\overline{X}}} = \frac{263 - 250}{5.00} = 2.60$$

Decision: Since the obtained z falls within the critical region (i.e., $260 > z_{0.01}$), we may reject H_0 at the 0.01 level of significance.

Thus, we conclude that the population from which the sample was drawn is different from the population with a mean equal to 255.

12.4 ESTIMATION OF PARAMETERS: POINT ESTIMATION

So far, we have been concerned with testing hypotheses when the population parameters are known. However, we have taken some pains in this book to point out that population values are rarely known, particularly when the population is extremely large. Every ten years, when the U.S. federal government undertakes that massive data collection effort called the census, we come close to knowing the parameters on the various response measures. But knowledge of parameters is not the usual case. However, the fact that we do not know the population values does not prevent us from using the logic developed in Section 12.3.

Whenever we make inferences about population parameters from sample data, we compare our sample results with the expected results that are given by the appropriate sampling distribution. A hypothetical sampling distribution of sample means is associated with any sample mean. This distribution has a mean, $\mu_{\overline{X}}$, and a standard deviation, $\sigma_{\overline{X}}$. So far, in order to obtain the values of $\mu_{\overline{X}}$ and $\sigma_{\overline{X}}$, we have required knowledge of μ and σ. In the absence of knowledge concerning the exact values of these parameters, we are forced to estimate μ and σ from the statistics calculated from sample data. Since in actual practice we rarely select more than one sample,

BOX 12.1

UNBIASED ESTIMATE OF THE POPULATION VARIANCE

Throughout this book, we have turned to a sampling experiment whenever we wanted to illustrate a concept of fundamental importance in statistical analysis. Let's take a look at the denominator of the variance formula, and show that $N - 1$ in the denominator provides an unbiased estimate of the population variance, whereas N in the denominator underestimates the population variance.

Imagine the following sampling experiment. You place the following population of four scores in a hat: 1, 2, 3, 4. The mean of this population is 2.5 and the variance is 1.25. You select, with replacement, all possible samples of $N = 2$ and calculate the variance of each sample, using N and $N - 1$ in the denominator. Just as we previously placed the mean of each sample in the cell corresponding to both draws, we now place the *variance* of each sample in the appropriate cell.

First, let's do this using N in the denominator when calculating each sample variance.

Let us now construct a frequency distribution of these variances, and calculate the mean variance.

The mean variance is found to be 10/16 = 0.625. Recall that the variance of the population is 1.25. In this sampling experiment, where N is used in the denominator of the variance formula, the mean variance of possible samples of $N = 2$ underestimates the population variance. Generalizing, sample variances that use N in the denominator provide a biased estimate of the population variance.

Now let us repeat the same procedures, using $N - 1$ to calculate the variance of each sample.

The frequency distribution and mean of the sample variances are shown in the fourth table.

Now the mean variance is 20/16 = 1.25. Note that this is identical to the variance of the original population. Thus, using $N - 1$ in the denominator provides an unbiased estimate of the population variance.

Variance of Each Sample when Using N in Denominator ($N = 2$)

| | | First Draw | | | |
		1	2	3	4
Second Draw	1	0.00	0.25	1.00	2.25
	2	0.25	0.00	0.25	1.00
	3	1.00	0.25	0.00	0.25
	4	2.25	1.00	0.25	0.00

s^2	f	fs^2
2.25	2	4.50
1.00	4	4.00
0.25	6	1.50
0.00	4	0.00
$\Sigma f = 16$		$\Sigma fs^2 = 10.00$

Variance of Each Sample when Using $N - 1$ in Denominator ($N = 2$)

| | | First Draw | | | |
		1	2	3	4
Second Draw	1	0.00	0.50	2.00	4.50
	2	0.50	0.00	0.50	2.00
	3	2.00	0.50	0.00	0.50
	4	4.50	2.00	0.50	0.00

s^2	f	fs^2
4.50	2	9.00
2.00	4	8.00
0.50	6	3.00
0.00	4	0.00
$\Sigma f = 16$		$\Sigma fs^2 = 20.00$

our estimates are generally based on the statistics calculated from a single sample. All such estimates involving the use of single sample values are known as **point estimates.**

Estimating $\sigma_{\bar{X}}$ From Sample Data

You will recall that we previously defined the variance of a sample as

$$s^2 = \frac{\Sigma(X - \bar{X})^2}{N}$$

in Formula (6.2). We obtained the standard deviation, s, by finding the square root of this value. These definitions are perfectly appropriate so long as we are interested only in *describing* the variability of a sample. However, when our interest shifts to *estimating* the population variance from a sample value, we find this definition inadequate, since $\Sigma(X - \bar{X})^2/N$ tends on the average to *underestimate* the population variance. In other words, it provides a **biased estimate** of the population variance, whereas an unbiased estimate is required.

We define an *unbiased estimate* as an estimate that equals, on the average, the value of the parameter. That is, when we make the statement that a statistic is an unbiased estimate of a parameter, we are saying that the mean of the distribution of an extremely large number of sample statistics, drawn from a given population, tends to center on the corresponding value of the parameter. We demonstrate in Box 12.1 that an unbiased estimate of the population variance may be obtained by dividing the sum of squares by $N - 1$. We now employ the symbol $\hat{s}^2$ to represent a sample variance[2] providing an *unbiased estimate of the population variance*, and $\hat{s}$ to represent a sample standard deviation based on the unbiased variance estimate. Thus

$$\text{Unbiased estimate of } \sigma^2 = \hat{s}^2 = \frac{\Sigma(X - \bar{X})^2}{N - 1} \qquad (12.4)$$

and

$$\text{Estimated } \sigma = \hat{s} = \sqrt{\hat{s}^2} \qquad (12.5)$$

We are now able to estimate $\sigma_{\bar{X}}^2$ and $\sigma_{\bar{X}}$ from sample data. We shall employ the symbols $s_{\bar{X}}^2$ and $s_{\bar{X}}$ to refer to the estimated variance and standard error of the mean, respectively. Since we do not know σ^2, we accept the unbiased variance estimate $\hat{s}^2$ as the best estimate we have of the population variance. Thus, the formula for determining the variance of the sampling distribution of the mean from sample data is

$$\text{Estimated } \sigma_{\bar{X}}^2 = s_{\bar{X}}^2 = \frac{\hat{s}^2}{N} \qquad (12.6)$$

Point Estimation: An estimate of a population parameter that involves a single value, selected by the criterion of "best estimate." (Contrast *interval estimation*.)

Biased Estimate of a Parameter: An estimate that does not equal, on the average, the value of the parameter.

We estimate the standard error of the mean by finding the square root of this value:

$$\text{Estimated } \sigma_{\bar{X}} = s_{\bar{X}} = \sqrt{\frac{\hat{s}^2}{N}} = \frac{\hat{s}}{\sqrt{N}} \qquad (12.7)$$

If the sample variance (not the unbiased estimate) is used, we may estimate $\sigma_{\bar{X}}$ as

$$\text{Estimated } \sigma_{\bar{X}} = s_{\bar{X}} = \frac{s}{\sqrt{N-1}} = \sqrt{\frac{\Sigma(X - \bar{X})^2}{N(N-1)}} = \sqrt{\frac{SS}{N(N-1)}} \qquad (12.8)*$$

Formula (12.8) is the formula most frequently employed in the behavioral sciences to estimate the standard error of the mean. We shall follow this practice.

Before proceeding further, let us review some of the symbols we have been discussing. Table 12.3 shows the various symbols for means, variances, and standard deviations depending on whether we are dealing with population parameters, unbiased population estimators, or sample statistics.

12.5 TESTING STATISTICAL HYPOTHESES WITH UNKNOWN PARAMETERS: STUDENT'S *t*

We previously pointed out that when the parameters of a population are known, it is possible to describe the form of the sampling distribution of sample means. It will be a normal distribution with $\sigma_{\bar{X}}$ equal to $\sigma/\sqrt{N}$. By

---

* The following algebraic proof demonstrates how we arrive at this estimate of $\sigma_{\bar{X}}$:

$$s^2 = \frac{\Sigma(X - \bar{X})^2}{N}$$

Multiplying both sides of the equation by $N/(N-1)$, we get

$$\frac{N}{N-1}s^2 = \frac{N\Sigma(X - \bar{X})^2}{N(N-1)} = \hat{s}^2 \qquad \text{[see Formula (12.4)]}$$

Thus, from Formula (12.7),

$$s_{\bar{X}} = \sqrt{\frac{\hat{s}^2}{N}}$$

Substituting

$$\hat{s}^2 = \frac{N}{N-1}s^2$$

we find

$$s_{\bar{X}} = \sqrt{\frac{Ns^2}{N(N-1)}} = \frac{s}{\sqrt{N-1}}$$

TABLE 12.3   Review of Symbols

	Population Parameters (Theoretical)	Parameters of Sampling Distribution of Mean (Theoretical)	Unbiased Population Estimators for Sampling Distribution of Mean (Empirical)	Sample Statistics (Empirical)
Means	μ, μ_0	$\mu_{\bar{x}}$	$\bar{X}$	$\bar{X}$
Variances	σ^2	$\sigma_{\bar{X}}^2$	$\hat{s}, s_{\bar{X}}^2$	s^2
Standard deviations	σ	$\sigma_{\bar{X}}$	$\hat{s}, s_{\bar{X}}$	s

employing the relationship between the z-scale and the normal distribution, we can test hypotheses using

$$z = \frac{(\bar{X} - \mu_0)}{\sigma_{\bar{X}}}$$

as a test statistic. When σ is not known, we are forced to estimate its value from sample data. Consequently, estimated $\sigma_{\bar{X}}$ (i.e., $s_{\bar{X}}$) must be based on the estimated σ (i.e., $\hat{s}$), as

$$s_{\bar{X}} = \frac{\hat{s}}{\sqrt{N}}$$

Now, if substituting $\hat{s}$ for σ provided a reasonably good approximation to the sampling distribution of means, we could continue to use z as our test statistic, and the normal curve as the model for our sampling distribution. As a matter of fact, however, this is not the case. At the turn of the century a statistician by the name of William Gosset, who published under the pseudonym of Student, noted that the approximation of $\hat{s}$ to σ is poor, particularly for small samples. This failure of approximation is due to the fact that, with small samples, $\hat{s}$ will tend to underestimate σ more than one-half the time. Compared to the normal distribution, the statistic

$$\frac{\bar{X} - \mu_0}{\hat{s}/\sqrt{N}}$$

will tend to be flatter in the central region and spread out more in extreme regions (see Figure 12.6).

Gosset's major contribution to statistics consisted of his description of a family of distributions that permits the testing of hypotheses with samples drawn from normally distributed populations when σ is not known. These distributions are referred to variously as the **t-distributions** or *Student's t*.

t-**Distributions:** Theoretical symmetrical sampling distributions with a mean of zero and a standard deviation that becomes smaller as degrees of freedom (df) increase. Employed in relation to Student's *t*-ratio.

STATISTICS IN ACTION 12.1

Type A heart-rate data: Calculating standard error from previously computed standard deviations

You may recall that we previously calculated the mean, range, variance, and standard deviation over one practice and four test trials for ten Type A subjects who received no feedback and were not penalized for failure. The results of these analyses are summarized here.

	Practice	Trial 1	Trial 2	Trial 3	Trial 4
Mean	85.10	88.76	83.23	83.22	82.28
Range	36.0	42.6	37.4	36.7	38.0
s^2	92.41	116.58	106.64	89.83	103.07
s	9.61	10.80	10.33	9.48	10.15

Recall that the sample standard deviations are based on biased estimates of the population variance. To obtain the standard error of the mean based on an unbiased estimate of the population variance, we must divide the standard deviation for each trial by the square root of $N - 1$ (i.e. $\sqrt{N-1}$). This is quite straightforward. Since $\sqrt{N-1} = \sqrt{9} = 3.00$, we divide each of the preceding sample standard deviations by 3.00 to obtain $s_{\bar{x}}$ for each trial.* These conversions are shown as follows:

	Practice	Trial 1	Trial 2	Trial 3	Trial
$s_{\bar{x}}$	9.61/3.00	10.80/3.00	10.33/3.00	9.48/3.00	10.15/3.00
	= 3.20	= 3.60	= 3.44	= 3.16	= 3.38

a. Using the standard deviations you calculated for the HR measures of Type B subjects (Statistics in Action 6.1), find the standard error of the mean for each of the five trials.

b. You previously calculated the sum of squares (SS) for each trial. Using the formula $s_{\bar{x}} = \sqrt{SS/N(N-1)}$, confirm that you obtain the same standard error of the mean.

* Since $s_{\bar{x}} = s/\sqrt{N-1}$ and $s = \sqrt{SS/N}$, $s_{\bar{x}} = \sqrt{SS/N}/\sqrt{N-1} = \sqrt{SS/N(N-1)}$.

ANSWERS

a.	Practice	Trial 1	Trial 2	Trial 3	Trial 4
$s_{\bar{X}}$	15.08/3.00	13.83/3.00	14.22/3.00	14.00/3.00	16.33/3.00
	= 5.03	= 4.61	= 4.74	= 4.67	= 5.44
b.	$\sqrt{2273.46/90}$	$\sqrt{1911.63/90}$	$\sqrt{2020.87/90}$	$\sqrt{1958.93/90}$	$\sqrt{2665.82/90}$
	= 5.03	= 4.61	= 4.74	= 4.67	= 5.44

Source: Based on data from K. A. Perkins, (1984), "Heart Rate Changes in Type A and Type B Males as a Function of Response Cost and Task Difficulty," Psychophysiology **21**, 14–21.

The ratio employed in the testing of hypotheses is known as the **t-ratio:**

$$t = \frac{\bar{X} - \mu_0}{s_{\bar{X}}}$$

(12.9)

where μ_0 is the value of the population mean under H_0.

Sampling distributions of $t = (\bar{X} = \mu_0)/s_{\bar{x}}$ when df = 3 and 10, compared to the standard normal curve.

t-Ratio: A test statistic for determining the significance of a difference between means (two-sample case) or for testing the hypothesis that a given sample mean was drawn from a population with the mean specified under the null hypothesis (one-sample case). Employed when population standard deviation (or standard deviations) is not known.

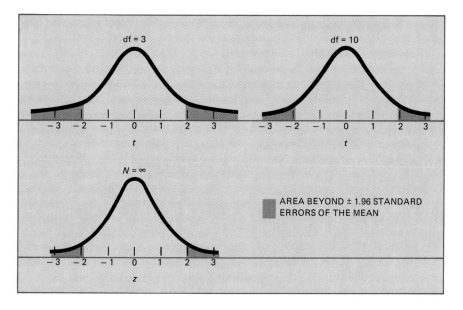

df = 3

df = 10

$N = \infty$

AREA BEYOND ± 1.96 STANDARD ERRORS OF THE MEAN

The *t*-statistic is similar in many respects to the previously discussed z-statistic. Both statistics are expressed as the deviation of a sample mean from a population mean (known or hypothesized) in terms of the standard error of the mean. By reference to the appropriate sampling distribution, we may express this deviation in terms of probability. When the z-statistic is used, the standard normal curve is the appropriate sampling distribution. For the *t*-statistic, there is a family of distributions that vary as a function of **degrees of freedom (df).**

Degree of Freedom (df): The number of values that are free to vary after we have placed certain restrictions upon our data.

The term "degrees of freedom" refers to the number of values that are free to vary after we have placed certain restrictions on our data. To illustrate, let us imagine that we have four numbers: 18, 23, 27, 32. The sum is 100 and the mean is $\overline{X} = 100/4 = 25$. Recall that if we subtract the mean from each score, we should obtain a set of four deviations that add up to zero. Thus

$$(18 - 25) + (23 - 25) + (27 - 25) + (32 - 25)$$
$$= (-7) + (-2) + 2 + 7 = 0$$

Note also that the four deviations are not independent. Once we have imposed the restriction that the deviations are taken from the mean, the values of only three deviations are free to vary. As soon as three deviations are known, the fourth is completely determined. Stated another way, the values of only three deviations are free to vary. For example, if we know three deviations to be -7, -2, and 7, we may calculate the unknown deviation by use of the equality

$$(X_1 - \overline{X}) + (X_2 - \overline{X}) + (X_3 - \overline{X}) + (X_4 - \overline{X}) = 0$$

Therefore

$$(X_4 - \overline{X}) = 0 - [(X_1 - \overline{X}) + (X_2 - \overline{X}) + (X_3 - \overline{X})]$$

In the present example,

$$(X_4 - \overline{X}) = 0 - [(-7) + (-2) + (2)]$$
$$= 0 + 7 + 2 - 2 = 7$$

To generalize: For any given sample on which we have placed a single restriction, the number of degrees of freedom is $N - 1$. In the preceding example, $N = 4$; therefore, degrees of freedom are $4 - 1 = 3$.

Note that when $s/\sqrt{N - 1}$ [Formula (12.8)] is employed to obtain $s_{\overline{X}}$, the quantity under the square root sign $(N - 1)$ is the degrees of freedom.

We noted previously that the use of Student's *t* depends on the assumption that the underlying population is normally distributed. This requirement stems from a unique property of normal distributions. *Given that observations are independent and random, the sample means and sample variances are independent only when the population is normally distributed.* As we previously pointed out, two scores or statistics are independent only when the values of one do not depend on the values of the other, and vice versa. Tests of significance of means demand that the means and the variances be independent of one another. They cannot vary together in some systematic way—for example, with the variances becoming larger as the means become larger. If they do vary in a systematic way, the underlying population cannot be normal, and tests of significance based on the assumption of normality may be invalid. It is for this reason that the assumption of normality underlies the use of Student's t-ratio.

One final note: Student's t-ratio is referred to as a *robust test*, meaning that statistical inferences are likely to be valid even when there are fairly large departures from normality in the population distribution. This robustness is another consequence of the central limit theorem. If we have serious doubts concerning the normality of the population distribution, it is wise to increase the N in each sample.

Characteristics of t-Distributions

Let us compare the characteristics of the t-distributions with those of the already familiar standard normal curve. First, both distributions are symmetrical about a mean of zero. Therefore, the proportion of area beyond a particular positive t-value is equal to the proportion of area below the corresponding negative t.

Second, the t-distributions are more spread out than the normal curve. Consequently, the proportion of area beyond a specific value of t is *greater* than the proportion of area beyond the corresponding value of z. However, the greater the df is, the more the t-distributions resemble the standard normal curve. In order that you may see the contrast between the t-distributions and the normal curve, we have reproduced three curves in Figure 12.6: the sampling distributions of t when df = 3 and df = 10, and the normal curve.

Inspection of Figure 12.6 permits several interesting observations. We have already seen that with the standard normal curve $|z| \geq 1.96$ defines the region of rejection at the 0.05 level of significance. However, when df = 3, a $|t| \geq 1.96$ includes approximately 15% of the total area. Consequently, if we were to employ the normal curve for testing hypotheses when N is small (therefore, df is small) and σ is unknown, we would be in serious danger of making a Type I error, that is, rejecting H_0 when it is true. Obviously, a much larger value of t is required to mark off the bounds of the critical region of rejection. Indeed, when df = 3, the absolute value of the obtained t must be equal to or greater than 3.18 to reject H_0 at the 0.05 level of significance (two-tailed test). However, as df increases, the differences in the proportions of area under the normal curve and Student's t-distributions become negligible.

In contrast to our use of the normal curve, the tabled values for t (see Table C, in the Table section) are **critical values,** that is, *those values that bound the critical rejection regions corresponding to varying levels of*

Critical Values of t: Those values that bound the critical rejection regions corresponding to varying levels of significance.

STATISTICS IN ACTION 12.2

Heart-rate data: Testing a statistical hypothesis

Let's look again at the heart-rate data of the study involving both Type A and Type B males. All the subjects were selected at random from a pool of male undergraduate students who were enrolled in an introductory psychology course at the University of Iowa. On the basis of the Jenkins Activity Survey, the subjects were assigned to either the Type A or the Type B category. We'll look at a small sample from this study, namely, the ten Type A subjects whose HR data were collected during the practice trial. This trial was introduced to familiarize the subjects with the apparatus. In Statistics in Action 12.1, we calculated and reported the following statistics:

$$\overline{X} = 85.10 \qquad s_{\overline{X}} = 3.20 \qquad N = 10$$

Let's imagine that the resting heart rate for the population from which the sample was drawn is known to be approximately normally distributed with a mean equal to 72. Our null hypothesis is that the sample was drawn at random from a population in which the mean HR is equal to or less than 72. Our alternative hypothesis reads: The mean heart rate of the population from which this sample was drawn is greater than 72. If we reject H_0, we assert H_1. Notice that we have used a directional hypothesis. This is due to the fact that activity is known to raise heart rates. It is also possible that the HRs of Type A subjects may be raised more by activity than those of the general population, but we cannot decide that issue with this one sample. Why not? In the parlance of experimental design, the two variables, Type A behavior and activity, are *confounded*, that is, the effects of the two variables are intermixed. This is due only to the fact that, for illustrative purposes, we selected a single group. Later, we'll conduct analyses in which the variables are "unconfounded."

Setting up the HR study in steps of hypothesis testing, we have the following:

1. *Null hypothesis (H_0):* The mean of the population from which the sample was drawn equals 72 or less ($\mu \leq \mu_0 = 72$), that is, the heart rates of active Type A subjects are equal to or less than the resting heart rates in the general population.
2. *Alternative hypothesis (H_1):* The mean of the population from which the sample was drawn is greater than 72 ($\mu > \mu_0$). [*Note:* That is a directional alternative.] Stated verbally, the heart rates of active Type A subjects are greater than the resting heart rates in the general population.
3. *Statistical test:* The Student's *t*-ratio is chosen because we are dealing with a normally distributed variable in which σ is unknown.
4. *Significance level:* $\sigma = 0.05$.
5. *Sampling distribution:* The sampling distribution is the Student's *t*-distribution with df = 9. [*Note:* df = $N - 1$.]

6. *Critical region:* $t_{0.05} \geq 1.833$. Since H_1 is directional, the critical region consists of all values of $t \geq 1.833$.

In the present example, to find the value of t corresponding to $\overline{X} = 85.10$, we use the following formula and find that

$$t = \frac{\overline{X} - \mu_0}{s_{\overline{X}}} = \frac{85.10 - 72}{3.20} = 4.09$$

Decision: The obtained t (4.09) is greater than the critical table value (1.833). Thus, the probability of getting a mean as high as 85.10 when the mean of the general population is 72 is unlikely to be a chance occurrence. Therefore, we reject H_0. In other words, the mean HR for the population from which this sample was drawn is greater than 72. The difference may be due to the fact that activity was involved, the subjects were Type A, or both.

a. Using the HR statistics of Type A subjects appearing in Statistics in Action 12.1, test the null hypotheses for trials 1 through 4.

b. Using the HR statistics of Type B subjects that you calculated in Statistics in Action 6.1 and 12.1, test the null hypotheses for the practice trial and trials 1 through 4.

ANSWERS

a.

	Trial 1	Trial 2	Trial 3	Trial 4	
t	3.27 reject H_0	3.26 reject H_0	3.55 reject H_0	3.04 reject H_0	

b.

	Practice	Trial 1	Trial 2	Trial 3	Trial 4
t	4.85 reject H_0	4.60 reject H_0	3.55 reject H_0	3.25 reject H_0	2.68 reject H_0

Source: Based on data from K. A. Perkins, (1984), "Heart Rate Changes in Type A and Type B Males as a Function of Response Cost and Task Difficulty," Psychophysiology **21,** 14–21.

significance. Thus, in using the table for the distribution of t, we locate the appropriate number of degrees of freedom in the left-hand column, then find the column corresponding to the chosen α. The tabled values represent the t-ratio required for significance. If the absolute value of our obtained t-ratio equals or exceeds this tabled value, we may reject H_0.

12.6 ESTIMATION OF PARAMETERS: INTERVAL ESTIMATION

Point Estimation: An estimate of a population parameter that involves a single value, selected by the criterion of "best estimate." (Contrast *interval estimation*.)

Interval Estimation: The determination of an interval within which the population parameter is presumed to fall. (Contrast *point estimation*.)

We have repeatedly pointed out that one of the basic problems in inferential statistics is the estimation of the parameters of a population from statistics calculated from a sample. This problem in turn involves two subproblems: (1) **point estimation** and (2) **interval estimation.**

When we estimate parameters employing single sample values, these estimates are known as *point estimates.* A single sample value drawn from a population provides an estimate of the population parameter. But how good an estimate is it? If a population mean were known to be 100, would a sample mean of 60 constitute a good estimate? How about a sample mean of 130, 105, 98, or 99.4? Under what conditions do we consider an estimate good? Since we know that the population parameters are virtually never known and that we generally employ samples to estimate these parameters, is there any way to determine the size of error we are likely to make? The answer to this question is a negative one. However, it is possible not only to estimate the population parameter (*point estimation*), but also to state a range of values within which we are confident that the parameter falls (*interval estimation*). Moreover, we may express our confidence in terms of probabilities.

Have you ever seen a weight-guesser at a carnival who promises to guess your correct weight to within a specified number of pounds? Suppose you are that weight-guesser and you are trying to estimate the weight of a man, basing the estimation on physical inspection. Let's assume that you are unable to place him on a scale, and that you cannot ask him his weight. This problem is similar to many you have faced throughout this text. You cannot know the population value (the man's true weight), and hence you are forced to estimate it. Let's say that you have the impression that he weighs about 200 pounds. If you are asked, "How confident are you that he weighs *exactly* 200 pounds?" You would probably reply. "I doubt that he weighs exactly 200 pounds. If he does, you can credit me with a fantastically lucky guess. However, I feel reasonably confident that he weighs between 190 and 210 pounds." In doing this, you have stated the interval within which you feel confident that his true weight falls. After a moment's reflection, you might hedge slightly, "Well, he is almost certainly between 180 and 220 pounds. In any event, I feel perfectly confident that his true weight falls somewhere between 170 and 230 pounds." Note that the greater the size of the interval is, the more certain you are that the true value lies between these limits. Note also that in stating these confidence limits, you are in effect making two statements: (1) You are stating the limits between which you feel our subject's true weight falls, and (2) you are rejecting the possibility that his true weight falls outside these limits. Thus, if someone asks, "Is it conceivable that your subject weighs as much as 240 pounds or as little as 160 pounds?" Your reply would be a negative one.

12.7 CONFIDENCE INTERVALS AND CONFIDENCE LIMITS

In the preceding example, we were in a sense concerning outselves with the problem of estimating *confidence limits*. In effect, we were attempting to determine the interval within which any hypotheses concerning the weight of the man might be considered tenable and outside which any hypotheses would be considered untenable. The interval within which we consider hypotheses tenable is known as the **confidence interval,** and the limits defining the interval are referred to as **confidence limits.**

Let's look at a sample problem and apply our statistical concepts to the estimation of confidence intervals.

A school district is trying to decide on the feasibility of setting up a vocational training program in its public high school curriculum. In part, the decision will depend on an estimate of the average IQ of high school students within the district. With only one school psychologist in the district, it is impossible to administer an individual test to each student. Consequently, we must content ourselves with testing a random sample of students and basing our estimate on this sample. We administer an IQ test to a random sample of 26 students and obtain the following results:

$$\overline{X} = 108 \qquad s = 15 \qquad N = 26$$

Our best estimate of the population mean (i.e., the mean IQ of children within the school district) is 108. However, even though sample statistics provide the best estimates of population values, we recognize that such estimates are subject to error. As with the weight problem, we would be fantastically lucky if the mean IQ of the high-school population were actually 108. On the other hand, if we have employed truly random selection procedures, we have a right to believe that our sample value is fairly close to the population mean. The critical question becomes: Between what limits will we entertain, as tenable, hypotheses concerning the value of the population mean (μ) in intelligence?

We have seen that the mean of the sampling distribution of sample means ($\mu_{\overline{X}}$) is equal to the mean of the population. We have also seen that since, for any given N, we may determine how far sample means are likely to deviate from any given or hypothesized value of μ, we may determine the likelihood that a particular $\overline{X}$ could have been drawn from a population with a mean of μ_0, where μ_0 represents the value of the population mean under H_0. Now, since we do not know the value of the population mean, we are free to hypothesize *any* value we desire.

It should be clear that we could entertain an unlimited number of hypotheses concerning the population mean and subsequently reject them, or fail to reject them, on the basis of the size of the *t*-ratios. For example, in the present problem, let us select a number of hypothetical population means. We may employ the 0.05 level of significance (two-tailed test), and

Confidence Interval: Interval within which we consider hypotheses about the population parameter tenable. Common confidence intervals are 95% and 99% ($1 - \alpha$ when $\alpha = 0.05$ and 0.01 respectively).

Confidence Limits: Limits defining the confidence interval.

test the hypothesis that $\mu_0 = 98$. The value of t corresponding to $\overline{X} = 108$ is

$$t = \frac{108 - 98}{15/\sqrt{25}} = 3.333$$

In Table C, we find that $t_{0.05}$ for 25 df is 2.060. Since our obtained t is greater than this critical value, we reject the hypothesis that $\mu_0 = 98$. In other words, it is unlikely that $\overline{X} = 108$ was drawn from a population with a mean of 98.

Our next hypothesis is that $\mu_0 = 100$, which gives a t of

$$t = \frac{108 - 100}{3} = 2.667$$

Since $2.667 > t_{0.05}$ (or 2.060), we may reject the hypothesis that the population mean is 100.

If we hypothesize $\mu_0 = 102$, the resulting t-ratio of 2.000 is less than $t_{0.05}$. Consequently, we may consider the hypothesis that $\mu_0 = 102$ tenable. Similarly, if we obtained the appropriate t-ratios, we would find that the hypothesis $\mu_0 = 114$ is tenable, whereas hypotheses of values greater than 114 are untenable. Thus, $\overline{X} = 108$ was probably drawn from a population whose mean falls in the interval 102–114 (note that these limits, 102 and 114, represent approximate limits, that is, the closest *integers*). The hypothesis that $\overline{X} = 108$ was drawn from a population with $\mu < 102$ or $\mu > 114$ may be rejected at the 0.05 level of significance. The interval within which the population mean probably lies is called the *confidence interval*. We refer to the limits of this interval as the *confidence limits*. Since we have been employing $\alpha = 0.05$, we call it the *95% confidence interval*. Similarly, if we employed $\alpha = 0.01$, we could obtain the *99% confidence interval*.

It was not necessary to perform all these calculations to establish the confidence limits. We may calculate the exact limits of the 95% confidence interval directly.

The determine the upper limit for the 95% confidence interval, we have

$$\text{Upper limit } \mu_0 = \overline{X} + (t_{0.05})(s_{\overline{X}}) \tag{12.10}$$

Similarly, for the lower limit,

$$\text{Lower limit } \mu_0 = \overline{X} - (t_{0.05})(s_{\overline{X}}) \tag{12.11}$$

For the 99% confidence interval, merely substitute $t_{0.01}$ in the preceding formulas.

You will note that these formulas are derived algebraically from Formula (12.9):

$$t_{0.05} = \frac{\overline{X} - \mu_0}{s_{\overline{X}}}$$

$$(t_{0.05})s_{\overline{X}} = \overline{X} - \mu_0$$

therefore,

$$\mu_0 = \overline{X} - (t_{0.05})(s_{\overline{X}})$$

Employing Formula (12.10), we find that the upper 95% confidence limit in the preceding problem is

$$\text{Upper limit } \mu_0 = 108 + (2.060)(3.0)$$
$$= 108 + 6.18 = 114.18$$

Similarly, employing Formula (12.11), we find that the lower confidence limit is

$$\text{Lower limit } \mu_0 = 108 - (2.060)(3.0)$$
$$= 108 - 6.18 = 101.82$$

Having established the lower and the upper limits as 101.82 and 114.18, respectively, we may now draw this conclusion: On the basis of our obtained mean and standard deviation, which were computed from scores drawn from a population in which the true mean is unknown, we assert that the population mean is likely to fall within the interval that we have established.

Some words of caution in interpreting the confidence interval. In establishing the interval within which we believe the population mean falls, we have *not* established any probability that our obtained mean is correct. In other words, we cannot claim that the chances are 95 to 100 that the population mean is 108. Our statements are valid only with respect to the interval and not with respect to any particular value of the sample mean. In addition, since the population mean is a fixed value and does not have a distribution, our probability statements never refer to μ. The probability we assert is about the interval—that is, the probability that the interval contains μ.

Finally, we have established the confidence interval of the mean, but we are not stating that the probability is 0.95 that the particular interval we have calculated contains the population mean. It should be clear that if we were to select repeated samples from a population, both the sample means and the standard deviations would differ from sample to sample. Consequently, our estimates of the confidence interval would also vary from sample to sample. When we have established the 95% confidence interval of the mean, then we are stating that if repeated samples of a given size are drawn from the population, 95% of the interval estimates will include the population mean.

12.8 TEST OF SIGNIFICANCE FOR PEARSON r: ONE-SAMPLE CASE

In Chapter 8, we discussed the calculation of two statistics—the Pearson r and r_s—commonly employed to describe the extent of the relationship between two variables. It will be recalled that the coefficient of correlation

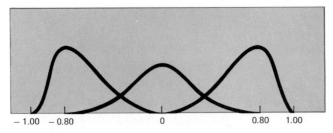

FIGURE 12.7 Illustrative sampling distributions of correlation coefficients when $\rho = -0.80$, $\rho = 0$, and when $\rho = +0.80$.

varies between ± 1.00, with $r = 0.00$ indicating the absence of a relationship. It is easy to overlook the fact that correlation coefficients based on sample data are only estimates of the corresponding population parameter and, as such, will be distributed about the population value. Thus, it is quite possible that a sample drawn from a population in which the true correlation is zero may yield a high positive or negative correlation by *chance*. The null hypothesis that is most often investigated in the one-sample case is that the *population correlation coefficient* (ρ, pronounced rho) is zero.

It is clear that a test of significance is called for. However, the test is complicated by the fact that the sampling distribution of ρ is usually nonnormal, particularly as ρ approaches the limiting values of ± 1.00. Consider the case in which ρ equals $+ 0.80$. It is clear that sample correlation coefficients drawn from this population will be distributed around $+ 0.80$ and can take on any value from $- 1.00$ to $+ 1.00$. It is equally clear, however, that there is a definite restriction in the range of values that sample statistics greater than $+ 0.80$ can assume, whereas the range of possible values less than $+ 0.80$ is greater: from $r < + 0.80$ to $r = - 1.00$, to be precise. The result is a negatively skewed sampling distribution. The departure from normality will usually be less as the number of paired scores in the sample increases. When the population correlation from which the sample is drawn is equal to zero, the sampling distribution is more likely to be normal. These relationships are demonstrated in Figure 12.7, which illustrates the sampling distribution of the correlation coefficient when $\rho = - 0.80$, 0, and $+ 0.80$.

Testing Other Null Hypotheses Concerning ρ

The t-test should not be used for testing hypothesis other than $\rho = 0.00$, since, as we pointed out earlier, the sampling distribution is not normal for values of ρ that are different from zero.

Fisher has described a procedure for transforming sample r's to a statistic z_r, which yields a sampling distribution that more closely approximates the normal curve, even for samples employing small N's.

The test statistic is the normal deviate, z, in which

$$z = \frac{z_r - Z_r}{\sqrt{1/(N-3)}} \qquad (12.12)$$

where

z_r = the transformed value of the sample r

Z_r = the transformed value of the population correlation
coefficient specified under H_0.

Using the example in Statistics in Action 12.3, let us test H_0 that the ρ for the population from which the sample was drawn is 0.50 or less. Recall that $r = 0.97$ and $N = 10$.

Obtaining z_r is greatly simplified by Table F in the Table section, which shows the value of z_r corresponding to each value of r, in steps of 0.01, between 0.00 and 0.99. Thus, referring to Table F, we see that an r of 0.97, for example, has a corresponding z_r of 2.092.

Similarly, a ρ of 0.50 has a corresponding Z_r, of 0.549. Substituting these values in the formula for z, we find

$$z = \frac{2.092 - 0.549}{\sqrt{1/(10-3)}} = \frac{1.543}{0.378} = 4.082$$

Decision: At the 0.05 level, one-tailed test, $z_{0.05} \geq 1.645$ is required for significance. Since $z = 4.082$ is greater than the critical value, we must reject H_0. It is quite unlikely that the sample was drawn from a population in which the true correlation is equal to or less than 0.50.

Let's carry this reasoning one step further. Suppose we wish to estimate the lowest possible value of the population correlation that we would consider tenable at a given α-level. By algebraically rearranging Formula (12.12) so that Z_r becomes the unknown, we can derive the following formula for obtaining the transformed value of the population correlation coefficient, Z_r at any α-level we chose. Thus

$$Z_r = z_r - z_\alpha (\sqrt{1/(N-3)})* \qquad (12.13)$$

where z_α = the z required for significance, under the normal probability curve, at any given α-level.

Suppose we wish to estimate the lower limit of a Pearson $r = 0.97$ at $\alpha = 0.05$, one-tailed test. Reference to Table F shows that the z_r corresponding to 0.97 equals 2.092. At $\alpha = 0.05$, the one-tailed $z = 1.645$. Substituting in Formula (12.13), we obtain

$$Z_r = 2.092 - 1.645 (\sqrt{1/(N-3)})$$
$$= 2.092 - (1.645)(0.378)$$
$$= 1.47$$

---

*We may also estimate the upper limit by changing the minus sign to plus in Formula (12.13). Thus, Z_r (upper limit) $= z_r + z_\alpha (\sqrt{1/(N-3)})$.

STATISTICS IN ACTION 12.3

Heart-rate data: Testing H_0: $\rho = 0$

In chapter 6, we noted a considerable amount of within-subject consistency among the heart-rate measures of both Type A and Type B subjects on the practice and four test trials. We found further support for this consistency in Statistics in Action 8.1 when we prepared a correlational matrix among these variables. However, the N was small (10), and it is conceivable that the intercorrelations might have occurred by chance. We would now like to subject these correlations to a test of the null hypothesis that the sample correlations were drawn from a population in which the true correlation is zero. The following correlation matrix was obtained from the ten Type A subjects.

Correlation Matrix

Various No.	1	2	3	4	5
1	10	0.970	0.963	0.979	0.960
2		10	0.977	0.985	0.971
3			10	0.986	0.985
4				10	0.991
5					10

When testing the null hypothesis that the population correlation coefficient is zero, the following t-test should be used:

$$t = \frac{r\sqrt{N-2}}{\sqrt{1-r^2}} \tag{12.12}$$

The number of degrees of freedom is equal to $N - 2$,* in which $N =$ the number of pairs.

There is a wealth of evidence that if repeated measures are taken on the same subjects, any observed correlations will be positive. For this reason, we'll use a directional test of the null hypothesis for each comparison. Note that the sample correlation between practice and the first trial equals 0.970. We'll test H_0 that the sample was drawn from a population in which the true correlation is zero.

Let us set up this problem in formal statistical terms.

1. *Null hypothesis* (H_0): The population correlation coefficient from which this sample was drawn is equal to or less than 0.00 ($\rho \leq 0.00$).

---

* Testing the significance of r from zero is the same as testing the slope of the regression line from zero. In a straight line, two points are fixed, that is, they are not free to vary. Thus, df = the number of paired observations minus 2.

2. *Alternative hypothesis* (H_1): The population correlation coefficient from which the sample was drawn is greater than 0.00 ($\rho > 0.00$).
3. *Statistical test:* The *t*-test, with $N - 2$ degrees of freedom.
4. *Significance level:* $\alpha = 0.05$ one-tailed test.
5. *Sampling distribution:* The Student's *t*-distribution with df $= 8$.
6. *Critical region:* $t_{0.05} \geq 1.860$. Since H_1 is directional, the critical region consists of all values of $t \geq 1.860$.

In the present example,

$$t = \frac{0.97 \sqrt{8}}{0.2431} = 11.286$$

Decision: Since the obtained $t > t_{0.05}$, it falls within the critical region for rejecting H_0. Thus, it may be concluded that the sample was drawn from a population in which $\rho > 0.00$.

Find the *t*-ratios for all the intercorrelations shown in the correlation matrix. Use $\alpha = 0.01$, one-tailed test.

ANSWERS

Variable	Practice	Trial 1	Trial 2	Trial 3	Trial 4
Practice	10	11.286	10.107	13.583	9.697
Trial 1	10	10	12.959	16.146	11.487
Trial 2	10	10	10	16.725	16.146
Trial 3	10	10	10	10	20.939
Trial 4	10	10	10	10	10

Source: Based on data from K. A. Perkins (1984), "Heart Rate Changes in Type A and Type B Males as a Function of Response Cost and Task Difficulty," Psychophysiology **21**, 14–21.

Now, looking in the body of Table F, we find that the value most closely approximating 1.47 is 1.472. The correlation coefficient corresponding to this value is 0.90. We may feel reasonably confident that the population correlation coefficient from which the sample was drawn is no less than 0.90.

Test of Significance of r_s: One-Sample Case

Table G, in the Table section, presents the critical values of r_s, one- and two-tailed tests, for selected values of N from 5 to 30.

In Section 8.5, we demonstrated the calculation of r_s from data consisting of 15 pairs of ranked scores and found a correlation of 0.64.

Since $N = 15$ is not listed in Table G, it is necessary to interpolate, employing the critical values for $N = 14$ and $N = 16$. The critical value at the 0.05 level, two-tailed test, for $N = 14$ is 0.544; at $N = 16$ it is 0.506. By employing linear interpolation, we may roughly approximate the critical value corresponding to $N = 15$.

With Table G, linear interpolation merely involves adding together the boundary values of r_s and dividing by 2. Thus

$$r_{s(0.05)} = \frac{0.544 + 0.506}{2} = 0.525$$

Since our obtained r_s of 0.64 exceeds the critical value at the 0.05 level, we may conclude that the population value of the Spearman correlation coefficient from which the sample was drawn is greater than 0.00.

12.9 PUTTING IT ALL TOGETHER

Suppose you are the personnel director at an electronics firm that employs hundreds of individuals to assemble miniature components for orbiting spacecraft. The work requires extremely fine eye/hand coordination.

During routine blood and urine testing for the presence of psychoactive drugs, 30 employees are identified who test positively for THC (delta-9-tetrahydrocannabinol), the most active of over 400 different chemicals in the *Cannabis sativa* or marijuana plant.

You have often wondered whether THC impairs performance on tasks requiring fine motor coordination. You recall a test of manual dexterity that is widely used as a selection device in the electronics field. You decide to administer this test to the 30 employees to see how their performance compares with the standards established, namely, $\mu = 100$ and $\sigma = 15$.

You find that your 30 positively testing employees obtained a mean equal to 92 with $s = 10$. The first question you ask: Is it likely that a sample mean as deviant as 8 from the population mean could have occurred by chance with an N as large as 30? You formulate null and alternative hypotheses, select a statistical test, decide on the significance level, and refer to the appropriate sampling distribution in order to make the statistical decision.

1. *Null hypothesis* (H_0): The population mean from which this sample was drawn is equal to 100.
2. *Alternative hypothesis* (H_1): The population mean from which this sample was drawn is not equal to 100.
3. *Statistical test:* z-statistic.
4. *Significance level:* $\alpha = 0.01$, two-tailed test.
5. *Sampling distribution:* The normal probability distribution.

6. *Critical region:* All values of $z \geq 2.58$ or ≤ -2.58.

The calculation of z is as follows:

$$z = 92 - 100 \, \sigma_{\overline{x}}$$

$$= \frac{-8}{15\sqrt{30}}$$

$$= \frac{-8}{2.74} = -2.92$$

Since the obtained z is more deviant than the critical value of -2.58, we reject H_0 and assert the alternative hypothesis. It appears that the employees testing positive performed poorer than would be expected if the sample were drawn at random from the broader population. However, a word of caution: Although the results are provocative and should be followed by a well-designed experiment, you should note that this study did not involve a control group, nor were the subjects assigned at random to their "experimental condition." They were self-selected. What has been demonstrated is that, for some reason as yet unknown, they performed at a statistically significant poorer level than expected.

The sample mean was 92 with $s = 10$. Find the confidence limits at the 95% confidence interval.

$$s_{\overline{x}} = 10/\sqrt{30 - 1}$$

$$= 1.86$$

Referring to Table C in Appendix D, we find that the critical value of t at the 0.05 level, two-tailed test, and df $= 29$ is 2.045.

The 95% confidence interval is, therefore, $92 \pm (2.045)(1.86) = 88.20$ to 95.80.

Imagine that you went one step further in your research. The medical tests yielded a score for each individual that indicated the degree of THC intoxication. You also had each individual's score on a manual dexterity test. You were consequently able to calculate a Pearson correlation between the two variables. When you did so, you found a Pearson r equal to 0.62. To test the null hypothesis that the population correlation equals zero at $\alpha = 0.01$, we employ

$$t = \frac{r\sqrt{N - 2}}{\sqrt{1 - r^2}} \qquad \text{width df} = N - 2 = 28$$

$$= \frac{3.281}{0.785} = 4.180$$

The critical value of t at $\alpha = 0.01$, two-tailed test, and df $= 28$ is 2.763. Since $t = 4.188$ exceeds this critical value, we reject H_0 and assert that the degree of impairment of dexterity and the level of THC in the blood are significantly and positively correlated. Although such a finding would not prove causation, it would be consistent with a causal relationship and provide further justification for a well-designed study.

CHAPTER SUMMARY

We have seen that if we take a number of samples from a given population, then:

1. The distribution of sample means tends to be normal.
2. The mean of these sample means ($\mu_{\bar{X}}$) is equal to the mean of the population (μ).
3. The standard error of the mean ($\sigma_{\bar{X}}$) is equal to $\sigma/\sqrt{N}$. As N increases, the variability decreases.

We used these relationships in the testing of hypotheses (e.g., $\mu = \mu_0$) when the standard deviation of a population was known, employing the familiar z-statistic and the standard normal curve.

For testing when σ is not known, we demonstrated the use of sample statistics to estimate these parameters. We used these estimates of the parameters to test hypotheses, employing Student's t-ratio and the corresponding sampling distributions. We compared these t-distributions, which vary as a function of degrees of freedom (df), with the standard normal curve.

We employed the t-ratio as a basis for establishing confidence intervals.

Finally, we demonstrated the test of significance for the Pearson r and the Spearman r_s, one-sample case.

TERMS TO REMEMBER

biased estimate of a parameter   **interval estimation**
central limit theorem   **point estimation**
confidence interval   **standard error of the mean**
confidence limits   **t-distributions**
critical region   **t-ratio**
critical values of t   **unbiased estimator**
degrees of freedom (df)

EXERCISES

1. Describe what happens to the distribution of sample means when you
   a. increase the size of each sample.   **b.** increase the number of samples.

2. Explain why the standard deviation of a sample will usually underestimate the standard deviation of a population. Give an example.

3. Given that $\bar{X} = 24$ and $s = 4$ for $N = 15$, use the t-distribution to find
   a. The 95% confidence limits for μ.   **b.** the 99% confidence limits for μ.

4. Given that $\bar{X} = 24$ and $s = 4$ for $N = 121$, use the t-distribution to find
   a. the 95% confidence limits for μ.   **b.** the 99% confidence limits for μ.

Compare the results with Exercise 3.

5. An instructor gives his class an examination that, as he knows from years of experience, yields $\mu = 78$ and $\sigma = 7$. His present class of 22 obtains a mean of 82. Is he correct in assuming that this is a superior class? Employ $\alpha = 0.01$, two-tailed test.

6. An instructor gives his class an examination that, as he knows from years of experience yields $\mu = 78$. His present class of 22 obtains $\bar{X} = 82$ and $s = 7$. Is he correct in assuming that this is a superior class? Employ $\alpha = 0.01$, two-tailed test.

7. Explain the difference between Exercises 5 and 6. What test statistic is employed in each case, and why? Why is the decision different?

Generalize: What is the effect of knowing σ upon the likelihood of a Type II error?

8. The superintendent of Zody school district claims that the children in her district are brighter, on the average, than the general population of students. In order to determine the IQ of school children in the district, a study was conducted. The results were as shown in the accompanying table. The mean of the general population of school children is 106. Set this up in formal statistical terms (i.e., H_0, H_1, etc.) and draw the appropriate conclusions. Employ a one-tailed test, $\alpha = 0.05$.

9. For a particular population with $\mu = 28.5$ and $\sigma = 5.5$, what is the probability that, in a sample of 100, the $\bar{X}$ will be
   a. equal to or less than 30.0?   **b.** equal to or less than 28.0?
   c. equal to or more than 29.5?   **d.** between 28.0 and 29.0?

10. Given that $\bar{X} = 40$ for $N = 24$ from a population in which $\sigma = 8$, find
   a. the 95% confidence limits for μ.
   b. the 99% confidence limits for μ.

11. It is axiomatic that when pairs of individuals are selected at random and the intelligence tests scores of the first members of the pairs are correlated with the second members, $\rho = 0.00$.
   a. Thirty-nine pairs of siblings are randomly selected and an $r = + 0.27$ is obtained between members of the pairs for intelligence. Are siblings more alike in intelligence than unrelated individuals? Use $\alpha = 0.05$.
   b. A study of 28 pairs of identical twins yields $r = + 0.91$ on intelligence test scores. What do you conclude? Use $\alpha = 0.05$.

12. Overton University claims that because of its superior facilities and close faculty supervision, its students complete the Ph.D. program earlier than usual. They base this assertion on the fact that the national mean age for completion is 32.11, whereas the mean age of their 26 Ph.D.s is 29.61 with $s = 6.00$. Test the validity of their assumption. Use $\alpha = 0.05$.

13. Employing the data in the preceding exercise, find the interval within which you are confident that the true population mean (average for Ph.D.s at Overton University) probably falls, using the 95% confidence interval.

Test scores
105
109
115
112
124
115
103
110
125
99

14. A sociologist asserts that the average length of courtship is longer before a second marriage than before a first. She bases this assertion on the fact that the average for first marriages is 265 days, whereas the average for second marriages (of her 626 subjects) is 268.5 days, with $s = 50$. Test the validity of her assumption, using $\alpha = 0.05$.

15. Employing the data in Exercise 14, find the interval within which you are 99% confident that the true population mean (average courtship days for a second marriage) probably falls.

16. Random samples of size 2 are selected from the following finite population of scores: 1, 3, 5, 7, 9, and 11.
   a. Calculate the mean and standard deviation of the population.
   b. Construct a histogram showing the sampling distribution of means when $N = 2$. Employ sampling *without* replacement.
   c. Construct a histogram showing the means of all possible samples that can be drawn, employing sampling *with* replacement.

17. Employing (b) in Exercise 16, answer the following: Selecting a sample with $N = 2$, what is the probability that
   a. a mean as high as 10 will be obtained?
   b. a mean as low as 2 will be obtained?
   c. a mean as deviant as 8 will be obtained?
   d. a mean as low as 1 will be obtained?

18. Employing (c) in Exercise 16, answer the following: Selecting a sample with $N = 2$, what is the probability that
   a. a mean as high as 10 will be obtained?
   b. a mean as low as 2 will be obtained?
   c. a mean as deviant as 8 will be obtained?
   d. a mean as low as 1 will be obtained?

19. A stock analyst claims that he has an unusually accurate method for forecasting price gains of listed common stocks. During a given period, stocks he advocated showed the following price gains: $1.25, $2.50, $1.75, $2.25, $3.25, $3.00, $2.00, $2.00. During the same period, the market as a whole showed a mean price gain of $1.83. Set up and test the H_0 that the stocks he selected have been randomly selected from the population of stock gains during the specified period, using $\alpha = 0.05$.

20. In a test of a gasoline additive, ten carefully engineered automobiles were run at a testing site under rigorously supervised conditions. The numbers of miles obtained from a single gallon of gasoline were 25, 22, 23, 26, 27, 21, 24, 25, 23, 24. Thousands of prior trials with the same gasoline without the additive had yielded the expectation of 22.63 miles per gallon. Using $\alpha = 0.05$, can it be concluded that the additive improved gasoline mileage?

21. A restaurant owner ranked her 17 waiters in terms of their speed and efficiency on the job. She correlated these ranks with the total amount of tips each of these waiters received for a one-week period, and obtained $r_s = 0.438$. What do you conclude? Use $\alpha = 0.05$.

22. The owner of a car-leasing company ranked 25 of this customers on their neatness and general care of their rented cars during a 3-month period. He correlated these ranks with the number of miles each customer drove during this same period. He obtained $r_s = -0.397$. Employing $\alpha = 0.05$, two-tailed test, what do you conclude?

23. As a requirement for admission to Blue Chip University, a candidate must take a standardized entrance examination. The correlation between performance on this examination and college grades is 0.43.

   a. The director of admissions claims that a better way to predict college success is by using high school grade averages. To test her claim, she randomly selects 52 students and correlates their college grades with their high school averages. She obtains $r = 0.54$. What do you conclude? Use $\alpha = 0.05$.

   b. The director's assistant constructs a test that he claims is better for predicting college success than the one currently used. He randomly selects 67 students and correlates their grade-point averages with performance on his test. He obtained $r = 0.61$. What do you conclude? Use $\alpha = 0.05$.

24. What are the statistics used to describe the distribution of a sample? The distribution of a sample statistic?

25. Is s^2 an unbiased estimate of σ^2? Explain.

26. Is $\hat{s}^2$ an unbiased estimate of σ^2? Explain.

27. What is a confidence interval?

28. Give an example to show the effect of the α-level on the precision of a confidence interval.

29. How do the t-distributions differ from the normal distribution? Are they ever the same?

*30. Imagine the following sampling experiment. You have two populations of means consisting of the following values:

Population 1:   3, 4, 5, 5, 6, 6, 6, 7, 7, 8, 9
Population 2:   0, 1, 2, 2, 3, 3, 3, 4, 4, 5, 6

| | | **Selection from Means in Population 1** | | | | | | | | | |
		3	4	5	5	6	6	6	7	7	8	9
	0	3	4	5	5	6	6	6	7	7	8	9
	1	2	3	4	4	5	5	5	6	6	7	8
	2	1	2	3	3	4	4	4	5	5	6	7
	2	1	2	3	3	4	4	4	5	5	6	7
Selection from Means in Population 2	**3**	0	1	2	2	3	3	3	4	4	5	6
	3	0	1	2	2	3	3	3	4	4	5	6
	3	0	1	2	2	3	3	3	4	4	5	6
	4	−1	0	1	1	2	2	2	3	3	4	5
	4	−1	0	1	1	2	2	2	3	3	4	5
	5	−2	−1	0	0	1	1	1	2	2	3	4
	6	−3	−2	−1	−1	0	0	0	1	1	2	3

You place tabs with these means into two separate hats—one for each population. You select a mean from population 1, replace it in the hat, and then select a mean from population 2 and replace it in the hat. You subtract mean 2 from mean 1 to obtain a difference between means. The cell entries in the preceding table show all possible differences between means that you could obtain.

Note that the mean of the means of population 1 is 6; the corresponding mean of population 2 is 3.

a. Construct a frequency and probability distribution of differences between means $(\overline{X}_1 - \overline{X}_2)$.

b. Intuitively, estimate what the mean of these differences should be. Now calculate the mean of the differences. How accurate was your estimate?

Generalize: What is the mean of the sampling distributions of differences between means?

*31. Vary the preceding sampling experiment slightly. Imagine that you know that hat 1 contains the population of means identified as population 1. However, the population of means in the second hat is a complete mystery. You select a sample mean from hat 1 and a sample mean from hat 2. By subtracting the second mean from the first mean, obtain a difference between sample means.

a. What statistical hypothesis are you most likely to test?

b. What is the sampling distribution against which you should test H_0: $\mu_1 = \mu_2$?

c. Construct a frequency and probability distribution of differences between means under the hypothesis H_0: $\mu_1 = \mu_2$. [*Hint*: Assume that population 2 is identical to population 1, and find all possible differences between means.] This probability distribution is known as the sampling distribution of differences between means, in which the null hypothesis is that you are sampling from identical populations.

*32. Employing the sampling distribution under H_0: $\mu_1 = \mu_2$ (Exercise 31), find the probability of obtaining a difference in sample means:

a. $\overline{X}_1 - \overline{X}_2 \leq 5$ or $\overline{X}_1 - \overline{X}_2 \geq 5$ **b.** $\overline{X}_1 - \overline{X}_2 \geq 6$ **c.** $\overline{X}_1 - \overline{X}_2 \leq -3$
d. $\overline{X}_1 - \overline{X}_2 \leq 6$ or $\overline{X}_1 - \overline{X}_2 \geq 6$ **e.** $\overline{X}_1 - \overline{X}_2 = -6$

*33. Imagine that the *true* situation is the sampling distribution of differences between means found in response to Exercise 30. Find the probability of obtaining a difference in sample means:

a. $\overline{X}_1 - \overline{X}_2 \leq -5$ or $\overline{X}_1 - \overline{X}_2 \geq 5$ **b.** $\overline{X}_1 - \overline{X}_2 \geq 6$ **c.** $\overline{X}_1 - \overline{X}_2 \leq -3$
d. $\overline{X}_1 - \overline{X}_2 \leq 6$ or $\overline{X}_1 - \overline{X}_2 \geq 6$ **e.** $\overline{X}_1 - \overline{X}_2 = -6$

*34. Compare the probability values obtained in response to Exercises 32 and 33. See if you can formulate any broad observations about the different answers you obtained.

35. Assume that the mean number of words typed per minute by secretaries is 50. A group of people who attended a certain secretarial school show the following typing speeds (words per minute):

| 55 | 50 | 45 | 75 | 80 | 75 | 80 | 80 |
| 85 | 60 | 50 | 65 | 60 | 50 | 80 | 50 |

Calculate the value of t. Can you conclude that the school produced secretaries with superior typing abilities?

36. A sports fan found a r_s of 0.15 between the batting averages of 20 baseball players and the amount of vitamins in their breakfast cereals. Can she conclude that this correlation is significant? Use $\alpha = 0.05$, two-tailed test.

37. Mr. Smith stated that his training program for selling life insurance enables a company to sell more insurance than the "average" company. The mean amount of life insurance sold by all salesmen per month is $100,000. A sample of ten people who have been through the training program show monthly selling rates (in thousands) of

$110	$120	$130	$120	$125
$ 90	$130	$135	$140	$110

If you were a supervisor of insurance salesmen, would you adopt Mr. Smith's training program? Calculate the value of t.

38. In a study of marital success and failure, Bentler and Newcomb (1978) gave a personality questionnaire to 162 newly married couples. Four years later 77 couples from the original sample were located; of these, 53 were still married, whereas 24 had separated or divorced. Among the still-married group it was found that the correlation between the husband's and wife's scores on an attractiveness scale was 0.59, and that the correlation between their scores on a generosity scale was 0.23. Among the divorced group the correlation between the ex-husbands and ex-wife's scores on the attractiveness scale was 0.07, and the correlation between their score on the generosity scale was 0.13.
   a. Using $\alpha = 0.05$, set up and test the null hypothesis that the correlation between the married couples' scores on attractiveness is equal to zero. Also set up and test the null hypothesis that the correlation between the divorced couples' scores on attractiveness is equal to zero.
   b. Using $\alpha = 0.05$, set up and test the null hypothesis that the correlation between the married couples' scores on generosity is equal to zero. Also set up and test the null hypothesis that the correlation between the divorced couples' scores on generosity is equal to zero.

39. Referring to the correlation matrix of the heart rates of Type B subjects that you prepared in Statistics in Action 8.1, test $H_0: \rho = 0.00$, using $\alpha = 0.01$, one-tailed test, for all ten intercorrelations.

40. Referring to the correlation matrix of the heart rates of Type A subjects shown in Statistics in Action 12.3, estimate the lowest value of the population correlation coefficients that you would find tenable at (a) $\alpha = 0.05$ and at (b) $\alpha = 0.01$, one-tailed test. [*Note:* Correlation coefficients should be rounded to the second decimal place prior to using Table F.)

13

Statistical Inference: Two-Sample Case

13.1 STATISTICAL COMPARISON OF TWO INDEPENDENT SAMPLES

Without the use of a drug that suppresses the immune system, the body would attack organ transplants as foreign invaders and cause the implanted organ to be rejected. Until 1989, cyclosporine was the drug of choice to inhibit the immune system. In late 1989, it was reported in *Lancet* that a new drug, FK506, obtained from a soil fungus in Japan, performed better than cyclosporine. How is such a claim substantiated?

Does the recidivism of male juvenile offenders who are provided with "father figures" differ from that of those without "father figures"?

Do students in "open" or ungraded classrooms differ in performance on standardized achievement tests from students in the typical graded classroom settings?

To answer each of these questions requires the comparison of at least two different samples. In Chapter 12, we restricted our examination of hypotheses to the one-sample case. However, most scientific research involves the comparison of two or more samples to determine whether or not these samples might reasonably have been drawn from the same population. Suppose we compare the means of two different samples and find that they differ. Must we conclude that these samples were drawn from two different populations? Not necessarily.

BOX 13.1

THE EYES: WINDOWS OF THE SOUL

The eyes have been referred to as the "windows of the soul." Research has demonstrated that changes in the size of the pupils may be taken as an indication of "what turns people on." The pupils of male subjects become larger when viewing pictures of women; and, conversely, the pupils of females become larger when viewing pictures of males.

Questions raised in one study were: "Do male homosexuals show a greater pupillary response to pictures of males than to pictures of females? How do their pupillary responses compare to those of heterosexual males?"

The accompanying graph shows a line drawing of the mean changes in pupil response obtained by two groups of subjects—homosexual males and heterosexual males—when viewing pictures of males and females.

A number of interesting questions involving inferential statistics may be raised. Consider these:

1. Is there a statistically significant difference between the mean pupil response of heterosexual vs. homosexual males when viewing the pictures of males?

2. Is there a statistically significant difference between the mean pupil response of hetero-

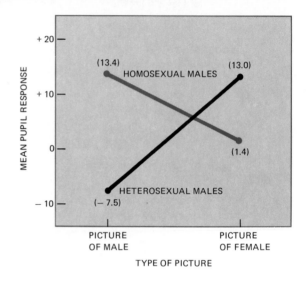

sexual vs. homosexual males when viewing the pictures of women?

Additional questions are taken up in the end-of-chapter exercises (Exercises 31 and 32).

Source: E. H. Hess, A. L. Selzer, and J. M. Shilen (1965), "Pupil Response of Hetero- and Homosexual Males to Pictures of Men and Women: A Pilot Study," *J. Abn. Psych* **70**, 166–168. Copyright 1965 by The American Psychological Association.

Recall our previous discussion on the sampling distribution of sample means (Section 12.2). We saw that some variability in the sample statistics is to be expected, even when these samples are drawn from the same population. We were able to describe this variability in terms of the sampling distribution of sample means. To conceptualize this distribution, we imagined drawing from a population an extremely large number of samples, of a fixed N, to obtain the distribution of sample means. In the two-sample case, we should imagine drawing pairs of samples, finding the *difference* between the means of each pair, and obtaining a distribution of these differences. The resulting distribution would be the *sampling distribution of the difference between means*.

To illustrate, imagine that from the population described in Table 12.1, in which $\mu = 5.00$ and $\sigma = 0.99$, we randomly draw (with replacement) two samples at a time. For illustrative purposes, let us draw two cases for the first sample (i.e., $N_1 = 2$) and three cases for the second sample (i.e., $N_2 = 3$). For example, we might draw scores of 5, 6 for our first sample and scores of 4, 4, 7 for our second sample. Thus, since $\bar{X}_1 = 5.5$ and $\bar{X}_2 = 5.0$, $\bar{X}_1 - \bar{X}_2 = 0.5$. Now suppose we continue to draw samples of $N_1 = 2$ and $N_2 = 3$ until we obtain an indefinitely large number of pairs of samples. If we calculate the differences between these pairs of sample means and treat each of these differences as a raw score, we may set up a frequency distribution of these differences.

Intuitively, what might we expect this distribution to look like? Since we are selecting pairs of samples at random from the *same* population, we would expect a normal distribution with a mean of zero.

Going one step further, we may describe the distribution of the difference between pairs of sample means, even when these samples are *not* drawn from the same population. It will be a normal distribution with a mean $(\mu_{\bar{X}_1-\bar{X}_2})$ equal to $\mu_1 - \mu_2$ and a standard deviation $\sigma_{\bar{X}_1-\bar{X}_2}$, referred to as the **standard error of the difference between means,** equal to $\sqrt{\sigma_{\bar{X}_1}^2 + \sigma_{\bar{X}_2}^2}$.

Standard Error of the Difference Between Means: Standard deviation of the sampling distribution of the difference between means.

Thus, the sampling distribution of the statistic

$$z = \frac{(\bar{X}_1 - \bar{X}_2) - (\mu_1 - \mu_2)}{\sigma_{\bar{X}_1-\bar{X}_2}}$$

is normal, and therefore we can employ the standard normal curve in testing hypotheses.

13.2 ESTIMATION OF $\sigma_{\bar{X}_1-\bar{X}_2}$ FROM SAMPLE DATA

The statistic z is employed only when the population standard deviations are known. Since it is rare that these parameters are known,* we are once again forced to estimate the standard error in which we are interested, that is, $\sigma_{\bar{X}_1-\bar{X}_2}$.

Historically, the estimated standard error of the difference between means was defined as follows:

$$s_{\bar{X}_1-\bar{X}_2} = \sqrt{s_{\bar{X}_1}^2 + s_{\bar{X}_2}^2}$$

---

*Many statisticians also recommend its use with large sample sizes ($N > 30$) because of the central limit theorem and the fact that the difference between the critical values of z (1.96 at the 0.05 level, two-tailed test) and t (2.045 at the same level with df = 29) are small. Others favor the use of z only when $N > 100$.

However, this formula provides a biased estimate whenever N_1 is not equal to N_2.

If we randomly select a sample of N_1 observations from a population with unknown variance and a second random sample of N_2 observations also from a population with unknown variance, the following is an unbiased estimate of the standard error of the difference. This estimate, which assumes that the two samples are drawn from a population with the same variance, pools the sum of squares and degrees of freedom of the two samples to obtain a pooled estimate of the standard error of the difference. Hence

$$s_{\bar{X}_1 - \bar{X}_2} = \sqrt{\left(\frac{SS_1 + SS_2}{N_1 + N_2 - 2}\right)\left(\frac{1}{N_1} + \frac{1}{N_2}\right)} \qquad (13.1)^*$$

However, if $N_1 = N_2 = N$, Formula (13.1) simplifies to

$$s_{\bar{X}_1 - \bar{X}_2} = \sqrt{\frac{SS_1 + SS_2}{N(N - 1)}} \qquad (13.2)^*$$

In order to obtain the sum of squares for our two groups, we apply Formula (6.6) to each sample and obtain

$$SS_1 = \sum X_1^2 - \frac{(\sum X_1)^2}{N_1} \qquad \text{and} \qquad SS_2 = \sum X_2^2 - \frac{(\sum X_2)^2}{N_2}$$

13.3 TESTING STATISTICAL HYPOTHESES: STUDENT'S *t*

The statistic employed in the testing of hypotheses when population standard deviations are not known is the familiar *t*-ratio:

$$t = \frac{(\bar{X}_1 - \bar{X}_2) - (\mu_1 - \mu_2)}{s_{\bar{X}_1 - \bar{X}_2}} \qquad (13.3)$$

in which $\mu_1 - \mu_2$ is the expected value as stated in the null hypothesis.

The most common null hypothesis tested is that both samples come from the same population of means, that is, $\mu_1 - \mu_2 = 0$. However, there are times when the null hypothesis may specify a difference between population means. As an example, let us imagine that we know (or have a reasonable estimate of) the difference in heights of male and female adults. Imagine that we have reason to believe that in a specific locality this difference may be affected by environmental factors such as smog or diet. In this case, the null hypothesis would specify the known difference in

---

*These formulas can be presented in terms of raw scores. Refer to the endpapers of this book.

heights. Thus, if the heights of males are known to be 5 inches greater than the heights of females on the average, the null hypothesis would read:

$$H_0 : \mu_M - \mu_F = 5 \text{ inches}$$

You will recall that Table C, in the Table section, provides the critical values of t that are required for significance at various levels of α. Since the degrees of freedom for each sample are $N_1 - 1$ and $N_2 - 1$, the total df in the two-sample case in $N_1 + N_2 - 2$.

Illustrative Problem: Student's t

In Case Example 5.1 we presented the results of research related to near-SIDS (Sudden Infant Death Syndrome). Many parents react to this tragedy with feelings of guilt mingled with accusations toward the spouse of carelessness and blame. Many researchers, however, are convinced that the fault lies in biological mechanisms within the infant. Orlowski (1982) has suggested one possible mechanism—higher than normal levels of the body's own narcotic-like substances, the endorphins and enkephalins. Recall that the β-endorphin levels in the cerebrospinal fluid of eight infants who had experienced near-SIDS were compared to the levels in two control infants. The results are reproduced in Table 13.1

Let's set up the test of significance in formal statistical terms.

1. *Null hypothesis* (H_0): The mean difference in β-endorphin levels between the infants experiencing near-SIDS and control infants is equal to or less than zero; that is, $\mu_1 \leq \mu_2$.

TABLE 13.1 Beta-endorphin Levels in Eight Infants Who Had Experienced Near-SIDS Compared to Levels in Two Control Infants

Group 1 Experimental		Group 2 Control	
X_1	X_1^2	X_2	X_2^2
52	2,704	1	1
52	2,704	10	100
66	4,356		
54	2,916		
47	2,209		
66	4,356		
90	8,100		
50	2,500		
$\Sigma = 477$	29,845	11	101

2. *Alternative hypothesis* (H_1): The mean difference in endorphin levels between the near-SIDS infants and control infants is greater than zero; that is, $\mu_1 > \mu_2$.

3. *Statistical test:* The t-ratio is used since the N in each group < 30. The assumptions of normality and equal variances are made.

4. *Significance level:* $\alpha = 0.05$, one-tailed test. If the difference between the two sample means is so large that its associated probability of occurrence under the sampling distribution is equal to or less than 0.05, we shall reject H_0.

5. *Sampling distribution:* Student's t-distribution at df $= 8$.

6. *Critical region for rejection of* H_0: $t_{0.05}$ (one-tailed) $= 1.860$.

The sum of squares for each condition is

$$SS_1 = 29{,}845 - \frac{477^2}{8} \qquad SS_2 = 101 - \frac{11^2}{2}$$
$$= 1{,}403.875 \qquad\qquad = 40.5$$

Since $N_1 \neq N_2$ and the population variances are assumed to be equal, we use Formula (13.1) to estimate the standard error of the difference between means.

$$s_{\bar{X}_1 - \bar{X}_2} = \sqrt{\left(\frac{1403.875 + 40.5}{8}\right)\left(\frac{10}{16}\right)}$$
$$= \sqrt{112.8418} = 10.62$$

The value of t in the present problem is

$$t = \frac{(\bar{X}_1 - \bar{X}_2) - (\mu_1 - \mu_2)}{s_{\bar{X}_1 - \bar{X}_2}}$$
$$= \frac{59.625 - 5.5}{10.62}$$
$$= 5.097$$

Decision: Since the obtained t falls within the critical region (i.e., $t \geq 1.860$) we reject H_0. From this we can conclude that the mean endorphin level is significantly greater among the near-SIDS children than among the control subjects. Note that this is not a true experiment. Therefore, a strong conclusion of causality cannot be drawn. It is possible that the endorphin levels are merely correlated with a variable that causes the near-SIDS or that the high levels of endorphins represent a consequence of the cessation of breathing during sleep.

Student's *t*-Ratio When Sample Means and Standard Deviations Are Known

When we read research reports in the literature of the behavioral sciences, we find that summary statements are usually given in terms of means and standard deviations rather than in terms of SS. Moreover, some statistical programs on the computer and on statistical calculators provide only means and standard deviations. When we do not know the sum of squares, Formula (13.4) should be used.

$$s_{\bar{X}_1 - \bar{X}_2} = \sqrt{\left[\frac{N_1 s_1^2 + N_2 s_2^2}{N_1 + N_2 - 2}\right]\left[\frac{N_1 + N_2}{N_1 N_2}\right]} \qquad (13.4)$$

when s_1^2 and s_2^2 are based on N in the denominator.

Note that Formula (13.4) assumes that we are using standard deviations based on the biased estimators of the population variance; that is, N was used in the denominator when we calculated the sample standard deviation. If the sample standard deviations are calculated with $N - 1$ in the denominator (as is the case with some computer programs and hand calculators), we should substitute $N_1 - 1$ for N_1 and $N_2 - 1$ for N_2 in Formula (13.4); that is,

$$s_{\bar{X}_1 - \bar{X}_2} = \sqrt{\left[\frac{(N_1 - 1)\hat{s}_1^2 + (N_2 - 1)\hat{s}_2^2}{N_1 + N_2 - 2}\right]\left[\frac{N_1 + N_2}{N_1 N_2}\right]}$$

when s_1^2 and s_2^2 are based on $N - 1$ in the denominator.

13.4   ESTIMATING THE DEGREE OF ASSOCIATION BETWEEN THE INDEPENDENT AND DEPENDENT VARIABLES

The finding of a statistically significant t-ratio means that some degree of association exists between the independent and dependent variables. However, the fact of statistical significance does not automatically confer "importance" to a finding. Given a sufficiently large N, even a trivial difference may be found to be statistically significant.

One way of clarifying the "significance" of a statistically significant difference is to ascertain the extent to which variations in the independent variable (the treatment administered) account for variations in the dependent measure. In general, the higher the degree of relationship is, the greater is the importance of the finding. A measure of association is ω^2 **(omega squared)**, which is estimated by

Omega Squared (ω^2): An estimate of the variance in the dependent variable accounted for by variations in the independent variable.

$$\text{est } \omega^{2*} = \frac{t^2 - 1}{t^2 + N_1 + N_2 - 1} \qquad (13.5)$$

*If $|t|$ is less than 1.00, ω^2 will be negative. Since a negative ω^2 is meaningless, we arbitrarily set $\omega^2 = 0$ when $|t| \leq 1.00$.

Example   In the near-SIDS study, we found $t = 5.097$ with $N_1 = 8$ and $N_2 = 2$. Therefore

$$\text{est } \omega^2 = \frac{25.98 - 1}{25.98 + 8 + 2 - 1}$$

$$= \frac{24.98}{34.98} = 0.714$$

This may be interpreted in very much the same way as the coefficient of determination (r_2), which was discussed in Chapter 9 (see Section 9.4). Recall that a coefficient of determination of 0.714 would mean that we estimate that 71.4% of the variance of Y is accounted for by variations in X. Similarly, $\omega^2 = 0.714$ may be interpreted to mean that approximately 71.4% of the variance in the dependent measure is accounted for by variations in the independent variable. When we consider the multitude of variables that usually influence the dependent measures, finding a single variable that accounts for 71.4% of the variance would appear to describe a real and important effect.

Note that we cannot judge the magnitude of the association by merely looking at the value of the t-ratio. For example, imagine that we had found the same t-ratio of 5.097 with $N_1 = N_2 = 75$. The difference is clearly statistically significant. However, does it also account for a high degree of association between the experimental and dependent variables? Let's see.

When $t = 5.097$ and $N_1 = N_2 = 75$

$$\text{est } \omega^2 = \frac{25.98 - 1}{25.98 + 75 + 75 - 1}$$

$$= \frac{24.98}{174.98}$$

$$= 0.143$$

In spite of the high t-ratio, we estimate the experimental variable to account for only about 14% of the variance in the dependent variable. These examples illustrate the fact that a significant t-ratio with a small N may well be describing a more *important* relationship between the independent and the dependent variables than a significant t-ratio with a large N.

Why is this so? Consider the following summary statistics and the Student's t-ratios obtained by two different investigators.

Investigator A: $\overline{X}_1 = 15$, $\overline{X}_2 = 10$, $s_{\overline{x}_1 - \overline{x}_2} = 2.244$, $N = 12$ (6 per group); $t = (15 - 10)/2.244 = 2.228$, df $= 10$. Critical value at $\alpha = 0.05$, two-tailed test $= 2.228$.

Investigator B: $\overline{X}_1 = 11$, $\overline{X}_2 = 10$, $s_{\overline{x}_1 - \overline{x}_2} = 0.494$, $N = 42$ (21 per group); $t = (11 - 10)/0.494 = 2.024$, df $= 40$. Critical value at $\alpha = 0.05$, two-tailed test $= 2.021$.

STATISTICS IN ACTION 13.1

Emotional contrast: Does humor before horror significantly increase the unpleasantness of horror?

Recall the fascinating study by Manstead and colleagues (1983) in which the emotional contrast effect was investigated. We looked at some of the data in Statistics in Action 5.1 and Exercises 16, 24, and 25 of Chapter 6. In Statistics in Action 5.1 we found that, for both males and females, the mean ratings of unpleasantness were higher when scenes of horror were preceded by scenes of humor than when horror was presented first. In Exercise 16 (Chapter 6) we calculated the standard deviations for each of these groups. The results of these analyses are summarized as follows:

Unpleasantness Ratings

Group	Horror Preceded by Humor			Horror First		
	Mean	**Stand. Dev.**	**N**	**Mean**	**Stand. Dev.**	**N**
Males	32.9	5.09	10	28.3	6.72	10
Females	38.4	5.55	10	35.0	4.49	10
Combined	35.65	5.99	20	31.65	6.63	20

Now let's investigate the statistical significance of the findings. Specifically, we'll calculate t-ratios to answer the following null hypotheses: There is no difference in the population mean unpleasantness ratings for either the males or the females. Note that we are using a nondirectional null hypothesis. This is done because we have no overwhelming theoretical basis nor empirical results for predicting the direction of the outcome of the results.

Using $\alpha = 0.05$, two-tailed test, with df $= 18$, we find that the absolute value of the t-ratio must exceed 2.101 to achieve statistical significance. The calculations of t for the male and female samples are summarized here:

Group	Horror Preceded by Humor	Horror First
Males	$\bar{X} = 32.9$	$\bar{X} = 28.3$
Sample size	$N = 10$	$N = 10$
Standard deviation	$s = 5.09$	$s = 6.72$

$$s_{\bar{X}_1 - \bar{X}_2} = \sqrt{\left[\frac{(10)(5.09)^2 + (10)(6.72)^2}{10 + 10 - 2}\right]\left[\frac{10 + 10}{100}\right]}$$

$$= \sqrt{\left(\frac{259.081 + 451.584}{18}\right)(0.2)} = \sqrt{7.896} = 2.81$$

$$t = (32.9 - 28.3)/2.81 = 1.637$$
$$\text{est } \omega^2 = 0.08$$

Group	Horror Preceded by Humor	Horror First
Females	$\bar{X} = 38.4$	$\bar{X} = 35.0$
Sample size	$N = 10$	$N = 10$
Standard deviation	$s = 5.55$	$s = 4.49$

$$s_{\bar{X}_1 - \bar{X}_2} = \sqrt{\left[\frac{(10)(5.55)^2 + (10)(4.49)^2}{10 + 10 - 2}\right]\left[\frac{10 + 10}{100}\right]}$$

$$= \sqrt{\left(\frac{308.025 + 201.601}{18}\right)(0.2)} = \sqrt{5.663} = 2.38$$

$$t = (38.4 - 35.0)/2.38 = 1.429$$
$$\text{est } \omega^2 = 0.05$$

Since both obtained t-ratios fall short of the critical value of t that is required to reject H_0, we cannot reject the null hypothesis. It should be noted, however, that this study involved two independent variables—the order of presentation of the horror scenes (a true independent variable) and the gender of the subjects (an organismic variable). The appropriate analysis when there are two or more independent variables involves the analysis of variance (ANOVA), factorial design. We'll reanalyze these data in Chapters 14 and 15, using ANOVA.

a. In each of the two conditions—horror preceded by humor and horror first—combine the males and females into single groups of 20 subjects each. Test H_0: The mean difference in the ratings of unpleasantness for the population(s) from which the two conditions were selected is equal to zero. Use $\alpha = 0.05$. What conclusion do you draw?

b. Are females more or less likely to rate scenes of horror as unpleasant? Looking only at the condition in which horror was preceded by humor, test for the significance of the difference between males and females, using $\alpha = 0.05$, two-tailed test.

c. Looking only at the condition in which horror was presented first, test for the significance of the difference between males and females, using $\alpha = 0.05$, two-tailed test.

d. Combine the male ratings of humor preceded by horror and horror first and the female ratings of both variables and administer the test of significance (males versus females) at $\alpha = 0.05$, two-tailed test.

ANSWERS

a.

Group	Horror Preceded by Humor	Horror First
Males and females combined	$\bar{X} = 35.65$	$\bar{X} = 31.65$
Sample size	$N = 20$	$N = 20$
Standard deviation	$s = 5.99$	$s = 6.63$

$$s_{\bar{x}_1 - \bar{x}_2} = \sqrt{\frac{(20)(5.99)^2 + (20)(6.63)^2}{(20 + 20 - 2)} \cdot \left[\frac{(20 + 20)}{400}\right]}$$

$$= \sqrt{\frac{(717.602 + 879.138)}{38} \times 0.1} = \sqrt{4.202} = 2.050$$

$$t = \frac{(35.65 - 31.65)}{2.050} = 1.951 \qquad df = 38$$

We cannot reject H_0 at $\alpha = 0.05$, two-tailed test.

$$\text{est } \omega^2 = 0.07$$

b.

Group	Females	Males
Horror preceded by humor	$\bar{X} = 38.4$	$\bar{X} = 32.9$
Sample size	$N = 10$	$N = 10$
Standard deviation	$s = 5.55$	$s = 5.09$

$$s_{\bar{x}_1 - \bar{x}_2} = \sqrt{\frac{(10)(5.55)^2 + (10)(5.09)^2}{(10 + 10 - 2)} \cdot \left[\frac{(10 + 10)}{100}\right]}$$

$$= \sqrt{\frac{(308.025 + 259.081)}{18} \times 0.2} = \sqrt{6.301} = 2.51$$

$$t = \frac{(38.4 - 32.9)}{2.51} = 2.191 \qquad df = 18$$

Critical value of $t_{0.05} = |2.101|$. Reject H_0. Ratings of unpleasantness among females are significantly higher than among males when horror is preceded by humor.

$$\text{est } \omega^2 = 0.16$$

c.

Group	Females	Males
Horror presented first	$\bar{X} = 35.0$	$\bar{X} = 28.3$
Sample size	$N = 10$	$N = 10$
Standard deviation	$s = 6.72$	$s = 4.49$

$$s_{\bar{x}_1 - \bar{x}_2} = \sqrt{\frac{(10)(6.72)^2 + (10)(4.49)^2}{(10 + 10 - 2)} \cdot \left[\frac{(10 + 10)}{100}\right]}$$

$$= \sqrt{\frac{(451.584 + 201.601)}{18}} \times 0.2 = \sqrt{7.257} = 2.694$$

$$t = \frac{(35.0 - 28.3)}{2.694} = 2.487 \qquad df = 18$$

Critical value of $t_{0.05} = |2.101|$. Reject H_0. Ratings of unpleasantness among females are significantly higher than among males when horror is presented first.

$$\text{est } \omega^2 = 0.206$$

d.

Group	Females	Males
Combined (humor-then-horror) and (horror first)	$\bar{X} = 36.7$	$\bar{X} = 30.6$
Sample size	$N = 20$	$N = 20$
Standard deviation	$s = 5.33$	$s = 6.39$

$$s_{\bar{x}_1 - \bar{x}_2} = \sqrt{\frac{(20)(5.33)^2 + (20)(6.39)^2}{(20 + 20 - 2)} \cdot \left[\frac{(20 + 20)}{400}\right]}$$

$$= \sqrt{\frac{(568.178 + 816.642)}{38}} \times 0.1 = \sqrt{3.644} = 1.909$$

$$t = \frac{(36.7 - 30.6)}{1.909} = 3.195 \qquad df = 38$$

Critical value of $t_{0.05} = |2.025|$ (by linear interpolation). Reject H_0. Ratings of unpleasantness among females are significantly higher than among males when horror preceded by humor is combined with horror first.

$$\text{est } \omega^2 = 0.187$$

Source: Manstead et al., 1983.

Note that both experimenters rejected H_0 at precisely the 0.05 α-level. However, we have already seen that: (1) the larger the N of pairs of samples that are drawn from a given population is, the smaller is the standard error of the difference between means; (2) the smaller the resulting denominator of the test statistic (z or t) is, the smaller is the difference between means required for statistical significance; and (3) the larger the sample size is, the smaller is the critical value of t that is required for significance at a given α-level. Thus, with large Ns, a smaller effect of the independent variable (i.e., a smaller difference between means) can be detected. Note that, in the preceding example, Experimenter A required a *difference in means exactly five times greater* than that obtained by Experimenter B to reject H_0 at the *same* α-level.

Finally, when estimated ω^2 is calculated for each study, we find that for Investigator A, est $\omega^2 = 0.248$, and for Investigator B, est $\omega^2 = 0.068$. Thus, with both studies achieving *equal* levels of significance, almost 25% of the variance in the dependent measure is accounted for by the independent variable in the study with the smaller N. In contrast, the independent variable in the study with the larger N accounts for only about 7% of the variance in the dependent measure.

13.5   THE *t*-RATIO AND HOMOGENEITY OF VARIANCE

The assumptions underlying the use of the *t*-distributions are as follows:

1. The sampling distribution of the difference between means is normally distributed.
2. Estimated $\sigma_{\bar{X}_1 - \bar{X}_2}$ (i.e., $s_{\bar{X}_1 - \bar{X}_2}$) is based on the unbiased estimate of the population variance.
3. Both samples are drawn from populations whose variances are equal. This assumption is referred to as **homogeneity of variance.**

Occasionally, for reasons that may not be very clear, the scores of one group may be far more widely distributed than the scores of another group. Such scores may indicate that we are sampling from two different distributions, but the critical question is this: Two different distributions of what? Means or variances?

To determine whether or not two variances differ significantly from one another, we must refer to yet another distribution: the *F*-distribution. Named after R. A. Fisher, the statistician who first described it, the *F*-distribution is unlike any other we have encountered so far; it is *tridimensional* in nature. To employ the *F* table (Table D_1, Table section), we must begin at the entry stating the number of degrees of freedom of

Homogeneity of Variance: The condition that exists when two or more sample variances have been drawn from populations with equal variances.

F-ratio: A ratio between sample variances.

the group with the larger variance, and move down the column until we find the entry for the number of degrees of freedom of the group with the smaller variance. At that point, we shall find the critical value of F required for rejecting the null hypothesis of no difference in variances. The **F-ratio** is defined as follows:

$$F = \frac{\hat{s}^2 \text{ (larger variance)}}{\hat{s}^2 \text{ (smaller variance)}} \tag{13.6}$$

The test is two-tailed, as we are interested in determining if either variance differs significantly from the other. It would be one-tailed *only* if we were interested in determining whether a specific variance is significantly greater than another. This is an unlikely comparison. Since Table D_1 is one-tailed, the use of the 0.025 critical value yields the 0.05 two-tailed significance level. In the preceding sample problem, the variance for group 1 is $(5.33)^2$ or 28.41 and that for group 2, $(6.39)^2$ or 40.83. The F-ratio becomes

$$F = \frac{40.83}{28.41} = 1.44 \qquad df = \frac{19}{19}$$

Referring to Table D_1 under 20 and 20 df (the nearest approximation to $df = 19/19$) we find that an $F \geq 2.46$ is significant at the 0.05 level. We may therefore conclude that it is reasonable to assume that both samples were drawn from populations with the same variance.

What if we found a significant difference in variances? Would it have increased our likelihood of rejecting the null hypothesis of no difference between means? Very little, in all probability; as we have already pointed out, the t-ratio is a robust test. Our conclusions are not likely to be altered by any but extremely large departures from the assumption of homogeneity of variances and normality.

Why, then, do we concern ourselves with an analysis of the variances? Frequently a significant difference in variances (particularly when the variance of the experimental group is significantly greater than that of the control group) is indicative of a *dual* effect of the experimental conditions. A larger variance indicates more extreme scores *at both ends* of a distribution. The alert researcher will seize upon these facts as a basis for probing into the possibility of dual effects.

For example, years ago the experimental question, "Does anxiety improve or hinder performance on complex psychological tasks?" was thoroughly studied, with rather ambiguous results. More recently, we have come to recognize that anxiety-induced conditions have dual effects, depending on a host of factors—for example, personality variables. An increase in anxiety causes some individuals to become better oriented to the task at hand, while others "come apart at the seams," so to speak. A study of the variances of our experimental groups may facilitate the uncovering of such interesting and theoretically important dual effects.

13.6 STATISTICAL COMPARISON OF TWO CORRELATED SAMPLES

One of the fundamental problems confronting behavioral scientists is the extreme variability of their data. Indeed, it is *because* of this variability that they are so concerned with the field of inferential statistics.

When an experiment is conducted, data comparing two or more groups are obtained and a difference in some measure of central tendency is found, and then we raise the question: Is the difference of such magnitude that it is unlikely to be due to chance factors? As we have seen, a visual inspection of the data is not usually sufficient to answer this question because there is so much overlapping of the experimental groups. The overlapping, in turn, is due to the fact that the experimental subjects themselves manifest widely varying aptitudes and proficiencies relative to the criterion measure. In an experiment the score of any subject on the criterion (dependent) variable may be thought to reflect at least three factors: (1) the subject's ability and/or proficiency on the criterion task; (2) the effects of the experimental variable; and (3) random error due to a wide variety of different causes, for example, minor variations from time to time in experimental procedures or conditions, or momentary fluctuations in such things as attention span and motivation of the experimental subjects. There is little we can do about *random error* except to maintain as close control as possible over experimental conditions. The *effects of the experimental variable* are, of course, what we are interested in assessing. In the majority of studies, the *individual differences between subjects* are by and large the most significant factor contributing to the scores and the variability of scores on the criterion variable. Anything we can do to take this factor into account or "statistically remove" its effects will improve our ability to estimate the effects of the experimental variable on the criterion scores. The next sections are concerned with a technique that is commonly employed to accomplish this objective: the employment of *correlated samples*.

13.7 STANDARD ERROR OF THE DIFFERENCE BETWEEN MEANS FOR CORRELATED GROUPS

In our earlier discussion of Student's *t*-ratio, we presented the formula for the unpooled estimate of the standard error of the difference between means as

$$s_{\bar{X}_1 - \bar{X}_2} = \sqrt{s_{\bar{X}_1}^2 + s_{\bar{X}_2}^2}$$

A more general formula for the standard error of the difference is

$$s_{\bar{X}_1 - \bar{X}_2} = \sqrt{s_{\bar{X}_1}^2 + s_{\bar{X}_2}^2 - 2rs_{\bar{X}_1}s_{\bar{X}_2}} \qquad (13.7)$$

BOX 13.2

AUTOMATIC TRANSMISSION: GUZZLE, GUZZLE

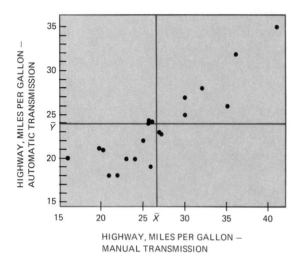

HIGHWAY, MILES PER GALLON — MANUAL TRANSMISSION

Earlier in this chapter we saw that $s_{\bar{x}_1 - \bar{x}_2}$ is a sort of benchmark against which we evaluate the difference between means. If $s_{\bar{x}_1 - \bar{x}_2}$ is large relative to the mean difference, we are less likely to reject H_0 than if $s_{\bar{x}_1 - \bar{x}_2}$ is small relative to the same difference between means.

If there were some way to legitimately reduce the size of the error term ($s_{\bar{x}_1 - \bar{x}_2}$), our benchmark would be more sensitive. Just such an opportunity is provided by correlational analysis. Recall from Chapter 9 that the higher the correlation between two variables is, the greater is the *explained variation* and the less the *unexplained* or random variation. Since the unexplained variation represents error, correlational analysis provides a legitimate way to lessen unexplained variation and thereby reduce error.

The table shows the highway miles-per-gallon scores achieved by 20 cars with manual transmission and 20 cars with automatic transmission. Each pair represents the same model car. In other words, both members of each pair are identical except for the type of transmission. When correlated samples are employed, the *difference* between the paired scores is used as the basis for calculating the error term. If

the correlation is low, these differences are large. So also is the error term based on these differences. When r is high, the differences are small. The higher the correlation is, the smaller are the differences between the paired scores. The error term is similarly reduced.

The accompanying scatter diagram suggests that the correlation between the paired observations is very high. As a matter of actual fact, $r = 0.89$. The resulting error term, referred to as the standard error of the mean difference $s_{\bar{D}}$, is much lower than the error term $s_{\bar{x}_1 - \bar{x}_2}$ that we would have used in the absence of correlated samples.

Car Model	Type of Transmission		Difference
	Manual	Automatic	
Gremlin	26	19	7
Hornet	16	20	−4
Audi Fox	36	32	4
Skyhawk	26	24	2
Vega	30	27	3
Datsun 210	41	35	6
Datsun 280	25	22	3
Fiat 131	30	25	5
Mustang II	24	20	4
Granada	20	21	−1
Capri II	27	23	4
Monarch	20	21	−1
Starfire	26	24	2
Valiant/ Duster	23	20	3
Sunbird	26	24	2
Lemans	21	18	3
Corolla	35	26	9
Corona MK. II	22	18	4
Volvo	27	23	4
LUV pickup	32	28	4

Highway mileage of 20 pairs of 1976 automobiles. Each pair consists of one car with manual transmission and the same model car with automatic transmission.

We drop the last term whenever our sample subjects are assigned to experimental conditions at *random*, for the simple reason that when scores are paired at random, the correlation between the two samples will average zero. Any observed correlation will be spurious, since it will represent a chance association. Consequently, when subjects are assigned to experimental conditions at random, the last term reduces to zero (since $r = 0$).

However, there are many experimental situations in which we do not randomly assign our subjects to each experimental condition. Most of these situations can be placed in one of two classes.

Before-After Design   A reading on the *same* subjects is taken both before and after the introduction of the experimental variable. It is presumed that each individual will remain relatively consistent. Thus, there will be a correlation between the scores made by subjects before and after the introduction of the independent variable. In other words, even if the independent variable causes changes in the dependent measures, the subjects will, by and large, retain the same relative position in both testings. Thus, in a reaction-time experiment, a quick responder will remain quick and a slow responder will remain slow. Note that each subject may have been *selected* at random from a subject pool, but since he or she participates in both conditions, we cannot say that the subjects have been *assigned* randomly to experimental conditions.

Before-After Design: A correlated-samples design in which each individual is measured on the criterion task both before and after the introduction of the experimental conditions.

Matched-Group Design   The subjects available for participation in the study are matched on some variable known to be correlated with the criterion or dependent variable. The result is a set of paired subjects in which each member of a given pair obtains approximately the same score on the matching variable. Then one member of each pair is randomly assigned to the experimental condition and the other is assigned to the control group. Thus, if we wanted to determine the effect of some drug on the ease of learning the solution to a mathematical problem, we might match individuals on the basis of IQ estimates, the amount of mathematical training, grades in statistics, or performance on other mathematics problems. Such a design has two advantages:

Matched-Group Design: A correlated-samples design in which pairs of subjects are matched on a variable correlated with the criterion measure. Each member of a pair receives different experimental conditions.

1. It ensures that the experimental groups are "equivalent" in initial ability.
2. It permits us to take advantage of the correlation based on initial ability and allows us in effect to remove one source of error from our measurements.

Fortunately, it is not necessary actually to determine the correlation between before-after or matched samples in order to find $s_{\bar{X}_1 - \bar{X}_2}$. Another method is available that permits the direct calculation of the standard error of the difference. We refer to this method as the *direct-difference method* and represent the standard error of the difference as $s_{\bar{D}}$.

In brief, the direct-difference method consists of finding the differences between the criterion scores that are obtained by each pair of correlated scores, and treating these *differences* as if they were raw scores. In effect, the direct-difference method transforms a two-sample case into a one-sample case. We find one sample mean and a standard error based on one standard deviation. The null hypothesis is that the obtained mean of the difference scores ($\Sigma D/N$, symbolized as $\mu_{\bar{D}}$) comes from a sampling distribution of mean differences (the population) in which the mean difference ($\mu_{\bar{D}}$) is some specified value. The *t*-ratio employed to test $H_0 : \mu_{\bar{D}} = 0$ is

$$t = \frac{\bar{D} - \mu_{\bar{D}}}{s_{\bar{D}}} = \frac{\bar{D}}{s_{\bar{D}}}$$ (13.8)

The raw score formula for calculating the sum of squares of the difference score is

$$SS_D = \sum D^2 - \frac{(\sum D)^2}{N}$$ (13.9)

where D is the difference between paired scores. It follows then that the standard deviation of the difference scores is

$$\hat{s}_{\bar{D}} = \sqrt{\frac{SS_D}{(N-1)}}$$ (13.10)

Furthermore, the **standard error of the mean difference** $s_{\bar{D}}$ may be obtained by dividing Formula (13.10) by $\sqrt{N}$. Thus

$$s_{\bar{D}} = \sqrt{\frac{SS_D}{N(N-1)}}$$ (13.11)

$$s_{\bar{D}} = \frac{\hat{s}_{\bar{D}}}{\sqrt{N}}$$ (13.12)*

CASE EXAMPLE 13.1

Evaluating a Possible Remedy for Treatment-Resistant Essential Hypertension

Seven patients suffering from treatment-resistant essential hypertension received long-term treatment with a drug called Captopril. No known cause has been

---

* An alternative formula for obtaining $s_{\bar{D}}$ is $s_{\bar{D}}/\sqrt{N-1}$, where $s_{\bar{D}} = \sqrt{SS_D/N}$.

found for essential hypertension. However, this lack of a known cause does not reduce its danger. If not treated successfully, it can lead to heart attacks, strokes, and kidney failure.

Based on preliminary studies, Captopril appeared to have the properties of an antitensive drug. Consequently, we use a directional null hypothesis in evaluating its effectiveness.

1. *Null hypothesis (H$_0$):* The mean diastolic blood pressure remains the same or becomes greater after the administration of Captopril, that is, $\mu_{\bar{D}} \geq 0$.
2. *Alternative hypothesis (H$_1$):* The mean diastolic blood pressure decreases after the administration of Captopril, that is, $\mu_{\bar{D}} < 0$.
3. *Statistical test:* Because we are dealing with a before-after design, Student's *t*-ratio, direct-difference method, is used. We assume that the variable is approximately normally distributed.
4. *Significance level:* $\alpha = 0.01$, one-tailed test. If the mean difference is positive and sufficiently above zero so that its associated probability of occurrence under the sampling distribution is equal to or less than 0.01, we reject H$_0$.
5. *Sampling distribution:* Student's *t*-distribution with df = $N - 1$ (number of paired values minus 1).
6. *Critical region for rejection of H$_0$:* The one-tailed critical value at $\alpha = 0.01$ and df = 6 is 3.143.

The following table shows the diastolic blood pressures of the seven patients both before and after treatment and the calculation of Student's *t*-ratio.

Patient	**Supine Diastolic Blood Pressure**		***D***	***D*^{2}**
	Before Drug	**After Drug**		
1	98	82	16	256
2	96	72	24	576
3	140	90	50	2500
4	120	108	12	144
5	130	72	58	3364
6	125	80	45	2025
7	110	98	12	144
	Sum = 819	602	217	9009

The following steps are involved in calculating Student's *t* by the direct-difference method.

Step 1.   The sum of squares of the difference scores is

$$SS_D = 9009 - \frac{(217)^2}{7} = 2282$$

Step 2.   The standard error of the mean difference is

$$s_{\overline{D}} = \sqrt{2282/(7)(6)} = \sqrt{54.333} = 7.371$$

Step 3.   The value of the mean difference is $\overline{D} = 217/7 = 31.00$. (To check the accuracy of $\Sigma\,D$, we subtract ΣX_2 from ΣX_1, that is, $\Sigma X_1 - \Sigma X_2 = \Sigma D$, $819 - 602 = 217$.)

Step 4.   The value of t in the present problem is

$$t = \frac{\overline{D}}{s_{\overline{D}}} = \frac{31.00}{7.371} = 4.206 \qquad df = 6$$

Decision: Since the obtained $t = 4.206$ falls within the critical region (i.e., $4.206 > t_{0.01}$), we reject H_0. Are we justified in concluding that Captopril produced a statistically significant change in diastolic blood pressure? Not necessarily. One of the problems with the before-after design is that there is no control for the possibility that the patients improved spontaneously or as a result of the placebo effect (i.e., they may have improved because their belief in the efficacy of the drug produced physiological changes signaling improvement). This problem is usually countered by the introduction of a control group that receives a placebo or, better still, a drug of known effectiveness. Difference scores are obtained for both groups, means and sums of squares are calculated, and the significance of the mean difference is evaluated by use of Student's t-ratio for independent samples. Why independent samples? The final analysis involves two separate groups of individuals (experimental and control subjects) who have not been paired in any way.

Source: Adapted from D. B. Case and S. A. Atlas (1982), Clinical Experience with Captropril in Moderate to Severe Hypertension." *Cardiovascular Reviews and Reports,* **3**(3), 435–453.

13.8   A COMPARISON OF INDEPENDENT-SAMPLES DESIGNS VERSUS CORRELATED-SAMPLES DESIGNS

If we ignored the fact that the preceding study involved correlated samples and used the t-ratio based on independent samples, we would have obtained the following results:

$$\overline{X}_1 - \overline{X}_2 = 31$$

$$s_{\overline{X}_1 - \overline{X}_2} = 8.033$$

$$t = \frac{31}{8.033} = 3.859$$

You will note that Formula (13.11), which takes correlation into account, provides a reduced error term for assessing the significance of the difference between means. In other words, it provides a more sensitive test of this difference and is more likely to lead to the rejection of the null hypothesis when it is false. Why is this so? You may have noted that the denominator of our various test statistics (t and z) is referred to as the standard error. We have encountered several standard errors so far, including the standard error of estimate, the standard error of the mean, and the standard error of the difference between means. Notice that the word "error" is common to them all. This is no accident. The denominator of the test statistic, be it z or t, may be thought of as an indicator of random or uncontrolled error. Indeed, it is often referred to as the "error term." This uncontrolled error reflects the random effects on the dependent variable of a wide assortment of uncontrolled and, often, unidentifiable variables. Those of you who have ever engaged in some skilled activity will surely appreciate the many factors that contribute to the variability of your performance. Your serves in tennis lack consistency, even though you practive many hours a week. Why? Here are but a few out of many possibilities. The wind changes from moment to moment, lighting conditions fluctuate, your elbow has developed a twinge, worries about personal matters intrude on your concentration, the tennis balls vary in quality, differences in relative humidity affect the tension on the strings of your tennis racket, the net is not always at the proper height, and your opponent's quality of play affects the types of serves you try. If you could identify these variables and control them, your serves would presumably take on an unprecedented consistency. In short, you would remove some of the error in your serving game.

One of the most important factors contributing to the error term in statistics consists of differences between and among individuals. Based on an assortment of such relatively stable factors as our biological, physical, mental, and emotional makeup, we exhibit consistent differences from one another. The differences between individual subjects contribute much to the magnitude of the error term. If, somehow, we could identify and quantify the contributions of individual differences to the error term, we could remove this source of "random error." The resulting error term would be smaller, permitting a more sensitive measure of the differences in the numerator (e.g., the differences between means).

Formula (13.11) takes into account this quantification of individual differences. The greater sensitivity of Formula (13.11) is directly related to our success in pairing subjects on a variable that is correlated with the dependent variable. When r is large, $s_{\overline{D}}$ will be correspondingly small. As r

approaches zero, the advantage of employing correlated samples becomes progressively smaller.

Balanced against the increased sensitivity of the standard error of the difference between means when r is large is the *loss* of degrees of freedom. Whereas the number of degrees of freedom for unmatched samples is $N_1 + N_2 - 2$, when correlated samples are employed the number of degrees of freedom is the number of pairs minus 1 (i.e. $N - 1$).* This difference can be critical when the number of degrees of freedom is small, since, as we saw in Section 12.5, larger t-ratios are required for significance when the numbers of degrees of freedom are small.

Furthermore, matching requires either testing beforehand or access to records that will provide data that are useful for matching purposes. Time and logistic and economic constraints may make testing unfeasible. More-over, preexisting records, when available, may be spotty and of questionable reliability. Matching may also pose problems when subject attrition is high. Whether subjects leave voluntarily or due to circumstances beyond their control, when we lose one subject, we must also exclude that subject's matched pair along with all the data contributed by both. Finally, it is not always possible to match subjects without distorting the "fit" between the sample and the target population. In some instances, extreme cases may be dropped because we can find no comparable subject to serve as a match. Selectively dropping subjects at the extremes artificially lowers variability, thereby producing a spuriously low error term. Because a smaller difference in means is then required for significance, we may inadvertently increase the risk of making a Type I error (falsely rejecting a true H_0).

All of this is not to argue against the use of matched-pair designs. However, their applicability to any experimental study must be evaluated in terms of competing designs that may or may not serve our purposes better.

13.9 PUTTING IT ALL TOGETHER

Suppose an organization devoted to developing programs for weight reduction wished to evaluate the effectiveness of a new regime that showed initial promise. They selected 24 overweight women between the ages of 40 and 50 for participation in a study. The initial weights of all subjects were listed in an array from highest to lowest. The two heaviest individuals were randomly assigned, one to the experimental condition and the other to the control condition. They constituted a matched pair. The same

---

* In independent-samples designs, each condition has $N - 1$ degrees of freedom. Thus, for two samples, df $= N_1 - 1 + N_2 - 1 = N_1 + N_2 - 2$. In correlated-samples designs, the differences between paired scores are the measures against which H_0 is being tested. All but one of these differences is free to vary. Thus, df $= N - 1$, where N is the number of pairs.

TABLE 13.2 Weights of 12 Matched Pairs 60 Days After the 12 Experimental Subjects Were Placed on a New Diet

Matched Ss	Weight			
	Control	Experimental	Difference	D^2
1	231	221	10	100
2	204	197	7	49
3	215	205	10	100
4	207	180	27	729
5	184	185	-1	1
6	215	196	19	361
7	196	187	9	81
8	187	180	7	49
9	173	186	-13	169
10	184	172	12	144
11	172	175	-3	9
12	164	158	6	36
	2332	2242	90	1828

procedures were repeated for the remaining 22 subjects. Thus, 12 matched pairs were obtained. The 12 experimental subjects were placed on the dietary regime, whereas their matched pairs in the control condition continued their regular diet. Sixty days later, all 24 subjects were weighed. The results are shown in Table 13.2. The control subjects are presented first for convenience—to avoid too many negative numbers. Let us test H_0: There is no difference in the population from which the samples were drawn. Use $\alpha = 0.05$, two-tailed test, in which the critical value is $t \geq 2.201$ at df $= 11$.

1. For each pair, subtract the experimental subject's weight from the weight of her matched control.
2. Sum the difference column and divide by N to obtain the mean difference:

$$\overline{D} = \frac{90}{12} = 7.5$$

3. Square and sum the difference column to obtain $\Sigma D^2 = 1828$.
4. Using the values obtained in steps 2 and 3, calculate the sum of squares of the difference scores:

$$SS_D = 1828 - \frac{(90)^2}{12} = 1153$$

5. Using Formula (13.11), find the standard error of the mean difference:

$$s_{\bar{D}} = \sqrt{\frac{1153}{(12)(11)}} = \sqrt{8.7348} = 2.955$$

6. Divide $\bar{D}$ (step 2) by $s_{\bar{D}}$ (step 5) to obtain t:

$$t = \frac{7.5}{2.955} = 2.538$$

Since $t = 2.538$ is greater than the critical value of 2.201, we reject H_0 and assert that the experimental subjects lost significantly more weight than their matched controls.

Now let's suppose that the 24 subjects in the weight control study had been assigned at random to the experimental conditions—in other words, no matching had been done. Test $H_0 : \mu_1 = \mu_2$, using $\alpha = 0.05$, two-tailed test, with df = 22. The critical value is 2.074.

1. For each condition, sum the weight measures. For the control condition, $\Sigma X_c = 2332$; for the experimental condition, $\Sigma X_e = 2242$.

2. Divide each sum in step 1 by N to obtain each condition mean:

$$\bar{X}_e = \frac{2332}{12} = 194.333 \qquad X_e = \frac{2242}{12} = 186.833$$

3. Square and sum each weight column to obtain the sum of the squared weights for each condition: $\Sigma X_c^2 = 457,782$; $\Sigma X_e^2 = 421,854$.

TABLE 13.3   Weights of 24 Independently Assigned Subjects 60 Days After the 12 Experimental Subjects Were Placed on a New Diet

Ss	Weight			
	Control	X_c^2	**Experimental**	X_e^2
1	231	53,361	221	48,841
2	204	41,616	197	38,809
3	215	46,225	205	42,025
4	207	42,849	180	32,400
5	184	33,856	185	34,225
6	215	46,225	196	38,416
7	196	38,416	187	34,969
8	187	34,969	180	32,400
9	173	29,929	186	34,596
10	184	33,856	172	29,584
11	172	29,584	175	30,625
12	164	26,896	158	24,964
	$\Sigma X_c = 2332$	$\Sigma X_c^2 = 457,782$	$\Sigma X_e = 2242$	$\Sigma X_e^2 = 421,854$

4. Using Formula (6.6), calculate the sum of squares (SS) for each condition:

$$SS_c = 457{,}782 - \frac{(2332)^2}{12} = 4596.667$$

$$SS_e = 421{,}844 - \frac{(2242)^2}{12} = 2963.667$$

5. Using Formula (13.2), find the standard error of the difference between means:

$$s_{\bar{x}_1 - \bar{x}_2} = \sqrt{\frac{(4596.667 + 2963.667)}{132}} = 7.568$$

6. Divide the difference between means (step 2) by the standard error of the difference between means (step 5) to obtain the t-ratio:

$$t = \frac{(194.333 - 186.833)}{7.568} = \frac{7.5}{7.568} = 0.991$$

Since the obtained t does not exceed the critical value of t, we fail to reject H_0.

So, analyzing the same set of data using two different forms of t-ratios, we reject H_0 in one case and fail to reject H_0 in the other. Why did this happen? The first solution used the fact that subjects were matched during their assignment to experimental conditions. The correlation introduced by matching subjects permitted the legitimate use of a dramatically reduced error term—2.955 as contrasted with 7.568. Thus, the same difference in means was being measured against a more sensitive error term.

CHAPTER SUMMARY

We have seen that if we take a number of pairs of samples from either the same population or two different populations, then

1. The distribution of differences between pairs of sample means tends to be normal.

2. The mean of these differences between means ($\mu_{\bar{x}_1 - \bar{x}_2}$) is equal to the difference between the population means, that is, $\mu_1 - \mu_2$.

3. The standard error of the difference between means ($\sigma_{\bar{x}_1 - \bar{x}_2}$) is equal to $\sqrt{\sigma_{\bar{x}_1}^2 + \sigma_{\bar{x}_2}^2}$.

We presented formulas for estimating $\sigma_{\bar{x}_1 - \bar{x}_2}$ from sample data. Employing estimated $\sigma_{\bar{x}_1 - \bar{x}_2}$ (i.e., $s_{\bar{x}_1 - \bar{x}_2}$), we demonstrated the use of Student's t to test hypotheses in the two-sample case.

Also presented was a method for estimating the degree of association between an experimental variable and the dependent measure. Omega squared (ω^2) provides an estimate of the variance in the dependent variable accounted for by variations in the independent variable.

An important assumption underlying the use of the t-distribution is that both samples are drawn from populations with equal variances. Although failure to find homogeneity of variance will probably not seriously affect our interpretations, the fact of heterogeneity of variance may have important theoretical implications.

A general formula for the standard error of the difference is

$$s_{\bar{X}_1 - \bar{X}_2} = \sqrt{s_{\bar{X}_1}^2 + s_{\bar{X}_2}^2 - 2rs_{\bar{X}_1}s_{\bar{X}_2}}$$

It is obvious that by matching samples on a variable correlated with the criterion variable, we may reduce the magnitude of the standard error of the difference and thereby provide a more sensitive test of the difference between means. The higher the correlation is, of course, the greater is the reduction in the standard error of the difference.

We demonstrated the use of the direct-difference method for determining the significance of the difference between the means of correlated samples.

TERMS TO REMEMBER

before-after design
F-ratio
homogeneity of variance
omega squared (ω^2)
matched-group design

**standard error of the
    difference between means**
**standard error of the mean
    difference**

EXERCISES

1. Two statistics classes of 25 students each obtained the following results on the final examination: $\bar{X}_1 = 82$, $SS_1 = 384.16$; $\bar{X}_2 = 77$, $SS_2 = 1536.64$. Test the hypothesis that the two classes are equal in ability, employing $\alpha = 0.01$.

2. In an experiment on the effects of a particular drug on the number of errors in the maze-learning behavior of rats, the following results were obtained:

Drug Group	Placebo Group
$\Sigma X_1 = 324$	$\Sigma X_2 = 256$
$\Sigma X_1^2 = 6516$	$\Sigma X_2^2 = 4352$
$N_1 = 18$	$N_2 = 16$

Set up this experiment in formal statistical terms, employing $\alpha = 0.05$, and draw the appropriate conclusions concerning the effect of the drug on the number of errors.

3. On a psychomotor task involving two target sizes, the following results were obtained:

Group 1	Group 2
9	6
6	7
8	7
8	9
9	8

Set up this experiment in formal statistical terms, employing $\alpha = 0.05$, and draw the appropriate conclusions.

4. A study was undertaken to determine whether or not the acquisition of a response is influenced by a drug. The criterion variable was the number of trials required to master the task (X_1 is the experimental group and X_2 is the control group).

X_1	6	8	14	9	10	4	7	
X_2	4	5	3	7	4	2	1	3

   a. Set up this study in formal statistical terms, and state the appropriate conclusions, employing $\alpha = 0.01$.
   b. Is there evidence of heterogeneity of variance?

5. Given two normal populations,

$$\mu_1 = 80, \sigma_1 = 6 \qquad \mu_2 = 77, \sigma_2 = 6$$

If a sample of 36 cases is drawn from population 1 and a sample of 36 cases from population 2, what is the probability that
   a. $\bar{X}_1 - \bar{X}_2 \geq 5$?   b. $\bar{X}_1 - \bar{X}_2 \geq 0$?
   c. $\bar{X}_1 - \bar{X}_2 \leq 0$?   d. $\bar{X}_1 - \bar{X}_2 \leq -5$?

6. Assuming the same two populations as in Exercise 5, calculate the probability that $\bar{X}_1 - \bar{X}_2 \geq 0$, when
   a. $N_1 = N_2 = 4$,   b. $N_1 = N_2 = 9$,
   c. $N_1 = N_2 = 16$,   d. $N_1 = N_2 = 25$.

7. Graph the preceding probabilities as a function of N. Can you formulate any generalization about the probability of finding a difference in the correct direction between sample means (i.e., $\bar{X}_1 - \bar{X}_2 \geq 0$, when $\mu_1 > \mu_2$) as a function of N?

8. A gasoline manufacturer runs tests to determine the relative performance of automobiles employing two different additives. The results are as follows (expressed in terms of miles per gallon of gasoline):

Additive 1:   12, 17, 15, 13, 11, 10, 14, 12
Additive 2:   16, 14, 18, 19, 17, 13, 11, 18

Set up and test the appropriate null hypothesis.

9. Each of two market analysts claim that her ability to forecast price gains in common stock is better than her rival's. Over a specified period, each analyst selected 10 common stocks that she predicted would show a gain. When increases in the prices of the stocks were later compiled, the results were as follows:

Analyst 1: $1.25, $2.50, $1.75, $2.25, $2.00, $1.75, $2.25, $1.00, $1.75, $2.00
Analyst 2: $1.25, $0.75, $1.00, $1.50, $2.00, $1.75, $0.50, $1.50, $0.25 $1.25

Set up and test the appropriate null hypothesis.

10. A toothpaste manufacturer claims that children brushing their teeth daily with his company's product (Brand A) will have fewer cavities than children using Brand X. In a carefully supervised study, the number of cavities in a sample of children using Brand A toothpaste was compared with the number of cavities among children using Brand X. The results were as follows:

Brand A: 1, 2, 0, 3, 0, 2, 1, 4, 2, 3, 1, 2, 1, 1
Brand X: 3, 1, 2, 4, 1, 5, 2, 0, 5, 6, 3, 2, 4, 3

Test the manufacturer's claim.

11. In a study of adolescent development, 582 male and 1052 female students in junior high school completed a questionnaire that included measures of personality and measures of drug use (Wingard, Huba, and Bentler: 1979). On the personality scale of "generosity," the following data were obtained:

Males	**Females**
$\Sigma X_1 = 10{,}371$	$\Sigma X_2 = 20{,}609$
$\Sigma X_1^2 = 198{,}503$	$\Sigma X_2^2 = 427{,}764$
$N_1 = 582$	$N_2 = 1{,}052$

Source: From Wingard, Huba, and Bentler, 1979.

a. Using $\alpha = 0.05$, set up and test the null hypothesis that males and females do not differ on the generosity scale. Find ω^2.

A five-point response scale that ranged from "never used the drug" (1) to "use the drug regularly" (5) yielded the following data:

Males	Females
$\Sigma X_1 = 1024$	$\Sigma X_2 = 1694$
$\Sigma X_1^2 = 2712$	$\Sigma X_2^2 = 4318$
$N_1 = 582$	$N_2 = 1052$

b. Using $\alpha = 0.05$, set up and test the null hypothesis that males and females do not differ in their frequency of marijuana use. Find ω^2.

12. In a study of the television viewing habits of preschool children, Friedrich and Stein (1973) asked 52 boys and 45 girls to name their favorite television programs. The authors then tabulated the number of programs that were considered violent and aggressive and obtained the following data:

Boys	Girls
$\Sigma X_1 = 71$	$\Sigma X_2 = 49$
$\Sigma X_1^2 = 185$	$\Sigma X_2^2 = 147$
$N_1 = 52$	$N_2 = 45$

Set up and test the null hypothesis that boys and girls do not differ in the number of violent programs they name as their favorites. Use $\alpha = 0.05$.

13. A training director in a large industrial firm claims that employees taking her training course perform better on the job than those not receiving training. Of 30 recently hired employees, 15 are randomly selected to receive training. The remaining 15 are employed as controls. Six months later, on-the-job test evaluations yield the following statistics for the training group: $\overline{X}_1 = 24.63$, $s_1 = 3.53$. The controls obtain $\overline{X}_2 = 21.45$ and $s_2 = 4.02$. Set up and test the appropriate null hypothesis, employing $\alpha = 0.05$.

14. A publisher claims that students who receive instruction in mathematics based on his newly developed textbook will score at least 5 points higher on end-of-term grades than those instructed using the old textbook. Thirty-six students are randomly assigned to two classes: The experimental group employs the new textbook for instruction, and the control group uses the old textbook. Students in the experimental group achieve $\overline{X}_1 = 83.05$ and $s_1 = 6.04$ as final grades, whereas the controls obtain $\overline{X}_2 = 76.85$ and $s_2 = 5.95$. Set up and test the appropriate null hypothesis employing $\alpha = 0.01$, one-tailed test. [*Note:* Remember that the numerator in the test statistic is: $(\overline{X}_1 - \overline{X}_2) - (\mu_1 - \mu_2)$.]

15. In a study of memory development, Wingard, Buchanan, and Burnell (1978) selected a set of pictures that could be classified into five semantic categories (food, clothes, toys, furniture, animals). The pictures were randomly presented to 64 four-year-olds and 64 five-year-olds, and the children were asked to recall as many of them as possible. The authors measured the children's tendency to cluster together pictures from the same semantic categories as they recalled them. Four-year-olds showed $\bar{X} = 0.192$ and $s = 0.302$ in semantic clustering, whereas five-year-olds showed $\bar{X} = 0.291$ and $s = 0.359$. Set up and test the null hypothesis that the five-year-olds showed no more semantic clustering than the four-year-olds. Since the alternative hypothesis was directional (five-year-olds were expected to show more clustering as a consequence of greater cognitive development), use $\alpha = 0.05$, one-tailed test. Calculate ω^2.

16. If we found a significant difference between means at the 5% level of significance, it would follow that (true or false):
a. This difference is significant at the 1% level of significance.
b. This difference is significant at the 10% level of significance.
c. The difference observed between means is the true difference.

For Exercises 17 through 21, the following two finite populations of scores are given:

Population 1:   2, 4, 6, 8
Population 2:   1, 3, 5, 7

*17. Random samples of size 2 are selected *(without replacement)* from each population. Construct a histogram showing the sampling distribution of differences between the sample means.

*18. What is the probability that
a. $\bar{X}_1 - \bar{X}_2 \geq 0$?   **b.** $\bar{X}_1 - \bar{X}_2 \geq 1$?   **c.** $\bar{X}_1 - \bar{X}_2 \leq 0$?
d. $\bar{X}_1 - \bar{X}_2 \leq -1$?   **e.** $\bar{X}_1 - \bar{X}_2 \geq 4$?   **f.** $\bar{X}_1 - \bar{X}_2 \leq -4$?
g. $\bar{X}_1 - \bar{X}_2 \geq 2$ or $\bar{X}_1 - \bar{X}_2 \leq -2$?

*19. Calculate the mean and standard deviation of each population.

*20. If a sample of 25 cases is drawn from population 1 and a sample of 25 cases from population 2, what is the probability that
a. $\bar{X}_1 - \bar{X}_2 \geq 0$?   **b.** $\bar{X}_1 - \bar{X}_2 \geq 1$?   **c.** $\bar{X}_1 - \bar{X}_2 \leq 0$?
d. $\bar{X}_1 - \bar{X}_2 \leq 1$?   **e.** $\bar{X}_1 - \bar{X}_2 \geq 4$?
f. $\bar{X}_1 - \bar{X}_2 \geq 1$ or $\bar{X}_1 - \bar{X}_2 \leq -1$?
g. $\bar{X}_1 - \bar{X}_2 \geq 2$ or $\bar{X}_1 - \bar{X}_2 \leq 2$?

*21. Calculate the probability that $\bar{X}_1 - \bar{X}_2 \leq 0$, when
a. $N_1 = N_2 = 4$ **b.** $N_1 = N_2 = 9$
c. $N_1 = N_2 = 16$ **d.** $N_1 = N_2 = 36$

22. A manufacturer sampled the number of dresses produced per day for ten days by a group of 26 workers (group A) who were operating on a fixed-wage plan. She then introduced a wage incentive plan to 26 other employees (group B) and recorded their output for 10 days. The number of dresses produced per day were as follows:

Group A: 75   72   73   76   78   72   80   74   76   75
Group B: 80   83   84   78   79   81   84   85   78   86

The wages paid to each group are equal. Can the manufactuer conclude that the wage incentive plan is more efficient? Calculate the value of t.

23. Company A finds that the mean number of burning hours of its light bulbs is 1200, with $\sigma_{\bar{X}_1}^2 = 100$; Company B shows a mean of 1250 burning hours, with $\sigma_{\bar{X}_2}^2 = 125$. Is it probable that the light bulbs at the two companies are from the same population of light bulbs? What is the value of z?

24. From records of past employees, two large companies sampled the number of years that secretaries stayed with the company. Using a sample of 25 employees each, Company A found that $SS_1 = 42$ and $\overline{X}_1 = 40$, and Company B found that $SS_2 = 58$ and $\overline{X}_2 = 50$. Is this difference significant at the 0.05 level? What is the value of t?

25. A manager finds that the number of employee errors increases as the day progresses, reaching a peak between 3:00 and 5:00. He divides a sample of 20 employees into two groups. One group proceeds on the same work schedule as before, but the other group gets a 15-minute coffee break from 2:45 to 3:00. The subsequent number of errors made between 3:00 and 5:00 are

No-break group: 5 6 7 4 8 9 6 5 7 6
   Break group: 2 3 4 3 4 4 3 1 5 4

Does the break significantly reduce the number of errors? Calculate the value of t.

26. Determine whether variances are homogeneous in Exercise 25. Calculate the value of F.

27. Banks A and B use two different forms for recording checks written. The banks found that the following number of checks had bounced for 15 customers during the last ten years.

Bank A: 4 8 3 0 3 5 3 4 0 5 2 4 6 2 0
Bank B: 2 0 1 2 1 1 3 3 4 3 1 4 0 5 0

Determine whether there is a significant difference between the number of checks bounced at each bank. Employ $\alpha = 0.05$.

28. State A finds that the mean number of cigarettes smoked per week by smokers of that state is 120, with a $\sigma_{\overline{X}_1}^2$ of 10. State B's cigarette tax is $0.05 greater per pack. The mean number smoked per week in State B is 110, with a $\sigma_{\overline{X}_2}^2$ of 9. Is there a significant difference in the number of cigarettes smoked between the two states? What is the value of z?

29. Two grocery store managers find that they have an overstock of spaghetti sauce. The price and usual amount sold in the two stores are identical. Manager A keeps the sauce in its regular place, while manager B piles the cans close to the checkout counters for a month. The managers record the number of cans sold during 10 days, with the following results:

A: 19 20 20 21 18 20 19 21 23 17
B: 26 24 25 23 25 24 22 26 27 25

Is there a significant difference in the number of cans sold? What is the value of t?

30. Determine whether the variances are homogeneous in Exercise 29. Calculate F.

31. In the displayed material at the start of this chapter, we showed a graph based on research into the pupil responses of heterosexual and homosexual males when viewing pictures of men and women. The following table shows the change in pupil size of five heterosexual and five homosexual males when viewing pictures of a male.

Subject	Heterosexuals	Subject	Homosexuals
1	− 00.4	6	+ 18.8
2	− 54.5	7	− 04.6
3	+ 12.5	8	+ 18.9
4	+ 06.3	9	+ 18.2
5	− 01.5	10	+ 15.8

Formulate H_0 and H_1, two-tailed test. Using Student's t-ratio for independent samples, determine whether H_0 may be rejected at $\alpha = 0.05$. [*Hint:* To facilitate calculations when negative numbers are involved, algebraically add 55 to each score. This procedure eliminates all the negative values and makes use of the generalization shown in Section 2.3.]

To calculate the mean for each group,

$$\frac{\sum\limits_{i=1}^{5} X_i}{N} = \frac{\sum\limits_{i=1}^{5} X_i - 5(55)}{N}$$

[*Note:* Adding 55 to all scores will not change the difference between means and the standard error of the difference, since the relative differences among scores are maintained. However, the mean for each group will increase by 55.]

32. The table shows the change in pupil size of five heterosexual and five homosexual males when viewing pictures of a female.

Subject	Heterosexuals	Subject	Homosexuals
1	+ 05.9	6	+ 11.2
2	− 22.4	7	− 38.0
3	+ 19.2	8	+ 18.1
4	+ 39.0	9	− 05.6
5	+ 23.1	10	+ 21.5

Formulate H_0 and H_1, two-tailed test. Using Student's t-ratio for independent samples, determine whether H_0 may be rejected at $\alpha = 0.05$. [*Hint:* To facilitate calculations when negative numbers are involved, algebraically add 39 to each score.]

33. In a study on the long-range effects of concentration camp internment on Nazi victims, Dor-Shav (1978) compared 43 survivors of the camps to 21 control subjects who were of similar age, background, and education but who had escaped imprisonment during World War II. Both groups were given a series of psychological tests, including the Rorschach Inkblot Test and the Sixteen Personality Factor Questionnaire. On the Rorschach Inkblot Test the following data were obtained.

Survivors	Controls
$\Sigma X_1 = 17$	$\Sigma X_2 = 39$
$\Sigma X_1^2 = 81$	$\Sigma X_2^2 = 357$
$N_1 = 43$	$N_2 = 21$

Source: Based on data from Dor-Shav, 1978.

a. Using $\alpha = 0.05$, set up and test the null hypothesis that the survivors do not differ from the control subjects in the number of abstract responses given on the Rorschach Inkblot Test. Find ω^2.

On the Personality Factor Questionnaire, 14 young survivors aged 50 and below and 5 young control subjects also aged 50 and below showed the following results on the shrewdness scale.

Survivors	Controls
$\Sigma X_1 = 182$	$\Sigma X_2 = 52$
$\Sigma X_1^2 = 2396$	$\Sigma X_2^2 = 552$
$N_1 = 14$	$N_2 = 5$

Source: Based on data from Dor-Shav, 1978.

b. Using $\alpha = 0.05$, set up and test the null hypothesis that the young survivors do not differ from the young control subjects on the shrewdness scale of the Personality Factor Questionnaire. Find ω^2.

34. Using the data in Table 13.1 calculate the standard deviations for each sample. Then calculate Student's t-ratio using Formula (13.4). Confirm that the same value of t is obtained.

35. The following table on page 392 shows the pleasantness of humor when presented first versus the pleasantness of humor when following horror. The ratings following each of six scenes were combined to produce a single score for each subject. The lower the score was, the greater was the pleasantness.

a. In each of the two conditions (humor first versus humor preceded by horror), combine the males and females into single groups of 20 subjects each. Test H_0: The mean difference in the ratings of pleasantness for the population(s) from which the two conditions were selected is equal to zero. Use $\alpha = 0.05$. Find ω^2. What conclusion do you draw?

b. Combine the male ratings of humor when following horror and humor first and the female ratings of both variables and administer a test of significance (males versus females) at $\alpha = 0.05$, two-tailed test. Find ω^2. What conclusion do you draw?

36. An experimenter named Laurie designs a study in which she matches subjects on a variable that she believes to be correlated with the criterion variable.

Humor First		Humor Preceded by Horror	
Male	**Female**	**Male**	**Female**
17	9	17	10
24	12	11	15
13	20	25	14
13	18	20	7
24	23	6	10
18	18	10	13
21	21	6	6
28	32	31	6
12	12	8	11
9	12	17	14

Assuming H_0 to be false, what is the likelihood of a Type II error (compare to the use of Student's t-ratio for uncorrelated samples) in the following situations?
a. The matching variable is uncorrelated with the criterion variable.
b. The matching variable is highly correlated with the criterion variable.

37. Numerous consumer organizations have criticized the automobile industry for employing odometers that show large variations in efficiency from one instrument to another and from one manufacturer to another. To test whether or not odometers from two competing manufacturers may be considered to have been drawn from a common population, 11 different cars were equipped with two odometers each, one from each manufacturer. All automobiles were driven over a measured course of 100 miles and their odometer readings were tabulated. Apply the appropriate test for the significance of the difference between the odometer readings of each manufacturer, employing $\alpha = 0.01$.

	Manufacturer			Manufacturer	
Automobile	**A**	**B**	**Automobile**	**A**	**B**
1	104	102	7	97	99
2	112	106	8	107	102
3	103	107	9	100	98
4	115	110	10	104	101
5	99	93	11	108	102
6	104	101			

38. Another complaint by consumer organizations is that the odometers are purposely constructed to *overestimate* the distance traveled in order to inflate the motorist's estimates of gasoline mileage. As a review of Chapter 12, conduct a one-sample test of $H_0: \mu_0 = 100$ miles for the product of *each* manufacturer.

39. A large discount house advertises that its prices are lower than its largest competitor's. To test the validity of this claim, we compare the prices of 15 randomly selected items. If the results are as shown in the accompanying table, what do you conclude?

Discount House	Competitor
$3.77	$3.95
7.50	7.75
4.95	4.99
3.18	3.25
5.77	5.98
2.49	2.39
8.77	9.49
6.99	6.49
2.99	2.95
1.98	2.49
0.49	0.52
5.50	5.62
0.99	0.98
6.49	6.66
5.49	5.55

40. A company has just switched to a 4-day workweek. It measured the number of units produced per week for ten employees before and after the change. Using the appropriate test statistics, test the null hypothesis at $\alpha = 0.05$ level of significance.

Employee	No. of Units	
	Before	After
A	25	23
B	26	24
C	27	26
D	22	23
E	29	30
F	25	24
G	29	26
H	30	32
I	25	25
J	28	29

41. Referring to Exercise 25, assume that the two groups had been matched on their abilities before the coffee break was instituted. Assume that the pairs are in identical order for the two groups. Determine the standard error of the difference between means and the *t*-scores. Compare the obtained value with that of Exercise 25.

42. A store owner wants to increase the number of people walking into his store. For a week, he records the number coming in per day. He then hires a designer to set up the window display and records the number the following week. The records show the following:

Day	Before	After
Monday	150	200
Tuesday	175	180
Wednesday	140	180
Thursday	180	175
Friday	170	190
Saturday	160	175

Did the new display help the owner? What is the value of *t*?

43. In an attempt to increase record sales, a manager advertises that five records are on sale. For a sample of ten albums not on sale, she finds the following amounts were sold a day before the sale and on a day during the sale:

Record	Before	After	Record	Before	After
A	25	30	F	5	5
B	15	17	G	0	1
C	10	13	H	40	45
D	25	30	I	50	45
E	30	25	J	35	40

Did the sale significantly increase the number of other records sold? What is the value of *t*?

44. In Exercise 40, Chapter 5, we examined the data of Rosenthal and his associates in which patients suffering from SAD were treated with light therapy. One group of six subjects was exposed to bright light during the first week and dim light during the third week.
a. What is the appropriate test of significance for these data?
b. Apply the appropriate test, using $\alpha = 0.05$, two-tailed test.

45. Refer to the data in Exercise 41, Chapter 5. One group of seven subjects was exposed to dim light during the first week and bright light during the third week.

a. What is the appropriate test of significance for these data?

b. Apply the appropriate test, using $\alpha = 0.05$, two-tailed test.

46. Refer to Exercise 27 in Chapter 8. Recall that, in the Sewich sleep study (1984), subjects were awakened from sleep by the ring of a telephone and the reaction time for a verbal response was obtained.

a. Conduct a test of significance of the difference between reaction times when the subjects thought they were awake and when they thought they were asleep. Use $\alpha = 0.05$, two-tailed test.

b. Recall that the variance estimates for the two conditions were 4.9351 and 41.4414. Conduct a test of homogeneity of variances, using $\alpha = 0.05$.

47. It has been noted that the means of reaction time scores and their associated variances are often correlated. That is, the larger the mean reaction time is, the larger is the associated variance. This correlation tends to produce heterogeneity of variances, since the mean and variance are not independent. Under these circumstances, it has been recommended that, prior to calculating Student's t, the scores should be transformed into reciprocals; that is, each score should be divided into 1 (Kirk, 1968). This transformation can be easily accomplished if you have a calculator with the key $\boxed{1/X}$. You enter a score and press the key $\boxed{1/X}$, and the reciprocal appears in the display.

a. Transform all the scores in Exercise 27, Chapter 8, into reciprocals.

b. What is the appropriate test of significance?

c. Conduct a test of significance of the transformed scores using $\alpha = 0.05$, two-tailed test.

48. Refer to Exercise 47.

a. Calculate the Pearson r for the transformed scores.

b. Compare with the previously calculated Pearson r (Exercise 27, Chapter 8).

c. Test the null hypothesis: $H_0: \rho = 0.00$, using $\alpha = 0.05$, one-tailed test.

An Introduction to the Analysis of Variance

14.1 MULTIGROUP COMPARISONS

We have reviewed the classic design of experiments on several different occasions in this text. The classic study consists of two groups, an experimental and a control. The purpose of statistical inference is to test specific hypotheses, for example, whether or not both groups could reasonably have been drawn from the same population (see Chapter 13).

Although this classical research design is still employed in many studies, its limitations should be apparent to you. To restrict our observations to two groups on all occasions is to overlook the wonderful complexity of the phenomena that the scientist investigates. Rarely do events in nature conveniently order themselves into two groups, an experimental and a control. More commonly the questions we pose to nature are of this variety: Which of several alternative schedules of reinforcement leads to the greatest resistance to experimental extinction? Which of five different methods of teaching the concepts of fractions to the primary grades leads to the greatest learning gains? Which form of psychotherapy leads to the greatest incidence of patient recovery?

Obviously the research design necessary to provide experimental answers to the preceding questions would require comparison of more than two groups. You may wonder: But why should multigroup comparisons provide any obstacles? Can we not simply compare the mean of each group with the mean of every other group and obtain Student's t-ratio for each comparison? For example, if we had four experimental groups, A, B, C, D, could we not calculate Student's t-ratios comparing A with B, C, and D; B with C and D; and C with D?

If you will think for a moment of the errors in inference that we have so frequently discussed, you will recall that our greatest concern has been to avoid Type I errors. When we establish the region of rejection at the 0.05 level, we are in effect acknowledging our willingness to take the risk of being wrong as often as 5% of the time in our rejection of the null hypothesis. Now what happens when we have numerous comparisons to make? For an extreme example, let us imagine that we have conducted a study involving the calculation of 1000 separate Student's t-ratios. Would we be terribly impressed if, say, 50 of the t's proved to be significant at the 0.05 level? Of course not. Indeed, we would probably murmur something such as, "With 1000 comparisons, we would be surprised if we didn't obtain approximately 50 comparisons that are significant *by chance* (i.e., due to predictable sampling error)."

The *analysis of variance* (sometimes abbreviated ANOVA) is a technique of statistical analysis that permits us to overcome the ambiguity involved in assessing significant differences when more than one comparison is made. It allows us to answer this question: Is there an overall indication that the experimental treatments are producing differences among the means of the various groups?

In this chapter we examine the single-variable case: three or more conditions or levels of a single independent variable. Because the statistical analysis involves only a single variable, it is often referred to as a **one-way ANOVA** (analysis of variance). Similarly, **two-way ANOVA** identifies the statistical analysis when there are two or more levels or conditions of two independent variables (Chapter 15).

As with Student's t-ratio, there are both independent- and correlated-samples designs. We look at the independent-samples design first.

One-Way Analysis of Variance: Statistical analysis of various categories or levels of a *single* treatment variable.

Two-Way Analysis of Variance: Statistical analysis of various categories or levels of two treatment variables.

14.2 SINGLE-VARIABLE DESIGN: INDEPENDENT SAMPLES

Variance Estimate: Sum of the squared deviations from the mean divided by degrees of freedom.

You will recall that we previously defined the unbiased **variance estimate** as

$$\hat{s}^2 = \frac{\Sigma(X - \overline{X})^2}{N - 1} = \frac{SS}{N - 1}$$

Also recall that when the deviation of scores from the mean $(X - \overline{X})$ is large, the variance, and therefore the variability of scores, is also large. When the deviations are small, the variance is correspondingly small.

BOX 14.1

COMPARISON OF SEVERAL GROUPS OF CHRONICALLY ILL PATIENTS ON A MENTAL HEALTH INDEX

The physical status of chronically ill patients is under almost constant supervision by care-giving professionals. But what about their psychological status— their emotional and social adjustment to a continuous state of illness? This side of their lives is often neglected in the struggle to bring about favorable changes in their physical status. The goals of one study were to obtain information on the psychological status of chronically ill patients (Cassileth et al., 1984). A Mental Health Index was obtained on a total of 758 patients in the following diagnostic categories: arthritis, cancer, depression, dermatological disorder, diabetes, and renal (kidney) disorder. The Index consists of five subscales (anxiety, depression, emotional ties, general positive affect, and loss of control) and a global score—the Mental Health Index.

The accompanying bar graph shows the mean scores obtained by the six diagnostic groups on the Mental Health Index. Since the diagnostic categories are qualitative rather than quantitative variables (that is, they differ in kind rather than "how much"), the categories are arranged alphabetically along the horizontal axis. Recall that line graphs of unordered variables are meaningless. A one-way analysis of variance is performed on these data in order to ascertain if there is an overall significant difference among the groups.

To construct the line graph, the scores of the patients in all six diagnostic categories were combined and the means obtained on the Mental Health Index by three different age groups were compared. A line graph is appropriate to display these data because age is a quantitative, ordered variable. As with the diagnostic category variable, age grouping is a single variable for which a one-way analysis of variance is the appropriate form of statistical analysis. Incidentally, the researchers found that mean scores on all six scales of the Mental Health Index improved significantly with increasing age. The older people appeared to be better able to handle the stress of chronic illness.

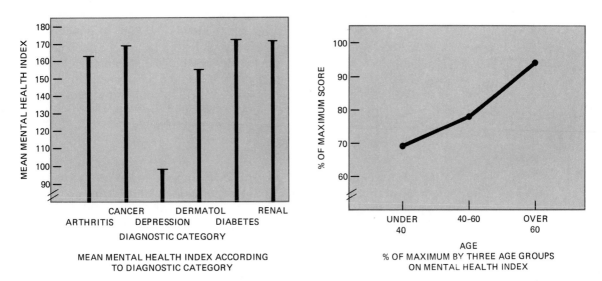

MEAN MENTAL HEALTH INDEX ACCORDING TO DIAGNOSTIC CATEGORY

% OF MAXIMUM BY THREE AGE GROUPS ON MENTAL HEALTH INDEX

Source: B. Cassileth, E. Lusk, T. Strouse, D. Miller, L. Brown, P. Cross, and A. Tenaglia (1984), "Psychosocial Status in Chance Illness," *New England Journal of Medicine,* **311,** 506–510.

Now if we think back to Student's t-ratio for a moment, we note that both the numerator and denominator give us some estimate of variability:

$$t = \frac{\overline{X}_1 - \overline{X}_2}{s_{\overline{X}_1 - \overline{X}_2}}$$

The denominator, which we referred to as the standard error of the difference between means, is based on the pooled estimate of the variability within each experimental group; that is,

$$s_{\overline{X}_1 - \overline{X}_2} = \sqrt{\frac{SS_1 + SS_2}{N_1 + N_2 - 2}\left(\frac{1}{N_1} + \frac{1}{N_2}\right)}$$

However, the numerator is also a measure of variability, that is, the variability between means. When the difference between means is large relative to $s_{\overline{X}_1 - \overline{X}_2}$, Student's t-ratio is large. When the difference between means is small relative to $s_{\overline{X}_1 - \overline{X}_2}$, the t-ratio is also small.

Between-Group Variance: Estimate of variance based upon variability between groups.

The analysis of variance consists of obtaining two independent estimates of variance, one based on variability between groups (**between-group variance**) and the other based on the variability within groups (**within-group variance**). The significance of the ratio of these two variance estimates is provided by Fisher's F-distributions. (We are already familiar with F-distributions from our prior discussion of homogeneity of variance, Section 13.5.) If the *between-group variance* estimate is large (i.e., the difference between means is large) relative to the *within-group variance* estimate, the F-ratio is large. Conversely, if the *between-group variance* estimate is small relative to the *within-group variance* estimate, the F-ratio will be small.

Within-Group Variance: Estimate of variance based upon the variability within groups.

Sum of Squares: Deviations from the mean squared and summed.

A basic concept in the analysis of variance is the **sum of squares**. We have already encountered the sum of squares in calculating the standard deviation, the variance, and the standard error of the difference between means. It is simply the numerator in the formula for variance, that is, SS. As you will recall, the raw score formula for calculating the sum of squares is

$$SS = \sum X^2 - \frac{(\sum X)^2}{N}$$

The advantage of the analysis of variance technique is that we can partition the total sum of squares (SS_{tot}) into two components, the *within-group sum of squares* (SS_w) and the *between-group sum of squares* (SS_{bet}). Before proceeding any further, let us clarify each of these concepts with a simple example.

Emotional Contrast: When Horror Follows Humor, Do Males and Females Differ in Rating Scenes of Horror as Unpleasant?

In Statistics in Action 13.1, Exercise b, we looked at the ratings of unpleasantness of horror by ten female subjects who viewed scenes of humor prior to seeing scenes of horror versus the unpleasantness ratings by males who viewed scenes in the same sequence. We found Student's t-ratio for the comparison of females versus males to be 2.191, df = 18. We rejected H_0 at $\alpha = 0.05$.

Now we'll look at the same data to illustrate the use of the analysis of variance when there are two treatment groups.

We previously found the mean unpleasantness ratings of the females and the males to be 38.4 and 32.9, respectively. The overall mean $\bar{X}_{tot}$ equals $(384 + 329)/20 = 35.65$.

Now, if we were to subtract the overall mean from each score and square, we would obtain the total sum of squares:

$$SS_{tot} = \Sigma(X - \bar{X}_{tot})^2 \qquad (14.1)$$

The alternative raw score formula is

$$SS_{tot} = \Sigma X_{tot}^2 - \frac{(\Sigma X_{tot})^2}{N} \qquad (14.2)$$

For the data in Table 14.1, the total sum of squares is

$$SS_{tot} = 26{,}137 - \frac{(713)^2}{20}$$

$$= 26{,}137 - 25{,}418.45$$

$$= 718.55$$

The within-group sum of squares is merely the sum of the sums of squares obtained within each group, that is,

$$SS_w = SS_1 + SS_2 \qquad (14.3)$$

$$SS_1 = \Sigma X_1^2 - \frac{(\Sigma X_1)^2}{N_1}$$

$$= 15{,}054 - \frac{(384)}{10} = 308.40$$

$$SS_2 = \Sigma X_2^2 - \frac{(\Sigma X_2)^2}{N_2}$$

$$= 11{,}083 - \frac{(329)^2}{10} = 258.90$$

$$SS_w = 308.40 + 258.90 = 567.30$$

TABLE 14.1 **Scores and squares of scores of females and males who rated unpleasantness of horror after viewing scenes of humor—the higher the score, the greater the unpleasantness**

	Females		Males	
X_1	X_1^2	X_2	X_2^2
42	1,764	36	1,296
26	676	31	961
40	1,600	36	1,296
31	961	20	400
37	1,369	41	1,681
37	1,369	34	1,156
43	1,849	32	1,024
43	1,849	34	1,156
44	1,936	32	1,024
41	1,681	33	1,089
Sum	384	15,054	329	11,083

$$N_1 = 10, \quad \bar{X}_1 = 38.4 \quad N_2 = 10, \quad \bar{X}_2 = 32.9$$

$$\Sigma X_{tot} = 384 + 329 = 713, \quad N = 20, \quad \bar{X}_{tot} = 35.65$$

Finally, the between-group sum of squares (SS_{bet}) may be obtained by subtracting the overall mean from each group mean, squaring the result, multiplying by the N in each group, and summing across all the groups. Thus

$$SS_{bet} = \Sigma N_i (\bar{X}_i - \bar{X}_{tot})^2 \tag{14.4}$$

where N_i is the number in the ith group, and $\bar{X}_i$ is the mean of the ith group.

$$SS_{bet} = 10(38.4 - 35.65)^2 + 10(32.9 - 35.65)^2$$

$$= 75.625 + 75.625 = 151.25$$

The raw score formula for calculating the between-group sum of squares is

$$SS_{bet} = \Sigma \frac{(\Sigma X_i)^2}{N_i} - \frac{(\Sigma X_{tot})^2}{N} \tag{14.5}$$

and

$$SS_{bet} = \left[\frac{(384)^2}{10} + \frac{(329)^2}{10} \right] - \frac{(713)^2}{20}$$

$$= (14,745.60 + 10,824.10) - 25,418.45$$

$$= 151.25$$

Note that the total sum of squares is equal to the sum of the between-group sum of squares and the within-group sum of squares. In other words,

$$SS_{tot} = SS_w + SS_{bet} \tag{14.6}$$

In our experimental example of two groups, $SS_{tot} = 718.55$, $SS_w = 567.30$, and $SS_{bet} = 151.25$. Thus, $718.55 = 567.30 + 151.25$.

Note that, when you calculate SS_w and SS_{bet} and add them together, the sum must equal SS_{tot}. If it does not, you have made an error.

Source: From Manstead et al. (1983), "A Contrast Effect in Judgments of Own Emotional State," *Motivation and Emotion,* **7,** 279–289.

14.3   OBTAINING VARIANCE ESTIMATES

Now, to arrive at variance estimates from between- and within-group sums of squares, all we need to do is divide each by the appropriate number of degrees of freedom.* The degrees of freedom of the between-group estimate is simply the number of cells (k) minus 1.

$$df_{bet} = k - 1 \qquad (14.7)$$

With two groups, $k = 2$. Therefore, $df = 2 - 1 = 1$. Thus, our between-group variance estimate for the problem at hand is

$$\hat{s}_{bet}^2 = \frac{SS_{bet}}{df_{bet}} = \frac{151.25}{1} = 151.25 \text{ df} = 1 \qquad (14.8)$$

The number of degrees of freedom of the within-group estimate is the total N minus the number of cells. Thus

$$df_w = N - k \qquad (14.9)$$

In the present problem, $df_w = 20 - 2 = 18$ and our within-group variance estimate becomes

$$\hat{s}_w^2 = \frac{SS_w}{df_w} = \frac{567.30}{18} = 31.52 \qquad df = 18 \qquad (14.10)$$

Now, all that is left is to calculate the *F*-ratio and determine whether or not our two variance estimates could have reasonably been drawn from the same population. If not, we shall conclude that the significantly larger between-group variance is due to the operation of the experimental conditions. In other words, we shall conclude that the experimental treatments produced a significant difference in means. The **F-ratio,** in analysis of variance, is the between-group variance estimate divided by the within-group variance estimate. Symbolically,

F-Ratio: The between-group variance estimate divided by the within-group variance estimate.

$$F = \frac{\hat{s}_{bet}^2}{\hat{s}_w^2} \qquad (14.11)$$

---

* The rationale for the degrees of freedom concept was presented in section 12.5. The same rationale applies here. Degrees of freedom represent the number of values that are free to vary once we have placed certain restrictions on our data.

For the preceding problem our F-ratio is

$$F = \frac{151.25}{31.52} = 4.799 \qquad df = 1, 18$$

Looking up the F-ratio under 1 and 18 degrees of freedom in Table D, in the Table section, we find that an F-ratio of 4.41 or larger is required for significance at the 0.05 level.

Since the obtained F is greater than the critical value at $\alpha = 0.05$, we may reject H_0. For the population sampled in this study, women rated horror following humor more unpleasant than did men.

Note that Table D provides two-tailed values. The analysis-of-variance test for significance is automatically two-tailed since *any* difference among the sample means will enlarge the entire value of F, not just the difference in the direction in which the researcher is interested.

14.4 FUNDAMENTAL CONCEPTS OF ANALYSIS OF VARIANCE

Analysis of Variance (ANOVA): A method, described initially by R. A. Fisher, partitioning the sum of squares for experimental data into known components of variation.

In these few pages, we have examined all the basic concepts that are necessary to understand simple **analysis of variance.** Before proceeding with an example involving three groups, let's briefly review these fundamental concepts.

1. We have seen that in an experiment involving two or more groups it is possible to identify two different bases for estimating the population variance: the between-group and the within-group.
   a. The between-group variance reflects changes in the dependent variable due to any systematic differences in the ways the groups were treated, including the independent variable and confounding, if it takes place.
   b. The within-group variance reflects changes in the dependent variable due to individual differences and/or other uncontrolled factors. In well-conducted research, the impact of these "other factors" is kept to a minimum.
2. The null hypothesis is that the samples were drawn from the same population, or that $\mu_1 = \mu_2 = \cdots = \mu_k$.
3. The alternative hypothesis is that the samples were not drawn from the same population, that is, $\mu_1 \neq \mu_2 \cdots \neq \mu_k$.
4. The F-ratio consists of the between-group variance estimate divided by the within-group variance estimate. By consulting Table D of the distribution of F, we can determine whether the null hypothesis of equal population means can reasonably be entertained. In the event of a significant F-ratio, we may conclude that the group means are not all estimates of a common population mean.

5. In the two-sample case, the F-ratio yields probability values that are identical to those of Student's t-ratio. Indeed, in the one-degree-of-freedom situation (i.e., $k = 2$), $t = \sqrt{F}$ or $t^2 = F$. To illustrate, in Case Example 14.1, we obtained an F-ratio equal to 4.799. The square root of 4.799 is 2.191. This is precisely the answer we obtained in Statistics in Action 13.1 (Exercise b) when we used Student's t-ratio to analyze these data.

14.5 AN EXAMPLE INVOLVING THREE GROUPS

Recall that in the Ortega and Pipal study of Type A and Type B behaviors (Section 3.1), there were two independent variables: type of behavior (A versus B, an organismic variable) and type of activity (a true independent variable). For purposes of examining the analysis of several categories of a single variable, we'll look at one-half the data from the Ortega and Pipal study, namely, the effects of three conditions on the diastolic blood pressure of type A subjects. The three conditions were: active, when the subjects were given a task to perform; passive, when the subjects sat quietly; and relaxed, when the subjects received guided relaxation instructions. Table 14.2 shows the mean diastolic blood pressures of 20 Type A subjects in each of these conditions as well as the squares of these values.

The design of a study in which the subjects are assigned at random to three or more levels or categories of a single independent variable is known as a randomized group design. As we'll see, randomized group designs often form the building blocks for more complex experimental designs. The following steps are employed in a three-group analysis of variance.

Step 1.   Employing Formula (14.2), the total sum of squares is

$$SS_{tot} = 271{,}456 - \frac{(4018)^2}{60} = 2383.94$$

Step 2.   Employing Formula (14.5) for three groups, we find that the between-group sum of squares is

$$SS_{bet} = \frac{(1407)^2}{20} + \frac{(1303)^2}{20} + \frac{(1308)^2}{20} - \frac{(4018)^2}{60} = 344.04$$

Step 3.   The within-group sum of squares may be obtained by employing Formula (14.3) for three groups:

$$SS_w = \left(99{,}723 - \frac{(1407)^2}{20} \right) + \left(85{,}479 - \frac{(1303)^2}{20} \right)$$

$$+ \left(86{,}254 - \frac{(1308)^2}{20} \right)$$

$$= 2{,}039.9$$

TABLE 14.2 Diastolic Blood Pressures and Squares of These Values. The BP Measures Taken during Three Activity Level Periods for Type A Subjects, 20 per Condition*

	Active		Passive		Relaxed	
	X_1	X_1^2	X_2	X_2^2	X_3	X_3^2
	81	6,561	58	3,364	62	3,844
	67	4,489	64	4,096	62	3,844
	73	5,329	60	3,600	65	4,225
	73	5,329	66	4,356	66	4,356
	77	5,929	68	4,624	74	5,476
	70	4,900	65	4,225	70	4,900
	68	4,624	67	4,489	64	4,096
	70	4,900	74	5,476	60	3,600
	64	4,096	66	4,356	63	3,969
	61	3,721	78	6,084	74	5,476
	70	4,900	67	4,489	81	6,561
	83	6,889	67	4,489	61	3,721
	71	5,041	63	3,969	63	3,969
	65	4,225	65	4,225	61	3,721
	68	4,624	64	4,096	59	3,481
	65	4,225	71	5,041	62	3,844
	71	5,041	53	2,809	57	3,249
	60	3,600	59	3,481	68	4,624
	70	4,900	61	3,721	73	5,329
	80	6,400	67	4,489	63	3,969
Sum	1,407	99,723	1,303	85,479	1308	86,254

$$N_1 = 20, \bar{X}_1 = 70.35 \qquad N_2 = 20, \bar{X}_2 = 65.15 \qquad N_3 = 20, \bar{X}_3 = 65.40$$
$$\Sigma X_{tot} = 1{,}407 + 1{,}303 + 1{,}308 = 4{,}018$$
$$\Sigma X_{tot}^2 = 99{,}723 + 85{,}479 + 86{,}254 = 271{,}456$$
$$N = 60$$

* Based on measurements taken every 3 minutes during a 15-minute activity session.
Source: Based on data from Ortega and Pipal, 1984.

Note that SS_w may also be obtained by subtraction. Thus

$$SS_w = SS_{tot} - SS_{bet} = 2383.94 - 344.04 = 2039.9$$

Step 4. The between-group variance estimate is

$$df_{bet} = k - 1 = 2 \qquad \hat{s}_{bet}^2 = \frac{344.04}{2} = 172.02$$

TABLE 14.3 Table for Summarizing Relevant Statistics Following Analysis of Variance

Source of Variation	Sum of Squares	Degrees of Freedom	Variance Estimate*	*F*-ratio
Between-groups	344.04	2	172.02	4.81
Within-groups	2039.90	57	35.79	
Total	2383.94	59		

* In many texts, the term "mean square" appears in this box. However, we prefer the term "variance estimate" since this term accurately describes the nature of the entries in the column.

Step 5. The within-group variance estimate is

$$\text{df}_w = N - k = 57 \qquad \hat{s}_w^2 = \frac{2039.9}{57} = 35.79$$

Step 6. Employing Formula (15.11), we find that the value of F is

$$F = \frac{172.02}{35.79} = 4.81 \qquad \text{df} = 2, 57$$

To summarize these steps, we employ the format shown in Table 14.3.

By employing the format recommended in Table 14.3, you have a final check upon your calculation of the sum of squares and your assignment of degrees of freedom. Thus, $SS_{bet} + SS_w$ must equal SS_{tot}. The degrees of freedom of the total are found by

$$\text{df}_{tot} = N - 1 \qquad\qquad (14.12)$$

In the present example, the number of degrees of freedom for the total is

$$\text{df}_{tot} = 60 - 1 = 59$$

14.6 THE INTERPRETATION OF F

When we look up the F required for significance with 2 and 57 degrees of freedom, we find that an F of 3.16 (interpolated) or larger is significant at the 0.05 level.

Since our F of 4.81 exceeds this value, we may conclude that the three group means are not all estimates of a common population mean. Now, do we stop at this point? Not really.

The truth of the matter is that our finding an overall significant F-ratio now permits us to investigate specific hypotheses. In the absence of a significant F-ratio, any significant differences between specific comparisons would have to be regarded as suspicious—very possibly representing a chance difference.

Over the past several years, behavioral scientists have developed a large number of tests that permit the researcher to investigate specific hypotheses concerning population parameters. Two broad classes of such tests exist:

A Priori or Planned Comparisons:
Comparisons planned in advance to investigate specific hypotheses concerning population parameters.

1. **A priori or planned comparisons:** When comparisons are planned in advance of the investigation, an a priori test is appropriate. For a priori tests, it is not necessary that the overall F-ratio be significant.
2. **A posteriori comparisons:** When the comparisons are not planned in advance, an a posteriori test is appropriate.

A Posteriori Comparisons:
Comparisons not planned in advance to investigate specific hypotheses concerning population parameters.

In the present example, we illustrate the use of an a posteriori test for making comparisons among pairs of means, also known as pairwise comparisons.

Tukey (1953) has developed such a test, which he named the HSD (honestly significant difference) test. To employ this test, the overall F-ratio must be significant.

A difference between two means is significant at a given α level if it equals or exceeds HSD, which is

$$\text{HSD} = q_\alpha \sqrt{\frac{\hat{s}_w^2}{n}} \tag{4.13}$$

in which

$\hat{s}_w^2$ = the within-group variance estimate
n = number of subjects in each condition
q_α = tabled value for a given α level found in Table O for df_w and k (number of means)

A Worked Example

Let us employ the data from Section 14.5 to illustrate the application of the HSD test. We shall employ $\alpha = 0.05$ for testing the significance of the difference between each pair of means.

Step 1. Prepare a matrix showing the mean of each condition and the differences between pairs of means. This is shown in Table 14.4.

TABLE 14.4   Difference among Means

	$\overline{X}_1 = 70.35$	$\overline{X}_2 = 65.15$	$\overline{X}_3 = 65.40$
$\overline{X}_1 = 70.35$	—	5.20	4.95
$\overline{X}_2 = 65.15$	—	—	-0.25
$\overline{X}_3 = 65.40$	—	—	—

Step 2.   Referring to Table O under error df $= 57$, $k = 3$ at $\alpha = 0.05$, we find $q_{0.05} = 3.41$ (interpolated).

Step 3.   Find HSD by multiplying $q_{0.05}$ by $\sqrt{\hat{s}_w^2/n}$. The quantity $\hat{s}_w^2$ is found in Table 14.3 under the within-group variance estimate. The n per condition is 20. Thus

$$\text{HSD} = 3.41 \sqrt{\frac{35.79}{20}} = 3.41(1.34) = 4.57$$

Step 4.   Referring to Table 14.4, we find that the differences between $\bar{X}_1$ versus $\bar{X}_2$ and $\bar{X}_1$ versus $\bar{X}_3$ both exceed HSD $= 4.57$. We may therefore conclude that these differences are statistically significant at $\alpha = 0.05$. Since the mean diastolic blood pressure in the active condition is higher than the mean of the other two conditions, we may conclude that this condition produced significantly higher diastolic blood pressures for the population represented by this sample (Table A males). We may also conclude that the passive and relaxed conditions did not differ significantly.

14.7   ESTIMATING THE DEGREE OF ASSOCIATION BETWEEN THE INDEPENDENT AND DEPENDENT VARIABLES

In Section 13.4, we saw the use of omega squared (ω^2) to estimate the proportion of variance in the dependent measure that may be attributed to variations in the treatment variable. A similar estimate is available in the one-way analysis of variance:

$$\text{est } \omega^2 = \frac{\text{SS}_{\text{bet}} - (k-1)\hat{s}_w^2}{\text{SS}_{\text{tot}} + \hat{s}_w^2} \tag{14.14}$$

In Table 14.3, we saw that $\text{SS}_{\text{bet}} = 344.04$, $k - 1 = 2$, $\hat{s}_w^2 = 35.79$, and $\text{SS}_{\text{tot}} = 2383.94$. Substituting in Formula (14.14), we find

$$\text{est } \omega^2 = \frac{344.04 - (2)(35.79)}{2383.94 + 35.79}$$

$$= \frac{272.46}{2419.73} = 0.11$$

Thus, the variations in the independent variable (activity level) account for approximately 11% of the variance in the dependent variable.

14.8 SINGLE-VARIABLE DESIGN: CORRELATED SAMPLES

In Chapter 13, we saw that many factors contribute to the variability of scores in behavioral research. Among the most important are factors like individual differences, which go unidentified and unquantified in an independent-samples design. Consequently, the error term is inflated, that is, it is larger than it would be if such sources of variability were identified, quantified, and "removed." A correlated-samples design represents one method for removing important sources of variability from the error term and thereby providing a more sensitive basis for evaluating differences among means.

As you may recall, we may achieve correlated samples by repeated measures on each subject (for example, before-after measures) or by matching subjects on some variable that is known or assumed to be correlated with the independent variable. We shall be looking at only matched-group designs in this text. This is due to the fact that repeated measures pose difficult design problems that are beyond the scope of this book. To illustrate, subjects who are repeatedly tested under different experimental conditions may show improvement or decrement independent of the experimental treatments. For example, they may show a learning effect or, under some circumstances, a fatigue effect. To keep these effects from contaminating our assessment of the experimental variable (technically called **confounding**), it is necessary to adopt designs that systematically vary the order in which each condition is presented to each subject. These designs have such exotic names as Latin square designs and Greco-Latin designs.

Confounding: When two or more variables are administered to subjects in such a way that their separate effects cannot be separated out.

Such is not the case with matched-group designs. In a matched-group design, subjects are assigned to matched groups or blocks according to their similarity on some measure known or assumed to be correlated with the dependent measure.

14.9 AN EXAMPLE INVOLVING THREE MATCHED GROUPS

Let us suppose that we wish to evaluate three different methods for training young basketball players to make shots from the foul line. Twenty-one junior high students were administered a pretest. Each was placed at the foul line and given 20 opportunities to shoot at the basket. Each player's score was the number of baskets made. On the basis of their scores, the students were divided into 7 blocks. Each block consisted of 3 players matched for pretest performing ability. In other words, block 1 consisted of the 3 best-scoring players, block 2 of the 3 players next in achievement, and so on to block 7, which consisted of the three poorest scorers. Thus,

TABLE 14.5 Scores (Number of Foul Shots Made in 20 Trials) Obtained by 3 Matched Groups After They Were Administered Different Training Conditions in Foul Shooting

Block	Training Condition			Sums
	X_1	X_2	X_3	
1	15	13	11	39
2	13	9	10	32
3	12	10	9	31
4	11	13	12	36
5	9	5	7	21
6	8	6	4	18
7	7	5	2	14
Sums	75	61	55	191

each of the 7·blocks of 3 students was matched for pretest performing ability. After this matching, a different form of foul-shot training was administered to each of the 3 groups of 7 players. After training, they were again permitted to attempt 20 foul shots. The scores are summarized in Table 14.5.

14.10 OBTAINING THE SUMS OF SQUARES AND THE VARIANCE ESTIMATES

Unlike the total sum of squares for the one-way independent-group design, the total sum of squares for correlated samples is partitioned into three, instead of two, components: the *treatment group sum of squares* (SS_{treat}), the *block sum of squares* (SS_{bl}), and the *residual sum of squares* (SS_{res}). Thus,

$$SS_{tot} = SS_{treat} + SS_{bl} + SS_{res} \qquad (14.15)$$

The total sum of squares is obtained by squaring each score, summing all the squares, and subtracting the square of the sum of all the scores divided by the total number of scores:

$$SS_{tot} = \Sigma X_{tot}^2 - \frac{(\Sigma X_{tot})^2}{nk} \qquad (14.16)$$

where

ΣX_{tot}^2 = the sum of all the squared scores

$(\Sigma X_{tot})^2$ = the square of the summed scores

n = sample size in each condition

k = number of levels of the independent variable (i.e., the number of conditions)

Correction Term (CT): The square of the sum of all the scores divided by the total number of scores, $(\Sigma X_{tot})^2/nk$.

The quantity $(\Sigma X_{tot})^2/nk$ is often referred to as the **correction term (CT)**.

The data for the foul-shooting experiment have been reproduced in Table 14.6. We can see that the sum of the 21 X^2 values is

$$\Sigma X_{tot}^2 = 225 + 169 + \cdots + 16 + 4 = 1973$$

From Table 14.6 we see that the correction term is

$$CT = \frac{191^2}{21} = 1737.19$$

Thus, the total sum of squares in this example is

$$SS_{tot} = \Sigma X_{tot}^2 - CT$$

$$= 1973 - 1737.19 = 235.81$$

The total sum of squares is a measure of the total variation in the data. The total degrees of freedom is equal to the total number of scores minus 1. Thus,

$$df_{tot} = nk - 1 \tag{14.17}$$

$$= (7)(3) - 1 = 20$$

TABLE 14.6   Computation of Sums of Squares for Foul-shooting Experiment

Block	X_1	X_1^2	X_2	X_2^2	X_3	X_3^2	Block Sum (bl_i)
1	15	225	13	169	11	121	39
2	13	169	9	81	10	100	32
3	12	144	10	100	9	81	31
4	11	121	13	169	12	144	36
5	9	81	5	25	7	49	21
6	8	64	6	36	4	16	18
7	7	49	5	25	2	4	14
Sum:	$T_1 = 75$		$T_2 = 61$		$T_3 = 55$		191

(Treatment Condition spans X_1, X_1^2, X_2, X_2^2, X_3, X_3^2)

$$\Sigma X_{tot}^2 = 225 + 169 + \cdots + 16 + 4 = 1973$$

$$\Sigma X_{tot} = 15 + 13 + \cdots + 4 + 2 = 191$$

$$\frac{(\Sigma X_{tot})^2}{nk} = \frac{191^2}{(7)(3)} = 1737.19 = CT$$

$$\frac{\Sigma T_i^2}{n} = \frac{75^2 + 61^2 + 55^2}{7} = 1767.29$$

$$\frac{\Sigma bl_i^2}{k} = \frac{39^2 + 32^2 + \cdots + 14^2}{3} = 1921$$

To find the treatment sum of squares, square each treatment sum, sum these squares, divide by the sample size (n), and subtract the correction term. Thus,

$$SS_{treat} = \frac{\Sigma T_i^2}{n} - CT \qquad (14.18)$$

$$= \frac{75^2 + 61^2 + 55^2}{7} - 1737.19$$

$$= \frac{12,\bar{3}71}{7} - 1737.19$$

$$= 30.10$$

The treatment sum of squares reflects the effects, if any, of the experimental treatments. In this example, the three treatment means contain only three independent pieces of information. Thus,

$$df_{treat} = k - 1 \qquad (14.19)$$

$$= 3 - 1 = 2$$

To obtain the treatment variance estimate, we divide the treatment sum of squares by its degrees of freedom:

$$\hat{s}_{treat}^2 = \frac{SS_{treat}}{df_{treat}} \qquad (14.20)$$

$$= \frac{30.10}{2} = 15.05$$

To find the block sum of squares, we square each block sum, sum these squares, divide by the number of treatments (k), and subtract the correction term. Thus,

$$SS_{bl} = \frac{\Sigma bl_i^2}{k} - CT \qquad (14.21)$$

$$= \frac{39^2 + 32^2 + \cdots + 14^2}{3} - CT$$

$$= \frac{5763}{3} - 1737.19$$

$$= 183.81$$

The block sum of squares (SS_{bl}) reflects the effects of the matching variable. Note in Table 14.5 that the block sum goes progressively down, suggesting successful matching. The subjects at the top scored more foul shots than those at the bottom.

The seven block means contain only seven independent pieces of information. Thus,

$$df_{bl} = bl - 1 \tag{14.22}$$

$$= 7 - 1 = 6$$

When we divide the block sum of squares by its degrees of freedom, we obtain the block variance estimate:

$$\hat{s}_{bl}^2 = \frac{SS_{bl}}{df_{bl}} \tag{14.23}$$

$$= \frac{183.81}{6} = 30.64$$

The residual sum of squares (SS_{res}) is what remains of the total sum of squares after the treatment and block sums of squares have been subtracted out. This residual represents random error and constitutes the basis for the error term (analogous to the standard error of the difference in the two-group design).

Recall that $SS_{tot} = SS_{treat} + SS_{bl} + SS_{res}$. Since we have already calculated SS_{tot}, SS_{treat}, and SS_{bl}, we may obtain SS_{res} by subtraction:

$$SS_{res} = SS_{tot} - SS_{treat} - SS_{bl}$$

In this example,

$$SS_{res} = 235.81 - 30.10 - 183.81 = 21.90$$

The residual degrees of freedom may also be obtained by subtraction:

$$df_{res} = df_{tot} - df_{treat} - df_{bl} \tag{14.24}$$

$$= 20 - 2 - 6$$

$$= 12$$

Dividing by the residual degrees of freedom yields the residual or error variance estimate:

$$\hat{s}_{res}^2 = \frac{SS_{res}}{df_{res}} \tag{14.25}$$

$$= \frac{21.90}{12}$$

$$= 1.82$$

We now enter the various values we have calculated into Table 14.7, the analysis of variance summary table. Since our primary interest is in evaluating the relative effectiveness of the training programs, we focus primarily on the F-ratio for the between-treatment condition. This F-ratio is obtained by dividing the treatment variance estimate by the residual or

TABLE 14.7 Summary Table for Presenting the Relevant Calculations and Statistics in a Randomized Block One-Way ANOVA

Source of Variation	Sum of Squares	Degrees of Freedom	Variance Estimate	F
Treatments	30.10	2	15.05	8.27
Blocks	183.81	6	30.64	16.84
Residual (error)	21.90	12	1.82	
Totals	235.81	20		

error variance. With 2 and 12 degrees of freedom, an F-ratio of 6.93 or greater is required for significance at the 0.01 level. Since our obtained $F = 8.27$, we may reject H_0 and assert that the training programs did produce different outcomes among the three experimental conditions.

Was the matching variable effective in reducing the error term? At 6 and 12 degrees of freedom, an F-ratio of 4.82 or greater is required to reject H_0. Since the obtained F is 16.84, we reject the null hypothesis and assert that matching effectively accounted for a significant portion of the total variance. Indeed, it accounted for $183.81/235.81 = 0.7795$ or about 78% of the total sum of squares.

14.11 APPLYING TUKEY'S HSD TEST OF SIGNIFICANCE BETWEEN MEANS

Recall that Tukey's HSD test [Formula (14.13)] may be applied to individual means when the overall F-ratio is significant. Since this is the case, let's ascertain the significance of the difference of the three possible comparisons—condition 1 versus condition 2, condition 1 versus condition 3, and condition 2 versus condition 3.

1. The means and differences among means are shown in Table 14.8.
2. Referring to Table O under error df $= 12$ and $k = 3$, we find that $q_{\alpha = 0.01} = 5.05$.
3. Find HSD by multiplying $q_{\alpha = 0.01}$ by $\sqrt{\hat{s}_{res}^2/n}$.

TABLE 14.8 Differences among Means

	$\bar{X}_1 = 75/7 = 10.71$	$\bar{X}_2 = 61/7 = 8.71$	$\bar{X}_3 = 55/7 = 7.86$
$\bar{X}_1 = 10.71$	—	2.00	2.85
$\bar{X}_2 = 8.71$	—	—	0.85
$\bar{X}_3 = 7.86$	—	—	—

In our present example, $q_\alpha\sqrt{\hat{s}^2_{res}/n} = 5.05\sqrt{1.82/7} = (5.05)(0.5099) = 2.58$. Thus, any difference between means equal to or greater than 2.58 is significant at the 0.01 level. Table 14.8 reveals that only the comparison between experimental conditions 1 and 3 is significant at the 0.01 level. Had the 0.05 significance level been used for the HSD test, the difference between means required for significance would naturally have been smaller. In fact, at the 0.05 level, HSD $= (3.77)(0.5099) = 1.92$. Consequently, the differences between the means of conditions 1 and 2 and 1 and 3 would have achieved statistical significance.

14.12 PUTTING IT ALL TOGETHER

At first sight, the calculations involved in ANOVA may appear to be complicated and confusing. In truth, they all follow an orderly and predictable progression in which even the most complex designs flow naturally out of simple models. As an example, take the calculations involved in one-way ANOVA, both independent-samples and correlated-samples designs. The independent-samples design involves basically four computational steps prior to obtaining variance estimates: finding SS_{tot}, SS_{bet}, SS_w, and the degrees of freedom associated with each. The SS_w can be simplified further by subtraction: $SS_w = SS_{tot} - SS_{bet}$.

The correlated-samples one-way ANOVA requires only five steps—finding SS_{tot}, SS_{treat}, SS_{bl}, SS_{res}, and df. Moreover, the calculation of SS_{bl} is computationally similar to that of SS_{treat}.

As with the error term in the independent-samples designs, the calculation of HSD uses the error term, $\hat{s}^2_w$ or $\hat{s}^2_{res}$, under the square root sign. To summarize:

One-Way Anova

Independent Samples

Step 1. Calculate total sum of squares.

$$SS_{tot} = \Sigma X^2 - CT \qquad \text{where } CT = \frac{(\Sigma X_{tot})^2}{nk}$$

Step 2. Calculate between or treatment sum of squares.

$$SS_{bet} = \frac{(\Sigma X_1)^2}{n_1} + \frac{(\Sigma X_2)^2}{n_2} + \cdots + \frac{(\Sigma X_N)^2}{n_N} - CT$$

or, for equal ns,

$$SS_{bet} = \frac{(\Sigma X_1)^2 + (\Sigma X_2)^2 + \cdots + (\Sigma X_n)^2}{n} - CT$$

Step 3. Calculate within sum of squares.

$$SS_w = \left(\sum X_1^2 - \frac{(\sum X_1)^2}{n_1}\right) + \left(\sum X_2^2 - \frac{(\sum X_2)^2}{n_2}\right) + \cdots + \left(\sum X_k^2 + \frac{(\sum X_k)^2}{n_k}\right)$$

or

$$SS_w = SS_{tot} - SS_{bet}$$

Step 4. Calculate degrees of freedom.

$$df_{tot} = N - 1 \qquad df_{bet} = k - 1 \qquad df_w = N - k$$

Correlated Samples

Step 1. Calculate total sum of squares.

$$SS_{tot} = \sum X^2 - CT \qquad \text{where } CT = \frac{(\sum X_{tot})^2}{nk}$$

Step 2. Calculate between or treatment sum of squares.

$$SS_{treat} = \frac{(\sum X_1)^2 + (\sum X_2)^2 + \cdots + (\sum X_N)^2}{n} - CT$$

Step 3. Calculate blocks sum of squares.

$$SS_{bl} = \frac{X^2{}_{bl_1} + X^2_{bl_2} + \cdots + X^2 bl_{bl}}{k} - CT$$

Step 4. Calculate residual sum of squares.

$$SS_{res} = SS_{tot} - SS_{treat} - SS_{bl}$$

Step 5. Calculate degrees of freedom.

$$df_{tot} = N - 1 \qquad df_{treat} = N - k \qquad df_{bl} = bl - 1$$

$$df_{res} = df_{tot} - df_{treat} - df_{bl}$$

CHAPTER SUMMARY

We began this chapter with the observation that the scientist is frequently interested in conducting studies that are more extensive than the classical two-group design. However, when more than two groups are involved in a study, we increase the risk of making a Type I error if we accept as significant *any* comparison that falls within the rejection region. In multi-group studies it is desirable to know whether or not there is an indication of any overall effect of the experimental treatments before we investigate specific hypotheses. The analysis-of-variance technique provides such a test.

In this chapter we presented a mere introduction to the basics of the analysis of variance. We showed that, in the independent-samples one-way ANOVA, the total sum of squares can be partitioned into two component sums of squares: the within-group and the between-group. These two sums of squares provide us, in turn, with independent estimates of the population variance. A between-group variance estimate (based on differences between group means) that is large relative to the within-group variance estimate suggests that the experimental treatments are responsible for the observed differences among the group means. The critical values of the ratio of the between-group variance estimate to the within-group variance estimate are obtained by reference to the F-table (Table D).

In the correlated-samples one-way ANOVA employing matched groups, the total sum of squares is partitioned into three components: treatments, blocks, and residual. The residual variance is used as the error term against which the treatment variance is evaluated.

When the overall F-ratio is statistically significant, we are free to investigate specific hypotheses, employing a multiple-comparison test. The test illustrated in this text is the Tukey HSD (honestly significant difference) test.

TERMS TO REMEMBER

analysis of variance (ANOVA)
a posteriori comparisons
a priori or planned
  comparisons
between-group variance
correction term (CT)
factorial design
F-ratio
HSD test
interaction

one-way analysis of variance
qualitative variables
quantitative variables
sum of squares
two-way analysis of variance
variance estimate
within-group variance

EXERCISES

1. Using the following data derived from the ten-year period 1955 to 1964, determine whether there is a significant difference at the 0.01 level in death rate among the various seasons. (*Note:* Assume death rates for any given year to be independent.)

Winter	Spring	Summer	Fall
9.8	9.0	8.8	9.4
9.9	9.3	8.7	9.4
9.8	9.3	8.8	10.3
10.6	9.2	8.6	9.8
9.9	9.4	8.7	9.4
10.7	9.1	8.3	9.6
9.7	9.2	8.8	9.5
10.2	8.9	8.8	9.6
10.9	9.3	8.7	9.5
10.0	9.3	8.9	9.4

2. Conduct an HSD test, comparing the death rate of each season with every other season. Employ the 0.01 level, two-tailed test for each comparison.

3. Conduct an analysis of variance on the data in Chapter 13, Exercise 3. Verify that in the two-group condition, $F = t^2$.

4. A manufacturer named Pass negotiates contracts with ten different independent research organizations to compare the effectiveness of his product with that of his leading competitor. A significant difference (0.05 level) in favor of Mr. Pass's product is found in one of the ten studies. He subsequently advertises that independent research has demonstrated the superiority of his product over the leading competitor. Criticize this conclusion.

5. Various drug companies make the claim that they manufacture an analgesic that releases its active ingredient "faster." A random selection of the products of each manufacturer revealed the following times, in seconds, required for the release of 50% of the analgesic agent. Test the null hypothesis that all the analgesics are drawn from a common population of means.

Brand A	Brand B	Brand C	Brand D
28	34	29	22
19	23	24	31
30	20	33	18
25	16	21	24

6. A consumer organization randomly selected several gas clothes dryers of three leading manufacturers for study. The time required for each machine to dry a standard load of clothes was tabulated. Set up and test the appropriate null hypothesis. Conduct an HSD test comparing each brand with every other brand, employing $\alpha = 0.05$.

Brand A	Brand B	Brand C
42	52	38
36	48	44
47	43	33
43	49	35
38	51	32

7. Automobile tires, selected at random from six different brands, required the following braking distances, in feet, when moving at 25 mi/hr.* Set up and test the appropriate null hypothesis. Conduct an HSD test comparing each brand with every other brand, employing $\alpha = 0.01$.

Brand A	Brand B	Brand C	Brand D	Brand E	Brand F
22	25	17	21	27	20
20	23	19	24	29	14
24	26	15	25	24	17
18	22	18	23	25	15

8. If the F-ratio is less than 1.00, what should you conclude?

9. Determine whether there is a significant difference in state gasoline taxes among the three geographical areas given.

New England		Mideast		Far West	
Maine	8	New York	7	Wash.	9
N.H.	7	New Jersey	7	Oregon	7
Vermont	8	Penn.	8	Nevada	6
Mass.	6.5	Delaware	7	Calif.	7
R.I.	8	Maryland	7	Alaska	8
Conn.	8	D.C.	7	Hawaii	5

10. Perform an analysis of variance, using the data given in Exercise 27, Chapter 13.

11. Suppose typing speeds (words per minute) are compared for a sample of 24 people who attended four different secretarial schools. The following data are obtained:

*Source: Federal Highway Administration. *The 1962 World Almanac and Book of Facts*. L. H. Long (ed.). New York: Newspaper Enterprise Association, Inc., 1971, p. 122.

School A	School B	School C	School D
50	55	50	70
50	60	65	80
55	65	75	65
60	55	55	70
45	70	60	75
55	65	65	60

Is there a significant difference in the typing speeds among the four groups?

12. A nutritional expert divides a sample of bicyclers into three groups. Group B is given a vitamin supplement and group C is given a diet of health foods. Group A is instructed to eat as they normally do. The expert subsequently records the number of minutes it takes each person to ride 6 miles. See the following table:

A	B	C
15	14	13
16	13	12
14	15	11
17	16	14
15	14	11

Set up the appropriate hypothesis and conduct an analysis of variance.

13. For Exercise 12, determine which diet or diets are superior.

14. In 1971 three baseball clubs showed the following numbers of home runs made by their players:

Chicago Cubs:	2	16	28	2	21	2	2	19	0	4	8	6
Houston Astros:	9	2	1	10	13	1	12	0	1	2	7	7
Cincinnati Reds:	13	39	25	9	3	0	13	27	5	1	2	

Test the hypothesis that all three clubs were drawn from the same population with respect to hitting home runs. (See *The 1972 World Almanac*, pp. 910–911.)

15. Assume that there are only four manufacturers of house paint, and manufacturer A states that his paint is superior to all the other paints. To test his claim, an investigator samples the number of years between the time a house is painted and the time it needs repainting, with the results shown in the accompanying table. Is manufacturer A's claim supported by the data? Compare the records of A and B.

A	B	C	D
4.5	4.0	2.5	3.5
5.5	4.5	3.0	3.0
5.0	4.0	3.0	4.0
5.5	3.5	3.5	3.0
6.0	3.0	4.0	4.5
5.0	4.5	2.5	3.0

16. Given the following scores on a matching variable, identify the subjects who are assigned to each of 4 treatments with 3 subjects per block.

Subject	Score	Subject	Score
A	120	G	98
B	119	H	105
C	114	I	104
D	115	J	100
E	109	K	116
F	106	L	122

17. Given the following scores on a matching variable, identify the subjects who are assigned to each of 3 blocks with 4 subjects per block.

Subject	Score	Subject	Score
A	24	G	12
B	17	H	18
C	20	I	22
D	17	J	14
E	16	K	21
F	11	L	10

18. In the following data, there are 4 treatment conditions and 20 subjects formed into 5 matched blocks. Use $\alpha = 0.01$ in the evaluation of the effectiveness of the treatment effects. Calculate HSD using $\alpha = 0.01$.

Block	X_1	X_2	X_3	X_4
1	16	18	18	20
2	14	17	19	26
3	12	13	18	17
4	10	14	13	15
5	8	7	9	11

19. The following scores were obtained in a study employing a randomized block design with 3 treatment groups and 6 blocks. Analyze the results using $\alpha = 0.01$.

Block	Treatment condition		
	X_1	X_2	X_3
1	26	18	23
2	22	14	21
3	18	19	20
4	14	12	16
5	10	6	11
6	8	7	9

20. Reanalyze the data in Exercise 19 assuming an independent-samples design, using $\alpha = 0.01$. If the results are not statistically significant, account for the different results of the two analyses.

Two-Way Analysis of Variance: Factorial Designs, Independent and Correlated Samples

15.1 INTRODUCTION

We have just been looking at independent- and correlated-samples one-way analysis of variance. Recall that these designs derive their name from the fact that the various treatment groups represent different levels or different categories of a *single* treatment variable. By making possible the simultaneous assessment of several levels or categories of an experimental variable, one-way ANOVA frees us from the limitations of the two-group, experimental versus control group design.

Advanced analysis-of-variance techniques introduce still more profound advantages: They (1) permit the evaluation of more than one variable at a time; (2) allow the assessment of possible interactive effects between and among variables; and (3) represent an efficient means of using research time and effort, since in many analysis-of-variance designs every observation provides information about each variable, interaction of variables, and error.

Moreover, the use of the randomized block factorial design incorporates the advantages plus the disadvantages (see Section 13.8) of using correlated samples. Recall that the main advantage is that, when matching is successful, an important source of variation is identified and removed from the error term. In this chapter, we'll be examining two-variable factorial designs based on independent and matched (correlated) groups.

15.2 TWO-WAY ANOVA, INDEPENDENT SAMPLES

Two-Way Analysis of Variance: Statistical analysis of various categories or levels of two-treatment variables.

When we were examining one-way analysis of variance with independent groups, we saw that the variability of the dependent measure is due to *both* the variability *between* the group treatment effects, if there are any, and the variability *within* groups (random effect differences; differences due to "chance"). In the **two-way analysis of variance**, the variability between groups may be further partitioned:

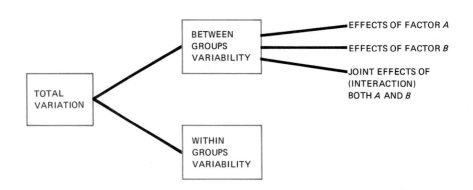

Qualitative Variables: Variables that differ in kind, such as gender.

Quantitative Variables: Variables that differ in "how much," such as level of intelligence.

In the two-way ANOVA, there are two different independent or treatment variables. One or both of these variables may be either qualitative or quantitative. Recall that **qualitative variables** differ in kind rather than "how much"; examples might be different methods of teaching or different types of psychotherapy. **Quantitative variables** differ in "how much," as in the level or amount of drug or amount of positive reinforcement administered to experimental subjects.

Although there are only two independent variables in a two-way analysis of variance, there may be any number of subclasses or levels of treatment of each variable. A given study might involve two levels of one variable and four levels of a second variable, or three levels of (each of) two variables, and so on. The traditional way of designating a two-way analysis of variance is by citing the number of levels (or subclasses) of each variable. To illustrate, a study with two levels of one variable and four levels of a second variable is referred to as having a 2 × 4 design. A study with three levels of each variable is referred to as having a 3 × 3 design. A study with three levels of one variable and four levels of a second variable is referred to as having a 3 × 4 design.

15.3 THE CONCEPT OF INTERACTION

Let's pause a moment and look at the concept of **interaction**. (See Box 15.1.) Two variables (or factors) are said to interact when the effect of one variable on some measure of behavior depends on either the presence or the amount of a second variable. For example, suppose a particular teaching method improved test scores for high-intelligence subjects but *not* for low-intelligence subjects. If the effects of the different teaching methods were the same across all intelligence levels, there would be no interaction. Let's look at another example. Refer back to the data presented in Box 13.1. Notice that the mean pupil response (dependent variable) to pictures of males and females (independent variable *A*) depended on the sexual orientation (independent variable *B*) of the male subjects. Thus, the variability in the dependent variable (pupil response) can best be understood by looking at the *joint* effect of the two independent variables, that is, the *interaction* between these factors. For still another example of interaction, look again at Case Example 3.1 (Bower, 1981) on the effects of a hypnotically induced mood and the emotional quality of past incidents on the recall of these experiences. The better recall of pleasant experiences when the mood is pleasant versus the superior recall of unpleasant experiences when the mood is unpleasant nicely describes interacting variables. Both the induced mood of the subject *and* the emotional quality of past experiences influenced the recall of the experiences.

The finding of a significant interaction is of great importance to our interpretation of the data. It means that we cannot claim that the effect of one variable is the same at all levels of a second variable. Indeed, we must look at each level of each variable to interpret our results. The interaction in the Bower study tells us that neither a pleasant nor an unpleasant mood at time of recall affects the recall in a unitary fashion. To understand the effect of mood on recall, you must look separately at both the pleasant and unpleasant past experiences.

> **Interaction:** The joint effect of two or more factors on the dependent variable, independent of the separate effects of either factor.

15.4 THE CONCEPT OF A TREATMENT COMBINATION

In a **factorial design**, some level of each treatment variable is administered to each experimental subject. The particular combination of experimental conditions is referred to as a treatment combination. For example, if in a 3×4 factorial design a given subject is administered the second level of variable *A* and the third level of variable *B*, the subject's treatment combination is A_2B_3.

> **Factorial Design:** A research design in which some level of each treatment variable is administered to each subject.

BOX 15.1

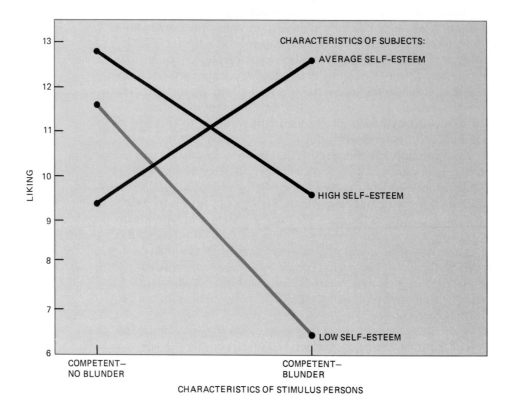

CHARACTERISTICS OF STIMULUS PERSONS

INTERACTIONS: THE SPICE OF RESEARCH

One of the strengths of the analysis-of-variance technique is that it frees the researcher from the constraints of the traditional two-group experimental design. Not only does it provide a method for analyzing the effects of an unlimited number of treatment levels of a single experimental variable, but it also provides a statistical basis for analyzing marvelously complex designs consisting of two or more independent variables. The research interest in such experiments often goes beyond the question, "What

are the effects of each experimental variable?" More often than not, the investigator is interested in knowing whether or not two or more independent variables *interact*. Two variables are said to interact if the effects of one variable are dependent on the level of a second variable. When trying to conceptualize interaction, it often helps to graph the experimental results.

The accompanying figure summarizes a set of experimental results in one part of a study concerned with the effects of seeing a stimulus person commit a blunder. The subjects were divided into three conditions—those of low, average, and high self-esteem. Some subjects in each esteem group saw a competent person make a blunder (spilling a cup of coffee). For the remaining subjects, the competent stimulus person did not commit any blunder. The dependent measure was a "liking" score of the stimulus person.

The figure shows a clear interaction. For subjects of low and high self-esteem, witnessing the stimulus person commit a blunder caused them to like that person less. In contrast, subjects of average self-esteem had a greater liking for the stimulus person

who committed a blunder. Interactions such as these add a bit of spice to the bland diet of many research efforts.

Attraction toward the competent stimulus person, with higher scores indicating greater attraction. (R. Helmreich, E. Aronson, and J. LeFan (1970), "To Err Is Human—Sometimes: Effects of Self-esteem, Competence, and a Prat-fall on Interpersonal Attraction," *Journal of Personality and Social Psychology* **16**, 262. Copyright 1970 by the American Psychological Association. Reprinted by permission.)

Example
  a. Treatment combinations in a 2×2 factorial design.

	A_1		A_2	
	B_1	B_2	B_1	B_2
Treatment combination	A_1B_1	A_1B_2	A_2B_1	A_2B_2

  b. Treatment combinations in a 2×3 factorial design.

	A_1			A_2		
	B_1	B_2	B_3	B_1	B_2	B_3
Treatment combination	A_1B_1	A_1B_2	A_1B_3	A_2B_1	A_2B_2	A_2B_3

The total number of treatment combinations or cells in any factorial design is equal to the product of the treatment levels of all factors or variables.

Earlier we noted that the randomized group design may serve as a building block for more complex designs. The factorial design is a case in point. Note that the 2×3 factorial design, illustrated here, consists of two randomized group designs, one headed by treatment A_1 and the other headed by treatment A_2. It is this fact that permitted us to treat, for illustrative purposes, one-half the data in the Ortega and Pipal study as a randomized group design.

Examples In a 2 × 2 factorial design, there are four treatment combinations or cells.

In a 2 × 3 factorial design, there are six treatment combinations or cells.

In more complex factorial designs, the same principle applies. In a 2 × 3 × 4 factorial design, there are 24 treatment combinations or cells.

15.5 PARTITIONING THE SUM OF SQUARES

Let us now look at the analysis of a 2 × 2 factorial design. However, the analysis may be readily generalized to any number of levels or subclasses of each of the two variables.

In a two-way analysis of variance, the total sum of squares is partitioned into two broad components—the within-group sum of squares and the between-group sum of squares:

$$SS_{tot} = SS_w + SS_{bet}$$

The between-group sum of squares is itself partitioned into three components—the sum of squares for the A variable (SS_A), the sum of squares for the B variable (SS_B), and the sum of squares for the interaction of the A and B variables $(SS_{A \times B})$:

$$SS_{bet} = SS_A + SS_B + SS_{A \times B}$$

When divided by the appropriate number of degrees of freedom, each of the treatment effects provides an independent estimate of the population variances:

$$\hat{s}_A^2 = \frac{SS_A}{df_A} \qquad df_A = A - 1$$

in which A is the number of levels of A

$$\hat{s}_B^2 = \frac{SS_B}{df_B} \qquad df_B = B - 1$$

in which B is the number of levels of B

$$\hat{s}_{A \times B}^2 = \frac{SS_{A \times B}}{df_{A \times B}} \qquad df_{A \times B} = df_A \times df_B$$

When divided by the appropriate degrees of freedom, the within-group sum of squares provides an independent estimate of the population variance:

$$\hat{s}_w^2(error) = \frac{SS_w}{df_w} \qquad df_w = N - k$$

in which k is the number of cells or treatment combinations.

STATISTICS IN ACTION 15.1

The effect on unpleasantness ratings of viewing horror first versus horror preceded by scenes of humor: Conducting a 2 × 2 analysis of variance

Unpleasantness of horror when presented first versus unpleasantness of horror when following humor.*

	A_1 Horror preceded by humor		A_2 Horror first	
	B_1 Male	B_2 Female	B_1 Male	B_2 Female
	36	42	29	30
	31	26	34	33
	36	40	27	37
	20	31	33	32
	41	37	10	30
	34	37	28	31
	32	43	26	45
	34	43	31	36
	32	44	30	38
	33	41	35	38
Treatment combination	A_1B_1	A_1B_2	A_2B_1	A_2B_2
Sum	329	384	283	350
Mean	32.9	38.4	28.3	35.0
ΣX^2	11,083	15,054	8,461	12,452

$$\Sigma X_{tot} = 1346$$

* Ratings following each of five horror scenes were combined to produce a score for each subject. The higher the score was, the greater was the unpleasantness.

Prior to beginning the analysis, we will find it helpful to construct a graph of the means of all the treatment combinations. By doing this, we can visually identify possible effects of the independent variable and interactions between these variables. If our calculations are at odds with the graphs, we are alerted to the possibility of calculation errors.

Note that the mean unpleasantness ratings for females is higher than that for males under both A_1 and A_2. Note also that the ratings for both males and females are higher when horror is preceded by humor. However, the slopes of the lines suggest little or no interaction between the two independent variables.

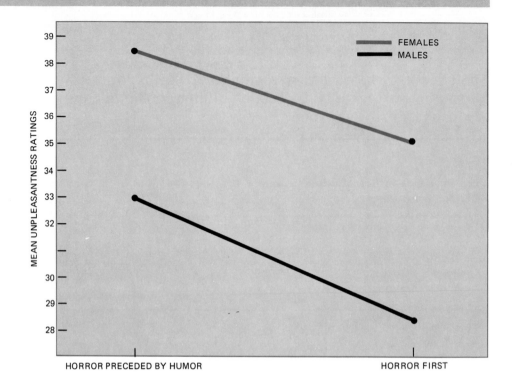

MEAN UNPLEASANTNESS RATINGS

FEMALES
MALES

HORROR PRECEDED BY HUMOR   HORROR FIRST

Let's now conduct an analysis of variance to determine if there is a significant effect of the A variable, the B variable, or an interaction between the two variables. We'll use α = 0.05.

Step 1. Find SS_{tot}. Square each score, sum all of the squared values, and subtract $(\Sigma X)^2/N$:

$$SS_{tot} = \sum X^2 - \frac{(\Sigma X)^2}{N}$$

In the present example,

$$SS_{tot} = 36^2 + 31^2 + 36^2 + \cdots + 38^2 - \frac{(1346)^2}{40}$$

$$= 47{,}050 - 45{,}292.9$$

$$= 1757.1$$

Step 2. Find df_{tot}.

$$df_{tot} = N - 1$$

$$= 40 - 1$$

$$= 39$$

Step 3. Enter SS_{tot} and df_{tot} into the summary table (Table 15.1).

TABLE 15.1 Summary Table for Two-Way Analysis of Variance

Source of Variation	Sum of Squares	Degrees of Freedom	Variance Estimate	F
Between-group	535.7	3		
A variable	160.0	1	160.0	4.72
B variable	372.1	1	372.1	10.97
$A \times B$	3.6	1	3.6	0.11
Within-group (error)	1221.4	36	33.93	
Total	1757.1	39		

Step 4. Find the between-group sum of squares. In the present problem,

$$SS_{bet} = \frac{(\Sigma A_1B_1)^2}{N_{A_1B_1}} + \frac{(\Sigma A_1B_2)^2}{N_{A_1B_2}} + \frac{(\Sigma A_2B_1)^2}{N_{A_2B_1}} + \frac{(\Sigma A_2B_2)^2}{N_{A_2B_2}} - \frac{(\Sigma X)^2}{N}$$

$$= \frac{(329)^2}{10} + \frac{(384)^2}{10} + \frac{(283)^2}{10} + \frac{(350)^2}{10} - 45,292.9$$

$$= 45,828.6 - 45,292.9 = 535.7$$

Since N is the same for each treatment combination, there will be less rounding error if the squares of the treatment combinations are summed and then divided by the N in each group (N_k):

$$SS_{bet} = \frac{(\Sigma A_1B_1)^2 + (\Sigma A_1B_2)^2 + (\Sigma A_2B_1)^2 + (\Sigma A_2B_2)^2}{N_k} - \frac{(\Sigma X)^2}{N}$$

$$= \frac{(329)^2 + (384)^2 + (283)^2 + (350)^2}{10} - 45,292.9$$

$$= 45,828.6 - 45,292.9$$

$$= 535.7$$

Step 5. Find the number of degrees of freedom for the between-group sum of squares:

$$df_{bet} = k - 1$$

in which k is the number of cells or treatment combinations. In the present example,

$$df_{bet} = 4 - 1 = 3$$

Step 6. Enter the between-group sum of squares and the corresponding degrees of freedom in Table 15.1.

Step 7. Begin the partitioning of the between-group sum of squares by finding the sum of squares for the A variable. Since N is the same for each A condition, there will be less rounding error if the squares of each level of A are summed and then divided by the N in each A condition:

$$SS_A = \frac{(\Sigma X_{A_1})^2 + (\Sigma X_{A_2})^2}{N_A} - \frac{(\Sigma X)^2}{N}$$

$$= \frac{(713)^2 + (633)^2}{N_A} - 45{,}292.9$$

$$= \frac{909{,}058}{20} - 45{,}292.9$$

$$= 160$$

Step 8.   Find the number of degrees of freedom for the A condition:

$$df_A = A - 1$$

in which A is the number of levels of A. In the present example,

$$df_A = 2 - 1 = 1$$

Step 9.   Enter the sum of squares for the A variable and the corresponding degrees of freedom in Table 15.1.

Step 10.   Find the sum of squares for the B variable:

$$SS_B = \frac{(\Sigma X_{B_1})^2}{N_{B_1}} + \frac{(\Sigma X_{B_2})^2}{N_{B_2}} - \frac{(\Sigma X)^2}{N}$$

Since N is the same for each B condition, there will be less rounding error if the squares of each level of B are summed and then divided by the N in each condition:

$$SS_B = \frac{(612)^2 + (734)^2}{20} - 45{,}292.9$$

$$= \frac{913{,}300}{20} - 45{,}292.9$$

$$= 45{,}665 - 45{,}292.9 = 372.1$$

Step 11.   Find the number of degrees of freedom for the B condition:

$$df_B = B - 1$$

in which B is the number of levels of B. In the present example,

$$df_B = 2 - 1 = 1$$

Step 12.   Enter the sum of squares for the B variable and the corresponding degrees of freedom in Table 15.1.

Step 13. Find the interaction sum of squares by subtraction:

$$SS_{A \times B} = SS_{bet} - (SS_A + SS_B)$$

$$= 535.7 - (160.0 + 372.1)$$

$$= 3.6$$

Step 14. Find the number of degrees of freedom for the interaction sum of squares:

$$df_{A \times B} = (A - 1)(B - 1)$$

$$= (1)(1) = 1$$

Step 15. Enter the interaction sum of squares and the corresponding degrees of freedom in Table 15.1.

Step 16. Find the within-group sum of squares. The within-group sum of squares may be obtained by subtraction:

$$SS_w = SS_{tot} - SS_{bet}$$

$$= 1757.1 - 535.7 = 1221.4$$

or by calculation:

$$SS_w = \left(11{,}083 - \frac{(329)^2}{10}\right) + \left(15{,}054 - \frac{(384)^2}{10}\right)$$

$$+ \left(8461 - \frac{(283)^2}{10}\right) + \left(12{,}452 - \frac{(350)^2}{10}\right)$$

$$= 258.9 + 308.40 + 452.10 + 202.00$$

$$= 1221.4$$

Step 17. Find the within-group degrees of freedom:

$$df_w = N - k$$

$$= 40 - 4$$

$$= 36$$

Step 18. Enter the within-group sum of squares and degrees of freedom in Table 15.1.

Step 19. Check to ascertain that

$$SS_{bet} + SS_w = SS_{tot}{}^*$$

---

*This provides a complete check on accuracy of calculations only when SS_w has been separately calculated rather than when obtained by subtraction.

and

$$SS_A + SS_B + SS_{A \times B} = SS_{bet}$$

and

$$df_{bet} + df_w = df_{tot}$$

and

$$df_A + df_B + df_{A+B} = df_{bet}$$

Step 20. Find the $A \times B$ interaction variance estimate by dividing the interaction sum of squares by $df_{A \times B}$:

$$\hat{s}^2_{A \times B} = \frac{SS_{A \times B}}{df_{A \times B}} = \frac{3.6}{1} = 3.6$$

Place in Table 15.1.

Step 21. Find the B-variance estimate by dividing the B-variable sum of squares by df_B:

$$\hat{s}^2_B = \frac{SS_B}{df_B} = \frac{372.1}{1} = 372.1$$

Step 22. Find the A-variable variance estimate by dividing the A-variable sum of squares by df_A:

$$\hat{s}^2_A = \frac{SS_A}{df_A} = \frac{160.0}{1} = 160.0$$

Step 23. Find the within-group variance estimate (error) by dividing the within-group sum of squares by df_w:

$$\hat{s}^2_w = \frac{SS_w}{df_w} = \frac{1221.4}{36} = 33.93$$

Step 24. Find the interaction F-ratio by dividing the interaction estimated variance by the within-group estimated variance:

$$F = \frac{\hat{s}^2_{A \times B}}{\hat{s}^2_w} = \frac{3.6}{33.93} = 0.11 \qquad df = 1, 36$$

Step 25. Consult Table D under 1 and 36 df to find the critical value of F required to reject H_0 at the $\alpha = 0.05$ level. Since $F_{0.05} \geq 4.11$, we fail to reject H_0.

Step 26. Find the B-variable F-ratio by dividing the estimated B-variance by the within-group estimated variance:

$$F = \frac{\hat{s}^2_B}{\hat{s}^2_w} = \frac{372.1}{33.93} = 10.97 \qquad df = 1, 36$$

Step 27. Consult Table D under 1 and 36 df to find the critical value of F required to reject H_0 at the $\alpha = 0.05$ level. Since $F_{0.05} \geq 4.11$, the obtained ratio of 10.97 is in the critical region for rejecting H_0. There is a significant effect of the B-variable.

Step 28. Find the A-variable F-ratio by dividing the estimated A-variance by the within-group estimated variance:

$$F = \frac{\hat{S}_A^2}{\hat{S}_w^2} = \frac{160.0}{33.93} = 4.72 \qquad df = 1, 36$$

Step 29. Consult Table D under 1 and 36 df to find the critical value required to reject H_0 at the $\alpha = 0.05$ level. Since $F_{0.05} \geq 4.11$, the obtained F of 4.72 is in the critical region. We reject H_0.

Conclusion: Of the three effects evaluated—A-variable, B-variable, and the interaction of A and B—both the A and the B variables are found to be statistically significant. The contrast hypothesis receives support. Humor preceding scenes of horror produced greater feelings of unpleasantness than scenes of horror being presented first. Moreover, females respond with higher feelings of unpleasantness than males.

Another aspect of the emotional contrast hypothesis is that scenes of humor following horror are likely to be perceived as funnier than scenes of humor without prior scenes of horror. The following table shows the ratings of funniness of humor when humorous scenes are presented first versus their presentation following scenes of horror.

	Humor First		Humor Preceded by Horror	
	B_1 Male	B_2 Female	B_1 Male	B_2 Female
	14	16	16	15
	16	17	13	15
	15	18	23	12
	20	17	22	7
	27	23	13	10
	22	20	11	12
	16	17	8	6
	22	32	24	7
	12	11	8	12
	12	11	16	13
Treatment combination	A_1B_1	A_1B_2	A_2B_1	A_2B_2

a. Prepare a graph of the means of the two independent variables and surmise about the possible effects of the two variables and their interactions.

b. Conduct the appropriate analysis of these data, using $\alpha = 0.05$, and draw the conclusions warranted by the analysis.

a.* ANSWERS

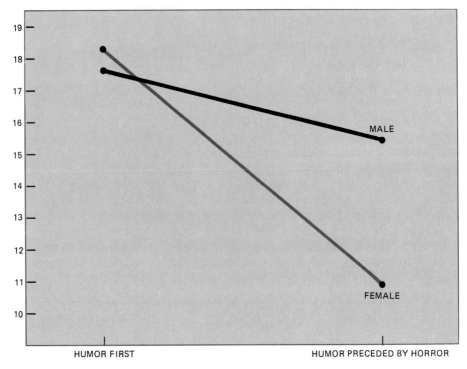

* The lower the score, the greater the funniness.

b.

	Humor First		Humor Preceded by Horror	
	Male	**Female**	**Male**	**Female**
Sum	176	182	154	109
Mean	17.6	18.2	15.4	10.9

$$\Sigma\, X_{\text{tot}} = 621$$

Source of Variation	Sum of Squares		Degrees of Freedom	Variance Estimate	F
Between		328.675	3		
A variable	225.6		1	225.6	8.43
B variable	38.0		1	38.0	1.42
A × B	65.0		1	65.0	2.43
Within-group		963.3	36	26.76	
Total		1291.975	39		

Only the A variable achieves statistical significance. This is additional support for the emotional contrast hypothesis. Individuals rated humor following scenes of horror as funnier than scenes of humor shown first. Note that the interaction does not achieve statistical significance.

From A. S. R. Manstead, H. L. Wagner, and C. J. MacDonald (1983). "A Contrast Effect in Judgments of Own Emotional State." *Motivation and Emotion,* **7,** 279–289.

15.6 TWO-WAY CORRELATED-SAMPLES ANOVA: RANDOMIZED BLOCK FACTORIAL DESIGN

Earlier we noted the architectural symmetry of factorial designs—more complex designs may be constructed by adding tiers of "building blocks" in a logical and orderly fashion. Happily, the data analyses (ANOVA) proceed in like fashion. When we advanced from one-way designs to two-way designs, each treatment variable was analyzed separately and independent variance estimates of their effects were obtained. At this point, a new "treatment effect" was introduced, the interaction between the independent variables. In both cases, the within-group error was the standard against which the treatment effects and interaction were interpreted.

The addition of matched groups to the one-way analysis added, in effect, a second variable—individual differences. In the independent-samples design, variations due to individual difference are inextricably bound into the within-group error term. Since individual differences often account for a sizable proportion of random error, the within-group error term in independent-samples designs is typically inflated and less sensitive to treatment effects than that in a correlated-samples design. The beauty of a matched-samples design is that, when we are able to use it—which we

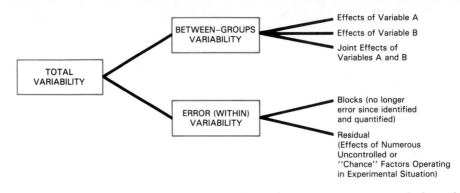

FIGURE 15.1 The partitioning of the total sum of squares in a two-way matched-samples factorial design.

often cannot do; see Section 13.8—the error due to individual differences is subtracted from within-group error, and the quantity that remains, the residual, becomes the basis for estimating error.

As illustrated in Figure 15.1, the only step added to the analysis of a two-way independent-samples design is the calculation of the block sum of squares, which is, in effect, subtracted from the error variations (within error) to yield a residual error term. Moreover, we have already performed the calculation of the block and residual sums of squares in the one-way matched-samples ANOVA.

15.7 A WORKED EXAMPLE

To illustrate the computations, we'll show the analysis of hypothetical data employing a 2 × 2 factorial design in which there are 28 subjects, matched in groups of 4 across both the A and the B variables. The raw data are shown in Table 15.2.

TABLE 15.2 **Hypothetical Data Involving a Factorial Randomized Block Design in which 4 Matched Individuals Were Randomly Assigned to Each Block**

| | | | *A* variable | | | Block |
| | | A_1 | | A_2 | | Sum |
B variable	B_1	B_2	B_1	B_2	
B 1	6	8	9	11	34
l 2	7	9	10	13	39
o 3	11	10	12	14	47
c 4	13	15	17	12	57
k 5	16	13	18	15	62
6	13	16	17	14	60
7	15	17	22	20	74
Sums	81	88	105	99	373

There are two separate and distinct stages in the analysis of data cast in the form of a randomized block factorial design. The first is the partitioning of the total sum of squares into three components: blocks, treatments, and residual. The second stage involves the partitioning of the treatment sum of squares into three components: A variable, B variable, and interaction of $A \times B$.

Partitioning SS_{tot} into $SS_{bl} + SS_{treat} + SS_{res}$, in which SS_{treat} Equals the Total Sum of Squares of the A and B Variables and the $A \times B$ interaction

1. $SS_{tot} = 6^2 + 8^2 + \cdots + 20^2 - \dfrac{373^2}{28}$

$= 5371 - 4968.89$

$= 402.11$

2. $SS_{bl} = \dfrac{34^2 + 39^2 + \cdots + 74^2}{4} - 4968.89$

$= 5263.75 - 4968.89$

$= \dfrac{294.86}{df_{bl}} = bl - 1 = 6$

3. $SS_{treat} = \dfrac{81^2 + 88^2 + 105^2 + 99^2}{7} - 4968.89$

$= \dfrac{35,131}{7} - 4968.89$

$= 49.82$

4. $SS_{res} = SS_{tot} - SS_{bl} - SS_{treat}$

$= 402.11 - 294.86 - 49.82$

$= 57.43, df_{res} = df_{tot} - df_{bl} - df_{treat} = 27 - 6 - 3 = 18$

Partitioning the Treatment Sum of Squares into SS_A, SS_B, and $SS_{A \times B}$

To partition the treatment sum of squares, set up Table 15.3.

TABLE 15.3 The Sum in Each Cell (Each Treatment Combination) and the Marginal Sums that Reflect the Effects of the A and the B Variables

		Variable		
		A_1	A_2	*B* Sums
	B_1	81	105	186
	B_2	88	99	187
A Sums		169	204	373

5. $SS_A = \dfrac{169^2 + 204^2}{14} - CT$

$= \dfrac{70{,}177}{14} - 4968.89$

$= 5012.64 - 4968.89$

$= 43.75 \qquad df_A = A - 1 = 1$

6. $SS_B = \dfrac{186^2 + 187^2}{14} - CT$

$= \dfrac{69{,}565}{14} - 4968.89$

$= 4968.93 - 4968.89$

$= 0.04 \qquad df_B = B - 1 = 1$

7. $SS_{A \times B} = SS_{treat} - SS_A - SS_B$

$= 49.82 - 43.75 - 0.04$

$= 6.03 \qquad df = df_A \times df_B = 1$

TABLE 15.4 Summary Table for Presenting the Relevant Calculations and Statistics in a Randomized Block Two-Way ANOVA

Source of Variation	Sum of Squares	Degrees of Freedom	Variance Estimate	F
Treatments	49.82	3		
A	43.75	1	43.75	13.71
B	0.04	1	0.04	0.01
A × B	6.03	1	6.03	1.89
Between blocks	294.86	6	49.14	
Residual (error)	57.43	18	3.19	
Totals	402.11	27		

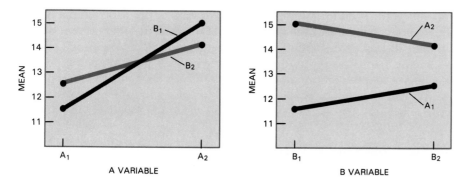

FIGURE 15.2 Graphing the means of a matched-groups two-way ANOVA. The graph on the left shows the means of the A variable at both levels of B. The graph on the right displays the means of the B variable at both levels of A.

We are interested in assessing the effects of the two treatment variables and the interaction between them. Using $\alpha = 0.01$ and referring to Table D in the Table section, we see that an F-ratio equal to or greater than 8.28 is required to reject H_0 at the 0.01 level. Only the F-ratio of the A variable meets this criterion. Thus, we assert that the A variable produced statistically significant effects on the dependent measures.

It is sometimes helpful to graph the results in terms of the cell means (see Figure 15.2). These means are readily obtainable from Table 15.3: Divide each cell entry (treatment combination) by the number of observations within each cell. Using these procedures, the following means are found:

$$\overline{A_1 B_1} = \frac{81}{7} = 11.57; \overline{A_1 B_2} = \frac{88}{7} = 12.57; \overline{A_2 B_1} = \frac{105}{7} = 15.00; \overline{A_2 B_2} = \frac{99}{7} = 14.14.$$

It is immediately apparent from the graph on the left that the means of A_1 are low at both levels of B, but the A_2 means are considerably higher at both levels of B. This is consonant with the finding of a significant effect of the A variable. As you can see from the graph on the right, there is no such consistency in the means of the B variable.

15.8 PUTTING IT ALL TOGETHER

In the comparable section of Chapter 14, we noted that the most complex-appearing research designs appropriate for ANOVA grow naturally out of simple models. Both the independent-group and matched-group two-way factorial designs superbly illustrate this point.

Going from One-Way to Two-Way Independent Factorial Designs

In the one-way ANOVA, the total sum of squares was partitioned into two components: the sum of squares between conditions and the sum of squares within conditions. The former provides the basis for estimating the treatment variance, and the latter permits the estimation of error variance. In the two-way analysis, the total between-conditions or treatment sum of squares is partitioned into three components: A, B, and interaction of $A \times B$. Otherwise, the computational procedures are only slightly altered. The within-conditions sum of squares can be obtained by subtracting the total between-conditions sum of squares (SS_{treat}) from the total sum of squares.

Going from One-Way to Two-Way Matched-Samples Factorial Designs

In the one-way ANOVA, the total sum of squares is partitioned into three components: between-conditions, blocks, and residual. The residual sum of squares, which provides the basis for estimating error variance, may be obtained by subtracting the between-condition sum of squares and the block sum of squares from the total sum of squares. In the first stage in a two-way analysis, the total sum of squares is partitioned into the total treatment sum of squares, the block sum of squares, and the residual. The residual is obtained by subtraction: $SS_{res} = SS_{tot} - SS_{treat}$. In the second stage, the total treatment sum of squares (SS_{treat}) is partitioned into three components: SS_A, SS_B, and $SS_{A \times B}$. The interaction sum of squares ($SS_{A \times B}$) is usually obtained by subtraction.

CHAPTER SUMMARY

In this chapter, we saw that ANOVA can be extended and applied to complex designs in which more than one independent variable is used. Specifically, we looked at two types of analysis of variance:

> Two-way independent-samples ANOVA, in which the subjects are assigned at random to the various treatment conditions
>
> Two-way matched-samples ANOVA, in which subjects, based on a variable that is known or presumed to be correlated with the dependent variable, are assigned to blocks and, within blocks, are randomly assigned to experimental or treatment conditions

Both analyses involve partitioning the total sum of squares into treatment sums of squares (such as treatments A and B and the interaction between these two variables) and a sum of squares that reflects random error. The independent-samples ANOVA bases this error on the within-group sum of squares. The matched-samples ANOVA, having identified and quantified a source of error (e.g., individual differences) through matching, is able to subtract the block sum of squares from the within-group sum of squares to produce a more sensitive error term (residual) whenever matching is successful.

The F-ratio is used to evaluate the effects of each of the experimental conditions as well as their interactions.

TERMS TO REMEMBER

factorial design　　　　　　**two-way analysis of variance with**
interaction　　　　　　　　　　**independent groups**
qualitative variables　　　　**two-way analysis of variance with**
quantitative variables　　　　**matched groups**

EXERCISES

1. Following are scores made by subjects in a 3 × 3 factorial experiment. Conduct the appropriate analysis of variance and show conclusions warranted by the analysis. Use $\alpha = 0.05$.

A_1			A_2			A_3		
B_1	B_2	B_3	B_1	B_2	B_3	B_1	B_2	B_3
8	10	12	5	9	16	6	10	17
1	7	9	3	10	11	5	7	9
7	9	11	8	10	12	4	11	12
9	7	5	8	6	4	10	8	6
4	8	15	6	8	10	8	10	12
12	14	15	10	12	13	13	14	14

2. Following are scores made by subjects in a 2 × 3 factorial experiment. Conduct the appropriate analysis of variance and show conclusions warranted by the analysis. Use $\alpha = 0.05$.

A_1			A_2		
B_1	B_2	B_3	B_1	B_2	B_3
4	5	4	8	6	11
6	8	6	7	9	9
7	3	2	9	12	13
9	7	5	11	8	7

3. The following table shows the scores on the Standard Challenging Task (SCT) made by 120 subjects in the study by Ortega and Pipal (1984). The SCT consisted of various perceptual, verbal, and arithmetic problems of moderate difficulty.

Scores on Standard Challenging Task (SCT)

Type A Subjects			Type B Subjects		
Active	Passive	Relaxed	Active	Passive	Relaxed
9	9	7	9	9	9
9	10	9	8	7	10
10	10	6	10	9	3
10	10	9	8	6	8
10	9	10	7	10	8
10	8	9	8	10	10
4	9	10	6	9	9
10	8	8	6	9	8
9	9	10	5	9	9
10	10	10	8	9	7
10	9	10	6	10	6
6	10	8	6	9	7
7	10	8	6	9	10
10	10	10	10	2	10
10	9	9	10	10	9
5	10	8	9	10	9
9	7	10	10	4	7
8	10	8	8	10	10
10	7	6	7	9	8
10	10	10	8	5	8

Source: Based on data from Ortega and Pipal, 1984.

  a. Construct a graph of the means and verbalize the findings at the descriptive level.
  b. Conduct the appropriate statistical analyses and draw the conclusions warranted by the analyses. Use $\alpha = 0.05$.

4. In Statistics in Action 5.1, we examined data on emotional contrast and mood. Twenty male and twenty female subjects viewed scenes of horror, half after viewing humorous scenes and half viewing horror first. The results are shown below. Note that the higher the score, the greater was the rating of unpleasantness.
  a. Formulate null and alternative hypotheses, using a two-tailed test.
  b. Perform appropriate ANOVA and draw the conclusions warranted by the analysis, using $\alpha = 0.05$. Review the figure in Statistics in Action 5.1. Note the visual support of the effects of both variables (gender and the effect of horror preceded by humor). Note also that there is no visual evidence of an interaction effect.

5. Using the data in Exercise 36, Chapter 5, conduct a 2×3 ANOVA of this factorial study involving Type A versus Type B behaviors under three different conditions of relaxation. Use $\alpha = 0.05$, two-tailed test.

Males (A_1)		Females (A_2)	
Horror Preceded by Humor (B_1)	Humor First (B_2)	Horror Preceded by Humor (B_1)	Humor First (B_2)
36	29	42	30
31	34	26	33
36	27	40	37
20	33	31	32
41	10	37	30
34	28	37	31
32	26	43	45
34	31	43	36
32	30	44	38
33	35	41	38

6. In Exercise 2 in this chapter, assume that subjects had been assigned to 4 blocks of 6 matched subjects per block. Conduct a randomized block ANOVA, using $\alpha = 0.05$. Are the conclusions changed? If so, why? If not, why not?

7. On the basis of a pretest, 40 subjects were assigned to matched groups of 4 subjects representing decreasing degrees of proficiency in completing a series of logical tasks. Two experimental variables were used in a 2 × 2 randomized block factorial design: knowledge of results (A variable: immediate feedback and no feedback) and prior explanation of the significance of the task versus no prior information (B variable). The dependent measure consisted of scores made on a test involving solutions to problems in logic. The results are shown below (the higher the score, the better the performance).

A_1 Knowledge of Results		A_2 No Knowledge of Results	
Prior Explanation	No Prior Explanation	Prior Explanation	No Prior Explanation
15	13	9	12
13	11	10	9
15	11	8	10
12	8	5	7
13	10	6	8
9	5	3	5
10	4	4	5
8	3	0	3
6	7	4	1
8	5	2	2

Set up and test appropriate null hypotheses, using $\alpha = 0.01$, two-tailed test.

PART IV

INFERENTIAL STATISTICS:
NONPARAMETRIC TESTS
OF SIGNIFICANCE

16

Power and Power Efficiency of a Statistical Test

16.1 THE CONCEPT OF POWER

Throughout the first two parts of this book, only fleeting references were made to the power and the power efficiency of a statistical test (although they were not identified as such). Before proceeding into nonparametric tests of significance, we need to examine these concepts in more detail.

While discussing Type I and Type II errors in Section 11.5, we pointed out that the basic conservatism of scientists causes them to set up a rejection level that is sufficiently low to make Type I errors less frequent than Type II errors. In other words, the scientist would rather make the mistake of accepting a false null hypothesis than the mistake of rejecting a true one. However, this conservatism should not be construed to mean that the scientist is happy about the prospect of making Type II errors. To the contrary, it is quite likely that many promising research projects have been abandoned because of the failure of the experimenter to reject the null hypothesis when it was actually false.

Now up to this point in the book, our concern has been to establish a level of significance that will reduce the likelihood of falsely rejecting the null hypothesis. In other words, we have been primarily concerned with avoiding Type I rather than Type II errors. However, the ideal statistical test is one that effects some sort of balance between these two types of error. Ideally, we should specify in advance of our study the probability of making both a Type I and a Type II error. In practice, however, most researchers content themselves with stating only the *p*-value, which they will employ to reject the null hypothesis. As we have seen, this *p*-value represents the probability of a Type I error (i.e., α).

When we begin to concern ourselves with effecting a balance beween Type I and Type II errors, we are dealing with the concept of the **power of a test.** The power of a test is defined simply as the probability of rejecting the null hypothesis when it is in fact false. Symbolically, power is defined as follows:

Power of a Test: The probability of rejecting the null hypothesis when it is in fact false.

$$\text{Power} = 1 - \text{probability of a Type II error}$$

If we let β represent the probability of a Type II error, the definition of power becomes

$$\text{Power} = 1 - \beta \qquad (16.1)$$

We can calculate the power of a test only when H_0 is false. Recall that if H_0 is true, we cannot make a Type II error (accepting a false H_0).

Before proceeding with a formal discussion of power, let us review a series of problems that appeared in the end-of-chapter exercises for Chapter 12 (Exercises 30 through 33). You will recall that we imagined drawing all possible pairs of samples from two populations of means.

Population 1 means: 3, 4, 5, 5, 6, 6, 6, 7, 7, 8, 9; $\mu_1 = 6$
Population 2 means: 0, 1, 2, 2, 3, 3, 3, 4, 4, 5, 6; $\mu_2 = 3$

We obtained the sampling distribution of differences between means shown in Table 16.1.

Then we pretended not to know the characteristics of the second population. We formulated the null hypothesis that the first and second populations are the same ($\mu_1 = \mu_2$). This sampling distribution of differences between means is shown in Table 16.2.

Note that, under the null hypothesis of no difference between population means, a difference equal to or greater than 5 or equal to or less than -5 would lead to the rejection of H_0 at $\alpha = 0.05$ ($0.0248 + 0.0248 = 0.0496$), two-tailed test.

Now we return to the *true* sampling distribution of differences between sample means (Table 16.1) and ask, "Under $H_0:\mu_1 = \mu_2$, how often would we have rejected this false null hypothesis when $\alpha = 0.05$, two-tailed test? How often would we have *failed* to reject this false H_0?" Stated another way, how often would we have made a Type II error?

Let's look at each of these questions in turn. Under $H_0:\mu_1 = \mu_2$, we would reject the null hypothesis at $\alpha = 0.05$, two-tailed test, whenever we obtained a difference in sample means equal to or greater than 5 or equal to or less than -5. Looking at Table 16.1, we see that under the *true*

TABLE 16.1 Frequency and Sampling Distributions of Differences between Means when All Possible Sample Means Are Selected, with Replacement, from Two Populations of Means in which $\mu_1 = 6$ and $\mu_2 = 3$*

$\overline{X}_1 - \overline{X}_2$	f	$p(\overline{X}_1 - \overline{X}_2)$
9	1	0.0083
8	2	0.0165
7	5	0.0413
6	10	0.0826
5	14	0.1157
4	18	0.1488
3	21	0.1736
2	18	0.1488
1	14	0.1157
0	10	0.0826
−1	5	0.0413
−2	2	0.0165
−3	1	0.0083
	$N_{\overline{X}_1 - \overline{X}_2} = 121$	$\Sigma\, p(\overline{X}_1 - \overline{X}_2) = 1.000$

* This represents the true sampling distribution of differences between means for the indicated populations of means.

TABLE 16.2 Sampling Distribution of Difference between Means under $H_0 : \mu_1 = \mu_2$*

$\overline{X}_1 - \overline{X}_2$	f	$p(\overline{X}_1 - \overline{X}_2)$	
6	1	0.0083	} 0.0248
5	2	0.0165	
4	5	0.0413	
3	10	0.0826	
2	14	0.1157	
1	18	0.1488	
0	21	0.1736	
−1	18	0.1488	
−2	14	0.1157	
−3	10	0.0826	
−4	5	0.0413	
−5	2	0.0165	} 0.0248
−6	1	0.0083	
	$N_{\overline{X}_1 - \overline{X}_2} = 121$	$\Sigma\, p(\overline{X}_1 - \overline{X}_2) = 1.0000$	

* *Note:* We have assumed that population 2 is identical to population 1, that is, $\mu_1 = \mu_2$, and found all possible differences between means.

sampling distribution of differences, we would obtain a difference in means equal to or greater than 5 about 26% of the time (0.1157 + 0.0826 + 0.0413 + 0.0165 + 0.0083 = 0.2644). Under the *true* distribution, we would never obtain a difference in means equal to or less than −5. Thus, the probability of correctly rejecting H_0 is 0.2644.

How often would we fail to reject H_0? Any difference in means less than 5 would not cause us to reject the null hypothesis. Since we know H_0 to be false, this entire region would represent a Type II error. The probability of a Type II error is therefore 1.000 − 0.2644 = 0.7356. In other words, we would *fail* to reject a false null hypothesis almost 74% of the time. The power of the test is 0.2644, which means that we would correctly reject a false null hypothesis only about 26% of the time.

Figure 16.1 graphically presents probability histograms for both the null and the *true* distributions of $\bar{X}_1 - \bar{X}_2$ for the sampling problem we have been discussing.

We might note that failure to reject H_0 when it is false is not only a statistical and research problem; it is also an economic one. Research costs both time and money. One must question the advisability of undertaking a project when the probability of making a Type II error is high. In this

FIGURE 16.1 Probability histograms for the null and true distributions of $\bar{X}_1 - \bar{X}_2$ for the sampling example given in the text.

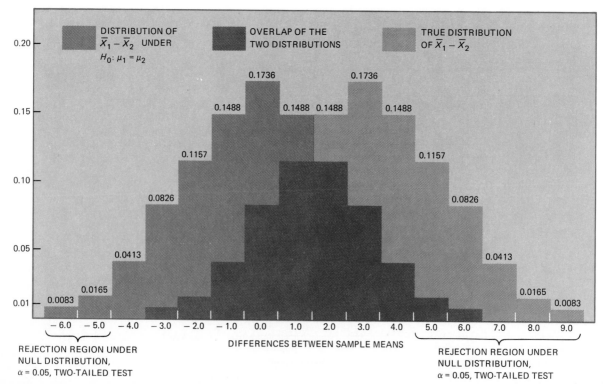

chapter, we discuss several strategies for reducing the risk of a Type II error.

The following section illustrates the calculation of power.

16.2 CALCULATION OF POWER: ONE-SAMPLE CASE

A psychologist working for a large industrial firm has constructed two aptitude scales, which he administers interchangeably to incoming groups of trainees. He knows that the mean performance on scale A is 70, and that on scale B is 72. Both scales have a standard deviation of 5. He is chagrined to discover that his assistant failed to record which scale was administered to a group of 16 trainees. Scanning the data and noticing a number of low scores, he believes that this sample came from a population in which $\mu = 70$ (i.e., the scale A test was administered to this group), or $H_0 : \mu = \mu_0 = 70$.

As a matter of fact, however, scale B had been administered. Thus, since we know that H_0 is false and we know the true value of μ under H_1 ($\mu = \mu_1 = 72$), we can calculate the power of the test (i.e., the probability that he will correctly reject the false null hypothesis).

Let's set up this problem in formal statistical terms.

1. *Null hypothesis (H_0):* The mean of the population from which this sample was drawn equals 70; that is, $\mu = \mu_0 = 70$.
2. *Alternative hypothesis (H_1):* The mean of the population from which this sample was drawn equals 72, that is, $\mu = \mu_1 = 72$.
3. *Statistical test:* Since σ is known, $z = (\overline{X} - \mu_0)/\sigma_{\overline{X}}$ is the appropriate test statistic.
4. *Significance level:* $\alpha = 0.01$ (one-tailed test).
5. *Sampling distribution:* The sampling distribution of the mean is known to be a normal distribution.
6. *Critical region:* $z_{0.01} = +2.33$. Since we are employing a one-tailed test, the critical region consists of all values of $z = (\overline{X} - \mu_0)/\sigma_{\overline{X}} \geq 2.33$.

Therefore, the critical value of the sample statistic (the minimum value of $\overline{X}$ leading to rejecting of H_0) is

$$\overline{X} = (2.33)\sigma_{\overline{X}} + \mu_0$$

Thus, the power equals the probability of obtaining this critical value in the distribution under H_1. The following steps are employed.

Step 1. Calculate the value of $\sigma_{\overline{X}}$:

$$\sigma_{\overline{X}} = \frac{\sigma}{\sqrt{N}} = \frac{5}{\sqrt{16}} = 1.25$$

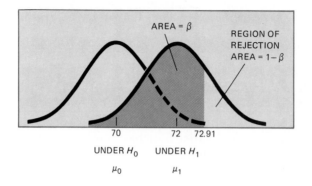

FIGURE 16.2 Region of rejection for H_0 in the distribution under H_1.

Step 2. Determine the critical value of $\overline{X}$ ($\alpha = 0.01$, one-tailed test):

$$\overline{X} = (2.33)(1.25) + 70 = 72.91$$

Step 3. Determine the probability of obtaining this critical value in the *true* sampling distribution under H_1. The critical value of $\overline{X}$ has a z-score, in the distribution under H_1, of

$$z = \frac{72.91 - \mu_1}{\sigma_{\overline{X}}} = \frac{72.91 - 72.00}{1.25} = 0.73$$

Referring to column C, Table A, in the Table section, we see that the probability of correctly rejecting H_0 is 23.27%. This probability is $1 - \beta$, or the power of the test. Incidentally, the probability of making a Type II error (β) is 76.73%.

Figure 16.2 clarifies these relationships by indicating the region of rejection for H_0 in the *true* distribution under H_1, $1 - \beta$ or power. The shaded area indicates β, which is the probability of falsely accepting H_0.

16.3 THE EFFECT OF SAMPLE SIZE ON POWER

Power varies as a function of several different factors. Let us examine the effect of varying the size of the sample on the power of the test. For example, let us employ $N = 25$ in the problem described in the previous section, and see what effect this has on the power of the test.

Employing the same procedures as described earlier, we test the hypothesis

$$H_0 : \mu = \mu_0 = 70$$

given that the true hypothesis is

$$H_1 : \mu = \mu_1 = 72$$

Since, with $\alpha = 0.01$ (one-tailed test), the critical region consists of all values of $z = (\overline{X} - \mu_0)/\sigma_{\overline{X}} \geq 2.33$, the critical value of $\overline{X} = (2.33)\sigma_{\overline{X}} + \mu_0$. Thus

Step 1. The value of $\sigma_{\overline{X}}$ is

$$\sigma_{\overline{X}} = \frac{\sigma}{\sqrt{N}} = \frac{5}{\sqrt{25}} = 1.00$$

Step 2. The critical value of $\overline{X}$ is

$$\overline{X} = (2.33)(1.00) + 70 = 72.33$$

Step 3 The critical value of $\overline{X}$ has a z-score in the distribution under H_1 of

$$z = \frac{72.33 - 72.00}{1.00} = 0.33$$

Referring to column C, Table A, we see that the power of the test is 37.07%.

We have seen in our illustrative problem that when $N = 16$, the power is 23.27%. When we increased our N to 25, power increased to 37.07%. Had we determined power for $N = 100$ for the preceding example, we would find that the power = 95.15%. Thus, we may conclude that the power of a test is a function of N.

16.4   THE EFFECT OF α-LEVEL ON POWER

In our previous discussion of Type I and Type II errors (Section 11.6), we indicated that the lower we set α, **the less** the likelihood of a Type I error and the more the likelihood of a Type II error. Since β is the probability that a Type II error will occur, and power = $1 - \beta$, the higher the α-level that is chosen, the greater is the power of the test. One can readily demonstrate this relationship between α and power by substituting a different α-level in the preceding problem and observing the change in power.

For example, employing $\alpha = 0.05$ (one-tailed test) with $N = 16$, we find that the critical region consists of all values of

$$z = \frac{\overline{X} - \mu_0}{\sigma_{\overline{X}}} \geq 1.65^*$$

---

*When $\alpha = 0.05$ (one-tailed test), the critical value of z is exactly halfway between 1.64 and 1.65. We employ z = 1.65 as the critical value so that $p < 0.05$, rather than z = 1.64, which results in $p > 0.05$.

Therefore, the critical value of $\overline{X} = (1.65)\sigma_{\overline{X}} + \mu_0 = 72.06$. Thus, power = 48.01% when $\alpha = 0.05$, as compared to 23.27% when $\alpha = 0.01$ in the example from Section 16.2.

16.5 THE EFFECT OF THE NATURE OF H_1 ON POWER

The power of a test is also a function of the nature of the alternative hypothesis. In the event that H_0 is actually false, the directional or one-tailed H_1 is more powerful than the two-tailed test so long as the parameter is in the predicted direction.

Inspection of Table 16.3 reveals that the higher the α-level is, the lower is the absolute value of z that is required to reject H_0. We have already seen that power increases with increasing α. It follows that power increases as the critical value of z decreases. Table 16.3 shows that for any given α-level, the critical value of z is lower for a one-tailed test than for a two-tailed test. Therefore, an obtained z that is not significant for a two-tailed test may be significant for a one-tailed test. Thus, the one-tailed test is more powerful than its two-tailed alternative, unless the parameter happens to lie in a direction opposite to the one predicted. In this case, the one-tailed test will be less powerful.

16.6 PARAMETRIC VERSUS NONPARAMETRIC TESTS: POWER

Another factor determining the power of a statistical test is the nature of the test itself. We can state as a general rule that for any given N, the parametric tests are more powerful than their nonparametric counterparts.

TABLE 16.3 Critical Values of z Required to Reject H_0 at Various α-levels as Function of the Nature of H_1

Nature of H_1	
Directional (one-tailed test)	Nondirectional (two-tailed test)
$\alpha = 0.005$ $z = 2.58$	$z = \pm 2.81$
$\alpha = 0.01$ $z = 2.33$	$z = \pm 2.58$
$\alpha = 0.025$ $z = 1.96$	$z = \pm 2.24$
$\alpha = 0.05$ $z = 1.65$	$z = \pm 1.96$

It is primarily for this reason that we have deferred the discussion of statistical power until the present section of the text. For any given N, the parametric tests of significance (those assuming normally distributed populations with the same variance) entail less risk of a Type II error. They are more likely to reject H_0 when H_0 is false. Thus, given the choice between a nonparametric and a parametric test of significance, the parametric test should be employed so long as its underlying assumptions are fulfilled. However, as we shall see in the following chapters, there are numerous situations in which the very nature of our data excludes the possibility of a parametric test of significance. We shall therefore be forced to employ less powerful nonparametric tests.[*]

Why do nonparametric tests have less power? Succinctly stated, the answer is that parametric statistical tests (as opposed to nonparametric tests) make maximum use of all the information that is inherent in the data when the populations are normally distributed. Let's look at a simple illustration. Imagine that we have obtained the following scores in the course of conducting a study: 50, 34, 21, 12, 10. Now, if we were to convert these scores into ranks (an operation basic to nonparametric statistics involving ordinal scales), we would obtain 1, 2, 3, 4, 5. Note that all the information concerning the *magnitudes* of the scores is lost when we convert to ranks. The difference between the scores of 50 and 34 becomes "equivalent," when expressed as ranks, to the difference between, say, 12 and 10. This greater sensitivity of the parametric tests to the magnitudes of scores makes them a more accurate basis for arriving at probability values when the basic assumptions of cardinality are met.

16.7 CALCULATION OF POWER: TWO-SAMPLE CASE

So far, we have examined the effect of various factors on power, employing the one-sample case. All the conclusions drawn apply equally to the two-sample case.

At this point, we would like to illustrate a sample problem in which we calculate the power of a test for the two-sample case.

Let us suppose that we have two populations with the following parameters:

$$\mu_1 = 80 \qquad \mu_2 = 75$$

$$\sigma_1 = 6 \qquad \sigma_2 = 6$$

---

[*] It must be reiterated that the parametric tests are more powerful only when the assumptions underlying their use are valid. When the assumptions are not met, a nonparametric treatment may be as powerful as the parametric.

If we draw a sample of nine cases from each of the two populations ($N_1 = 9$, $N_2 = 9$), we may test for the significance of the difference between the two sample means obtained. First, let us set up this problem in formal statistical terms.

1. *Null hypothesis (H_0):* The two samples were drawn from populations with equal means, that is, $\mu_1 = \mu_2$.
2. *Alternative hypothesis (H_1):* The two samples were drawn from populations with different means, that is $\mu_1 \neq \mu_2$.
3. *Statistical test:* Since we are comparing two sample means drawn from normally distributed populations with known variances, z is the appropriate test statistic.
4. *Significance level:* $\alpha = 0.01$.
5. *Sampling distribution:* The sampling distribution of the statistic $(\overline{X}_1 - \overline{X}_2)$ is known to be a normal distribution.
6. *Critical region:* $|z_{0.01}| \geq 2.58$.

In other words, when

$$|z| = \left| \frac{(\overline{X}_1 - \overline{X}_2) - (\mu_1 - \mu_2)}{\sigma_{\overline{X}_1 - \overline{X}_2}} \right| \geq 2.58$$

we will reject H_0. Since H_0 means that $\mu_1 - \mu_2 = 0$, the lower critical value of $(\overline{X}_1 - \overline{X}_2) = (-2.58)\sigma_{\overline{X}_1 - \overline{X}_2}$, and the upper critical value of $(\overline{X}_1 - \overline{X}_2) = (+2.58)\sigma_{\overline{X}_1 - \overline{X}_2}$.

Now, since we know H_0 to be false (i.e., $\mu_1 - \mu_2 \neq 0$), the power of the test is equal to the probability of obtaining these critical values. Any obtained sample difference that is less than these critical values will lead to a Type II error (i.e., acceptance of a false H_0).

We employ the following steps to calculate power:

Step 1. Calculate the value of $\sigma_{\overline{X}_1 - \overline{X}_2}$:

$$\sigma_{\overline{X}_1} = \frac{\sigma_1}{\sqrt{N_1}} = 2 \qquad \sigma_{\overline{X}_2} = \frac{\sigma_2}{\sqrt{N_2}} = 2$$

$$\sigma_{\overline{X}_1 - \overline{X}_2} = \sqrt{\sigma_{\overline{X}_1}^2 + \sigma_{\overline{X}_2}^2} = 2.828$$

Step 2. Determine the critical values of $(\overline{X}_1 - \overline{X}_2)$, $\alpha = 0.01$, two-tailed test. The lower critical value is $(\overline{X}_1 - \overline{X}_2) = (-2.58)(2.828) = -7.296$. The upper critical value is $(\overline{X}_1 - \overline{X}_2) = 7.296$.

Step 3. Determine the probability of obtaining these critical values in the *true* sampling distribution under H_1. The upper critical value of $(\overline{X}_1 - \overline{X}_2)$ has a z-score, in the distribution under H_1, of

$$z = \frac{7.296 - \mu_{\overline{X}_1 - \overline{X}_2}}{\sigma_{\overline{X}_1 - \overline{X}_2}} = \frac{7.296 - 5.0}{2.828} = 0.81$$

Referring to column (C), Table A, we see that the area beyond a z of 0.81 is 20.90%. The lower critical value of $(\bar{X}_1 - \bar{X}_2)$ has a z-score of

$$z = \frac{-7.296 - 5.0}{2.828} = -4.35$$

A z of -4.35 is so large that only a negligible proportion of area falls beyond it ($<0.003\%$). Thus, the power $= 20.90\%$. This is quite low, since the probability of detecting a true difference is only about 1 in 5. One must question the advisability of embarking on the time, labor, and expense of research which has such a small chance of bearing fruit.

16.8   THE EFFECT OF CORRELATED MEASURES ON POWER

In Section 13.7, we indicated that when subjects have been successfully matched on a variable correlated with the criterion variable, a statistical test that takes this correlation into account provides a more powerful test than one that does not. This is due to the fact that a major source of error has been identified, quantified, and "removed" from the error term. Thus, any difference in means is more readily measured. This may be readily demonstrated.

Employing the data in the preceding problem, let us assume that the nine subjects drawn from population 1 are matched on a related variable with the nine subjects drawn from population 2 and that the correlation between these two variables is 0.80.

Since, with $\alpha = 0.01$ (two-tailed test), the critical region consists of all values of

$$|z| = \left| \frac{(\bar{X}_1 - \bar{X}_2) - (\mu_1 - \mu_2)}{\sigma_{\bar{X}_1 - \bar{X}_2}} \right| \geq 2.58$$

the critical values of $(\bar{X}_1 - \bar{X}_2) = (\pm 2.58)\sigma_{\bar{X}_1 - \bar{X}_2}$.

Step 1.   The value of $\sigma_{\bar{X}_1 - \bar{X}_2}$ is

$$\sigma_{\bar{X}_1 - \bar{X}_2} = \sqrt{\sigma_{\bar{X}_1}^2 + \sigma_{\bar{X}_2}^2 - 2r\sigma_{\bar{X}_1}\sigma_{\bar{X}_2}}$$

$$= \sqrt{4 + 4 - (2)(0.8)(2)(2)}$$

$$= \sqrt{1.6} = 1.26$$

Step 2.   The critical values of $(\bar{X}_1 - \bar{X}_2)$ are

$$(\bar{X}_1 - \bar{X}_2) = (\pm 2.58)(1.26) = \pm 3.25$$

Step 3. The lower critical value of $(\overline{X}_1 - \overline{X}_2)$ has a z-score, in the distribution under H_1, of

$$z = \frac{(-3.25 - 5.00)}{1.26} = -6.55$$

Referring to Table A, we find that the area beyond a z of -6.55 is negligible. Therefore, power will be determined according to the upper critical value.

The upper critical value of $(\overline{X}_1 - \overline{X}_2)$ has a z of

$$z = \frac{3.25 - 5.00}{1.26} = -1.39$$

To find the probability of obtaining $(\overline{X}_1 - \overline{X}_2) \geq 3.25$, we refer to Table A to find the area *above* a z of -1.39. This comes to 41.77% + 50% = 91.77%. Since $\beta = 1 -$ power, the probability of a Type II error (β) is 1 − 91.77% = 8.23%. Thus, our chances are fairly small (about 8 in 100) of failing to reject a false null hypothesis. Recall that when we assumed, for purpose of argument, that the two groups were independent, we found a low index of power (20.9%). However, when matching produced a high correlation (0.80), the power of the test was increased enormously and the risk of a Type II error was substantially reduced.

16.9 POWER AND TYPE I AND TYPE II ERRORS

Let us take a moment to tie together some of our observations about power and Type I and Type II errors. To begin, we must emphasize the fact that there are only two possibilities with respect to the null hypothesis; that is, either it is true (e.g., $\mu_1 = \mu_2$) or it is not true (e.g., $\mu_1 \neq \mu_2$). These are two mutually exclusive situations. Now, since a Type I error is defined as the probability of rejecting H_0 when it is true, two points should immediately be obvious.

1. If H_0 is *false*, the probability of a Type I error is zero.
2. It is only when we *reject* H_0 that any possibility exists for a Type I error. Such an error will be made only when H_0 is true, in which case the probability of a Type I error is α.

Further, since a Type II error is defined as the probability of accepting H_0 when it is false, we arrive at the following conclusions.

1. If H_0 is *true*, the probability of a Type II error is zero.
2. It is only when we *accept* H_0 that any possibility exists for a Type II error. Such an error will be made only when H_0 is false, in which

TABLE 16.4   Type of Error Made as Function of True Status of H_0 and Statistical Decision Made*

		True Status of H_0	
		H_0 True	H_0 False
Decision {	Accept H_0	Correct $1 - \alpha$	Type II error β
	Reject H_0	Type I error α	Correct $1 - \beta$

* To illustrate, if H_0 is true (column 1) and we have rejected H_0 (row 2), we have made a Type I error. If H_0 is false (column 2) and we have rejected H_0, we have made a correct decision.

case the probability of a Type II error is β. It should be clear, then, that the concept of power, which is defined in terms of a Type II error $(1 - \beta)$, applies only when H_0 is not true.

Table 16.4 summarizes the probabilities associated with acceptance or rejection of H_0 depending on the true state of affairs. (Recall that this table was presented in Section 11.5.)

16.10 POWER EFFICIENCY OF A STATISTICAL TEST

In Section 16.6, we pointed out that when the underlying assumptions can be considered valid, parametric tests are more powerful than nonparametric tests for any given N. However, it is also true that when nonparametric tests are to be utilized, we can make any specific nonparametric test as powerful as a parametric test by employing a larger sample size. Thus, test A may be more powerful than test B when the Ns are equal, but B may be as powerful as A when an N of, say, 40 is used as compared to an N of 30 with test A. Such a reduction may arise when different instruments are available to measure the behavior that interests us. One may be a precise quantitative measure that, unfortunately, is expensive and time-consuming to administer. A second may not be as precise—perhaps using ordinal or nominal scales—but has the virtue of permitting many observations at dramatically reduced cost and time commitment. The increased sample size permitted by the alternative measuring instrument may even yield equal or greater power. This is what the concept of **power efficiency** is all about. It is concerned with the increase in sample size that is required to make one test as powerful as a competing test. Let us assume that test

Power Efficiency: The increase in sample size required to make one test as powerful as a competing test.

A is the most powerful for the type of data that we are analyzing. Let us also assume that test B is equal in power to test A when their Ns are 40 and 30, respectively. We let N_b represent the N required to make it as powerful as test A *when N_a is used*. The power efficiency of test B may now be stated:

$$\text{Power efficiency of test B} = 100\,\frac{N_a}{N_b}\% \qquad (16.2)$$

Thus, the power efficiency of test B relative to test A is $100(^{30}\!/_{40})$ or 75%. Therefore, given that all the assumptions for employing test A are met, we shall have to use four cases of test B for every three cases of test A to achieve equal power. Of course, if the assumptions underlying test A are not met, the concept of power efficiency has no meaning, since test A should not be employed.

CHAPTER SUMMARY

In this chapter, we discussed two important concepts: power and power efficiency. Power is defined as the probability of rejecting H_0 when it is actually false; that is, *power* $= 1 - \beta$.

We demonstrated the calculation of power for the one-sample and the two-sample cases when H_0 is known to be false and the true value of the parameter under H_1 is known.

The calculation of power requires that we compute

1. The standard error of the sampling distribution under both H_0 and H_1.
2. The critical value of the sample statistic—$\bar{X}$ in the one-sample case, $\bar{X}_1 - \bar{X}_2$ in the two-sample case.
3. The probability of obtaining this critical value in the sampling distribution under H_1. This probability is the power of the test.

We showed that power varies as a function of

1. Sample size
2. α-level
3. The nature of H_1
4. The nature of the statistical test
5. The use of correlated measures

Power efficiency is concerned with the increase in sample size for a given test that is necessary to make it as powerful as another test employing a smaller N. Symbolically, the power efficiency of test B relative to test A may be represented as

$$\text{Power efficiency of test B} = 100\,\frac{N_a}{N_b}\%$$

TERMS TO REMEMBER

power efficiency   **power of a test**

EXERCISES

1. Test A has a power efficiency of 80% relative to test B. If in test B we employed a total of 24 subjects, what is the N required to achieve equal power with test A?

2. Employing the sample problem in Section 16.3, calculate power when $N = 100$.

3. Employing the sample problem in Section 16.7, demonstrate the effect of the nature of H_1 on power by calculating the power when $\alpha = 0.01$, *one*-tailed test—that is, $H_1 : \mu_1 > \mu_2$.

4. Employ $\alpha = 0.01$, two-tailed test, with the following two normal populations:

$$\mu_1 = 100 \qquad \mu_2 = 90$$

$$\sigma_1 = 10 \qquad \sigma_2 = 10$$

    a. If a sample of 25 cases is drawn from each population, find:
        i. the probability of a Type I error
        ii. the probability of a Type II error
        iii. the power of the test
    b. If two samples of 25 cases each are drawn from population 1, find:
        i. the probability of a Type I error
        ii. the probability of a Type II error
        iii. the power of the test

5. For Problem 6, Chapter 13, calculate the power for each of the four examples, employing $\alpha = 0.01$, one-tailed test. Which of the factors influencing power do these examples illustrate?

6. Occasionally the use of correlated samples produce a t-ratio that is farther removed from the region of rejection than the t-ratio based on independent samples. This would appear to contradict Section 16.8. What could cause this disparity?

7. Explain why power is an economic as well as a research and statistical problem.

8. Why doesn't the concept of power apply when the null hypothesis is true?

9. Explain why a Type I error cannot be made when the null hypothesis is false.

10. Assume that test A is the most powerful test for the data we are analyzing. What is the power efficiency of test B when $N_a = 20$ and the following values of N_b are required to make test B equally powerful?
    a. 25   **b.** 30   **c.** 35   **d.** 40   **e.** 50

11. Summarize the various factors affecting the power of a test. Enumerate the various ways in which power may be increased.

17

Statistical Inference: Categorical Variables

17.1 INTRODUCTION

In recent years there has been a broadening in both the scope and the penetration of research in the behavioral and social sciences. Much provocative and stimulating research has been initiated in diverse areas, such as personality, psychotherapy, group processes, economic forecasts, and so forth. New variables have been added to the arsenal of the researcher, many of which do not lend themselves to traditional parametric statistical treatment, because of either the scales of measurement employed or the flagrant violations of the assumptions of these parametric tests. For these reasons, many new statistical techniques have been developed. In this chapter and the following one, we present a few choice dishes in the extensive nonparametric menu. See the table on page 468 for nonparametric tests that appear in Chapters 17 and 18 as well as several parametric tests of significance that appeared earlier in the text. Tests in parentheses are not covered.

> A nonparametric test of significance is defined as one that makes no assumptions concerning the shape of the parent distribution or population, and accordingly is commonly referred to as a distribution-free test of significance.

Scale of Measurement	One-Sample Case	Two-Sample Case	
		Related Samples	Independent Samples
Nominal	Binomial test Sections 17.2–17.3 χ² test Section 17.4	(McNemar test for significance of change)	χ² test Sections 17.5–17.6
Ordinal	(Kolmogorov-Smirnov one-sample test)	Sign test Section 18.4	
	(One-sample runs test)	Wilcoxon matched-pairs signed-rank test Section 18.5	Mann-Whitney U Section 18.2
Interval/Ratio	Student's t Section 12.5	Student's t Section 13.7	Student's t Section 13.3 z-statistic Section 13.1

Parametric techniques are usually preferable because of their greater sensitivity, that is, they are more likely to lead to the rejection of H_0 when it is actually false. This generalization is not true, however, when the underlying assumptions are seriously violated. Indeed, under certain circumstances (e.g., badly skewed distributions, particularly with small sample sizes), a nonparametric test may well be as powerful as its parametric counterpart.* Consequently, the researcher is frequently faced with the difficult choice of a statistical test appropriate for his or her data.

At this point let us interject a word of caution with respect to the choice of statistical tests of inference. For heuristic purposes, we take a few sample problems and subject them to statistical analyses employing several different tests of significance. This procedure will serve to clarify points of difference among the various tests. However, you may inadvertently draw an erroneous conclusion, namely, that researchers first collect their data, then "shop around" for a statistical test that will be the most sensitive to any differences that exist. Actually, nothing could be further from the truth. The null hypothesis, alternative hypothesis, statistical test, sampling distribution, and level of significance should all be specified in *advance* of the collection of data. If we "shop around," so to speak, after the collection of the data,

---

* Numerous investigators have demonstrated the robustness of the t and F tests; that is, even substantial departures from the assumptions underlying parametric tests do not seriously affect the validity of statistical inferences. For articles dealing with this topic, see Haber, Runyon, and Badia, *Readings in Statistics*. Reading, Mass.: Addison-Wesley Publishing Co., Inc. 1970.

BOX 17.1

DOGS: THE BEST FRIEND OF A CORONARY PATIENT?

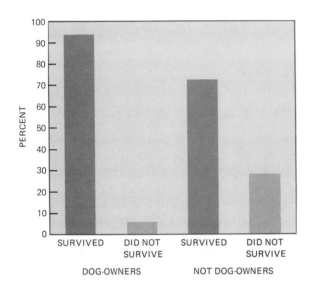

The cliché "Dog is man's best friend" is celebrated in both song and legend. Recent evidence suggests that the presence of a dog may also be therapeutic (Friedman, 1978). A group of coronary patients were studied for one year following their release from the hospital. Of these patients, 53 owned dogs and 39 did not. One year later, 11 of the patients who did not own dogs had died, whereas only three of the dog owners succumbed.

In this study there are two nominal variables—status with respect to ownership of a pet dog and survival record after suffering a coronary heart dis-ease. There are two values of each variable: owning vs. not owning a dog, and surviving vs. not surviving a heart condition. At the descriptive level, we could determine the percent of pet owners versus the percent of non-pet owners who survived and failed to survive at least one year following hospitalization. These results are summarized in the bar graph at the left.

At the inferential level, the data can be cast in the form of a 2 × 2 contingency table. Reading downward, we see that 50 of 53 dog owners survived at least one year. In contrast, only 28 of 39 non-dog owners enjoyed a similar survival record. The appropriate test of significance—the chi square test—permits us to ascertain whether or not dog ownership and survival are related.

2 × 2 Contingency Table Showing Number of Dog Owners and Number of Non-Dog Owners Who Survived at Least One Year Following Onset of a Coronary Disease

Survival Status	Status of Dog Ownership		
	Owners	Not Owners	Totals
Survived one year	50	28	78
Did not survive	3	11	14
Totals	53	39	92

Source: Friedman, E. "Pet Ownership and Coronary Heart Disease Patient Survival." *Circulation,* 1978, *168,* 57–58.

we tend to maximize the effects of any chance differences that favor one test over another. As a result, the possibility of a Type I error (rejecting the null hypothesis when it is true) is substantially increased.

Usually, we do not have the problem of choosing statistical tests in relation to categorical variables because nonparametric tests alone are suitable for enumerative data. Even here, however, parametric estimation tests are available when N is sufficiently large.

When our scales of measurement are either interval or ratio, the problem of choosing a statistical treatment usually arises when we employ small samples* and/or when there is doubt concerning the normality of the underlying population distribution. In Chapter 18, we shall demonstrate several nonparametric statistical tests employed when such doubts arise.

17.2 THE BINOMIAL TEST

Two-Category (Dichotomous) Population: Simplest form of nominal scale, containing two classes or categories.

In Section 2.4, when discussing various scales of measurement, we pointed out that the observation of unordered variables constitutes the lowest level of measurement. In turn, the simplest form of nominal scale is one that contains only two classes or categories, and is referred to variously as a **two-category** or **dichotomous population.** Examples of two-category populations are numerous: male and female, right and wrong on a test item, married and single, juvenile delinquent and nondelinquent, literate and illiterate. Some of these populations may be thought of as inherently dichotomous (e.g., male versus female) and therefore are not subject to measurement on a higher-level numerical scale, whereas others (e.g., literate and illiterate) may be thought of as continuous, varying from the absence of the quality under observation to different degrees of its manifestation. Obviously, whenever possible, the data we collect should be at the highest level of measurement that we can achieve. However, for a variety of reasons, we cannot always scale a variable at the ordinal level or higher. Nevertheless, we are often called upon to collect nominally scaled data and to draw inferences from these data.

In a two-category population, we define P as the proportion of cases in one class and $Q = 1 - P$ as the proportion in the other class.

Use of the binomial sampling distribution to test hypotheses concerning the value of P under H_0 was demonstrated in Chapter 11. For illustrative purposes, we restricted our discussion to $H_0 : P = Q = \frac{1}{2}$. However, it is possible to test hypotheses concerning *any* value of P.

The probabilities associated with specific outcomes may be obtained by employing Formula (17.1):

$$p(x) = \frac{N!}{x!\,(N - x)!}\,P^x Q^{N-x} \tag{17.1}$$

---

*When large samples are employed, the parametric tests are almost always appropriate because of the *central limit theorem* (Section 12.2).

where

x = the number of objects in one category or the number of successes

$N - x$ = the number of objects in the remaining category or the number of failures

N = the total number of objects or total number of trials

$p(x)$ = the probability of x objects in one category

$!$ = the factorial sign, directing us to multiply the indicated value by all integers less than it but greater than zero; for example, if $N = 5$, $N!* = 5 \cdot 4 \cdot 3 \cdot 2 \cdot 1 = 120$

A sample problem should serve to illustrate the use of Formula (17.1) in the testing of hypotheses.

Sample Problem

The dean of students in a large university claims that since the sale of cigarettes was prohibited on campus, the proportion of students who smoke has dropped to 0.30. However, previous observations at other institutions where the sale of cigarettes had been banned found little effect on smoking behavior; that is, far greater than 0.30 of the students continue to smoke.

Nine students, selected at random, are asked to indicate whether or not they smoke. Six of these students respond in the affirmative.

To test the validity of the dean's claim, we let P represent the proportion of students in the population who smoke, and Q, the proportion of students who do not smoke.

1. *Null hypothesis* (H_0): $P \leq 0.30$, $Q \geq 0.70$.
2. *Alternative hypothesis* (H_1): $P > 0.30$, $Q < 0.70$. Note that H_1 is directional.
3. *Statistical test:* Since we are dealing with a two-category population, the binomial test is appropriate.
4. *Significance level:* $\alpha = 0.05$.
5. *Sampling distribution:* The sampling distribution is given by the binomial expansion, Formula (17.1).
6. *Critical region:* The critical region consists of all values of x that are so large that the probability of their occurrence under H_0 is less than or equal to 0.05. Since H_1 is directional, the critical region is one-tailed.

In order to determine whether the obtained x lies in the critical region, we must obtain the sum of the probabilities associated with $x = 9$, $x = 8$, $x = 7$, and $x = 6$.

---

* In obtaining the binomial probabilities, we must remember that $0! = 1$ and that any value other than zero raised to the zero power equals 1, that is, $X^0 = 1$.

To illustrate, employing Formula (17.1) we find that the probability of $x = 9$—that is, if $P = 0.3$ (under H_0), the probability that all the 9 students smoke—is

$$p(9) = \frac{9!}{9!(9-9)!}(0.3)^9(0.7)^{9-9}$$

$$= 0.3^9 = 0.000019683$$

The probability of $x = 8$ is

$$p(8) = 9(0.3)^8(0.7)^1 = 0.000413343$$

The probability of $x = 7$ is

$$p(7) = 36(0.3)^7(0.7)^2 = 0.003857868$$

Finally, the probability of $x = 6$ is

$$p(6) = 84(0.3)^6(0.7)^3 = 0.021003948$$

Thus, the probability that at least 6 out of 9 students smoke when $P = 0.30$ is the sum of the preceding probabilities, that is, $p(x \geq 6) = 0.025$.

Decision. Since the obtained probability is less than 0.05, we may reject H_0. In other words, the dean's claim would appear to be in error.

The preceding example was offered to illustrate the application of Formula (17.1) when $P \neq Q \neq \frac{1}{2}$. However, when $N \leq 49$, and $P \neq Q \neq \frac{1}{2}$, Table N, in the Table section, may be employed to obtain the critical values of x directly for selected values of P and Q. Referring to Table N, for $N = 9$ and $P = 0.30$, we find that x must be equal to or greater than 6 to reject H_0 at $\alpha = 0.05$.

Incidentally, when $P = Q = \frac{1}{2}$ and $N \leq 50$, Table M provides both one- and two-tailed critical values of x, at $\alpha = 0.01$ and $\alpha = 0.05$, when x is defined as the larger of the observed frequencies. For example, if we toss a coin ten times $(N = 10)$, we find that a critical value of $x = 9$ is required for rejection of H_0 $(P = Q = \frac{1}{2})$ at $\alpha = 0.05$, two-tailed test.

The Probability of No Events Favoring an Outcome

You may recall the display in Table 10.7, the probability that Charleston and its environs would again be struck by at least one hurricane during the next year, or 10, 20, 50, 75, or 100 years into the future. These were empirical probability estimates, based on historical records that showed two hurricanes in slightly less than 100 years. From this we estimated that the single-year probability of a hurricane is 0.02 and the single-year probability of no hurricane (i.e., the probability of nonoccurrence) is 0.98. To determine the probability that at least one hurricane (i.e., one or more) will occur during a specific time period, you calculate the probability that none will strike during that period. Then, you subtract this probability from 1 to obtain the probability that one or more hurricanes will occur during this period.

To illustrate, what is the probability that Charleston will have at least one hurricane during the next 15-year period? The probability that none will occur is $0.98^{15} = 0.74$. Therefore, the probability that at least one will occur is $1 - 0.74 = 0.26$. Incidentally, if you have a calculator that includes the exponential function (displayed variously as x^n, y^n, y^x, etc.), the calculations are simple. Enter the probability of the nonoccurrence of the event (0.98), depress the exponential key, enter the number of years of interest (15), then depress the equals $(=)$ key. You should see 0.7385691025 in the display. Now strike the $+/-$ key to change this value to negative. Then depress $+1$. You should obtain 0.2614308974, which rounds to 0.26. Thus, if the single-year estimate is accurate, the chances are about 1 in 4 that Charleston will experience another hurricane within the next decade and a half.

A word of caution is in order. The probability estimate is based on observing hurricanes over only one 100-year period and may or may not accurately reflect the long-term probabilities. But, as is often the case, it is the best we can do with the amount of information available. As more information is added to our data base, our ability to predict future events will presumably improve commensurately.

17.3 NORMAL-CURVE APPROXIMATION TO BINOMIAL VALUES

As N increases, the binomial distribution approaches the normal distribution. The approximation is more rapid as P and Q approach $\frac{1}{2}$. On the other hand, as P or Q approaches 0, the approximation to the normal curve becomes poorer for any given N. A good rule of thumb to follow, when considering the normal-curve approximation to the binomial, is that the product NPQ should equal at least 9 when P approaches 0 or 1, and N should equal 25 or greater when $P = Q = \frac{1}{2}$. Even with somewhat smaller Ns, however, the approximation is excellent. Accepting these restrictions, we see that the sampling distribution of x, defined as the number of objects in one category, is normal, with a mean equal to NP and a standard deviation equal to $\sqrt{NPQ}$.

To test the null hypothesis, we put x into standardized form:

$$z = \frac{x - NP}{\sqrt{NPQ}} \tag{17.2}$$

The distribution of the z-scores is approximately normal, with a mean equal to zero and a standard deviation equal to one. Thus, the probability of any given x equals the probability of its corresponding z-score.

Let us look at an example in which $x = 5$, $N = 20$, $P = Q = \frac{1}{2}$, and $\alpha = 0.05$, two-tailed test. To obtain the probability of $x \leq 5$, we put x into standardized form and we have

$$z = \frac{5 - 10}{\sqrt{(20)(0.5)(0.5)}}$$

$$= \frac{-5.00}{\sqrt{5.00}} = \frac{-5.00}{2.236} = -2.24$$

Recall that $|z| \geq |1.96|$ is required for significance at $\alpha = 0.05$, two-tailed test. Since our obtained z of -2.24 exceeds the critical value, we may reject H_0.

Note that if we look up the result in Table M under $N = 20$ and $\alpha = 0.05$, two-tailed test, we find that $N - x \geq 15$ is required to reject H_0. In the present problem, $N - x = 15$, so we reject the null hypothesis and assert H_1. This is precisely the same decision we make when using the normal approximation to binomial values. Since Table M presents critical values through $N = 50$, we recommend using the normal approximation to the binomial only when N exceeds 50.

17.4 THE χ^2 ONE-VARIABLE CASE

Following a course in research methods, 86 nursing students completed a course-evaluation questionnaire that was administered to the entire class (Van Bree, 1981). One item in the questionnaire dealt with the importance of research to the nursing profession. The following results were obtained:

| | | | Student Response | | |
	Item	Strongly Agree	Agree	Undecided	Disagree	Strongly Disagree
Research is important to nursing profession		34	41	7	3	1

Source: N. S. Van Bree. "Undergraduate Research." *Nursing Outlook,* January 1981, 39–41.

One-Variable Test ("Goodness-of-Fit") Technique): Test of whether or not a significant difference exists between the *observed* number of cases falling into each category and the *expected* number of cases, based on the null hypothesis.

This is the type of problem for which the χ^{2*} **one-variable test** is ideally suited. In single-variable applications, the χ^2 test has been described as a **"goodness-of-fit" technique:** It permits us to determine whether or not a significant difference exists between the *observed* number of cases falling into each category and the *expected* number of cases, based on the null

---

* The symbol χ^2 will be used to denote the test of significance as well as the quantity obtained from applying the test to observed frequencies, whereas the word "chi-square" will refer to the theoretical chi-square distribution.

hypothesis. In other words, it permits us to answer the question, "How well does our observed distribution fit the theoretical distribution?"

What we require, then, is a null hypothesis that allows us to specify the expected frequencies in each category and, subsequently, a test of this null hypothesis. The null hypothesis may be tested by

$$\chi^2 = \sum_{i=1}^{k} \frac{(f_0 - f_e)^2}{f_e} \tag{17.3}$$

where

$$f_0 = \text{the observed number in a given category}$$
$$f_e = \text{the expected number in that category}$$
$$\sum_{i=1}^{k} = \text{directs us to sum this ratio over all } k \text{ categories}$$

As is readily apparent, if there is close agreement between the observed frequencies and the expected frequencies, the resulting χ^2 will be small, leading to a failure to reject the null hypothesis. As the discrepancy $(f_0 - f_e)$ increases, the value of χ^2 increases. The larger the χ^2 is, the more likely we are to reject the null hypothesis.

In our example, the null hypothesis would be that there is an equal preference for each response category; that is, $\frac{86}{5} = 17.2$ is the expected frequency in each category. Thus

$$\chi^2 = \frac{(34 - 17.2)^2}{17.2} + \frac{(41 - 17.2)^2}{17.2} + \frac{(7 - 17.2)^2}{17.2} + \frac{(3 - 17.2)^2}{17.2} + \frac{(1 - 17.2)^2}{17.2}$$

$$= 16.409 + 32.933 + 6.049 + 11.723 + 15.258$$

$$= 82.372$$

In studying Student's t-ratio (Section 12.5), we saw that the sampling distributions of t varied as a function of degrees of freedom. The same is true for χ^2. However, assignments of degrees of freedom with the t-ratio are based on N, whereas for χ^2 the degrees of freedom are a function of the number of categories (k). In the one-variable case, df $= k - 1$.* Table B lists the critical values of χ^2 for various α levels. If the obtained χ^2 value exceeds the critical value at a given probability level, the null hypothesis may be rejected at that level of significance.

In this example, $k = 5$. Therefore, df $= 4$. Employing $\alpha = 0.01$, we find that Table B indicates that a χ^2 value of 13.277 or greater is required for significance. Since our obtained value of 82.372 is greater than 4.604, we may reject the null hypothesis and assert instead that each response

---

* Since the marginal total is fixed, only $k - 1$ categories are free to vary. Given that the total is 86, as soon as four cells or categories are filled, the fifth is completely determined. Thus, there are only four degrees of freedom.

category was not equally preferred. Incidentally, we are free to investigate any form of hypothetical distribution suggested by prior research or theoretical considerations. If we had prior reason to suspect that the distribution might be 0.25, 0.25, 0.20, 0.20, 0.10, we could investigate this H_0 by multiplying each hypothesized proportion by N in order to obtain the expected frequency in each cell.

17.5   THE χ^2 TEST OF THE INDEPENDENCE OF CATEGORICAL VARIABLES*

So far in this chapter, we have been concerned with the one-variable case. In practice, we do not encounter the one-variable case too frequently when employing categorical variables. More often we ask questions concerning the interrelationships between and among variables. For example, we may ask:

1. Is there a difference in the crime rate of children coming from different socioeconomic backgrounds? (In other words, is crime rate independent of socioeconomic background, or does it depend in part on this background?)
2. If we are conducting an opinion poll, can we determine whether there is a difference between males and females in their opinions about a given issue? (Stated another way, does the opinion on a given issue depend to any extent on the gender of the respondent?)

These are but two examples of problems for which the χ^2 technique has an application. You could undoubtedly extend this list to include many campus activities, such as attitudes of fraternity brothers versus nonfraternity students toward certain basic issues (e.g., cheating on exams), or differences in grading practices among professors in various departments of study. All these problems have some things in common: (1) They deal with two or more nominal categories in which (2) the data consist of a frequency count that is tabulated and placed in the appropriate cells.

These examples also share an additional and more important characteristic: (3) There is no immediately obvious way to assign expected frequency values to each category. However, as we shall point out shortly, what we must do is base our expected frequencies on the obtained frequencies themselves.

Let's take a look at an actual example. Visitors to developing nations frequently experience an acute intestinal affliction that is variously referred

---

* Most textbooks recommend the Yates correction for continuity and that expected cell frequencies equal or exceed 5 when df = 1. Based on convincing evidence (Dunlap, 1974; Camilli and Hopkins, 1978), we have dropped these recommendations in this edition. This correction consists of subtracting 0.5 from the absolute value of $f_o - f_e$ prior to squaring.

to as Montezuma's Revenge, Delhi Belly, Galloping Gollies, or mundanely, Traveler's Diarrhea. Indeed, the anticipation of traveling to distant lands is often dimmed by the relatively high risk of spending much of the vacation sightseeing in the toilet. A team of medical researchers recently evaluated the effectiveness of a drug called doxycycline in curbing the incidence of this disorder. A total of 39 Peace Corps volunteers in Kenya participated in the study. Over a 3-week period, 18 received the actual drug, whereas the remaining 21 volunteers were given a placebo—an inert substance that resembled the drug. The results of this study are summarized in Table 17.1. We must now apply a test of significance. In formal statistical terms:

1. *Null hypothesis* (H_0): There is no difference in the incidence of Traveler's Diarrhea among those receiving the drug and those receiving the placebo.
2. *Alternative hypothesis* (H_1): There is a difference in the incidence of the disorder among drug and placebo subjects.
3. *Statistical test:* Since the two groups (drug and placebo) are independent and the data are in terms of frequencies in discrete categories, the χ^2 test of independence is the appropriate statistical test.
4. *Significance level:* $\alpha = 0.05$.
5. *Sampling distribution:* The sampling distribution is the chi-square distribution with df $= (r - 1)(c - 1)$.

   Since marginal totals are fixed, the frequency of only one cell is free to vary. Therefore, we have a one-degree-of-freedom situation. The general rule for finding df in the two-variable case is $(r - 1)(c - 1)$, in which r = number of rows and c = number of columns. Thus, in the present example, df $= (2 - 1)(2 - 1) = 1$.

TABLE 17.1 2 × 2 Contingency Table, Showing Number of Volunteers in Drug and Placebo Groups Contracting Traveler's Diarrhea over 3-Week Period

Experimental Condition	Outcome of Study		Totals
	Contracted Disorder	Failed to Contract Disorder	
Drug group	(a) 1	(b) 17	18
Placebo group	(c) 9	(d) 12	21
Totals	10	29	39

6. *Critical region:* Table B shows that for df $= 1$, $\alpha = 0.05$, the critical region consists of all values of $\chi^2 \geq 3.84$. χ^2 is calculated from the formula

$$\chi^2 = \sum_{r=1}^{r} \sum_{c=1}^{c} \frac{(f_o - f_e)^2}{f_e} \qquad (17.4)$$

where

$$\sum_{r=1}^{r} \sum_{c=1}^{c}$$

directs us to sum this ratio over both rows and columns.

The *main problem* now is to decide on a basis for determining the expected cell frequencies. Let us concentrate for a moment on cell (a). The two marginal totals common to cell (a) are row 1 marginal and column 1 marginal. If the null hypothesis is correct, and the incidence of the disorder is independent of condition, we would expect the same proportion of subjects in the drug group to contract the disorder as subjects in the placebo group. Since 18 of the total sample of 39 are in the drug condition, we would expect that (18/39) × 10 would be found in cell (a). This figure comes to 4.62.

Since we have a one-degree-of-freedom situation, the expected frequencies in all the remaining cells are determined as soon as we have calculated one expected cell frequency. Consequently, we obtain all the remaining expected cell frequencies by subtracting from the appropriate marginal totals. Thus, cell (b) is 18 − 4.62 or 13.38, cell (c) is 10 − 4.62 or 5.38, and cell (d) is 29 − 13.38 or 15.62. To make certain that no error was made in our original calculation of the expected frequency for cell (a), we independently calculate the expected frequency for *any* of the remaining cells. If this figure agrees with the result we obtained by subtraction, we may feel confident that we made no error. Thus, the expected frequency for cell (d), obtained through direct calculation, is

$$\frac{21}{39} \times 29 = 15.62$$

Since this figure does agree with the result obtained by subtraction, we may proceed with our calculation of the χ^2 value.

Incidentally, you may have noted that there is a simple rule that may be followed in determining expected frequency of a given cell: You multiply the marginal frequencies that are common to that cell and divide by N.

Table 17.2 presents the obtained data, with the expected cell frequencies in the lower right-hand corner of each cell.

TABLE 17.2   Number of Volunteers in Drug and Placebo Groups Contracting Traveler's Diarrhea over 3-Week Period*

Experimental Condition	Outcome of Study		Totals
	Contracted Disorder	Failed to Contract Disorder	
Drug group	1 (4.62)	17 (13.38)	18
Placebo group	9 (5.38)	12 (15.62)	21
Totals	10	29	

* Expected frequencies are within parentheses.

Now, all that remains is to calculate the χ^2 value.

It can be seen that a total of ten subjects became ill. Of these, only one was in the drug condition. The remaining nine were in the control or placebo group. Is this difference sufficiently large to justify the conclusion that the drug was effective?

$$\chi^2 = \frac{(1 - 4.62)^2}{4.62} + \frac{(17 - 13.38)^2}{13.38} + \frac{(9 - 5.38)^2}{5.38} + \frac{(12 - 15.62)^2}{15.62} = 7.09$$

Since the χ^2 value of 7.09 is greater than 3.84, which is required for significance at the 0.05 level, we may reject H_0. In other words, we may conclude that the drug is effective in curbing the incidence of Traveler's Diarrhea.*

In research we often find that we have more than two subgroups within a nominal class. For example, we might have three categories in one scale and four in another, resulting in a 3 × 4 contingency table. The procedure for obtaining the expected frequencies is the same as the one for the 2 × 2 contingency table. Of course, the degrees of freedom will be greater than 1 (e.g., for a 3 × 4 contingency table, df = 6).

---

* Had the correction for continuity been applied, the obtained χ^2 would have been

$$\chi^2 = \frac{(|1 - 4.62| - 0.5)^2}{4.62} + \frac{(|17 - 13.38| - 0.5)^2}{13.38} + \frac{(|9 - 5.38| - 0.5)^2}{5.38} + \frac{(|12 - 15.62| - 0.5)^2}{15.62}$$

$$= 2.107 + 0.728 + 1.809 + 0.623 = 5.267$$

CASE EXAMPLE 17.1

The Successful Women

With the relatively recent changes in the traditional female sex roles, much attention has been directed to the possible impact of these changes on various aspects of the behavior and emotions of contemporary women. In this study, 33 women completed Horner's scale of fear of success (FOS), as well as other questionnaires aimed at tapping attitudes about sex-role traditionalism, political beliefs, and educational levels.

In one facet of the study, the women were subdivided into two groups—those with fear of success (FOS) and those without fear of success (no-FOS). They were further subdivided in terms of educational level. The results are summarized in Table 17.3.

Let's test the null hypothesis that there is no difference in fear of success by educational level against the alternative hypothesis that there is a difference. We shall use $\alpha = 0.05$.

TABLE 17.3 Relationship between FOS and Educational Level

Educational Level	FOS	No-FOS	Total
Less than BA	6	8	14
BA degree	6	1	7
Some graduate school	10	1	11
Column totals	22	10	32

TABLE 17.4 Expected Cell Frequencies in Study of Relationship between FOS and Educational Level

Educational Level	FOS	No-FOS	Total
Less than BA	9.62	4.38	14
BA degree	4.81	2.19	7
Some graduate school	7.57	3.43	11
Column totals	22	10	32

$$\chi^2 = \frac{(6 - 9.62)^2}{9.62} + \frac{(8 - 4.38)^2}{4.38} + \cdots + \frac{(1 - 3.43)^2}{3.43}$$

$$= 7.797$$

$$df = (r - 1)(c - 1) = 2$$

The expected cell frequencies are shown in Table 17.4.

The critical value at $\alpha = 0.05$ with df $= 2$ is 5.991. Since the obtained χ^2 exceeds this value, we may reject H_0 and assert H_1. Examination of the data reveals a clear-cut tendency for fear of success to increase with increasing educational level. Note that this study is not a true experiment, but is more in the nature of a correlational investigation. Although we can conclude that there is a statistically significant increase in FOS with educational level, we cannot make a strong statement of causality. Several possibilities present themselves, one of which is that the more educated women are employed at levels that put them into competition with men, the more they may demand of themselves.

Source: Based on Carmen M. Caballero, Patricia Giles, and Phillip Shaver (1975), "Sex-Role Traditionalism and Fear of Success," *Sex Roles*, **1**(4), 319–326.

17.6 LIMITATIONS IN THE USE OF χ^2

A fundamental assumption in the use of χ^2 is that each observation or frequency is independent of all other observations. Consequently, one may not make several observations of the same individual and treat each as though it were independent of all the other observations. Such an error produces what is referred to as an **inflated N,** that is, you are treating the data as though you had a greater number of independent observations than you actually have. This error is extremely serious and may easily lead to the rejection of the null hypothesis when it is in fact true.

Consider the following hypothetical example. Imagine that you are a student in a sociology course and that as a class project you decide to poll the student body to determine whether male and female students differ in their opinions on an issue of contemporary significance. Each of 15 members of the class is asked to obtain replies from 10 respondents, 5 male and 5 female. The results are listed in Table 17.5.

Inflated N: An error produced whenever several observations are made on the same individual and treated as though they were independent observations.

TABLE 17.5

Sex	Response to Question		
	Approve	Disapprove	
Male	30	45	75
	(40)	(35)	
Female	50	25	75
	(40)	(35)	
	80	70	150

$$\chi^2 = 10.71$$

TABLE 17.6

Sex	Response to Question		
	Approve	Disapprove	
Male	28	37	65
	(32.5)	(32.5)	
Female	32	23	55
	(27.5)	(27.5)	
	60	60	120

$$\chi^2 = 2.72$$

Employing $\alpha = 0.05$, we find that the critical region consists of all the values of $\chi^2 \geq 3.84$. Since the obtained χ^2 of 10.71 > 3.84, you reject the null hypothesis of no difference in the opinions of male and female students on the issue in question. You conclude instead that approval of the issue is dependent on the sex of the respondent.

Subsequent to the study, you discover that a number of students were inadvertently polled as many as two or three times by different members of the class. Consequently, the frequencies within the cells are not independent since some individuals had contributed as many as two or three responses. In a reanalysis of the data, in which only one frequency per respondent was permitted, you obtain the results shown in Table 17.6.

Note that now the obtained χ^2 of 2.72 < 3.84; thus, you must accept H_0. The failure to achieve independence of responses resulted in a serious error in the original conclusion. Incidentally, you should note that the requirement of independence within a cell or condition is basic to *all* statistical tests. We have mentioned this specifically in connection with the χ^2 test because violations may be very subtle and not easily recognized.

17.7 PUTTING IT ALL TOGETHER

In Chapters 1 and 2 (Sections 1.7 and 2.8), we looked at an impressive bit of statistical sleuthing in the mysterious case of dental enamel erosion among some members of a private club in Charlottesville, Virginia. Recall that a survey and follow-up dental examination ascertained the frequency of dental enamel erosion of frequent versus nonfrequent swimmers. The results are shown in Table 17.7. We wish to test the null hypothesis that the incidence of dental enamel erosion is the same among frequent and nonfrequent swimmers. Use $\alpha = 0.01$, two-tailed test to ascertain the validity of H_0.

1. Find the expected number in any cell by multiplying together the marginal frequencies common to that cell and dividing by N. To

TABLE 17.7   **Relative Frequency Table of Frequent and Nonfrequent Swimmers Evidencing and Failing to Evidence Erosion of Dental Enamel***

	Evidence of Dental Enamel Erosion		Row Totals
	No	**Yes**	
Frequent swimmers	383 (404.80)	69 (47.20)	452
Nonfrequent swimmers	286 (264.20)	9 (30.80)	295
Column totals	669	78	747

* Expected numbers shown in parentheses.
Source: Erosion and Dental Enamel among Competitive Swimmers—Virginia (1983), *Morbidity and Mortality Weekly Report,* July 22, **32**(20).

obtain the expected frequency in the cell in the upper left-hand quadrant, for example, multiply 452 by 669 and divide by 747. This comes to 404.80.

2. The remaining expected frequencies may be obtained in the same way or by subtraction. Thus, to obtain the expected frequency in the lower left-hand quadrant, subtract 404.80 from 669 to obtain 264.20 [also, as a check, $(295 \times 669)/747 = 264.20$]. The remaining expected frequencies are shown in Table 17.7.

3. Subtract the expected frequency in each cell from the obtained frequency for that cell, square, and divide by the expected frequency. Add the four values together to obtain χ^2:

$$\frac{(383 - 404.80)^2}{404.80} + \frac{(69 - 47.20)^2}{47.20} + \frac{(286 - 264.20)^2}{264.20}$$
$$+ \frac{(9 - 30.80)^2}{30.80} = 28.48 \qquad df = 1$$

Referring to Table B in the Table section, we find that the critical value of χ^2 at $\alpha = 0.01$ is 6.635. Since the obtained χ^2 exceeds this value, we reject H_0 and assert that enamel erosion is significantly higher among frequent swimmers.

CHAPTER SUMMARY

In this chapter, we have discussed four tests of significance employed with categorical variables—that is, the binomial test, the normal approximation to the binomial, the χ^2 one-variable test, and the χ^2 two-variable test.

1. We saw that the binomial may be employed to test null hypotheses when frequency counts are distributed between two categories or cells. When $P = Q = \frac{1}{2}$ and when $N \leq 50$, Table M provides both one- and two-tailed critical values for $\alpha = 0.05$ and $\alpha = 0.01$. When $P \neq Q$, probabilities may be obtained by employing Formula (17.1), which is based on the binomial expansion. When $N \leq 49$, Table N provides the critical values for the selected values of P and Q. A rule of thumb is that NPQ must equal or exceed 9 as P approaches 0 or 1, to permit the use of the normal approximation to the binomial.

2. The χ^2 one-variable test has been described as a goodness-of-fit technique, permitting us to determine whether or not a significant difference exists between the *observed* number of cases appearing in each category and the *expected* number of cases specified under the null hypothesis.

3. The χ^2 two-variable case may be employed to determine whether two variables are related or independent. If the χ^2 value is significant, we may conclude that the variables are dependent, or related. In this chapter, we restricted our discussion to the 2×2 contingency table. However, the procedures are easily extended to include more than two categories within each variable.

4. Finally, we discussed an important limitation on the use of the χ^2 test: The frequency counts must be independent of one another. Failure to meet this requirement results in an error known as the *inflated N* and may well lead to the rejection of the null hypothesis when it is true (Type I error).

TERMS TO REMEMBER

inflated *N*

one-variable test (goodness-of-fit technique)

two-category (dichotomous) population

EXERCISES

1. In 9 tosses of a single coin:
   a. What is the probability of obtaining exactly 7 heads?
   b. What is the probability of obtaining as many as 8 heads?
   c. What is the probability of obtaining a result as rare as 8 heads?

2. A revelation to many students is the surprisingly low probability of obtaining a passing grade on multiple-choice examinations when the selection of alternatives is made purely on a chance basis (i.e., without any knowledge of the material covered on the exam). If 60% is considered a passing grade on a 40-item multiple-choice test, determine the probability of passing when there are
   a. four alternatives   **b.** three alternatives   **c.** two alternatives

3. In reference to Exercise 4, Chapter 14, show how Table N might be employed to determine the critical values of various numbers of successes (i.e., rejection of H_0 at $\alpha = 0.05$) out of ten attempts.

4. A study was conducted in which three groups of rats (5 per group) were reinforced under three different schedules of reinforcement (100% reinforcement, 50% reinforcement, 25% reinforcement). The number of bar-pressing responses obtained during extinction are shown as follows:

100%	50%	25%
615	843	545

Criticize the use of chi-square as the appropriate statistical technique.

5. The World Series may last from four to seven games. During the period 1922 to 1989, the distribution of the number of games played per series was as follows:

Number of games	4	5	6	7
Frequency of occurrence	11	15	13	29

For these data, test the hypothesis that each number of games is equally likely to occur.

6. In a large eastern university, a study of the composition of the student council reveals that 6 of its 8 members are political science majors. In the entire student body of 1200 students, 400 are political science majors. Set up this study in formal statistical terms and draw the appropriate conclusions.

7. A study was conducted to determine if there is a relationship between socioeconomic class and attitudes toward a new urban-renewal program. The results are listed as follows:

Socioeconomic Class	Disapprove	Approve
Middle	90	60
Lower	200	100

Set up this study in formal statistical terms and draw the appropriate conclusion.

8. Construct the sampling distribution of the binomial when $P = 0.20$, $Q = 0.80$, and $N = 6$.

9. Out of 300 castings on a given mold, 27 were found to be defective. Another mold produced 31 defective castings in 500. Determine whether there is a significant difference in the proportion of defective castings produced by the two molds.

10. Employ the χ^2 test, one-variable case for the example shown in Section 17.3 of the text. Verify that $\chi^2 = z^2$ in the one-degree-of-freedom situation.

11. In a study concerned with preferences of packaging for potato chips, 100 people in a high-income group and 200 people in a lower-income group were interviewed. The results of their choices follow:

Preference Stated	Upper-Income Group	Lower-Income Group
Prefer metallic package	36	84
Prefer waxed-paper package	39	51
Prefer cellophane package	16	44
Have no preference	9	21

What conclusions would you draw from these data?

12. Suppose that 100 random drawings with replacement from a deck of cards produced 28 hearts, 19 clubs, 31 diamonds, and 22 spades. Would you consider these results unusual?

13. In polling 46 interviewees drawn at random from a specified population, we find that 28 favor and 18 oppose a certain routing of a highway. Test the hypothesis that the sample was drawn from a population in which $P = Q = \frac{1}{2}$. Use $\alpha = 0.05$, two-tailed test.

14. Suppose a study was conducted that compared the types of investments made by 115 persons who were considered conservative and 125 individuals who were judged as likely to take risks. What can you conclude from the following results:

Type of Investment	Type of Investor	
	Conservative	Risk-taker
Government bonds	75	45
Stocks	40	80

15. Suppose a company manufactured an equal number of three different file cabinets. The capacity of each cabinet was equal, but the designs were different. The first 300 buyers ordered 125 of Type A, 100 of Type B, and 75 of Type C. Should the company continue to produce an equal number of each design?

16. In Exercise 15, if the first 300 buyers ordered 115 cabinets of Type A, 95 of Type B, and 90 of Type C, should the company continue its present production policy?

17. Assume you are testing a die to determine if it is biased. With 90 tosses, you obtain 13 ones, 18 twos, 13 threes, 23 fours, 9 fives, and 14 sixes. What would you conclude?

18. In Exercise 17, suppose you wanted to compare the number of times a toss shows an odd number with the number of times it is even. Using the z-score, can you conclude that the die is unbiased?

19. Use the χ^2 test to determine the answers for Exercise 18.

20. Suppose that a recording company is interested in the type of cover to put on an album. It sends the same record with three different covers to a store. At the end of a month, it has found that the following number of albums have been sold:

Type A Cover	Type B Cover	Type C Cover
41	50	20

Is the company in a position to determine which type of cover it should use?

21. In Chapter 1, Exercise 4, we reported a study by Professor Yetman showing the number of white and black athletes who had an opportunity to appear in commercials. The following 2 × 2 table summarizes the results:

Racial Background of Athletes	Appearance in Commercials	
	No Opportunity	Opportunity
White	3	8
Nonwhite	11	2

Test the null hypothesis that opportunity to appear in commercials is independent of racial background (i.e., whites and nonwhites have an equal opportunity to appear).

22. Using the data presented at the beginning of this chapter, test the null hypothesis that ownership of a dog is unrelated to survival.

23. In the preceding exercise, we found a significant relationship between dog ownership and survival following coronary heart disease. Critique the conclusion, "Dog ownership leads to better survival rates of coronary victims," in the light of what we know about correlation and causation.

24. In the study reported in Case Example 17.1 (Caballero et al., 1975), the political beliefs of FOS subjects were compared with those of no-FOS subjects. The results are summarized in the following table:

Political Categories	FOS	No-FOS
Radical or liberal	14	4
Moderate or conservative	2	8

Note: Five subjects failed to provide political information.

Set up and test H_0 that political beliefs and FOS are independent, using $\alpha = 0.01$.

25. A field study tested the hypothesis that "complex social behavior that appears to be enacted mindfully instead may be performed without conscious attention to relevant semantics."* The experimenter requested that another person step aside to allow the experimenter to use the machine. In the no-information condition, the experimenter gave no reason for the request. In the placebic condition, the experimenter said, "Excuse me, I have 5 (20) pages. May I use the Xerox machine, because I have to make copies?" In the information condition, the reason given for the request was that the experimenter was in a rush. A small favor was a request to make five copies of a single page, as compared to a big favor, which was to make 20 copies. For instructional purposes, we have divided the analyses into three separate comparisons as shown in the following table.

Set up and test three separate null hypotheses, using $\alpha = 0.05$.

Response of Subjects	Conditions					
	(a) No Information		(b) Placebic Information		(c) Information	
	Small Request	Large Request	Small Request	Large Request	Small Request	Large Request
Complied	9	6	14	6	15	5
Did not comply	6	9	1	9	9	1

26. Refer to Exercise 25, and graph the proportions complying in each condition. Is there evidence of an interaction between compliance and size of request?

27. In Case Example 2.2, we looked at a study by Peter Benson and his colleagues (1976) which explored the effects of physical attractiveness on receiving help. In one part of the study, the researchers tabulated the number of males helping when the applicant was an attractive or unattractive female. These results are presented in the table that follows:

Helping Response	Characteristics of Target		Total
	Attractive	Unattractive	
Helped	52	35	87
Did not help	62	71	133

a. What is the appropriate test of significance?
b. Conduct a test of significance using $\alpha = 0.05$.

28. The following table shows the number of female subjects helping an attractive or an unattractive male applicant.

---

* Ellen Langer, Arthur Blank, and Benzoin Chanowitz (1978), "The Mindlessness of Ostensibly Thoughtful Action: The Role of Placebic Information in Interpersonal Interaction," *J. Pers. and Soc. Psych.,* **36**(6) 635–642, the quotation from 635.

Helping Response	Characteristics of Target		Total
	Attractive	Unattractive	
Helped	17	13	30
Did not help	24	27	51

a. What is the appropriate test of significance?
b. Conduct a test of significance using $\alpha = 0.05$.

29. Infections acquired while the patient is hospitalized are a continuing problem in hospitals. One study traced the mortality rates of patients with urinary-tract infections who had a catheter inserted by medical doctors, by registered nurses, and by others. The results are shown in the following table:

Catheter Inserted By	Survived	Died	Total
Medical doctor	510	11	521
Registered nurse	542	38	580
Others	345	28	373

Source: From R. Platt, B. F. Polk, B. Murdock, and B. Rosner. "Mortality Associated with Nosocomial Urinary-Tract Infection." *New England Journal of Medicine* (1982), **307**, 637–641.

a. Find the percentages across. Which group experienced the highest mortality rates?
b. What is the appropriate test of significance?
c. Using $\alpha = 0.01$, test H_0 that mortality is independent of the professional inserting the catheter.

Statistical Inference: Ordinally Scaled Variables

18.1 INTRODUCTION

In the previous chapter, we pointed out that the researcher is frequently faced with a choice as to which statistical test is appropriate for the data. You will recall that this was not really a problem in relation to categorical variables because nonparametric tests alone are suitable for nominally scaled data.

In this chapter, we discuss several statistical techniques that are frequently employed as alternatives to parametric tests.

Before examining them in detail, let's look at a brief summary of the situations in which their use is appropriate.

Mann-Whitney U: Used in two-group designs in which the groups are independent, that is, the subjects are not matched in any way, nor are before-after measures involved. The subjects are randomly assigned to the experimental conditions. The scale of the independent measures is either ordinal or interval/ratio. If it is interval/ratio, the Mann-Whitney U is used as a substitute for Student's t-ratio when the validity of the assumption of normality is questionable.

Sign Test: Used in two-group correlated-samples designs, when before-after measures are employed or pairs of subjects are matched on some basis. Although the underlying scale of the dependent measures is ordinal, we are unwilling to assume that the scores have any precise quantitative properties. We ignore the amount of difference between scores and concentrate only on the direction of the differences (larger than or smaller than).

Wilcoxon Matched-Pairs Signed-Rank Test: Used in matched-pair two-group designs in which we assume the scores are quantitative and that the differences in scores achieve an ordinal level of measurement, that is, the differences in scores may legitimately be ranked from smallest to largest or vice versa.

18.2 MANN-WHITNEY *U*-TEST

Mann-Whitney *U*-Test: Powerful nonparametric statistical test commonly employed as an alternative to Student's *t*-ratio when the measurements fail to achieve interval scaling.

The **Mann-Whitney *U*-test** is one of the most powerful nonparametric statistical tests, since it utilizes most of the quantitative information that is inherent in the data. It is most commonly employed as an alternative to Student's *t*-ratio when the measurements fail to achieve interval scaling or when the researcher wishes to avoid the assumptions of the parametric counterpart.

Imagine that we have drawn two independent samples of N_1 and N_2 observations. The null hypothesis is that both samples are drawn from populations with the same distributions. The two-tailed alternative hypothesis, against which we test the null hypothesis, is that the parent populations from which the samples were drawn are different. Imagine further that we combine the $N_1 + N_2$ observations and assign a rank of 1 to the smallest value, a rank of 2 to the next smallest value, and so on until we have assigned ranks to all the observations. Let us refer to our two groups as E and C, respectively. If we were to count the number of times each C precedes an E in the ranks, we would expect under the null hypothesis that it would equal the number of times each E precedes a C. In other words, if there is no difference between the two groups, the order of Es preceding Cs, and vice versa, should be random. However, if the null hypothesis is not true, we would expect a bulk of the E-scores or the C-scores to precede their opposite number.

For example, suppose you have the hypothesis that leadership is a trainable quality. You set up two groups, one to receive special training in leadership (E) and the other to receive no special instruction (C). Following the training, independent estimates of the leadership qualities of all the subjects are obtained. The results are

E-scores	12	18	31	45	47
C-scores	2	8	15	19	38

In employing the Mann-Whitney test, we are concerned with the sampling distribution of the statistic "U." To find U, we must first rank all the scores

TABLE 18.1

Rank	1	2	3	4	5	6	7	8	9	10
Score	2	8	12	15	18	19	31	38	45	47
Condition	C	C	E	C	E	C	E	C	E	E

from the lowest to the highest, retaining the identity of each score as *E* or *C* (Table 18.1).

You note that the number of *E*s preceding *C*s is less than the number of *C*s preceding *E*s. The next step is to count the number of times each *E* precedes a *C*. Note that the first *E* (score of 12) precedes three *C*s (scores of 15, 19, and 38, respectively). The second *E* (score of 18) precedes two *C*s (scores of 19 and 38). The third *E* (score of 31) precedes one *C* (score of 38). Finally, the last two *E*s precede no *C*s. *U* is the sum of the number of times each *E* precedes a *C*. Thus, in our hypothetical problem, $U = 3 + 2 + 1 + 0 + 0 = 6$. Had we concentrated on the number of times *C*s precede *E*s, we would have obtained a sum of $5 + 5 + 4 + 3 + 2 = 19$. We shall refer to this greater sum as U'. Under the null hypothesis, U and U' should be equal. The question is whether the magnitude of the observed difference is sufficient to warrant the rejection of the null hypothesis.

The sampling distribution of U under the null hypothesis is known. Tables I_1 through I_4 show the values of U and U' which are significant at various α levels. To be significant at a given α level, the obtained U must be equal to or *less* than the tabled value, or the obtained U' must be equal to or *greater* than its corresponding critical value. Employing $\alpha = 0.05$, two-tailed test, we find (Table I_3) that for $N_1 = 5$ and $N_2 = 5$, either $U \leq 2$ or $U' \geq 23$ is required to reject H_0. Since our obtained U of $6 > 2$, we may not reject the null hypothesis.

Formula (18.1) may be employed as a check on the calculation of U and U':

$$U = N_1 N_2 - U' \qquad (18.1)$$

The counting technique for arriving at U can become tedious, particularly with large *N*s, and frequently leads to error. An alternative procedure, which provides identical results, is to *assign ranks* to the combined groups as we did before, and then to employ either of the following formulas to arrive at U and/or U':

$$U = N_1 N_2 + \frac{N_1(N_1 + 1)}{2} - R_1 \qquad (18.2)$$

or

$$U' = N_1 N_2 + \frac{N_2(N_2 + 1)}{2} - R_2 \qquad (18.3)$$

where

R_1 = the sum of ranks assigned to the group with a sample size of N_1

R_2 = the sum of ranks assigned to the group with a sample size of N_2

Suppose we conducted a study to determine the effects of a drug on the reaction time to a visual stimulus. Since reaction time and related measures (such as latency, time to traverse a runway, etc.) are commonly skewed to the right because of a restriction on the left of the distribution (i.e., no score can be less than zero) and no restrictions on the right (i.e., the score can take on *any* value greater than zero), the Mann-Whitney *U*-test was selected in preference to Student's *t*-ratio. The results of the hypothetical study and the computational procedures are shown in Table 18.2.

To check the following calculations, we should first obtain the value of U', employing Formula (18.3):

$$U' = N_1 N_2 + \frac{N_2(N_2 + 1)}{2} - 39 = 45$$

We employ Formula (18.1) as a check of our calculations:

$$U = N_1 N_2 - U'$$
$$= 56 - 45 = 11$$

As a check on our calculations of the sums of the ranks, the total sum of the ranks R_T is given by

$$R_T = \left(\frac{N_1 + N_2}{2}\right)(N_1 + N_2 + 1) \tag{18.4}$$

TABLE 18.2 Calculation of Mann-Whitney *U* Employing Formula (18.2) (Hypothetical Data)

Experimental		Control		
Time (milliseconds)	Rank	Time (milliseconds)	Rank	Computation
140	4	130	1	$U = N_1 N_2 + \dfrac{N_1(N_1 + 1)}{2} - 81$
147	6	135	2	
153	8	138	3	$= 56 + \dfrac{8(9)}{2} - 81$
160	10	144	5	
165	11	148	7	$= 56 + 36 - 81$
170	13	155	9	$= 11$
171	14	168	12	
193	15			
	$R_1 = 81$		$R_2 = 39$	
	$N_1 = 8$		$N_2 = 7$	

In the present example, $R_1 + R_2 = (15/2)(16) = 120$. In our calculations, we found $R_1 = 81$ and $R_2 = 39$. Note that $R_1 + R_2 = 81 + 39 = 120$. Employing $\alpha = 0.01$, two-tailed test, for $N_1 = 8$ and $N_2 = 7$, we find (in Table I_1) that a $U \le 6$ is required to reject H_0. Since the obtained U of 11 is greater than this value, we accept H_0. We do not have a valid statistical basis for asserting that the drug affected reaction time.

Tables I_1 through I_4 have been constructed so that it is not necessary to calculate both U and U'. Indeed, it is not even necessary to identify which of these statistics has been calculated. For any given N_1 and N_2, at a specific α level, the tabled values represent the upper and the lower limits of the critical region. The obtained statistic, whether it is actually U or U', must fall *outside* these limits to be significant. Thus, you need not be concerned about labeling which of the statistics you have calculated.

Mann-Whitney U-Test with Tied Ranks

A problem that often arises with data is that several scores may be exactly the same. Although the underlying dimension on which we base our measures may be continuous, our measures are, for the most part, quite crude. Even though, theoretically, there should be no ties (if we had sufficiently sensitive measuring instruments), we do in fact obtain ties quite often. The procedures for converting tied scores to ranks are the same as we used with the Spearman r_s (Section 8.5). We assign the mean of the tied ranks to each of the tied scores, with the next rank in the array receiving the rank that is normally assigned to it. Although ties within a group do not constitute a problem (U is unaffected), we do face some difficulty when ties occur between two or more observations that involve both groups. There is a formula available that corrects for the effects of ties. Unfortunately, the use of this formula is rather involved and is beyond the scope of this introductory textbook.* However, the failure to correct for ties results in a test that is more "conservative," that is, decreases the probability of a Type I error (rejecting the null hypothesis when it should not be rejected). Correcting for ties is recommended only when their proportion is high and when the uncorrected U approaches our previously set level of significance.

In the event that several ties occur, we recommend that you calculate the Mann-Whitney without correcting for ties. If the uncorrected U approaches but does not achieve the α level we have set for rejecting the null hypothesis, consult the source shown in the footnote and recalculate the Mann-Whitney U, correcting for ties.

Mann-Whitney U-Test when N_1 and/or N_2 Exceeds 20

Tables I_1 through I_4 provide critical values of U for sample sizes up to and including $N_1 = 20$ and $N_2 = 20$. What test of significance should be used

---

* See Siegel and Castellan (1988) for corrections when a large number of ties occur.

when either N_1 or N_2 exceeds 20? As with many other statistics, the sampling distribution approaches the normal curve as the sample size becomes larger. As long as both Ns are approximately equal in number and one exceeds 20, the normal curve and the z-statistic may be used to evaluate the significance of the difference between ranks. The z-statistic takes the following form:

$$z = \frac{U_1 - U_E}{s_U}$$

in which U_1 is the sum of ranks of group 1, U_E is the sum expected under H_0, and s_U is the standard error of the U-statistic.

In turn,

$$U_E = \frac{N_1(N_1 + N_2 + 1)}{2}$$

and

$$s_U = \sqrt{\frac{N_1 N_2(N_1 + N_2 + 1)}{12}}$$

Imagine that an investigator has completed a study in which $N_1 = 22$ and $N_2 = 22$. The sum of the ranks of group 1 was found to be 630.* At $\alpha = 0.05$, test the null hypothesis that both groups were drawn from populations with the same mean rank. The critical value of z is ± 1.96.

The standard error of the ranks is

$$s_U = \sqrt{\frac{(22)(22)(22 + 22 + 1)}{12}}$$

$$= \sqrt{\frac{21{,}780}{12}} = 42.60$$

The expected rank under H_0 is

$$U_E = \frac{22(22 + 22 + 1)}{2} = \frac{990}{2} = 495$$

The test statistic z becomes

$$z = \frac{630 - 495}{42.60} = 3.17$$

---

* Using Formula (18.4), we find that the sum of all the ranks equals $[(22 + 22)/2)](22 + 22 + 1) = (44/2)(45) = 990$. By subtraction, $R_2 = R_T - R_1 = 990 - 630 = 360$. Note that $U_1 - U_E$ equals $U_2 - U_E$. Thus, we could just as easily have used $z = (U_1 - U_E)/s_U$. However, *if the sample sizes differ*, U_E must be changed to

$$U_E = N_2 \frac{(N_1 + N_2 + 1)}{2}$$

in order to use U_2 in the formula for z. Both yield identical probability values, and both test $H_0{:}\mu_1 = \mu_2$.

Since our obtained z of 3.17 exceeds the critical value of 1.96, we may reject the null hypothesis and assert that the experimental treatment produced a significant difference between conditions.

18.3   NONPARAMETRIC TESTS INVOLVING CORRELATED SAMPLES

In Section 13.6, when discussing Student's *t*-ratio for correlated samples, we noted the advantages of employing correlated samples wherever feasible. The same advantages accrue to nonparametric tests involving matched or correlated samples. In the following sections, we discuss two such tests for ordinally scaled variables—the *sign test* and the *Wilcoxon signed-rank test*.

18.4   THE SIGN TEST

Suppose that we are repeating the leadership experiment with which we introduced the chapter, employing larger samples. On the expectation that intelligence and leadership ability are correlated variables, we set up two groups, an experimental and a control, that are matched on the basis of intelligence. On completion of the leadership training course, independent observers are asked to rate the leadership qualities of each subject on a 50-point scale. The results are listed in Table 18.3.

TABLE 18.3   Ratings of Two Groups of Matched Subjects on Qualities of Leadership (Hypothetical Data)

Matched Pair	Leadership Score		Sign of Difference $(E - C)$
	Experimental	Control	
A	47	40	+
B	43	38	+
C	36	42	−
D	38	25	+
E	30	29	+
F	22	26	−
G	25	16	+
H	21	18	+
I	14	8	+
J	12	4	+
K	5	7	−
L	9	3	+
M	5	5	(0)

Polonium-210, smoking, and cancer in directly exposed tissue: Calculating Mann-Whitney U

The recent discovery of a radioelement in cigarettes (polonium-210) suggests the possibility that smokers may be put at greater risk for the development of cancer at directly exposed sites (e.g., buccal cavity, pharynx, etc.). Health data for various risk groups are frequently expressed as an o/e ratio (observed to expected). On the surface, it might appear that these are the type of data that are made for the use of Student's t-ratio. But notice that the o/e ratios appear to be extremely skewed, the N is small, and the validity of the assumption of normality might well be raised. Moreover, it is clear at a glance that the variances of the two groups are markedly different. In fact, the computed F-ratio of variances is 73.17. At 4 and 10 degrees of freedom, an F-ratio ≥ 4.47 permits the rejection at the 0.01 level of the null hypothesis of equal variances. Therefore, the Mann-Whitney U is chosen over its parametric counterpart (Student's t-ratio for independent samples). However, the decision to use the Mann-Whitney U is not engraved in stone. Some researchers would use Student's t-ratio based on the robustness of the t-test.

The following table shows the observed/expected (o/e) ratios for indirectly exposed and directly exposed tissues, the conversion to ranks, and the application of the Mann-Whitney U-test. An o/e ratio greater than 1 means a higher-than-average risk.

Based on the known carcinogenic properties of radioelements, we'll use a directional test of H_0 at $\alpha = 0.01$. Since a two-tailed $\alpha = 0.02$ yields a one-tailed $\alpha = 0.01$, we'll use Table I_2 to evaluate the significance of the results.

Cancer of Indirectly Exposed Tissue	O/E Ratio	Rank	Cancer of Directly Exposed Tissue	O/E Ratio	Rank
Stomach	1.52	7	Buccal cavity	4.23	12
Intestines	1.11	3.5	Pharynx	13.14	16
Rectum	1.11	3.5	Larynx	11.75	15
Liver/biliary ducts	2.35	11	Lung and		
Pancreas	1.79	9	bronchus	11.29	14
Prostate	1.31	5	Esophagus	6.5	13
Kidney	1.41	6			
Bladder	2.16	10			
Brain	1.05	1			
Malignant lymphomas	1.07	2			
Leukemias	1.61	8			
Sum of ranks	66				70

$$U = (11)(5) + \frac{11(12)}{2} - 66$$
$$= 55 + 66 - 66$$
$$= 55$$

Reference to Table I_2 shows the one-tailed critical value of U at $\alpha = 0.01$ to be 48. Since obtained U exceeds this value, we reject H_0 and assert that directly exposed tissues are at a greater risk for the development of cancer.

Can we conclude that polonium-210 caused the greater risk of cancer at directly exposed sites?

Analyze these data with Student's t-ratio for independent samples, using $\alpha = 0.01$, one-tailed test. Compare the conclusion drawn from the two different tests of significance.

ANSWERS

a. Not necessarily. There may be other carcinogens in cigarette smoke that increase the risk of cancer in directly exposed tissue.

b. $\bar{X}_1 = 1.50$, $\bar{X}_2 = 9.38$, $t = -7.05$ with df $= 14$. Critical value $\alpha = -2.624$. Reject H_0 at $\alpha = 0.01$, one-tailed test.

Source: Based on R. T. Ravenholt, letter to the editor. *New England Journal of Medicine* (1982), **307,** 312.

The rating scales seem to be extremely crude, and we are unwilling to affirm that the scores have any precise quantitative properties. The only assumption we feel justified in making is that any existing difference between two paired scores is a valid indicator of the direction and not the magnitude of the difference.

There are 13 pairs of observations in Table 18.3. Since pair M is tied and there is consequently no indication of a difference one way or another, we drop these paired observations. Of the remaining 12 pairs, we would expect, on the basis of the null hypothesis, half the changes to be in the positive direction and half the changes to be in the negative direction. In other words, under H_0, the probability of any difference being positive is equal to the probability that it will be negative. Since we are dealing with a two-category population (positive differences and negative differences), H_0 may be expressed in precisely the same fashion as in the binomial test when $P = Q = \frac{1}{2}$. That is, in the present problem, $H_0 : P = Q = \frac{1}{2}$. Indeed, the **sign test** is merely a variation of the binomial test introduced in Section 17.2.

Out of 12 comparisons showing a difference ($N = 12$) in the present example, 9 are positive, and 3 are negative. Since $P = Q = \frac{1}{2}$, we refer to Table M, under $x = 9$, $N = 12$, and find that the critical value at $\alpha = 0.05$, two-tailed test, is 10. Since x is less than the critical value, we fail to reject H_0.

The assumptions underlying the use of the sign test are that the pairs of measurements must be independent of each other and that these measurements must represent at least ordinal scaling.

Sign Test:
Nonparametric statistical test for ordinally scaled variables, used with matched or correlated samples. The sign test simply utilizes information concerning the *direction* of the differences between pairs of scores.

One of the disadvantages of the sign test is that it completely eliminates any quantitative information that may be inherent in the data (e.g., $-8 = -7 = -6$, etc.). The sign test treats all plus differences as if they were the same and all minus differences as if they were the same.

If this is the only assumption warranted by the scale of measurement employed, we have little choice but to employ the sign test. If, on the other hand, the data *do* permit us to make such quantitative statements as "a difference of $8 > 7 > 6 > \cdots$," we lose power when we employ the sign test.

18.5 WILCOXON MATCHED-PAIRS SIGNED-RANK TEST

Wilcoxon Matched-Pairs Signed-Rank Test:
Nonparametric statistical test for ordinally scaled variables used with matched or correlated samples; more powerful than the sign test since it utilizes information concerning the *magnitude* of the differences between pairs of scores.

We have seen that the sign simply utilizes information concerning the direction of the differences between pairs. If the *magnitude* as well as the *direction* of these differences may be considered, a more powerful test may be employed. The **Wilcoxon matched-pairs signed-rank test** achieves greater power by utilizing the quantitative information that is inherent in the ranking of the differences.

For heuristic purposes, let us return to the data in Table 18.3 and make a different assumption about the scale of measurement employed. Suppose the rating scale is not so crude as we had imagined; that is, not only do the measurements achieve ordinal scaling, but also the differences between measures achieve ordinality. Table 18.4 reproduces these data, with an additional entry indicating the magnitude of the differences.

Note that the difference column represents differences in scores rather than in ranks. The following column represents the ranking of these differences from the smallest to largest without regard to the algebraic sign. We have placed the negative sign in parentheses so that we can keep track of the differences bearing positive and negative signs. Now, if the null hypothesis were correct, we would expect the sum of the positive and that of the negative ranks to more or less balance each other. The more the sums of the ranks are preponderantly positive or negative, the more likely we are to reject the null hypothesis.

The statistic T is the sum of the ranks with the smaller sum. In this problem, T is equal to -13. Table J presents the critical values of T for sample sizes up to 50 pairs. All entries are for the absolute value of T. In the present example, we find that a T of 13 or less is required for significance at the 0.05 level (two-tailed test) when $N = 12$. Note that we dropped the M pair from our calculations since, as with the sign test, a zero difference in scores cannot be considered as either a negative or a positive change. Since our obtained T was 13, we may reject the null hypothesis. We may conclude that the leadership training produced higher ratings for the experimental subjects.

TABLE 18.4 Ratings of Two Groups of Matched Subjects on Qualities of Leadership (Hypothetical Data)

Matched Pair	Leadership Score		Difference	Rank of Difference	Ranks with Smaller Sum
	Experimental	Control			
A	47	40	+7	9	
B	43	38	+5	5	
C	36	42	−6	(−)7	−7
D	38	25	+13	12	
E	30	29	+1	1	
F	22	26	−4	(−)4	−4
G	25	16	+9	11	
H	21	18	+3	3	
I	14	8	+6	7	
J	12	4	+8	10	
K	5	7	−2	(−)2	−2
L	9	3	+6	7	
M	5	5	(0)		

$$T = -13$$

You will recall that the sign test applied to these same data did not lead to the rejection of the null hypothesis. The reason should be apparent; that is, we were not taking advantage of all the information inherent in our data when we employed the sign test.

Assumptions Underlying the Wilcoxon Matched-Pairs Signed-Rank Test

An assumption involved in the use of the Wilcoxon signed-rank test is that the scale of measurement is at least ordinal in nature. In other words, the assumption is that the scores permit the ordering of the data into relationships of greater than and less than. However, the signed-rank test makes one additional assumption, which may rule it out for some potential applications; namely, it assumes that the differences in scores also constitute an ordinal scale. It is not always clear whether or not this assumption is valid for a given set of data. Take, for example, a personality scale purported to measure "manifest anxiety" in a testing situation. Can we validly claim that a difference between matched pairs of, say, 5 points on one part of the scale is greater than a difference of 4 points on another part of the scale? If we cannot validly make this assumption, we must employ another form of statistical analysis, even if it requires that we move to a less sensitive test of significance. Once again, our basic conservatism as scientists makes us more willing to risk a Type II rather than a Type I error.

TABLE 18.5 **Three Ordinal Tests of Significance that May Be Used to Replace Indicated Statistical Tests when the Validity of the Assumptions of These Tests Is Questionable**

Test of Significance	Experimental Design	Number of Conditions	Type of Data	Test Statistic	Test Replaced
Mann-Whitney U	Independent samples	2	Ordinal, interval, ratio	U or U'	Student's t-ratio for independent samples
Sign test	Correlated samples	2	Ordinal, but only direction of difference ($+$ or $-$)	Binomial	Student's t-ratio, Wilcoxon signed-rank test
Wilcoxon matched-pairs signed-rank test	Correlated samples	2	Obtains ranks of differences between scores or ranks	T	Student's t-ratio for correlated samples

18.6 PUTTING IT ALL TOGETHER

In this chapter, we have looked at three tests for ordinally scaled variables that are commonly used in place of their parametric counterparts whenever there are serious doubts concerning the validity of meeting the assumptions of the parametric tests. Table 18.5 summarizes the conditions under which each of these tests might be advantageously employed.

CHAPTER SUMMARY

In this chapter, we have pointed out that the behavioral scientist does not first collect data and then "shop around" for a statistical test to determine the significance of differences between experimental conditions. *The research must specify in advance of the experiment* the null hypothesis, the alternative hypothesis, the test of significance, and the probability value that is acceptable as the basis for rejecting the null hypothesis.

We demonstrated the use of the Mann-Whitney U-test as an alternative to Student's t-ratio when the measurements fail to achieve interval scaling or when the researcher wishes to avoid the assumptions of the parametric counterpart. It is one of the most powerful of the nonparametric tests, since it utilizes most of the quantitative information that is inherent in the data.

We have seen that by taking into account correlations between subjects on a variable correlated with the criterion measure, we can increase the sensitivity of our statistical test.

The sign test accomplishes this objective by employing before-after measures on the same individuals.

We have also seen that the sign test, although taking advantage of the *direction* of differences involved in ordinal measurement, fails to make use of information concerning *magnitudes* of differences.

The Wilcoxon matched-pairs signed-rank test takes advantage of both *direction* and *magnitude* implicit in ordinal measurement with correlated samples. When the assumptions underlying the test are met, the Wilcoxon paired-replicates technique is an extremely sensitive basis for obtaining probability values.

TERMS TO REMEMBER

Mann-Whitney *U*-test
sign test

Wilcoxon matched-pairs
signed-rank test

EXERCISES

1. From the data presented in the accompanying table, determine whether there is a significant difference in the number of stolen bases obtained by two leagues, employing
   a. the sign test
   b. the Wilcoxon matched-pairs test
   c. the Mann-Whitney *U*-test.
   Which is the best statistical test for these data? Why?

| | **Number of Stolen Bases** | |
Team Standing	**League 1**	**League 2**
1	91	81
2	46	51
3	108	63
4	99	51
5	110	46
6	105	45
7	191	66
8	57	64
9	34	90
10	81	28

2. In a study to determine the effect of a drug on aggressiveness, group A received a drug and group B received a placebo. A test of aggressiveness was applied

following the drug administration. The scores obtained were as follows (the higher the score, the greater is the aggressiveness):

Group A	10	8	12	16	5	9	7	11	6
Group B	12	15	20	18	13	14	9	16	

Set up this study in formal statistical terms and state the conclusion that is warranted by the statistical evidence.

3. The personnel director at a large insurance office claims that insurance agents who are trained in personal-social relations make more favorable impressions on prospective clients. To test this hypothesis, 22 individuals are randomly selected from those most recently hired and half are assigned to the personal-social relations course. The remaining 11 individuals constitute the control group. Following the training period, all 22 individuals are observed in a simulated interview with a client, and they are rated on a 10-point scale (0–9) for their ease in establishing relationships. The higher the score is, the better is the rating. Set up and test H_0, employing the appropriate test statistic. Use $\alpha = 0.01$.

Experimentals:	8	7	9	4	7	9	3	7	8	9	3
Controls:	5	6	2	6	0	2	6	5	1	0	5

4. Assume that the subjects in Exercise 3 were matched on a variable known to be correlated with the criterion variable. Employ the appropriate test statistic to test $H_0 : \alpha = 0.01$.

5. Fifteen husbands and their wives were administered an opinion scale to assess their attitudes about a particular political issue. The results were as follows (the higher the score is, the more favorable is the attitude):

Husband	Wife	Husband	Wife
37	33	32	46
46	44	35	32
59	48	39	29
17	30	37	45
41	56	36	29
36	30	45	48
29	35	40	35
38	38		

What do you conclude?

6. Suppose that during the last track season, there was no difference in the mean running speeds of the runners from two schools. Assume that the same people are on the teams this year.

School A trains as usual for this season. However, the coach at school B introduces bicycle riding in the training classes. During a meet, the following times (in seconds) were recorded for the runners of the two schools:

A	10.2	11.1	10.5	10.0	9.7	12.0	10.7	10.9	11.5	10.4
B	9.9	10.3	11.0	10.1	9.8	9.5	10.8	10.6	9.6	9.4

Test the hypothesis that bicycle riding does not affect running speed.

7. Suppose that in Exercise 6 the people on each team had been previously matched on running speed for the 50-yard dash. The matches are as listed in Exercise 6. Using the sign test and the Wilcoxon matched-pairs signed-rank test, set up and test the null hypothesis.

8. An investigator wants to measure the effectiveness of an advertisement that promotes his brand of toothpaste. He matched subjects (all of whom had never bought his brand of toothpaste) according to the number of tubes of toothpaste they usually buy in 6 months. He then divided the sample into two groups and showed one group the advertisement. After 6 months, he found that the number of tubes of his brand of toothpaste the people bought during that time was:

Advertisement group	4	4	3	1	2	0	1	0
No-advertisement group	1	2	0	2	0	1	0	1

Was the advertisement effective?

Review of Basic Mathematics

ARITHMETIC OPERATIONS

You already know that addition is indicated by the sign "+"; subtraction by the sign "−"; multiplication in one of three ways: 2×4, $2(4)$, or $2 \cdot 4$; and division by a slash, "/," an overbar, "—," or the symbol "÷." However, it is not unusual to forget the rules concerning addition, subtraction, multiplication, and division, particularly when these operations occur in a single problem.

Addition and Subtraction

When numbers are added together, the order in which the numbers are added has no influence on the sum. Thus, we may add $2 + 5 + 3$ in any of the following ways:

$$2 + 5 + 3 \qquad 5 + 2 + 3 \qquad 2 + 3 + 5$$
$$5 + 3 + 2 \qquad 3 + 2 + 5 \qquad 3 + 5 + 2$$

When a series of numbers containing both positive and negative signs are added, the order in which the numbers are added has no influence on the sum. However, it is often desirable to group together the numbers preceded by positive signs, group together the numbers preceded by negative signs, add each group separately, and subtract the latter sum from the former. Thus

$$-2 + 3 + 5 - 4 + 2 + 1 - 8$$

may best be added by grouping in the following ways:

$$
\begin{array}{ll}
+3 & \\
+5 & -2 \\
+2 & -4 \\
\underline{+1} & \underline{-8} \\
+11 & -14 = -3
\end{array}
$$

Incidentally, to subtract a larger numerical value from a smaller numerical value, as in the preceding example $(11 - 14)$, we ignore the signs, subtract the small number from the larger, and affix the sign of the larger to the sum. Thus $-14 + 11 = -3$.

Multiplication

The order in which numbers are multiplied has no effect on the product. In other words,

$$2 \times 3 \times 4 = 2 \times 4 \times 3 = 3 \times 2 \times 4$$
$$= 3 \times 4 \times 2 = 4 \times 2 \times 3 = 4 \times 3 \times 2 = 24$$

When addition, subtraction, and multiplication occur in the same expression, we must develop certain procedures governing *which* operations are to be performed first.

In the expression

$$2 \times 4 + 7 \times 3 - 5$$

multiplication is performed first. Thus, this expression is equal to

$$2 \times 4 = 8$$
$$7 \times 3 = 21$$
$$-5 = -5 \qquad \text{Thus, } 8 + 21 - 5 = 24$$

We may *not* add first and then multiply. Thus, $2 \times 4 + 7$ is *not* equal to $2(4 + 7)$ or 22.

If a problem involves finding the product of one term multiplied by a second expression that includes two or more terms either added or subtracted, we may multiply first and then add, or add first and then multiply. Thus, the solution to the following problems becomes

$$8(6 - 4) = 8 \times 6 - 8 \times 4$$
$$= 48 - 32$$
$$= 16$$

or

$$8(6 - 4) = 8(2)$$
$$= 16$$

In most cases, however, it is more convenient to reduce the expression within the parentheses first. Thus, generally speaking, the second of these solutions will be more frequently employed.

Finally, if numbers having like signs are multiplied, the product is always positive; for example,

$$(+2) \times (+4) = +8 \qquad (-2) \times (-4) = +8$$

If numbers bearing unlike signs are multiplied, the product is always negative; for example,

$$(+2) \times (-4) = -8 \qquad (-2) \times (+4) = -8$$

The same rule applies also to division: When we obtain the quotient of two numbers of like signs, it is always positive; when the numbers differ in sign, the quotient is always negative.

Multiplication as Successive Addition   Many students tend to forget that multiplication is a special form of successive addition. Thus

$$15 + 15 + 15 + 15 + 15 = 5(15)$$

and

$$(15 + 15 + 15 + 15 + 15) + (16 + 16 + 16 + 16) = 5(15) + 4(16)$$

This formulation is useful in understanding the advantages of "grouping" scores into what is called a frequency distribution. In obtaining the sum of an array of scores, some of which occur a number of times, we would find it desirable to multiply each score by the frequency with which it occurs, and then add the products. Thus, if we were to obtain the following distribution of scores:

12, 13, 13, 13, 14, 14, 14, 14, 15, 15, 15, 15,
15, 15, 15, 16, 16, 16, 17, 17, 17, 17, 18

and wanted the sum of these scores, it would be advantageous to form the following frequency distribution:

X	f	fX
12	1	12
13	3	39
14	4	56
15	7	105
16	3	48
17	4	68
18	1	18

$$N = 23 \quad \Sigma fX = 346$$

ALGEBRAIC OPERATIONS

Transposing

To transpose a term from one side of an equation to another, you merely have to *change the sign* of the transposed term. All the following are equivalent statements:

$$a + b = c$$
$$a = c - b$$
$$b = c - a$$
$$0 = c - a - b$$
$$0 = c - (a + b)$$

Solving Equations Involving Fractions   Much of the difficulty encountered in solving equations that involve fractions can be avoided by remembering one important mathematical principle:

Equals multiplied by equals are equal.

Let's look at a few sample problems.

1. Solve the following equation for x:

$$b = \frac{a}{x}$$

In solving for x, we want to express the value of x in terms of a and b. In other words, we want our final equation to read, $x = $ _____ .

Note that we may multiply both sides of the equation by x/b and obtain the following:

$$b \cdot \frac{x}{b} = \frac{a}{x} \cdot \frac{x}{b}$$

This reduces to

$$x = \frac{a}{b}$$

2. Solve the equation in the problem for a.

Similarly, if we wanted to solve the equation in terms of a, we could multiply both sides of the equation by x. Thus

$$b \cdot x = \frac{a}{x} \cdot x$$

becomes $bx = a$, or $a = bx$.

In each of the previous solutions, you will note that the net effect of multiplying by a constant has been to rearrange the terms in the numerator and the denominator of the equations. In fact, we may state two general rules that will permit us to solve these problems without having to employ multiplication by equals (although multiplication by equals is implicit in the arithmetic operations):

a. A term in the denominator on one side of the equation may be moved to the other side of the equation by multiplying it by the numerator on the other side. Thus

$$\frac{x}{a} = b \qquad \text{becomes} \qquad x = ab$$

b. A term in the numerator on one side of an equation may be moved to the other side of the equation by dividing the numerator on the other side by it. Thus

$$ab = x \qquad \text{may become} \qquad a = \frac{x}{b} \qquad \text{or} \qquad b = \frac{x}{a}$$

Thus, we have seen that all the following are equivalent statements:

$$b = \frac{a}{x} \qquad a = bx \qquad x = \frac{a}{b}$$

Similarly,

$$\frac{\Sigma X}{N} = \bar{X} \qquad \sum X = N\bar{X} \qquad \text{and} \qquad \frac{\Sigma X}{\bar{X}} = N$$

Dividing by a Sum or a Difference   It is true that

$$\frac{x + y}{z} = \frac{x}{z} + \frac{y}{z} \qquad \text{and} \qquad \frac{x - y}{z} = \frac{x}{z} - \frac{y}{z}$$

We cannot, however, simplify the following expressions as easily:

$$\frac{x}{y + z} \quad \text{or} \quad \frac{x}{y - z}$$

Thus

$$\frac{x}{y + z} \neq \frac{x}{y} + \frac{x}{z}$$

in which $\neq$ means "not equal to."

REDUCING FRACTIONS TO SIMPLEST EXPRESSIONS

This is corollary to the rule that equals multiplied by equals are equal:

Unequals multiplied by equals remain proportional.

Thus, if we were to multiply ¼ by ⅝, the product, ⅝₂, is in the same proportion as ¼. This corollary is useful in reducing complex fractions to their simplest expression. Let us look at an example.

Example Reduce

$$\frac{a/b}{c/d} \quad \text{or} \quad \frac{a}{b} \div \frac{c}{d}$$

to its simplest expression.

Note that if we multiply both the numerator and the denominator by

$$\frac{bd/1}{bd/1}$$

we obtain

$$\frac{(a/b) \cdot (bd/1)}{(c/d) \cdot (bd/1)}$$

which becomes ad/bc.

However, we could obtain the same result if we were to *invert the divisor* and multiply. Thus

$$\frac{a/b}{c/d} = \frac{a}{b} \cdot \frac{d}{c} = \frac{ad}{bc}$$

We may now formulate a general rule for dividing one fraction into another fraction. In dividing fractions, we *invert the divisor and multiply*. Thus

$$\frac{x/y}{a^2/b} \quad \text{becomes} \quad \frac{x}{y} \cdot \frac{b}{a^2} \quad \text{which equals} \quad \frac{bx}{a^2y}$$

To illustrate: If $a = 5$, $b = 2$, $x = 3$, and $y = 4$, the preceding expressions become

$$\frac{3/4}{5^2/2} = \frac{3}{4} \cdot \frac{2}{5^2} = \frac{2 \cdot 3}{4 \cdot 5^2} = \frac{6}{100}$$

A general practice you should follow when substituting numerical values into fractional expressions is to reduce the expression to its simplest form *prior* to substitution.

Multiplication and Division of Terms Having Exponents

An exponent indicates how many times a number is to be multiplied by itself. For example, X^5 means that X is to be multiplied by itself 5 times, or

$$X^5 = X \cdot X \cdot X \cdot X \cdot X$$

If $X = 3$,

$$X^5 = 3 \cdot 3 \cdot 3 \cdot 3 \cdot 3 = 243 \qquad \text{and} \qquad \left(\frac{1}{X}\right)^5 = \frac{1^5}{X^5} = \frac{1 \cdot 1 \cdot 1 \cdot 1 \cdot 1}{3 \cdot 3 \cdot 3 \cdot 3 \cdot 3} = \frac{1}{243}$$

To multiply X raised to the ath power (X^a) times X raised to the bth power, you simply *add the exponents*, thus raising X to the $(a + b)$th power. The reason for the addition of exponents may be seen from the following illustration.

If $a = 3$ and $b = 5$, then

$$X^a \cdot X^b = X^3 X^5 = (X \cdot X \cdot X)/(X \cdot X \cdot X \cdot X \cdot X)$$

which equals X^8.

Now, if $X = 5$, $a = 3$, and $b = 5$, then

$$X^a \cdot X^b = X^{a+b} = X^{3+5} = X^8 = 5^8 = 390{,}625$$

If $X = \frac{1}{6}$, $a = 2$, and $b = 3$,

$$X^a \cdot X^b = X^{a+b} = \left(\frac{1}{6}\right)^{2+3} = \left(\frac{1}{6}\right)^5 = \frac{1^5}{6^5} = \frac{1}{7776}$$

To divide X raised to the ath power by X raised to the bth power, you simply *subtract* the exponent in the denominator from the exponent in the numerator.* The reason for the subtraction is made clear in the following illustration. If $X = 3$, $a = 5$, and $b = 2$, then

$$\frac{X^a}{X^b} = \frac{X^5}{X^2} = \frac{X \cdot X \cdot X \cdot X \cdot X}{X \cdot X} = X^3 = 3^3 = 27$$

---

* This leads to an interesting exception to the rule that an exponent indicates the number of times a number is multiplied by itself; that is,

$$\frac{X^N}{X^N} = X^{N-N} = X^0$$

however,

$$\frac{X^N}{X^N} = 1 \qquad \text{therefore} \qquad X^0 = 1$$

Any number raised to the zero power is equal to 1.

If $X = 5/6$, $a = 4$, and $b = 2$, then

$$\frac{X^a}{X^b} = X^{a-b} = X^{4-2} = X^2$$

Substituting $5/6$ for X, we have

$$X^2 = \left(\frac{5}{6}\right)^2 = \frac{5^2}{6^2} = \frac{25}{36}$$

EXTRACTING SQUARE ROOTS

The square root of a number is the value that, when multiplied by itself, equals that number. Table P contains square roots.

The usual difficulty encountered in calculating square roots is the decision as to how many digits precede the decimal, for example, $\sqrt{25{,}000{,}000} = 5000$, not 500 or 50,000; that is, there are four digits before the decimal. In order to calculate the number of digits preceding the decimal, simply count the number of *pairs* to the left of the decimal:

$$\text{Number of pairs} = \text{Number of digits}$$

However, if there is an odd number of digits, then the number of digits preceding the decimal equals the number of pairs $+1$. The following examples illustrate this point:

$$\text{a. } \overset{50.0}{\sqrt{2500.00}} \qquad \overset{5.0}{\sqrt{25.00}} \qquad \text{b. } \overset{15.8}{\sqrt{250.00}} \qquad \overset{1.58}{\sqrt{2.5000}}$$

Handling Nonnormal Distributions

TRANSFORMING NONNORMAL FREQUENCY DISTRIBUTIONS INTO AREAS OF THE STANDARD NORMAL CURVE

There are several techniques for normalizing a frequency distribution of scores. All yield more or less the same results. The method shown here is the one preferred by the authors.

To illustrate the procedures for normalizing frequency distributions, we employ a grouped frequency distribution ($i = 2$) of miles-per-gallon ratings of sixty 1976 cars. These are reproduced below. Note the extreme positive skew.

Real Limits on Class	f	Cum f
27.5–29.5	1	60
25.5–27.5	1	59
23.5–25.5	2	58
21.5–23.5	3	56
19.5–21.5	7	53
17.5–19.5	6	46
15.5–17.5	10	40
13.5–15.5	6	30
11.5–13.5	10	24
9.5–11.5	14	14

Step A. List all the integers from the highest in the upper class ($X = 29$) to the lowest in the bottom class ($X = 10$). See column (A) of Table 1 in this appendix.

Step B. Select a value near the upper real limit of the highest class (29.4) and one near the lower real limit of the lowest class (9.6). This is done to provide "anchor" points for drawing the graph.

Step C. Find the score with a corresponding percentile rank of 50. In the present example:

a. $50 \times 60 \div 100 = 30$

b. The 30th score is found at the upper real limit of the class 13.5 to 15.5. Thus, the score at the 50th percentile is 15.5. This score will correspond to the mean, median, and mode in the normalized distribution. It should be placed between 15 and 16 in Table 1.

Step D. Use the procedure learned in Chapter 4 to find the percentile rank of each of the scores.

Examples The percentile rank of a score of 29.4 is

$$\frac{(1.9/2)1 + 59}{60} \times 100 = \frac{59.95}{60} \times 100$$

$$= 99.92$$

The percentile rank of a score of 19 is

$$\frac{(1.5/2)6 + 40}{60} \times 100 = \frac{44.5}{60} \times 100$$

$$= 74.17$$

TABLE 1

(A) Score	(B) Percentile Rank	(C) Corresponding z under Standard Normal Curve	(D) Height of Ordinate
29.4	99.92	3.14	0.0029
29	99.58	2.64	0.0122
28	98.75	2.24	0.0325
27	97.92	2.04	0.0498
26	97.08	1.89	0.0669
25	95.83	1.73	0.0893
24	94.17	1.57	0.1163
23	92.08	1.41	0.1476
22	89.58	1.26	0.1804
21	85.42	1.05	0.2299
20	79.58	0.83	0.2827
19	74.17	0.65	0.3230
18	69.17	0.50	0.3521
17	62.50	0.32	0.3790
16	54.17	0.10	0.3970
15.5	50.00	0.00	0.3989
15	47.50	−0.06	0.3988
14	42.50	−0.19	0.3918
13	35.83	−0.36	0.3739
12	27.50	−0.60	0.3332
11	17.50	−0.93	0.2589
10	05.83	−1.57	0.1163
9.6	01.17	−2.27	0.0303

Step E.   Turn to Table A in the Table section. Find in the body of the table the percentile rank that most closely approximates the percentile ranks listed in column (B) of Table 1. For example, a score of 12 has a percentile rank of 27.50. The closest value to this is 27.43. The z corresponding to 27.43 is -0.60. Record each z in column (C).

Examples

1. A score of 28 is at the 98.75th percentile. The z corresponding to this percentile rank is 2.24.
2. A score of 15 is at the 47.50th percentile. The value closest to this in the body of the table is 47.61. This corresponds to a z of -0.06.

TRANSFORMING TO *T*-SCORES

We have now transformed the nonnormal frequency distribution into a normal distribution with a mean of 0 and a standard deviation of 1. However, most scores involve decimal values, and all scores below the mean are negative. It is usually desirable to express values for a normally distributed variable in terms of a positive number. This can be accomplished by a simple transformation:

$$T = a + bz$$

The selection of the constants *a* and *b* depends upon which mean and standard deviation you want in the final transformed distribution. For example, if you want the mean of the transformed distribution to be 500, you set *a* equal to 500. If you want the scores of the transformed distribution to be whole numbers, you set *b* equal to 100 or more.

Examples   Show the *T*-transformation that is necessary to produce a mean equal to 50 and a standard deviation equal to 5:

$$T = a + bz$$
$$= 50 + 5z$$

Show the transformation that is necessary to produce a mean of 500 and a standard deviation of 100:

$$T = a + bz$$
$$= 500 + 100z$$

Let us now transform the miles-per-gallon scores into a *T*-score so that we obtain a mean equal to 50 and a standard deviation equal to 10.

Step A.   Take the z corresponding to each score and multiply by $b = 10$.

Examples   The z of a score of 29.4 is 3.14:

$$b \times 3.14 = 10 \times 3.14$$
$$= 31.4$$

The z of the mean score, 15.5, is 0:

$$b \times 0 = 10 \times 0$$
$$= 0$$

Step B. Add the constant $a = 50$ to each bz to yield the transformed score, T. The score of 29.4 becomes

$$T = a + bz$$
$$= 50 + 31.4$$
$$= 81.4$$

(*Note:* In many practical applications of the T-score transformation, the number is rounded to the nearest integer so that the T is expressed as a positive *whole* number.)

Examples The T of the mean becomes

$$T = a + bz$$
$$= 50 + 0$$
$$= 50$$

The T of a score of 11 becomes

$$T = a + bz$$
$$= 50 + 10(-0.93)$$
$$= 40.7$$

Shown here are the T-score transformations of all the normalized values of the miles-per-gallon data.

Score	Corresponding z under Standard Normal Curve	T-Transformation $(T = 50 + 10z)$	Rounded to Nearest Whole number
29.4	3.14	81.4	81
29	2.64	76.4	76
28	2.24	72.4	72
27	2.04	70.4	70
26	1.89	68.9	69
25	1.73	67.3	67
24	1.57	65.7	66
23	1.41	64.1	64
22	1.26	62.6	63
21	1.05	60.5	60
20	0.83	58.3	58
19	0.65	56.5	56
18	0.50	55.0	55
17	0.32	53.2	53
16	0.10	51.0	51
15.5	0.00	50.0	50
15	-0.06	49.7	50
14	-0.10	48.1	48
13	-0.36	46.4	46
12	-0.60	44.0	44
11	-0.93	40.7	41
10	-1.57	34.3	34
9.6	-2.27	27.3	27

Any transformed score can be readily interpreted by converting to units of the standard normal curve.

Examples

1. A score of 81.9 yields the following:

$$z = \frac{81.9 - 50}{10} = \frac{31.9}{10} = 3.19$$

Table A reveals that the corresponding percentile rank is 99.93.

2. A score of 37.8 yields the following:

$$z = \frac{37.8 - 50}{10} = \frac{-12.2}{10} = -1.22$$

Table A reveals that the corresponding percentile rank is 11.12.

PLOTTING A GRAPH OF A NORMALIZED DISTRIBUTION

To illustrate the procedures for constructing a graph of a normalized distribution of z-scores, we shall use the previously calculated transformed miles-per-gallon scores. These are reproduced here.

(A) Score	(B) Corresponding z under Standard Normal Curve	(C) Height of Y-Axis
29.4	3.15	
29	2.64	
28	2.24	
27	2.04	
26	1.89	
25	1.73	
24	1.57	
23	1.41	
22	1.26	
21	1.05	
20	0.83	
19	0.65	
18	0.50	
17	0.32	
16	0.10	
15.5	0.00	
15	-0.06	
14	-0.19	
13	-0.36	
12	-0.60	
11	-0.93	
10	-1.57	
9.6	-2.27	

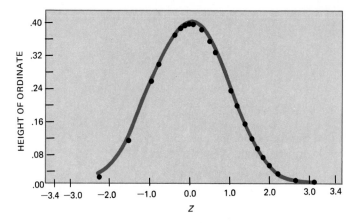

FIGURE A.1 Graph showing a normalized distribution of miles-per-gallon figures of sixty 1976 cars.

> **Step A.** Refer to column (D) of Table 1. This shows the height of the ordinate corresponding to each z-score. Find the height of the ordinate corresponding to each z in the preceding table and place it in column (c).

Examples

> **1.** The height of the ordinate corresponding to $z = 3.14$ is 0.0029.
> **2.** The height of the ordinate corresponding to $z = 0$ is 0.3989.
> **3.** The height of the ordinate corresponding to $z = -1.57$ is 0.1163.

> **Step B.** On a piece of graph paper, draw the horizontal or X-axis so that values between -3.4 and 3.4 are equally spaced.
> **Step C.** Draw the vertical or Y-axis so that two-place decimal values from 0.00 to 0.40 are represented.
> **Step D.** Locate each z-score along the horizontal axis and move vertically until you find the corresponding value representing the height of the ordinate. Place a dot at this point.
> **Step E.** When you have completed all the values and joined the dots, you will have a normal distribution of your transformed scores. You may also add the corresponding original scores and their transformed T-scores to the legend along the X-axis (see Fig. A.1).

Appendix C

Symbol Glossary

The following are symbols and their definitions as used in this textbook, followed by the page number.

English letters and Greek letters are listed separately in their approximate alphabetical order. Mathematical operators are also listed separately.

Symbol	Definition	Page
MATHEMATICAL OPERATORS		
$\neq$	Not equal to	33
$a < b$	a is less than b	34
$a > b$	a is greater than b	34
$\leq$	Less than or equal to	263
$\geq$	Greater than or equal to	263
$\sqrt{}$	Square root	26
X^a	X raised to the ath power	27
$N!$	Factorial: multiply N by all integers less than it but greater than zero:	
	$$(N)(N-1)(N-2)\cdots(2)(1)$$	471
$|X|$	Absolute value of X	147
Σ	Sum all quantities or scores that follow	26
$\displaystyle\sum_{i=1}^{N} X_i$	Sum all quantities X_1 through X_N:	
	$$X_1 + X_2 + \cdots + X_N$$	24
GREEK LETTERS		
α	Probability of a Type 1 error; probability of rejecting H_0 when it is true	303
β	Probability of a Type II error; probability of accepting H_0 when it is false	307
χ^2	Chi-square	474
μ	Population mean	7
μ_0	Value of the population mean under H_0	304
μ_1	Value of the population mean under H_1	304
$\mu_{\bar{x}}$	Mean of the distribution of sample means	300

Symbol	Definition	Page
$\mu_{\bar{x}_1 - \bar{x}_2}$	Mean of the distribution of the difference between pairs of sample means	335
$\mu_{\bar{D}}$	Mean of the difference between paired scores	350
σ^2	Population variance	149
σ	Sigma; population standard deviation	149
$\sigma_{\bar{x}}^2 = \dfrac{\sigma^2}{N}$	Variance of the sampling distribution of the mean	326
$\sigma_{\bar{x}}^2 = \dfrac{\sigma}{\sqrt{N}}$	True standard error of the mean given random samples of a fixed N	326
$\sigma_{\bar{x}_1 - \bar{x}_2}$	True standard error of the difference between means	361
ω^2	Omega squared; degree of association between the dependent and the independent variables	365
ρ	Rho; population correlation	320

ENGLISH LETTERS

Symbol	Definition	Page
a	Constant term in a regression equation	227
b_y	Slope of a line relating values of Y to values of X	226
c	Number of columns in a contingency table	477
cum f	Cumulative frequency	66
cum $f_{\parallel}$	Cumulative frequency at the lower real limit of the interval containing X	100
cum %	Cumulative percentage	67
D	1. Rank on X-variable $-$ rank on Y-variable (r_s formula)	205
	2. Score on X-variable–score on Y-variable ($X - Y$)	351
$\bar{D}$	Mean of the differences between the paired scores	350
df	Degrees of freedom; number of values free to vary after certain restrictions have been placed on the data	338
F	A ratio of two variances	404
f	Frequency	63
f_i	Number of cases within the class containing X	100
f_e	Expected number in a given category	475
f_o	Observed number in a given category	475
fX	A score multiplied by its corresponding frequency	120

Symbol	Definition	Page
H_0	The null hypothesis; hypothesis actually tested	303
H_1	The alternative hypothesis; hypothesis entertained if H_0 is rejected	303
i	Width of the class	64
k	Number of groups or categories or cells	475
k^2	Coefficient of nondetermination	240
M.D.	Mean deviation	147
N	1. Number of pairs	377
	2. Number in either sample	26
	3. Total number of scores or quantities	26
N_s	Total number of means obtained in a sampling experiment	327
p	Probability	256
$p(A)$	Probability of event A	261
$p(B|A)$	Probability of B given that A has occurred	272
P	1. Probability of the occurrence of an event	269
	2. Proportion of cases in one class in a two-category population	470
Q	1. Probability of the nonoccurrence of an event	269
	2. Proportion of cases in the other class in a two-category population	470
Q_1	First quartile, 25th percentile	145
Q_3	Third quartile, 75th percentile	145
r	1. Pearson product-moment correlation coefficient	222
	2. Number of rows in a contingency table	477
r^2	Coefficient of determination	239
r_s	Spearman rank-order correlation coefficient	201
R_1	Sum of ranks assigned to the group with a sample size of N_1 (Mann-Whitney U-formula)	494
R_2	Sum of ranks assigned to the group with a sample size of N_2 (Mann-Whitney U-formula)	494
$s^2 = \dfrac{SS}{N}$	Variance of a sample	150
$s = \sqrt{\dfrac{SS}{N}}$	Standard deviation of a sample	150
$\hat{s}^2 = \dfrac{\Sigma(X - \bar{X}^2)}{N - 1} = \dfrac{SS}{N - 1}$	Unbiased estimate of the population variance	333

Symbol	Definition	Page
$\hat{s} = \sqrt{\dfrac{SS}{N-1}}$	Sample standard deviation based on unbiased variance estimate	332
$s_{\bar{X}}^2$	Estimated variance of the sampling distribution of the mean	333
$s_{\bar{X}} = \dfrac{\hat{s}}{\sqrt{N}} = \dfrac{s}{\sqrt{N-1}}$	Estimated standard error of the mean	323
$s_{\bar{X}_1 - \bar{X}_2}$	Estimated standard error of the difference between means	361
$\hat{s}_D$	Standard deviation of the difference scores	376
$s_{\bar{D}}$	Estimated standard error of the difference between means, direct-difference method	375
$\hat{s}_{bet}^2$	Between-group variance estimate	403
$\hat{s}_w^2$	Within-group variance estimate	403
$\hat{s}_{A \times B}$	Interaction variance estimate	436
$s_{\text{est } y}$	Standard error of estimate when predictions are made from X to Y	235
$s_{\text{est } x}$	Standard error of estimate when predictions are made from Y to X	235
$SS = \Sigma(X - \bar{X})^2$	Sum of squares, sum of the squared deviations from the mean	150
$SS_{A \times B}$	Interaction sum of squares	435
SS_{tot}	Total sum of squares; sum of the squared deviations of each score (X) from the overall mean $(\bar{X}_{tot})$	401
SS_w	Within-group sum of squares; sum of the squared deviations of each score (X) from the mean of its own group $(\bar{X}_i)$	401
SS_{bet}	Between-group sum of squares; sum of the squared deviations of each group mean $(\bar{X}_i)$ from the overall mean $(\bar{X}_{tot})$, multiplied by the N in each group	402
T	Sum of the ranks with the least frequent sign	500
t	Statistic employed to test hypotheses when σ is unknown	334
U, U'	Statistics in the Mann-Whitney test	492
X, Y	Variables; quantities or scores of variables	26
X_i, X_i	Specific quantities indicated by the subscript i	28
$\bar{X}, \bar{Y}$	Arithmetic means	117
$\bar{X}_i$	Mean of the ith group	402
$\bar{X}_{tot} = \dfrac{\Sigma X_{tot}}{N}$	Overall mean	402

Symbol	Definition	Page
$(X - \bar{X})$	Deviation of a score from its mean	126
x	Number of objects in one category or the number of successes	471
ΣX^2	Sum of the squares of the raw scores	151
$(\Sigma X)^2$	Sum of the raw scores, the quantity squared	151
$X_{\parallel}$	Score at lower real limit of class containing X	100
X', Y'	Scores predicted by regression equations	227
Y_T	Interval around the regression line within which the true value probably occurs	237
z	1. Deviation of a specific score from the mean, expressed in standard deviation units	168
	2. Statistic employed to test hypotheses when σ is known	304
$z_{0.01} = \pm 2.58$	Critical value of z; minimum value of z required to reject H_0 at the 0.01 level of significance, two-tailed test	304
$z_{0.05} = \pm 1.96$	Critical value of z; minimum value of z required to reject H_0 at the 0.05 level of significance, two-tailed test	305
$z_{y'}$	Y' expressed in terms of a z-score	227

Appendix D

Tables

TABLE A **Proportions of Area under the Normal Curve**

The Use of Table A

The use of Table A requires that the raw score be transformed into a z-score and that the variable be normally distributed.

The values in Table A represent the proportion of area in the standard normal curve, which has a mean of 0, a standard deviation of 1.00, and a total area also equal to 1.00.

Since the normal curve is symmetrical, it is sufficient to indicate only the areas corresponding to positive z-values. Negative z-values will have precisely the same proportions of area as their positive counterparts.

Column B represents the proportion of area between the mean and a given z. Column C represents the proportion of area beyond a given z.

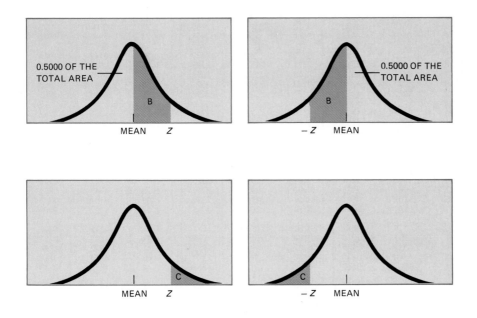

TABLE A

(A) z	(B) area between mean and z	(C) area beyond z	(A) z	(B) area between mean and z	(C) area beyond z	(A) z	(B) area between mean and z	(C) area beyond z
0.00	.0000	.5000	0.55	.2088	.2912	1.10	.3643	.1357
0.01	.0040	.4960	0.56	.2123	.2877	1.11	.3665	.1335
0.02	.0080	.4920	0.57	.2157	.2843	1.12	.3686	.1314
0.03	.0120	.4880	0.58	.2190	.2810	1.13	.3708	.1292
0.04	.0160	.4840	0.59	.2224	.2776	1.14	.3729	.1271
0.05	.0199	.4801	0.60	.2257	.2743	1.15	.3749	.1251
0.06	.0239	.4761	0.61	.2291	.2709	1.16	.3770	.1230
0.07	.0279	.4721	0.62	.2324	.2676	1.17	.3790	.1210
0.08	.0319	.4681	0.63	.2357	.2643	1.18	.3810	.1190
0.09	.0359	.4641	0.64	.2389	.2611	1.19	.3830	.1170
0.10	.0398	.4602	0.65	.2422	.2578	1.20	.3849	.1151
0.11	.0438	.4562	0.66	.2454	.2546	1.21	.3869	.1131
0.12	.0478	.4522	0.67	.2486	.2514	1.22	.3888	.1112
0.13	.0517	.4483	0.68	.2517	.2483	1.23	.3907	.1093
0.14	.0557	.4443	0.69	.2549	.2451	1.24	.3925	.1075
0.15	.0596	.4404	0.70	.2580	.2420	1.25	.3944	.1056
0.16	.0636	.4364	0.71	.2611	.2389	1.26	.3962	.1038
0.17	.0675	.4325	0.72	.2642	.2358	1.27	.3980	.1020
0.18	.0714	.4286	0.73	.2673	.2327	1.28	.3997	.1003
0.19	.0753	.4247	0.74	.2704	.2296	1.29	.4015	.0985
0.20	.0793	.4207	0.75	.2734	.2266	1.30	.4032	.0968
0.21	.0832	.4168	0.76	.2764	.2236	1.31	.4049	.0951
0.22	.0871	.4129	0.77	.2794	.2206	1.32	.4066	.0934
0.23	.0910	.4090	0.78	.2823	.2177	1.33	.4082	.0918
0.24	.0948	.4052	0.79	.2852	.2148	1.34	.4099	.0901
0.25	.0987	.4013	0.80	.2881	.2119	1.35	.4115	.0885
0.26	.1026	.3974	0.81	.2910	.2090	1.36	.4131	.0869
0.27	.1064	.3936	0.82	.2939	.2061	1.37	.4147	.0853
0.28	.1103	.3897	0.83	.2967	.2033	1.38	.4162	.0838
0.29	.1141	.3859	0.84	.2995	.2005	1.39	.4177	.0823
0.30	.1179	.3821	0.85	.3023	.1977	1.40	.4192	.0808
0.31	.1217	.3783	0.86	.3051	.1949	1.41	.4207	.0793
0.32	.1255	.3745	0.87	.3078	.1922	1.42	.4222	.0778
0.33	.1293	.3707	0.88	.3106	.1894	1.43	.4236	.0764
0.34	.1331	.3669	0.89	.3133	.1867	1.44	.4251	.0749
0.35	.1368	.3632	0.90	.3159	.1841	1.45	.4265	.0735
0.36	.1406	.3594	0.91	.3186	.1814	1.46	.4279	.0721
0.37	.1443	.3557	0.92	.3212	.1788	1.47	.4292	.0708
0.38	.1480	.3520	0.93	.3238	.1762	1.48	.4306	.0694
0.39	.1517	.3483	0.94	.3264	.1736	1.49	.4319	.0681
0.40	.1554	.3446	0.95	.3289	.1711	1.50	.4332	.0668
0.41	.1591	.3409	0.96	.3315	.1685	1.51	.4345	.0655
0.42	.1628	.3372	0.97	.3340	.1660	1.52	.4357	.0643
0.43	.1664	.3336	0.98	.3365	.1635	1.53	.4370	.0630
0.44	.1700	.3300	0.99	.3389	.1611	1.54	.4382	.0618
0.45	.1736	.3264	1.00	.3413	.1587	1.55	.4394	.0606
0.46	.1772	.3228	1.01	.3438	.1562	1.56	.4406	.0594
0.47	.1808	.3192	1.02	.3461	.1539	1.57	.4418	.0582
0.48	.1844	.3156	1.03	.3485	.1515	1.58	.4429	.0571
0.49	.1879	.3121	1.04	.3508	.1492	1.59	.4441	.0559
0.50	.1915	.3085	1.05	.3531	.1469	1.60	.4452	.0548
0.51	.1950	.3050	1.06	.3554	.1446	1.61	.4463	.0537
0.52	.1985	.3015	1.07	.3577	.1423	1.62	.4474	.0526
0.53	.2019	.2981	1.08	.3599	.1401	1.63	.4484	.0516
0.54	.2054	.2946	1.09	.3621	.1379	1.64	.4495	.0505

TABLE A (*continued*)

(A) z	(B) area between mean and z	(C) area beyond z	(A) z	(B) area between mean and z	(C) area beyond z	(A) z	(B) area between mean and z	(C) area beyond z
1.65	.4505	.0495	2.22	.4868	.0132	2.79	.4974	.0026
1.66	.4515	.0485	2.23	.4871	.0129	2.80	.4974	.0026
1.67	.4525	.0475	2.24	.4875	.0125	2.81	.4975	.0025
1.68	.4535	.0465	2.25	.4878	.0122	2.82	.4976	.0024
1.69	.4545	.0455	2.26	.4881	.0119	2.83	.4977	.0023
1.70	.4554	.0446	2.27	.4884	.0116	2.84	.4977	.0023
1.71	.4564	.0436	2.28	.4887	.0113	2.85	.4978	.0022
1.72	.4573	.0427	2.29	.4890	.0110	2.86	.4979	.0021
1.73	.4582	.0418	2.30	.4893	.0107	2.87	.4979	.0021
1.74	.4591	.0409	2.31	.4896	.0104	2.88	.4980	.0020
1.75	.4599	.0401	2.32	.4898	.0102	2.89	.4981	.0019
1.76	.4608	.0392	2.33	.4901	.0099	2.90	.4981	.0019
1.77	.4616	.0384	2.34	.4904	.0096	2.91	.4982	.0018
1.78	.4625	.0375	2.35	.4906	.0094	2.92	.4982	.0018
1.79	.4633	.0367	2.36	.4909	.0091	2.93	.4983	.0017
1.80	.4641	.0359	2.37	.4911	.0089	2.94	.4984	.0016
1.81	.4649	.0351	2.38	.4913	.0087	2.95	.4984	.0016
1.82	.4656	.0344	2.39	.4916	.0084	2.96	.4985	.0015
1.83	.4664	.0336	2.40	.4918	.0082	2.97	.4985	.0015
1.84	.4671	.0329	2.41	.4920	.0080	2.98	.4986	.0014
1.85	.4678	.0322	2.42	.4922	.0078	2.99	.4986	.0014
1.86	.4686	.0314	2.43	.4925	.0075	3.00	.4987	.0013
1.87	.4693	.0307	2.44	.4927	.0073	3.01	.4987	.0013
1.88	.4699	.0301	2.45	.4929	.0071	3.02	.4987	.0013
1.89	.4706	.0294	2.46	.4931	.0069	3.03	.4988	.0012
1.90	.4713	.0287	2.47	.4932	.0068	3.04	.4988	.0012
1.91	.4719	.0281	2.48	.4934	.0066	3.05	.4989	.0011
1.92	.4726	.0274	2.49	.4936	.0064	3.06	.4989	.0011
1.93	.4732	.0268	2.50	.4938	.0062	3.07	.4989	.0011
1.94	.4738	.0262	2.51	.4940	.0060	3.08	.4990	.0010
1.95	.4744	.0256	2.52	.4941	.0059	3.09	.4990	.0010
1.96	.4750	.0250	2.53	.4943	.0057	3.10	.4990	.0010
1.97	.4756	.0244	2.54	.4945	.0055	3.11	.4991	.0009
1.98	.4761	.0239	2.55	.4946	.0054	3.12	.4991	.0009
1.99	.4767	.0233	2.56	.4948	.0052	3.13	.4991	.0009
2.00	.4772	.0228	2.57	.4949	.0051	3.14	.4992	.0008
2.01	.4778	.0222	2.58	.4951	.0049	3.15	.4992	.0008
2.02	.4783	.0217	2.59	.4952	.0048	3.16	.4992	.0008
2.03	.4788	.0212	2.60	.4953	.0047	3.17	.4992	.0008
2.04	.4793	.0207	2.61	.4955	.0045	3.18	.4993	.0007
2.05	.4798	.0202	2.62	.4956	.0044	3.19	.4993	.0007
2.06	.4803	.0197	2.63	.4957	.0043	3.20	.4993	.0007
2.07	.4808	.0192	2.64	.4959	.0041	3.21	.4993	.0007
2.08	.4812	.0188	2.65	.4960	.0040	3.22	.4994	.0006
2.09	.4817	.0183	2.66	.4961	.0039	3.23	.4994	.0006
2.10	.4821	.0179	2.67	.4962	.0038	3.24	.4994	.0006
2.11	.4826	.0174	2.68	.4963	.0037	3.25	.4994	.0006
2.12	.4830	.0170	2.69	.4964	.0036	3.30	.4995	.0005
2.13	.4834	.0166	2.70	.4965	.0035	3.35	.4996	.0004
2.14	.4838	.0162	2.71	.4966	.0034	3.40	.4997	.0003
2.15	.4842	.0158	2.72	.4967	.0033	3.45	.4997	.0003
2.16	.4846	.0154	2.73	.4968	.0032	3.50	.4998	.0002
2.17	.4850	.0150	2.74	.4969	.0031	3.60	.4998	.0002
2.18	.4854	.0146	2.75	.4970	.0030	3.70	.4999	.0001
2.19	.4857	.0143	2.76	.4971	.0029	3.80	.4999	.0001
2.20	.4861	.0139	2.77	.4972	.0028	3.90	.49995	.00005
2.21	.4864	.0136	2.78	.4973	.0027	4.00	.49997	.00003

TABLE B   Two-Tailed Critical Ratios of χ^2

Degrees of freedom df	.10	.05	.02	.01
1	2.706	3.841	5.412	6.635
2	4.605	5.991	7.824	9.210
3	6.251	7.815	9.837	11.341
4	7.779	9.488	11.668	13.277
5	9.236	11.070	13.388	15.086
6	10.645	12.592	15.033	16.812
7	12.017	14.067	16.622	18.475
8	13.362	15.507	18.168	20.090
9	14.684	16.919	19.679	21.666
10	15.987	18.307	21.161	23.209
11	17.275	19.675	22.618	24.725
12	18.549	21.026	24.054	26.217
13	19.812	22.362	25.472	27.688
14	21.064	23.685	26.873	29.141
15	22.307	24.996	28.259	30.578
16	23.542	26.296	29.633	32.000
17	24.769	27.587	30.995	33.409
18	25.989	28.869	32.346	34.805
19	27.204	30.144	33.687	36.191
20	28.412	31.410	35.020	37.566
21	29.615	32.671	36.343	38.932
22	30.813	33.924	37.659	40.289
23	32.007	35.172	38.968	41.638
24	33.196	36.415	40.270	42.980
25	34.382	37.652	41.566	44.314
26	35.563	38.885	42.856	45.642
27	36.741	40.113	44.140	46.963
28	37.916	41.337	45.419	48.278
29	39.087	42.557	46.693	49.588
30	40.256	43.773	47.962	50.892

TABLE C   Critical Values of *t*

For any given df, the table shows the values of *t* corresponding to various levels of probability. The obtained *t* is significant at a given level if it is equal to or *greater than* the value shown in the table.

df	Level of significance for one-tailed test					
	.10	.05	.025	.01	.005	.0005
	Level of significance for two-tailed test					
	.20	.10	.05	.02	.01	.001
1	3.078	6.314	12.706	31.821	63.657	636.619
2	1.886	2.920	4.303	6.965	9.925	31.598
3	1.638	2.353	3.182	4.541	5.841	12.941
4	1.533	2.132	2.776	3.747	4.604	8.610
5	1.476	2.015	2.571	3.365	4.032	6.859
6	1.440	1.943	2.447	3.143	3.707	5.959
7	1.415	1.895	2.365	2.998	3.499	5.405
8	1.397	1.860	2.306	2.896	3.355	5.041
9	1.383	.1.833	2.262	2.821	3.250	4.781
10	1.372	1.812	2.228	2.764	3.169	4.587
11	1.363	‹1.796	2.201	2.718	3.106	4.437
12	1.356	1.782	2.179	2.681	3.055	4.318
13	1.350	1.771	2.160	2.650	3.012	4.221
14	1.345	1.761	2.145	2.624	2.977	4.140
15	1.341	1.753	2.131	2.602	2.947	4.073
16	1.337	1.746	2.120	2.583	2.921	4.015
17	1.333	1.740	2.110	2.567	2.898	3.965
18	1.330	1.734	2.101	2.552	2.878	3.922
19	1.328	1.729	2.093	2.539	2.861	3.883
20	1.325	1.725	2.086	2.528	2.845	3.850
21	1.323	1.721	2.080	2.518	2.831	3.819
22	1.321	1.717	2.074	2.508	2.819	3.792
23	1.319	1.714	2.069	2.500	2.807	3.767
24	1.318	1.711	2.064	2.492	2.797	3.745
25	1.316	1.708	2.060	2.485	2.787	3.725
26	1.315	1.706	2.056	2.479	2.779	3.707
27	1.314	1.703	2.052	2.473	2.771	3.690
28	1.313	1.701	2.048	2.467	2.763	3.674
29	1.311	1.699	2.045	2.462	2.756	3.659
30	1.310	1.697	2.042	2.457	2.750	3.646
40	1.303	1.684	2.021	2.423	2.704	3.551
60	1.296	1.671	2.000	2.390	2.660	3.460
120	1.289	1.658	1.980	2.358	2.617	3.373
∞	1.282	1.645	1.960	2.326	2.576	3.291

Table C is taken from Table III (page 46) of Fisher and Yates, *Statistical Tables for Biological, Agricultural, and Medical Research*, 6th ed., published by Longman Group Ltd., 1974. London (previously published by Oliver and Boyd, Edinburgh), and by permission of the authors and publishers.

TABLE D Critical Values of F

The obtained *F* is significant at a given level if it is equal to or *greater than* the value shown in the table. 0.05 (light row) and 0.01 (dark row) points for the distribution of *F*.

The values shown are the right tail of the distribution obtained by dividing the larger variance estimate by the smaller variance estimate. To find the complementary left or lower tail for a given df and α-level, reverse the degrees of freedom and find the reciprocal of that value in the *F*-table. For example, the value cutting off the top 5% of the area for 7 and 12 df is 2.85. To find the cutoff point of the bottom 5% of the area, find the tabled value of the α = 0.05 level for 12 and 7 df. This is found to be 3.57. The reciprocal is 1/3.57 = 0.28. Thus 5% of the area falls *at or below an F* = 0.28.

Each cell shows the 0.05 (light row) value over the 0.01 (dark row) value.

Degrees of freedom for numerator

df (denom)	1	2	3	4	5	6	7	8	9	10	11	12	14	16	20	24	30	40	50	75	100	200	500	∞
1	161 / 4052	200 / 4999	216 / 5403	225 / 5625	230 / 5764	234 / 5859	237 / 5928	239 / 5981	241 / 6022	242 / 6056	243 / 6082	244 / 6106	245 / 6142	246 / 6169	248 / 6208	249 / 6234	250 / 6258	251 / 6286	252 / 6302	253 / 6323	253 / 6334	254 / 6352	254 / 6361	254 / 6366
2	18.51 / 98.49	19.00 / 99.01	19.16 / 99.17	19.25 / 99.25	19.30 / 99.30	19.33 / 99.33	19.36 / 99.34	19.37 / 99.36	19.38 / 99.38	19.39 / 99.40	19.40 / 99.41	19.41 / 99.42	19.42 / 99.43	19.43 / 99.44	19.44 / 99.45	19.45 / 99.46	19.46 / 99.47	19.47 / 99.48	19.47 / 99.48	19.48 / 99.49	19.49 / 99.49	19.49 / 99.49	19.50 / 99.50	19.50 / 99.50
3	10.13 / 34.12	9.55 / 30.81	9.28 / 29.46	9.12 / 28.71	9.01 / 28.24	8.94 / 27.91	8.88 / 27.67	8.84 / 27.49	8.81 / 27.34	8.78 / 27.23	8.76 / 27.13	8.74 / 27.05	8.71 / 26.92	8.69 / 26.83	8.66 / 26.69	8.64 / 26.60	8.62 / 26.50	8.60 / 26.41	8.58 / 26.30	8.57 / 26.27	8.56 / 26.23	8.54 / 26.18	8.54 / 26.14	8.53 / 26.12
4	7.71 / 21.20	6.94 / 18.00	6.59 / 16.69	6.39 / 15.98	6.26 / 15.52	6.16 / 15.21	6.09 / 14.98	6.04 / 14.80	6.00 / 14.66	5.96 / 14.54	5.93 / 14.45	5.91 / 14.37	5.87 / 14.24	5.84 / 14.15	5.80 / 14.02	5.77 / 13.93	5.74 / 13.83	5.71 / 13.74	5.70 / 13.69	5.68 / 13.61	5.66 / 13.57	5.65 / 13.52	5.64 / 13.48	5.63 / 13.46
5	6.61 / 16.26	5.79 / 13.27	5.41 / 12.06	5.19 / 11.39	5.05 / 10.97	4.95 / 10.67	4.88 / 10.45	4.82 / 10.27	4.78 / 10.15	4.74 / 10.05	4.70 / 9.96	4.68 / 9.89	4.64 / 9.77	4.60 / 9.68	4.56 / 9.55	4.53 / 9.47	4.50 / 9.38	4.46 / 9.29	4.44 / 9.24	4.42 / 9.17	4.40 / 9.13	4.38 / 9.07	4.37 / 9.04	4.36 / 9.02
6	5.99 / 13.74	5.14 / 10.92	4.76 / 9.78	4.53 / 9.15	4.39 / 8.75	4.28 / 8.47	4.21 / 8.26	4.15 / 8.10	4.10 / 7.98	4.06 / 7.87	4.03 / 7.79	4.00 / 7.72	3.96 / 7.60	3.92 / 7.52	3.87 / 7.39	3.84 / 7.31	3.81 / 7.23	3.77 / 7.14	3.75 / 7.09	3.72 / 7.02	3.71 / 6.99	3.69 / 6.94	3.68 / 6.90	3.67 / 6.88
7	5.59 / 12.25	4.74 / 9.55	4.35 / 8.45	4.12 / 7.85	3.97 / 7.46	3.87 / 7.19	3.79 / 7.00	3.73 / 6.84	3.68 / 6.71	3.63 / 6.62	3.60 / 6.54	3.57 / 6.47	3.52 / 6.35	3.49 / 6.27	3.44 / 6.15	3.41 / 6.07	3.38 / 5.98	3.34 / 5.90	3.32 / 5.85	3.29 / 5.78	3.28 / 5.75	3.25 / 5.70	3.24 / 5.67	3.23 / 5.65
8	5.32 / 11.26	4.46 / 8.65	4.07 / 7.59	3.84 / 7.01	3.69 / 6.63	3.58 / 6.37	3.50 / 6.19	3.44 / 6.03	3.39 / 5.91	3.34 / 5.82	3.31 / 5.74	3.28 / 5.67	3.23 / 5.56	3.20 / 5.48	3.15 / 5.36	3.12 / 5.28	3.08 / 5.20	3.05 / 5.11	3.03 / 5.06	3.00 / 5.00	2.98 / 4.96	2.96 / 4.91	2.94 / 4.88	2.93 / 4.86
9	5.12 / 10.56	4.26 / 8.02	3.86 / 6.99	3.63 / 6.42	3.48 / 6.06	3.37 / 5.80	3.29 / 5.62	3.23 / 5.47	3.18 / 5.35	3.13 / 5.26	3.10 / 5.18	3.07 / 5.11	3.02 / 5.00	2.98 / 4.92	2.93 / 4.80	2.90 / 4.73	2.86 / 4.64	2.82 / 4.56	2.80 / 4.51	2.77 / 4.45	2.76 / 4.41	2.73 / 4.36	2.72 / 4.33	2.71 / 4.31
10	4.96 / 10.04	4.10 / 7.56	3.71 / 6.55	3.48 / 5.99	3.33 / 5.64	3.22 / 5.39	3.14 / 5.21	3.07 / 5.06	3.02 / 4.95	2.97 / 4.85	2.94 / 4.78	2.91 / 4.71	2.86 / 4.60	2.82 / 4.52	2.77 / 4.41	2.74 / 4.33	2.70 / 4.25	2.67 / 4.17	2.64 / 4.12	2.61 / 4.05	2.59 / 4.01	2.56 / 3.96	2.55 / 3.93	2.54 / 3.91
11	4.84 / 9.65	3.98 / 7.20	3.59 / 6.22	3.36 / 5.67	3.20 / 5.32	3.09 / 5.07	3.01 / 4.88	2.95 / 4.74	2.90 / 4.63	2.86 / 4.54	2.82 / 4.46	2.79 / 4.40	2.74 / 4.29	2.70 / 4.21	2.65 / 4.10	2.61 / 4.02	2.57 / 3.94	2.53 / 3.86	2.50 / 3.80	2.47 / 3.74	2.45 / 3.70	2.42 / 3.66	2.41 / 3.62	2.40 / 3.60
12	4.75 / 9.33	3.88 / 6.93	3.49 / 5.95	3.26 / 5.41	3.11 / 5.06	3.00 / 4.82	2.92 / 4.65	2.85 / 4.50	2.80 / 4.39	2.76 / 4.30	2.72 / 4.22	2.69 / 4.16	2.64 / 4.05	2.60 / 3.98	2.54 / 3.86	2.50 / 3.78	2.46 / 3.70	2.42 / 3.61	2.40 / 3.56	2.36 / 3.49	2.35 / 3.46	2.32 / 3.41	2.31 / 3.38	2.30 / 3.36
13	4.67 / 9.07	3.80 / 6.70	3.41 / 5.74	3.18 / 5.20	3.02 / 4.86	2.92 / 4.62	2.84 / 4.44	2.77 / 4.30	2.72 / 4.19	2.67 / 4.10	2.63 / 4.02	2.60 / 3.96	2.55 / 3.85	2.51 / 3.78	2.46 / 3.67	2.42 / 3.59	2.38 / 3.51	2.34 / 3.42	2.32 / 3.37	2.28 / 3.30	2.26 / 3.27	2.24 / 3.21	2.22 / 3.18	2.21 / 3.16
14	4.60 / 8.86	3.74 / 6.51	3.34 / 5.56	3.11 / 5.03	2.96 / 4.69	2.85 / 4.46	2.77 / 4.28	2.70 / 4.14	2.65 / 4.03	2.60 / 3.94	2.56 / 3.86	2.53 / 3.80	2.48 / 3.70	2.44 / 3.62	2.39 / 3.51	2.35 / 3.43	2.31 / 3.34	2.27 / 3.26	2.24 / 3.21	2.21 / 3.14	2.19 / 3.11	2.16 / 3.06	2.14 / 3.02	2.13 / 3.00
15	4.54 / 8.68	3.68 / 6.36	3.29 / 5.42	3.06 / 4.89	2.90 / 4.56	2.79 / 4.32	2.70 / 4.14	2.64 / 4.00	2.59 / 3.89	2.55 / 3.80	2.51 / 3.73	2.48 / 3.67	2.43 / 3.56	2.39 / 3.48	2.33 / 3.36	2.29 / 3.29	2.25 / 3.20	2.21 / 3.12	2.18 / 3.07	2.15 / 3.00	2.12 / 2.97	2.10 / 2.92	2.08 / 2.89	2.07 / 2.87

Degrees of freedom for denominator

Degrees of freedom for denominator

df																								
16	2.01/2.75	2.02/2.77	2.04/2.80	2.07/2.86	2.09/2.89	2.13/2.96	2.16/3.01	2.20/3.10	2.24/3.18	2.28/3.25	2.33/3.37	2.37/3.45	2.42/3.55	2.45/3.61	2.49/3.69	2.54/3.78	2.59/3.89	2.66/4.03	2.74/4.20	2.85/4.44	3.01/4.77	3.24/5.29	3.63/6.23	4.49/8.53
17	1.96/2.65	1.97/2.67	1.99/2.70	2.02/2.76	2.04/2.79	2.08/2.86	2.11/2.92	2.15/3.00	2.19/3.08	2.23/3.16	2.29/3.27	2.33/3.35	2.38/3.45	2.41/3.52	2.45/3.59	2.50/3.68	2.55/3.79	2.62/3.93	2.70/4.10	2.81/4.34	2.96/4.67	3.20/5.18	3.59/6.11	4.45/8.40
18	1.92/2.57	1.93/2.59	1.95/2.62	1.98/2.68	2.00/2.71	2.04/2.78	2.07/2.83	2.11/2.91	2.15/3.00	2.19/3.07	2.25/3.19	2.29/3.27	2.34/3.37	2.37/3.44	2.41/3.51	2.46/3.60	2.51/3.71	2.58/3.85	2.66/4.01	2.77/4.25	2.93/4.58	3.16/5.09	3.55/6.01	4.41/8.28
19	1.88/2.49	1.90/2.51	1.91/2.54	1.94/2.60	1.96/2.63	2.00/2.70	2.02/2.76	2.07/2.84	2.11/2.92	2.15/3.00	2.21/3.12	2.26/3.19	2.31/3.30	2.34/3.36	2.38/3.43	2.43/3.52	2.48/3.63	2.55/3.77	2.63/3.94	2.74/4.17	2.90/4.50	3.13/5.01	3.52/5.93	4.38/8.18
20	1.84/2.42	1.85/2.44	1.87/2.47	1.90/2.53	1.92/2.56	1.96/2.63	1.99/2.69	2.04/2.77	2.08/2.86	2.12/2.94	2.18/3.05	2.23/3.13	2.28/3.23	2.31/3.30	2.35/3.37	2.40/3.45	2.45/3.56	2.52/3.71	2.60/3.87	2.71/4.10	2.87/4.43	3.10/4.94	3.49/5.85	4.35/8.10
21	1.81/2.36	1.82/2.38	1.84/2.42	1.87/2.47	1.90/2.51	1.93/2.58	1.96/2.63	2.00/2.72	2.05/2.80	2.09/2.88	2.15/2.99	2.20/3.07	2.25/3.17	2.28/3.24	2.32/3.31	2.37/3.40	2.42/3.51	2.49/3.65	2.57/3.81	2.68/4.04	2.84/4.37	3.07/4.87	3.47/5.78	4.32/8.02
22	1.78/2.31	1.80/2.33	1.81/2.37	1.84/2.42	1.87/2.46	1.91/2.53	1.93/2.58	1.98/2.67	2.03/2.75	2.07/2.83	2.13/2.94	2.18/3.02	2.23/3.12	2.26/3.18	2.30/3.26	2.35/3.35	2.40/3.45	2.47/3.59	2.55/3.76	2.66/3.99	2.82/4.31	3.05/4.82	3.44/5.72	4.30/7.94
23	1.76/2.26	1.77/2.28	1.79/2.32	1.82/2.37	1.84/2.41	1.88/2.48	1.91/2.53	1.96/2.62	2.00/2.70	2.04/2.78	2.10/2.89	2.14/2.97	2.20/3.07	2.24/3.14	2.28/3.21	2.32/3.30	2.38/3.41	2.45/3.54	2.53/3.71	2.64/3.94	2.80/4.26	3.03/4.76	3.42/5.66	4.28/7.88
24	1.73/2.21	1.74/2.23	1.76/2.27	1.80/2.33	1.82/2.36	1.86/2.44	1.89/2.49	1.94/2.58	1.98/2.66	2.02/2.74	2.09/2.85	2.13/2.93	2.18/3.03	2.22/3.09	2.26/3.17	2.30/3.25	2.36/3.36	2.43/3.50	2.51/3.67	2.62/3.90	2.78/4.22	3.01/4.72	3.40/5.61	4.26/7.82
25	1.71/2.17	1.72/2.19	1.74/2.23	1.77/2.29	1.80/2.32	1.84/2.40	1.87/2.45	1.92/2.54	1.96/2.62	2.00/2.70	2.06/2.81	2.11/2.89	2.16/2.99	2.20/3.05	2.24/3.13	2.28/3.21	2.34/3.32	2.41/3.46	2.49/3.63	2.60/3.86	2.76/4.18	2.99/4.68	3.38/5.57	4.24/7.77
26	1.69/2.13	1.70/2.15	1.72/2.19	1.76/2.25	1.78/2.28	1.82/2.36	1.85/2.41	1.90/2.50	1.95/2.58	1.99/2.66	2.05/2.77	2.10/2.86	2.15/2.96	2.18/3.02	2.22/3.09	2.27/3.17	2.32/3.29	2.39/3.42	2.47/3.59	2.59/3.82	2.74/4.14	2.96/4.64	3.37/5.53	4.22/7.72
27	1.67/2.10	1.68/2.12	1.71/2.16	1.74/2.21	1.76/2.25	1.80/2.33	1.84/2.38	1.88/2.47	1.93/2.55	1.97/2.63	2.03/2.74	2.08/2.83	2.13/2.93	2.16/2.98	2.20/3.06	2.25/3.14	2.30/3.26	2.37/3.39	2.46/3.56	2.57/3.79	2.73/4.11	2.96/4.60	3.35/5.49	4.21/7.68
28	1.65/2.06	1.67/2.09	1.69/2.13	1.72/2.18	1.75/2.22	1.78/2.30	1.81/2.35	1.87/2.44	1.91/2.52	1.96/2.60	2.02/2.71	2.06/2.80	2.12/2.90	2.15/2.95	2.19/3.03	2.24/3.11	2.29/3.23	2.36/3.36	2.44/3.53	2.56/3.76	2.71/4.07	2.95/4.57	3.34/5.45	4.20/7.64
29	1.64/2.03	1.65/2.06	1.68/2.10	1.71/2.15	1.73/2.19	1.77/2.27	1.80/2.32	1.85/2.41	1.90/2.49	1.94/2.57	2.00/2.68	2.05/2.77	2.10/2.87	2.14/2.92	2.18/3.00	2.22/3.08	2.28/3.20	2.35/3.32	2.43/3.50	2.54/3.73	2.70/4.04	2.93/4.54	3.33/5.42	4.18/7.60
30	1.62/2.01	1.64/2.03	1.66/2.07	1.69/2.13	1.72/2.16	1.76/2.24	1.79/2.29	1.84/2.38	1.89/2.47	1.93/2.55	1.99/2.66	2.04/2.74	2.09/2.84	2.12/2.90	2.16/2.98	2.21/3.06	2.27/3.17	2.34/3.30	2.42/3.47	2.53/3.70	2.69/4.02	2.92/4.51	3.32/5.39	4.17/7.56
32	1.59/1.96	1.61/1.98	1.64/2.02	1.67/2.08	1.69/2.12	1.74/2.20	1.76/2.25	1.82/2.34	1.86/2.42	1.91/2.51	1.97/2.62	2.02/2.70	2.07/2.80	2.10/2.86	2.14/2.94	2.19/3.01	2.25/3.12	2.32/3.25	2.40/3.42	2.51/3.66	2.67/3.97	2.90/4.46	3.30/5.34	4.15/7.50
34	1.57/1.91	1.59/1.94	1.61/1.98	1.64/2.04	1.67/2.08	1.71/2.15	1.74/2.21	1.80/2.30	1.84/2.38	1.89/2.47	1.95/2.58	2.00/2.66	2.05/2.76	2.08/2.82	2.12/2.89	2.17/2.97	2.23/3.08	2.30/3.21	2.38/3.38	2.49/3.61	2.65/3.93	2.88/4.42	3.28/5.29	4.13/7.44

TABLE D (continued)

Degrees of freedom for numerator — Degrees of freedom for denominator

Each cell shows the upper (.05) value over the lower (.01) value.

df (denom.)	1	2	3	4	5	6	7	8	9	10	11	12	14	16	20	24	30	40	50	75	100	200	500	∞
36	4.11 / 7.39	3.26 / 5.25	2.86 / 4.38	2.63 / 3.89	2.48 / 3.58	2.36 / 3.35	2.28 / 3.18	2.21 / 3.04	2.15 / 2.94	2.10 / 2.86	2.06 / 2.78	2.03 / 2.72	1.98 / 2.62	1.93 / 2.54	1.87 / 2.43	1.82 / 2.35	1.78 / 2.26	1.72 / 2.17	1.69 / 2.12	1.65 / 2.04	1.62 / 2.00	1.59 / 1.94	1.56 / 1.90	1.55 / 1.87
38	4.10 / 7.35	3.25 / 5.21	2.85 / 4.34	2.62 / 3.86	2.46 / 3.54	2.35 / 3.32	2.26 / 3.15	2.19 / 3.02	2.14 / 2.91	2.09 / 2.82	2.05 / 2.75	2.02 / 2.69	1.96 / 2.59	1.92 / 2.51	1.85 / 2.40	1.80 / 2.32	1.76 / 2.22	1.71 / 2.14	1.67 / 2.08	1.63 / 2.00	1.60 / 1.97	1.57 / 1.90	1.54 / 1.86	1.53 / 1.84
40	4.08 / 7.31	3.23 / 5.18	2.84 / 4.31	2.61 / 3.83	2.45 / 3.51	2.34 / 3.29	2.25 / 3.12	2.18 / 2.99	2.12 / 2.88	2.07 / 2.80	2.04 / 2.73	2.00 / 2.66	1.95 / 2.56	1.90 / 2.49	1.84 / 2.37	1.79 / 2.29	1.74 / 2.20	1.69 / 2.11	1.66 / 2.05	1.61 / 1.97	1.59 / 1.94	1.55 / 1.88	1.53 / 1.84	1.51 / 1.81
42	4.07 / 7.27	3.22 / 5.15	2.83 / 4.29	2.59 / 3.80	2.44 / 3.49	2.32 / 3.26	2.24 / 3.10	2.17 / 2.96	2.11 / 2.86	2.06 / 2.77	2.02 / 2.70	1.99 / 2.64	1.94 / 2.54	1.89 / 2.46	1.82 / 2.35	1.78 / 2.26	1.73 / 2.17	1.68 / 2.08	1.64 / 2.02	1.60 / 1.94	1.57 / 1.91	1.54 / 1.85	1.51 / 1.80	1.49 / 1.78
44	4.06 / 7.24	3.21 / 5.12	2.82 / 4.26	2.58 / 3.78	2.43 / 3.46	2.31 / 3.24	2.23 / 3.07	2.16 / 2.94	2.10 / 2.84	2.05 / 2.75	2.01 / 2.68	1.98 / 2.62	1.92 / 2.52	1.88 / 2.44	1.81 / 2.32	1.76 / 2.24	1.72 / 2.15	1.66 / 2.06	1.63 / 2.00	1.58 / 1.92	1.56 / 1.88	1.52 / 1.82	1.50 / 1.78	1.48 / 1.75
46	4.05 / 7.21	3.20 / 5.10	2.81 / 4.24	2.57 / 3.76	2.42 / 3.44	2.30 / 3.22	2.22 / 3.05	2.14 / 2.92	2.09 / 2.82	2.04 / 2.73	2.00 / 2.66	1.97 / 2.60	1.91 / 2.50	1.87 / 2.42	1.80 / 2.30	1.75 / 2.22	1.71 / 2.13	1.65 / 2.04	1.62 / 1.98	1.57 / 1.90	1.54 / 1.86	1.51 / 1.80	1.48 / 1.76	1.46 / 1.72
48	4.04 / 7.19	3.19 / 5.08	2.80 / 4.22	2.56 / 3.74	2.41 / 3.42	2.30 / 3.20	2.21 / 3.04	2.14 / 2.90	2.08 / 2.80	2.03 / 2.71	1.99 / 2.64	1.96 / 2.58	1.90 / 2.48	1.86 / 2.40	1.79 / 2.28	1.74 / 2.20	1.70 / 2.11	1.64 / 2.02	1.61 / 1.96	1.56 / 1.88	1.53 / 1.84	1.50 / 1.78	1.47 / 1.73	1.45 / 1.70
50	4.03 / 7.17	3.18 / 5.06	2.79 / 4.20	2.56 / 3.72	2.40 / 3.41	2.29 / 3.18	2.20 / 3.02	2.13 / 2.88	2.07 / 2.78	2.02 / 2.70	1.98 / 2.62	1.95 / 2.56	1.90 / 2.46	1.85 / 2.39	1.78 / 2.26	1.74 / 2.18	1.69 / 2.10	1.63 / 2.00	1.60 / 1.94	1.55 / 1.86	1.52 / 1.82	1.48 / 1.76	1.46 / 1.71	1.44 / 1.68
55	4.02 / 7.12	3.17 / 5.01	2.78 / 4.16	2.54 / 3.68	2.38 / 3.37	2.27 / 3.15	2.18 / 2.98	2.11 / 2.85	2.05 / 2.75	2.00 / 2.66	1.97 / 2.59	1.93 / 2.53	1.88 / 2.43	1.83 / 2.35	1.76 / 2.23	1.72 / 2.15	1.67 / 2.06	1.61 / 1.96	1.58 / 1.90	1.52 / 1.82	1.50 / 1.78	1.46 / 1.71	1.43 / 1.66	1.41 / 1.64
60	4.00 / 7.08	3.15 / 4.98	2.76 / 4.13	2.52 / 3.65	2.37 / 3.34	2.25 / 3.12	2.17 / 2.95	2.10 / 2.82	2.04 / 2.72	1.99 / 2.63	1.95 / 2.56	1.92 / 2.50	1.86 / 2.40	1.81 / 2.32	1.75 / 2.20	1.70 / 2.12	1.65 / 2.03	1.59 / 1.93	1.56 / 1.87	1.50 / 1.79	1.48 / 1.74	1.44 / 1.68	1.41 / 1.63	1.39 / 1.60
65	3.99 / 7.04	3.14 / 4.95	2.75 / 4.10	2.51 / 3.62	2.36 / 3.31	2.24 / 3.09	2.15 / 2.93	2.08 / 2.79	2.02 / 2.70	1.98 / 2.61	1.94 / 2.54	1.90 / 2.47	1.85 / 2.37	1.80 / 2.30	1.73 / 2.18	1.68 / 2.09	1.63 / 2.00	1.57 / 1.90	1.54 / 1.84	1.49 / 1.76	1.46 / 1.71	1.42 / 1.64	1.39 / 1.60	1.37 / 1.56
70	3.98 / 7.01	3.13 / 4.92	2.74 / 4.08	2.50 / 3.60	2.35 / 3.29	2.23 / 3.07	2.14 / 2.91	2.07 / 2.77	2.01 / 2.67	1.97 / 2.59	1.93 / 2.51	1.89 / 2.45	1.84 / 2.35	1.79 / 2.28	1.72 / 2.15	1.67 / 2.07	1.62 / 1.98	1.56 / 1.88	1.53 / 1.82	1.47 / 1.74	1.45 / 1.69	1.40 / 1.62	1.37 / 1.56	1.35 / 1.53
80	3.96 / 6.96	3.11 / 4.88	2.72 / 4.04	2.48 / 3.56	2.33 / 3.25	2.21 / 3.04	2.12 / 2.87	2.05 / 2.74	1.99 / 2.64	1.95 / 2.55	1.91 / 2.48	1.88 / 2.41	1.82 / 2.32	1.77 / 2.24	1.70 / 2.11	1.65 / 2.03	1.60 / 1.94	1.54 / 1.84	1.51 / 1.78	1.45 / 1.70	1.42 / 1.65	1.38 / 1.57	1.35 / 1.52	1.32 / 1.49
100	3.94 / 6.90	3.09 / 4.82	2.70 / 3.98	2.46 / 3.51	2.30 / 3.20	2.19 / 2.99	2.10 / 2.82	2.03 / 2.69	1.97 / 2.59	1.92 / 2.51	1.88 / 2.43	1.85 / 2.36	1.79 / 2.26	1.75 / 2.19	1.68 / 2.06	1.63 / 1.98	1.57 / 1.89	1.51 / 1.79	1.48 / 1.73	1.42 / 1.64	1.39 / 1.59	1.34 / 1.51	1.30 / 1.46	1.28 / 1.43
125	3.92 / 6.84	3.07 / 4.78	2.68 / 3.94	2.44 / 3.47	2.29 / 3.17	2.17 / 2.95	2.08 / 2.79	2.01 / 2.65	1.95 / 2.56	1.90 / 2.47	1.86 / 2.40	1.83 / 2.33	1.77 / 2.23	1.72 / 2.15	1.65 / 2.03	1.60 / 1.94	1.55 / 1.85	1.49 / 1.75	1.45 / 1.68	1.39 / 1.59	1.36 / 1.54	1.31 / 1.46	1.27 / 1.40	1.25 / 1.37
150	3.91 / 6.81	3.06 / 4.75	2.67 / 3.91	2.43 / 3.44	2.27 / 3.13	2.16 / 2.92	2.07 / 2.76	2.00 / 2.62	1.94 / 2.53	1.89 / 2.44	1.85 / 2.37	1.82 / 2.30	1.76 / 2.20	1.71 / 2.12	1.64 / 2.00	1.59 / 1.91	1.54 / 1.83	1.47 / 1.72	1.44 / 1.66	1.37 / 1.56	1.34 / 1.51	1.29 / 1.43	1.25 / 1.37	1.22 / 1.33
200	3.89 / 6.76	3.04 / 4.71	2.65 / 3.88	2.41 / 3.41	2.26 / 3.11	2.14 / 2.90	2.05 / 2.73	1.98 / 2.60	1.92 / 2.50	1.87 / 2.41	1.83 / 2.34	1.80 / 2.28	1.74 / 2.17	1.69 / 2.09	1.62 / 1.97	1.57 / 1.88	1.52 / 1.79	1.45 / 1.69	1.42 / 1.62	1.35 / 1.53	1.32 / 1.48	1.26 / 1.39	1.22 / 1.33	1.19 / 1.28
400	3.86 / 6.70	3.02 / 4.66	2.62 / 3.83	2.39 / 3.36	2.23 / 3.06	2.12 / 2.85	2.03 / 2.69	1.96 / 2.55	1.90 / 2.46	1.85 / 2.37	1.81 / 2.29	1.78 / 2.23	1.72 / 2.12	1.67 / 2.04	1.60 / 1.92	1.54 / 1.84	1.49 / 1.74	1.42 / 1.64	1.38 / 1.57	1.32 / 1.47	1.28 / 1.42	1.22 / 1.32	1.16 / 1.24	1.13 / 1.19
1000	3.85 / 6.66	3.00 / 4.62	2.61 / 3.80	2.38 / 3.34	2.22 / 3.04	2.10 / 2.82	2.02 / 2.66	1.95 / 2.53	1.89 / 2.43	1.84 / 2.34	1.80 / 2.26	1.76 / 2.20	1.70 / 2.09	1.65 / 2.01	1.58 / 1.89	1.53 / 1.81	1.47 / 1.71	1.41 / 1.61	1.36 / 1.54	1.30 / 1.44	1.26 / 1.38	1.19 / 1.28	1.13 / 1.19	1.08 / 1.11
∞	3.84 / 6.63	2.99 / 4.60	2.60 / 3.78	2.37 / 3.32	2.21 / 3.02	2.09 / 2.80	2.01 / 2.64	1.94 / 2.51	1.88 / 2.41	1.83 / 2.32	1.79 / 2.24	1.75 / 2.18	1.69 / 2.08	1.64 / 1.99	1.57 / 1.87	1.52 / 1.79	1.46 / 1.69	1.40 / 1.59	1.35 / 1.52	1.28 / 1.41	1.24 / 1.36	1.17 / 1.25	1.11 / 1.15	1.00 / 1.00

TABLE D₁   Critical Values of F that Cut Off the Upper and Lower 2.5% of the F-distributions

A difference in variances is significant at $\alpha = 0.05$ with df_1 and df_2 if it equals or exceeds the upper value in each cell or is *less than or equal to* the lower value in that cell. For example, if $\hat{s}_1^2 = 8.69$, $df = 12$ and $\hat{s}_2^2 = 2.63$, $df = 9$, $F = 3.30$. The critical values at df_{12} and df_9 are .291 and 3.87. Since the obtained F is between these values, we fail to reject the hypothesis of homogeneity of variances. *Note:* Had we calculated F with $\hat{s}_1^2$ in the denominator, the critical lower and upper values at 9 and 12 df would have been .259 and 3.44.

df		1	2	3	4	5	6	7	8	9	10	11	12	15	20	24	30	40	50	60	100	200	500
1		.002	.026	.057	.082	.100	.113	.124	.132	.139	.144	.149	.153	.161	.170	.175	.180	.184	.187	.189	.193	.196	.198
		648	800	864	900	922	937	948	957	963	969	973	977	985	993	997	1000	1010	1010	1010	1010	1020	1020
2		.001	.026	.062	.094	.119	.138	.153	.165	.175	.183	.190	.196	.210	.224	.232	.239	.247	.251	.255	.261	.266	.269
		38.5	39.0	39.2	39.2	39.3	39.3	39.4	39.4	39.4	39.4	39.4	39.4	39.4	39.4	39.5	39.5	39.5	39.5	39.5	39.5	39.5	39.5
3		.001	.026	.065	.100	.129	.152	.170	.185	.197	.207	.216	.224	.241	.259	.269	.279	.289	.295	.299	.308	.314	.318
		17.4	16.0	15.4	15.1	14.9	14.7	14.6	14.5	14.5	14.4	14.4	14.3	14.3	14.2	14.1	14.1	14.0	14.0	14.0	14.0	13.9	13.9
4		.001	.026	.066	.104	.135	.161	.181	.198	.212	.224	.234	.243	.263	.284	.296	.308	.320	.327	.332	.342	.351	.356
		12.2	10.6	9.98	9.60	9.36	9.20	9.07	8.98	8.90	8.84	8.79	8.75	8.66	8.56	8.51	8.46	8.41	8.38	8.36	8.32	8.29	8.27
5		.001	.025	.067	.107	.140	.167	.189	.208	.223	.236	.248	.257	.280	.304	.317	.330	.344	.353	.359	.370	.380	.386
		10.0	8.43	7.76	7.39	7.15	6.98	6.85	6.76	6.68	6.62	6.57	6.52	6.43	6.33	6.28	6.23	6.18	6.14	6.12	6.08	6.05	6.03
6		.001	.025	.068	.109	.143	.172	.195	.215	.231	.246	.258	.268	.293	.320	.334	.349	.364	.375	.381	.394	.405	.415
		8.81	7.26	6.60	6.23	5.99	5.82	5.70	5.60	5.52	5.46	5.41	5.37	5.27	5.17	5.12	5.07	5.01	4.98	4.96	4.92	4.88	4.86
7		.001	.025	.068	.110	.146	.176	.200	.221	.238	.253	.266	.277	.304	.333	.348	.364	.381	.392	.399	.413	.426	.433
		8.07	6.54	5.89	5.52	5.29	5.12	4.99	4.90	4.82	4.76	4.71	4.67	4.57	4.47	4.42	4.36	4.31	4.28	4.25	4.21	4.18	4.16
8		.001	.025	.069	.111	.148	.179	.204	.226	.244	.259	.273	.285	.313	.343	.360	.377	.395	.407	.415	.431	.442	.450
		7.57	6.06	5.42	5.05	4.82	4.65	4.53	4.43	4.36	4.30	4.24	4.20	4.10	4.00	3.95	3.89	3.84	3.81	3.78	3.74	3.70	3.68
9		.001	.025	.069	.112	.150	.181	.207	.230	.248	.265	.279	.291	.320	.352	.370	.388	.408	.420	.428	.446	.459	.467
		7.21	5.71	5.08	4.72	4.48	4.32	4.20	4.10	4.03	3.96	3.91	3.87	3.77	3.67	3.61	3.56	3.51	3.47	3.45	3.40	3.37	3.35
10		.001	.025	.069	.113	.151	.183	.210	.233	.252	.269	.283	.296	.327	.360	.379	.398	.419	.431	.441	.459	.474	.483
		6.94	5.46	4.83	4.47	4.24	4.07	3.95	3.85	3.78	3.72	3.66	3.62	3.52	3.42	3.37	3.31	3.26	3.22	3.20	3.15	3.12	3.09

TABLE D₁ *(continued)*

df	1	2	3	4	5	6	7	8	9	10	11	12	15	20	24	30	40	50	60	100	200	500
11	.001	.025	.069	.114	.152	.185	.212	.236	.256	.273	.288	.301	.332	.368	.386	.407	.429	.442	.450	.472	.485	.495
	6.72	5.26	4.63	4.28	4.04	3.88	3.76	3.66	3.59	3.53	3.47	3.43	3.33	3.23	3.17	3.12	3.06	3.03	3.00	2.96	2.92	2.90
12	.001	.025	.070	.114	.153	.186	.214	.238	.259	.276	.292	.305	.337	.374	.394	.416	.437	.450	.461	.481	.498	.508
	6.55	5.10	4.47	4.12	3.89	3.73	3.61	3.51	3.44	3.37	3.32	3.28	3.18	3.07	3.02	2.96	2.91	2.87	2.85	2.80	2.76	2.74
15	.001	.025	.070	.116	.156	.190	.219	.244	.265	.284	.300	.315	.349	.389	.410	.433	.458	.474	.485	.508	.526	.538
	6.20	4.76	4.15	3.80	3.58	3.41	3.29	3.20	3.12	3.06	3.01	2.96	2.86	2.76	2.70	2.64	2.59	2.55	2.52	2.47	2.44	2.41
20	.001	.025	.071	.117	.158	.193	.224	.250	.273	.292	.310	.325	.363	.406	.430	.456	.484	.503	.514	.541	.562	.575
	5.87	4.46	3.86	3.51	3.29	3.13	3.01	2.91	2.84	2.77	2.72	2.68	2.57	2.46	2.41	2.35	2.29	2.25	2.22	2.17	2.13	2.10
24	.001	.025	.071	.117	.159	.195	.227	.253	.277	.297	.315	.331	.370	.415	.441	.468	.498	.518	.531	.562	.585	.599
	5.72	4.32	3.72	3.38	3.15	2.99	2.87	2.78	2.70	2.64	2.59	2.54	2.44	2.33	2.27	2.21	2.15	2.11	2.08	2.02	1.98	1.95
30	.001	.025	.071	.118	.161	.197	.229	.257	.281	.302	.321	.337	.378	.426	.453	.482	.515	.535	.551	.585	.610	.625
	5.57	4.18	3.59	3.25	3.03	2.87	2.75	2.65	2.57	2.51	2.46	2.41	2.31	2.20	2.14	2.07	2.01	1.97	1.94	1.88	1.84	1.81
40	.001	.025	.071	.119	.162	.199	.232	.260	.285	.307	.327	.344	.387	.437	.466	.498	.533	.556	.573	.610	.641	.662
	5.42	4.05	3.46	3.13	2.90	2.74	2.62	2.53	2.45	2.39	2.33	2.29	2.18	2.07	2.01	1.94	1.88	1.83	1.80	1.74	1.69	1.66
60	.001	.025	.071	.120	.163	.202	.235	.264	.290	.313	.333	.351	.396	.450	.481	.515	.555	.581	.600	.641	.680	.704
	5.29	3.93	3.34	3.01	2.79	2.63	2.51	2.41	2.33	2.27	2.22	2.17	2.06	1.94	1.88	1.82	1.74	1.70	1.67	1.60	1.54	1.51
120	.001	.025	.072	.120	.165	.204	.238	.268	.295	.318	.340	.359	.406	.464	.498	.536	.580	.611	.633	.684	.729	.762
	5.15	3.80	3.23	2.89	2.67	2.52	2.39	2.30	2.22	2.16	2.10	2.05	1.95	1.82	1.76	1.69	1.61	1.56	1.53	1.45	1.39	1.34

TABLE E Random Digits

Row number										
00000	10097	32533	76520	13586	34673	54876	80959	09117	39292	74945
00001	37542	04805	64894	74296	24805	24037	20636	10402	00822	91665
00002	08422	68953	19645	09303	23209	02560	15953	34764	35080	33606
00003	99019	02529	09376	70715	38311	31165	88676	74397	04436	27659
00004	12807	99970	80157	36147	64032	36653	98951	16877	12171	76833
00005	66065	74717	34072	76850	36697	36170	65813	39885	11199	29170
00006	31060	10805	45571	82406	35303	42614	86799	07439	23403	09732
00007	85269	77602	02051	65692	68665	74818	73053	85247	18623	88579
00008	63573	32135	05325	47048	90553	57548	28468	28709	83491	25624
00009	73796	45753	03529	64778	35808	34282	60935	20344	35273	88435
00010	98520	17767	14905	68607	22109	40558	60970	93433	50500	73998
00011	11805	05431	39808	27732	50725	68248	29405	24201	52775	67851
00012	83452	99634	06288	98033	13746	70078	18475	40610	68711	77817
00013	88685	40200	86507	58401	36766	67951	90364	76493	29609	11062
00014	99594	67348	87517	64969	91826	08928	93785	61368	23478	34113
00015	65481	17674	17468	50950	58047	76974	73039	57186	40218	16544
00016	80124	35635	17727	08015	45318	22374	21115	78253	14385	53763
00017	74350	99817	77402	77214	43236	00210	45521	64237	96286	02655
00018	69916	26803	66252	29148	36936	87203	76621	13990	94400	56418
00019	09893	20505	14225	68514	46427	56788	96297	78822	54382	14598
00020	91499	14523	68479	27686	46162	83554	94750	89923	37089	20048
00021	80336	94598	26940	36858	70297	34135	53140	33340	42050	82341
00022	44104	81949	85157	47954	32979	26575	57600	40881	22222	06413
00023	12550	73742	11100	02040	12860	74697	96644	89439	28707	25815
00024	63606	49329	16505	34484	40219	52563	43651	77082	07207	31790
00025	61196	90446	26457	47774	51924	33729	65394	59593	42582	60527
00026	15474	45266	95270	79953	59367	83848	82396	10118	33211	59466
00027	94557	28573	67897	54387	54622	44431	91190	42592	92927	45973
00028	42481	16213	97344	08721	16868	48767	03071	12059	25701	46670
00029	23523	78317	73208	89837	68935	91416	26252	29663	05522	82562
00030	04493	52494	75246	33824	45862	51025	61962	79335	65337	12472
00031	00549	97654	64051	88159	96119	63896	54692	82391	23287	29529
00032	35963	15307	26898	09354	33351	35462	77974	50024	90103	39333
00033	59808	08391	45427	26842	83609	49700	13021	24892	78565	20106
00034	46058	85236	01390	92286	77281	44077	93910	83647	70617	42941
00035	32179	00597	87379	25241	05567	07007	86743	17157	85394	11838
00036	69234	61406	20117	45204	15956	60000	18743	92423	97118	96338
00037	19565	41430	01758	75379	40419	21585	66674	36806	84962	85207
00038	45155	14938	19476	07246	43667	94543	59047	90033	20826	69541
00039	94864	31994	36168	10851	34888	81553	01540	35456	05014	51176
00040	98086	24826	45240	28404	44999	08896	39094	73407	35441	31880
00041	33185	16232	41941	50949	89435	48581	88695	41994	37548	73043
00042	80951	00406	96382	70774	20151	23387	25016	25298	94624	61171
00043	79752	49140	71961	28296	69861	02591	74852	20539	00387	59579
00044	18633	32537	98145	06571	31010	24674	05455	61427	77938	91936
00045	74029	43902	77557	32270	97790	17119	52527	58021	80814	51748
00046	54178	45611	80993	37143	05335	12969	56127	19255	36040	90324
00047	11664	49883	52079	84827	59381	71539	09973	33440	88461	23356
00048	48324	77928*	31249	64710	02295	36870	32307	57546	15020	09994
00049	69074	94138	87637	91976	35584	04401	10518	21615	01848	76938
00050	09188	20097	32825	39527	04220	86304	83389	87374	64278	58044
00051	90045	85497	51981	50654	94938	81997	91870	76150	68476	64659
00052	73189	50207	47677	26269	62290	64464	27124	67018	41361	82760
00053	75768	76490	20971	87749	90429	12272	95375	05871	93823	43178
00054	54016	44056	66281	31003	00682	27398	20714	53295	07706	17813
00055	08358	69910	78542	42785	13661	58873	04618	97553	31223	08420
00056	28306	03264	81333	10591	40510	07893	32604	60475	94119	01840
00057	53840	86233	81594	13628	51215	90290	28466	68795	77762	20791
00058	91757	53741	61613	62669	50263	90212	55781	76514	83483	47055
00059	89415	92694	00397	58391	12607	17646	48949	72306	94541	37408

TABLE F **Transformation of r to z_r**

r	z_r	r	z_r	r	z_r
.01	.010	.34	.354	.67	.811
.02	.020	.35	.366	.68	.829
.03	.030	.36	.377	.69	.848
.04	.040	.37	.389	.70	.867
.05	.050	.38	.400	.71	.887
.06	.060	.39	.412	.72	.908
.07	.070	.40	.424	.73	.929
.08	.080	.41	.436	.74	.950
.09	.090	.42	.448	.75	.973
.10	.100	.43	.460	.76	.996
.11	.110	.44	.472	.77	1.020
.12	.121	.45	.485	.78	1.045
.13	.131	.46	.497	.79	1.071
.14	.141	.47	.510	.80	1.099
.15	.151	.48	.523	.81	1.127
.16	.161	.49	.536	.82	1.157
.17	.172	.50	.549	.83	1.188
.18	.181	.51	.563	.84	1.221
.19	.192	.52	.577	.85	1.256
.20	.203	.53	.590	.86	1.293
.21	.214	.54	.604	.87	1.333
.22	.224	.55	.618	.88	1.376
.23	.234	.56	.633	.89	1.422
.24	.245	.57	.648	.90	1.472
.25	.256	.58	.663	.91	1.528
.26	.266	.59	.678	.92	1.589
.27	.277	.60	.693	.93	1.658
.28	.288	.61	.709	.94	1.738
.29	.299	.62	.725	.95	1.832
.30	.309	.63	.741	.96	1.946
.31	.321	.64	.758	.97	2.092
.32	.332	.65	.775	.98	2.298
.33	.343	.66	.793	.99	2.647

TABLE G Critical Values of r_s

A given value of r_s is statistically significant if it equals or exceeds the tabled value at the designated α-level at a given N. To interpolate, sum the critical values above and below the N of interest and divide by 2. Thus, the critical value at $\alpha = 0.05$, two-tailed test, when $N = 21$, is $(0.450 + 0.428)/2 = 0.439$.

	Level of significance for one-tailed test			
	.05	.025	.01	.005
	Level of significance for two-tailed test			
N^*	.10	.05	.02	.01
5	.900	1.000	1.000	--
6	.829	.886	.943	1.000
7	.714	.786	.893	.929
8	.643	.738	.833	.881
9	.600	.683	.783	.833
10	.564	.648	.746	.794
12	.506	.591	.712	.777
14	.456	.544	.645	.715
16	.425	.506	.601	.665
18	.399	.475	.564	.625
20	.377	.450	.534	.591
22	.359	.428	.508	.562
24	.343	.409	.485	.537
26	.329	.392	.465	.515
28	.317	.377	.448	.496
30	.306	.364	.432	.478

$^* N$ = number of pairs.

TABLE H Functions of r

r	$\sqrt{r}$	r^2	$\sqrt{r-r^2}$	$\sqrt{1-r}$	$1-r^2$	$\sqrt{1-r^2}$	$100(1-k)$	r
						k	% Eff.	
1.00	1.0000	1.0000	0.0000	0.0000	0.0000	0.0000	100.00	1.00
.99	.9950	.9801	.0995	.1000	.0199	.1411	85.89	.99
.98	.9899	.9604	.1400	.1414	.0396	.1990	80.10	.98
.97	.9849	.9409	.1706	.1732	.0591	.2431	75.69	.97
.96	.9798	.9216	.1960	.2000	.0784	.2800	72.00	.96
.95	.9747	.9025	.2179	.2236	.0975	.3122	68.78	.95
.94	.9695	.8836	.2375	.2449	.1164	.3412	65.88	.94
.93	.9644	.8649	.2551	.2646	.1351	.3676	63.24	.93
.92	.9592	.8464	.2713	.2828	.1536	.3919	60.81	.92
.91	.9539	.8281	.2862	.3000	.1719	.4146	58.54	.91
.90	.9487	.8100	.3000	.3162	.1900	.4359	56.41	.90
.89	.9434	.7921	.3129	.3317	.2079	.4560	54.40	.89
.88	.9381	.7744	.3250	.3464	.2256	.4750	52.50	.88
.87	.9327	.7569	.3363	.3606	.2431	.4931	50.69	.87
.86	.9274	.7396	.3470	.3742	.2604	.5103	48.97	.86
.85	.9220	.7225	.3571	.3873	.2775	.5268	47.32	.85
.84	.9165	.7056	.3666	.4000	.2944	.5426	45.74	.84
.83	.9110	.6889	.3756	.4123	.3111	.5578	44.22	.83
.82	.9055	.6724	.3842	.4243	.3276	.5724	42.76	.82
.81	.9000	.6561	.3923	.4359	.3439	.5864	41.36	.81
.80	.8944	.6400	.4000	.4472	.3600	.6000	40.00	.80
.79	.8888	.6241	.4073	.4583	.3759	.6131	38.69	.79
.78	.8832	.6084	.4142	.4690	.3916	.6258	37.42	.78
.77	.8775	.5929	.4208	.4796	.4071	.6380	36.20	.77
.76	.8718	.5776	.4271	.4899	.4224	.6499	35.01	.76
.75	.8660	.5625	.4330	.5000	.4375	.6614	33.86	.75
.74	.8602	.5476	.4386	.5099	.4524	.6726	32.74	.74
.73	.8544	.5329	.4440	.5196	.4671	.6834	31.66	.73
.72	.8485	.5184	.4490	.5292	.4816	.6940	30.60	.72
.71	.8426	.5041	.4538	.5385	.4959	.7042	29.58	.71
.70	.8367	.4900	.4583	.5477	.5100	.7141	28.59	.70
.69	.8307	.4761	.4625	.5568	.5239	.7238	27.62	.69
.68	.8246	.4624	.4665	.5657	.5376	.7332	26.68	.68
.67	.8185	.4489	.4702	.5745	.5511	.7424	25.76	.67
.66	.8124	.4356	.4737	.5831	.5644	.7513	24.87	.66
.65	.8062	.4225	.4770	.5916	.5775	.7599	24.01	.65
.64	.8000	.4096	.4800	.6000	.5904	.7684	23.16	.64
.63	.7937	.3969	.4828	.6083	.6031	.7766	22.34	.63
.62	.7874	.3844	.4854	.6164	.6156	.7846	21.54	.62
.61	.7810	.3721	.4877	.6245	.6279	.7924	20.76	.61
.60	.7746	.3600	.4899	.6325	.6400	.8000	20.00	.60
.59	.7681	.3481	.4918	.6403	.6519	.8074	19.26	.59
.58	.7616	.3364	.4936	.6481	.6636	.8146	18.54	.58
.57	.7550	.3249	.4951	.6557	.6751	.8216	17.84	.57
.56	.7483	.3136	.4964	.6633	.6864	.8285	17.15	.56
.55	.7416	.3025	.4975	.6708	.6975	.8352	16.48	.55
.54	.7348	.2916	.4984	.6782	.7084	.8417	15.83	.54
.53	.7280	.2809	.4991	.6856	.7191	.8480	15.20	.53
.52	.7211	.2704	.4996	.6928	.7296	.8542	14.58	.52
.51	.7141	.2601	.4999	.7000	.7399	.8602	13.98	.51
.50	.7071	.2500	.5000	.7071	.7500	.8660	13.40	.50

TABLE H *(continued)*

r	$\sqrt{r}$	r^2	$\sqrt{r-r^2}$	$\sqrt{1-r}$	$1-r^2$	$\sqrt{1-r^2}$	$100(1-k)$	r
						k	% Eff.	
.50	.7071	.2500	.5000	.7071	.7500	.8660	13.40	.50
.49	.7000	.2401	.4999	.7141	.7599	.8717	12.83	.49
.48	.6928	.2304	.4996	.7211	.7696	.8773	12.27	.48
.47	.6856	.2209	.4991	.7280	.7791	.8827	11.73	.47
.46	.6782	.2116	.4984	.7348	.7884	.8879	11.21	.46
.45	.6708	.2025	.4975	.7416	.7975	.8930	10.70	.45
.44	.6633	.1936	.4964	.7483	.8064	.8980	10.20	.44
.43	.6557	.1849	.4951	.7550	.8151	.9028	9.72	.43
.42	.6481	.1764	.4936	.7616	.8236	.9075	9.25	.42
.41	.6403	.1681	.4918	.7681	.8319	.9121	8.79	.41
.40	.6325	.1600	.4899	.7746	.8400	.9165	8.35	.40
.39	.6245	.1521	.4877	.7810	.8479	.9208	7.92	.39
.38	.6164	.1444	.4854	.7874	.8556	.9250	7.50	.38
.37	.6083	.1369	.4828	.7937	.8631	.9290	7.10	.37
.36	.6000	.1296	.4800	.8000	.8704	.9330	6.70	.36
.35	.5916	.1225	.4770	.8062	.8775	.9367	6.33	.35
.34	.5831	.1156	.4737	.8124	.8844	.9404	5.96	.34
.33	.5745	.1089	.4702	.8185	.8911	.9440	5.60	.33
.32	.5657	.1024	.4665	.8246	.8976	.9474	5.25	.32
.31	.5568	.0961	.4625	.8307	.9039	.9507	4.93	.31
.30	.5477	.0900	.4583	.8367	.9100	.9539	4.61	.30
.29	.5385	.0841	.4538	.8426	.9159	.9570	4.30	.29
.28	.5292	.0784	.4490	.8485	.9216	.9600	4.00	.28
.27	.5196	.0729	.4440	.8544	.9271	.9629	3.71	.27
.26	.5099	.0676	.4386	.8602	.9324	.9656	3.44	.26
.25	.5000	.0625	.4330	.8660	.9375	.9682	3.18	.25
.24	.4899	.0576	.4271	.8718	.9424	.9708	2.92	.24
.23	.4796	.0529	.4208	.8775	.9471	.9732	2.68	.23
.22	.4690	.0484	.4142	.8832	.9516	.9755	2.45	.22
.21	.4583	.0441	.4073	.8888	.9559	.9777	2.23	.21
.20	.4472	.0400	.4000	.8944	.9600	.9798	2.02	.20
.19	.4359	.0361	.3923	.9000	.9639	.9818	1.82	.19
.18	.4243	.0324	.3842	.9055	.9676	.9837	1.63	.18
.17	.4123	.0289	.3756	.9110	.9711	.9854	1.46	.17
.16	.4000	.0256	.3666	.9165	.9744	.9871	1.29	.16
.15	.3873	.0225	.3571	.9220	.9775	.9887	1.13	.15
.14	.3742	.0196	.3470	.9274	.9804	.9902	.98	.14
.13	.3606	.0169	.3363	.9327	.9831	.9915	.85	.13
.12	.3464	.0144	.3250	.9381	.9856	.9928	.72	.12
.11	.3317	.0121	.3129	.9434	.9879	.9939	.61	.11
.10	.3162	.0100	.3000	.9487	.9900	.9950	.50	.10
.09	.3000	.0081	.2862	.9539	.9919	.9959	.41	.09
.08	.2828	.0064	.2713	.9592	.9936	.9968	.32	.08
.07	.2646	.0049	.2551	.9644	.9951	.9975	.25	.07
.06	.2449	.0036	.2375	.9695	.9964	.9982	.18	.06
.05	.2236	.0025	.2179	.9747	.9975	.9987	.13	.05
.04	.2000	.0016	.1960	.9798	.9984	.9992	.08	.04
.03	.1732	.0009	.1706	.9849	.9991	.9995	.05	.03
.02	.1414	.0004	.1400	.9899	.9996	.9998	.02	.02
.01	.1000	.0001	.0995	.9950	.9999	.9999	.01	.01
.00	.0000	.0000	.0000	1.0000	1.0000	1.0000	.00	.00

TABLE I. Critical Values of U and U' for a One-Tailed Test at $\alpha = 0.005$ or a Two-Tailed Test at $\alpha = 0.01$

To be significant for any given N_1 and N_2, obtained U must be equal to or *less than* the value shown in the table. Obtained U' must be equal to or *greater than* the value shown in the table. *Example:* If $\alpha = 0.01$, two-tailed test, $N_1 = 13$, $N_2 = 15$, and obtained $U = 150$, we cannot reject H_0 since obtained U is within the upper (153) and lower (42) critical values.

Each cell shows U (upper) over U' (lower), written as U/U'.

N_2＼N_1	1	2	3	4	5	6	7	8	9	10	11	12	13	14	15	16	17	18	19	20
1	--	--	--	--	--	--	--	--	--	--	--	--	--	--	--	--	--	--	--	--
2	--	--	--	--	--	--	--	--	--	--	--	--	--	--	--	--	--	--	0/38	0/40
3	--	--	--	--	--	--	--	--	0/27	0/30	0/33	1/35	1/38	1/41	2/43	2/46	2/49	2/52	3/54	3/57
4	--	--	--	--	--	0/24	0/28	1/31	1/35	2/38	2/42	3/45	3/49	4/52	5/55	5/59	6/62	6/66	7/69	8/72
5	--	--	--	--	0/25	1/29	1/34	2/38	3/42	4/46	5/50	6/54	7/58	7/63	8/67	9/71	10/75	11/79	12/83	13/87
6	--	--	--	0/24	1/29	2/34	3/39	4/44	5/49	6/54	7/59	9/63	10/68	11/73	12/78	13/83	15/87	16/92	17/97	18/102
7	--	--	--	0/28	1/34	3/39	4/45	6/50	7/56	9/61	10/67	12/72	13/78	15/83	16/89	18/94	19/100	21/105	22/111	24/116
8	--	--	--	1/31	2/38	4/44	6/50	7/57	9/63	11/69	13/75	15/81	17/87	18/94	20/100	22/106	24/112	26/118	28/124	30/130
9	--	--	0/27	1/35	3/42	5/49	7/56	9/63	11/70	13/77	16/83	18/90	20/97	22/104	24/111	27/117	29/124	31/131	33/138	36/144
10	--	--	0/30	2/38	4/46	6/54	9/61	11/69	13/77	16/84	18/92	21/99	24/106	26/114	29/121	31/129	34/136	37/143	39/151	42/158
11	--	--	0/33	2/42	5/50	7/59	10/67	13/75	16/83	18/92	21/100	24/108	27/116	30/124	33/132	36/140	39/148	42/156	45/164	48/172
12	--	--	1/35	3/45	6/54	9/63	12/72	15/81	18/90	21/99	24/108	27/117	31/125	34/134	37/143	41/151	44/160	47/169	51/177	54/186
13	--	--	1/38	3/49	7/58	10/68	13/78	17/87	20/97	24/106	27/116	31/125	34/125	38/144	42/153	45/163	49/172	53/181	56/191	60/200
14	--	--	1/41	4/52	7/63	11/73	15/83	18/94	22/104	26/114	30/124	34/134	38/144	42/154	46/164	50/174	54/184	58/194	63/203	67/213
15	--	--	2/43	5/55	8/67	12/78	16/89	20/100	24/111	29/121	33/132	37/143	42/153	46/164	51/174	55/185	60/195	64/206	69/216	73/227
16	--	--	2/46	5/59	9/71	13/83	18/94	22/106	27/117	31/129	36/140	41/151	45/163	50/174	55/185	60/196	65/207	70/218	74/230	79/241
17	--	--	2/49	6/62	10/75	15/87	19/100	24/112	29/124	34/148	39/148	44/160	49/172	54/184	60/195	65/207	70/219	75/231	81/242	86/254
18	--	--	2/52	6/66	11/79	16/92	21/105	26/118	31/131	37/143	42/156	47/169	53/181	58/194	64/206	70/218	75/231	81/243	87/255	92/268
19	--	0/38	3/54	7/69	12/83	17/97	22/111	28/124	33/138	39/151	45/164	51/177	56/191	63/203	69/216	74/230	81/242	87/255	93/268	99/281
20	--	0/40	3/57	8/72	13/87	18/102	24/116	30/130	36/144	42/158	48/172	54/186	60/200	67/213	73/227	79/241	86/254	92/268	99/281	105/295

(Dashes in the body of the table indicate that no decision is possible at the stated level of significance.)

TABLE I₂ Critical Values of U and U' for a One-Tailed Test at $\alpha = 0.01$ or a Two-Tailed Test at $\alpha = 0.02$

To be significant for any given N_1 and N_2, obtained U must be equal to or *less than* the value shown in the table. Obtained U' must be equal to or *greater than* the value shown in the table.

Each cell below is given as U / U' (where U' is the underlined value).

N_2 \ N_1	1	2	3	4	5	6	7	8	9	10	11	12	13	14	15	16	17	18	19	20
1	--	--	--	--	--	--	--	--	--	--	--	--	--	--	--	--	--	--	--	--
2	--	--	--	--	--	--	--	--	--	--	--	--	0/26	0/28	0/30	0/32	0/34	0/36	1/37	1/39
3	--	--	--	--	--	--	0/21	0/24	1/26	1/29	1/32	2/34	2/37	2/40	3/42	3/45	4/47	4/50	4/53	5/55
4	--	--	--	--	0/20	1/23	1/27	2/30	3/33	3/37	4/40	5/43	5/47	6/50	7/53	7/57	8/60	9/63	9/67	10/70
5	--	--	--	0/20	1/24	2/28	3/32	4/36	5/40	6/44	7/48	8/52	9/56	10/60	11/64	12/68	13/72	14/76	15/80	16/84
6	--	--	--	1/23	2/28	3/33	4/38	6/42	7/47	8/52	9/57	11/61	12/66	13/71	15/75	16/80	18/84	19/89	20/94	22/98
7	--	--	0/21	1/27	3/32	4/38	6/43	7/49	9/54	11/59	12/65	14/70	16/75	17/81	19/86	21/91	23/96	24/102	26/107	28/112
8	--	--	0/24	2/30	4/36	6/42	7/49	9/55	11/61	13/67	15/73	17/79	20/84	22/90	24/96	26/102	28/108	30/114	32/120	34/126
9	--	--	1/26	3/33	5/40	7/47	9/54	11/61	14/67	16/74	18/81	21/87	23/94	26/100	28/107	31/113	33/120	36/126	38/133	40/140
10	--	--	1/29	3/37	6/44	8/52	11/59	13/67	16/74	19/81	22/88	24/96	27/103	30/110	33/117	36/124	38/132	41/139	44/146	47/153
11	--	--	1/32	4/40	7/48	9/57	12/65	15/73	18/81	22/88	25/96	28/104	31/112	34/120	37/128	41/135	44/143	47/151	50/159	53/167
12	--	--	2/34	5/43	8/52	11/61	14/70	17/79	21/87	24/96	28/104	31/113	35/121	38/130	42/138	46/146	49/155	53/163	56/172	60/180
13	--	0/26	2/37	5/47	9/56	12/66	16/75	20/84	23/94	27/103	31/112	35/121	39/130	43/139	47/148	51/157	55/166	59/175	63/184	67/193
14	--	0/28	2/40	6/50	10/60	13/71	17/81	22/90	26/100	30/110	34/120	38/130	43/139	47/149	51/159	56/168	60/178	65/187	69/197	73/207
15	--	0/30	3/42	7/53	11/64	15/75	19/86	24/96	28/107	33/117	37/128	42/138	47/148	51/159	56/169	61/179	66/189	70/200	75/210	80/220
16	--	0/32	3/45	7/57	12/68	16/80	21/91	26/102	31/113	36/124	41/135	46/146	51/157	56/168	61/179	66/190	71/201	76/212	82/222	87/233
17	--	0/34	4/47	8/60	13/72	18/84	23/96	28/108	33/120	38/132	44/143	49/155	55/166	60/178	66/189	71/201	77/212	82/224	88/234	93/247
18	--	0/36	4/50	9/63	14/76	19/89	24/102	30/114	36/126	41/139	47/151	53/163	59/175	65/187	70/200	76/212	82/224	88/236	94/248	100/260
19	--	1/37	4/53	9/67	15/80	20/94	26/107	32/120	38/133	44/146	50/159	56/172	63/184	69/197	75/210	82/222	88/235	94/248	101/260	107/273
20	--	1/39	5/55	10/70	16/84	22/98	28/112	34/126	40/140	47/153	53/167	60/180	67/193	73/207	80/220	87/233	93/247	100/260	107/273	114/286

(Dashes in the body of the table indicate that no decision is possible at the stated level of significance.)

TABLE I₃ Critical Values of *U* and *U'* for a One-Tailed Test at α = 0.025 or a Two-Tailed Test at α = 0.05

To be significant for any given N_1 and N_2, obtained *U* must be equal to or *less than* the value shown in the table. Obtained *U'* must be equal to or *greater than* the value shown in the table.

Each cell shows *U* (top) / *U'* (bottom).

N_2 \ N_1	1	2	3	4	5	6	7	8	9	10	11	12	13	14	15	16	17	18	19	20
1	--	--	--	--	--	--	--	--	--	--	--	--	--	--	--	--	--	--	--	--
2	--	--	--	--	--	--	--	0/16	0/18	0/20	0/22	1/23	1/25	1/27	1/29	1/31	2/32	2/34	2/36	2/38
3	--	--	--	--	0/15	1/17	1/20	2/22	2/25	3/27	3/30	4/32	4/35	5/37	5/40	6/42	6/45	7/47	7/50	8/52
4	--	--	--	0/16	1/19	2/22	3/25	4/28	4/32	5/35	6/38	7/41	8/44	9/47	10/50	11/53	11/57	12/60	13/63	13/67
5	--	--	0/15	1/19	2/23	3/27	5/30	6/34	7/38	8/42	9/46	11/49	12/53	13/57	14/61	15/65	17/68	18/72	19/76	20/80
6	--	--	1/17	2/22	3/27	5/31	6/36	8/40	10/44	11/49	13/53	14/58	16/62	17/67	19/71	21/75	22/80	24/84	25/89	27/93
7	--	--	1/20	3/25	5/30	6/36	8/41	10/46	12/51	14/56	16/61	18/66	20/71	22/76	24/81	26/86	28/91	30/96	32/101	34/106
8	--	0/16	2/22	4/28	6/34	8/40	10/46	13/51	15/57	17/63	19/69	22/74	24/80	26/86	29/91	31/97	34/102	36/108	38/111	41/119
9	--	0/18	2/25	4/32	7/38	10/44	12/51	15/57	17/64	20/70	23/76	26/82	28/89	31/95	34/101	37/107	39/114	42/120	45/126	48/132
10	--	0/20	3/27	5/35	8/42	11/49	14/56	17/63	20/70	23/77	26/84	29/91	33/97	36/104	39/111	42/118	45/125	48/132	52/138	55/145
11	--	0/22	3/30	6/38	9/46	13/53	16/61	19/69	23/76	26/84	30/91	33/99	37/106	40/114	44/121	47/129	51/136	55/143	58/151	62/158
12	--	1/23	4/32	7/41	11/49	14/58	18/66	22/74	26/82	29/91	33/99	37/107	41/115	45/123	49/131	53/139	57/147	61/155	65/163	69/171
13	--	1/25	4/35	8/44	12/53	16/62	20/71	24/80	28/89	33/97	37/106	41/115	45/124	50/132	54/141	59/149	63/158	67/167	72/175	76/184
14	--	1/27	5/37	9/47	13/57	17/67	22/76	26/86	31/95	36/104	40/114	45/123	50/132	55/141	59/151	64/160	67/171	74/178	78/188	83/197
15	--	1/29	5/40	10/50	14/61	19/71	24/81	29/91	34/101	39/111	44/121	49/131	54/141	59/151	64/161	70/170	75/180	80/190	85/200	90/210
16	--	1/31	6/42	11/53	15/65	21/75	26/86	31/97	37/107	42/118	47/129	53/139	59/149	64/160	70/170	75/181	81/191	86/202	92/212	98/222
17	--	2/32	6/45	11/57	17/68	22/80	28/91	34/102	39/114	45/125	51/136	57/147	63/158	67/171	75/180	81/191	87/202	93/213	99/224	105/235
18	--	2/34	7/47	12/60	18/72	24/84	30/96	36/108	42/120	48/132	55/143	61/155	67/167	74/178	80/190	86/202	93/213	99/225	106/236	112/248
19	--	2/36	7/50	13/63	19/76	25/89	32/101	38/114	45/126	52/138	58/151	65/163	72/175	78/188	85/200	92/212	99/224	106/236	113/248	119/261
20	--	2/38	8/52	13/67	20/80	27/93	34/106	41/119	48/132	55/145	62/158	69/171	76/184	83/197	90/210	98/222	105/235	112/248	119/261	127/273

(Dashes in the body of the table indicate that no decision is possible at the stated level of significance.)

TABLE I₄ Critical Values of U and U' for a One-Tailed Test at $\alpha = 0.05$ or a Two-Tailed Test at $\alpha = 0.10$

To be significant for any given N_1 and N_2, obtained U must be equal to or *less than* the value shown in the table. Obtained U' must be equal to or *greater than* the value shown in the table.

Each cell shows U (upper value) and U' (lower value).

N_2 \ N_1	1	2	3	4	5	6	7	8	9	10	11	12	13	14	15	16	17	18	19	20
1	--	--	--	--	--	--	--	--	--	--	--	--	--	--	--	--	--	--	0 / 19	0 / 20
2	--	--	--	--	0 / 10	0 / 12	0 / 14	1 / 15	1 / 17	1 / 19	1 / 21	2 / 22	2 / 24	2 / 26	3 / 27	3 / 29	3 / 31	4 / 32	4 / 34	4 / 36
3	--	--	0 / 9	0 / 12	1 / 14	2 / 16	2 / 19	3 / 21	3 / 24	4 / 26	5 / 28	5 / 31	6 / 33	7 / 35	7 / 38	8 / 40	9 / 42	9 / 45	10 / 47	11 / 49
4	--	--	0 / 12	1 / 15	2 / 18	3 / 21	4 / 24	5 / 27	6 / 30	7 / 33	8 / 36	9 / 39	10 / 42	11 / 45	12 / 48	14 / 50	15 / 53	16 / 56	17 / 59	18 / 62
5	--	0 / 10	1 / 14	2 / 18	4 / 21	5 / 25	6 / 29	8 / 32	9 / 36	11 / 39	12 / 43	13 / 47	15 / 50	16 / 54	18 / 57	19 / 61	20 / 65	22 / 68	23 / 72	25 / 75
6	--	0 / 12	2 / 16	3 / 21	5 / 25	7 / 29	8 / 34	10 / 38	12 / 42	14 / 46	16 / 50	17 / 55	19 / 59	21 / 63	23 / 67	25 / 71	26 / 76	28 / 80	30 / 84	32 / 88
7	--	0 / 14	2 / 19	4 / 24	6 / 29	8 / 34	11 / 38	13 / 43	15 / 48	17 / 53	19 / 58	21 / 63	24 / 67	26 / 72	28 / 77	30 / 82	33 / 86	35 / 91	37 / 96	39 / 101
8	--	1 / 15	3 / 21	5 / 27	8 / 32	10 / 38	13 / 43	15 / 49	18 / 54	20 / 60	23 / 65	26 / 70	28 / 76	31 / 81	33 / 87	36 / 92	39 / 97	41 / 103	44 / 108	47 / 113
9	--	1 / 17	3 / 24	6 / 30	9 / 36	12 / 42	15 / 48	18 / 54	21 / 60	24 / 66	27 / 72	30 / 78	33 / 84	36 / 90	39 / 96	42 / 102	45 / 108	48 / 114	51 / 120	54 / 126
10	--	1 / 19	4 / 26	7 / 33	11 / 39	14 / 46	17 / 53	20 / 60	24 / 66	27 / 73	31 / 79	34 / 86	37 / 93	41 / 99	44 / 106	48 / 112	51 / 119	55 / 125	58 / 132	62 / 138
11	--	1 / 21	5 / 28	8 / 36	12 / 43	16 / 50	19 / 58	23 / 65	27 / 72	31 / 79	34 / 87	38 / 94	42 / 101	46 / 108	50 / 115	54 / 122	57 / 130	61 / 137	65 / 144	69 / 151
12	--	2 / 22	5 / 31	9 / 39	13 / 47	17 / 55	21 / 63	26 / 70	30 / 78	34 / 86	38 / 94	42 / 102	47 / 109	51 / 117	55 / 125	60 / 132	64 / 140	68 / 148	72 / 156	77 / 163
13	--	2 / 24	6 / 33	10 / 42	15 / 50	19 / 59	24 / 67	28 / 76	33 / 84	37 / 93	42 / 101	47 / 109	51 / 118	56 / 126	61 / 134	65 / 143	70 / 151	75 / 159	80 / 167	84 / 176
14	--	2 / 26	7 / 35	11 / 45	16 / 54	21 / 63	26 / 72	31 / 81	36 / 90	41 / 99	46 / 108	51 / 117	56 / 126	61 / 135	66 / 144	71 / 153	77 / 161	82 / 170	87 / 179	92 / 188
15	--	3 / 27	7 / 38	12 / 48	18 / 57	23 / 67	28 / 77	33 / 87	39 / 96	44 / 106	50 / 115	55 / 125	61 / 134	66 / 144	72 / 153	77 / 163	83 / 172	88 / 182	94 / 191	100 / 200
16	--	3 / 29	8 / 40	14 / 50	19 / 61	25 / 71	30 / 82	36 / 92	42 / 102	48 / 112	54 / 122	60 / 132	65 / 143	71 / 153	77 / 163	83 / 173	89 / 183	95 / 193	101 / 203	107 / 213
17	--	3 / 31	9 / 42	15 / 53	20 / 65	26 / 76	33 / 86	39 / 97	45 / 108	51 / 119	57 / 130	64 / 140	70 / 151	77 / 161	83 / 172	89 / 183	96 / 193	102 / 204	109 / 214	115 / 225
18	--	4 / 32	9 / 45	16 / 56	22 / 68	28 / 80	35 / 91	41 / 103	48 / 114	55 / 123	61 / 137	68 / 148	75 / 159	82 / 170	88 / 182	95 / 193	102 / 204	109 / 215	116 / 226	123 / 237
19	0 / 19	4 / 34	10 / 47	17 / 59	23 / 72	30 / 84	37 / 96	44 / 108	51 / 120	58 / 132	65 / 144	72 / 156	80 / 167	87 / 179	94 / 191	101 / 203	109 / 214	116 / 226	123 / 238	130 / 250
20	0 / 20	4 / 36	11 / 49	18 / 62	25 / 75	32 / 88	39 / 101	47 / 113	54 / 126	62 / 138	69 / 151	77 / 163	84 / 176	92 / 188	100 / 200	107 / 213	115 / 225	123 / 237	130 / 250	138 / 262

(Dashes in the body of the table indicate that no decision is possible at the stated level of significance.)

TABLE J Critical Values of *T*

The symbol *T* denotes the smaller sum of ranks associated with differences that are all of the same sign. For any given *N* (number of ranked differences), the obtained *T* is significant at a given level if it is equal to or *less than* the value shown in the table. All entries are for the *absolute* value of *T*.

	Level of significance for one-tailed test					Level of significance for one-tailed test			
	.05	.025	.01	.005		.05	.025	.01	.005
	Level of significance for two-tailed test					Level of significance for two-tailed test			
N	.10	.05	.02	.01	*N*	.10	.05	.02	.01
5	0	--	--	--	28	130	116	101	91
6	2	0	--	--	29	140	126	110	100
7	3	2	0	--	30	151	137	120	109
8	5	3	1	0	31	163	147	130	118
9	8	5	3	1	32	175	159	140	128
10	10	8	5	3	33	187	170	151	138
11	13	10	7	5	34	200	182	162	148
12	17	13	9	7	35	213	195	173	159
13	21	17	12	9	36	227	208	185	171
14	25	21	15	12	37	241	221	198	182
15	30	25	19	15	38	256	235	211	194
16	35	29	23	19	39	271	249	224	207
17	41	34	27	23	40	286	264	238	220
18	47	40	32	27	41	302	279	252	233
19	53	46	37	32	42	319	294	266	247
20	60	52	43	37	43	336	310	281	261
21	67	58	49	42	44	353	327	296	276
22	75	65	55	48	45	371	343	312	291
23	83	73	62	54	46	389	361	328	307
24	91	81	69	61	47	407	378	345	322
25	100	89	76	68	48	426	396	362	339
26	110	98	84	75	49	446	415	379	355
27	119	107	92	83	50	466	434	397	373

Slight discrepancies will be found between the critical values appearing in the table above and those in Table 2 of the 1964 revision of F. Wilcoxon and R. A. Wilcox, *Some Rapid Approximate Statistical Procedures*, New York: Lederle Laboratories. The disparity reflects the latter's policy of selecting the critical value nearest a given significance level, occasionally overstepping that level. For example, for *N* = 8,

$$\text{the probability of a } T \text{ of } 3 = 0.0390 \text{ (two-tail)}$$

and

$$\text{the probability of a } T \text{ of } 4 = 0.0546 \text{ (two-tail)}$$

Wilcoxon and Wilcox selects a *T* of 4 as the critical value at the 0.05 level of significance (two-tail), whereas Table J reflects a more conservative policy by setting a *T* of 3 as the critical value at this level.

TABLE K Factorials of Numbers 1 to 20

N	N!
0	1
1	1
2	2
3	6
4	24
5	120
6	720
7	5040
8	40320
9	362880
10	3628800
11	39916800
12	479001600
13	6227020800
14	87178291200
15	1307674368000
16	20922789888000
17	355687428096000
18	6402373705728000
19	121645100408832000
20	2432902008176640000

TABLE L Binomial Coefficients

N	$\binom{N}{0}$	$\binom{N}{1}$	$\binom{N}{2}$	$\binom{N}{3}$	$\binom{N}{4}$	$\binom{N}{5}$	$\binom{N}{6}$	$\binom{N}{7}$	$\binom{N}{8}$	$\binom{N}{9}$	$\binom{N}{10}$	Sum of Coefficients
1	1	1										2
2	1	2	1									4
3	1	3	3	1								8
4	1	4	6	4	1							16
5	1	5	10	10	5	1						32
6	1	6	15	20	15	6	1					64
7	1	7	21	35	35	21	7	1				128
8	1	8	28	56	70	56	28	8	1			256
9	1	9	36	84	126	126	84	36	9	1		612
10	1	10	45	120	210	252	210	120	45	10	1	1,024
11	1	11	55	165	330	462	462	330	165	55	11	2,048*
12	1	12	66	220	495	792	924	792	495	220	66	4,096
13	1	13	78	286	715	1287	1716	1716	1287	715	286	8,192
14	1	14	91	364	1001	2002	3003	3432	3003	2002	1001	16,384
15	1	15	105	455	1365	3003	5005	6435	6435	5005	3003	32,768
16	1	16	120	560	1820	4368	8008	11440	12870	11440	8008	65,536
17	1	17	136	680	2380	6188	12376	19448	24310	24310	19448	131,072
18	1	18	153	816	3060	8568	18564	31824	43758	48620	43758	262,144
19	1	19	171	969	3876	11628	27132	50388	75582	92378	92378	524,288
20	1	20	190	1140	4845	15504	38760	77520	125970	167960	184756	1,048,576

* From this point and below, not all the coefficients are shown in the table. However, the column "Sum of Coefficients" includes all values up to $N = 20$.

TABLE M   Critical Values of x or $N - x$ (Whichever Is Larger) at 0.05 and 0.01 Levels when $P = Q = 1/2$

x is the frequency in the P category, and $N - x$ is the frequency in the Q category. The obtained x or $N - x$ must be *equal to or greater than* the value shown for significance at the chosen level. Dashes indicate that no decision is possible for N at the given α-level.

N	ONE-TAILED TEST		TWO-TAILED TEST	
	0.05	0.01	0.05	0.01
5	5	—	—	—
6	6	—	6	—
7	7	7	7	—
8	7	8	8	—
9	8	9	8	9
10	9	10	9	10
11	9	10	10	11
12	10	11	10	11
13	10	12	11	12
14	11	12	12	13
15	12	13	12	13
16	12	14	13	14
17	13	14	13	15
18	13	15	14	15
19	14	15	15	16
20	15	16	15	17
21	15	17	16	17
22	16	17	17	18
23	16	18	17	19
24	17	19	18	19
25	18	19	18	20
26	18	20	19	20
27	19	20	20	21
28	19	21	20	22
29	20	22	21	22
30	20	22	21	23
31	21	23	22	24
32	22	24	23	24
33	22	24	23	25
34	23	25	24	25
35	23	25	24	26
36	24	26	25	27
37	24	27	25	27
38	25	27	26	28
39	26	28	27	28
40	26	28	27	29
41	27	29	28	30
42	27	29	28	30
43	28	30	29	31
44	28	31	29	31
45	29	31	30	32
46	30	32	31	33
47	30	32	31	33
48	31	33	32	34
49	31	34	32	35
50	32	34	33	35

TABLE N   Critical Values of x at α = 0.05 (Lightface) and α = 0.01 (Boldface) at Varying Values of P and Q for N's Equal to 2 through 49

The Use of Table N

This table was prepared to expedite decision making when dealing with binomial populations in which $P \neq Q$. *Example:* A researcher has conducted 12 independent repetitions of the same study, using α = 0.01. Four of these studies achieved statistical significance. Is this result (4 out of 12 statistically significant outcomes) itself statistically significant, or is it within chance expectations? Looking in the column headed .01 opposite N = 12, we find that two or more differences significant at α = 0.01 is in itself significant at α = 0.01. Thus, the researcher may conclude that the overall results of his or her investigations justify rejecting H_0.

A given value of x is significant at a given α-level if it equals or exceeds the critical value shown in the table. All values shown are one-tailed. Since the binomial is not symmetrical when $P \neq Q \neq 1/2$, there is no straightforward way to obtain two-tailed values.

TABLE N

N	P / Q	.01 / .99	.02 / .98	.03 / .97	.04 / .96	.05 / .95	.06 / .94	.07 / .93	.08 / .92	.09 / .91	.10 / .90	.11 / .89	.12 / .88	.13 / .87	.14 / .86	.15 / .85	.16 / .84	.17 / .83	.18 / .82	.19 / .81	.20 / .80	.21 / .79	.22 / .78	.23 / .77	.24 / .76	.25 / .75
2	P	1	1	2	2	2	2	2	2	2	2	2	2	2	2	2	2	2	2	2	2	2	2	—	—	—
	Q	1	2	2	2	2	2	2	2	2	2	—	—	—	—	—	—	—	—	—	—	—	—	—	—	—
3	P	1	2	2	2	2	2	2	2	2	2	2	2	2	3	3	3	3	3	3	3	3	3	3	3	3
	Q	2	2	2	2	2	3	3	3	3	3	3	3	3	3	3	3	3	3	3	3	3	—	—	—	—
4	P	1	2	2	2	2	2	2	2	2	3	3	3	3	3	3	3	3	3	3	3	3	3	3	3	4
	Q	2	2	2	2	3	3	3	3	3	3	3	3	3	4	4	4	4	4	4	4	4	4	4	4	4
5	P	1	2	2	2	2	2	2	3	3	3	3	3	3	3	3	3	3	3	4	4	4	4	4	4	4
	Q	2	2	2	3	3	3	3	3	3	3	4	4	4	4	4	4	4	4	4	4	4	4	5	5	5
6	P	2	2	2	2	2	2	3	3	3	3	3	3	3	3	3	4	4	4	4	4	4	4	4	5	5
	Q	2	2	3	3	3	3	3	3	4	4	4	4	4	4	4	4	4	5	5	5	5	5	5	5	5
7	P	2	2	2	2	2	3	3	3	3	3	3	3	4	4	4	4	4	4	4	4	4	5	5	5	5
	Q	2	2	3	3	3	3	3	4	4	4	4	4	4	4	5	5	5	5	5	5	6	6	6	6	6
8	P	2	2	2	2	3	3	3	3	3	3	3	4	4	4	4	4	4	4	5	5	5	5	5	5	5
	Q	2	3	3	3	3	3	4	4	4	4	4	4	5	5	5	5	5	5	6	6	6	6	6	6	6
9	P	2	2	2	2	3	3	3	3	3	4	4	4	4	4	4	4	5	5	5	5	5	5	5	5	5
	Q	2	3	3	3	3	4	4	4	4	4	5	5	5	5	5	5	5	6	6	6	6	6	6	6	6
10	P	2	2	2	3	3	3	3	3	4	4	4	4	4	4	4	5	5	5	5	5	5	5	6	6	6
	Q	2	3	3	3	4	4	4	4	4	5	5	5	5	5	5	6	6	6	6	6	6	7	7	7	7
11	P	2	2	2	3	3	3	3	4	4	4	4	4	4	5	5	5	5	5	5	6	6	6	6	6	6
	Q	2	3	3	3	4	4	4	4	5	5	5	5	5	6	6	6	6	6	6	7	7	7	7	7	7
12	P	2	2	2	3	3	3	3	4	4	4	4	4	5	5	5	5	5	5	6	6	6	6	6	6	7
	Q	2	3	3	4	4	4	4	5	5	5	5	6	6	6	6	6	7	7	7	7	7	7	7	8	8
13	P	2	2	3	3	3	3	4	4	4	4	4	5	5	5	5	5	6	6	6	6	6	6	7	7	7
	Q	2	3	3	4	4	4	5	5	5	5	6	6	6	6	7	7	7	7	7	7	8	8	8	8	8
14	P	2	2	3	3	3	3	4	4	4	4	5	5	5	5	5	6	6	6	6	6	7	7	7	7	7
	Q	2	3	3	4	4	4	5	5	5	5	6	6	6	6	7	7	7	7	7	8	8	8	8	8	9
15	P	2	2	3	3	3	4	4	4	4	5	5	5	5	5	6	6	6	6	6	7	7	7	7	7	8
	Q	2	3	3	4	4	5	5	5	5	6	6	6	6	7	7	7	7	8	8	8	8	8	9	9	9
16	P	2	2	3	3	3	4	4	4	4	5	5	5	5	6	6	6	6	7	7	7	7	7	8	8	8
	Q	3	3	4	4	4	5	5	5	6	6	6	6	7	7	7	7	8	8	8	8	8	9	9	9	9
17	P	2	2	3	3	4	4	4	4	5	5	5	5	6	6	6	6	7	7	7	7	7	8	8	8	8
	Q	3	3	4	4	4	5	5	5	6	6	6	7	7	7	7	8	8	8	8	9	9	9	9	9	10
18	P	2	2	3	3	4	4	4	5	5	5	5	6	6	6	6	7	7	7	7	8	8	8	8	8	9
	Q	3	3	4	4	5	5	5	6	6	6	7	7	7	7	8	8	8	8	9	9	9	9	10	10	10
19	P	2	3	3	3	4	4	4	5	5	5	6	6	6	6	7	7	7	7	8	8	8	8	9	9	9
	Q	3	3	4	4	5	5	5	6	6	6	7	7	7	8	8	8	8	9	9	9	9	10	10	10	10
20	P	2	3	3	3	4	4	4	5	5	5	6	6	6	7	7	7	7	8	8	8	8	9	9	9	9
	Q	3	3	4	4	5	5	6	6	6	7	7	7	8	8	8	8	9	9	9	9	10	10	10	10	11
21	P	2	3	3	3	4	4	5	5	5	6	6	6	6	7	7	7	8	8	8	8	9	9	9	9	10
	Q	3	3	4	4	5	5	6	6	6	7	7	7	8	8	8	9	9	9	10	10	10	10	11	11	11
22	P	2	3	3	4	4	4	5	5	5	6	6	6	7	7	7	8	8	8	8	9	9	9	9	10	10
	Q	3	3	4	5	5	5	6	6	7	7	7	8	8	8	9	9	9	10	10	10	10	11	11	11	11
23	P	2	3	3	4	4	4	5	5	6	6	6	6	7	7	7	8	8	8	9	9	9	9	10	10	10
	Q	3	4	4	5	5	6	6	6	7	7	7	8	8	9	9	9	9	10	10	10	11	11	11	12	12
24	P	2	3	3	4	4	5	5	5	6	6	6	7	7	7	8	8	8	9	9	9	9	10	10	10	11
	Q	3	4	4	5	5	6	6	7	7	7	8	8	8	9	9	9	10	10	10	11	11	11	12	12	12

.26	.27	.28	.29	.30	.31	.32	.33	.34	.35	.36	.37	.38	.39	.40	.41	.42	.43	.44	.45	.46	.47	.48	.49	.50
.74	.73	.72	.71	.70	.69	.68	.67	.66	.65	.64	.63	.62	.61	.60	.59	.58	.57	.56	.55	.54	.53	.52	.51	.50
—	—	—	—	—	—	—	—	—	—	—	—	—	—	—	—	—	—	—	—	—	—	—	—	—
—	—	—	—	—	—	—	—	—	—	—	—	—	—	—	—	—	—	—	—	—	—	—	—	—
3	3	3	3	3	3	3	3	3	3	3	—	—	—	—	—	—	—	—	—	—	—	—	—	—
—	—	—	—	—	—	—	—	—	—	—	—	—	—	—	—	—	—	—	—	—	—	—	—	—
4	4	4	4	4	4	4	4	4	4	4	4	4	4	4	4	4	4	4	4	4	—	—	—	—
4	4	4	4	4	4	—	—	—	—	—	—	—	—	—	—	—	—	—	—	—	—	—	—	—
4	4	4	4	4	4	4	4	4	5	5	5	5	5	5	5	5	5	5	5	5	5	5	5	5
5	5	5	5	5	5	5	5	5	5	5	5	5	5	5	—	—	—	—	—	—	—	—	—	—
5	5	5	5	5	5	5	5	5	5	5	5	5	5	5	5	6	6	6	6	6	6	6	6	6
5	5	5	5	6	6	6	6	6	6	6	6	6	6	6	6	6	6	6	6	6	—	—	—	—
5	5	5	5	5	5	5	5	5	6	6	6	6	6	6	6	6	6	6	6	6	6	7	7	7
6	6	6	6	6	6	6	6	6	6	6	7	7	7	7	7	7	7	7	7	7	7	7	7	7
5	5	5	6	6	6	6	6	6	6	6	6	6	6	6	6	7	7	7	7	7	7	7	7	7
6	6	6	6	7	7	7	7	7	7	7	7	7	7	7	7	8	8	8	8	8	8	8	8	8
6	6	6	6	6	6	6	6	6	7	7	7	7	7	7	7	7	7	7	8	8	8	8	8	8
7	7	7	7	7	7	7	7	7	8	8	8	8	8	8	8	8	8	8	8	9	9	9	9	9
6	6	6	6	6	7	7	7	7	7	7	7	7	7	8	8	8	8	8	8	8	8	8	8	9
7	7	7	7	8	8	8	8	8	8	8	8	8	9	9	9	9	9	9	9	9	9	9	9	10
6	6	7	7	7	7	7	7	7	8	8	8	8	8	8	8	8	8	9	9	9	9	9	9	9
7	8	8	8	8	8	8	8	9	9	9	9	9	9	9	9	9	9	10	10	10	10	10	10	10
7	7	7	7	7	7	8	8	8	8	8	8	8	8	9	9	9	9	9	9	9	10	10	10	10
8	8	8	8	8	9	9	9	9	9	9	9	10	10	10	10	10	10	10	10	10	11	11	11	11
7	7	7	8	8	8	8	8	8	8	9	9	9	9	9	9	10	10	10	10	10	10	10	10	10
8	8	9	9	9	9	9	9	10	10	10	10	10	10	10	10	11	11	11	11	11	11	11	11	12
7	8	8	8	8	8	9	9	9	9	9	9	9	9	10	10	10	10	10	10	11	11	11	11	11
9	9	9	9	9	10	10	10	10	10	10	10	11	11	11	11	11	11	11	12	12	12	12	12	12
8	8	8	8	9	9	9	9	9	9	10	10	10	10	10	10	10	11	11	11	11	11	11	12	12
9	9	9	10	10	10	10	10	10	11	11	11	11	11	11	12	12	12	12	12	12	13	13	13	13
8	8	9	9	9	9	9	9	10	10	10	10	10	10	11	11	11	11	11	11	12	12	12	12	12
9	10	10	10	10	10	11	11	11	11	11	11	12	12	12	12	12	12	13	13	13	14	14	14	14
8	9	9	9	9	9	10	10	10	10	10	11	11	11	11	11	12	12	12	12	12	13	13	13	13
10	10	10	10	11	11	11	11	11	12	12	12	12	12	13	13	13	13	13	13	14	14	14	14	14
9	9	9	9	10	10	10	10	10	11	11	11	11	11	12	12	12	12	13	13	13	13	13	13	13
10	10	11	11	11	11	12	12	12	12	12	13	13	13	13	13	13	14	14	14	14	14	14	15	15
9	9	10	10	10	10	10	11	11	11	11	11	12	12	12	12	12	13	13	13	13	13	14	14	14
11	11	11	11	12	12	12	12	12	13	13	13	13	13	14	14	14	14	15	15	15	15	15	15	15
10	10	10	10	10	11	11	11	11	12	12	12	12	12	13	13	13	13	13	14	14	14	14	14	15
11	11	11	12	12	12	12	13	13	13	13	14	14	14	14	14	15	15	15	15	15	16	16	16	16
10	10	10	11	11	11	11	12	12	12	12	13	13	13	13	13	14	14	14	14	14	15	15	15	15
11	12	12	12	12	13	13	13	13	14	14	14	14	15	15	15	15	16	16	16	16	16	16	17	17
10	10	11	11	11	11	12	12	12	12	13	13	13	13	14	14	14	14	14	15	15	15	15	16	16
12	12	12	13	13	13	13	14	14	14	14	15	15	15	15	15	16	16	16	16	17	17	17	17	17
11	11	11	11	12	12	12	12	13	13	13	13	14	14	14	14	15	15	15	15	16	16	16	16	16
12	12	13	13	13	13	14	14	14	15	15	15	15	15	16	16	16	16	17	17	17	17	18	18	18
11	11	11	12	12	12	13	13	13	13	14	14	14	15	15	15	15	16	16	16	16	17	17	17	17
13	13	13	13	14	14	14	14	15	15	15	15	16	16	16	16	17	17	17	17	18	18	18	18	19

TABLE N (continued)

N	P / Q	.01 / .99	.02 / .98	.03 / .97	.04 / .96	.05 / .95	.06 / .94	.07 / .93	.08 / .92	.09 / .91	.10 / .90	.11 / .89	.12 / .88	.13 / .87	.14 / .86	.15 / .85	.16 / .84	.17 / .83	.18 / .82	.19 / .81	.20 / .80	.21 / .79	.22 / .78	.23 / .77	.24 / .76	.25 / .75
25	P	2	3	3	4	4	5	5	5	6	6	6	7	7	8	8	8	8	9	9	9	10	10	10	11	11
	Q	3	4	4	5	5	6	6	7	7	7	8	8	9	9	9	10	10	10	11	11	11	12	12	12	13
26	P	2	3	3	4	4	5	5	6	6	6	7	7	7	8	8	8	9	9	9	10	10	10	11	11	11
	Q	3	4	4	5	5	6	6	7	7	8	8	9	9	9	10	10	10	11	11	11	12	12	12	13	13
27	P	2	3	3	4	4	5	5	6	6	6	7	7	8	8	8	9	9	9	10	10	10	11	11	11	12
	Q	3	4	4	5	6	6	6	7	7	8	8	9	9	9	10	10	11	11	11	12	12	12	13	13	13
28	P	2	3	4	4	4	5	5	6	6	7	7	7	8	8	8	9	9	10	10	10	11	11	11	12	12
	Q	3	4	4	5	6	6	7	7	8	8	8	9	9	10	10	10	11	11	12	12	12	13	13	13	14
29	P	2	3	4	4	5	5	5	6	6	7	7	8	8	8	9	9	9	10	10	10	11	11	12	12	12
	Q	3	4	5	5	6	6	7	7	8	8	9	9	9	10	10	11	11	11	12	12	13	13	13	14	14
30	P	2	3	4	4	5	5	6	6	6	7	7	8	8	8	9	9	10	10	10	11	11	11	12	12	13
	Q	3	4	5	5	6	6	7	7	8	8	9	9	10	10	10	11	11	12	12	12	13	13	14	14	14
31	P	2	3	4	4	5	5	6	6	7	7	7	8	8	9	9	9	10	10	11	11	11	12	12	12	13
	Q	3	4	5	5	6	6	7	7	8	8	9	9	10	10	11	11	12	12	12	13	13	14	14	14	15
32	P	2	3	4	4	5	5	6	6	7	7	8	8	8	9	9	10	10	10	11	11	12	12	12	13	13
	Q	3	4	5	5	6	7	7	8	8	9	9	10	10	10	11	11	12	12	13	13	13	14	14	15	15
33	P	2	3	4	4	5	5	6	6	7	7	8	8	9	9	9	10	10	11	11	12	12	12	13	13	13
	Q	3	4	5	5	6	7	7	8	8	9	9	10	10	11	11	12	12	12	13	13	14	14	15	15	15
34	P	2	3	4	4	5	6	6	7	7	7	8	8	9	9	10	10	11	11	11	12	12	13	13	13	14
	Q	3	4	5	6	6	7	7	8	8	9	9	10	10	11	11	12	12	13	13	14	14	14	15	15	16
35	P	2	3	4	5	6	6	6	7	7	8	8	9	9	9	10	10	11	11	12	12	12	13	13	14	14
	Q	3	4	5	6	6	7	7	8	9	9	10	10	11	11	12	12	13	13	13	14	14	15	15	16	16
36	P	3	3	4	5	5	6	6	7	7	8	8	9	9	10	10	11	11	11	12	12	13	13	14	14	14
	Q	3	4	5	6	6	7	8	8	9	9	10	10	11	11	12	12	13	13	14	14	15	15	15	16	16
37	P	3	3	4	5	5	6	6	7	7	8	8	9	9	10	10	11	11	12	12	13	13	13	14	14	15
	Q	3	4	5	6	6	7	8	8	9	9	10	11	11	12	12	13	13	13	14	14	15	15	16	16	17
38	P	3	3	4	5	5	6	6	7	8	8	9	9	10	10	10	11	11	12	12	13	13	14	14	15	15
	Q	3	4	5	6	7	7	8	8	9	10	10	11	11	12	12	13	13	14	14	15	15	16	16	17	17
39	P	3	3	4	5	5	6	6	7	8	8	9	9	10	10	11	11	12	12	13	13	14	14	14	15	15
	Q	3	4	5	6	7	7	8	9	9	10	10	11	11	12	12	13	13	14	14	15	15	16	16	17	17
40	P	3	3	4	5	5	6	7	7	8	8	9	9	10	10	11	11	12	12	13	13	14	14	15	15	16
	Q	3	4	5	6	7	7	8	9	9	10	10	11	12	12	13	13	14	14	15	15	16	16	17	17	18
41	P	3	3	4	5	6	6	7	7	8	8	9	10	10	11	11	12	12	13	13	14	14	15	15	15	16
	Q	3	4	5	6	7	8	8	9	9	10	11	11	12	12	13	13	14	14	15	16	16	17	17	18	18
42	P	3	4	4	5	6	6	7	7	8	9	9	10	10	11	11	12	12	13	13	14	14	15	15	16	16
	Q	3	4	5	6	7	8	8	9	10	10	11	11	12	12	13	14	14	15	15	16	16	17	17	18	18
43	P	3	4	4	5	6	6	7	8	8	9	9	10	10	11	11	12	13	13	14	14	15	15	16	16	17
	Q	3	5	5	6	7	8	8	9	10	10	11	12	12	13	13	14	14	15	16	16	17	17	18	18	19
44	P	3	4	4	5	6	6	7	8	8	9	9	10	11	11	12	12	13	13	14	14	15	15	16	16	17
	Q	3	5	5	6	7	8	9	9	10	11	11	12	12	13	14	14	15	15	16	16	17	17	18	18	19
45	P	3	4	4	5	6	7	7	8	8	9	10	10	11	11	12	12	13	13	14	15	15	16	16	17	17
	Q	4	5	6	6	7	8	9	9	10	11	11	12	13	13	14	14	15	15	16	17	17	18	18	19	19
46	P	3	4	4	5	6	7	7	8	9	9	10	10	11	11	12	13	13	14	14	15	15	16	16	17	17
	Q	4	5	6	6	7	8	9	9	10	11	11	12	13	13	14	15	15	16	16	17	17	18	19	19	20
47	P	3	4	5	5	6	7	7	8	9	9	10	10	11	12	12	13	13	14	15	15	16	16	17	17	18
	Q	4	5	6	7	7	8	9	10	10	11	12	12	13	14	14	15	15	16	17	17	18	18	19	19	20
48	P	3	4	5	5	6	7	7	8	9	9	10	11	11	12	12	13	14	14	15	15	16	16	17	18	18
	Q	4	5	6	7	7	8	9	10	10	11	12	12	13	14	14	15	16	16	17	17	18	19	19	20	20
49	P	3	4	5	5	6	7	8	8	9	10	10	11	11	12	13	13	14	14	15	16	16	17	17	18	18
	Q	4	5	6	7	8	8	9	10	11	11	12	13	13	14	15	15	16	16	17	18	18	19	19	20	21

| .26 | .27 | .28 | .29 | .30 | .31 | .32 | .33 | .34 | .35 | .36 | .37 | .38 | .39 | .40 | .41 | .42 | .43 | .44 | .45 | .46 | .47 | .48 | .49 | .50 |
.74	.73	.72	.71	.70	.69	.68	.67	.66	.65	.64	.63	.62	.61	.60	.59	.58	.57	.56	.55	.54	.53	.52	.51	.50
11	12	12	12	12	13	13	13	13	14	14	14	15	15	15	15	16	16	16	16	17	17	17	17	18
13	**13**	**13**	**14**	**14**	**14**	**15**	**15**	**15**	**15**	**16**	**16**	**16**	**17**	**17**	**17**	**17**	**18**	**18**	**18**	**18**	**19**	**19**	**19**	**19**
12	12	12	12	13	13	13	14	14	14	14	15	15	15	16	16	16	16	17	17	17	17	18	18	18
13	**14**	**14**	**14**	**14**	**15**	**15**	**15**	**16**	**16**	**16**	**16**	**17**	**17**	**17**	**18**	**18**	**18**	**18**	**19**	**19**	**19**	**19**	**20**	**20**
12	12	12	13	13	13	14	14	14	15	15	15	15	16	16	16	17	17	17	17	18	18	18	18	19
14	**14**	**14**	**15**	**15**	**15**	**15**	**16**	**16**	**16**	**17**	**17**	**17**	**18**	**18**	**18**	**18**	**19**	**19**	**19**	**19**	**20**	**20**	**20**	**20**
12	13	13	13	13	14	14	14	15	15	15	16	16	16	16	17	17	17	18	18	18	18	19	19	19
14	**14**	**15**	**15**	**15**	**16**	**16**	**16**	**17**	**17**	**17**	**17**	**18**	**18**	**18**	**19**	**19**	**19**	**19**	**20**	**20**	**20**	**21**	**21**	**21**
13	13	13	14	14	14	14	15	15	15	16	16	16	17	17	17	18	18	18	18	19	19	19	20	20
14	**15**	**15**	**15**	**16**	**16**	**16**	**17**	**17**	**17**	**18**	**18**	**18**	**19**	**19**	**19**	**19**	**20**	**20**	**20**	**21**	**21**	**21**	**21**	**22**
13	13	14	14	14	15	15	15	16	16	16	17	17	17	17	18	18	18	19	19	19	20	20	20	20
15	**15**	**15**	**16**	**16**	**16**	**17**	**17**	**17**	**18**	**18**	**18**	**19**	**19**	**19**	**20**	**20**	**20**	**21**	**21**	**21**	**21**	**22**	**22**	**22**
13	14	14	14	15	15	15	16	16	16	17	17	17	18	18	18	19	19	19	20	20	20	20	21	21
15	**15**	**16**	**16**	**16**	**17**	**17**	**17**	**18**	**18**	**19**	**19**	**19**	**19**	**20**	**20**	**20**	**21**	**21**	**21**	**22**	**22**	**22**	**23**	**23**
14	14	14	15	15	15	16	16	16	17	17	17	18	18	18	19	19	19	20	20	20	21	21	21	22
15	**16**	**16**	**16**	**17**	**17**	**18**	**18**	**18**	**19**	**19**	**19**	**20**	**20**	**20**	**21**	**21**	**21**	**22**	**22**	**22**	**22**	**23**	**23**	**24**
14	14	15	15	15	16	16	16	17	17	17	18	18	19	19	19	20	20	20	21	21	21	22	22	22
16	**16**	**16**	**17**	**17**	**18**	**18**	**18**	**19**	**19**	**19**	**20**	**20**	**20**	**21**	**21**	**21**	**22**	**22**	**22**	**23**	**23**	**23**	**24**	**24**
14	15	15	15	16	16	16	17	17	18	18	18	19	19	19	20	20	20	21	21	21	22	22	22	23
16	**16**	**17**	**17**	**17**	**18**	**18**	**19**	**19**	**20**	**20**	**20**	**21**	**21**	**21**	**22**	**22**	**22**	**23**	**23**	**23**	**24**	**24**	**24**	**25**
14	15	15	16	16	16	17	17	18	18	18	19	19	19	20	20	21	21	21	22	22	22	23	23	23
16	**17**	**17**	**18**	**18**	**18**	**19**	**19**	**20**	**20**	**20**	**21**	**21**	**21**	**22**	**22**	**23**	**23**	**23**	**24**	**24**	**25**	**25**	**25**
15	15	16	16	16	17	17	18	18	18	19	19	20	20	20	21	21	21	22	22	22	23	23	24	24
17	**17**	**18**	**18**	**18**	**19**	**19**	**20**	**20**	**20**	**21**	**21**	**22**	**22**	**22**	**23**	**23**	**23**	**24**	**24**	**25**	**25**	**25**	**26**	**26**
15	16	16	16	17	17	18	18	18	19	19	20	20	20	21	21	22	22	22	23	23	23	24	24	24
17	**18**	**18**	**18**	**19**	**19**	**20**	**20**	**20**	**21**	**21**	**22**	**22**	**22**	**23**	**23**	**24**	**24**	**24**	**25**	**25**	**25**	**26**	**26**	**27**
15	16	16	17	17	18	18	18	19	19	20	20	20	21	21	22	22	22	23	23	24	24	24	25	25
17	**18**	**18**	**19**	**19**	**20**	**20**	**20**	**21**	**21**	**22**	**22**	**23**	**23**	**23**	**24**	**24**	**24**	**25**	**25**	**26**	**26**	**26**	**27**	**27**
16	16	17	17	17	18	18	19	19	20	20	20	21	21	22	22	22	23	23	24	24	24	25	25	26
18	**18**	**19**	**19**	**20**	**20**	**20**	**21**	**21**	**22**	**22**	**23**	**23**	**23**	**24**	**24**	**25**	**25**	**25**	**26**	**26**	**27**	**27**	**27**	**28**
16	17	17	17	18	18	19	19	20	20	20	21	21	22	22	23	23	23	24	24	25	25	25	26	26
18	**19**	**19**	**20**	**20**	**20**	**21**	**21**	**22**	**22**	**23**	**23**	**23**	**24**	**24**	**25**	**25**	**26**	**26**	**26**	**27**	**27**	**28**	**28**	**28**
16	17	17	18	18	19	19	20	20	20	21	21	22	22	23	23	23	24	24	25	25	26	26	26	27
18	**19**	**19**	**20**	**20**	**21**	**21**	**22**	**22**	**23**	**23**	**23**	**24**	**24**	**25**	**25**	**26**	**26**	**26**	**27**	**27**	**28**	**28**	**28**	**29**
17	17	18	18	19	19	19	20	20	21	21	22	22	23	23	23	24	24	25	25	26	26	26	27	27
19	**19**	**20**	**20**	**21**	**21**	**22**	**22**	**23**	**23**	**23**	**24**	**24**	**25**	**25**	**26**	**26**	**27**	**27**	**27**	**28**	**28**	**29**	**29**	**29**
17	18	18	18	19	19	20	20	21	21	22	22	23	23	24	24	24	25	25	26	26	27	27	27	28
19	**20**	**20**	**21**	**21**	**22**	**22**	**23**	**23**	**23**	**24**	**24**	**25**	**25**	**26**	**26**	**27**	**27**	**28**	**28**	**28**	**29**	**29**	**30**	**30**
17	18	18	19	19	20	20	21	21	22	22	23	23	24	24	24	25	25	26	26	27	27	28	28	28
19	**20**	**21**	**21**	**21**	**22**	**22**	**23**	**23**	**24**	**24**	**25**	**25**	**26**	**26**	**27**	**27**	**28**	**28**	**28**	**29**	**29**	**30**	**30**	**31**
18	18	19	19	20	20	21	21	22	22	23	23	24	24	24	25	25	26	26	27	27	28	28	29	29
20	**20**	**21**	**21**	**22**	**22**	**23**	**23**	**24**	**24**	**25**	**25**	**26**	**26**	**27**	**27**	**28**	**28**	**29**	**29**	**29**	**30**	**30**	**31**	**31**
18	18	19	20	20	21	21	22	22	22	23	23	24	24	25	25	26	26	27	27	28	28	29	29	30
20	**21**	**21**	**22**	**22**	**23**	**23**	**24**	**24**	**25**	**25**	**26**	**26**	**27**	**27**	**28**	**28**	**29**	**29**	**30**	**30**	**30**	**31**	**31**	**32**
18	19	19	20	20	21	21	22	22	23	23	24	24	25	25	26	26	27	27	28	28	29	29	30	30
21	**21**	**22**	**22**	**23**	**23**	**24**	**24**	**25**	**25**	**26**	**26**	**27**	**27**	**28**	**28**	**29**	**29**	**30**	**30**	**31**	**31**	**31**	**32**	**32**
19	19	20	20	21	21	22	22	23	23	24	24	25	25	26	26	27	27	28	28	29	29	30	30	31
21	**21**	**22**	**22**	**23**	**24**	**24**	**25**	**25**	**26**	**26**	**27**	**27**	**28**	**28**	**29**	**29**	**30**	**30**	**31**	**31**	**32**	**32**	**33**	**33**
19	19	20	21	21	22	22	23	23	24	24	25	25	26	26	27	27	28	28	29	29	30	30	31	31
21	**22**	**22**	**23**	**23**	**24**	**24**	**25**	**26**	**26**	**27**	**27**	**28**	**28**	**29**	**29**	**30**	**30**	**31**	**31**	**32**	**32**	**33**	**33**	**34**

TABLE O Percentage Points of the Studentized Range

Error df	α	\multicolumn{10}{c}{k = number of means or number of steps between ordered means}
		2	3	4	5	6	7	8	9	10	11
5	.05	3.64	4.60	5.22	5.67	6.03	6.33	6.58	6.80	6.99	7.17
	.01	5.70	6.98	7.80	8.42	8.91	9.32	9.67	9.97	10.24	10.48
6	.05	3.46	4.34	4.90	5.30	5.63	5.90	6.12	6.32	6.49	6.65
	.01	5.24	6.33	7.03	7.56	7.97	8.32	8.61	8.87	9.10	9.30
7	.05	3.34	4.16	4.68	5.06	5.36	5.61	5.82	6.00	6.16	6.30
	.01	4.95	5.92	6.54	7.01	7.37	7.68	7.94	8.17	8.37	8.55
8	.05	3.26	4.04	4.53	4.89	5.17	5.40	5.60	5.77	5.92	6.05
	.01	4.75	5.64	6.20	6.62	6.96	7.24	7.47	7.68	7.86	8.03
9	.05	3.20	3.95	4.41	4.76	5.02	5.24	5.43	5.59	5.74	5.87
	.01	4.60	5.43	5.96	6.35	6.66	6.91	7.13	7.33	7.49	7.65
10	.05	3.15	3.88	4.33	4.65	4.91	5.12	5.30	5.46	5.60	5.72
	.01	4.48	5.27	5.77	6.14	6.43	6.67	6.87	7.05	7.21	7.36
11	.05	3.11	3.82	4.26	4.57	4.82	5.03	5.20	5.35	5.49	5.61
	.01	4.39	5.15	5.62	5.97	6.25	6.48	6.67	6.84	6.99	7.13
12	.05	3.08	3.77	4.20	4.51	4.75	4.95	5.12	5.27	5.39	5.51
	.01	4.32	5.05	5.50	5.84	6.10	6.32	6.51	6.67	6.81	6.94
13	.05	3.06	3.73	4.15	4.45	4.69	4.88	5.05	5.19	5.32	5.43
	.01	4.26	4.96	5.40	5.73	5.98	6.19	6.37	6.53	6.67	6.79
14	.05	3.03	3.70	4.11	4.41	4.64	4.83	4.99	5.13	5.25	5.36
	.01	4.21	4.89	5.32	5.63	5.88	6.08	6.26	6.41	6.54	6.66
15	.05	3.01	3.67	4.08	4.37	4.59	4.78	4.94	5.08	5.20	5.31
	.01	4.17	4.84	5.25	5.56	5.80	5.99	6.16	6.31	6.44	6.55
16	.05	3.00	3.65	4.05	4.33	4.56	4.74	4.90	5.03	5.15	5.26
	.01	4.13	4.79	5.19	5.49	5.72	5.92	6.08	6.22	6.35	6.46
17	.05	2.98	3.63	4.02	4.30	4.52	4.70	4.86	4.99	5.11	5.21
	.01	4.10	4.74	5.14	5.43	5.66	5.85	6.01	6.15	6.27	6.38
18	.05	2.97	3.61	4.00	4.28	4.49	4.67	4.82	4.96	5.07	5.17
	.01	4.07	4.70	5.09	5.38	5.60	5.79	5.94	6.08	6.20	6.31
19	.05	2.96	3.59	3.98	4.25	4.47	4.65	4.79	4.92	5.04	5.14
	.01	4.05	4.67	5.05	5.33	5.55	5.73	5.89	6.02	6.14	6.25
20	.05	2.95	3.58	3.96	4.23	4.45	4.62	4.77	4.90	5.01	5.11
	.01	4.02	4.64	5.02	5.29	5.51	5.69	5.84	5.97	6.09	6.19
24	.05	2.92	3.53	3.90	4.17	4.37	4.54	4.68	4.81	4.92	5.01
	.01	3.96	4.55	4.91	5.17	5.37	5.54	5.69	5.81	5.92	6.02
30	.05	2.89	3.49	3.85	4.10	4.30	4.46	4.60	4.72	4.82	4.92
	.01	3.89	4.45	4.80	5.05	5.24	5.40	5.54	5.65	5.76	5.85
40	.05	2.86	3.44	3.79	4.04	4.23	4.39	4.52	4.63	4.73	4.82
	.01	3.82	4.37	4.70	4.93	5.11	5.26	5.39	5.50	5.60	5.69
60	.05	2.83	3.40	3.74	3.98	4.16	4.31	4.44	4.55	4.65	4.73
	.01	3.76	4.28	4.59	4.82	4.99	5.13	5.25	5.36	5.45	5.53
120	.05	2.80	3.36	3.68	3.92	4.10	4.24	4.36	4.47	4.56	4.64
	.01	3.70	4.20	4.50	4.71	4.87	5.01	5.12	5.21	5.30	5.37
∞	.05	2.77	3.31	3.63	3.86	4.03	4.17	4.29	4.39	4.47	4.55
	.01	3.64	4.12	4.40	4.60	4.76	4.88	4.99	5.08	5.16	5.23

TABLE P **Squares, Square Roots, and Reciprocals of Numbers from 1 to 1000**

N	N²	√N	1/N	N	N²	√N	1/N	N	N²	√N	1/N
1	1	1.0000	1.000000	61	3721	7.8102	.016393	121	14641	11.0000	.00826446
2	4	1.4142	.500000	62	3844	7.8740	.016129	122	14884	11.0454	.00819672
3	9	1.7321	.333333	63	3969	7.9373	.015873	123	15129	11.0905	.00813008
4	16	2.0000	.250000	64	4096	8.0000	.015625	124	15376	11.1355	.00800452
5	25	2.2361	.200000	65	4225	8.0623	.015385	125	15625	11.1803	.00800000
6	36	2.4495	.166667	66	4356	8.1240	.015152	126	15876	11.2250	.00793651
7	49	2.6458	.142857	67	4489	8.1854	.014925	127	16129	11.2694	.00787402
8	64	2.8284	.125000	68	4624	8.2462	.014706	128	16384	11.3137	.00781250
9	81	3.0000	.111111	69	4761	8.3066	.014493	129	16641	11.3578	.00775194
10	100	3.1623	.100000	70	4900	8.3666	.014286	130	16900	11.4018	.00769231
11	121	3.3166	.090909	71	5041	8.4261	.014085	131	17161	11.4455	.00763359
12	144	3.4641	.083333	72	5184	8.4853	.013889	132	17424	11.4891	.00757576
13	169	3.6056	.076923	73	5329	8.5440	.013699	133	17689	11.5326	.00751880
14	196	3.7417	.071429	74	5476	8.6023	.013514	134	17956	11.5758	.00746269
15	225	3.8730	.066667	75	5625	8.6603	.013333	135	18225	11.6190	.00740741
16	256	4.0000	.062500	76	5776	8.7178	.013158	136	18496	11.6619	.00735294
17	289	4.1231	.058824	77	5929	8.7750	.012987	137	18769	11.7047	.00729927
18	324	4.2426	.055556	78	6084	8.8318	.012821	138	19044	11.7473	.00724638
19	361	4.3589	.052632	79	6241	8.8882	.012658	139	19321	11.7898	.00719424
20	400	4.4721	.050000	80	6400	8.9443	.012500	140	19600	11.8322	.00714286
21	441	4.5826	.047619	81	6561	9.0000	.012346	141	19881	11.8743	.00709220
22	484	4.6904	.045455	82	6724	9.0554	.012195	142	20164	11.9164	.00704225
23	529	4.7958	.043478	83	6889	9.1104	.012048	143	20449	11.9583	.00699301
24	576	4.8990	.041667	84	7056	9.1652	.011905	144	20736	12.0000	.00694444
25	625	5.0000	.040000	85	7225	9.2195	.011765	145	21025	12.0416	.00689655
26	676	5.0990	.038462	86	7396	9.2736	.011628	146	21316	12.0830	.00684932
27	729	5.1962	.037037	87	7569	9.3274	.011494	147	21609	12.1244	.00680272
28	784	5.2915	.035714	88	7744	9.3808	.011364	148	21904	12.1655	.00675676
29	841	5.3852	.034483	89	7921	9.4340	.011236	149	22201	12.2066	.00671141
30	900	5.4772	.033333	90	8100	9.4868	.011111	150	22500	12.2474	.00666667
31	961	5.5678	.032258	91	8281	9.5394	.010989	151	22801	12.2882	.00662252
32	1024	5.6569	.031250	92	8464	9.5917	.010870	152	23104	12.3288	.00657895
33	1089	5.7446	.030303	93	8649	9.6437	.010753	153	23409	12.3693	.00653595
34	1156	5.8310	.029412	94	8836	9.6954	.010638	154	23716	12.4097	.00649351
35	1225	5.9161	.028571	95	9025	9.7468	.010526	155	24025	12.4499	.00645161
36	1296	6.0000	.027778	96	9216	9.7980	.010417	156	24336	12.4900	.00641026
37	1369	6.0828	.027027	97	9409	9.8489	.010309	157	24649	12.5300	.00636943
38	1444	6.1644	.026316	98	9604	9.8995	.010204	158	24964	12.5698	.00632911
39	1521	6.2450	.025641	99	9801	9.9499	.010101	159	25281	12.6095	.00628931
40	1600	6.3246	.025000	100	10000	10.0000	.010000	160	25600	12.6491	.00625000
41	1681	6.4031	.024390	101	10201	10.0499	.00990099	161	25921	12.6886	.00621118
42	1764	6.4807	.023810	102	10404	10.0995	.00980392	162	26244	12.7279	.00617284
43	1849	6.5574	.023256	103	10609	10.1489	.00970874	163	26569	12.7671	.00613497
44	1936	6.6332	.022727	104	10816	10.1980	.00961538	164	26896	12.8062	.00609756
45	2025	6.7082	.022222	105	11025	10.2470	.00952381	165	27225	12.8452	.00606061
46	2116	6.7823	.021739	106	11236	10.2956	.00943396	166	27556	12.8841	.00602410
47	2209	6.8557	.021277	107	11449	10.3441	.00934579	167	27889	12.9228	.00598802
48	2304	6.9282	.020833	108	11664	10.3923	.00925926	168	28224	12.9615	.00595238
49	2401	7.0000	.020408	109	11881	10.4403	.00917431	169	28561	13.0000	.00591716
50	2500	7.0711	.020000	110	12100	10.4881	.00909091	170	28900	13.0384	.00588235
51	2601	7.1414	.019608	111	12321	10.5357	.00900901	171	29241	13.0767	.00584795
52	2704	7.2111	.019231	112	12544	10.5830	.00892857	172	29584	13.1149	.00581395
53	2809	7.2801	.018868	113	12769	10.6301	.00884956	173	29929	13.1529	.00578035
54	2916	7.3485	.018519	114	12996	10.6771	.00877193	174	30276	13.1909	.00574713
55	3025	7.4162	.018182	115	13225	10.7238	.00869565	175	30625	13.2288	.00571429
56	3136	7.4833	.017857	116	13456	10.7703	.00862069	176	30976	13.2665	.00568182
57	3249	7.5498	.017544	117	13689	10.8167	.00854701	177	31329	13.3041	.00564972
58	3364	7.6158	.017241	118	13924	10.8628	.00847458	178	31684	13.3417	.00561798
59	3481	7.6811	.016949	119	14161	10.9087	.00840336	179	32041	13.3791	.00558659
60	3600	7.7460	.016667	120	14400	10.9545	.00833333	180	32400	13.4164	.00555556

TABLE P (*continued*)

N	N²	√N	1/N	N	N²	√N	1/N	N	N²	√N	1/N
181	32761	13.4536	.00552486	241	58081	15.5242	.00414938	301	90601	17.3494	.00332226
182	33124	13.4907	.00549451	242	58564	15.5563	.00413223	302	91204	17.3781	.00331126
183	33489	13.5277	.00546448	243	59049	15.5885	.00411523	303	91809	17.4069	.00330033
184	33856	13.5647	.00543478	244	59536	15.6205	.00409836	304	92416	17.4356	.00328947
185	34225	13.6015	.00540541	245	60025	15.6525	.00408163	305	93025	17.4642	.00328947
186	34596	13.6382	.00537634	246	60516	15.6844	.00406504	306	93636	17.4929	.00326797
187	34969	13.6748	.00534759	247	61009	15.7162	.00404858	307	94249	17.5214	.00325733
188	35344	13.7113	.00531915	248	61504	15.7480	.00403226	308	94864	17.5499	.00324675
189	35721	13.7477	.00529101	249	62001	15.7797	.00401606	309	95481	17.5784	.00323625
190	36100	13.7840	.00526316	250	62500	15.8114	.00400000	310	96100	17.6068	.00322581
191	36481	13.8203	.00523560	251	63001	15.8430	.00398406	311	96721	17.6352	.00321543
192	36864	13.8564	.00520833	252	63504	15.8745	.00396825	312	97344	17.6635	.00320513
193	37249	13.8924	.00518135	253	64009	15.9060	.00395257	313	97969	17.6918	.00319489
194	37636	13.9284	.00515464	254	64516	15.9374	.00393701	314	98596	17.7200	.00318471
195	38025	13.9642	.00512821	255	65025	15.9687	.00392157	315	99225	17.7482	.00317460
196	38416	14.0000	.00510204	256	65536	16.0000	.00390625	316	99856	17.7764	.00316456
197	38809	14.0357	.00507614	257	66049	16.0312	.00389105	317	100489	17.8045	.00315457
198	39204	14.0712	.00505051	258	66564	16.0624	.00387597	318	101124	17.8326	.00314465
199	39601	14.1067	.00502513	259	67081	16.0935	.00386100	319	101761	17.8606	.00313480
200	40000	14.1421	.00500000	260	67600	16.1245	.00384615	320	102400	17.8885	.00312500
201	40401	14.1774	.00497512	261	68121	16.1555	.00383142	321	103041	17.9165	.00311526
202	40804	14.2127	.00495050	262	68644	16.1864	.00381679	322	103684	17.9444	.00310559
203	41209	14.2478	.00492611	263	69169	16.2173	.00380228	323	104329	17.9722	.00309598
204	41616	14.2829	.00490196	264	69696	16.2481	.00378788	324	104976	18.0000	.00308642
205	42025	14.3178	.00487805	265	70225	16.2788	.00377358	325	105625	18.0278	.00307692
206	42436	14.3527	.00485437	266	70756	16.3095	.00375940	326	106276	18.0555	.00306748
207	42849	14.3875	.00483092	267	71289	16.3401	.00374532	327	106929	18.0831	.00305810
208	43264	14.4222	.00480769	268	71824	16.3707	.00373134	328	107584	18.1108	.00304878
209	43681	14.4568	.00478469	269	72361	16.4012	.00371747	329	108241	18.1384	.00303951
210	44100	14.4914	.00476190	270	72900	16.4317	.00370370	330	108900	18.1659	.00303030
211	44521	14.5258	.00473934	271	73441	16.4621	.00369004	331	109561	18.1934	.00302115
212	44944	14.5602	.00471698	272	73984	16.4924	.00367647	332	110224	18.2209	.00301205
213	45369	14.5945	.00469484	273	74529	16.5227	.00366300	333	110889	18.2483	.00300300
214	45796	14.6287	.00467290	274	75076	16.5529	.00364964	334	111556	18.2757	.00299401
215	46225	14.6629	.00465116	275	75625	16.5831	.00363636	335	112225	18.3030	.00298507
216	46656	14.6969	.00462963	276	76176	16.6132	.00362319	336	112896	18.3303	.00297619
217	47089	14.7309	.00460829	277	76729	16.6433	.00361011	337	113569	18.3576	.00296736
218	47524	14.7648	.00458716	278	77284	16.6733	.00359712	338	114244	18.3848	.00295858
219	47961	14.7986	.00456621	279	77841	16.7033	.00358423	339	114921	18.4120	.00294985
220	48400	14.8324	.00454545	280	78400	16.7332	.00357143	340	115600	18.4391	.00294118
221	48841	14.8661	.00452489	281	78961	16.7631	.00355872	341	116281	18.4662	.00293255
222	49284	14.8997	.00450450	282	79524	16.7929	.00354610	342	116964	18.4932	.00292398
223	49729	14.9332	.00448430	283	80089	16.8226	.00353357	343	117649	18.5203	.00291545
224	50176	14.9666	.00446429	284	80656	16.8523	.00352113	344	118336	18.5472	.00290698
225	50625	15.0000	.00444444	285	81225	16.8819	.00350877	345	119025	18.5742	.00289855
226	51076	15.0333	.00442478	286	81796	16.9115	.00349650	346	119716	18.6011	.00289017
227	51529	15.0665	.00440529	287	82369	16.9411	.00348432	347	120409	18.6279	.00288184
228	51984	15.0997	.00438596	288	82944	16.9706	.00347222	348	121104	18.6548	.00287356
229	52441	15.1327	.00436681	289	83521	17.0000	.00346021	349	121801	18.6815	.00286533
230	52900	15.1658	.00434783	290	84100	17.0294	.00344828	350	122500	18.7083	.00285714
231	53361	15.1987	.00432900	291	84681	17.0587	.00343643	351	123201	18.7350	.00284900
232	53824	15.2315	.00431034	292	85264	17.0880	.00342466	352	123904	18.7617	.00284091
233	54289	15.2643	.00429185	293	85849	17.1172	.00341297	353	124609	18.7883	.00283286
234	54756	15.2971	.00427350	294	86436	17.1464	.00340136	354	125316	18.8149	.00282486
235	55225	15.3297	.00425532	295	87025	17.1756	.00338983	355	126025	18.8414	.00281690
236	55696	15.3623	.00423729	296	87616	17.2047	.00337838	356	126736	18.8680	.00280899
237	56169	15.3948	.00421941	297	88209	17.2337	.00336700	357	127449	18.8944	.00280112
238	56644	15.4272	.00420168	298	88804	17.2627	.00335570	358	128164	18.9209	.00279330
239	57121	15.4596	.00418410	299	89401	17.2916	.00334448	359	128881	18.9473	.00278552
240	57600	15.4919	.00416667	300	90000	17.3205	.00333333	360	129600	18.9737	.00277778

TABLE P *(continued)*

N	N²	√N	1/N	N	N²	√N	1/N	N	N²	√N	1/N
361	130321	19.0000	.00277008	421	177241	20.5183	.00237530	481	231361	21.9317	.00207900
362	131044	19.0263	.00276243	422	178084	20.5426	.00236967	482	232324	21.9545	.00207469
363	131769	19.0526	.00275482	423	178929	20.5670	.00236407	483	233289	21.9773	.00207039
364	132496	19.0788	.00274725	424	179776	20.5913	.00235849	484	234256	22.0000	.00206612
365	133225	19.1050	.00273973	425	180625	20.6155	.00235294	485	235225	22.0227	.00206186
366	133956	19.1311	.00273224	426	181476	20.6398	.00234742	486	236196	22.0454	.00205761
367	134689	19.1572	.00272480	427	182329	20.6640	.00234192	487	237169	22.0681	.00205339
368	135424	19.1833	.00271739	428	183184	20.6882	.00233645	488	238144	22.0907	.00204918
369	136161	19.2094	.00271003	429	184041	20.7123	.00233100	489	239121	22.1133	.00204499
370	136900	19.2354	.00270270	430	184900	20.7364	.00232558	490	240100	22.1359	.00204082
371	137641	19.2614	.00269542	431	185761	20.7605	.00232019	491	241081	22.1585	.00203666
372	138384	19.2873	.00268817	432	186624	20.7846	.00231481	492	242064	22.1811	.00203252
373	139129	19.3132	.00268097	433	187489	20.8087	.00230947	493	243049	22.2036	.00202840
374	139876	19.3391	.00267380	434	188356	20.8327	.00230415	494	244036	22.2261	.00202429
375	140625	19.3649	.00266667	435	189225	20.8567	.00229885	495	245025	22.2486	.00202020
376	141376	19.3907	.00265957	436	190096	20.8806	.00229358	496	246016	22.2711	.00201613
377	142129	19.4165	.00265252	437	190969	20.9045	.00228833	497	247009	22.2935	.00201207
378	142884	19.4422	.00264550	438	191844	20.9284	.00228311	498	248004	22.3159	.00200803
379	143641	19.4679	.00263852	439	192721	20.9523	.00227790	499	249001	22.3383	.00200401
380	144400	19.4936	.00263158	440	193600	20.9762	.00227273	500	250000	22.3607	.00200000
381	145161	19.5192	.00262467	441	194481	21.0000	.00226757	501	251001	22.3830	.00199601
382	145924	19.5448	.00261780	442	195364	21.0238	.00226244	502	252004	22.4054	.00199203
383	146689	19.5704	.00261097	443	196249	21.0476	.00225734	503	253009	22.4277	.00198807
384	147456	19.5959	.00260417	444	197136	21.0713	.00225225	504	254016	22.4499	.00198413
385	148225	19.6214	.00259740	445	198025	21.0950	.00224719	505	255025	22.4722	.00198020
386	148996	19.6469	.00259067	446	198916	21.1187	.00224215	506	256036	22.4944	.00197628
387	149769	19.6723	.00258398	447	199809	21.1424	.00223714	507	257049	22.5167	.00197239
388	150544	19.6977	.00257732	448	200704	21.1660	.00223214	508	258064	22.5389	.00196850
389	151321	19.7231	.00257069	449	201601	21.1896	.00222717	509	259081	22.5610	.00196464
390	152100	19.7484	.00256410	450	202500	21.2132	.00222222	510	260100	22.5832	.00196078
391	152881	19.7737	.00255754	451	203401	21.2368	.00221729	511	261121	22.6053	.00195695
392	153664	19.7990	.00255102	452	204304	21.2603	.00221239	512	262144	22.6274	.00195312
393	154449	19.8242	.00254453	453	205209	21.2838	.00220751	513	263169	22.6495	.00194932
394	155236	19.8494	.00253807	454	206116	21.3073	.00220264	514	264196	22.6716	.00194553
395	156025	19.8746	.00253165	455	207025	21.3307	.00219870	515	265225	22.6936	.00194175
396	156816	19.8997	.00252525	456	207936	21.3542	.00219298	516	266256	22.7156	.00193798
397	157609	19.9249	.00251889	457	208849	21.3776	.00218818	517	267289	22.7376	.00193424
398	158404	19.9499	.00251256	458	209764	21.4009	.00218341	518	268324	22.7596	.00193050
399	159201	19.9750	.00250627	459	210681	21.4243	.00217865	519	269361	22.7816	.00192678
400	160000	20.0000	.00250000	460	211600	21.4476	.00217391	520	270400	22.8035	.00192308
401	160801	20.0250	.00249377	461	212521	21.4709	.00216920	521	271441	22.8254	.00191939
402	161604	20.0499	.00248756	462	213444	21.4942	.00216450	522	272484	22.8473	.00191571
403	162409	20.0749	.00248139	463	214369	21.5174	.00215983	523	273529	22.8692	.00191205
404	163216	20.0998	.00247525	464	215296	21.5407	.00215517	524	274576	22.8910	.00190840
405	164025	20.1246	.00246914	465	216225	21.5639	.00215054	525	275625	22.9129	.00190476
406	164836	20.1494	.00246305	466	217156	21.5870	.00214592	526	276676	22.9347	.00190114
407	165649	20.1742	.00245700	467	218089	21.6102	.00214133	527	277729	22.9565	.00189753
408	166464	20.1990	.00245098	468	219024	21.6333	.00213675	528	278784	22.9783	.00189394
409	167281	20.2237	.00244499	469	219961	21.6564	.00213220	529	279841	23.0000	.00189036
410	168100	20.2485	.00243902	470	220900	21.6795	.00212766	530	280900	23.0217	.00188679
411	168921	20.2731	.00243309	471	221841	21.7025	.00212314	531	281961	23.0434	.00188324
412	169744	20.2978	.00242718	472	222784	21.7256	.00211864	532	283024	23.0651	.00187970
413	170569	20.3224	.00242131	473	223729	21.7486	.00211416	533	284089	23.0868	.00187617
414	171396	20.3470	.00241546	474	224676	21.7715	.00210970	534	285156	23.1084	.00187266
415	172225	20.3715	.00240964	475	225625	21.7945	.00210526	535	286225	23.1301	.00186916
416	173056	20.3961	.00240385	476	226576	21.8174	.00210084	536	287296	23.1517	.00186567
417	173889	20.4206	.00239808	477	227529	21.8403	.00209644	537	288369	23.1733	.00186220
418	174724	20.4450	.00239234	478	228484	21.8632	.00209205	538	289444	23.1948	.00185874
419	175561	20.4695	.00238663	479	229441	21.8861	.00208768	539	290521	23.2164	.00185529
420	176400	20.4939	.00238095	480	230400	21.9089	.00208333	540	291600	23.2379	.00185185

TABLE P *(continued)*

N	N²	√N	1/N	N	N²	√N	1/N	N	N²	√N	1/N
541	292681	23.2594	.00184843	601	361201	24.5153	.00166389	661	436921	25.7099	.00151286
542	293764	23.2809	.00184502	602	302404	24.5357	.00166113	662	438244	25.7294	.00151057
543	294849	23.3024	.00184162	603	363609	24.5561	.00165837	663	439569	25.7488	.00150830
544	295936	23.3238	.00183824	604	364816	24.5764	.00165563	664	440896	25.7682	.00150602
545	297025	23.3452	.00183486	605	366025	24.5967	.00165289	665	442225	25.7876	.00150376
546	298116	23.3666	.00183150	606	367236	24.6171	.00165017	666	443556	25.8070	.00150150
547	299209	23.3880	.00182815	607	368449	24.6374	.00164745	667	444889	25.8263	.00149925
548	300304	23.4094	.00182482	608	369664	24.6577	.00164474	668	446224	25.8457	.00149701
549	301401	23.4307	.00182149	609	370881	24.6779	.00164204	669	447561	25.8650	.00149477
550	302500	23.4521	.00181818	610	372100	24.6982	.00163934	670	448900	25.8844	.00149254
551	303601	23.4734	.00181488	611	373321	24.7184	.00163666	671	450241	25.9037	.00149031
552	304704	23.4947	.00181159	612	374544	24.7386	.00163399	672	451584	25.9230	.00148810
553	305809	23.5160	.00180832	613	375769	24.7588	.00163132	673	452929	25.9422	.00148588
554	306916	23.5372	.00180505	614	376996	24.7790	.00162866	674	454276	25.9615	.00148368
555	308025	23.5584	.00180180	615	378225	24.7992	.00162602	675	455625	25.9808	.00148148
556	309136	23.5797	.00179856	616	379456	24.8193	.00162338	676	456976	26.0000	.00147929
557	310249	23.6008	.00179533	617	380689	24.8395	.00162075	677	458329	26.0192	.00147710
558	311364	23.6220	.00179211	618	381924	24.8596	.00161812	678	459684	26.0384	.00147493
559	312481	23.6432	.00178891	619	383161	24.8797	.00161551	679	461041	26.0576	.00147275
560	313600	23.6643	.00178571	620	384400	24.8998	.00161290	680	462400	26.0768	.00147059
561	314721	23.6854	.00178253	621	385641	24.9199	.00161031	681	463761	26.0960	.00146843
562	315844	23.7065	.00177936	622	386884	24.9399	.00160772	682	465124	26.1151	.00146628
563	316969	23.7276	.00177620	623	388129	24.9600	.00160514	683	466489	26.1343	.00146413
564	318096	23.7487	.00177305	624	389376	24.9800	.00160256	684	467856	26.1534	.00146199
565	319225	23.7697	.00176991	625	390625	25.0000	.00160000	685	469225	26.1725	.00145985
566	320356	23.7908	.00176678	626	391876	25.0200	.00159744	686	470596	26.1916	.00145773
567	321489	23.8118	.00176367	627	393129	25.0400	.00159490	687	471969	26.2107	.00145560
568	322624	23.8328	.00176056	628	394384	25.0599	.00159236	688	473344	26.2298	.00145349
569	323761	23.8537	.00175747	629	395641	25.0799	.00158983	689	474721	26.2488	.00145138
570	324900	23.8747	.00175439	630	396900	25.0998	.00158730	690	476100	26.2679	.00144928
571	326041	23.8956	.00175131	631	398161	25.1197	.00158479	691	477481	26.2869	.00144718
572	327184	23.9165	.00164825	632	399424	25.1396	.00158228	692	478864	26.3059	.00144509
573	328329	23.9374	.00174520	633	400689	25.1595	.00157978	693	480249	26.3249	.00144300
574	329476	23.9583	.00174216	634	401956	25.1794	.00157729	694	481636	26.3439	.00144092
575	330625	23.9792	.00173913	635	403225	25.1992	.00157480	695	483025	26.3629	.00143885
576	331776	24.0000	.00173611	636	404496	25.2190	.00157233	696	484416	26.3818	.00143678
577	332929	24.0208	.00173310	637	405769	25.2389	.00156986	697	485809	26.4008	.00143472
578	334084	24.0416	.00173010	638	407044	25.2587	.00156740	698	487204	26.4197	.00143266
579	335241	24.0624	.00172712	639	408321	25.2784	.00156495	699	488601	26.4386	.00143062
580	336400	24.0832	.00172414	640	409600	25.2982	.00156250	700	490000	26.4575	.00142857
581	337561	24.1039	.00172117	641	410881	25.3180	.00156006	701	491401	26.4764	.00142653
582	338724	24.1247	.00171821	642	412164	25.3377	.00155763	702	492804	26.4953	.00142450
583	339889	24.1454	.00171527	643	413449	25.3574	.00155521	703	494209	26.5141	.00142248
584	341056	24.1661	.00171233	644	414736	25.3772	.00155280	704	495616	26.5330	.00142045
585	342225	24.1868	.00170940	645	416025	25.3969	.00155039	705	497025	26.5518	.00141844
586	343396	24.2074	.00170648	646	417316	25.4165	.00154799	706	498436	26.5707	.00141643
587	344569	24.2281	.00170358	647	418609	25.4362	.00154560	707	499849	26.5895	.00141443
588	345744	24.2487	.00170068	648	419904	25.4558	.00154321	708	501264	26.6083	.00141243
589	346921	24.2693	.00169779	649	421201	25.4755	.00154083	709	502681	26.6271	.00141044
590	348100	24.2899	.00169492	650	422500	25.4951	.00153846	710	504100	26.6458	.00140845
591	349281	24.3105	.00169205	651	423801	25.5147	.00153610	711	505521	26.6646	.00140647
592	350464	24.3311	.00168919	652	425104	25.5343	.00153374	712	506944	26.6833	.00140449
593	351649	24.3516	.00168634	653	426409	25.5539	.00153139	713	508369	26.7021	.00140252
594	352836	24.3721	.00168350	654	427716	25.5734	.00152905	714	509796	26.7208	.00140056
595	354025	24.3926	.00168067	655	429025	25.5930	.00152672	715	511225	26.7395	.00139860
596	355216	24.4131	.00167785	656	430336	25.6125	.00152439	716	512656	26.7582	.00139665
597	356409	24.4336	.00167504	657	431649	25.6320	.00152207	717	514089	26.7769	.00139470
598	357604	24.4540	.00167224	658	432964	25.6515	.00151976	718	515524	26.7955	.00139276
599	358801	24.4745	.00166945	659	434281	25.6710	.00151745	719	516961	26.8142	.00139082
600	360000	24.4949	.00166667	660	435600	25.6905	.00151515	720	518400	26.8328	.00138889

TABLE P *(continued)*

N	N²	√N	1/N	N	N²	√N	1/N	N	N²	√N	1/N
721	519841	26.8514	.00138696	781	609961	27.9464	.00128041	841	707281	29.0000	.00118906
722	521284	26.8701	.00138504	782	611524	27.9643	.00127877	842	708964	29.0172	.00118765
723	522729	26.8887	.00138313	783	613089	27.9821	.00127714	843	710649	29.0345	.00118624
724	524176	26.9072	.00138122	784	614656	28.0000	.00127551	844	712336	29.0517	.00118483
725	525625	26.9258	.00137931	785	616225	28.0179	.00127389	845	714025	29.0689	.00118343
726	527076	26.9444	.00137741	786	617796	28.0357	.00127226	846	715716	29.0861	.00118203
727	528529	26.9629	.00137552	787	619369	28.0535	.00127065	847	717409	29.1033	.00118064
728	529984	26.9815	.00137363	788	620944	28.0713	.00126904	848	719104	29.1204	.00117925
729	531441	27.0000	.00137174	789	622521	28.0891	.00126743	849	720801	29.1376	.00117786
730	532900	27.0185	.00136986	790	624100	28.1069	.00126582	850	722500	29.1548	.00117647
731	534361	27.0370	.00136799	791	625681	28.1247	.00126422	851	724201	29.1719	.00117509
732	535824	27.0555	.00136612	792	627264	28.1425	.00126263	852	725904	29.1890	.00117371
733	537289	27.0740	.00136426	793	628849	28.1603	.00126103	853	727609	29.2062	.00117233
734	538756	27.0924	.00136240	794	630436	28.1780	.00125945	854	729316	29.2233	.00117096
735	540225	27.1109	.00136054	795	632025	28.1957	.00125786	855	731025	29.2404	.00116959
736	541696	27.1293	.00135870	796	633616	28.2135	.00125628	856	732736	29.2575	.00116822
737	543169	27.1477	.00135685	797	635209	28.2312	.00125471	857	734449	29.2746	.00116686
738	544644	27.1662	.00135501	798	636804	28.2489	.00125313	858	736164	29.2916	.00116550
739	546121	27.1846	.00135318	799	638401	28.2666	.00125156	859	737881	29.3087	.00116414
740	547600	27.2029	.00135135	800	640000	28.2843	.00125000	860	739600	29.3258	.00116279
741	549081	27.2213	.00134953	801	641601	28.3019	.00124844	861	741321	29.3428	.00116144
742	550564	27.2397	.00134771	802	643204	28.3196	.00124688	862	743044	29.3598	.00116009
743	552049	27.2580	.00134590	803	644809	28.3373	.00124533	863	744769	29.3769	.00115875
744	553536	27.2764	.00134409	804	646416	28.3549	.00124378	864	746496	29.3939	.00115741
745	555025	27.2947	.00134228	805	648025	28.3725	.00124224	865	748225	29.4109	.00115607
746	556516	27.3130	.00134048	806	649636	28.3901	.00124069	866	749956	29.4279	.00115473
747	558009	27.3313	.00133869	807	651249	28.4077	.00123916	867	751689	29.4449	.00115340
748	559504	27.3496	.00133690	808	625864	28.4253	.00123762	868	753424	29.4618	.00115207
749	561001	27.3679	.00133511	809	654481	28.4429	.00123609	869	755161	29.4788	.00115075
750	562500	27.3861	.00133333	810	656100	28.4605	.00123457	870	756900	29.4958	.00114943
751	564001	27.4044	.00133156	811	657721	28.4781	.00123305	871	758641	29.5127	.00114811
752	565504	27.4226	.00132979	812	659344	28.4956	.00123153	872	760384	29.5296	.00114679
753	567009	27.4408	.00132802	813	660969	28.5132	.00123001	873	762129	29.5466	.00114548
754	568516	27.4591	.00132626	814	662596	28.5307	.00122850	874	763876	29.5635	.00114416
755	570025	27.4773	.00132450	815	664225	28.5482	.00122699	875	765625	29.5804	.00114286
756	571536	27.4955	.00132275	816	665856	28.5657	.00122549	876	767376	29.5973	.00114155
757	573049	27.5136	.00132100	817	667489	28.5832	.00122399	877	769129	29.6142	.00114025
758	574564	27.5318	.00131926	818	669124	28.6007	.00122249	878	770884	29.6311	.00113895
759	576081	27.5500	.00131752	819	670761	28.6182	.00122100	879	772641	29.6479	.00113766
760	577600	27.5681	.00131579	820	672400	28.6356	.00121951	880	774400	29.6848	.00113636
761	579121	27.5862	.00131406	821	674041	28.6531	.00121803	881	776161	29.6816	.00113507
762	580644	27.6043	.00131234	822	675684	28.6705	.00121655	882	777924	29.6985	.00113379
763	582169	27.6225	.00131062	823	677329	28.6880	.00121507	883	779689	29.7153	.00113250
764	583696	27.6405	.00130890	824	678976	28.7054	.00121359	884	781456	29.7321	.00113122
765	585225	27.6586	.00130719	825	680625	28.7228	.00121212	885	783225	29.7489	.00112994
766	586756	27.6767	.00130548	826	682276	28.7402	.00121065	886	784996	29.7658	.00112867
767	588289	27.6948	.00130378	827	683929	28.7576	.00120919	887	786769	29.7825	.00112740
768	589824	27.7128	.00130208	828	685584	28.7750	.00120773	888	788544	29.7993	.00112613
769	591361	27.7308	.00130039	829	687241	28.7924	.00120627	889	790321	29.8161	.00112486
770	592900	27.7489	.00129870	830	688900	28.8097	.00120482	890	792100	29.8329	.00112360
771	594441	27.7669	.00129702	831	690561	28.8271	.00120337	891	793881	29.8496	.00112233
772	595984	27.7849	.00129534	832	692224	28.8444	.00120192	892	795664	29.8664	.00112108
773	597529	27.8029	.00129366	833	693889	28.8617	.00120048	893	797449	29.8831	.00111982
774	599076	27.8209	.00129199	834	695556	28.8791	.00119904	894	799236	29.8998	.00111857
775	600625	27.8388	.00129032	835	697225	28.8964	.00119760	895	801025	29.9166	.00111732
776	602176	27.8568	.00128866	836	698896	28.9137	.00119617	896	802816	29.9333	.00111607
777	603729	27.8747	.00128700	837	700569	28.9310	.00119474	897	804609	29.9500	.00111483
778	605284	27.8927	.00128535	838	702244	28.9482	.00119332	898	806404	29.9666	.00111359
779	606841	27.9106	.00128370	839	703921	28.9655	.00119190	899	808201	29.9833	.00111235
780	608400	27.9285	.00128205	840	705600	28.9828	.00119048	900	810000	30.0000	.00111111

TABLE P *(continued)*

N	N²	√N	1/N	N	N²	√N	1/N	N	N²	√N	1/N
901	811801	30.0167	.00110988	936	876096	30.5941	.00106838	971	942841	31.1609	.00102987
902	813604	30.0333	.00110865	937	877969	30.6105	.00106724	972	944784	31.1769	.00102881
903	815409	30.0500	.00110742	938	879844	30.6268	.00106610	973	946729	31.1929	.00102775
904	817216	30.0666	.00110619	939	881721	30.6431	.00106496	974	948676	31.2090	.00102669
905	819025	30.0832	.00110497	940	883600	30.6594	.00106383	975	950625	31.2250	.00102564
906	820836	30.0998	.00110375	941	885481	30.6757	.00106270	976	952576	31.2410	.00102459
907	822649	30.1164	.00110254	942	887364	30.6920	.00106157	977	954529	31.2570	.00102354
908	824464	30.1330	.00110132	943	889249	30.7083	.00106045	978	956484	31.2730	.00102249
909	826281	30.1496	.00110011	944	891136	30.7246	.00105932	979	958441	31.2890	.00102145
910	828100	30.1662	.00109890	945	893025	30.7409	.00105820	980	960400	31.3050	.00102041
911	829921	30.1828	.00109769	946	894916	30.7571	.00105708	981	962361	31.3209	.00101937
912	831744	30.1993	.00109649	947	896809	30.7734	.00105597	982	964324	31.3369	.00101833
913	833569	30.2159	.00109529	948	898704	30.7896	.00105485	983	966289	31.3528	.00101729
914	835396	30.2324	.00109409	949	900601	30.8058	.00105374	984	968256	31.3688	.00101626
915	837225	30.2490	.00109290	950	902500	30.8221	.00105263	985	970225	31.3847	.00101523
916	839056	30.2655	.00109170	951	904401	30.8383	.00105152	986	972196	31.4006	.00101420
917	840889	30.2820	.00109051	952	906304	30.8545	.00105042	987	974169	31.4166	.00101317
918	842724	30.2985	.00108932	953	908209	30.8707	.00104932	988	976144	31.4325	.00101215
919	844561	30.3150	.00108814	954	910116	30.8869	.00104822	989	978121	31.4484	.00101112
920	846400	30.3315	.00108696	955	912025	30.9031	.00104712	990	980100	31.4643	.00101010
921	848241	30.3480	.00108578	956	913936	30.9192	.00104603	991	982081	31.4802	.00100908
922	850084	30.3645	.00108460	957	915849	30.9354	.00104493	992	984064	31.4960	.00100806
923	851929	30.3809	.00108342	958	917764	30.9516	.00104384	993	986049	31.5119	.00100705
924	853776	30.3974	.00108225	959	919681	30.9677	.00104275	994	988036	31.5278	.00100604
925	855625	30.4138	.00108108	960	921600	30.9839	.00104167	995	990025	31.5436	.00100503
926	857476	30.4302	.00107991	961	923521	31.0000	.00104058	996	992016	31.5595	.00100402
927	859329	30.4467	.00107875	962	925444	31.0161	.00103950	997	994009	31.5753	.00103842
928	861184	30.4631	.00107759	963	927369	31.0322	.00103842	998	996004	31.5911	.00100200
929	863041	30.4795	.00107643	964	929296	31.0483	.00103734	999	998001	31.6070	.00100100
930	864900	30.4959	.00107527	965	931225	31.0644	.00103627	1000	1000000	31.6228	.00100000
931	866761	30.5123	.00107411	966	933156	31.0805	.00103520				
932	868624	30.5287	.00107296	967	935089	31.0966	.00103413				
933	870489	30.5450	.00107181	968	937024	31.1127	.00103306				
934	872356	30.5614	.00107066	969	938961	31.1288	.00103199				
935	874225	30.5778	.00106952	970	940900	31.1448	.00103093				

Acknowledgments

The authors are grateful to the authors and publishers listed below for permission to adapt from the following tables.

TABLE B   R. A. Fisher, *Statistical Methods for Research Workers*, 14th ed. Reprinted with permission of Macmillan Publishing Company, Inc. Copyright © 1970, University of Adelaide.

TABLE C   Table III of R. A. Fisher and F. Yates, *Statistical Tables for Biological, Agricultural, and Medical Research*, 6th ed. London: Longman Group Ltd., 1974. (Previously published by Oliver and Boyd, Ltd., Edinburgh.)

TABLE D   G. W. Snedecor and William G. Cochran, *Statistical Methods*, 7th ed. Ames, Iowa: Iowa State University Press, copyright © 1980.

TABLE E   Rand Corporation, *A Million Random Digits*. Glencoe, Ill. Free Press of Glencoe, 1955.

TABLE F   Q. McNemar, Table B of *Psychological Statistics*. New York: John Wiley, 1962.

TABLE G   E. G. Olds (1949), "The 5 Percent Significance Levels of Sums of Squares of Rank Differences and a Correction," *Ann. Math. Statist.*, **20,** 117–118.
E. G. Olds, (1938), "Distribution of Sums of Squares of Rank Differences for Small Numbers of Individuals," *Ann. Math. Statist.*, **9,** 133–148.

TABLE H   W. V. Bingham, Table XVII of *Aptitudes and Aptitude Testing*. New York: Harper and Bros., 1937.

TABLE I   H. B. Mann and D. R. Whitney (1947), "On a Test of Whether One of Two Random Variables Is Stochastically Larger Than the Other," *Ann. Math. Statist.*, **18,** 52–54.
D. Auble (1953), "Extended Tables for the Mann-Whitney Statistic," *Bulletin of the Institute of*

TABLE J   F. Wilcoxon, S. Katti, and R. A. Wilcox, *Critical Values and Probability Levels for the Wilcoxon Rank Sum Test and the Wilcoxon Signed Rank Test*. New York: American Cyanamid Co., 1963.
F. Wilcoxon and R. A. Wilcox, *Some Rapid Approximate Statistical Procedures*. New York: Lederle Laboratories, 1964.

TABLE L   S. Siegel. *Nonparametric Statistics*. New York: McGraw-Hill, 1956.

TABLE M   R. P. Runyon, Table A of *Nonparametric Statistics*. Reading, Mass.: Addison-Wesley, 1977.

TABLE N   R. P. Runyon, Table B of *Nonparametric Statistics*. Reading, Mass.: Addison-Wesley, 1977.

TABLE O   E. S. Pearson and H. O. Hartley, *Biometrika Tables for Statisticians*, vol. 1, 2d ed. New York: Cambridge, 1958.

TABLE P   A. L. Edwards, *Statistical Analysis*, 3d ed. New York: Holt, Rinehart and Winston, 1969.
J. W. Dunlap and A. K. Kurtz, *Handbook of Statistical Nomographs, Tables, and Formulas*. New York: World Book Company, 1932.

Answers to Selected Exercises

In problems involving many steps, you may occasionally find a discrepancy between the answers you obtained and those shown here. Where the discrepancies are small, they are probably due to rounding errors. These disparities are more common today because of the wide differences in methods employed, that is, varying degrees of sophistication among calculators, adding machines, and hand calculations.

Chapter 1

1. a. statistic   **b.** inference from statistics   **c.** data   **d.** data
    e. inference from statistics

3. a. constant   **b.** variable   **c.** variable   **d.** variable
    e. constant   **f.** variable   **g.** constant   **h.** variable

5. These are not statistics; they are data. Statistics that may be calculated from these data include proportion or percentage of passes completed by each team, proportion or percentage of yards gained on the ground or in the air, proportion or percentage of time of possession. (See Chapter 2 for a discussion of proportions and percentages.)

7. (b)   **9.** (b)   **11.** (a)

13.

Under experimenter control	Organismic	Physical
a. amount of drug administered	**e.** gender of subjects	**b.** season of the year
f. amount of noise	**d.** diagnostic category	**c.** time of day
g. method of instruction	**i.** scores on IQ test	
h. hours of deprivation	**h.** age of previous toilet training*	
j. age toilet training will be introduced*	**k.** mood of subjects†	
k. mood of subjects†		

* If the experimenter has access to infants before the beginning of toilet training, he or she can control the age at which training begins. If the subjects have already been toilet trained, the experimenter can only select subjects on the basis of the age at which training took place. The experimenter has no control over the introduction of the variable in the second case.
† If procedures are used to induce mood changes in order to ascertain their effects on a dependent measure, the mood would be under the experimenter's control. If subjects are selected according to their mood at the time of their participation in the study, the experimenter has exercised no control over the independent variable, mood.

Chapter 2

1. a.

	Proportion*	Percentage*
Too little	0.77	77
About right	0.21	21
Too much	0.02	2
No opinion	0.01	1

* The slight disparity from 1.00 and 100 is due to rounding error.

b.

	Proportion	Percentage
Too little	0.71	71
About right	0.24	24
Too much	0.03	3
No opinion	0.02	2

c.

	Proportion	Percentage
Too little	0.83	83
About right	0.13	13
Too much	0.02	2
No opinion	0.02	2

d.

	Proportion*	Percentage*
Too little	0.25	25
About right	0.28	28
Too much	0.43	43
No opinion	0.03	3

* The slight disparity from 1.00 and 100 is due to rounding error.

The majority of the respondents appear to want more information about earthquakes and how to prepare for them. Thus, the results appear to contradict the view that California would prefer not to think about earthquakes.

3. $y = 22$ **5.** $N = 4$ **7.** $s^2 = 20$

9. a. 79% and 21%   **b.** 94%   **c.** 75% and 25%. The number of whites in the general population of the United States is much greater than the number of blacks. Even if the suicide rates among whites and blacks were the same, both the number and the percent of suicides would be much greater among whites than among blacks. A valid measure of suicide rates would compare the percent of white suicides within the white population versus the percent of black suicides within the black population.

11. suicides $= 0.5445$; homicides $= 0.4555$

13. a. 25   **b.** 60   **c.** 37   **d.** 31   **e.** 60   **f.** 44

15. a. ratio   **b.** ratio   **c.** nominal   **d.** ordinal

17. a. 12.65   **b.** 4.00   **c.** 1.26   **d.** 0.40   **e.** 0.13

19. $$\sum_{i=1}^{N} X_i^2 = 4^2 + 5^2 + 7^2 + 9^2 + 10^2 + 11^2 + 14^2 = 588$$

$$\left(\sum_{i=1}^{N} X_i\right)^2 = (4 + 5 + 7 + 9 + 10 + 11 + 14)^2$$

$$= 60^2 = 3600$$

$$588 \neq 3600$$

21. a.

		b. 38.10	**c.** 13.33	**d.** 58.33
Business administration	20.00%	4.76	20.00	males
Education	75.00%	14.29	26.67	41.67%
Humanities	57.14%	23.81	13.33	females
Science	28.57%	19.05	26.67	**e.** 20%
Social science	50.00%			**f.** 71.43%

23.

Year	% Males	% Females
1950	51.31	48.69
1955	51.24	48.76
1960	51.20	48.80
1965	51.25	48.75
1970	51.33	48.67

25.

	Berkeley	Yale
Firearms	35	40
Poisoning	26	12
Asphyxiation	17	20
Hanging	9	24
Jumping from high places	9	4
Cutting instruments	4	0

27. a. 37.0%   **b.** 41.5 and 58.5   **c.** 32.5 and 67.5

29. a. Percentages in Terms of Totals

	White Males	White Females	Black Males	Black Females	Row Totals
Neither a black nor a female	3.11	4.07	0.00	0.18	7.36
A female but not a black	4.25	4.11	0.04	0.21	8.61
A black but not a female	3.79	5.58	1.00	0.68	11.04
Both a black and a female	28.98	35.06	3.54	5.40	72.98
Column totals	40.14	48.82	4.57	6.47	100

b. Percentages in Terms of Rows

Would Vote For	White Males	White Females	Black Males	Black Females	Row Totals
Neither a black nor a female	42.23	55.34	0.00	2.43	100.00
A female but not a black	49.38	47.72	0.41	2.49	100.00
A black but not a female	34.30	50.49	9.06	6.15	100.00
Both a black and a female	39.72	48.04	4.85	7.39	100.00

c. **Percentages in Terms of Columns**

Would Vote For	White Males	White Females	Black Males	Black Females
Neither a black nor a female	7.75	8.35	0.00	2.76
A female but not a black	10.60	8.42	0.78	3.31
A black but not a female	9.44	11.42	21.88	10.50
Both a black and a female	72.22	71.82	77.34	83.43
Column totals	100.00	100.00	100.00	100.00

d. The extremely large proportion of white males and females in the sample distorts the perception of all the percentages when the percentages are obtained in terms of totals and across rows. However, when the percentages are obtained in terms of the column variables (gender and race), a valid comparison may be obtained in terms of the relative numbers of white/ black males and females who are willing to vote for each class of candidates.

30. Percentage of RSI Reported among Government Employees through January 1985

Employment Category	Number of Operators	Reported Cases	%
Secretary stenographers	397	70	17.6
Typists	1163	137	11.7
Clerk typists	838	60	7.1
Word-processing operators	340	99	19.1
Data-processing operators	379	84	22.1
Telephonists	172	6	3.4
Accounting machinists	72	7	9.7
Computer programmers	749	9	1.2
Clerks	1190	40	3.3
Clerical assistants	193	9	4.6
Telex operators	49	0	0.0
Journalists	12	0	0.0
Hansard/court reporters	32	7	21.8
Other keyboard operators	938	32	3.4
Total	6524	560	8.6

Chapter 3

1.

	True Limits	Midpoint	Width
a.	7.5–12.5	10	5
b.	5.5–7.5	6.5	2
c.	$(-0.5)–(+2.5)$	1	3
d.	4.5–14.5	9.5	10
e.	$(-8.5)–(-1.5)$	-5	7
f.	2.45–3.55	3	1.1
g.	1.495–1.755	1.625	0.26
h.	$(-3.5)–(+3.5)$	0	7

3.

Classes	True Limits	Midpoint	f	Cum. f	Cum. %
95–99	94.5–99.5	97	1	40	100.0%
90–94	89.5–94.5	92	3	39	97.5
85–89	84.5–89.5	87	4	36	90.0
80–84	79.5–84.5	82	8	32	80.0
75–79	74.5–79.5	77	11	24	60.0
70–74	69.5–74.5	72	4	13	32.5
65–69	64.5–69.5	67	3	9	22.5
60–64	59.5–64.5	62	3	6	15.0
55–59	54.5–59.5	57	0	3	7.5
50–54	49.5–54.5	52	1	3	7.5
45–49	44.5–49.5	47	1	2	5.0
40–44	39.5–44.5	42	1	1	2.5

5.

Classes	True Limits	Midpoint	f
9.6–9.9	9.55–9.95	9.75	1
9.2–9.5	9.15–9.55	9.35	3
8.8–9.1	8.75–9.15	8.95	1
8.4–8.7	8.35–8.75	8.55	4
8.0–8.3	7.95–8.35	8.15	7
7.6–7.9	7.55–7.95	7.75	10
7.2–7.5	7.15–7.55	7.35	2
6.8–7.1	6.75–7.15	6.95	4
6.4–6.7	6.35–6.75	6.55	2
6.0–6.3	5.95–6.35	6.15	3
5.6–5.9	5.55–5.95	5.75	0
5.2–5.5	5.15–5.55	5.35	1
4.8–5.1	4.75–5.15	4.95	0
4.4–4.7	4.35–4.75	4.55	1
4.0–4.3	3.95–4.35	4.15	1

Width = 0.4

7.

Classes	f
65–69	1
60–64	2
55–59	3
50–54	4
45–49	5
40–44	6
35–39	8
30–34	6
25–29	5
20–24	4
15–19	3
10–14	2
5–9	1

9.

Classes	f
66–67	1
64–65	1
62–63	1
60–61	0
58–59	0
56–57	2
54–55	3
52–53	2
50–51	0
48–49	0
46–47	2
44–45	7
42–43	2
40–41	0
38–39	0
36–37	7
34–35	4
32–33	3
30–31	0
28–29	0
26–27	4
24–25	3
22–23	2
20–21	0
18–19	0
16–17	2
14–15	2
12–13	1
10–11	0
8–9	0
6–7	0
4–5	1

17. a. positively skewed   **b.** normal   **c.** normal   **d.** bimodal

19.

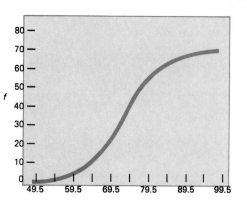

21.

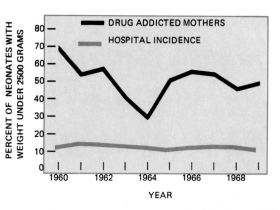

23.

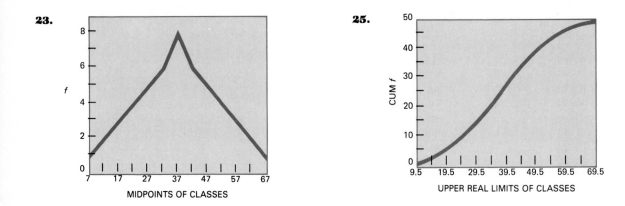

MIDPOINTS OF CLASSES

25.

UPPER REAL LIMITS OF CLASSES

27. a.

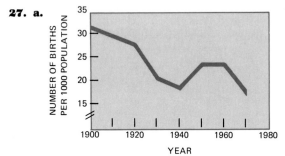

YEAR

b. There does appear to be a generally declining trend.

*28. a.

Sum of Two Scores	f
12	1
11	2
10	3
9	4
8	5
7	6
6	7
5	6
4	5
3	4
2	3
1	2
0	1
	$N = 49$

b.

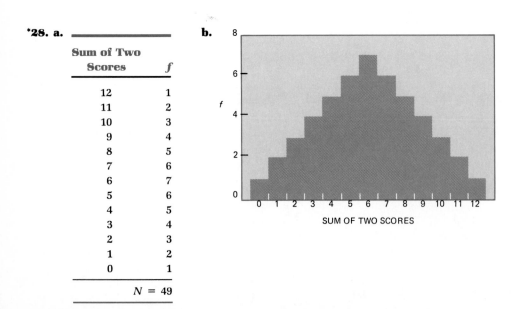

SUM OF TWO SCORES

29.

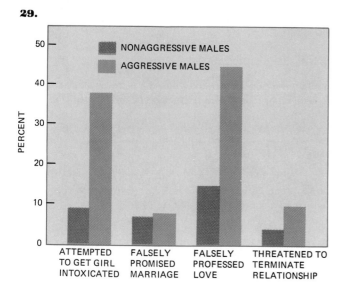

31.

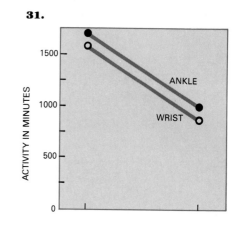

32.

Age	Proportion of White Suicides	Proportion of White Homicides	Proportion of Black Suicides	Proportion of Black Homicides
15–24	0.2273	0.2400	0.1852	0.2089
25–34	0.4545	0.5200	0.5926	0.6329
35–44	0.2045	0.2000	0.1852	0.1266
45–54	0.0682	0.0400	0.0370	0.0253
55–64	0.0227	0.0000	0.0000	0.0063
65–74	0.0227	0.0000	0.0000	0.0000
Totals	1.0000	1.0000	1.0000	1.0000

33.

Job Category	Percent
Secretary stenographers	XXXXXXXXXXXXXXXXXXXX (17.6)
Typists	XXXXXXXXXXXXXX (11.7)
Clerk typists	XXXXXXX (7.1)
Word-processing operators	XXXXXXXXXXXXXXXXXXXXXXX (19.1)
Data-processing operators	XXXXXXXXXXXXXXXXXXXXXXXXXXX (22.1)
Telephonists	XXXX (3.4)
Accounting machinists	XXXXXXXXXXX (9.7)
Computer programmers	XX (1.2)
Clerks	XXX (3.3)
Clerical assistants	XXXXX (4.6)
Telex operators	(0)
Journalists	(0)
Hansard/court reporters	XXXXXXXXXXXXXXXXXXXXXXXXXX (21.8)
Other keyboard operators	XXXX (3.4)

Chapter 4

5. The mean and the median, the population on which the test was standardized, the percentile of his score when compared to his age group.

*7. **a.** $\dfrac{22.5}{120} \times 100 = 18.75\%$ **b.** $\dfrac{97.5}{120} \times 100 = 18.25\%$ **c.** 10%

d. 1.11%   **e.** 85.97%   **f.** 16.25%

9. The score value = 72 $N = 140$ $i = 5$ Number of cases within class = 20   Score at lower real limit = 71.45   Cum f to lower real limit 61   The percentile rank of a score of 72 equals 45.1429

11. The score value = 95 $N = 140$ $i = 5$ Number of cases within class = 5   Score at lower real limit = 91.45   Cum f to lower real limit 128   The percentile rank of a score of 95 equals 93.9643

13. The score value = 101 $N = 140$ $i = 5$ Number of cases within class = 3   Score at lower real limit = 96.45   Cum f to lower real limit 133   The percentile rank of a score of 101 equals 96.95

15. The cumulative frequency of the score is 14 $N = 140$ $i = 5$ Score at lower limit = 56.45   Score units within class = 3.07692   The score at the 10th percentile equals 59.5269

17. The cumulative frequency of the score is 105 $N = 140$ $i = 5$ Score at lower limit = 81.45   Score units within class = 0.384615   The score at the 75th percentile equals 81.8346

19. The cumulative frequency of the score is 117.6 $N = 140$ $i = 5$ Score at lower limit = 86.45   Score units within class = 0.272727   The score at the 84th percentile = 62.6643

21. and **22**.

A. 88.8	F. 42.0	K. 77.2	P. 42.0	U. 42.0
B. 77.2	G. 96.4	L. 61.6	Q. 25.6	V. 13.2
C. 25.6	H. 61.6	M. 4.8	R. 4.8	W. 61.6
D. 61.6	I. 77.2	N. 25.6	S. 0.4	X. 25.6
E. 42.0	J. 13.2	O. 88.8	T. 13.2	Y. 42.0

The answers to 21 and 22 are the same because a constant of 10 has been subtracted from each score in Exercise 21. The subtraction of a constant does not change the relative position or percentile rank of each individual score.

*23.

Sum	f	Cum f	Cum %
12	1	49	100
11	2	48	98
10	3	46	94
9	4	43	88
8	5	39	80
7	6	34	69
6	7	28	57
5	6	21	43
4	5	15	31
3	4	10	20
2	3	6	12
1	2	3	6
0	1	1	2

$N = 49$

*24. a. 98%   **b.** 45%   **c.** 12%   **d.** 12%   **e.** 24%

25. b. Maria   **c.** Matthew   **e.** Alicia

27. All of the following are obtained by visual inspection and are subject to error. Thus, all values shown are approximate.   **a.** 25th %ile   **b.** 25th %ile   **c.** 50 %ile   **d.** 50th %ile   **e.** 80th %ile   **f.** 90th %ile.

Chapter 5

1. a. $\overline{X} = 5.0$ median = 5.5   mode = 8
   b. $\overline{X} = 5.0$ median = 5.0   mode = 5.0
   c. $\overline{X} = 17.5$ median = 3.83   mode = 4

5. All measures of central tendency will be divided by 16.

7. $\overline{X} = 5.0$; median unchanged, mode unchanged

9. 8 (c) symmetrical   8 (d) bimodal

11. group A: median; group B: mean

13. The distribution is symmetrical.

15. a. 0.89   **b.** −5.11   **17.** $\overline{X} = 164.94$

19. a. $\overline{X} = -16.50$ **b.** The difference between means is the same as the mean difference.

21. All scores contribute to the calculation of the mean. Extreme scores "draw" the mean toward them.

23. 1.83%   **25. a.** mean = 30   median = 30   mode = 30
   b. mean = 30   median = 30   mode = 25; 30; 35
   c. mean = 26.0   median = 27.5   mode = 25; 30

27. mean = 6.1   median = 6.5   mode = 7

29. manufacturer A: either mean, median, or mode;   manufacturer B: mode

*31.

		First Draw						
		0	**1**	**2**	**3**	**4**	**5**	**6**
Second Draw	**0**	0	0.5	1.0	1.5	2.0	2.5	3.0
	1	0.5	1.0	1.5	2.0	2.5	3.0	3.5
	2	1.0	1.5	2.0	2.5	3.0	3.5	4.0
	3	1.5	2.0	2.5	3.0	3.5	4.0	4.5
	4	2.0	2.5	3.0	3.5	4.0	4.5	5.0
	5	2.5	3.0	3.5	4.0	4.5	5.0	5.5
	6	3.0	3.5	4.0	4.5	5.0	5.5	6.0

*32.

$\bar{X}$	f
6.0	1
5.5	2
5.0	3
4.5	4
4.0	5
3.5	6
3.0	7
2.5	6
2.0	5
1.5	4
1.0	3
0.5	2
0	1
$N = 49$	

*33. a. 2%   **b.** 6%   **c.** 43%   **d.** 12%

*34. The two means are identical.

35.

	Type A	Type B
Active	24.2	18.9
Passive	22.9	19.8
Relaxed	21.45	20.3

37. a. Type A   **37. b.** Type B

Real Limits	f	fX	Cum f	f	fX	Cum f
27.5–28.5	1	28	60	1	28	60
26.5–27.5	2	54	59	0	0	59
25.5–26.5	9	234	57	0	0	59
24.5–25.5	8	200	48	4	100	59
23.5–24.5	10	240	40	3	72	55
22.5–23.5	6	138	30	9	207	52
21.5–22.5	5	110	24	4	88	43
20.5–21.5	8	168	19	5	105	39
19.5–20.5	3	60	11	4	80	34
18.5–19.5	3	57	8	7	133	30
17.5–18.5	2	36	5	8	144	23
16.5–17.5	1	17	3	5	85	15
15.5–16.5	1	16	2	3	48	10
14.5–15.5	0	0	1	1	15	7
13.5–14.5	0	0	1	2	28	6
12.5–13.5	1	13	1	2	26	4
11.5–12.5	0	0	0	0	0	2
10.5–11.5	0	0	0	1	11	2
9.5–10.5	0	0	0	1	10	1

a. $\bar{X} = 22.85$, median $= 22.5$ **b.** $\bar{X} = 19.67$, median $= 19.5$

39.

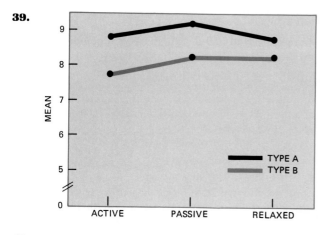

41. a.

	Baseline	1 Dim	2 WD-1	3 Bright	4 WD-2
Mean	26.86	23.29	26.93	9.79	17.00
Standard dev.	6.32	8.14	5.19	8.37	7.56

b.

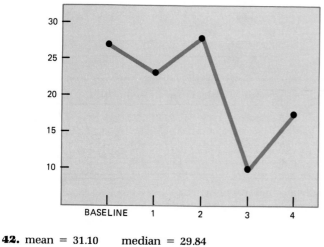

42. mean = 31.10   median = 29.84

43. mean = 29.93   median = 29.10

Chapter 6

1. $s^2 = 1.66$, $s = 1.29$
   a. no change   **b.** no change   **c.** increase
   d. increase   **e.** decrease
3. Only the standard deviation satisfies these conditions. However, if the properties included *powers* of the constant, the variance would qualify as a measure of dispersion.

5. All scores have the same value.

7. The distribution is extremely skewed to the right. Extreme deviations increase the size of the standard deviation.

9. a. $s^2 = 16.77$, $s = 4.10$ **b.** $s^2 = 34.77$, $s = 5.90$
   c. $s^2 = 26.44$, $s = 5.14$

11. a. $\bar{X} = 63.10$ **b.** range $= 35$, semi-interquartile range $= 4.00$, M.D. $= 5.61$
   c. $s = 7.89$, $s^2 = 62.25$

13. $\bar{X} = 68.25$, $s = 7.61$

17. $0.40; $0.40

19. a. The rows correspond to the within-subject measures, with each city representing a single "subject." In this context, we may regard Barrow as a subject "who" has been repeatedly measured over the course of the year, with each monthly precipitation total constituting one measure (similar to trials in a repeated measures study).

b.

	Mean	Range	Variance	Standard Deviation
Barrow, Alaska	0.36	0.8	0.07	0.27
Burlington, Vermont	2.78	2.1	0.42	0.65
Honolulu, Hawaii	1.82	3.5	1.30	1.14
Seattle–Takoma, Washington	3.25	5.5	3.33	1.82

c.

	Jan.	Feb.	Mar.	Apr.	May	Jun.	Jul.	Aug.	Sep.	Oct.	Nov.	Dec.
Mean	2.92	2.38	2.22	1.60	1.45	1.45	1.48	1.55	1.75	2.32	2.60	2.90
Range	5.5	4.0	3.7	2.5	2.90	3.2	3.50	2.5	2.7	3.5	5.2	6.1
Variance	4.19	2.31	1.87	1.00	1.12	1.66	1.99	1.14	1.10	1.72	3.44	4.88
Standard dev.	2.05	1.52	1.37	1.00	1.06	1.29	1.41	1.07	1.05	1.31	1.85	2.21

d. The "between-subject" (months of the year) measures of variability generally yielded larger ranges, variances, and standard deviations than the "within-subject" (cities) measures. In this small sample of four cities, precipitation data within a given city were more consistent than precipitation data across different cities.

e. Barrow, with the smallest mean, also had the smallest range, variance, and standard deviation. In contrast, Seattle–Takoma was highest on all these measures.

20. $s = 1.41$ **21. a.** $s^2 = 471.04$, $s = 21.70$
   b. $s^2 = 287.37$, $s = 16.95$
   c. $s^2 = 133.31$, $s = 11.55$

23. Median $= 53$, $\bar{X} = 59.62$, skew $= 19.875/13.2471 = 1.5$. The skew is positive and too large to consider the distribution symmetrical.

25. a.

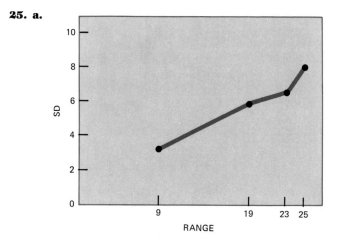

b. and. **c.** Yes. Indeed, in the Student Guide and Solutions Manual, we present a useful approximation method for estimating the standard deviation from knowledge of the range.

26. $s^2 = 102.20$, $s = 10.11$

27. $s^2 = 81.75$, $s = 9.04$

28. $sk_w = 0.37$; $sk_{bl} = 0.28$; no

Chapter 7

1. a. 0.94 **b.** -0.40 **c.** 0.00 **d.** -1.32 **e.** 2.23 **f.** -2.53

3. a. i. 0.3413; 341 **ii.** 0.4772; 477 **iii.** 0.1915; 192 **iv.** 0.4938; 494
  b. i. 0.1587; 159 **ii.** 0.0228; 23 **iii.** 0.6915; 692 **iv.** 0.9938; 994 **v.** 0.5000; 500
  c. i. 0.1359; 136 **ii.** 0.8351; 835 **iii.** 0.6687; 669 **iv.** 0.3023; 302

5. a. 40.13; 57.93 **b.** 60.26

7. a. $z = -0.67$ **b.** $z = 0.67$
    $X = 63.96$ $X = 80.04$
  c. $z = 1.28$ **d.** $z = 0.67$
    $X = 87.36$ 25.14% score above
  e. $z = -0.5$ **f.** $z = -0.67$ and $z = 0.67$
    30.85% score below   63.96–80.04
  g. $z = \pm 1.64$ **h.** $z = \pm 2.58$
    below 52.32, above 91.68   below 41.04, above 102.96

9. test 2, test 1

11. The normal distribution includes a family of bell-shaped curves of which the standard normal distribution ($\mu = 0$, $\sigma = 1.0$) is one.

13. a. -2.7 **b.** 0.0 **c.** 2.8 **d.** 1.4 **e.** -0.4

15. a. Females: $z = -0.5$, 30.85%; $z = -2.5$, 0.62% (less than 1%) **b.** Females: $z = 2.0$, 97.72%; $z = 0$, 50%

17. a. A, $z = 2.00$, percentile rank $= 97.72$ **b.** D, $z = -1.50$, percentile rank $= 6.68$

Chapter 8

1. $r = 0.85$ **3.** $r_s = 0.91$

5. a. nonlinear relationship **b.** truncated range **c.** truncated range

7. $r = 0$; $r_s = 0.50$

9. Nonlinear relationships give rise to spuriously low Pearson r correlation coefficients.

11. $r = 0.7614$

13. $r = 0.85$, $r_s = 0.79$. There appears to be a high positive correlation between the blood pressures of subjects during control and conditioning sessions.

15. The degree of relationship is the same in both cases. In the first, however, the relationship is positive; it is negative in the second.

17. a. $r = -0.9536$ **b.** $r_s = -0.9406$

19. $r = -0.598$; truncated range **21.** 1

23. a. (c) **b.** (a) **c.** (d) **d.** (b)

25. a. 0.23 **b.** The clientele of most hairdressers consists of women, whereas for bartenders it is men. The low correlation probably reflects different focuses of daily activities.

27. a. Awake: $\overline{X} = 4.29$, $s = 2.2215$; Asleep: $\overline{X} = 7.62$, $s = 6.4375$

b. Pearson r because scale of data is ratio.

c.

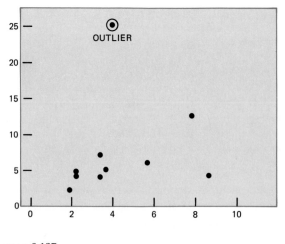

d. $r = 0.197$
e. $r = 0.557$

Chapter 9

1. $Y' = 5.70 + (-0.9)X$; $a = 5.70$; $b = -0.9$; $r = -0.90$

3. a. 1.59   **b.** $s_{esty} = 0.4745$, $s_{estx} = 11.387$

5. 9.0. The standard deviation for a group with the same IQ is the standard error of estimate: $s_{esty} = s_y \sqrt{1 - r^2} = 9$

7. a. $Y' = 89.17$ **b.** The proportion (p) of area corresponding to a score of 110 or higher is 0.0031.
    c. $X = 31.54$ **d.** $p = 0.4129$ **e.** $p < 0.00003$ **f.** $X = 68.64$
    g. 500, 93, 93, 907

11. a. $r = -0.8450$ **b.** 3.78

13. b. $r = 0.966$ **d.** Chile: 429.9   Ireland: 831.4   Belgium: 1390.6

15. Since $Y = a + b_y X$ and $a = \bar{Y} - b_y \bar{X}$, therefore

$$Y' = \bar{Y} - b_y \bar{X} + b_y X \quad \text{or} \quad Y' = \bar{Y} + b_y (X - \bar{X})$$

Since

$$b_y = \frac{N\Sigma XY - (\Sigma X)(\Sigma Y)}{N\Sigma X^2 - (\Sigma X)^2}$$

by substitution

$$Y' = \bar{Y} + \left(\frac{N\Sigma XY - (\Sigma X)(\Sigma Y)}{N\Sigma X^2 - (\Sigma X)^2} \right)(X - \bar{X})$$

17. a. 5.56   **b.** 4.16   **c.** 0.857

19.

a = 1.953
b$_y$ = 0.029
r = 0.158

(continued)

19. *(cont.)*

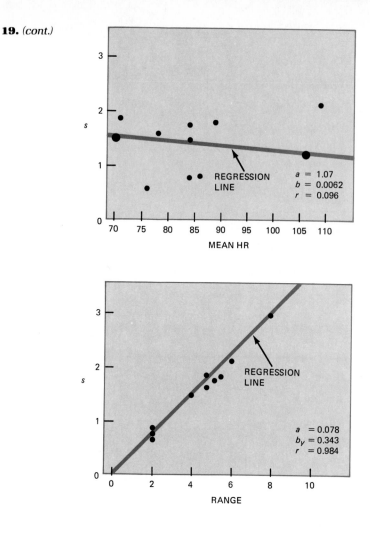

Chapter 10

*1. a.

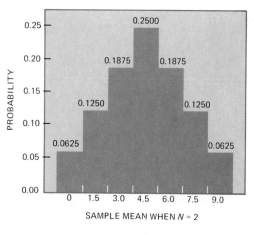

(a)

b.

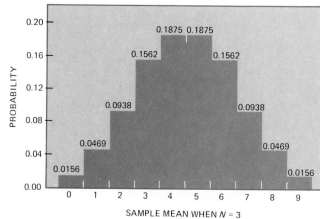

(b)

*2. An extreme deviation is rarer as sample size increases.

*3. **a.** 0.0625; 0.0156   **b.** 0.1250; 0.0312   **c.** 0.3750; 0.3125
   d. 0.7500; 0.6250

*4. **a.** 0.6250   **b.** 0.1875   **c.** 0.2500

*5. **a.** 0.6874   **b.** 0.3750   **c.** 0.1407

*6. **a.** and **b.**

$\overline{X}$	f	$p(\overline{X})$
4	1	0.0123
3	4	0.0494
2	10	0.1235
1	16	0.1975
0	19	0.2346
−1	16	0.1975
−2	10	0.1235
−3	4	0.0494
−4	1	0.0123
	$N_{\overline{x}} = 81$	$\Sigma p(\overline{X}) = 1.000$

   c. Mean = 0.00;
      standard deviation = 1.63

*7. **a.** 0.2346   **b.** 0.6296   **c.** 0.0123   **d.** 0.0246
   e. 0.0617   **f.** 0.0617   **g.** 0.1234   **h.** 0.8766

9. **a.** 0.0192   **b.** 0.0769   **c.** 0.3077   **d.** 0.4231

11. **a.** 0.1667   **b.** 0.1667   **c.** 0.2778   **d.** 0.5000

13. **a.** 0.0129   **b.** 0.4135   **c.** 0.0100

15. **a.** 0.0838   **b.** 126.40   **c.** <68.64 and >131.36   **d.** 0.4648

   e. **i.** 0.0070   **ii.** 0.2160   **iii.** 0.03895

17. $p = \frac{1}{24}$

19. **a.** 0.6561   **b.** 0.0001   **c.** 0.3438

21. **a.** ⅓   **b.** ½   **c.** ⅙   **d.** 0

23. **a.** ⅛   **b.** ⅓₆   **c.** ¹⁶⁄₈₁

25. **a.** $p = 0.3085$ **b.** $p = 0.2266$ **c.** $p = 0.4649$
   d. $p = 0.2564$ **e.** $p = 0.2934$ **f.** $p = 0.0947$ **g.** $p = 0.3296$

27.

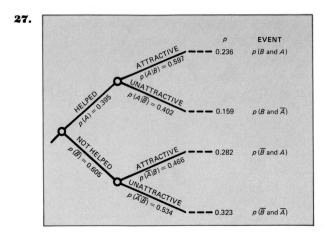

Chapter 11

3. The null hypothesis cannot be proved. Failure to reject the null hypothesis does not constitute proof that the null hypothesis is correct.

5. H_0: There is no difference in running speed of organisms operating under different drive levels.
H_1: There is a difference in running speed of organisms operating under different drive levels.

7. a. Type II   **b.** Type I   **c.** no error   **d.** no error

9. It is more likely that he is accepting a false H_0, since the probability that the observed event occurred by chance is still quite low ($p = 0.02$).

11. By chance, one would expect five (give or take a few) statistically significant differences when $\alpha = 0.01$.

13. Yes. Two-tailed H_1: There is a difference in running speed of organisms operating under different drive levels. One-tailed H_1: The running speed is greater for organisms operating under stronger drive levels.

15. a. (b)

17. a. (h)   **b.** (a)

19. The probability of making a Type I error is equal to α. In the present case, $\alpha = 0.05$.

21. Failure to detect a potentially serious condition in a client (e.g., suicidal tendency) may lead to the false conclusion that nothing need be done to intervene in the client's behalf. Similarly, failure to detect possible unfavorable reactions to a treatment (e.g., thalidomide) may lead to the certification of the treatment as safe.

23. On the basis of the data, we would fail to reject H_0. Since H_0 is true, we have made the correct decision.

25. We reject H_0. Since H_0 is false, we have made a correct decision.

Chapter 12

1. a. As sample size increases, the dispersion of sample means decreases.

   b. As you increase the number of samples, you are more likely to obtain extreme values of the sample mean. For example, suppose the probability of obtaining a sample mean of a given value is 0.01. If the number of samples drawn is 10, you probably will not obtain any sample means with that value. However, if you draw as many as 1000 samples, you would expect to obtain approximately 10 sample means with values so extreme that the probability of their occurrence is 0.01.

3. a. 21.71–26.29   **b.** 20.82–27.18

5. Reject H_0; $z = 2.68$ and $z_{0.01} = \pm 2.58$

7. In Problem 5 the value of the population standard deviation is known; thus, we may employ the z-statistic and determine probability values in terms of areas under the normal curve. In Problem 6, the value of the population standard deviation is not known and must be estimated from the sample data. Thus, the test statistic is the t-ratio.

   Since the t-distributions are more spread out than the normal curve, the proportion of area beyond a specific value of t is greater than the proportion of area beyond the corresponding value of z. Thus, a larger value of t is required to mark off the bounds of the critical region of rejection. In Problem 5, the absolute value of the obtained z must equal or exceed 2.58. In Problem 6, the absolute value of the obtained t must equal or exceed 2.83.

   To generalize: The probability of making a Type II error is less when we know the population standard deviation.

9. a. $z = 2.73$, $p = 0.9968$ **b.** $z = -0.91$, $p = 0.1814$

   c. $z = 1.82$, $p = 0.0344$ **d.** $p = 0.6372$

11. a. $t = 1.706$, reject H_0 **b.** $t = 11.19$, significant positive correlation

13. 27.14–32.08

15. 263.34–273.66

17. a. $p = \frac{1}{15}$ **b.** $p = \frac{1}{15}$ **c.** $p = \frac{8}{15}$ **d.** $p = 0$

19. $\bar{X} - \mu_0 = 0.42$, $s_{\bar{X}} = 0.2315$, $t = 1.814$, df $= 7$

21. The conclusion we draw depends on the nature of the alternative hypothesis. If H_1 is directional and we employ $\alpha = 0.05$, we reject H_0, since the obtained r_s of 0.438 exceeds the value required (interpolating for $N = 17$, the critical value of r_s for $\alpha = 0.05$, one-tailed test, is 0.412). However, if we employ a two-tailed test, we must accept H_0.

23. a. $z = 1.01$, not significant   **b.** $z = 1.99$, significant at 0.05 level

25. s^2 is not an unbiased estimate of σ^2. When we use N in the denominator of the variance formula, we underestimate the population variance $(s^2 = SS/N)$.

27. The interval within which the population mean probably lies is called the confidence interval.

29. The t-distributions are more spread out than the normal curve. Thus, the proportion of area beyond a specific value of t is greater than the proportion of area beyond the corresponding value of z. As df increases, the t-distributions more closely resemble the normal curve.

*30. a.

$X_1 - X_2$	f	$p(X_1 - X_2)$
9	1	0.0083
8	2	0.0165
7	5	0.0413
6	10	0.0826
5	14	0.1157
4	18	0.1488
3	21	0.1736
2	18	0.1488
1	14	0.1157
0	10	0.0826
−1	5	0.0413
−2	2	0.0165
−3	1	0.0083

$$N_{\bar{x}_1 - \bar{x}_2} = 121 \qquad \Sigma p(\bar{X}_1 - \bar{X}_2) = 1.0000$$

b. The mean of the differences = 3. The mean of the sampling distribution of differences between means is equal to the difference between the means of the population from which these samples were drawn.

*31. a. $H_0 : \mu_1 = \mu_2$; that is, the two populations of means from which we are drawing samples are the same.

b. The sampling distribution of differences between means under the null hypothesis.

c.

$X_1 - X_2$	f	$p(X_1 - X_2)$
6	1	0.0083
5	2	0.0165
4	5	0.0413
3	10	0.0826
2	14	0.1157
1	18	0.1488
0	21	0.1736
−1	18	0.1488
−2	14	0.1157
−3	10	0.0826
−4	5	0.0413
−5	2	0.0165
−6	1	0.0083

*32. a. 0.0496   **b.** 0.0083   **c.** 0.1487   **d.** 0.0166   **e.** 0.0083

*33. a. 0.2644   **b.** 0.1487   **c.** 0.0083   **d.** 0.1487   **e.** 0.0000

35. $t = 4.28$ **37.** $t = 4$

Variable	Practice	Trial 1	Trial 2	Trial 3	Trial 4
Practice	10	6.289	6.372	6.092	5.405
Trial 1	10	10.000	13.583	12.160	7.865
Trial 2	10	10.000	10.000	22.226	12.411
Trial 3	10	10.000	10.000	10.000	15.143
Trial 4	10	10.000	10.000	10.000	10.000

Reject all null hypotheses at the 0.01 level since all the t-ratios exceed the critical value of $t = 12.896$.

1. $t = 2.795$, reject H_0 **3.** $t = 0.802$, accept H_0

5. a. $z = 1.41, p = 0.0793$ **b.** $z = -2.12, p = 0.9830$
   c. $z = -2.12, p = 0.0170$ **d.** $z = -5.66, p < 0.00003$

7.

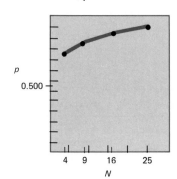

The probability of finding a difference in the correct direction between sample means increases as N increases.

9. $t = 2.968$, df $= 18$

11. a.

$SS_1 = 13,696.06$	$SS_2 = 24,027.66$
$\bar{X} = 17.82$	$\bar{X}_2 = 19.59$
$t = 7.080$	df $= 1632$

$\omega^2 = 0.029$

b.

$SS_1 = 910.32$	$SS_2 = 1590.21$
$\bar{X}_1 = 1.76$	$\bar{X}_2 = 1.61$
$t = 2.333$	df $= 1632$

$\omega^2 = 0.003$

13. $t = 2.224$, df $= 28$, reject H_0

15. $t = 1.688$, df $= 126, p < 0.05$, one-tailed test, $\omega_2 = 0.014$

17.

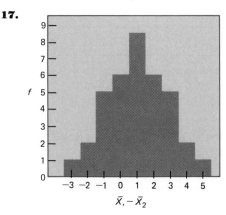

$\bar{X}_1 - \bar{X}_2$	f
5	1
4	2
3	5
2	6
1	8
0	6
-1	5
-2	2
-3	1

*18. a. $p = 0.7778$ **b.** $p = 0.6111$ **c.** $p = 0.3889$ **d.** $p = 0.2222$
   e. $p = 0.0833$ **f.** $p = 0$ **g.** $p = 0.4722$

*19. $\mu_1 = 5.0$, $\sigma_1 = 2.24$; $\mu_2 = 4.0$, $\sigma_2 = 2.24$

*20. a. $z = -1.59$, $p = 0.9441$ **b.** $z = 0.00$, $p = 0.5000$ **c.** $z = -1.59$,
   d. $z = 0$, $p = 0.50$ **e.** 4.76, $p = 0.00003$ $p = 0.0559$
   g. $p = 0.0559$ **f.** $p = 0.5007$

*21. a. $z = -0.63$, $p = 0.2643$ **b.** $z = -0.94$, $p = 0.1736$ **c.** $z = -1.27$,
   d. $z = -1.89$, $p = 0.0294$ $p = 0.1020$

23. $z = 3.33$ **25.** $t = 5.02$ **27.** $t = 1.76$

29. $t = -6.88$

31. $t = 1.63$, df $= 8$; accept H_0.

33. a. $SS_1 = 74.28$ $SS_2 = 284.57$ **b.** $SS_1 = 30.00$ $SS_2 = 11.2$
   $\bar{X}_1 = 0.40$ $\bar{X}_2 = 1.86$ $\bar{X}_1 = 13.00$ $\bar{X}_2 = 10.40$
   $t = 2.281$ $df = 62$ $t = 3.206$ $df = 17$
   $\omega^2 = 0.062$ $\omega^2 = 0.328$

35. a.

Group	Humor First	Humor after Horror
Males and females combined	$\bar{X} = 17.80$	$\bar{X} = 12.85$
Sample size	$N = 20$	$N = 20$
Standard deviation	$s = 6.21$	$s = 6.51$

$$s_{\bar{X}_1 - \bar{X}_2} = \sqrt{[(20)(6.21)^2 + (20)(6.51)^2]/(20 + 20 - 2) \times [(20 + 20)/400]}$$
$$= \sqrt{(771.282 + 847.602)/38 \times 0.1} = \sqrt{4.260} = 2.064$$
$$\omega^2 = 0.106$$
$$t = (17.80 - 12.85)/2.064 = 2.398$$

We reject H_0 at $\alpha = 0.05$, two-tailed test. In support of the emotional contrast hypothesis, humorous scenes following scenes of horror are apparently rated more pleasant than humorous scenes that are not preceded by either humor or horror.

b.

Group	Males	Females
Ratings of humor-after-horror combined with humor first	$\bar{X} = 16.50$	$\bar{X} = 14.15$
Sample size	$N = 20$	$N = 20$
Standard deviation	$s = 7.17$	$s = 6.24$

$$s_{\bar{X}_1 - \bar{X}_2} = \sqrt{[(20)(7.17)^2 + (20)(6.24)^2]/(20 + 20 - 2) \cdot [(20 + 20)/400]}$$
$$= \sqrt{(1028.178 + 778.752)/38 \times 0.1} = \sqrt{4.755} = 2.181$$
$$t = (16.50 - 14.15)/2.181 = 1.077$$

We cannot reject H_0 at $\alpha = 0.05$, two-tailed test. There is no significant difference among males and females in rating the pleasantness of humorous scenes.

$$\text{est } \omega^2 = 0.004$$

36. Manufacturer A: $t = \dfrac{104.82 - 100}{1.63} = 2.96$, df $= 10$

Manufacturer B: $t = \dfrac{101.91 - 100}{1.39} = 1.37$, df $= 10$

39. $t = 0.422$

41. $t = 8.22$

43. $t = -1.24$

45. a. The design involves repeated measures on the same individuals. Therefore, Student's t-ratio for correlated samples is appropriate.
  b. $\bar{D} = 13.5$; $s_{\bar{D}} = 4.244$; $t = 3.181$. Critical value with df $= 6$ equals 2.447. Since $t = 3.181 \geq |2.447|$, we reject H_0. The depressed mood was significantly improved when the same subjects were exposed to bright as opposed to dim light.

47. a.

Subjects	Subject Reported Being Awake	Subject Reported Being Asleep
1	0.1754	0.1613
2	0.1163	0.2326
3	0.5263	0.4545
4	0.2703	0.1923
5	0.4545	0.2128
6	0.1282	0.0775
7	0.2941	0.1370
8	0.4545	0.2381
9	0.2500	0.0398
10	0.2941	0.2439

  b. Student's t-ratio for correlated samples. The transformation does not change the fact that the scores were based on repeated measures. Note, however, that the reciprocal transformation reverses the relative magnitudes of the reaction times. Thus, a large reaction time (e.g., 25.1) becomes a small reciprocal (0.0398) and a small reaction time (e.g., 1.9) becomes a relatively large reciprocal (0.5263). Because of this reversal, it is common to treat the reciprocals of reaction times as the speed score. Thus, the faster (shorter duration) the reaction time is, the *larger* or *faster* is the speed score.
  c. $\bar{X}_1 = 0.2964$, $\bar{X}_2 = 0.1990$, $t = 2.794$, df $= 9$. Reject H_0 and assert the alternative hypothesis for the transformed means. The transformed reaction times (speed scores) were faster when the subjects reported being awake.

Chapter 14

1. $F = 47.02$; reject H_0

3. $F = 0.643$

5. $F = 0.30$, df $= \frac{3}{12}$

7. $F = 12.99$, df $= \frac{5}{18}$, HSD $= 6.02$

9.

Source of Variation	Sum of Squares	Degrees of Freedom	Variance Estimate	F
Between-groups	1.083	2	0.5415	0.6228
Within-groups	13.042	15	0.8695	
Total	14.125	17		

11.

Source of Variation	Sum of Squares	Degrees of Freedom	Variance Estimate	F
Between-groups	919.793	3	306.598	6.43
Within-groups	954.167	20	47.708	
Total	1873.96	23		

13. The only comparison significant at 0.01 level is between Group C and Group A.

15.

Source of Variation	Sum of Squares	Degrees of Freedom	Variance Estimate	F
Between-groups	15.8645	3	5.288	15.57
Within-groups	6.7917	20	0.3396	
Total	22.6562	23		

17. Block 1: A, C, I, K; Block 2: B, D, E, H; Block 3: F, G, J, L, shown in alphabetical order. Remember that, within each block, subjects are assigned at random.

19.

Summary Table

Variable	Sum of Squares	Degrees of Freedom	Variance Estimate	F-Ratio
Treatment	59.1108	2	29.5554	7.86987
Blocks	514.446	5	102.889	27.3968
Residual	37.5552	10	3.75552	
Total	611.112	17		

19.

	$\bar{X}_1 = 98/6 = 16.33$	$\bar{X}_2 = 76/6 = 12.67$	$\bar{X}_3 = 100/6 = 16.67$
$\bar{X}_1 = 16.33$	—	3.66	-0.34
$\bar{X}_2 = 12.67$	—	—	-4.00
$\bar{X}_3 = 16.67$	—	—	—

HSD $= 5.70 \sqrt{3.76/6} = 3.59$. Any difference in means equal to or greater than the absolute value of 3.59 leads to the rejection of H_0. The differences between means 1 versus 2 and 2 versus 3 are statistically significant at the 0.01 level.

20.

Summary Table

Variable	Sum of Squares	Degrees of Freedom	Variance Estimate	F
Treatment	59.1106	2	29.5553	0.803131
Within	552.001	15	36.8001	
Total	611.112	17		

Note that the F-ratio is not significant at either the 0.05 or the 0.01 level. This is due to the fact that, in the independent-groups design, the SS_{bl} are not identified and subtracted from "error" but are incorporated within the SS_w. Note that, in the correlated-samples design, $SS_{bl} + SS_{res}$ is equal to SS_w in the independent-samples design. The proportion SS_{bl}/SS_w tells us the proportion of SS_w that is accounted for by the SS_{bl}. It is $514.45/552 = 0.93$.

Chapter 15

1.

Source of Variation	Sum of Squares	Degrees of Freedom	Variance Estimate	F
Treatment combinations	169.04	8		
A-variable	7.37	2	3.68	0.35
B-variable	161.37	2	80.68	7.64*
$A \times B$	0.30	4	0.08	0.01
Within (error)	475.33	45	10.56	
Total	644.37	53		

* Reject H_0 at $\alpha = 0.01$.

HSD	$\bar{X}_{B_1} = 7.06$	$\bar{X}_{B_2} = 9.44$	$\bar{X}_{B_3} = 11.28$
$\bar{X}_{B_1} = 7.06$	—	2.38	4.22*
$\bar{X}_{B_2} = 9.44$	—	—	1.84
$\bar{X}_{B_3} = 11.28$	—	—	—

$$\text{HSD}_{0.05} = 3.43 \sqrt{\frac{10.56}{18}} = 2.64$$

* Reject at $\alpha = 0.05$.

2.

Source of Variation	Sum of Squares	Degrees of Freedom	Variance Estimate	F
Treatment combinations	95.33	5		
A-variable	80.66	1	80.66	17.31
B-variable	1.13	2	0.56	00.12
A × B	13.54	2	6.77	1.45
Within (error)	84.00	18	4.66	
Total	179.33	23		

3.

Source of Variation	Sum of Squares	Degrees of Freedom	Variance Estimate	F
Treatments	25.16	5		
A	15.26	1	15.26	4.58
B	4.91	2	2.46	0.74
A × B	4.99	2	2.49	0.75
Within (error)	379.45	114	3.33	
Totals	404.61	119		

At $\alpha = 0.05$ and df $= \frac{1}{114}$, an F-ratio equal to or greater than 3.93 (interpolated) is required for significance. The mean score on the Standard Challenging Task is significantly higher for the Type A (8.80) than for the Type B subjects (8.08).

4.

Summary Table

Variable	Sum of Squares	Degrees of Freedom	Variance Estimate	F
Treatment Comb.	399.867	5		
Variable A	304.023	1	304.023	27.835
Variable B	9.64063	2	4.82031	0.441325
Interaction	86.2031	2	43.1016	3.94618
Within (error)	1245.15	114	10.9224	
Total	1645.15	119		

A_1, A_2 means $= 22.85 \quad 19.6667$

B_1, B_2, B_3 means $= 21.55 \quad 21.35 \quad 20.875$

5.

Source of Variation	Sum of Squares	Degrees of Freedom	Variance Estimate	F
Treatments	399.87	5		
A	304.02	1	304.02	27.83
B	9.64	2	4.82	0.44
A × B	86.21	2	43.10	3.95
Within (error)	1245.15	114	10.92	
Totals	1645.02	119		

At $\alpha = 0.05$ and df $= \frac{1}{114}$, an F-ratio equal to or greater than 3.93 (interpolated) is required for significance. The mean score on the Standard Challenging Task is significantly higher for the Type A (8.80) than for the Type B subjects (8.08). However, the interaction between the A and B variables is also significant at the 0.05 level (critical value of F at $\frac{2}{119}$ df $= 3.08$). For this reason, the interpretation of the effects of the A variable (Type A versus Type B) must include the qualification that, in this study, the effects of personality type are dependent on the activity level of the subjects.

6.

Source of Variation	Sum of Squares	Degrees of Freedom	Variance Estimate	F
Treatments	95.33	5		
A	80.67	1	80.67	16.01
B	1.08	2	0.54	0.11
A × B	13.58	2	6.79	1.35
Blocks	8.33	3	2.78	
Residual (error)	75.67	15	5.04	
Totals	179.33	119		

Although the blocking variable failed to account for much of the error, the conclusions remain essentially unchanged because of the very large effect of the A variable.

7.

Source of Variation	Sum of Squares	Degrees of Freedom	Variance Estimate	F
Treatments	190.48	3		
A	133.23	1	133.23	93.82
B	11.03	1	11.03	7.77
A × B	46.23	1	46.23	33.56
Between blocks	365.23	9	40.58	
Residual (error)	38.27	27	1.42	
Totals	593.98	39		

These results pose a problem in interpretation. Using the residual as error, there is a statistically significant effect of the A variable, the B variable, and the interaction between the A and B variables. Ordinarily, in the absence of a significant interaction, we infer that the difference in sample means reflects a similar difference in the population means from which the samples were drawn. Thus, we conclude that there is an overall effect of the treatment variable. However, a significant interaction implies that the observed effect of the treatment variable is not uniform over different levels of a second variable. In other words, the effect of condition A is dependent on the level of condition B and vice versa. Our conclusions should reflect this qualification. It is analogous to stating that penicillin is not effective against all types of bacterial infections. Its effectiveness depends on the type of bacteria involved.

Chapter 16

1. $N_a = 30$

3. 28.77%

5. a. 5.26%   **b.** 10.20%   **c.** 17.88%   **d.** 28.77%

7. It takes time, effort, and money to conduct research. When the power to reject a false null hypothesis is low, we are in effect sending good money after bad. A small increase in time, effort, and funding may sometimes be sufficient to raise the power of a test to levels that justify the risk.

9. When the null hypothesis is false, a rejection of the null hypothesis is the correct statistical decision. The concept of Type I error simply does not apply.

11. Factors affecting power:
  a. Sample size: As N increases, power increases.
  b. α-level: The higher the α-level we set, the greater is the power of the test.
  c. Nature of the alternative hypothesis: One-tailed test is more powerful than two-tailed alternative (unless the parameter lies in a direction opposite to the one predicted).
  d. Nature of the statistical test: Parametric tests are more powerful than their nonparametric counterparts (assuming assumptions underlying the use of the parametric test are valid).
  e. Correlated measures: When subjects have been successfully matched on a variable correlated with the criterion, a statistical test that takes this correlation into account is more powerful than one that does not.
  Power may be increased by:
  a. Increasing sample size.
  b. Setting α high (e.g., 0.05 as opposed to 0.01).
  c. Employing a one-tailed alternative hypothesis.
  d. Employing parametric tests rather than nonparametric.
  e. Employing correlated measures, if appropriate.

Chapter 17

1. a. $p = 0.070$ **b.** $p = 0.020$ **c.** $p = 0.040$

5. $\chi^2 = 11.765$, df $= 3$

7. $\chi^2 = 1.941$, df $= 1$

9. $\chi^2 = 2.185$, df $= 1$

11. $\chi^2 = 6.00$, df $= 3$

13. $x = 28$, $N = 46$ (Table M), critical value $= 31$; we fail to reject H_0

15. $\chi^2 = 12.5$, df $= 2$ **17.** $\chi^2 = 7.86$, df $= 5$

19. $\chi^2 = 4.44$, df $= 1$ **21.** $\chi^2 = 8.077$, df $= 1$

25. a. $\chi^2 = 1.2$. When no information was given, there was no statistically acceptable evidence that compliance depended on the size of the request.
  b. $\chi^2 = 9.6$. Reject H_0. With placebic information, there was significantly greater compliance when the request was small.
  c. $\chi^2 = 0.938$. Do not reject H_0.

27. a. The χ^2 test of independence   **b.** $\chi^2 = 3.645$. The obtained χ^2 falls short of the critical value of 3.841 at $\alpha = 0.05$, df $= 1$.

29. a. MDs: 97.9% survived, 2.1% died; RNs: 93.4% survived, 6.6% died; Others: 92.5% survived, 7.5% died.
  b. Chi-square test of independence.
  c. Obtained $\chi^2 = 16.186$; critical value at $\alpha = 0.01$ level $= 9.210$; df $= 2$. Reject H_0. The mortality rate is related to the care-giver who inserts the catheter.

Chapter 18

1. a. sign test $N = 10$, $x = 7$ **b.** $N = 10$, $T = 10$ **c.** $U = 23$, $U' = 77$

3. $U = 18$, $U' = 103$ **5.** $T = 48$

7. sign test $N = 10$, $x = 6$; Wilcoxon $T = -12$

9. $U' = 89$, $U = 11$

References

"Additional Recommendations to Reduce Sexual and Drug Abuse-Related Transmission of Human T-Lymphotropic Virus Type III/Lymphadenopathy-Associated Virus" (1986), *Morbidity and Mortality Report,* **35**(10), 152–155.

Anas, N., V. Namasthoni, and M. Ginsburg (1981), "Criteria for Hospitalizing Children Who Have Ingested Products Containing Hydrocarbons," *Journal of the American Medical Association,* **246**(8).

Auble, D. (1953), "Extended Tables for the Mann–Whitney Statistic," *Bulletin of the Institute of Educational Research at Indiana University,* **1**(2).

Barkley, R. A., and C. E. Cunningham (1979), "The Effects of Methylphenidate on the Mother-Child Interactions of Hyperactive Children," *Archives of General Psychiatry,* **36**, 201–208.

Benson, H., D. Shapiro, B. Tursky, and G. E. Schwartz (1971), "Decreased Systolic Blood Pressure Through Operant Conditioning Techniques in Patients with Essential Hypertension," *Science,* **173**, 740–742.

Benson, P. L., S. A. Karabenick, and R. M. Lerner (1976), "Pretty Pleases: The Effects of Physical Attractiveness, Race, and Sex on Receiving Help," *Journal of Experimental Social Psychology,* **12**, 409–415.

Bentler, P. M., and M. D. Newcomb (1978), "Longitudinal Study of Marital Success and Failure," *Journal of Consulting and Clinical Psychology,* **46**, 1053–1070.

Bingham, W. V., *Aptitudes and Aptitude Testing.* New York: Harper and Bros., 1937.

Bower, G. H. (1981), "Mood and Memory," *American Psychologist,* **36**(2), 129–148.

Camilli, G., and K. D. Hopkins (1978), "Applicability of Chi-square to 2 × 2 Contingency Tables with Small Expected Cell Frequencies," *Psychological Bulletin,* **85**, 163–167.

Carmen, M., P. G. Caballero, and P. Shaver (1975), "Sex-Role Traditionalism and Fear of Success," *Sex Roles* **1**(4), 319–326

Case, D. B., and S. A. Atlas (1982), "Clinical Experience with Captopril in Moderate to Severe Hypertension," *Cardiovascular Reviews and Reports,* **3**(3), 435–453.

Cassileth, B., E. Lusk, T. Strouse, D. Miller, L. Brown, P. Cross, and A. Tenaglia (1984), "Psychosocial Status in Chance Illness," *New England Journal of Medicine,* **311**, 506–510.

Cowens, E. L. (1982), "Help Is Where You Find It," *American Psychologist,* **37**(4), 385–395.

Dingle, J. H. (1973), "The Ills of Man," *Scientific American,* **229**(3), 77–84.

Dor-Shav, N. K. (1978), "On the Long-range Effects of Concentration Camp Internment on Nazi Victims: 25 Years Later," *Journal of Consulting and Clinical Psychology,* **46**, 1–11.

Dunlap, J. W., and A. K. Kurtz, *Handbook of Statistical Nomographs, Tables, and Formulas.* New York: World Book Company, 1932.

Dusek, D., and D. A. Girdano, *Drugs, A Factual Account,* 3d ed. Reading, Mass.: Addison-Wesley, 1980.

Edwards, A. L., *Statistical Analysis,* 3d ed. New York: Holt, Rinehart and Winston, 1969.

———, *Experimental Design in Pyschological Research,* 3d ed. New York: Rinehart, 1950.

Feinstein, A. R., D. M. Sosin, and C. K. Wells (1985), "The Will Rogers Phenomenon: Stage Migration and New Diagnostic Techniques as a Source of Misleading Statistics for Survival in Cancer," *The New England Journal of Medicine* **312**(25), 1604–1608.

Fisher, R. A., *Statistical Methods for Research Workers.* Edinburgh: Oliver and Boyd, Ltd., 1935.

———, *The Design of Experiments*. Edinburgh: Oliver and Boyd, Ltd., 1935.

Fisher, R. A., and F. Yates, *Statistical Tables for Biological, Agricultural, and Medical Research*. Edinburgh: Oliver and Boyd, Ltd., 1948.

Friedrich, L. K., and A. H. Stein (1973), "Aggressive and Prosocial Television Programs and the Natural Behavior of Preschool Children," *Monographs of the Society for Research in Child Development*, Serial no. 151, 38.

Grinspoon, L. (1969), "Marihuana," *Scientific American* **221**(6), 17–25.

Haber, A., R. P. Runyon, and P. Badia, *Readings in Statistics*. Reading, Mass.: Addison-Wesley, 1970.

Hess, E. H., A. L. Seltzer, and J. J. Shlien (1965), "Pupil Response of Hetero- and Homosexual Males to Pictures of Men and Women: A Pilot Study," *Journal of Abnormal Social Psychology*, **70,** 165–168.

Huff, D., *How to Lie with Statistics*. New York: W. W. Norton, 1954.

Jenkins, C. D., R. H. Rosenman, and M. Friedman, (1967), "Development of an Objective Psychological Test for the Determination of the Coronary-Prone Behavior Pattern in Employed Men," *Journal of Chronic Diseases*, **20,** 371–379.

Kanin, E. J. (1967), "An Examination of Sexual Aggression as a Response to Sexual Frustration," *Journal of Marriage and the Family*, **29,** 428–433.

Kirk, R. E., *Experimental Design: Procedures for the Behavioral Sciences*. California: Brooks/Cole, 1968.

Klein, A. (1981), "Adolescent Hypertention," *Therapia*, September, 37–41.

Langan, P. A., and C. A. Innes (1985), "The Risk of Violent Crime," *Bureau of Justice Statistics Special Report*, NCJ-97119.

Latané, B. (1981), "The Psychology of Social Impact," *American Psychologist*, **36**(4), 342–356.

Lipson, G., and D. Wolman (1972), "Polling Americans on Birth Control and Population," *Family Planning Perspectives*, **4**(1), 39–42.

Mann, H. B., and D. R. Whitney (1947), "On a Test of Whether One of Two Random Variables Is Stochastically Larger Than the Other," *Annals of Mathematical Statistics*, **18**, 52–54.

Manstead, A. S. R., H. L. Wagner, and C. J. MacDonald (1983), "A Contrast Effect in Judgments of Own Emotional State," *Motivation and Emotion*, **7**, 279–289.

McFadden, D., and E. G. Pasanen (1975), "Binaural Beats at High Frequencies," *Science*, **190,** 394–396.

McNemar, Q., *Psychological Statistics*. New York: John Wiley, 1962.

Merrington, M., and C. M. Thompson (1943), "Tables of Percentage Points of the Inverted Beta Distribution," *Biometrika*, **33**(1), 73.

Meyer, G. E., and K. Hilterbrand (1984), "Does It Pay to Be 'Bashful'?: The Seven Dwarfs and Long-Term Memory," *American Journal of Psychology*, **97,** 47–55.

NIOSH Recommendations for Occupational Safety and Health Standards (1985), *Morbidity and Mortality Weekly Report*, Supplement, 34/No. 1S.

Olds, E. G. (1949), "The 5 Percent Significance Levels of Sums of Squares of Rank Differences and a Correction," *Annuals of Mathematical Statistics*, **20,** 117–118.

Orlowski, J. P. (1982), "Endorphins in Infant Apnea," *New England Journal of Medicine*, **307**(3), 186–187.

Ortega, D. F., and J. E. Pipal (1984), "Challenge Seeking and Type A Coronary-Prone Behavior Pattern," **46**(6), 1328–1334.

Pearson, E. S., and H. O. Hartley, *Biometrika Tables for Statisticians*, vol. 1, 2d ed. New York: Cambridge University Press, 1958.

Perkins, K. A. (1984), "Heart Rate Changes in Type A and Type B Males as a Function of Response Cost and Task Difficulty, *Journal of Personality and Social Psychology*, **21,** 14–21.

Pope, K. S., P. Keith-Spiegel, and B. G. Tabachnick (1986), "Sexual Attraction to Client: The Human Therapist and the (Sometimes) Inhuman Training System," *American Psychologist*, **41**(2), 147–158.

Rabies in the United States and Canada, 1983. *Morbidity and Mortality Weekly Report* (1985), **34,** #1SS, 11SS–27SS.

Rand Corporation, *A Million Random Digits*. Glencoe, Ill.: Free Press of Glencoe, 1955.

Rocks, L., and R. P. Runyon, *The Energy Crisis*. New York: Crown Publishers, 1972.

Rosenman, A. H. (1978), "History and Definition of the Type A Coronary-Prone Behavior Pattern," in T. M. Dembroski, S. M. Weiss, J. L. Shields, S. G. Haynes, and M. Feinleib (eds.), *Coronary Prone Behavior* (pp. 55–69). New York: Springer Verlag.

Rosenthal, N. E., D. A. Sack, C. J. Carpenter, B. L.

Parry, W. B. Mendelson, T. A. Wehr (1984–1985), "Antidepressant Effects of Light in Seasonal Affective Disorder," *American Journal of Psychiatry*, **21**, 234–239.

Runyon, R. P., *Winning with Statistics*. Reading, Mass.: Addison-Wesley, 1977.

———, *Non-Parametric Statistics*. Reading, Mass.: Addison-Wesley, 1977.

——— (1968), "Note on Use of the *A*-statistic as a Substitute for *t* in the One-Sample Case," *Psychological Reports*, **22**, 361–362.

Runyon, R. P., and M. Kosacoff, "Olfactory Stimuli as Reinforcers of Bar Pressing Behavior." Paper presented at meeting of Eastern Psych. Assn., Philadelphia, 1965.

Runyon, R. P., and W. J. Turner, *A Study of the Effects of Drugs on the Social Behavior of White Rats*. New York: Long Island University, 1964.

Russo, N. F., E. L. Olmedo, J. Stapp, and R. Fulcher (1981), "Women and Minorities in Psychology," *American Psychologist*, **35**(11), 1315–1363.

Salk, L. (1973), "The Role of the Heartbeat in the Relations Between Mother and Infant," *Scientific American*, **228**(5), 26–29.

Sbordone, R. J., J. A. Wingard, M. L. Elliott, and J. Jervey (1978), "Mescaline Produces Pathological Aggression in Rats Regardless of Age or Strain," *Pharmacology, Biochemistry and Behavior*, **8**, 542–546.

Seiden, R. H. (1966), "Campus Tragedy: A Story of Student Suicide," *Journal of Abnormal Social Psychology*, **71**, 389–399.

Sewich, D. E. (1984), "The Perceptual Uncertainty of Having Slept," *Psychophysiology*, **21**, 243–259.

Siegel, S., and Castellan, Jr., *Non-Parametric Statistics*, 2d ed. New York: McGraw-Hill, 1988.

Snedecor, G. W., and W. G. Cochran, *Statistical Methods*, 6th ed. Ames, Iowa: Iowa State University Press, 1956.

Thorton, B. (1977), "Toward a Linear Prediction Model of Marital Happiness," *Personality and Social Psychology Bulletin*, **3**, 674–676.

Tukey, J. W. (1953), "The Problem of Multiple Comparisons." Princeton University. Unpublished manuscript, 396 pp.

Tukey, John W., *Exploratory Data Analysis*. Reading, Mass.: Addison-Wesley, 1977.

Update: Acquired Immunodeficiency Syndrome—Europe (1986), *Morbidity and Mortality Report*, **35**(3), 35–46.

Van Bree, N. S., "Undergraduate Research." *Nursing Outlook*, January 1981, 39–41.

Walker, H., and J. Lev, *Statistical Inference*. New York: Henry Holt, 1953.

Wilcoxon, F., and R. A. Wilcox, *Some Rapid Approximate Statistical Procedures*. New York: Lederle Laboratories, 1964.

———, *Critical Values and Probability Levels for the Wilcoxon Rank-Sum Test and the Wilcoxon Signed-Rank Test*. New York: American Cyanamid Co., 1963.

Wingard, J. A., J. P. Buchanan, and A. Burnell (1978), "Organizational Changes in the Memory of Young Children," *Perceptual and Motor Skills*, **46**, 735–742.

Wingard, J. A., G. J. Huba, and P. M. Bentler (1979), "The Relationship of Personality Structure to Patterns of Adolescent Substance Use," *Journal of Multivariate Behavioral Research*, **14**, 131–143.

Winkler, R. C., and R. A. Winett (1983), "Behavioral Interventions in Resource Conservation: A Systems Approach Based on Behavioral Economics," *American Psychologist*, **37**(4), 421–435.

Zelson, C., E. Rubio, and E. Wasserman (1971), "Neonatal Narcotic Addiction: 10-Year Observation," *Pediatrics*, **48**(2), 178–188.

Index